The Chinese Gazette in European Sources

Sinica Leidensia

Edited by

Barend J. ter Haar
Maghiel van Crevel

In co-operation with

P.K. Bol, D.R. Knechtges, E.S. Rawski,
W.L. Idema, H.T. Zurndorfer

VOLUME 155

The titles published in this series are listed at *brill.com/sinl*

The Chinese Gazette in European Sources

Joining the Global Public in the Early and Mid-Qing Dynasty

By

Nicolas Standaert

BRILL

LEIDEN | BOSTON

Cover illustration: Drawing of A-gui 阿桂 by Giuseppe Panzi (c. 1780): BnF, Bréquigny 114, fol. 177r (© Bibliothèque nationale de France, Paris).

Library of Congress Cataloging-in-Publication Data

Names: Standaert, N., author.
Title: The Chinese gazette in European sources : joining the global public in the early and mid-Qing dynasty / by Nicolas Standaert.
Description: Leiden ; Boston : Brill, [2022] | Series: Sinica leidensia, 0169-9563 ; volume 155 | Includes bibliographical references and index.
Identifiers: LCCN 2021052216 (print) | LCCN 2021052217 (ebook) | ISBN 9789004472709 (hardback) | ISBN 9789004505001 (ebook)
Subjects: LCSH: Jing bao. | Gazettes—China—History | Law—China—History—Sources. | China—Politics and government—1644-1912—Sources. | China—History—Qing dynasty, 1644-1912—Study and teaching—Europe.
Classification: LCC KNN7 .S73 2022 (print) | LCC KNN7 (ebook) | DDC 349.51—dc23/eng/20211223
LC record available at https://lccn.loc.gov/2021052216
LC ebook record available at https://lccn.loc.gov/2021052217

Typeface for the Latin, Greek, and Cyrillic scripts: "Brill". See and download: brill.com/brill-typeface.

ISSN 0169-9563
ISBN 978-90-04-47270-9 (hardback)
ISBN 978-90-04-50500-1 (e-book)

Contents

Acknowledgments

This book started with a random search for references to the Chinese gazette in eighteenth-century European sources. The quest for these references was part of a larger research project on the intercultural communication circuit of books between China and Europe of the seventeenth and eighteenth centuries. Originally, I had assumed that there were not many references to the gazette to be found. I expected to spend only a few days on this search, or at most a week or two. However, the unexpected discovery of a wealth of sources made it so that the topic preoccupied me for more than three years.

During this whole period, I benefited enormously from the help, support, and friendship of many colleagues. I express my gratitude to colleagues who generously provided extra material for this book: Chen Tuo 陈拓, Noël Golvers, Eugenio Menegon, Nii Yōko 新居洋子, Pierre-Emmanuel Roux, Benedicte Vaerman, and the colleagues of the Interlibrary Loan Service of KU Leuven and of the Max Planck Institute for the History of Science (Berlin). Special thanks go to Ad Dudink for sharing his material on the Chinese sources in the Archivio Storico "de Propaganda Fide" and to Martin Heijdra for introducing the *tizou shijian* 题奏事件 to me and for sharing his material on this subject. I am grateful to those who critically read earlier versions of this text and provided suggestions to improve it: Hilde De Weerdt, Marie-An Knops, Silvia Toro, Katlijne Van der Stighelen, Yang Hongfan 杨虹帆, and the anonymous reviewers of the initial versions of the article and the book. I thank especially Valentina Yang 杨灵艳 for her precious input to the first section of the second chapter. I am particularly grateful to Moira De Graef for her careful revision of and many insightful suggestions to the different versions of the entire manuscript, which greatly improved its quality. Special thanks also to Carine Defoort who not only read and commented upon the manuscript, but once again strongly encouraged its publication as a book. I express my deep appreciation to all the colleagues of the Department of Chinese Studies at KU Leuven, for creating a unique academic and social environment in which research can flourish. Gratitude also to Chu Ping-yi 祝平一, Lu Miau-fen 吕妙芬, and Wang Hung-tai 王鴻泰 for organizing a workshop about this topic at the Academia Sinica (Taipei) and for their positive input, as well as to the participants of the workshop organized by the Institute of Advanced Humanistic Studies (Fudan University) for their feedback. I particularly want to thank Ge Zhaoguang 葛兆光 and Ding Chennan 丁晨楠 for their encouragement and valuable suggestions which led to the publication of a tailored version of the second chapter published in Chinese in *Fudan xuebao* 复旦学报. I thank the editors of *T'oung*

Pao for printing a preliminary version of chapter three on the gazette during the Qianlong era and Patricia Radder (Brill) for efficiently guiding the whole publication process. I was lucky to be able to obtain Emily Mokros' new book on the Peking gazette in late imperial China just before sending this manuscript to the editor. I can recommend her work as the broader context of the topic of this book, since my work merely focuses on the intercultural use of the Chinese gazette in the early and mid-Qing. The subtitle of this book is inspired by the collective work edited in 2007 by the late Rudolf Wagner, whose scholarship stimulated many young scholars. I wish to thank FWO Vlaanderen and the KU Leuven Onderzoeksraad for supporting this research.

I hope readers will enjoy "reading the gazette" as much as I did over the past few years. Maybe they will be equally amazed at the extent to which Europe was informed about China in the seventeenth and eighteenth centuries. They might even long for the time when many European scholars and savants were willing to learn from other cultures, including China. Modern-day scholars may still find themselves heeding the advice that one of their eighteenth-century predecessors gave with some enthusiasm but also with farsightedness:

> Il n'y a pas de meilleur moyen de s'instruire de la Chine, que par la Chine même: car par là on est sûr de ne se point tromper, dans la connoissance du génie, & des usages de cette Nation.[1]

> There is no better way to learn about China, than through China itself: because in this way one is sure not to be mistaken, in the knowledge of the genius and of the customs of this Nation.

1 *Description … de la Chine* (1735), vol. 2, p. 258; also quoted on the title page of *Hau Kiou Choaan* (1761).

Figures

GAZETTE, ſ. f. (*Hiſt. mod.*) relation des affaires publiques. Ce fut au commencement du xvij^e^ ſiecle que cet uſage utile fut inventé à Veniſe, dans le tems que l'Italie étoit encore le centre des négociations de l'Europe, & que Veniſe étoit toûjours l'aſyle de la liberté. On appella ces feuilles qu'on donnoit une fois par ſemaine, *gazettes*, du nom de *gazetta*, petite monnoie revenante à un de nos demi-ſous, qui avoit cours alors à Veniſe. Cet exemple fut enſuite imité dans toutes les grandes villes de l'Europe.

De tels journaux étoient établis à la Chine de tems immémorial; on y imprime tous les jours la *gazette* de l'empire par ordre de la cour. Si cette *gazette* eſt vraie, il eſt à croire que toutes les vérités n'y ſont pas. Auſſi ne doivent-elles pas y être.

Le medecin Théophraſte Renaudot donna en France les premieres *gazettes* en 1631; & il en eut le privilége, qui a été long-tems un patrimoine de ſa famille. Ce privilége eſt devenu un objet important dans Amſterdam; & la plûpart des *gazettes* des Provinces-Unies ſont encore un revenu pour pluſieurs familles de magiſtrats, qui payent les écrivains. La ſeule ville de Londres a plus de douze *gazettes* par ſemaine. On ne peut les imprimer que ſur du papier timbré, ce qui n'eſt pas une taxe indifférente pour l'état.

Les *gazettes* de la Chine ne regardent que cet empire; celles de l'Europe embraſſent l'univers. Quoiqu'elles ſoient ſouvent remplies de fauſſes nouvelles, elles peuvent cependant fournir de bons matériaux pour l'Hiſtoire; parce que d'ordinaire les erreurs d'une *gazette* ſont rectifiées par les ſuivantes, & qu'on y trouve preſque toutes les pieces auten-

ILLUSTRATION 1 Voltaire, beginning of the lemma "Gazette" with reference to the Chinese Gazette: *Encyclopédie*, vol. VII (1757), p. 534

Introduction

The well-known French *Encyclopédie*, edited by Denis Diderot and Jean Le Rond d'Alembert between 1751 and 1772, defined the term 'gazette' as an "account of public affairs." It points out that the term, created in Venice, was only used since the early seventeenth century. Voltaire, author of this lemma, added that "such journals have been established in China from time immemorial, and the gazette of the empire is printed there every day by order of the court."[1] Though Voltaire was not aware that the gazettes in fact circulated in China already in Song times, he acknowledged the existence of a specific account of public affairs in China much earlier than in Europe. Moreover, to a certain extent, he established the European term that since then has been used as translation for a variety of Chinese terms, of which *dibao* 邸報 (officials' liaison gazette) and *jingbao* 京報 (capital gazette) are the most common ones. This publicly available Chinese government gazette that was published, distributed, and sold in a variety of print and manuscript formats has recently caught new academic interest both in China and in the West. Most of these studies focus on the *Peking Gazette* (*jingbao*) in the (late) nineteenth century, from which the generic term "Peking gazette" is derived, and study the topic in the context of the history of journalism and newspapers. Yet while the nineteenth century is relatively well documented through descriptions, editions, or even translations of primary sources, information about the gazette for earlier times remains very scarce. A very limited number of original copies from before 1800 is still extant, and those that exist, especially the *tizou quanlu* 題奏全錄 (complete record of memorials) from the Yongzheng period (1723–1735) and the *tizou shijian* 題奏事件 (memorialised documents) from the late Qianlong period (1736–1795), have hardly been studied. Especially for Song, Ming, and early Qing times, one has to rely on other sources, such as references in private jottings, letters, and poems. Because of the scarcity of sources, there has been a tendency to project the characteristics of the nineteenth century gazette on the early and mid-Qing (seventeenth and eighteenth centuries), without discussing the latter in its own right.

Other – so far barely explored – sources for the gazette of the pre-1800 period are the European texts mostly compiled by missionaries who lived in China in the early and mid-Qing. These include manuscript texts (private letters, reports, translations,...) composed in China and sent to Europe, where

1 Voltaire, "Gazette," in *Encyclopédie*, vol. VII (1757), pp. 534–535; see also: Voltaire, *Œuvres alphabétiques I* (OCV 33) (1987), pp. 113–114.

 | DOI:10.1163/9789004505001_002

they were published in the eighteenth century, especially in substantial collections of texts about Chinese culture. They comprise translations of (extracts of) gazettes, which account for about half of the preserved Chinese gazettes. Though coloured by their own times and interests, these sources add significantly to our knowledge of the gazettes. On the one hand, they shed light on the early existence, form, structure, content, and use of the Chinese gazette, especially the *tizou shijian*, and they may contain information that is not provided by any Chinese source of those times. On the other hand, they afford insight into how contemporary Europeans read the gazette within China, and how they, as global agents, informed Europe about China. They thus made the Chinese gazette part of a remarkable and lively global information network.

By providing a view from the periphery and approaching the topic of the gazette from an intercultural perspective, this book intends to be a guide to these documents. As a kind of source reader, it will present and analyse the documents from the Kangxi, Yongzheng, and Qianlong periods as extensively as possible, while leaving enough space for detailed analysis to others. For this purpose, an extensive overview of the European primary sources together with the identification of Chinese sources has been included at the end of this book.

Brief Presentation of the Chinese Gazette

What did the 'gazette,' or more accurately 'gazettes,' look like in the early and mid-Qing dynasty, roughly from the mid-seventeenth until the end of the eighteenth century? By way of introduction, the following general description of the gazette can be given, temporarily putting aside the many variations that existed and the changes that occurred even during the period under discussion.[2] In its various forms, the gazette was composed exclusively of official documents, the distribution of which had been authorised by the central administration. Many of these documents, such as the memorials, had originally been submitted for consideration to the emperor by the office of

2 This general description is based on, among others, Fang Hanqi (1992–1999), vol. 1, chap. 1, esp. on the Qing dynasty (pp. 188–245); Fang Hanqi (2013), chap. 1; Shi Yuanyuan (2008), chap. 3 and 5; Ma Ting (2002) and (2004); Mittler (2004), pp. 173–242; Kong Zhengyi & Wang Shuchuan (2015a); Harris (2018), pp. 5–8; Mokros (2016), pp. 29–37; Mokros (2021), esp. chap. 1, and passim; Yin Qing (2018); for references to the Song dynasty: De Weerdt (2015), chap. two: "Court Gazettes and Short Reports," pp. 76–104 (earlier version, see De Weerdt (2009)); for the Ming dynasty: Yin Yungong (1990); Fang Hanqi (1992–1999), vol. 1, chap. 1, esp. on the Ming dynasty (pp. 121–187). For a description of the circulation of the documents by Bourgeois, see BnF, Bréquigny 10, pp. 1–2.

transmission (*tongzheng shisi* 通政使司) and subsequently subjected to an imperial decision in the form of an edict, rescript, or endorsement. After this decision, some documents were released for dissemination (*fachao* 發抄). In periods when the imperial authority was strong, such as during the reigns of the Kangxi 康熙 (1662–1722), Yongzheng 雍正 (1723–1735), and Qianlong 乾隆 (1736–1795) emperors, the emperor himself often decided which edicts and memorials should be copied for wider distribution.

Nevertheless, the gazette was strictly speaking not a government publication but a copy of documents posted daily on placards in a hall by the Grand Secretariat (Neige 內閣, hence the term *gechao* 閣抄), and by the Six Offices of Scrutiny (Liuke 六科, hence the term *kechao* 科抄 (manuscript of the Offices)). The Six Offices were responsible for maintaining censorial surveillance over the six ministries and were attached to the Censorate (Duchayuan 都察院 after 1723), which entirely controlled the flow of documents passing through the ministries and checked them for possible errors. The work of copying the documents that had been released for dissemination was carried out by the agents of the provincial courier office (*titang guan* 提塘官). In the Qing, there were sixteen provincial courier offices in the capital, which were founded by the different provinces and maintained the connection between their respective province and the capital. Besides transmitting official documents from and to the provinces, the offices participated in publishing the gazette, including the process of recording, screening, editing, compiling, and delivering them to the provinces. It was one of their most important daily duties to visit the hall in order to copy down the documents related to their provinces or materials of general interest. These authorised documents were in principle included in the gazette without comments, judgment, or information provided by any "editor." At most they were arranged under certain subtitles, such as "edicts" or "memorials."

The gazette destined for the provinces was produced by hand-copying (hence the term *dichao* 邸鈔 (officials' liaison manuscript) or *jingchao* 京鈔 (capital manuscript)) and printing. The agents of the provincial courier office delivered the copies they had made to the reporting offices (*baofang* 報房), which had probably been established in the Yongzheng reign and were formally recognised in 1756 (QL21). Following extremely rudimentary procedures, the reporting offices printed a few copies of the gazette and sent them to the provincial capitals, where they were reprinted in much larger numbers for local distribution. There they were also marketed and could be acquired by anyone – not only highly educated government officials, but also people from the general public. This included, as will be shown, foreigners such as missionaries. As the number of copies to be sent out steadily grew in the course of the eighteenth century, the percentage of the printed copies also gradually increased. In fact, in the course of the eighteenth century and increasingly in the early nineteenth century, the work was also subcontracted to a small number of specialized private publishers and bookshop owners in Beijing. One accredited bookseller at the end of the eighteenth century, the Gongshen tang 公慎堂, published the gazette that became known as *tizou shijian* 題奏事件. It was not until the middle of the nineteenth century that such private publishers began stamping the title *Jingbao* 京報, in English literature translated as "Peking Gazette," on the cover of their publications.

The gazette was also recopied by hand or reprinted at various stages – by the agents of the courier office themselves, the Beijing booksellers, or the provincial administrations, and varying in the selection of its contents depending on the target readership. Thus, there existed also versions of the gazette produced by the local provincial couriers in the provincial capitals, sometimes supplemented by news or even commentaries collected by the copiers themselves. One special genre, not to be confused with the regular gazette, was the *tangbao* 塘報 (military post courier gazette), which originated in the Ming dynasty and was a bottom-up document used by the local governments to report military situations to the imperial court.

Finally, there were certain non-accredited by-products, the content of which partly escaped the control of the administration, including the "small gazettes" or "short reports" (*xiaobao* 小報, *xiaochao* 小抄, sometimes translated as "tabloids"). At times, these included memorials published without the consent of the Six Offices – in certain cases falsified memorials and edicts – or contained information that was considered secret or misleading. For this reason, several attempts were undertaken during the Kangxi, Yongzheng, and Qianlong reigns to monitor or prohibit the publication activities of the provincial couriers and unofficial booksellers.

Contrary to the general impression one may have of the gazette being one specific medium communicating official documents and accounts of public affairs with one continuous history, its history is in fact one of diversity and variety, also during the early and mid-Qing. There were various ways of reproducing the gazette (by handwriting and different printing methods), various formats of the documents (longer and shorter versions), various contents depending on the documents that were released for dissemination and that were actually copied, and various degrees of accredited and non-accredited publishers that reproduced official or sometimes non-official news. These often existed at the same time and add to the complexity of the study of the 'gazette.'

A Question of Terms

Another factor that may conceal this historical diversity is the term used to designate the 'gazette,' because the use of one single term may seem to imply that there was only one type of 'gazette' throughout history. In English, the term that is most often used is *Peking Gazette*, a term that originated in the nineteenth century, but that is also used as a generic term for the earlier centuries. In Chinese, one faces a similar problem with the usage of limited terms. For instance, the most common terms in scholarly publications are *dibao* 邸報 and *jingbao* 京報, while terms such as *tizou quanlu* 題奏全錄 and *tizou shijian* 題奏事件 are rarely used.[3] However, a closer look at the history of the gazette shows that different terms should be used for different periods in history. Already in 1992, Pan Tianzhen 潘天禎 quite convincingly showed that the term *dibao* 邸報 was utilised in the Song, Ming, and early Qing dynasty. Furthermore, he points out that under the late Qianlong reign, the gazettes became known as *tizou shijian* 題奏事件. In their layout these gazettes started immediately with the date followed by the name of the publisher, the above-mentioned Gongshen tang. In these booklets, the title *tizou shijian* appears in the fishtail margin on the outside of the page. It can be ascertained that this *tizou shijian* was published with this name as a mobile character text at the Gongshen tang during the late Qianlong and early Jiaqing 嘉慶 reigns (1796–1820), in 1760 and between 1770 (QL35) and 1801 (JQ6).[4] Ma Ting 馬挺, whose early study appeared around the same time as Pan Tianzhen's, in particular studied the layout of *tizou shijian* and also insisted on the recognition of *tizou shijian* as such.[5] In addition, under the Yongzheng emperor, the booklets of a few pages that included the gazette carried the title *tizou quanlu* 題奏全錄 immediately followed by the date. This *tizou quanlu* appears to be the predecessor of the *tizou shijian*. The title of both *tizou quanlu* and *tizou shijian* seems to imply that the memorials (*tizou* 題奏) were the focus of the gazette, rather than only the imperial decisions themselves. Finally, *jingbao* 京報 was employed for the gazette during the Daoguang 道光 (1821–1850) and Xianfeng 咸豐 reigns (1851–1861), and

3 For the different names, see also Fang Hanqi (1992–1999), p. 192; Fang Hanqi (2007), pp. 10–11; Mittler (2004), p. 178; Fang Hanqi (2013), pp. 33, 36; Mokros (2016), p. 29. *Dibao* is probably the most often used. Ge Gongzhen (1964, pp. 35–37) traces the term back to the Han. Most scholars (including Ge) think that the practice of referring to the gazette as *dibao* really originated in the Tang (or Song) (see Ma Ting (2004), p. 138; Mittler (2004), p. 178; Xu Zilin (2019)).

4 Pan Tianzhen (1992), esp. p. 90. The formal *guanbao* 官報 (official gazette) was only used since 1877 (GX33). For the early publication in 1760 referenced in Korean sources, see Ding Chennan (2018), pp. 144–154.

5 Ma Ting (1993); see also Ma Ting (2002), p. 80 and (2004), pp. 141–146.

possibly first used as formal title in 1852 (XF2). In other words, the gazette of the mid and late eighteenth century did not yet carry the nineteenth-century title *Jingbao*. However, as Pan Tianzhen has pointed out, the late Qing term *jingbao* has often been projected onto earlier times, when it did not yet exist as a generic term, even if it was sporadically used.[6]

This projection of the nineteenth century onto the eighteenth century is understandable given the lack of primary sources, but it tends to neglect the specificities of earlier developments of the gazette. For example most scholars, basing themselves on concrete examples of the *jingbao* in the second half of the nineteenth century, explain that the gazette was basically divided into three sections: court news, including the activities of the emperor (e.g. audiences, rituals) and personnel records such as appointments and dismissals (*gongmen chao* 宮門抄); edicts and rescripts by the emperor (*shangyu* 上諭, *zhi* 旨); and memorials (*tiben* 題本 and *zouben* 奏本) submitted by officials in the capital or in the provinces. Certain issues included a fourth section with a list of examination results.[7] While most of these topics can also be found in earlier gazettes, several sources reveal that such a relatively clear division did not yet exist in these earlier gazettes – especially regarding the first section of the *gongmen chao* ("palace gate jottings"). Moreover, earlier gazettes tend to present the imperial decisions in response to the proposals and memorials by high officials. This appears from descriptions found in original secondary sources, and concrete copies of surviving *tizou quanlu* and *tizou shijian*. For the Qianlong period, the *tizou shijian* was indeed the main source for the missionaries, and for the Yongzheng period it was the *tizou quanlu*. For all the reasons outlined above, this book discusses the Chinese gazette of the early and mid-Qing in its own right, hence avoiding the term *jingbao* and its equivalent *Peking Gazette*, which became the common denomination in Western literature.

Regarding the early European terms for the Chinese gazette, terms equivalent with *Peking Gazette* were almost never used in European texts before 1800 – only two exceptions could be found. In general, Europeans explaining the genre tended to translate the term rather than transcribe it. Examples of

---

6 On the early use of the term *jingbao* in the Yuan and Ming dynasties, see Kong Zhengyi & Chen Chen (2012).

7 Ge Gongzhen (1964), pp. 44–49; Britton (1976), pp. 11–12; Fang Hanqi (1992–1999), vol. 1, pp. 211–214; Fang Hanqi (2013), pp. 36–38; Shi Yuanyuan (2008), p. 78; Mittler (2004), pp. 187–188; Kong Zhengyi & Wang Shuchuan (2015a), pp. 99–100; Harris (2018), pp. 4–5; Mokros (2016), pp. 32–34.

transcriptions are *pao* (= *bao*)[8] and once *kin pao* (= *jingbao*),[9] but they were rarely used. When authors opted for a translation, they used denominations in different European languages:[10] *Gazetas* (Portuguese),[11] *Gazettae* (Latin),[12] *coninglijcke coura[n]ten* (Dutch),[13] *Stampa*,[14] *Gazzette* (Italian).[15] Likewise, in the French texts, which contain numerous references and therefore will predominate in this book, the common name is *Gazette*.[16] This name was settled on relatively early on and was also new in Europe.[17] It had originated in the late sixteenth or early seventeenth century in Venice, where sheets of news produced once a week were named after *gazetta*, a coin of small value then common in Venice for which they were bought.[18] One of the most common qualifications of these 'gazettes' in the missionaries' texts is that they are 'public gazettes': *publicis regni gazettis*,[19] *litteris publicis*,[20] *novis publicis*/

8 Letter by F. Verbiest (Beijing, 3 July 1680) to Francesco Saverio Filippucci, Provincial (Canton), in Golvers (2017), letter no. 38, p. 327.

9 Letter by Francesco Saverio Filippucci (Canton, 5 February 1688) to Ferdinand Verbiest (Beijing), in Golvers (2017), letter no. 127, p. 788.

10 F. Verbiest uses in one of his letters the term "gazettis nostris Europaeis," besides the generic denomination for contemporary newspapers (Letter by F. Verbiest (Beijing, 20 August 1670) to Philippe Couplet (Canton), in Golvers (2017), letter no. 19, p. 188).

11 Letter by F. Verbiest (Beijing, 1 January 1671) to Antonio de Gouveia, Vice-Provincial (Canton), in Golvers (2017), letter no. 23, p. 207; Letter by F. Verbiest (Beijing, 7 January 1684) to Francesco Saverio Filippucci (Canton), in Golvers (2017), letter no. 62, p. 527.

12 F. Verbiest, "Responsium Apologeticum" (Beijing, 1681), in Golvers (2017), letter no. 39bis, p. 377 (memorials).

13 Letter by Philippe Couplet (Canton, 1669) to Hendrick van Alckemade S.J. and Clement Verschoor S.J. (Amsterdam), Barten (1970), p. 113.

14 Letter by Christian Wolfgang Herdtrich (Canton, 23 November 1670) to Prospero Intorcetta, in Intorcetta, *Compendiosa narratione dello stato della missione Cinese* (1672), p. 117; *stampe*: P. Intorcetta, *Compendiosa narratione dello stato della missione Cinese* (1672), p. 70.

15 "Memorie della Cina del 1727 per la S. Congregazione di Propaganda Fide," AFP, SOCP: vol. 33 (dall'Anno 1727 al 1728), fol. 262r.

16 Early reference in Annual Letter of 1669 by Adrien Grelon (Canton, 10 November 1669), in Bosmans (1912), p. 53. Term used by Contancin: *LEC* (1729), vol. 19, pp. 266–267; *LEC* (1810–1811), vol. 21, p. 7; term also used by Amiot in his articles in *MCC* and by Bourgeois in the manuscript BnF, Bréquigny 10.

17 For a short overview of the origin of newspapers in Europe, see Pettegree (2014), esp. chapter 9; Blair & Fitzgerald (2015), pp. 256–258.

18 Voltaire, "Gazette," in *Encyclopédie*, vol. VII (1757), p. 534; see also: Voltaire, *Œuvres alphabétiques I* (*OCV* 33) (1987), pp. 113–114.

19 Letter by F. Verbiest (Beijing, 25 October 1684) to Nicolas Avancini (Vienna), in Golvers (2017), letter no. 76, p. 601.

20 de Rougemont, *Historia Tartaro-Sinica Nova* (1673), p. 316.

nova publica,[21] *Gazulis publicis*,[22] *gazetis publicis* (Latin),[23] *gazette publiche* (Italian),[24] *Gazettes publiques* (French).[25] If there is a link with Peking in the terminology, it is because they are "printed in Beijing": *Gazzette impresse in Pekino*,[26] *Gazulis publicis Pekini impressis*,[27] *Gazette qui s'imprime à Pékin*.[28] Only twice could the expression "gazettes of Beijing" (in plural) be found in missionaries' texts: *impresso nelle gazette di Pekino*[29] and *le gazzette di Pekino del presente anno*.[30] The one time that the term occurs in the singular, *la gazette de Pekin imprimée chaque jour*,[31] is a reformulation not by a missionary but by an Enlightenment thinker who clearly had no access to Chinese sources to translate a term such as *jingbao*.[32] Also *la gazette de la cour*[33] is used once, while the "gazette of the empire" (*la gazette de l'empire*,[34] *Gazettes de l'Empire*,[35] *la gazette du gouvernement intérieur de l'empire*[36]) is used a bit more regularly. The more common qualification is the link with China: *gazzette della Cina*,[37] *gazzette di Cina*,[38] *Gazette de la Chine*,[39] *les gazettes de la Chine*,[40] *les*

21 *Brevis relatio* (1701), p. 14b, in Standaert (2012), p. 429.
22 APF, SC, Indie orientali e Cina, vol. 18 (anno 1726), fol. 532r.
23 APF, SOCP: vol. 47 (dall'Anno 1748 al 1750), tomo primo, fol. 102r.
24 APF, SOCP: vol. 33 (dall'Anno 1727 al 1728), fols. 326v–327r.
25 *Description ... de la Chine* (1735), vol. 1, p. 547; vol 2, p. 11.
26 APF, SOCP: vol. 33 (dall'Anno 1727 al 1728), fol. 262r; see also fol. 326r.
27 APF, SC, Indie orientali e Cina, vol. 18 (anno 1726), fol. 532r.
28 *LEC* (1729), vol. 19, p. 270; *LEC* (1810–1811), vol. 21, p. 78; *MCC*, vol. 5, p. 39.
29 APF, SOCP: vol. 33 (dall'Anno 1727 al 1728), fol. 351v.
30 APF, SC, Indie orientali e Cina, vol. 19 (dal 1727 al 1728), fol. 717r.
31 Montesquieu, *Geographica* (2007), p. 214; it refers to *Description ... de la Chine* (1735), vol. 2, p. 43; which was based on *LEC* (1729), vol. 19, pp. 268–269; *LEC* (1810–1811), vol. 21, p. 77.
32 Montesquieu, *Geographica* (2007), p. 214; it refers to *Description ... de la Chine* (1735), vol. 2, p. 43.
33 Montesquieu, *Esprit des lois* (1849), pp. 160–161 (Livre XII, Chapitre VII: Du crime de lèse-majesté); Montesquieu, *The Spirit of Laws* (1777), vol. 1, pp. 249–250.
34 Voltaire, "Gazette," in *Encyclopédie*, vol. VII (1757), p. 534; *MCC*, vol. 1, p. 11.
35 BnF, Bréquigny 10, p. 1. The first line refers to "Les Gazettes de Chine"; in the text they are usually referred to as "Gazette." Letter of Bourgeois to Bertin (Beijing, 10 October 1788) in BnF, Bréquigny 2, fol. 209r also uses "gazettes de l'Empire."
36 Quesnay, "Despotisme de la Chine," *Éphémérides du citoyen, ou Chronique de l'esprit national* (1767): Tome IV.1, pp. 20–21; "Despotisme de la Chine" (1965), p. 597.
37 APF, SOCP: vol. 33 (dall'Anno 1727 al 1728), fol. 262r.
38 APF, SOCP: vol. 33 (dall'Anno 1727 al 1728), fol. 326r.
39 *LEC* (1728), vol. 18, pp. 434–435; *LEC* (1810–1811), vol. 20, pp. 301–302.
40 Voltaire, "Gazette," in *Encyclopédie*, vol. VII (1757), p. 534.

Gazettes de Chine,[41] *la gazette Chinoise*,[42] or *les gazettes chinoises*.[43] These are contrasted with the *Gazettes d'Europe*. It can be noticed that certainly in the eighteenth century, missionaries in China had regular access to these European newspapers and journals, especially those published in Holland (in Dutch or in French), and less frequently to those from France, Germany, Portugal, and England.[44] Yet, this subject is beyond the scope of this book.

In fact, missionaries were aware of the limitations of the use of a European term: as will be explained further, readers who are confronted with the term 'gazette' for what is produced in China automatically associate it with European gazettes, in which different credible and less credible news sources were indiscriminately mixed together. In China, on the other hand, the information came directly from the central government:

> ... at the mere word of gazette they hear, they [= the European Missionaries] imagine that it resembles certain gazettes of Europe, in which one puts or has put everything one wants, good and bad, without any distinction. Now, by reasoning thus on the gazette of China, they are strongly mistaken; for nothing is printed here which has not been presented to the Emperor, or which does not come from the Emperor himself.[45]

> The name of Gazettes, which we are accustomed to give them, might make you believe that they are almost similar to the Gazettes of Europe, in which the Composers bring pell-mell all that they think about to insert.[46]

These warnings by eighteenth-century authors are probably still valid for twenty-first century readers. Conscious of the limitations that are linked to using a European term, this book uses the term 'gazette' or 'Chinese gazette' as a contrast to the European one.

---

41 BnF, Bréquigny 10, p. 1; Letter of Bourgeois to Bertin (Beijing, 10 October 1788): BnF, Bréquigny 2, fol. 209r.

42 *LEC* (1728), vol. 18, pp. 440–441; *LEC* (1810–1811), vol. 20, pp. 304–305.

43 Letter of Amiot to Bertin (Beijing, 16 September 1779): Inst. 1516, p. 236, fol. 1v.

44 On the spread of European newspapers and journals in the China mission, see Golvers (2015), n. 5.4.23, pp. 461ff, esp. pp. 469–473.

45 *LEC* (1729), vol. 19, pp. 267–269; *LEC* (1810–1811), vol. 21, pp. 76–77.

46 *MCC*, vol. 14, p. 524: Extrait d'une lettre de M. Amiot, Missionnaire, Ecrite de Péking, le 25 Janvier 1787 (Extract from a letter by Mr. Amiot, Missionary, Written from Peking, 25 January 1787).

Short Historiography of the Study of the Chinese Gazette of the Early and Mid-Qing Dynasty

If the study of the Chinese gazette based on European sources of the seventeenth and eighteenth century is relatively new, it still follows the traces of the study of this gazette that has already a much longer history.

In a short overview of the historiography of the study of the Chinese gazette, Emily Mokros has shown that "interest in the gazettes of late imperial China comes from three directions: the history of the press, the history of the state, and the history of information in society."[47] In fact, these three approaches also represent to a certain extent a chronology. The first direction originated with seminal works in the 1920s and 1930s and placed the gazette within the history of journalism, viewing it as a predecessor of the modern newspaper.[48] Until the 1990s and early 2000s, most descriptions of the gazette can be found in such works, both in Chinese and Western languages, even if these do not necessarily adopt the same teleological approach.[49] The second, more recent direction frames the gazette as an instrument of bureaucratic administration. With studies analysing the standardisation, centralisation, and regularisation of the official communication from as early as the Song dynasty, this approach helps to understand the role of the gazette in the imperial bureaucracy as a means to integrate the empire and give the central government control over the circulation of information about official documents.[50] The third, even more recent direction focuses on the gazette as a medium for the circulation of information in society. While mining private writings, novels, and plays, this scholarship investigates the wider readership and demonstrates the cultural and social function of the gazette and its role in connecting the populace to state politics.[51]

Though there is an increasing number of publications on the gazette in the Song, Ming, and early Qing, most publications concern the developments in

---

47 Mokros (2016), pp. 14–21; quotation from p. 20; for a good review article of Chinese publications before 2000, see Ma Ting (2002); and for a review article of mainly recent mainland publications, see Gu Keyong 顾克勇 & Ding Xin 丁鑫 (2016).

48 Ge Gongzhen 戈公振, *Zhongguo baoxue shi* 中國報學史, Shanghai: Commercial Press, 1927 (reprint 1928 and 1931); Roswell S. Britton, *The Chinese Periodical Press, 1800–1912*, Shanghai: Kelly & Walsh, 1933.

49 E.g. Yin Yungong (1990); Fang Hanqi (1992–1999), vol. 1; Mittler (2004), pp. 173–242; Fang Hanqi (2013), chap. 1.

50 E.g. De Weerdt (2015), chap. two: "Court Gazettes and Short Reports," pp. 76–104 (earlier version, see De Weerdt (2009)). For an example of the Qing, see Yin Qing (2018).

51 An example about late Ming times, that will also be quoted in the conclusion, is Wang Hung-tai (2009) and (2010).

the late Qing (nineteenth century). This is largely due to the availability of primary sources in Chinese and in English. A clear example is the primary source reader compiled by Lane J. Harris, *The Peking Gazette: A Reader in Nineteenth-Century Chinese History* (2018). This source reader has a companion database, "Translations of the Peking Gazette Online," which is a comprehensive database of approximately 8,500 pages of English-language renderings of official edicts and memorials from the Qing dynasty between 1799 and 1912.[52]

On the whole, information about the gazette before 1800 in general, and of the gazette during the early and mid-Qing in particular, remains limited, especially in Western languages. *Zhongguo xinwen shiye tongshi* 中国新闻事业通史 (3 vols., 1992–1999), the comprehensive work on the history of journalism in China (also partially translated into English), edited by one of the well-known Chinese historians of Chinese newspapers, Fang Hanqi 方汉奇, contains a general overview of the news genres, institutions, and activities in the early and mid-Qing dynasty and considers them mainly as a continuation of the Ming activities.[53] His student, Shi Yuanyuan 史媛媛, is the first and thus far only researcher to have devoted a monograph to the topic of circulation of news specifically in the early and mid-Qing (Ph.D. obtained at Renmin University in 2003 and published in 2008). By relying on administrative texts, she was able to reconstruct a much more precise view of the complex communication circuit between the office of transmission, the Six Offices of Scrutiny, and the provincial courier superintendents.[54] The contents of the gazette, mainly from the Kangxi and Yongzheng period, are reconstructed on the basis of official sources (memorials which refer to the reading of the *dibao*) and private sources.[55] Another scholar with a Ph.D. on the *dibao* in the Qing is Kong Zhengyi 孔正毅 (also obtained at Renmin University in 2011).[56] He has co-authored several publications on the different types of *dibao* and the distribution system of the *dibao* in the Qing (and Ming).[57] He also co-authored the first systematic review of the copies remaining from before 1800.[58] Taking an intercultural approach, Ding Chennan 丁晨楠 (Ph.D. degree at Yonsei

52 BrillOnline Primary Sources: https://primarysources.brillonline.com/browse/the-peking-gazette.
53 Fang Hanqi (1992–1999), vol. 1, chap. 1, esp. on the Ming (pp. 121–187) and the Qing (pp. 188–245); Fan Hanqi (2000), vol. 1, pp. 173–242; Fang Hanqi (2013), chap. 1.
54 See esp. Shi Yuanyuan (2008), chap. 3, sections 2–3.
55 Shi Yuanyuan (2008), chap. 3, section 4.
56 Kong Zhengyi, *Qingdai dibao yanjiu* 清代邸报研究, Ph.D. diss. Zhongguo renmin daxue Qingshi yanjiusuo 中国人民大学清史研究所, 2011.
57 Kong Zhengyi & Wang Shuchuan (2015a) and (2015b).
58 Kong Zhengyi & Zhang Lu (2014).

University in 2018) collected much new information in her dissertation, which investigates how Korean envoys to China gathered intelligence on the basis of gazettes during the Ming and early and mid-Qing dynasties.[59]

Finally, the latest English publication in the field, Emily Mokros' *The Peking Gazette in Late Imperial China: State News and Political Authority*, is the revised version of her Ph.D. dissertation "Communication, Empire, and Authority in the Qing Gazette." As a result of additional research, her book contains quite a bit more on the pre-1800 circumstances of the gazette than her dissertation did. Mokros' research positions itself at the intersection of the three directions she described (history of the press, the state, and information in society), and offers a chronology of policy, publishing, and reception. Throughout, she remains attentive to both continuities and changes in the political, administrative, and cultural role of gazettes during the entire Qing dynasty.[60] She particularly investigates the role of the gazettes as a medium for disseminating "state news" within a coherent "information policy" of the Qing administration. Central in this policy was the institution of the Qing "information order," "the set of communications pathways by which social intelligence was gathered, organized, and disseminated by the Qing state." This information policy valued both control and publicity, secrecy and transparency. Mokros refers to the latter as a "curated transparency," put in practice through the widespread circulation of selected imperial documents among the bureaucracy. The court and the members of the central bureaucracy shared the idea that this transparency could improve the administrative efficiency and moral coherence of the bureaucracy, and could even be used as an instrument for disciplining officials. In general, in her analysis, the gazettes advanced the Qing state's "documentary authority," in the sense that "the state constructed rules concerning the redaction, filing, release to or restriction from public view, with an eye toward protecting and enhancing its perceived authority."[61] As will appear from the European sources presented in this book, the missionaries' interpretations of the gazette communicate insights into its role and significance that are very similar to those represented by these notions, despite relying on a different vocabulary.

Adding on to this existing scholarship, this book investigates the descriptions of and quotations from the gazette in European sources of the seventeenth and eighteenth centuries. Aside from manuscript sources, mainly kept in Paris and Rome, there are some relevant printed collections that were compiled in the eighteenth century. Given the shift in interest from European to Chinese

59 Ding Chennan (2018).
60 Mokros (2016), p. 21; Mokros (2021), p. 4.
61 See especially Mokros (2021), pp. 12–17.

sources in the study of the Sino-European intercultural contacts of that time (a shift that took place in the 1970s and 1980s), basic research on these collections still often depends on solid publications from the 1960s and early 1970s. These collections, however, have drawn new interest recently because they appear to contain an enormous wealth of information on Chinese and Manchu primary sources that they quote or translate. At a time when the complementarity of European and Chinese/Manchu sources is increasingly valued, they shed a new light not only on the European knowledge about the Qing but also on the Chinese/Manchu sources themselves.[62]

Three eighteenth century French sources, which informed Europe about China at that time, will be quoted in this book. First, *Description géographique, historique, chronologique, politique, et physique de l'empire de la Chine et de la Tartarie chinoise*, which is the best known of the three. It was compiled by Jean-Baptiste Du Halde (1674–1743) and published for the first time in 1735. Researchers can benefit from the rich study by Isabelle Landry-Deron (2002), who identified many of the Chinese sources that are at the origin of the translations in Du Halde's compilation.[63] Recent publications include also a study about the French Jesuits' work of translation itself by Wu Huiyi 吴蕙仪.[64] Second, this book also quotes from the famous collection *Lettres édifiantes et curieuses*, of which Du Halde was also one of the editors. It consists of 34 volumes published between 1702 and 1776, in which 98 of the 259 reproduced letters were sent by missionaries from China.[65] Joseph Dehergne (1903–1990) already pleaded for a critical edition of these letters in 1973, around the time when the last selected publication of China letters appeared with an introduction by Isabelle and Jean-Louis Vissière in 1979.[66] Especially noteworthy are the modern translations in Asian languages. Besides a translation of the China letters into Modern Chinese in the 1990s, there is an earlier annotated translation into Japanese by Yazawa Toshihiko 矢澤利彥 (1914–2008), which appeared in the 1970s and which corresponds to a certain extent to the appeal made by Dehergne.[67] New interest for the textual history of the *Lettres* appears in a recent study by Sarah Barthélemy (2019). She studied its editorial enterprise

62 In the CCT-database (Ad Dudink and Nicolas Standaert, Chinese Christian Texts Database: http://www.arts.kuleuven.be/sinology/cct), one will find many identifications of the Chinese sources that are at the origin of these European translations or paraphrases.

63 Landry-Deron (2002); for other identifications that have been made since then by Frédéric Obringer, by Wu Huiyi, and by Shan Lin 單琳 & Han Qi 韩琦, see CCT-database.

64 Wu Huiyi (2017).

65 Barthélemy (2019), p. 229.

66 Dehergne made the plea in 1973, but his text was published in 1977; Vissière & Vissière (1979).

67 These translations rearrange the letters thematically. This book uses the volume on 'society,' see Yazawa (1973). For the correspondence between these letters and the original

and identified the remaining original manuscript letters.[68] Finally, probably most neglected of the three sources is the monumental collection *Mémoires concernant l'histoire, les sciences, les arts, les moeurs, les usages, &c. des Chinois, par les missionnaires de Pékin* (17 vols.: 15 vols.: 1776–1791; 2 vols.: 1814). After Dehergne's detailed table of contents with identification of the European primary sources,[69] the work as such has only recently received some interest in a study on its illustrations by Lee Chao Ying 李招瑩,[70] and specific sections of the collection have also been the subject of new studies.

Regarding the presence of the Chinese gazette in these European sources, there has been only a limited number of publications. In 2015, Wu Boya 吴伯娅 wrote an article in Chinese on Cyr Contancin's (1670–1732) letters on the Chinese gazette published in *Lettres édifiantes et curieuses*.[71] In a short section on the "Qing *dibao* in the eyes of eighteenth-century Europeans," Shi Yuanyuan only makes reference to the reception by François Quesnay (1694–1774), and so did a short article by Yin Yungong 尹韵公 (already in 1993).[72] Noël Golvers also found scattered references in various European sources.[73] In Japanese, on the other hand, the theme of the Qing gazette is present in the notes of the Japanese translation of Contancin's letters by Yazawa for the Yongzheng period.[74] In her rich and extensive study of Joseph-Marie Amiot (1718–1793), Nii Yōko 新居洋子 is the first one to discuss the use of gazettes by Amiot during the Qianlong period, making use of *Mémoires concernant les Chinois*.[75] In her recent book on the Peking Gazette in late imperial China, Emily Mokros included a chapter on the Qing gazette going abroad, which refers to many of the sources that will be discussed in more detail in this book.[76]

French version (in different editions), as well as with the early Italian, Spanish, and German translations, see CCT-database.

68 Barthélemy (2019).

69 Dehergne (1983); this is to a certain extent a follow-up of his thesis on the "two Chinese of Bertin" (1965), about two Chinese who contributed to the *Mémoires concernant les Chinois*.

70 Lee Chao Ying (2016).

71 There is also a short reference in an earlier article on the *Peking Gazette* by Yin Wenjuan (2005).

72 Shi Yuanyuan (2008), pp. 80–82; Yin Yungong (1993).

73 Golvers (2015), (2016), and (2017).

74 Yazawa Toshihiko (1973). Notwithstanding what the title seems to indicate, the article by Koito Chūgo (1978) is not really devoted to this topic.

75 See Nii Yōko (2011) and her book on the translation of China by Amiot (2017), chap. 6; see also her notes to chap. 4 to her revised and annotated edition of Goto Sueo, *Kenryu tei den* 乾隆帝伝 (2016; originally 1942).

76 Mokros (2021), pp. 116–128.

Another development is the study of China in the European newspapers. There have been initial studies on the presence of the fall of the Ming, the Manchu conquest, and the Chinese Rites Controversy in Dutch newspapers and other media of the late seventeenth and early eighteenth century by Edwin J. Van Kley, Paize Keulemans, and Trude Dijkstra.[77] Ma Li 马丽 investigated the "Chinese art of governing" in French-language periodicals from 1750 to 1789.[78] This fascinating research on the reception history, however, is beyond the scope of this publication. Some reference will be made to it, but it would be worthwhile to investigate into further detail the presence of information from the Chinese gazettes in European gazettes at that time.

Quasi Absence of Chinese Copies of the Gazette from the Early and Mid-Qing Dynasty

One of the major problems in the study of the gazette in the early and mid-Qing, in contradistinction with the late Qing, is the quasi absence of the most important Chinese primary sources, more precisely issues of the Chinese gazette. What the secondary publications share, is that they are not based on original or translated copies of the *dibao* because these are extremely scarce for the time before 1800. Concerning the period of the early and mid-Qing, the situation is as follows. For the Kangxi period, no *dibao* copy is preserved except for a five-page list of successful candidates at the *jinshi* 進士 examination in 1697 (KX36).[79] For the Yongzheng reign, so far around four documents that carry on their covers an etiquette with the title *dibao* (each likely covering more than one day) could be identified. However, there is no indication of the place where these documents might be preserved and to what extent they are copies of the daily published gazettes.[80] Moreover, there exists one known copy of the *tizou quanlu* 題奏全錄, which is a list of short references to memorials and

77 Van Kley (1973); Keulemans (2015) on the fall of the Ming; Dijkstra (2016) on the Chinese Rites Controversy; and Dijkstra (2017) on the Tournon legation (1705–1710).

78 Ma Li (2019): this work includes also multiple references to texts of Amiot in *Mémoires concernant les Chinois*.

79 "Cang jia tao de Kanxi shi *dibao*: Jilu shang bang jinshi xingming zhuzhi" 藏家淘得康熙时《邸报》：记录上榜进士姓名住址, web.archive.org/web/20210526091525/http://www.chinanews.com/cul/2014/08-22/6519158.shtml. It was discovered by Miao Shiming 苗世明. It carries in the fish tail margin on the outside of the page the text *timing beilu* 題名碑錄. It is not entirely clear whether this is a *dibao* in the strict sense of the word, or rather a supplement to it.

80 For further details, see the chapter on the Yongzheng era.

their respective imperial decisions.[81] As confirmed by Korean sources, '*tizou quanlu*' is a title under which the Chinese gazette appeared at that time. For the Qianlong period, there are only two identified copies of *dibao* from the 1760s and possibly still a few more unidentified copies in a private collection.[82] However, there are more copies of the *tizou shijian* 題奏事件, which, according to Martin Heijdra, in origin possibly belonged to a same set that was dispersed in the early twentieth century and ended up in different libraries around the world.[83] In total, they represent c. 384 days of gazette between 1770 (QL35) and 1778 (QL42).[84] In addition, ten more days of *tizou shijian* have been preserved for the years 1778–1779 (QL43–QL44). These were sent as samples by Jean Joseph-Marie Amiot (1718–1793) to France.[85] This adds up to around 394 days, which is just over one year and one month in a reign that lasted sixty years. Moreover, there is a manuscript in Korea entitled *Hwanbo sanjeol* 環報删節, which contains a selective transcript of the Chinese gazette of nearly one year: from Joseon Yeongjo 朝鮮英祖 (Qianlong 25 = 14 March 1760 to 31 January 1761), covering 181 different days.[86]

The material presented in this reader considerably expands these resources, though it is in translation. There exists a quasi-full manuscript translation of sixty-four days of the *tizou shijian* (February–April 1788 (QL53)) by François Bourgeois (1723–1792). Though it is difficult to count the exact number of *dibao* that the other translations or long translated excerpts represent, they may well constitute an additional 130 days (c. fifty from the Yongzheng reign 1723–1728 (YZ1–YZ6) and c. eighty from the Qianlong reign 1777–1787 (QL42–QL52)). In total, this amounts to over 180 days of new material about the Chinese gazette.

81 YZ9/8/18 (18 September 1731): preserved in Österreichische Nationalbibliothek, Vienna: Sin. 251; for further details, see the chapter on the Yongzheng era.

82 Kong Zhengyi & Zhang Lu (2014), pp. 171–172:
QL26/8/23 (21 September 1761): in private collection Anhui Hefei 安徽合肥 Runze dongfang laobao fang 润泽东方老报馆 (with the title *Qianlong jingbao* 乾隆京報 but not clear whether this is original)
QL32/11/23 (12 January 1768): at an auction of Zhongguo shudian 中国书店挂拍: (with the title *Qianlong jingbao* 乾隆京報 but not clear whether this is original)
The unidentified copies belong to the collection of Fang Hanqi 方汉奇 (acquired in 1946 and 1950).

83 I thank Martin Heijdra (Princeton) for pointing out the importance of the *tizou shijian*. For the different libraries with the corresponding dates, see the chapter on the Qianlong era and the "Guide to the sources" at the end of this book.

84 In addition there are still 31 days for the year 1801 (JQ6).

85 In France: Bibliothèque nationale de France: BnF, Chinois 2216. The first references to these *tizou shijian* can be found in Britton (1976; originally 1933), plates 2–3.

86 Ding Chennan (2018), pp. 144–154. For further details, see the chapter on the Qianlong era.

Except for the ten days of the Qianlong period for which the original *tizou shijian* has been preserved, and the c. ten days of the Yongzheng period for which the Chinese transcribed excerpts were added to the Italian or Latin translations, the other translations can quite evidently not be directly compared with the original gazettes, which appear to be lost. Still, the Chinese source can be searched for in order to link the available translations to original sources. A first step in this search was usually to find the related passage in the full-search database of the *Qing shilu* 清實錄 (Qing veritable records) on the basis of a few indications in the translated text, being well aware that the *Qing shilu* itself is not the primary source of the gazette.[87] This detailed daily chronicle of affairs of state was compiled by Qing court historians, consulting a wide variety of original documents, long after their publication in the gazette. Moreover, it was never meant to be published, but was intended solely for consultation by the emperor and his ministers. As it did not include all memorials and edicts, it was also necessarily a selection.[88] Still, this search was helpful in identifying basic information about events described by the missionaries, as well as the texts in the gazettes on which they had based themselves. Once the event, date, and names of officials were identified, an attempt was made to find the information in original sources closer to the texts on which the gazettes were based. One of these sources is the *Shangyu dang* 上諭檔 (Record book of imperial edicts), a record book of the Grand Council in which imperial edicts were copied.[89] A second source is the *Qijuzhu* 起居注 (Court diaries), which not only includes records on the daily activities taking place in the court, but also records of imperial decrees and memorials.[90] These sources, however, do not always record the original memorials of officials, since they are often summarized in the imperial decision. More sporadically, references to these memorials

---

87 *Qing shilu* 清實錄 (1982). Scripta Sinica: Hanji dianzi wenxian 漢籍電子文獻, Academia Sinica. Other databases that were used are: (Wenyuange) Siku quanshu (文淵閣) 四庫全書; Zhongguo fangzhi ku 中國方志庫; Zhongguo jiben guji ku 中國基本古籍庫; Diaolong Full-text Database of Chinese & Japanese Ancient Books 雕龙中日古籍全文检索数据库; CCT-Database (Ad Dudink and Nicolas Standaert, Chinese Christian Texts Database).

88 Elliott (2009), pp. 179–180; Wilkinson (2018), pp. 928–929.

89 *Qianlong chao shangyu dang* 乾隆朝上諭檔 (2008). For the Yongzheng period there are various sources: *Yongzheng chao hanwen yuzhi huibian* 雍正朝漢文諭旨匯編 (1999); *Shizong xianhuangdi shangyu baqi* 世宗憲皇帝上諭八旗 (1731); *Shizong xianhuangdi shangyu neige* 世宗憲皇帝上諭內閣 (1731); *Shizong xianhuangdi shengxun* 世宗憲皇帝聖訓 (1744); *Shizong xianhuangdi zhupi yuzhi* 世宗憲皇帝硃批諭旨 (1738). Wilkinson (2018), pp. 922–923.

90 *Qianlong di qijuzhu* 乾隆帝起居注 (2002); *Yongzheng chao qijuzhu ce* 雍正朝起居注冊 (1993). Wilkinson (2018), p. 928.

could be found in the collections from the Ming-Qing archives.[91] In case no reference was found, the record registers of the Grand Council (as they come at hand) (*Junjichu suishou dengji dang* 軍機處隨手登記檔) were consulted. These registers list all memorials received and edits or orders sent out during the Qianlong period, usually with a brief summary of the contents.[92] In certain cases sources were found in local gazetteers (*difangzhi* 地方志) or private jottings (*biji* 筆記). Other modern chronologies were occasionally consulted, as well as reference works helpful for the identification of names and functions.[93] In this way the content of the Chinese gazettes was to a certain extent "reconstructed." All the references in the French and Italian texts and in the Chinese sources can be found in the notes and the table at the end of this volume.

About This Book

This book focuses on European sources about the Chinese gazette from the early and mid-Qing dynasty. The choice for the early Qing rather than the late Ming is due to the fact that very little is known about the *dibao* in the late Ming. At that time, the imperial gazette was probably released on a daily basis and copied manually by copiers for distribution to the provinces, but apparently no physical copies have been preserved.[94] One has to rely on other sources for information about them, as is also the case with the scarce references related to Christianity. An early example concerns the news of the death of Matteo Ricci (1552–1610). It is a reference in the collected texts by the essayist and poet Yuan Zhongdao 袁中道 (1570–1627), who had made the acquaintance of Matteo Ricci. While residing in his native province of Huguang two months after Ricci's death (who died on 11 May 1610), Yuan wrote a note in his *biji*: "When I read the *bao*, I got [to see] the obituary of Western vassal Matteo Ricci," thus

91 *Ming Qing dang'an* 明清檔案 (1986–1995). Wilkinson (2018), p. 922.

92 *Qianlong chao junjichu suishou dengji dang* 乾隆朝軍機處隨手登記檔 (2000). Wilkinson (2018), p. 922.

93 These include *Qingshi biannian* 清史编年 (1985–2000): *di* 2–3 *juan* 第 2–3 卷: *Kangxi chao* 康熙朝 (*shang* 上, *xia* 下); *di* 4 *juan* 第 4 卷: *Yongzheng chao* 雍正朝; *di* 5–6 *juan* 第 5–6 卷: *Qianlong chao* 乾隆朝 (*shang* 上, *xia* 下); and further *Qingdai zhiguan nianbiao* 清代職官年表 (1980); *Qingdai renwu shengzu nianbiao* 清代人物生卒年表 (2005); *Ch'ing Administrative Terms* (1960); *A Dictionary of Official Titles in Imperial China* (1985).

94 The only gazettes to survive are copies (excerpts) of late Ming ones covering the period 1573.1 to 1617.6 (*Wanli dichao* 萬曆邸鈔) (copied version of *dibao* from the Wanli reign), Taipei: Guoli Zhongyang tushuguan, 1963. See Wilkinson (2018), p. 303; see also p. 944: until 1638, the gazettes were normally hand-copied. After that date, they were printed with movable type. Mittler (2004), p. 180 points out that the date of the printed version is a subject of debate.

indicating that Ricci's death was announced in the *dibao* or another type of gazette.[95] References to *dibao* also appear in the Chinese documents related to the anti-Christian incident in Nanjing in 1616–1617. They ascertain that memorials concerning this incident were published in the public gazette.[96] Direct references to *dibao* in late Ming European missionary sources are rare as well. Still, it seems that missionaries had direct or indirect access to *dibao*, as can be observed from the *Litterae Annuae*. These annual letters were sent to the Jesuit General in Rome and were sometimes re-edited and printed for a wider public. They normally contain a first chapter on the general political situation of the country that is informed by sources that go beyond the local level, possibly gazettes. This is a topic that needs more investigation.

Regarding the early Qing dynasty, by contrast, there are three types of European sources related to the gazettes: some documents inform the reader *about* gazettes without quoting them; other sources clearly refer to Chinese events, edicts, or memorials and *explicitly* mention that these are adopted from gazettes; finally, some do the same but without mentioning the gazettes, though they may well have been used as source. Since it is often difficult to prove the link with the gazettes for the latter group, here the focus is on the first two groups, which often appear in the same text. In this book, these sources are divided into three periods, which more or less correspond to the three reigns of the Kangxi 康熙 (1662–1722), Yongzheng 雍正 (1723–1735), and Qianlong 乾隆 (1736–1795) emperors. This intends in the first place to be a source book, leading the reader to the sources. While doing so, for each period two interrelated questions are answered: What do these sources tell us about the form, structure, and content of the gazette? And what do they tell us about the way the Europeans used and read them? As such, it hopes to shed an intercultural perspective on the Chinese gazette.

---

95 Yuan Zhongdao 袁中道, *Kexuezhai ji* 珂雪斋集 (2007), vol. 3, p. 1200: 看報，得西洋陪臣利瑪竇之訃.

96 Xu Guangqi 徐光啓, *Bianxue zhangshu* 辨學章疏 (A Memorial in Defense of [Christian] Learning), in *Xu Guangqi ji* 徐光啓集 (1984), vol. 2, pp. 431–437: p. 431: 臣見邸報： 南京禮部參西洋陪臣龐迪我等， 内言...: "Your servant has read in the *dibao* that the Nanjing Ministry of Rites has impeached the Western vassals Diego de Pantoja and others, stating that ..." (Kelly (1971), p. 294 (slightly adapted)); Shen Que 沈㴶, *Zai can yuanyi shu* 再參遠夷疏 (A Memorial Impeaching the Distant Barbarians [by Shen Que, vice-minister in the Nanjing Ministry of Rites]), in *Shengchao poxieji* 聖朝破邪集, *juan* 1, pp. 10b–14a: p. 12b; *Shengchao poxieji* (1996), p. 64: 更可駭者，臣疏向未發抄，頃七月初，纔有邸報: "It is even more surprising that your servant's memorial [impeaching the Western barbarians] was not issued for duplication until early in the seventh lunar month [about 12 August 1616] when it was published in the *dibao*." (Kelly (1971), p. 285 (The second memorial)).

The first chapter on the Kangxi period draws on scattered references in the letters of the missionaries to show how information from the gazettes was used for circulation of information within China, not only by Chinese officials but also by foreigners. Moreover, news was also sent to Europe, as is the case of the news about the Tancheng 郯城 earthquake (1668). These European sources disclose information that is no longer preserved in Chinese sources. The second chapter on the Yongzheng period first focuses on manuscripts in the Archivio Storico "de Propaganda Fide" in Rome, as they are the only Chinese transcripts of gazettes that have so far been discovered in Europe. These include the reports and translations by Domenico Perroni O.M.D. (1674–1729). They prove that the official gazette was an important and reliable source for reports about the state of affairs (of Christianity) in China. The next part of the chapter discusses in detail the letters by the Jesuit Cyr Contancin (1670–1732) (more than 300 pages in the printed version) as published in the well-known collection *Lettres édifiantes et curieuses*. One can prove that this was the main source for the ideas about the Chinese way of governing developed by Enlightenment thinkers such as Voltaire (1694–1778), Montesquieu (1689–1755), and Quesnay (1694–1774), as well as for several Swedish politicians who advocated the freedom of writing and the press. Their use of the gazette is subsequently discussed. The third chapter on the Qianlong period focuses on the large collection *Mémoires concernant ... les Chinois* (15 volumes), which contains many references to the gazette, mainly by Joseph-Marie Amiot (1718–1793), as well as by François Bourgeois (1723–1792), of whom also a manuscript is preserved that contains a full translation of two months of the gazette (now lost in the original Chinese version). In addition to a description of the text management in terms of selection and translation, and a general overview of the contents, this chapter analyses into depth the information about the *Siku quanshu* 四庫全書, the imperial book collection, that was communicated to Europe on the basis of reports in the gazettes. Finally, it demonstrates how the gazettes were interpreted as news in service of imperial truth and the public good, and how the European translations presented a certain view on the emperor and his art of governing. The conclusion links the analysis to present-day (Chinese) scholarship on the gazette and approaches the topic as a case of interconnected cultural history. It shows how the gazettes were not only read by the Chinese bureaucracy but reached a wider public beyond the strict literati network by the early Qing. This included Europeans in China, some of whom not only actively read the gazette, but also became writers and translators in a global information network. Through their translations of gazettes that were sent to Europe, it appears that information about China joined the global public much earlier than so far assumed.

CHAPTER 1

The Kangxi Period (1662–1722)

The Kangxi reign was the longest reign in late imperial China.[1] It is during this reign that the first significant number of European sources that refer to the Chinese gazette appeared, but they remain limited in number and are scattered. Moreover, they mainly date from the 1660s and the early 1670s, the earliest years of the Kangxi era. These texts originated in the particular context of the Chinese mission during these years. After an initially smooth transition to the Qing dynasty, these years were rather difficult for the Christian mission in China. The prospects for Christianity had improved considerably when the Jesuit missionary Johann Adam Schall von Bell (1592–1666) became head of the Imperial Astronomical Bureau (Qintianjian 欽天監) in 1645. In that capacity, he enjoyed the favour of the Shunzhi emperor (1644–1661). Lacking the necessary contacts with the Manchu elite, however, he became more vulnerable during the Oboi regency (1661–1669). He first came under fire in 1657, when one of the astronomers of the Muslim section of the Astronomical Bureau falsely accused Schall of having made faulty predictions. Next, starting in 1660, Yang Guangxian 楊光先 (1597–1669) attacked Schall in the name of Confucian orthodoxy. Yang succeeded in bringing a case against Schall to court in 1664, accusing him of deliberately choosing an inauspicious date for the funeral of a prince. The missionaries lost their case and were condemned together with their collaborators. As a result of this so-called "Calendar Case," only four Jesuits – Schall von Bell, Ferdinand Verbiest (1623–1688), Lodovico Buglio (1607–1682), and Gabriel de Magalhães (1610–1677) – were allowed to remain in Beijing. The other missionaries were exiled to Canton, where they remained during the period 1665–1671.[2] Still, the Beijing and Canton missionaries remained in epistolary contact with each other and sent letters and reports to Europe, some of which were published. Aside from Ferdinand Verbiest in Beijing, the authors of these publications were: Philippe Couplet (1622–1693), Adrien Grelon (1618–1696), Prospero Intorcetta (1625–1696), Christian Wolfgang Herdtrich (1625–1684), and François de Rougemont (1624–1676), who all were in exile in Canton in the period 1665–1671; and Francesco Saverio Filippucci (1632–1692), who was in Canton in the subsequent years.[3]

1 For a general overview of the Kangxi reign in English, see Spence (2002).

2 See Ad Dudink, "Opponents," in *HCC*, pp. 513–515.

3 For basic biographical references of these and other Jesuits mentioned in this book, see Dehergne (1973) and Pfister (1932–1934).

DOI:10.1163/9789004505001_003

When these missionaries refer to the gazette in their letters and reports, they usually describe it as coming forth from the court, printed in Beijing, and distributed all over the country.[4] It is precisely because of the gazette's wide circulation that the Jesuits who were exiled in Canton could remain informed about events in Beijing and other places, even at times when communication was scarce with the other missionaries left in Beijing. The existence of such internal communication and the missionaries' usage of the gazettes appear from scattered references in their letters, but also from information that was sent to Europe, including reports about the major earthquake of Tancheng 郯城. Moreover, there are some indications of the missionaries' contacts with the publishers of the gazettes.

1.1 Scattered References

The relevant letters by the missionaries do not provide a systematic presentation of the Chinese gazette, but they do contain scattered references to it. These show that the missionaries looked to the gazette as a source of official news, such as the appointment of officials to new positions.[5] Examples include the appointment of new *tianwensheng* 天文生 (junior members) in the Astronomical Bureau, where the Jesuits had been active themselves. In a letter to Antonio de Gouveia, Vice-Provincial in Canton, Ferdinand Verbiest refers to these appointments and tells de Gouveia that "he will be able to know about it in the gazettes."[6] A few years later, in a letter to Francesco Saverio Filippucci, Provincial in Canton, Verbiest mentions that "he saw in the pao [= *bao* 報] the name of the new *anchashi* 按察使 (Surveillance Commissioner)

---

4 See e.g. letter by Philippe Couplet (Canton, 1669) to Hendrick van Alckemade S.J. and Clement Verschoor S.J. (Amsterdam), in Barten (1970), pp. 112–113: "… the story of these signs, which came fresh from the court, printed in the royal gazettes, which are spread throughout all provinces and lands." See also: Letter by Christian Wolfgang Herdtrich (Canton, 23 November 1670) to Prospero Intorcetta, in Intorcetta, *Compendiosa narratione dello stato della missione Cinese* (1672), p. 70: "and spread throughout the Empire"; Intorcetta, *Compendiosa narratione dello stato della missione Cinese* (1672), p. 117: "and disseminated throughout the Empire."

5 Martino Martini (1614–1661), in his *Novus atlas Sinensis* (Amsterdam: Joan Blaeu, 1655: preface p. 12), mentions that "every three months a book is published in which are listed the names [of officials], their place of origin, office and degree, which is clearly necessary and convenient for those who, according to Chinese custom, want to go to friends for a courtesy visit or, if they have obtained a higher rank, to congratulate them by letter." This was identified by G. Bertuccioli as a reference to the *jingbao* (Martini (2002), p. 313 n. 70). However, it refers instead to the lists of officeholders (*jinshen lu* 縉紳錄) that were published every three months (see Wilkinson (2018), 66.4.4. p. 936; see also chapter three of this book).

6 Letter by F. Verbiest (Beijing, 1 January 1671) to Antonio de Gouveia, Vice-Provincial (Canton), in Golvers (2017), letter no. 23, p. 207.

of Guangdong."[7] News about appointments or promotions also concerned the missionaries themselves. For instance, in Ferdinand Verbiest's *Cixian wenda* 辭銜問答 (Dialogue [between Ferdinand Verbiest and two of his students] concerning the refusal of a promotion, 1678), which was published when the exile was lifted, one finds the following short reference:

> 康熙十七年十月初八日，本監門人來謁云:今日午右，閱邸報，内列先生辭銜一疏

> On KX7/10/8 (= 21 November 1678), disciples in our office called upon me saying: "Today at noon, while reading the *dibao*, [we saw] in it your demand refusing a promotion."[8]

As another example, gazettes also played a role in informing the missionaries of the revision of the court case in the above-mentioned Johann Adam Schall von Bell – Yang Guangxian controversy, initiated at the request of the Ministry of Rites (Libu 禮部) in 1668. As reported by Adrien Grelon, the missionaries in Canton learned the outcome of this case through the gazette, rather than through their communication with other missionaries:

> (…) here is sad news that we received from the court, not through the letters of our Fathers (since it is already a long time that we did not receive any) but through the gazette.[9]

Finally, gazettes were not only relied on for news that was related to the missionaries themselves. For instance, in a letter to Intorcetta, Christian Wolfgang Herdtrich cites the gazette as a source on the emperor's response to a letter sent by King of Portugal Afonso VI (1643–r. 1656–1683) and transmitted to the Chinese court by the Portuguese Embassy led by Manuel de Saldanha (which arrived in Beijing 30 June 1670).[10]

---

7 Letter of F. Verbiest (Beijing, 3 July 1680) to Francesco Saverio Filippucci, Provincial (Canton), in Golvers (2017), letter no. 38, p. 327: the letter mentions *ngan chu su Quam hun* which may be a corruption of *ngan cha su Quam tum* (Golvers (2017), p. 327 n. 935). It remains difficult to identify who this could be, as there was no change of *anchashi* in Guangdong in 1680 (or 1679); see *Qingdai zhiguan nianbiao*, vol. 3, p. 2000.

8 ARSI: Jap. Sin. II, 156, see CCT ARSI, vol. 12, pp. 369–378: p. 371. With thanks to Chen Tuo for this reference.

9 Annual Letter of 1669 by Adrien Grelon (Canton, 10 November 1669), in Bosmans (1912), p. 53.

10 Letter by Christian Wolfgang Herdtrich (Canton, 23 November 1670) to Prospero Intorcetta, in Intorcetta, *Compendiosa narratione dello stato della missione Cinese* (1672), p. 115ff.

These subjects, such as appointments, decisions provided by the six ministries, and imperial edicts, belong to the regular topics included in the gazette.[11] The examples mentioned above, quoted from various Jesuit letters, illustrate that the authors not only had access to the information contained in the gazettes, but were also familiar enough with them to actively share information from the gazettes with each other.

1.2 The Tancheng 郯城 Earthquake

The following section examines three documents (by Couplet, Intorcetta, and de Rougemont) which together present an interesting case study on the content and use of the gazettes. The documents in question report on the well-known earthquake that occurred in Shandong on KX7/6/17 (= 25 July 1668), and the ominous events that accompanied it. Sometimes called the Tancheng 郯城 earthquake, it had an estimated magnitude of 8.5 on the Richter scale.[12] It was one of the most damaging earthquakes in Chinese late imperial history, with possibly more than 50.000 casualties.[13] It not only led to the destruction of buildings and houses, but also to the collapse of mountains, fissures of rocks, and cleaving of the earth accompanied by floods of mud, the results of which can still be seen in the natural environment today.

Three Jesuit documents report about these disasters and the locations in which they occurred. The first document is a description of the earthquake included in François de Rougemont's *Historia Tartaro-Sinica Nova* (New Tartar-Chinese History), which is an eyewitness report of the Manchu conquest and the subsequent first decades of Qing rule. The text is dated 16 December 1668 in Canton and was published in Leuven in 1673.[14] The second document is a letter in Dutch by Philippe Couplet (also written in Canton, 1669) to Hendrick van Alckemade and Clement Verschoor, two Jesuits in Amsterdam. In this letter, Couplet reports on the past year, including the earthquake.[15] The third

11 Cf. Fang Hanqi (1992–1999), vol. 1, p. 81ff. (Song); p. 134ff. (Ming); p. 192 (Qing).

12 Zhou Cuiying, e.a., "Fault Plane Parameters of Tancheng M8½ Earthquake on the Basis of Present-day Seismological Data," *Earthquake Science* 23 (2010), pp. 567–576.

13 Baidu: 郯城地震, web.archive.org/web/20210526124019/https://baike.baidu.com/item/%E9%83%AF%E5%9F%8E%E5%9C%B0%E9%9C%87/4051449?fromtitle=%E9%83%AF%E5%9F%8E%E5%A4%A7%E5%9C%B0%E9%9C%87&fromid=9655620.

14 de Rougemont (1673), pp. 316–327.

15 See modern transcript in Barten (1970), pp. 112–116. In fact, the source used by Barten was already a transcript of the original letter, made by the Dutch East Asian Company and preserved in The Hague: Rijksarchief, Koloniaal Archief 1162, fols 1225ff.; see Barten, p. 90 n.1.

document is a report that Prospero Intorcetta wrote for the Cardinals of the Congregation of the Propaganda Fide, signed in Rome 18 April 1671. Like de Rougemont and Couplet, Intorcetta was one of the missionaries exiled to Canton, and in 1668 he had been sent back to Europe to report about the state of the Chinese mission. The Italian translation of his text was published as *Compendiosa narratione dello stato della missione Cinese comincia[n]do dall'anno 1581. fino al 1669* (Compendious narration of the state of the Chinese mission starting from the year 1581 until 1669) (Roma: Francesco Tizzoni, 1672).[16]

Given the similarities in the details provided in the three texts, one can assert with relative certainty that the authors based themselves on the same sources, but adapted them with their own characteristics.[17] Aside from describing the damage done by the earthquake, they also mention the ominous events that accompanied it: the enormous noise, the bells of monasteries that started to sound by themselves (bells often not having a clapper), the continuous crowing of cocks and barking of dogs.[18] There was also the reported appearance of a dragon in Zhangdefu 彰德府, Wu'anxian 武安縣 (Henan),[19] and the mysterious discovery of two stones with enigmatic texts – one of which was found at the Lugou bridge 蘆溝橋.[20]

As an illustration of the contents of these documents, a full translation of the Dutch letter by Couplet is included below. It was chosen because, out of the three, Couplet's text provides the longest report about the earthquake itself. Couplet starts with a general remark on the "terrible signs in heaven and on earth" by which "the omnipotent God continues to show his anger and

---

16 Intorcetta (1672), pp. 59–74. The first part of the report is signed in Rome 18 April 1671 (p. 34); the second part, to which the narration of the earthquake belongs, is dated 25 January 1672 (p. 76).

17 Intorcetta certainly had access to the text by de Rougemont, since he brought the manuscript to Europe (Golvers (2016), p. 324).

18 Barten (1970), pp. 113–114; Intorcetta (1672), pp. 61–64; de Rougemont (1673), pp. 317–318.

19 Intorcetta (1672), p. 66ff: Zhangdefu (Henan), 25 July 1668 (KX7/6/17 instead of 27). Intorcetta writes that it was first mentioned in private letters and then spread through all the provinces. It was also referred to by Domingo Sarpetri OP (1623–1683) and Antonio de Santa Maria Caballero (1602–1669) in a letter to the Sacred Congregation of Propaganda Fide (Canton, 9 November 1668); Barten (1970), p. 115: Couplet mentions that according to the custom the high officials of the province informed the court about it.

20 Barten (1970), pp. 114–115; Intorcetta (1672), p. 73 (with transcription of the Lugou bridge text); de Rougemont (1673), p. 322ff (with characters). This bridge, originally completed in 1192, was praised by Marco Polo (1254–1324), hence the Western name Marco Polo Bridge. It is the same bridge at which an incident took place in 1937 that marked the beginning of the Second Sino-Japanese War (1937–1945).

his justice."[21] In his eyes, this earthquake was directly related to the condemnation of Johann Adam Schall von Bell and other Jesuits and Christians, and to the exile of the missionaries to Canton. In addition, he points out that the "gazettes" (*couranten* in Dutch) are his main source.

> Meanwhile the omnipotent God continues to show his anger and his justice through terrible signs in heaven and on earth, in order to move these hearts and to make known that the Lord of Hosts should be honoured and feared. I will finish this letter with the story of these signs, which came fresh from the court, printed in the royal gazettes, which are spread throughout all provinces and lands; the content is as follows.

In the first part of his report Couplet describes what happened before and during the earthquake, as well as the damage that was caused in different places:

> On the seventeenth day of the sixth month of the current year 1668 – that is 25 July, day of St. James, there was a terrible earthquake in Xantum,[22] starting at 6 p.m. until 2 p.m. of the next day, the eighteenth day of the sixth month or 26 July. In the capital Cisnau[23] and six other cities, which are mentioned in the gazettes, the earth has cracked, and deep pits have opened. In fifteen other cities the earth trembled three times and once during the day of 26 July. In the city of Faigum[24] a white cloud erupted from the earth and climbed upwards with an enormous noise like drums, and the earth has sunk, making the noise like a thunder under one's feet. This lasted until 10 a.m. on 26 July. At 8 p.m. the noise had doubled. In six other cities,[25] even the drums and the clocks sounded, which nevertheless do not have a clapper here. Again on 25 July the earth has trembled three times from 8 p.m. onwards in eight other cities, and the next day it started again from 8 a.m. and continued the whole day. In four other cities,[26] at 8 p.m., while there was a pure clear sky and a clean moonlight without clouds, it suddenly started to rain. In the air people heard the beating of drums and when the rain stopped, it was followed by earthquakes. On

21 Barten (1970), p. 112; see also de Rougemont (1673), p. 315; Intorcetta (1672), pp. 58, 74.
22 = Shandong 山東.
23 = Ji'nan 濟南; Intorcetta (1672), p. 60: Ci-nan-fu. The romanisation got distorted in the course of transcription.
24 = Tai'an 泰安; Intorcetta (1672), p. 60: Tai-ngan-cheu; de Rougemont (1673), p. 316: Táignán.
25 According to Intorcetta (1672), p. 61 it was in Te-cheu = Dezhou 德州 and five other cities.
26 According to de Rougemont (1673), p. 317 this was in Ló-ngán = Luo'an 濼安 and three other cities.

the seventh day, i.e. 26 July, in the city of Liucheu,[27] at 8 p.m., the earth cracked with the noise of a thunder due to the earthquake. People saw the earth revolving from one side to the other. From these cracks in the earth rivers of sand erupted, flying through the air. Hereafter, due to the power of stones, an enormous amount of yellow water has flowed into the palace of the governor of the city. Eighteen people were killed in the palace of the field commander. And also two in the house of the one who takes care of the royal rice, the puiya. [And in addition] seven persons with two lower officials. Five other towns[28] have been damaged by the abundance of water, with all the places of residence flooded by four palms of water; the rib of mountain Mumjju[29] is torn in half from top to bottom. In four other towns[30] the earth started trembling on 25 July at 8 p.m. and it lasted without ceasing until 10 a.m. of 27 July. In two other cities[31] one heard in the air strange voices, without knowing from where they came. In four other towns people heard an enormous noise like a thunder. A cloud has risen so thick that it could be touched with the hand. The roosters crowed and the dogs barked and howled without ceasing. In the city of Pim-tu[32] the earth opened and from the opening dirty smelly water spouted out. In four other cities, more than a thousand people were immediately overtaken and buried under the walls that fell to the ground. In all houses or palaces of officials, the public residences, all the towers, walls, and uncountable large and small houses [collapsed]. The people who have died are innumerable. The viceroy of the province of Xamtum has spent a large sum of money to bury the dead. The earthquake has also been felt in three other provinces, namely Pekin, Nankin, Kiamsij,[33] with the collapse of many houses and the loss of many human lives.

In the town of Liucheu[34] the height or top of a mountain has been opened nine palms wide; from this opening a river of mud has sprung,

27 Intorcetta (1672), p. 62 has also Liu-cheu, should be Lüzhou but this place could not be found; if Liu is a misspelling for Kiu it could be Juzhou/xian 莒州/縣. In de Rougemont (1673), p. 317 it appears as Luí chéu = Leizhou, but this place also could not be found, unless it is = ? Laizhou 萊州.

28 According to de Rougemont (1673), p. 317 this was in Ngán kiéu = Anqiu 安丘.

29 According to de Rougemont (1673), p. 318: Múm yn = Mengyin 蒙陰.

30 According to de Rougemont (1673), p. 318: Càoyuén = Gaoyuan 高苑, Nhí xuí = Yishui 沂水, Gécháo = Rizhao 日照, Ngànló = Anluo cun 安落村.

31 According to de Rougemont (1673), p. 318 in Luí chéu = Laizhou ? 萊州 and Chàm yé = Changyi 昌邑.

32 = Pingdu 平度.

33 = Jiangxi 江西.

34 Should be Lüzhou but this place could not be found, unless it is Luzhou 廬州; de Rougemont (1673), p. 319 mentions Liu hsien, a town in the Nanjing Province; Intorcetta

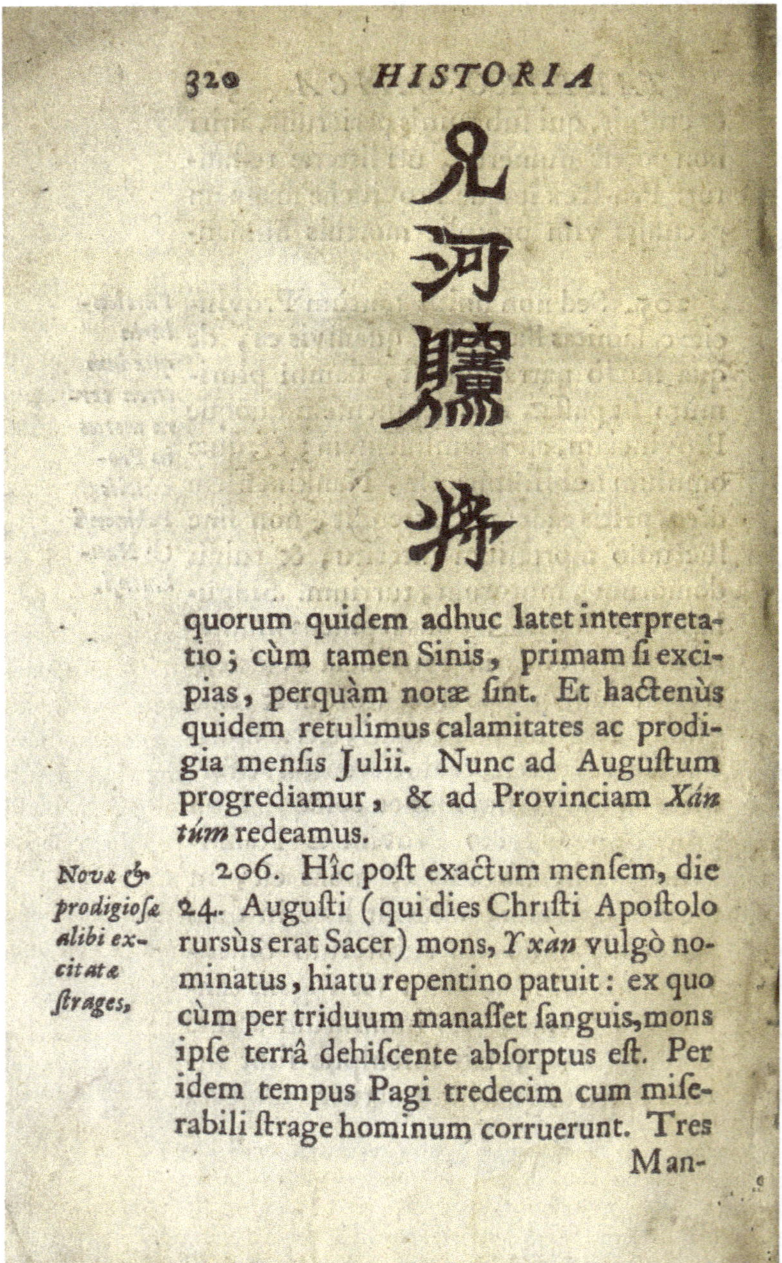
320 HISTORIA

凡

河

贖

將

quorum quidem adhuc latet interpretatio; cùm tamen Sinis, primam si excipias, perquàm notæ sint. Et hactenùs quidem retulimus calamitates ac prodigia mensis Julii. Nunc ad Augustum progrediamur, & ad Provinciam *Xán túm* redeamus.

Novæ & prodigiosæ alibi excitatæ strages.

206. Hîc post exactum mensem, die 24. Augusti (qui dies Christi Apostolo rursùs erat Sacer) mons, *Y xàn* vulgò nominatus, hiatu repentino patuit: ex quo cùm per triduum manasset sanguis, mons ipse terrâ dehiscente absorptus est. Per idem tempus Pagi tredecim cum miserabili strage hominum corruerunt. Tres Man-

ILLUSTRATION 2 Chinese inscription on a stone that emerged from the top of a mountain which had broken open due to the earthquake of 1668: François de Rougemont, *Historia Tartaro-Sinica Nova*, printed in Leuven, 1673, p. 320

and among the stones, which emerged from it, there was a stone with four Chinese characters, of which the meaning is still unknown. The next month, i.e. the seventeenth day of the seventh month, which corresponds to 24 August, day of St. Bartholomeus, mount IJxau[35] burst open and during three days bloody-like water was seen running from this opening. Shortly afterwards the whole mountain has sunk into the ground. Thirteen beautiful surrounding villages have fallen into decay with the loss of countless people. In the village of Li-kia-Thuan,[36] three Manchu officials were struck by lightning. The city of Ngankieu[37] is completely covered by water and in the place of the houses and walls one saw a large pond. The capital Nankin is also seriously damaged by the earthquake, and part of its walls collapsed. The city of Socieu,[38] belonging to the province of Nankin, through which we passed coming back from the court, is likewise overtaken by the flood of waters. The nineteenth of the seventh month, that is 26 August, a renowned stone bridge, called Lukeu-kao,[39] 蘆溝橋 built a thousand years ago, and one third of an Italian mile long, collapsed under the abundance of water. Among the stones, people found one with an inscription of twenty letters [= characters], which I do not provide here, because its meaning is obscure and unknown. Near the city of Caotani,[40] one side of a tower collapsed, and the other side remains bent and cursed as if it wanted to collapse. The above-mentioned earthquakes caused a lot of damage to twelve larger cities and forty-eight lesser towns. On 11 August it rained in Beijing for five days and five nights, so terrible that more than one thousand houses collapsed. The river, which is the river that flows through the imperial palace, has risen so high that a large number of the city gates collapsed. In the city of Hoeij-cheu[41] in the province of Nankin, in the month of July snow fell until five cubits high, as was told to us by those who came from there. The above-mentioned signs are drawn from the gazettes of the court and translated nearly word for word.

(1672), p. 66 only mentions that it was in the Nanjing province, without a reference to the name. If Liu is a misspelling for Kiu it could be Juzhou/xian 莒州/縣, where a high mountain collapsed (see Baidu: 莒县地震, web.archive.org/web/20210526152859/https://baike.baidu.com/item/%E8%8E%92%E5%8E%BF%E5%9C%B0%E9%9C%87).

35 Intorcetta (1672), p. 71: Yxan; de Rougemont (1673), p. 320: Yxàn = Yishan 沂山.

36 = Lijia 李家?

37 = Anqiu 安丘.

38 = Suzhou 蘇州?

39 = Lugouqiao 蘆溝橋.

40 = Gaotang 高唐?

41 = Huizhou 徽州.

The repetitive character of the text is striking, with the date of the earthquake repeated several times for events in different places. It gives the impression that Couplet's description of the earthquake was in fact a collection of excerpts collated from different sources, possibly indicating that it was based on different gazettes. After the description in which Couplet primarily focuses on the damage to humans, buildings, and nature, he devotes a special section to the ominous events that accompanied the earthquake.

> Yet, what is beyond the foregoing stories and probably cannot be found in any of our histories and subsequently will be considered unbelievable, is that in the city called Ungan,[42] belonging to the larger city of Cham te Fu[43] in the most renowned province of Honan, the seventeenth day of the Chinese sixth month, that is 25 July, at 6 [a.m.] a dragon fell out of heaven, so it is reported, and it is described as having four feet, claws, a tail, scales, but headless. It is said that the length is extraordinary, so that the official of the place had wrapped this terrible monster in one hundred fifty mats, and had it buried as such. The highest officials of the capital of the province have been informed about it, in order to inform the court about it according to the customs. This was the first miraculous sign, after which at 8 p.m. on the same day the above-mentioned earthquakes in the province of Xantum occurred.
>
> It is also written, though the day and the month are not mentioned, that in the province of Chekian[44] in the capital Hanckeu[45] a rain of white hair fell down, like the beasts have, covering the lands nearly two palms high. About the latter we have not yet an assured notice, but the others are beyond any doubt, even if we still expect more assurances from the court concerning this monster. The Chinese consider all this, but especially the last two, as infallible signs of a major change and revolution. After all, it is sure that in the eighth month of the tenth year of the last emperor of the previous family Taimum,[46] a sea monster with four feet had stranded on the seashore of the province of Chekiam – I think that it was a crocodile – which was more than six Chinese fathoms long (one of theirs constitutes two of ours), from his ribs and bones tables and chairs were made and seven eight years later a Manchu made himself emperor.

42 = Wu'an 武安.
43 = Zhangdefu 彰德府.
44 = Zhejiang 浙江.
45 = Hangzhou 杭州.
46 = Daming 大明.

Describing both natural and seemingly supernatural phenomena, Couplet's letter thus offers a vivid description of the Tancheng earthquake. Together with the texts by Intorcetta and de Rougemont, it is notable because the reports provide complementary information to the Chinese sources that have been preserved. Indeed, there is a sharp contrast between the narratives provided by the missionaries, such as the one cited above, and the silence from other official sources. The *Qing shilu* 清實錄 from the Kangxi reign, for example, hardly contains any contemporary information about the earthquake, except for brief references to tax exemptions to remediate the consequences of the disaster one month and more after the event.[47]

Comparatively more information about the disaster and its destruction can be found in various *difangzhi* 地方志 and in some private sources, some of which were used by Jonathan Spence in his book *The Death of Woman Wang*, which starts with a short description of this earthquake.[48] They all converge in some common descriptive elements, such as the frightening roar that accompanied the earthquake, the uncountable number of deaths, the collapse of houses, city walls and other buildings, the fissures opening up with jets of water spurting up, the breaking open of mountains and streams of mud pouring down, etc. But these sources are relatively brief and of a later date, and none give as wide an overview as the one in the Jesuit reports.

Moreover, these sources hardly report on the more inexplicable phenomena that accompanied the earthquake. Still, at least some of these more enigmatic events mentioned by the Jesuits seem to have been reported on at that time, as appears from a note in *Chibei outan* 池北偶談 (Casual Conversations in the Chibei Library), the private jottings (*biji* 筆記) by the scholar, poet,

47 *Qing shilu*, vol. 4, p. 366 (*juan* 26), KX7/7/丙辰[= 18] (= 26 August 1668); vol. 4, p. 381 (*juan* 27), KX7/10/戊寅[= 13] (= 16 November 1668); vol. 4, pp. 434–435 (*juan* 32), KX9/閏2/壬子[= 25] (= 14 April 1670). The *Kangxi qijuzhu* 康熙起居注 (1984) and (2009) of these years are not preserved.

48 Spence (1980), p. 1ff.; for an overview of these sources with quotations, especially various *difangzhi*, see 郯城大地震文献辑录(书虫 286 的博客), http://blog.sina.com.cn/s/blog_64370dc30102e1bx.html; see also Baidu: 郯城地震, https://web.archive.org/web/20210526124019/https://baike.baidu.com/item/%E9%83%AF%E5%9F%8E%E5%9C%B0%E9%9C%87/4051449?fromtitle=%E9%83%AF%E5%9F%8E%E5%A4%A7%E5%9C%B0%E9%9C%87&fromid=9655620.
See e.g. *Tancheng xianzhi* (1763; repr. 1976), which contains a short description, *juan* 3, pp. 6a–b (pp. 99–100); and a text entitled *Zaimin ge* 災民歌 by Feng Kecan 馮可參 (*jinshi* 1661), *juan* 11, pp. 10a–b (pp. 537–538).
One of the private sources is Pu Songling's 蒲松齡 (1640–1715) *Liaozhai zhiyi* 聊齋誌異, which contains a short eyewitness report of the earthquake in Jixia 稷下. See [Pu Songling], *Strange Stories from a Chinese Studio*, 2 vols., trans. Herbert A. Giles, London: Thos. De la Rue, 1880, vol. 2, pp. 263–264 (n. 127).

and bibliophile Wang Shizhen 王士禛 (1634–1711). The enormous noise, the self-striking bells, and the appearance of a dragon (though in a different place than in the Jesuit reports) are all mentioned in it.[49]

> 康熙戊申六月十七日戌刻，山東、江南、浙江、河南諸省，同時地大震，而山東之沂、莒、郯三州縣尤甚。郯之馬頭鎮，死傷數千人，地裂山潰，沙水湧出水中多有魚蟹之屬。又天鼓鳴，鐘鼓自鳴。淮北沭陽人白日見一龍騰起，金鱗爛然，時方晴明無雲氣云
>
> On KX7/6/17 (25 July 1668) between 7–9 p.m., there was an enormous earthquake simultaneously in the provinces of Shandong, Jiangnan, Zhejiang, and Henan, and it was strongest in the districts of Yizhou 沂州, Juzhou 莒州, and Tancheng 郯城. In the town of Matou 馬頭 in the Tancheng district, several thousands of people were killed and wounded, the earth cracked and mountains collapsed, mud gushed out, and in it there were all kinds of fish and crabs. In heaven there was thunder, and the bells and drums resonated by themselves. The people of Shuyang 沭陽 (to the north of Huai[an] 淮北) saw in daytime a dragon rising, bright with golden scales; at that time the sky was clear and there were no clouds.

While Wang Shizhen's jottings touch upon some of the more ominous events described in the Jesuit reports, they do not mention the stones with characters that were allegedly found. Regarding the four characters found on a stone that came out of the fissure of a mountain in Liucheu/hsien, Couplet mentions the events, but does not provide any translation "because the meaning is unknown"; Intorcetta adds the romanisation of the inscription[50] and de Rougemont the characters,[51] but neither can provide a translation. Regarding the twenty characters found on a stone at the Lugou bridge, Couplet again does not provide a translation because of the obscure meaning, Intorcetta has the romanisation and translation,[52] and de Rougemont adds the characters.[53] The characters that de Rougemont provides in his description of both inscriptions

49 Wang Shizhen 王士禛, *Chibei outan* 池北偶談, vol. 2, pp. 523–524 (no. 1015: "Dizhen" 地震).

50 Intorcetta (1672), p. 66: Hium Hò Quam Giam = *xiong he guang/kuang jiang*.

51 de Rougemont (1673), p. 320: 兄河？將.

52 Intorcetta (1672), pp. 73–74.

53 de Rougemont (1673), pp. 322–323.

are among the earliest examples of Chinese characters printed in the Southern Low Countries.[54]

七輛筐車過
壓倒蘆溝橋
食了南來米
燒盡西山煤

When the seven chariots loaded with baskets will have passed
They will have crushed down the Lugou bridge
People will have finished eating the rice that comes from the south
And will have burned all the coal that comes from the western mountains

This is an example of an incident on which European sources contain more detailed information than the surviving Chinese sources. So far, no other written source concerning these stone inscriptions has been found. They do not appear in any of the multiple electronic versions and databases of official texts that were consulted.

The question remains exactly what source the Jesuits used for their detailed information about the Tancheng earthquake. The reason to raise this question is that it is often assumed that earthquakes were a topic that usually was not included in the Chinese gazette, since they were traditionally considered signs from Heaven that could threaten the position of the emperor. Natural disasters, such as floods and droughts, were only reported on when they presented an occasion to exhibit relief efforts, tax exemptions, and other charitable acts by the emperor and the officials.[55] Yet Couplet clearly mentions that the stories he recounts "came fresh from the court, printed in the royal gazettes, which are spread throughout all provinces and lands." Moreover, the Jesuit sources indicate that they faithfully translated from the gazettes: "nearly word by word,"[56] according to Couplet. In case the Tancheng earthquake was mentioned in the gazettes, it is still inexplicable why so little of it appears in these official Chinese sources, which usually contain information parallel to the gazettes.

54 See Golvers (2016).

55 Fang Hanqi (1992–1999), vol. 1, p. 91ff.; Fang Hanqi (2013), pp. 14–15 (starting from the Song); Mokros (2016), p. 34. Yet, according to Mittler (2004), pp. 190–191, natural disasters were favourite topics in the gazettes of the late nineteenth century, as they provided an opportunity to showcase positive behaviour.

56 Letter by Philippe Couplet (Canton, 1669) to Hendrick van Alckemade S.J. and Clement Verschoor S.J. (Amsterdam), in Barten (1970), p. 115.

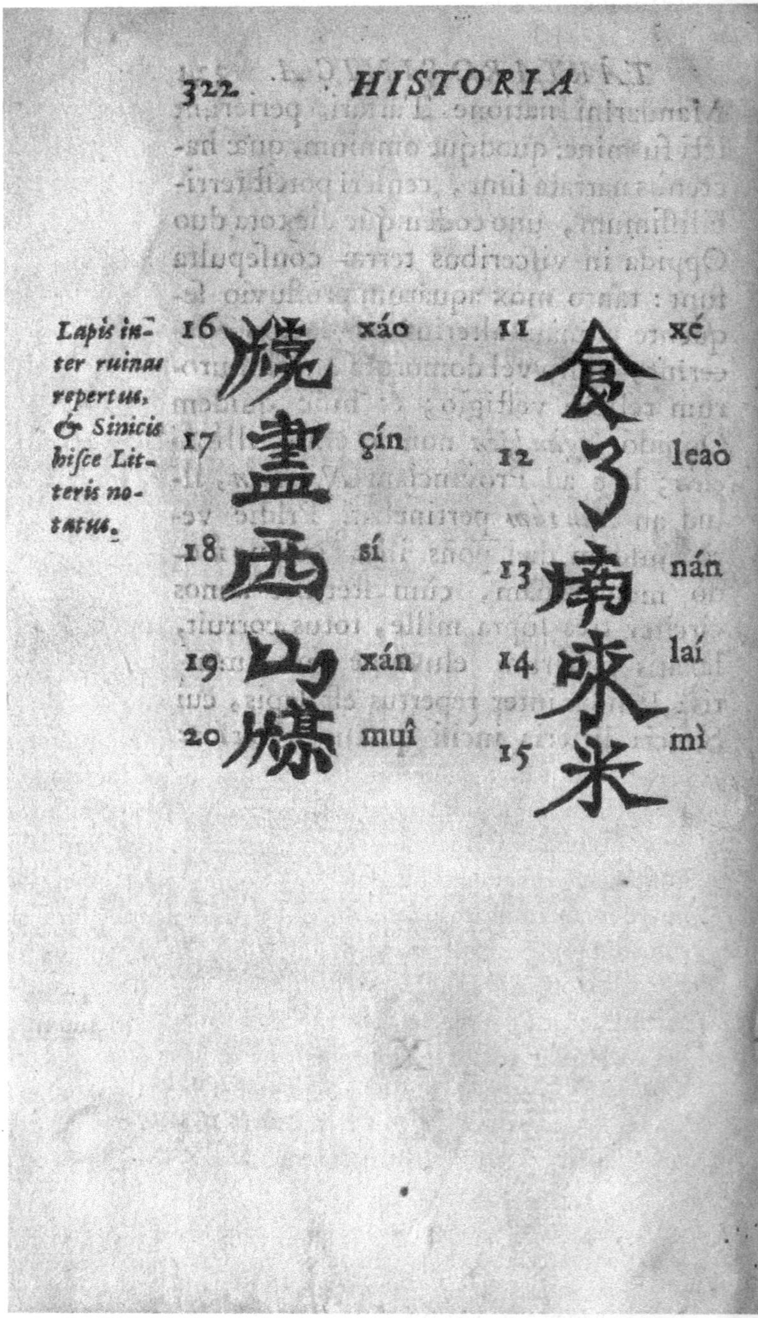

322 *HISTORIA*

Lapis inter ruinas repertus, & Sinicis hisce Litteris notatus.

11 食 xé
12 了 leaò
13 南 nán
14 來 laí
15 米 mì
16 燒 xáo
17 盡 çín
18 西 sí
19 山 xán
20 煤 muî

ILLUSTRATION 3 Chinese inscription found at the Lugou bridge 蘆溝橋 (Beijing), 1668: François de Rougemont, *Historia Tartaro-Sinica Nova*, printed in Leuven, 1673, pp. 322–323

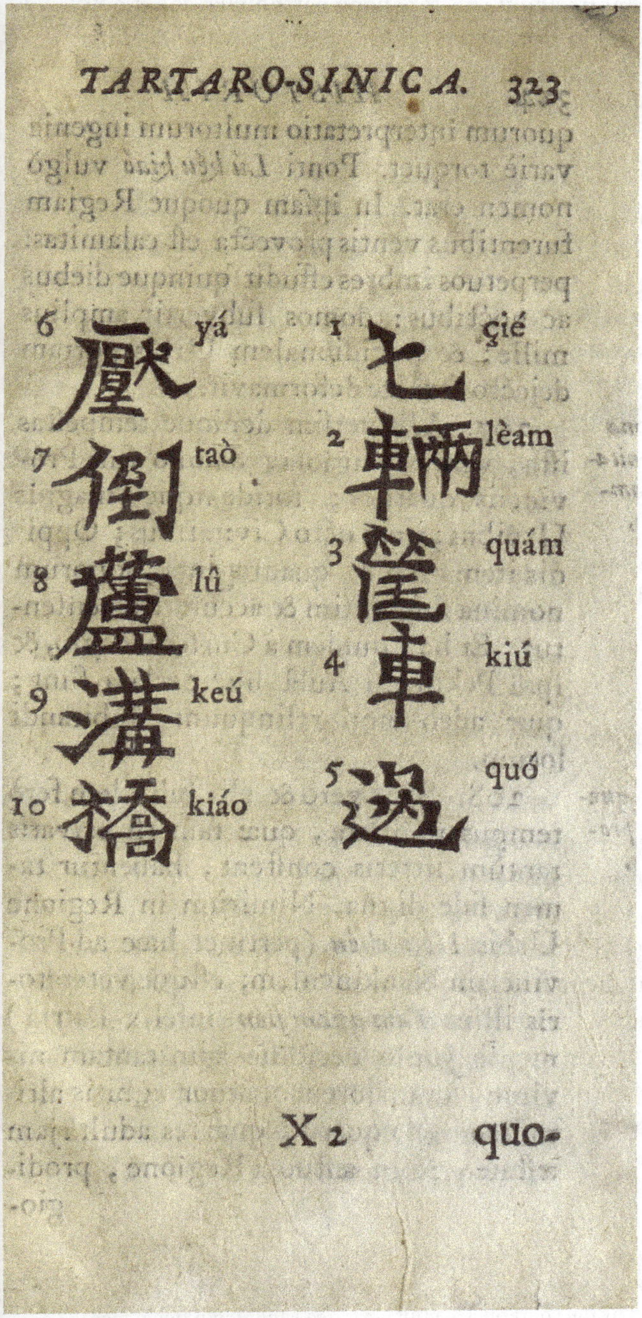
TARTARO-SINICA. 323

1 七 çie
2 輛 lèam
3 筐 quám
4 車 kiú
5 過 quó
6 壓 yá
7 倒 taò
8 蘆 lû
9 溝 keú
10 橋 kiáo

X 2 quo-

At the same time, their reports about the Tancheng earthquake show how cautious the missionaries were in passing on information about the disaster. De Rougemont, for instance, explains that they would not publish or write about these events if they had not appeared in the press distributed in the whole empire:

> And since these [events] are so new to us, and portentous, that they can be considered incredible by many, here I first affirm that there is nothing that will be narrated by me, that I did not take from the public letters published at the Court itself, which the royal postmen commonly brought here [= Canton].[57]

He also insists that the information is reliable – a recurrent viewpoint in the Jesuit sources on the Chinese gazettes. For instance, regarding the characters from the Lugou bridge, he writes:

> And these things were brought [i.e. reported] hither [i.e. to Canton] by an Imperial postman and from the Peking Court; for this they leave no place for any doubt.[58]

Intorcetta, for his part, explains that the Jesuits used to wait for confirmation of the news out of fear of incurring the death penalty for spreading deceitful information:[59]

> For this reason the Fathers, before writing about it [in letters], waited for the news that came from the other Provinces; and when they had seen that this was uniform, even given to the press, and divulged in the whole empire, without being forbidden by the Mandarins, and Governors of the Cities, at that moment they wrote it down, and joined it with the other prodigies that occurred on the same day, all the more because they knew well that the death penalty was established by the Chinese laws for those who divulge in the empire or in writing or in print deceitful news, especially in such a sensitive matter, as this was.[60]

---

57 de Rougemont, *Historia Tartaro-Sinica Nova* (1673), p. 316. See Golvers (2016), p. 326.

58 de Rougemont, *Historia Tartaro-Sinica Nova* (1673), p. 324. See Golvers (2016), p. 326 n. 18.

59 On the restrictions imposed by the court on deceitful news, see Fang Hanqi (1992–1999), vol. 1, p. 174ff. (Ming), p. 231ff. (Qing).

60 Intorcetta, *Compendiosa narratione dello stato della missione Cinese* (1672), p. 70.

These comments suggest that the Jesuits had access to provincial gazettes rather than only the gazette that was sent from Beijing. In this regard, it can be pointed out that local scholar officials, and maybe also missionaries, gathered news through different channels. Besides the official gazette sent by the provincial couriers in the capital, these officials ordered the locally-reproduced capital gazette from the provincial couriers or their local offices. In addition, they probably bought local gazettes, such as the *yuanmen* gazette (*yuanmen chao* 轅門抄, named after the office of the provincial governor(-general)), from local printing offices or newspaper copiers. These *yuanmen* gazettes included not only documents from the capital, but also local official information, such as appointments and resignations of local officials. In addition, some of the provincial couriers randomly published single-page "small gazettes" or "short reports" (*xiaobao* 小報 or *xiaochao* 小抄, sometimes translated as "tabloids"). These documents had no title, no headline, and no fixed issue date. They mainly reported breaking news, such as earthquakes, floods, droughts, and other major political and military events.[61] The comments by Intorcetta are too brief to decide which gazette he is referring to exactly, but they are at least clear enough to indicate that the news came from different types of (provincial) gazettes. However, there is no direct indication that these "small gazettes" were among the sources used by the Jesuits, as these documents were not necessarily well-spread in the Qing.

1.3 Contacts with Publishers

The documents and references cited above already give some insights into the missionaries' reading practices of the gazette, both in Beijing (as in the case of Ferdinand Verbiest) and in the provinces. They indicate that at least some missionaries had regular access to the information published in the gazettes. Other references can not only provide further insight into their use and evaluation of the gazettes, but also into their possible contacts with the publishers.

A first example is a short reference to the gazette that appeared about thirty years after the earthquake in *Brevis relatio* (Brief account), edited by Antoine Thomas (1644–1709) in 1701. The longer title of this text is: *Brevis Relatio eorum, quæ spectant ad Declarationem Sinarum Imperatoris Kam Hi circa Cœli, Cumfucii, et Avorũ cultũ, datam anno 1700* (Brief account of those who witnessed the declaration by the emperor of the Chinese, Kangxi, concerning Heaven, Confucius, and the cult of the ancestors, dated the year 1700).

61 See Fang Hanqi (1992–1999), vol. 1, pp. 202–203; Fang Hanqi (2013), pp. 39–40.

The text reports on the audience that the Emperor granted to several Jesuits on 30 November 1700, during which he expressed his opinion on some issues in the Chinese Rites Controversy. *Brevis relatio* contains the Manchu version of the memorial and imperial rescript issued at that moment, as well as the Chinese and Latin translation. The missionaries reported that the Chinese version was published in the gazettes. Moreover, it can be ascertained that it was also published "corresponding to the copy printed in Beijing" (*iuxta Exemplar Pekini impressum*) in Canton, Nanjing, and Fujian,[62] though it is not entirely clear whether this was done with the local printing office. If this is the case, it could indicate that the missionaries and the Chinese collaborators were in contact with the local publishers to have a favourable edict reprinted. The description of this decree in *Brevis relatio* makes a comparison between the Chinese gazettes and those of Europe, and insists on both the close link with the court and the dissemination in the provinces.

> After several days the decree of the Emperor appeared in the public newsletters (*in novis publicis*), which are disseminated throughout the provinces; it was received everywhere, as far as we know, with approval. The public newsletters (*nova publica*) in China, however, are not like the ones in Europe, where accounts of different nature are brought together. In those of China, which come forth from the Court, one can hardly read anything else than the deeds and the decrees of the Emperor. Since, however, the printed decision of the Emperor comes forth in the various provinces, and in the many cities, it is expedient to bring forward a genuine authentic copy or text, as it was sent to and disseminated in the Provinces, in the Chinese idiom, 'as it came forth.'[63]

The statement that in the Chinese gazettes "one can hardly read anything else than the deeds and the decrees of the Emperor" will be repeated in all the subsequent comparisons between the Chinese and European gazettes.

Missionaries themselves occasionally had official texts that were considered favourable to them printed not only in Beijing, but also in the provinces. In addition, there seem to have been several other instances when missionaries used print to spread official news independent from or in connection to the

---

62 Several different copies have been preserved and can be found in ARSI (Rome). For details, see Standaert (2012), p. 17, p. 18 n. 13. The "Edict of tolerance," which had been printed a few years earlier, may have been distributed across China in a similar way. Of this last edict, an imperial copy has been preserved. See Standaert (2012b).

63 *Brevis relatio* (1701), p. 14b, in Standaert (2012), p. 429.

official gazette. For instance, in 1703, the papal legate Charles-Thomas Maillard de Tournon (1668–1710) was sent to China to announce the latest Roman decisions concerning the Chinese Rites Controversy. At the occasion of his visit to Beijing in January 1706, the Kangxi emperor decided to dispatch two missionaries, de Tournon's auditor Sabino Mariani (1665–1721) and the Jesuit Joachim Bouvet (1656–1730), to Rome in order to offer presents to the pope. The two missionaries then arranged for the news announcing this imperial delegation to be published in the gazette. The titles for these delegates used in this text and the order in which they appeared became the cause of an internal dispute with de Tournon.[64]

It is unclear to what extent and in which period the missionaries had regular contacts with the provincial courier offices (*titang* 提塘) and the reporting offices (*baofang* 報房). These offices were in charge of copying the documents that had been released for dissemination, and of transmitting them to the provinces. In the Qing, there were sixteen provincial courier offices in the capital, which maintained the connection between their respective province and the capital.[65] Again, one relies on scattered references, which at least reveal that these contacts existed. In a notebook (that also functioned as an account book) by Jean-François Foucquet (1665–1741), one finds the reference "江西提塘萬 住正陽門外蝎子廟 / 廣東報房 住前門外虎坊橋兒," which indicates the address of the Jiangxi courier office (at the Xiezi temple outside the Zhengyang gate) and the Guangdong reporting office (at the Hufang bridge, outside the Qian gate). Though it is not clear why the addresses of these two places in Beijing are mentioned, at least it shows that Foucquet was informed about these institutions.[66]

That sometimes a direct intervention by the missionaries took place, appears from the following episode that happened in the 1730s–no longer in the Kangxi era. It concerns memorials and imperial responses that were exchanged at the occasion of anti-Christian incidents in 1737.[67] In the annual report on these events, it is mentioned that

> Father André Pereira [1689–1743], vice-provincial of the Portuguese Jesuits, who knew the *zongdu* [總督] or Governor-General of the province of

64 Stumpf (2015), pp. 120–121; Collani (1985), p. 286.

65 On this topic, see i.a. Shi Yuanyuan (2008), chap. 3, sections 2–3.

66 BAV (Biblioteca Apostolica Vaticana), Borgia Cinese 377, fol. 145v. With thanks to Chen Tuo for this reference.

67 It concerns memorials and edicts that have also been included in *Ruijianlu* 睿鑑錄 (1738), some of which were printed and spread separately. On this text see Marinescu (2006), esp. p. 22 (see also *Qing shilu*, vol. 10, pp. 697–698 (*juan* 115), QL5/4/29 (24 May 1740)).

> Beizhili [北直隸], sent a catechist to his hostel in Peking, where he was then, in order to communicate to him the last memorial offered to the Emperor, with the reply of His Majesty, and to beg him not to allow the Christians under his authority to be ill-treated.
>
> This Mandarin asked why the Missionaries had not managed to have this Memorial and the answer be put in the public gazettes, where he had seen that of Yin-ji-shan [尹繼善 (1694–1771)[68]], because one did not need many more [of these] to restrain the Mandarins of the Provinces. The catechist replied that they had wanted very much to have it put there, but that the gazetier had refused it, because this Memorial had not been sent by the Emperor to the Court of Ministers of State for registration. Whereupon Li Wei [李衛 (1686–1738)[69]], which is the name of this *zongdu*, summoned one of his secretaries, and he ordered to take the memorial and the Emperor's reply, and to have them put into the public gazettes as early as that night, in order to have them passed incessantly into all the provinces of the Empire.[70]

This case not only illustrates that at that moment the missionaries actively sought to get documents published in the gazette, but also helps to understand the procedures used to get documents published, both from the perspective of the officials refusing the publication and the officials ordering documents to be published.

Conclusion

The information about the gazettes in European sources from the Kangxi period was not only provided by Jesuits in the capital, but also by those in the provinces. This gives an insight in what information reached and circulated between the provinces. The news about the Tancheng earthquake is significant in this regard, because it can hardly be found in other Chinese sources that usually contain information similar to that published in the gazette.

The Jesuit letters and reports show that already in the early Qing the missionaries were regular readers of the Chinese gazette, and that they effectively

68 *ECCP*, vol. 2, pp. 920–921.

69 *ECCP*, vol. 2, pp. 720–721; Huang Pei (1974), pp. 234–235; see also *HCC*, pp. 524–525.

70 [Anon.], "État de la religion de l'Empire de la Chine, en l'année 1738," in *LEC* (1741), vol. 25, pp. 234–298: pp. 286–288; *LEC* (1810–1811), vol. 22, pp. 197–231: pp. 225–226.

used them as a source of information. Gazettes were referred to both in internal communication among Jesuits in China and in external communication with Europe, though often in a fragmented way. Moreover, information contained in the gazettes was printed in Europe to inform Europe about specific events in China.

Among the scattered references of this period, one also finds the first comparisons between the Chinese gazettes and the Europeans newspapers. Missionaries observed that Chinese public newsletters were "not like the ones in Europe, where accounts of different nature are brought together," while in the Chinese gazettes "one can hardly read anything else than the deeds and the decrees of the Emperor."[71] This comparison highlights a contrast between the two types of gazettes that was repeated time and again in all the subsequent comparisons between the Chinese and European gazettes. The juxtaposition was influenced by the development of the European newspapers, which at the time had only a short history since this new genre of news publication dated from the early seventeenth century.[72] Even if European gazettes most often operated under official license, they initially drew a lot of their content from the personal networks and correspondence of the editors, through which the gathered information. Depending on the networks, the newsletters included a wide variety of both local and transnational news, varying from domestic murders to international wars. In addition, the content was determined by commercial gains and market requests. At times, political events would also elicit a mass of pamphlets, debating and advocating different positions.

Soon, government control was installed, against "excess of lavish and licentious speech in matters of state."[73] Despite the implementation of various control strategies to regulate the press, ranging from pre-publication censorship to post-publication punishment, the newspaper market expanded rapidly and widely all over Europe in the seventeenth century.[74] Newspapers continued to cultivate in their readers what Andrew Pettegree has called "a habit of news," accustoming their audience to the regular consumption of news items.[75] With varying intensity and regularity from country to country, newspapers had

71 *Brevis relatio* (1701), p. 14b; in Standaert (2012), p. 429.

72 On the European invention of news, see Pettegree (2014), esp. chap. 9.

73 Pettegree (2014), pp. 194–195 (from a proclamation of 1620 by the Scottish king).

74 Pettegree (2014), p. 185, gives the example of Germany. One can document the existence of around 200 titles published in Germany by the end of the seventeenth century: a total of some 70.000 surviving issues (possibly a total output of around 70 million copies, taking into account the issues that have been lost).

75 Pettegree (2014), p. 207.

become the method par excellence for conveying political information by the end of the seventeenth century.[76] But as the market grew, so did the search for truth, which was often contested. "As the newspaper passed the end of its first century," Pettegree remarks, "the serial press presented an awkward paradox: the more the newspaper extended their readership and their political influence, the less they were trusted."[77] This is the background that explains much of the reaction of the European missionaries regarding the Chinese gazette: the official Chinese government gazette was indeed quite unique compared to most of the European news pamphlets and serials in circulation around the same time.

76 Dooley & Baron (2001), p. 9.
77 Pettegree (2014), p. 268.

CHAPTER 2

The Yongzheng Period (1723–1735)

Compared to the Kangxi and Qianlong reigns, the Yongzheng reign was relatively short.[1] Yet in comparison to the Kangxi reign, the European sources about the Chinese gazette were significantly more numerous. For the missionaries, the transition of reign had considerable effects on their activities since rather shortly after his accession, the Yongzheng emperor proscribed Christianity. This was probably a consequence of the deteriorating relations as a result of the failure of the visit by the papal legation, and the presence of Christians within the family of Sunu 蘇努 (1648?–1725), a fourth cousin of the emperor, and their link with the emperor's brothers who had been considered rivals for the succession of the throne. As a result, in October 1724, a large number of missionaries was deported to Canton, while only a small number of them remained in Beijing.[2]

Information about the Chinese gazette during this reign can be found in two major categories of European sources: 1) manuscript sources, including transcriptions of the Chinese originals, that have been preserved in the Archivio Storico "de Propaganda Fide" (Historical Archives of the Propaganda Fide) in Rome and were originally sent by, among others, Domenico Perroni O.M.D. (1674–1729), procurator of Propaganda Fide at Canton (1721–1729); 2) several letters that specifically discuss the gazette, written by the Jesuit Cyr Contancin (1670–1732) and published in the French collection *Lettres édifiantes et curieuses*. In both cases the senders were in Canton, where they lived in exile.

Unfortunately, no significant work on the gazettes by Jesuit missionaries who resided in Beijing at that time has been preserved.[3] This would have allowed a comparison of the views on the gazette of the missionaries in Canton with those of the courtiers. Jesuits such as François-Xavier Dentrecolles (1664–1741) and Dominique Parrenin (1665–1741) were very active translators, but do not seem to have left a substantial introduction to the Chinese gazette.[4] It can be ascertained, however, that already during the final years of the Kangxi period they were readers of the gazette, and they referred to it in their

1 For a general overview of the Yongzheng reign in English, see Huang Pei (1974) and Zelin (2002).

2 See Ad Dudink, "Opponents," in *HCC*, pp. 521–522.

3 For a list of the missionaries in Beijing in October 1727, see the letter of Gaubil to the Jesuit Louis Gaillard (1676–1740), in Gaubil (1970), pp. 180–181.

4 On their translations, see i.a. Wu Huiyi (2017).

 | DOI:10.1163/9789004505001_004

correspondence with each other.[5] Moreover, in his letters, Parrenin regularly translated official documents that were most probably taken from the gazette.[6] Similar references can be found in the letters by Joseph Marie Anne de Moyriac de Mailla (1669–1748), who is known for his texts on Chinese history.[7] Another well-known Jesuit is Antoine Gaubil (1689–1759), who only arrived in Beijing in 1723. From his letters to Europe, it appears that he was eager to be kept informed about European news through French gazettes and journals.[8] He also wrote a letter with a chronological overview of events that happened in Beijing in 1727, mainly related to actions of the emperor towards Christianity and the

5 E.g. Letter of Dentrecolles to the Jesuit de Broissia (Raozhou 饒州, 10 May 1715), *LEC* (1728), vol. 13, pp. 370–372; *LEC* (1810–1811), vol. 18, pp. 313–314: In the context of the attempt by censor Fan Shaozuo 樊紹祚 (*jinshi* 1691) to proscribe Christianity in December 1711-January 1712, Dentrecolles mentions that Parrenin informed him that the censor's request to investigate the matter would appear in the "Gazette publique," together with the corresponding imperial instruction to the Ministry of Rites (Libu 禮部). On this case see *HCC*, p. 518. Dentrecolles reports that the next letter by Parrenin also makes reference to another imperial decision that can be read in the "Gazette." These references indicate that both had access and read the gazettes, while being far removed from one another (Beijing and Raozhou 饒州 (Jiangxi)).

6 On several occasions, Parrenin also makes explicit reference to the gazette: e.g. letter of Parrenin to an unidentified Jesuit (Beijing, 20 July 1725), *LEC* (1728), vol. 18, p. 119; *LEC* (1810–1811), vol. 20, p. 51: reference to the publication in the gazette of a statement by the emperor concerning Sunu a few days earlier (on this case, see further in this chapter); letter of Parrenin to Jean-Baptiste Du Halde (Beijing, 26 September 1727), *LEC* (1728), vol. 19, p. 119; *LEC* (1810–1811), vol. 20, p. 149: reference to the publication in the gazette of the emperor's statement concerning Christianity at the occasion of the audience with the Portuguese ambassador (in May 1727) (see also further in this chapter).

7 (Second) letter of de Mailla to the Jesuit de Colonia (Beijing, 1 June 1717), *LEC* (1728), vol. 14, p. 87; *LEC* (1810–1811), vol. 19, p. 6: refers to the publication in the gazette of an imperial edict that prohibits vessels to travel in the seas south of China under the pretext of commerce (on this case, see Fu Lo-shu (1966), vol. 1, pp. 122–123); *LEC* (1728), vol. 14, p. 190; *LEC* (1810–1811), vol. 19, p. 59: reference to the publication in the gazette of a memorial by Chen Mao 陳昴 (c. 1651–c. 1719), brigade-general in Guangdong, proposing to proscribe Christianity in May 1717 (on this case, see also Dudink, "Opponents," in *HCC*, pp. 518–519; Fu Lo-shu (1966), vol. 1, pp. 123–124).

8 In a letter to an anonymous recipient (14 October 1729), Gaubil writes that he learned from Parrenin that it was decided to no longer send gazettes from France because they were considered to be too expensive. Gaubil argues that it should not be difficult to collect gazettes of the current year free of charge from the Jesuit houses, and that he would be astonished if one dares to charge a large sum for their mailing. Gaubil (1970), p. 238. See also in other letters: p. 327 (Gaubil to Theophile Siegfried Bayer (1694–1738) in St. Petersburg (3 July 1732): thanking him in advance for sending him French gazettes via St. Petersburg or Moscow); p. 375 (Gaubil to Joseph Nicolas Delisle (1688–1768) in St. Petersburg (13 July 1734): gazettes from Europe are welcome); p. 855 (Gaubil to Thomas Birch in London (31 October 1758): he has received the gazettes from 1757).

Jesuits, and the visit of the Portuguese ambassador Alexandre Metelo de Sousa e Meneses (1687–1766). However, no reference is made to the gazette.[9]

After discussing the two major sources for the Yongzheng period, additional attention will be paid to the reception history, since the texts by Contancin were used extensively by some Enlightenment thinkers.

2.1 Reports by Perroni in the Archivio Storico "de Propaganda Fide"

In 1622, Pope Gregory XV founded the "Sacra Congregatio de Propaganda Fide" (The Holy Congregation for the Propagation of the Faith), through which the full responsibility for missionary work all over the earth resorted under the Pope. The Congregation is not a missionary order, but at times missionaries of various orders were sent by the Congregation to mission areas, including China. Since the seventeenth century, much correspondence between Rome and the missionaries about mission issues passed through the Congregation and was preserved in its archives, the Archivio Storico "de Propaganda Fide," including communication about the Chinese Rites Controversy. Though mainly written in European languages, the archival documents also contain texts in Chinese.[10]

This archive contains a unique source regarding the gazettes in the Yongzheng period: the set of folios folded as a kind of booklet that Dominico Perroni added to his annual report for Propaganda Fide in the years 1727 and 1728.[11] Domenico Perroni O.M.D., from a small religious order called Ordine della Madre di Dio, arrived in China in 1710. He was part of a delegation sent by pope Clement XI to deliver the cardinal's hat to Charles-Thomas Maillard de Tournon, the papal legate during the Chinese Rites Controversy, as a reward for his actions.[12] Perroni became procurator of Propaganda Fide in Canton (1721–1729), regularly reporting to Rome about the state of the mission.

9 Letter from Gaubil to Louis Gaillard (1676–1740) in Tournon (8 October 1727), in Gaubil (1970), pp. 171–180.

10 Ad Dudink prepared a catalogue of these documents and generously shared his material for the references that follow. See Dudink (2022).

11 "Memorie della Cina del 1727 per la S. Congregazione di Propaganda Fide," APF, SOCP, vol. 33 (dall'Anno 1727 al 1728), fols. 262r–315r; "Memorie del 1727 concernenti varie occurrenze delle Missioni per la S. Cong[regazio]ne di Propag[an]da Fide" APF, SOCP, vol. 33 (dall'Anno 1727 al 1728), fols. 316r–325v (dated Canton, 16 October 1727). These and the following examples include explicit references to the gazette, which does not exclude that other materials may also be (partly) based on the gazettes.

12 Rosso (1948), p. 184; see also D'Arelli (1997), p. 444 n. 64.

2.1.1 *Selection of Various News*

The first booklet by Perroni is entitled: "Ristretto di varie notizie cavate dalle Gazzette impresse in Pekino nel 1727, in supplimento delle Memorie della Cina del medesmo Anno per la S. Congregazione di Propaganda Fide" (Selection of various news extracted from the Gazettes imprinted in Pekin in 1727, in supplement to the Reports from China of the same Year for the Sacred Congregation of Propaganda Fide).[13] This booklet was added because the news included in the gazettes "is very useful to those who are interested in the progress of our Holy Religion."[14] The focus of Perroni's reports is indeed the state of the Catholic Church in China, which was the responsibility of the Propaganda Fide. This is also the reason why he started to read the Chinese gazette, something he had not done earlier:

> The interests of Religion obliged me last year not to neglect the reading of the said public gazettes, no less in order to know with certainty which Mandarins are to be found in the Government in the Provinces, whether they are known and benevolent towards the Missionaries, or whether they are hostile and contrary to them; as well as to find out the Emperor's attitudes towards us. And to know in time the accidents that can occur to Christian communities: news that, in the circumstances of these evil times, is necessary to be able to seize the opportunity to introduce in the Provinces Missionaries attentive to the relief of the desolate Christians; and for other purposes, about which I wrote to this Sacred Congregation last year, [all these reasons] have led me to read these gazettes, which I had never read before.[15]

Unlike previous years, Perroni gave priority to these gazettes when preparing his new report and deemed them "most necessary to enter in depth into the superstitious system of the sect of Confucius, as it is professed by the Emperor, the great [personalities], and by the literati of the Empire."[16] He mentions that in order to make the extracts, he was helped by the Italian Franciscan Francesco Iovino da Ottaviano (1677–1737). The latter arrived in China in 1716 and spent most of his subsequent life in the Shaanxi province, until he was forced to move to Canton in 1726. Francesco da Ottaviano's reading ability of

---

13 APF, SOCP, vol. 33 (dall'Anno 1727 al 1728), fols. 326r–359r.
14 APF, SOCP, vol. 33 (dall'Anno 1727 al 1728), fol. 262r.
15 APF, SOCP, vol. 33 (dall'Anno 1727 al 1728), fols. 326v–327r.
16 APF, SOCP, vol. 33 (dall'Anno 1727 al 1728), fol. 327r.

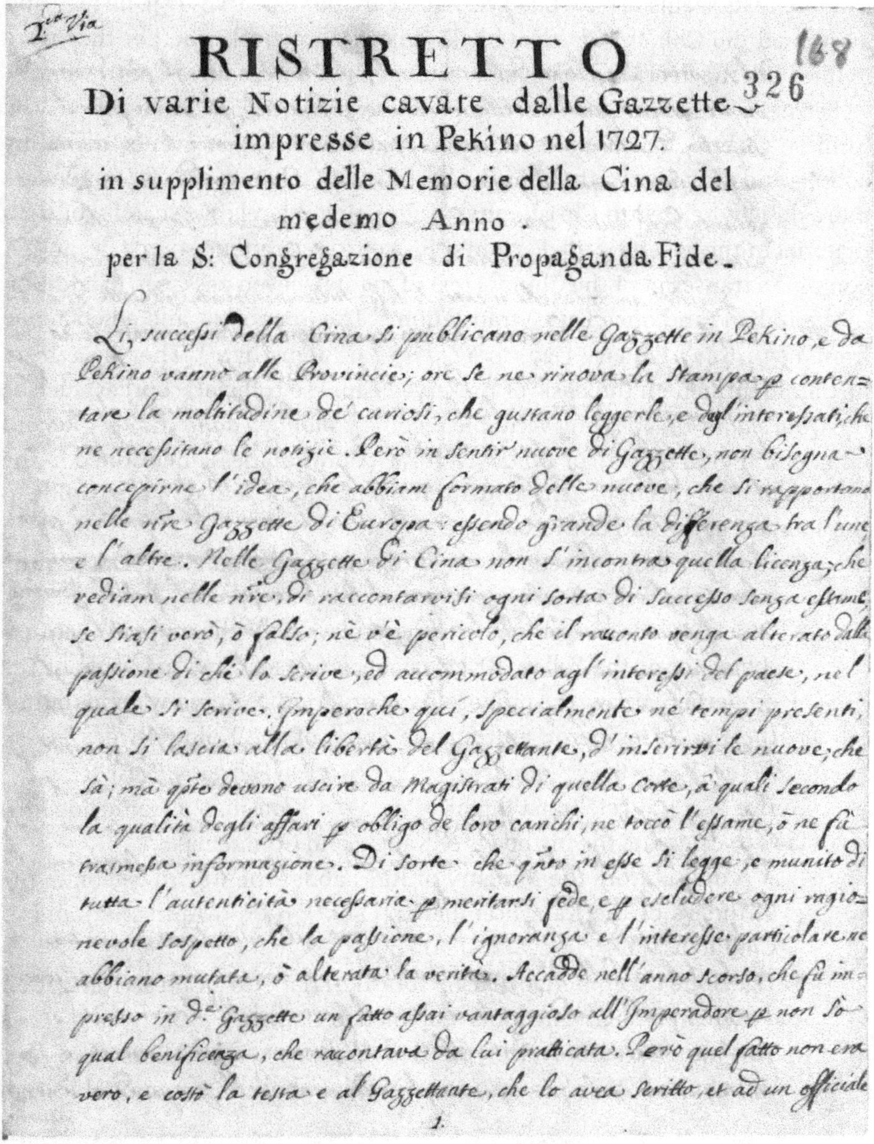

1.ma Via

168

326

RISTRETTO

Di varie Notizie cavate dalle Gazzette impresse in Pekino nel 1727. in supplimento delle Memorie della Cina del medemo Anno. per la S: Congregazione di Propaganda Fide.

Li successi della Cina si publicano nelle Gazzette in Pekino, e da Pekino vanno alle Provincie; ove se ne rinova la Stampa per contentare la moltitudine de' curiosi, che gustano leggerle, e degl'interessati, che ne necessitano le notizie. Però in sentir nuove di Gazzette, non bisogna concepirne l'idea, che abbiam formato delle nuove, che si rapportano nelle nostre Gazzette di Europa: essendo grande la differenza tra l'une e l'altre. Nelle Gazzette di Cina non s'incontra quella licenza, che vediam nelle nostre, di raccontarvisi ogni sorta di successo senza esame, se stiasi vero, ò falso; nè v'è pericolo, che il racconto venga alterato dalla passione di chi lo scrive, ed accommodato agl'interessi del paese, nel quale si scrive. Imperoche qui, specialmente ne' tempi presenti, non si lascia alla libertà del Gazzettante, d'inserirvi le nuove, che sà; mà queste devono uscire da Magistrati di quella Corte, à quali secondo la qualità degli affari per obligo de loro carichi, ne toccò l'essame, ò ne fù trasmessa informazione. Di sorte che quanto in esse si legge, è munito di tutta l'autenticità necessaria per meritarsi fede, e per escludere ogni ragionevole sospetto, che la passione, l'ignoranza e l'interesse particolare ne abbiano mutata, ò alterata la verità. Accadde nell'anno scorso, che fù impresso in d.e Gazzette un fatto assai vantaggioso all'Imperadore per non sò qual benificenza, che raccontava da lui praticata. Però quel fatto non era vero, e costò la testa e al Gazzettante, che lo avea scritto, et ad un officiale

1.

ILLUSTRATION 4 First page of Domenico Perroni's "Ristretto di varie notizie cavate dalle Gazzette impresse in Pekino nel 1727": APF, SOCP, vol. 33 (dall'Anno 1727 al 1728), fol. 326r

Chinese texts seems to have been very good. In the years 1728–1731, he read and annotated 169 Chinese Catholic books, in order to check whether they were in line with the decisions taken as a result of the Chinese Rites Controversy.[17]

Perroni's "Ristretto" for 1727 comprises seven notices extracted from the Chinese gazette, which concern various natural and state events, including actions and decisions by the Yongzheng emperor. Only two of these notices are more directly related to Christianity – suggesting the relative scarcity of such material in the gazette. Still, Perroni's "Ristretto" is a unique source because it contains a transcript of the Chinese text of in total eleven passages, in addition to the Italian (and once Latin) translation.[18] The memorials and edicts range from YZ5/1/6 (27 January 1727) to YZ5/7/3 (19 August 1727). They have been further identified on the basis of preserved Chinese (official) sources, such as the *Qing shilu* 清實錄 (Qing veritable records), *Shangyu dang* 上諭檔 (Record book of imperial edicts), or *Qijuzhu* 起居注 (Court diaries), mentioned in the introduction to this book. These identifications can be found in the "Guide to the sources" at the end of this book.

1. L'acque del fiume croceo di gialle divengono cristalline, e chiare (The waters of the Yellow River become crystalline and clear)
   - Officials want a ceremony of congratulation for the emperor because the water of the Yellow River has become clear; two rescripts of the emperor rejecting the proposals and ordering a ceremony for his father, the Kangxi emperor, and for the Spirit of the Yellow River (*heshen* 河神) (YZ5/1/6 = 27 January 1727; YZ5/1/17 = 6 February 1727)[19]
2. Nuova legge di celebrarsi il giorno natale a Kam-hi, e a Confusio (New laws to celebrate the birthdays of Kangxi and Confucius)
   - A proposal from the Ministry of Rites about the way to celebrate the birthdays of the Kangxi emperor ([YZ5/]3/18 = 9 April 1727) and of Confucius ([YZ5/]8/27 = 11 October 1727)[20]
3. Navigazione e commercio a Regni forastieri riaperto a Cinesi (Navigation and trade in foreign kingdoms reopened to Chinese)
   - The imperial approval of the deliberations of the Ministry of War (Bingbu 兵部) on YZ5/3/10 (1 April 1727) about the memorial of Gao

17 D'Arelli (1997), pp. 445–452.

18 APF, SOCP, vol. 33 (dall'Anno 1727 al 1728), fols. 326r–359v.

19 APF, SOCP, vol. 33 (dall'Anno 1727 al 1728), fols. 327r–333r; Chinese: fols. 328v–329r (edict); fols. 330v–331v (imperial rescript); transl.: fols. 329v–330r; 332r–333r (Italian).

20 APF, SOCP, vol. 33 (dall'Anno 1727 al 1728), fols. 334v–336r; Chinese: fols. 335r–v; transl.: fols. 335v–336r (Italian).

Qizhuo 高其倬 (1676–1738),[21] Governor of Fujian, asking for the reopening of foreign trade for Chinese merchants[22]

4. Spese superflue vietate dal Imperadore a suoi popoli, e sue Massime concernenti tal materia (Superfluous expenses forbidden by the Emperor to his peoples, and his Maxims concerning this matter)
   – The emperor's admonition addressed to the new *jinshi* 進士 of that year showing his aversion to superfluous, extravagant, and useless spending (YZ5/4/5 = 22 June 1727)[23]
   – Similar admonitions that the emperor gave on other days (e.g. YZ5/5/7 = 25 June 1727)[24]
5. Ceremonie di arar la terra, costumata dal sol'Imperadore in Pekino, deve farsi in tutte le Città di Cina da Mandarini che in esse presiedono (Ceremonies of ploughing the land, performed by only the Emperor in Pekin, must be executed in all the cities of China by Mandarins who preside in them)
   – Memorial of the Ministry of Rites concerning the rite of ploughing the land at the Xiannong 先農 altar (also called 'tillage rite' (*gengji li* 耕耤禮)), to be practised by officials in the provinces (YZ5/7/3 = 19 August 1727)[25]
6. Discorso dell' Imper.e ingiurioso alla Religione Cristiana impresso nelle Gazzette (Speech of the emperor, which was insulting to the Christian Religion, imprinted in the Gazettes)
   – Anti-Christian sermon of the emperor given to the head of the Portuguese Embassy to China (Alexandre Metelo de Sousa e Meneses (1687–1766)), which happened to take place on the birthday of the Buddha (*fodan* 佛誕) (YZ5/4/8 = 28 May 1727)[26]

---

21 *ECCP*, vol. 2, p. 735.

22 APF, SOCP, vol. 33 (dall'Anno 1727 al 1728), fols. 336v–340r; Chinese: fols. 339r–340r; transl. / summary: fols. 337r–339r.

23 APF, SOCP, vol. 33 (dall'Anno 1727 al 1728), fols. 340v–343v; Chinese: fols. 342v–343v; transl.: fols. 341r–342v (Italian).

24 APF, SOCP, vol. 33 (dall'Anno 1727 al 1728), fols. 344r–347v; Chinese: fols. 346 r–v; transl.: fols. 344r–346r (Italian).

25 APF, SOCP, vol. 33 (dall'Anno 1727 al 1728), fols. 347v–351r; Chinese: fols. 350r–351r; transl.: fols. 348v–349v (Italian); not yet found (in various databases).

26 APF, SOCP, vol. 33 (dall'Anno 1727 al 1728), fols. 351r–356r; Chinese: fols. 355r–356r; transl.: fols. 351v–354v (Latin); APF, SOCP, vol. 33 (dall'Anno 1727 al 1728), fol. 418: other copy (Chinese); fol. 422: other copy (Chinese). On this embassy, see also Gaubil (1970), p. 140ff (including an audience of the missionaries with the emperor on 21 July 1727).

7. Prencipi del sangue perseguitati dall'Imperadore, tra gli parecchi sono Christiani: & alcuni d'essi condennati a morte per non voler renunciare alla Religione (Blood princes persecuted by the Emperor, among whom many are Christians: & some of them sentenced to death for not wanting to renounce the Religion)
   - Persecution of imperial family members – including Christians – of the family of Sunu 蘇努 (1648?–1725),[27] a fourth cousin of the Yongzheng emperor. In this case: Sunu's third son Su-er-jin 蘇爾金, his eleventh son Ku-er-cheng 庫爾成, and others (YZ5/3/5 = 27 March 1727; YZ5/3/- = ? March-April 1727; YZ5/6/21 = 8 August 1727); in total three Chinese texts.[28]

For these extracts, Perroni explicitly mentions his source: the passages "are taken from the originals printed in Peking, and not from the copies, which are reprinted in the Provinces; although there is no difference among them, except for some characters that are changed, or the narration that is sometimes reported in succinct form."[29]

A similar "selection of various news" exists for the report of the next year, 1728: "Ristretto di varie notizie cavate dalle Gazzette impresse in Pekino nel 1728, in supplimento delle Memorie della Cina del medesmo anno per la S. Congregazione di Propaganda Fide" (Selection of various news extracted from the Gazettes imprinted in Pekin in 1728, in supplement to the Reports

27 *ECCP*, vol. 2, pp. 692–694; *HCC*, pp. 444–447.

28 APF, SOCP, vol. 33 (dall'Anno 1727 al 1728), fols. 356r–359r; Sentenza di Morte in Cinese di sopra menz[ion]ata (Above mentioned death sentence in Chinese): Chinese: fols. 356v–357r; transl.: fols. 356r–356v (Italian); English transl. in Fu Lo-shu (1966), vol. 1, pp. 157–158. APF, SOCP, vol. 33 (dall'Anno 1727 al 1728), fol. 357v: L'imperadore non approvò la sud.a sentenza, benche à seconda del suo gusto, e ordinò la gita d'un Regolo a quei Prencipi Xrani per esortarli ad abbandonar la Relig.e che se non si arrendepero, erano degni di morte. Il decreto Imp.le secondo fu sparso fuora, è come segue (The emperor did not approve the aforementioned sentence, although it was according to his taste, and ordered the visit of a Regulus to those Christian princes to exhort them to abandon the Religion; that if they did not surrender, they were worthy of death. The second imperial decree was spread outside, it is as follows); Chinese: fol. 357v; (YZ5/3/- = ? March-April 1727); APF, SOCP, vol. 33 (dall'Anno 1727 al 1728), fols. 358r–v: Supplica fatta all'Imp.re dal Tribunale soprastante à Regoli, e Prencipi del sangue acciò totalm.te estingua la famiglia de soprad.i Prencipi senza distinzione de Xr.ani, e gentili, che sono in essa (A petition made to the Emperor by the aforementioned Tribunal for the Regoli, and Blood Princes so that the family of the aforementioned Princes be completely extinguished, without distinction between Christians and gentiles, who are among them); Chinese: fols. 358r–v; (YZ5/6/21 = 8 Aug. 1727); see also the letters of Gaubil to the Jesuit Pierre Jean Cayron (1672–1754), 4–7 Oct. 1727 in Gaubil (1970), pp. 145–171.

29 APF, SOCP, vol. 33 (dall'Anno 1727 al 1728), fol. 327r.

from China of the same year for the Sacred Congregation of Propaganda Fide).[30] Just as in the case of the previous year, Perroni laments the relative lack of notices related to religion: "the gazettes of Pekin of the present year give us very little material to make the report: it is not so that every two days a booklet according to custom has not come out, but because the news they provide is out of our intent; since they have no relation to the Christian Religion or the Religion of the Chinese."[31] Yet he takes the occasion to further present the contents of the gazettes in order to "satisfy the European curiosity."[32] The term "curiosity" – used here as "desire for knowledge" – had acquired a morally good or at least neutral quality in the seventeenth century. As Neil Kenny has shown, curiosity was considered to be something inside a person making him or her desire certain objects, while at the same time signalling that something about those objects was making them desirable. Moreover, to call something "curious" was not only to represent it as "rare" or "exotic" as it is often used today, but also as "excellent," "elegant," "noteworthy," "worth buying," etc., as will appear from its use in Perroni's and later texts. Since the eighteenth century, it was gradually displaced by the word "interesting."[33]

The "Ristretto" of 1728 consists of four items. The first is a summary of various news items (fourteen rubrics in total) mentioned in the gazettes. They are intended to present the wide variety of topics included in the gazettes. The items are relatively short, they do not contain translations or Chinese texts, but rather summarize a case and put it in context for the European reader.[34] Next, there are three additional Chinese transcripts for passages in the gazette, each with an Italian translation, treated in a way similar to the "Ristretto" of 1727. Again, the corresponding Chinese sources can be found in the "Guide to the sources" at the end of this book.

1. Succinta Raccolta di nuove che occupano le Gazzette di Cina (A succinct collection of news that occupies the Gazettes of China)
   - in Shandong: after verification, Ran Tianlin 冉天琳, a descendant in the sixty-seventh generation of Confucius' disciple ?Jen-zu (= Ranzi 冉子 = Ran Yong 冉雍) is conferred the title *Wujing boshi* 五經博士,

30 APF, SC, Indie orientali e Cina, vol. 19 (dal 1727 al 1728), fols. 717r–731r.

31 APF, SC, Indie orientali e Cina, vol. 19 (dal 1727 al 1728), fol. 717r.

32 APF, SC, Indie orientali e Cina, vol. 19 (dal 1727 al 1728), fol. 718r: "contentar la curiosità Europea."

33 Kenny (1998). This work was followed by a second extensive study by the same author: *The Uses of Curiosity in Early Modern France and Germany*, Oxford: Oxford Univ. Press, 2004.

34 APF, SC, Indie orientali e Cina, vol. 19 (dal 1727 al 1728), fols. 718r–722v (summary).

which is the same title as the one granted to four other families of descendants of Confucius (since 1724)[35]

- in Henan: a peasant (Cui Shiyou 翟世有 from the Mengjin district 孟津縣) is commended because he gave back a large amount of money lost by merchant Qin Tai 秦泰 (from Shaanxi)[36]
- in Nanjing: as a wind, which used to blow and impede boat traffic on the rivers that converged into the lake of Hum-ze (= Hongzi hu 洪澤湖), had ceased blowing for four years, an honorary title is asked and sacrifices are made to thank the Spirit of this Wind (*fengshen* 風神) for such a blessing[37]
- in Shaanxi: Shuo-se 碩色, Surveillance Commissioner and Salt Supervisor 陝西西安按察使兼管河東鹽政, had written a memorial reporting that a large amount of high-quality salt had formed by itself during the winter, when normally it required great human efforts and could only be produced in summer. In response, a temple is built to the Spirit of Salt (= *yanshen* 鹽神) to make sacrifices twice a year[38]
- memorials reporting on elderly people who reach a very high age (60, 70, 80, 90, or 100 years) and presents that are given (30 taels to erect an epitaph with four characters, offered by the Ministry of Rites) and celebrations that are organised on such an occasion[39]
- reward (5 *shi* 石 of rice and 10 *pi* 疋 of cloth) for the birth of male triplets (*yichan sannan* 一產三男), which is a sign of felicity (unlike in Europe, where it is a shame)[40]
- in Tibet: suppression of a rebellion (led by A-er-bu-ba 阿爾布巴, i.e. Ngaphöpa Dorje Gyalpo (?–1728), one of the Tibetan ministers) after

35 APF, SC, Indie orientali e Cina, vol. 19 (dal 1727 al 1728), fols. 718r–v.

36 APF, SC, Indie orientali e Cina, vol. 19 (dal 1727 al 1728), fol. 718v; this is the same case as the one mentioned by Contancin: *LEC* (1736), vol. 22, pp. 299–324; *LEC* (1810–1811), vol. 21, pp. 292–304.

37 APF, SC, Indie orientali e Cina, vol. 19 (dal 1727 al 1728), fols. 718v–719r.

38 APF, SC, Indie orientali e Cina, vol. 19 (dal 1727 al 1728), fol. 719r.

39 APF, SC, Indie orientali e Cina, vol. 19 (dal 1727 al 1728), fols. 719r–719v; there are many of such examples, e.g. a man of 118 years old who received the 30 taels: *Qing shilu*, vol. 7, p. 703 (*juan* 46) (YZ4/7/己未 [= 29] = 26 Aug. 1726).

40 APF, SC, Indie orientali e Cina, vol. 19 (dal 1727 al 1728), fols. 719v–720r. The rule of *mi wushi bu shipi* 米五石布十疋 (5 *shi* or rice and 10 *pi* of cloth) as reward was decreed in KX2 (1663): *DaQing huidian* (*Yongzheng chao*) 大清會典 (雍正朝), *juan* 68, fol. 32a. (*yichan sannan* 一產三男), see *DaQing wuchao huidian*, vol. 5 (*Yongzheng huidian* 雍正會典), p. 1085. It is not clear what is the specific case here. One finds a list of male triplets born during the Yongzheng period in *Qingshi gao* 清史稿 (*juan* 40, *zhi* 志 15), vol. 6, pp. 1521–1522.

the king asks the emperor for help; at the sight of the Chinese troops, the rebels immediately surrendered without any fight; the emperor attributes the success to his father[41]
- in order to stimulate agriculture, the emperor orders a reward for old peasants who have spent their lives cultivating the land; 559 are rewarded[42]
- instruction to collect objects made of brass, in order to limit the use of such metals to the production of money, and to control its distribution[43]
- condemnation of Muslims and butchers who secretly slaughter cows or buffalo, which should only be used for the cultivation of the fields; stronger punishment for Muslims in Beijing where the rules are stricter[44]
- condemnation of Yan-xin 延信 (1673–1728),[45] General in Shaanxi, who thought of usurpation, following the prognostication of an old witch; also accused of association with the party of Sunu 穌努 and Yinsi 胤禩 (1681–1726),[46] brother of the emperor[47]
- imperial measures to reduce personal interventions in the judicial courts when treating conflicts between officials[48]
- a new law passed by the emperor to relieve the people suffering as a result of bad harvests[49]
- other topics that are mentioned in the gazettes: homicides, adulteries, thefts, and other offenses and how they were handled; punishments of gamblers and merchants engaged in gambling, and of the officials of the regions where the incidents occurred; inundations; ...[50]

2. L'Imperadore attribuisce la fertilità della raccolta, alla cerimonia da lui istituita d'arar la terra (The Emperor attributes the fertility of the harvest to the ceremony he instituted to work the land)

41 APF, SC, Indie orientali e Cina, vol. 19 (dal 1727 al 1728), fol. 720r.
42 APF, SC, Indie orientali e Cina, vol. 19 (dal 1727 al 1728), fol. 720r.
43 APF, SC, Indie orientali e Cina, vol. 19 (dal 1727 al 1728), fols. 720r–v. Concerning this issue, see Huang Pei (1974), pp. 245ff., 289–290.
44 APF, SC, Indie orientali e Cina, vol. 19 (dal 1727 al 1728), fols. 720v–721r.
45 *ECCP*, vol. 2, pp. 907–908.
46 *ECCP*, vol. 2, pp. 926–927.
47 APF, SC, Indie orientali e Cina, vol. 19 (dal 1727 al 1728), fols. 721r–721v.
48 APF, SC, Indie orientali e Cina, vol. 19 (dal 1727 al 1728), fol. 721v.
49 APF, SC, Indie orientali e Cina, vol. 19 (dal 1727 al 1728), fols. 721v–722r.
50 APF, SC, Indie orientali e Cina, vol. 19 (dal 1727 al 1728), fols. 722r–v.

- Edict about the ceremony of ploughing land (*gengji li* 耕耤禮) by officials of rank 1–3 in imitation of the Emperor in Beijing (YZ5/8/16 = 30 September 1727)[51]

3. Sacrificii ordinati in ringraziamento per essersi ritirate l'acque del fiume croceo da un gran tratto di paese, che solevano inondare e render inutile alla coltura (Sacrifices ordered in thanksgiving for the withdrawal of the waters of the Yellow River from a large stretch of land, which used to become flooded and rendered useless for cultivation)
   - Edict about sacrifices to be made in gratitude for the fact that an impending inundation did not take place (YZ5/11/9 = 21 December 1727)[52]
4. L'amore de figli à loro Genitori e della Moglie al Marito deve avere i suoi limiti (The love of children for their Parents and of the Wife for the Husband must have its limits)
   - Edict about the limits that there should be in the expression of love of children towards their parents (*xiao* 孝) and of wives towards their husbands. For instance, the rejection of *gegan* 割肝 ("cutting the liver," which refers to the preparation of a medicinal soup out of one's own flesh as an extreme effort to cure one's parents) (YZ6/3/12 = 20 April 1728)[53]

These supplements indicate Perroni's attempt to substantiate the report with original sources, at least during these years.

2.1.2 *Description and Use of the Gazettes*

The introductions to the "Ristretto" of 1727 and 1728 give a good idea of Perroni's knowledge of the nature of the Chinese gazettes. He provides a precise description of the contents of the common gazette, which, according to him, appears as a booklet every two days:[54] they include the decrees of the emperor, the memorials (offered to him from all parts of the empire), his answers, his exhortations to the magistrates and to the populace, the changes in positions of the Mandarins, the rewards and punishments, and "other similar things, which are

51 APF, SC, Indie orientali e Cina, vol. 19 (dal 1727 al 1728), fols. 722v–725r; Chinese: fols. 724v–725r; transl.: fols. 723r–724v (partial, Italian).

52 APF, SC, Indie orientali e Cina, vol. 19 (dal 1727 al 1728), fols. 725v–727v; Chinese: fols. 727r–v; transl.: fols. 725v–727r (partial, Italian).

53 APF, SC, Indie orientali e Cina, vol. 19 (dal 1727 al 1728), fols. 728r–731r; Chinese: fols. 730r–731r; transl.: fols. 728r–730r (partial, Italian).

54 APF, SC, Indie orientali e Cina, vol. 19 (dal 1727 al 1728), fol. 717r: ogni due giorni ... un libretto; fol. 718r: ogni due giorni un libro.

referred to their Prince, and to the public government."[55] In the eyes of Perroni, the gazettes are destined to a wide audience:

> The successes of China are published in the gazettes in Peking and from Peking they go to the Provinces; their press is continuously renewed in order to satisfy the multitude of the curious, who enjoy reading them, and of those interested, who need their news (*le notizie*).[56]

But he insists that in getting a sense of the news in the Chinese gazettes, Europeans should not start from the idea that they have formed about news in "gazettes from Europe," as there is a great difference between the one and the other. In this context, one may notice that the place of comparison is "Europe" and not a particular European country, a way of comparing that is characteristic of most reports of that time.

> In the gazettes of China we do not encounter that license, which we see in ours, to tell without examination all sorts of successes, whether they are true or false; nor is there any danger that the story will be altered by the passion of the writer, and accommodated to the interests of the region, from where one writes. For here, especially in the present times, it is not left to the liberty of the *gazzettante* to insert news, which he [himself] knows; but this [news] must come from the magistrates of that court, by whom, according to the quality of the business due to the obligation of their charges, the examination of them is made, or the information is transmitted.[57]

Perroni refers here to the exact copying by the agents of the provincial courier office of documents that were posted by the Grand Secretariat and the Six Offices.

This comparison with European gazettes, which recurs in several other descriptions included in this book, points to the fact that the information included in Chinese gazettes is about the court and emanates from the court. In addition, it is also related to the question of the reliability and truthfulness of the news that is reported:

---

55 APF, SOCP, vol. 33 (dall'Anno 1727 al 1728), fol. 326v; see also APF, SC, Indie orientali e Cina, vol. 19 (dal 1727 al 1728), fol. 718r.

56 APF, SOCP, vol. 33 (dall'Anno 1727 al 1728), fol. 326r.

57 APF, SOCP, vol. 33 (dall'Anno 1727 al 1728), fol. 326r.

> As a result, what is written in them is equipped with all the authenticity (*autenticità*) necessary to deserve faith and to exclude any reasonable suspicion that passion, ignorance, and particular interest may have changed or altered the truth (*verità*).[58]

Perroni refers briefly to the capital punishment that was imposed one year earlier on a "gazzettante" and an official of the supreme magistrate of the royal treasury for having introduced in the gazettes a false fact, even though the fabricated information was very advantageous to the Emperor.

> It happened last year, that was published in these gazettes a very advantageous fact to the Emperor regarding I do not know what good deed, which was told that was done by him. But that fact was not true, and cost the head both to the *gazzettante*, who had written it, and to an official of the supreme magistrate of the royal treasury who during a visit [to the *gazzettante*] made this compliment about the emperor, when to have fun he was asked what stories were running and he put on the said achievement.[59]

The focus on the interests of the emperor and the verification system through officials and the court ensure that no "strange and curious things, pertaining to private persons" can be read in the gazettes unless they were transmitted by mandarins from the provinces to the court. In addition, the *gazzettante* have no freedom to put more in them than is provided.[60] There is one exception, however, and this is the secret gazette:

> To supply this defect, there are the secret gazettes (*le Gazzette segrete*); but these do not spread except under the eyes of a few, who, for the business they have, can afford the payment that is necessary in order to obtain them.[61]

It is not entirely clear what is meant here by "secret gazette," but it may be a description of "small gazettes" or "short reports" (*xiaobao* 小報 or *xiaochao* 小抄, sometimes translated as "tabloids"), the content of which partly escaped the control of the central administration.

---

58 APF, SOCP, vol. 33 (dall'Anno 1727 al 1728), fol. 326r.
59 APF, SOCP, vol. 33 (dall'Anno 1727 al 1728), fols. 326r–v.
60 APF, SOCP, vol. 33 (dall'Anno 1727 al 1728), fol. 326r.
61 APF, SOCP, vol. 33 (dall'Anno 1727 al 1728), fol. 326r.

The first case in the "Ristretto" of 1727 – concerning the clear waters of the Yellow River – is a good example of the way Perroni presents the information contained in the gazettes. It is also one of the most extensive cases he developed. The narrative basically includes three components: the core is the original edict in Chinese characters taken from the gazette; this is followed by a literal translation in Italian; both are framed by the explanation of the case, including its background and Perroni's own interpretation. In the case of the Yellow River, he transcribed two edicts.

The narrative starts with a description of the Yellow River, clearly intended for a public not acquainted with its existence. Perroni explains its name – yellow because of the yellow mud it transports – and its course – from the source "in Tibet" to the sea, passing through the provinces of Shaanxi, Shanxi, Henan, Shandong, and Nanjing. In this context, he refers also to the cartographic expeditions of the missionaries during the Kangxi reign and to Ferdinand Verbiest's map printed in Chinese.[62]

Next, Perroni recounts the occasion that caused the successive memorials and edicts to be published in the gazette. In the beginning of 1727, the water of the river became clear, "to the amazement and contentment of all of China."[63] It first happened in some places, and a bit later in others. When the water had turned clear on previous occasions, it had only remained that way for a short period of time and in small stretches of the country. This time, however, the river water remained limpid for a whole month, and in all the aforementioned five provinces – with some places preserving the crystalline waters for longer than others.[64] In the eyes of Perroni, this was

> such a rare accident that it would have given our philosophers an occasion to investigate the cause, but to the Chinese, more active for superstitious observations than for philosophizing, it has been an occasion for innumerable superstitions, attributing it to an extraordinary favour of Heaven, and of the spirits which presided over the said river; and the

62 APF, SOCP, vol. 33 (dall'Anno 1727 al 1728), fols. 327r–v.

63 APF, SOCP, vol. 33 (dall'Anno 1727 al 1728), fol. 327v.

64 The statistics can be found in a memorial by Qi-su-le 齊蘇勒 (?–1729), director-general of waterways, and others submitted later in the year (YZ5/6/丙戌 [= 1] = 19 July 1727). The clearing of the water started on the eighth or ninth day of the twelfth month of YZ4 (30–31 Dec. 1726) and lasted well into the first month of YZ5, depending on the province. Counted together, the number of days with clear water are reported as follows: Shaanxi: 36; Shanxi: 35; Henan: 31; Shandong: 14; Jiangnan: 7. See *Qing shilu*, vol. 7, p. 878 (*juan* 58) (YZ5/6/丙戌 [= 1] = 19 July 1727).

> reigning Emperor even recognizing it as a blessing (as one will see below) that came to them from his late father Kam-hi.[65]

In the above paragraph, Perroni has summarized the results of the successive attempts of the officials to plead with the emperor that he should claim the fortuitous event for himself: the emperor refused, instead attributing the occurrence to the Spirit of the Yellow River (i.e. *heshen* 河神) and to the Kangxi emperor.

Perroni points out that the belief in the auspicious nature of this rare phenomenon was not just based on rumours. In fact, it was founded on predictions that can be found in ancient books, which link the clarity of the water to prosperity for the nation or the coming of a great saint. Illustrating this, he quotes sentences from two works: a commentary on the *Yijing* 易經 (Book of Changes) entitled *Kien-zo-tu*, and a historical work entitled *Sci-i-ki*. They can be identified as respectively the Han dynasty apocryphal commentary, *Yi Qian zuodu* 易乾鑿度 (The Changes: Penetrating the Regularities of Qian), and the mythological-historical treatise compiled by the Taoist scholar Wang Jia 王嘉 (300–386), *Shiyi ji* 拾遺記 (Record of Picked-Up Leftovers). Perroni includes the Chinese characters of the two quotes:

> 天降嘉應河水先清 Quando il cielo invia prosperità, innanzi l'acqua del fiume [croceo] divien, chiara.
>
> When the sky sends prosperity, first the water of the [yellow] river becomes clear.

> 黄河千年一清此聖人之大瑞也 Una volta in mille anni [cioè assai di raro] si rischiara il fiume croceo: il che è grande pronostico d'un huomo Santo.
>
> Once in a thousand years [that is, very rarely] the yellow river clears up: which is a great prediction of a holy man.[66]

Since these are very specific quotes from works that are not well known, and since they do not appear in the edicts in his report, one may assume Perroni took them either from the memorials by the governors that appeared in the gazettes, or from other sources – possibly provided by Chinese collaborators. He concludes from these quotes that "it is beyond doubt that every time the waters of the said river became clear, all of China always exalted with joy."[67]

65 APF, SOCP, vol. 33 (dall'Anno 1727 al 1728), fol. 328r.
66 APF, SOCP, vol. 33 (dall'Anno 1727 al 1728), fol. 328r.
67 APF, SOCP, vol. 33 (dall'Anno 1727 al 1728), fol. 328r.

Yet, he refers to an opposite interpretation as well, which can be found in a chronological table by Philippe Couplet, which contains a record describing a previous clearing of the water in the Han dynasty. This shows how Perroni also brings European sources into the discussion:

> Therefore it seems quite strange that Fr. Couplet in his *Chronological Table of the Chinese Monarchy*, narrating the clearing of these waters which occurred in the year of Our Salvation 167, added by himself that this is considered by the Chinese as a sign of bad luck *quod illis* [these are his words] *mali ominis instar est*.[68]

Next, Perroni relates the responses of the officials to this phenomenon. First, the mandarins of the provinces through which the Yellow River passes immediately gave notice of it to the emperor, and

> they did not lose the opportunity to flatter him (*adularlo*), attributing to him the prosperity, which it presaged, and [stating] that he was the Holy man, and virtuous man, that Heaven offered them with such change.[69]

Perroni insists on this flattery or adulation. For example, some mandarins of these provinces

> sent him their congratulatory memorials; exposing in them the strength no less of their eloquence than of Chinese flattery (*adulazione Cinese*). So that for several months the Gazettes were laden with a good part of the aforementioned memorials.[70]

The next stage was a joint memorial by the grand secretaries and high officials on 23 January 1727 (YZ5/1/2), congratulating the emperor on the fortuitous prediction and begging him to decide on a day for a solemn ceremony of prostrations while he would be seated on the throne. "The Emperor did not accede to the plea and the answer, which he gave them, is as follows in Chinese characters."[71] Perroni underscores that he provides the Chinese text "with the

68 Couplet (1686/87), p. 41: Anno 43 [this is the year of the cycle, which should be the year 166, during the reign of emperor Huan 桓 of Han] *Croceus fluvius semper turidus, limpidissimis fluxit aquis, quod illis mali ominis instar est*: The yellow river [which] is always turbid (muddy), flowed with very limpid waters, which is for them the sign of a bad omen.

69 APF, SOCP, vol. 33 (dall'Anno 1727 al 1728), fols. 328r–v.

70 APF, SOCP, vol. 33 (dall'Anno 1727 al 1728), fol. 328v.

71 APF, SOCP, vol. 33 (dall'Anno 1727 al 1728), fol. 328v.

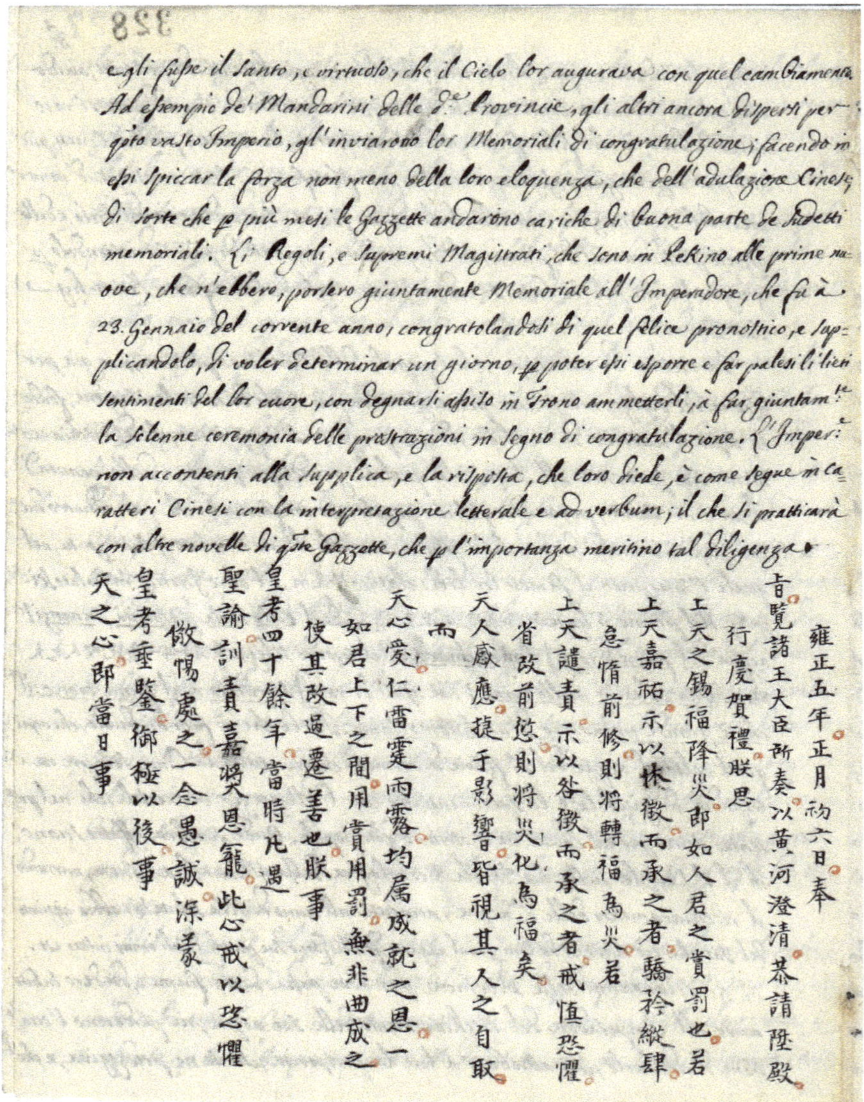

e gli fusse il Santo, e virtuoso, che il Cielo lor augurava con quel cambiamento.
Ad esempio de' Mandarini delle d.te Provincie, gli altri ancora dispersi per
q.to vasto Imperio, gl'inviarono lor Memoriali di congratulazione, facendo in
essi spiccar la forza non meno della loro eloquenza, che dell'adulazione Cinese;
di sorte che p più mesi le Gazzette andarono cariche di buona parte de sudetti
memoriali. Li Regoli, e supremi Magistrati, che sono in Pekino alle prime nuove, che n'ebbero, portero giuntamente Memoriale all'Imperadore, che fu à
23. Gennaio del corrente anno, congratolandosi di quel felice pronostico, e supplicandolo, di voler determinar un giorno, p poter essi esporre e far palesi li lieti
sentimenti del lor cuore, con degnarsi assiso in Trono ammetterli, à far giuntam.te
la solenne ceremonia delle prostrazioni in segno di congratulazione. L'Imper.e
non acconsentì alla supplica, e la risposta, che loro diede, è come segue in caratteri Cinesi con la interpretazione letterale e ad verbum; il che si prattiicarà
con altre novelle di q.te Gazzette, che p l'importanza meritino tal diligenza.

雍正五年正月初六日奉
旨覽諸王大臣所奏以黃河澄清恭請陞殿
行慶賀禮朕思
上天之錫福降災即如人君之賞罰也君
上天嘉祐示以休徵而承之者驕矜縱肆
怠惰前修則將轉福為災君
上天譴責示以咎徵而承之者戒慎恐懼
省改前愆則將災化為福矣
天人感應捷于影響皆視其人之自取
而
天心愛仁雷霆雨露均屬成就之恩一
如君上下之間用賞用罰無非曲成之
使其改過遷善也朕事
皇考四十餘年當時凡遇
聖諭訓責嘉獎恩寵此心戒以恐懼
儆惕處之一念愚誠深蒙
皇考垂鑒御極以後事
天之心即當日事

ILLUSTRATION 5 Rescript by the Yongzheng emperor about the waters of the Yellow River becoming clear, transcribed from a gazette (YZ5/1/6 = 27 January 1727): APF, SOCP, vol. 33 (dall'Anno 1727 al 1728), fols. 328v–329r

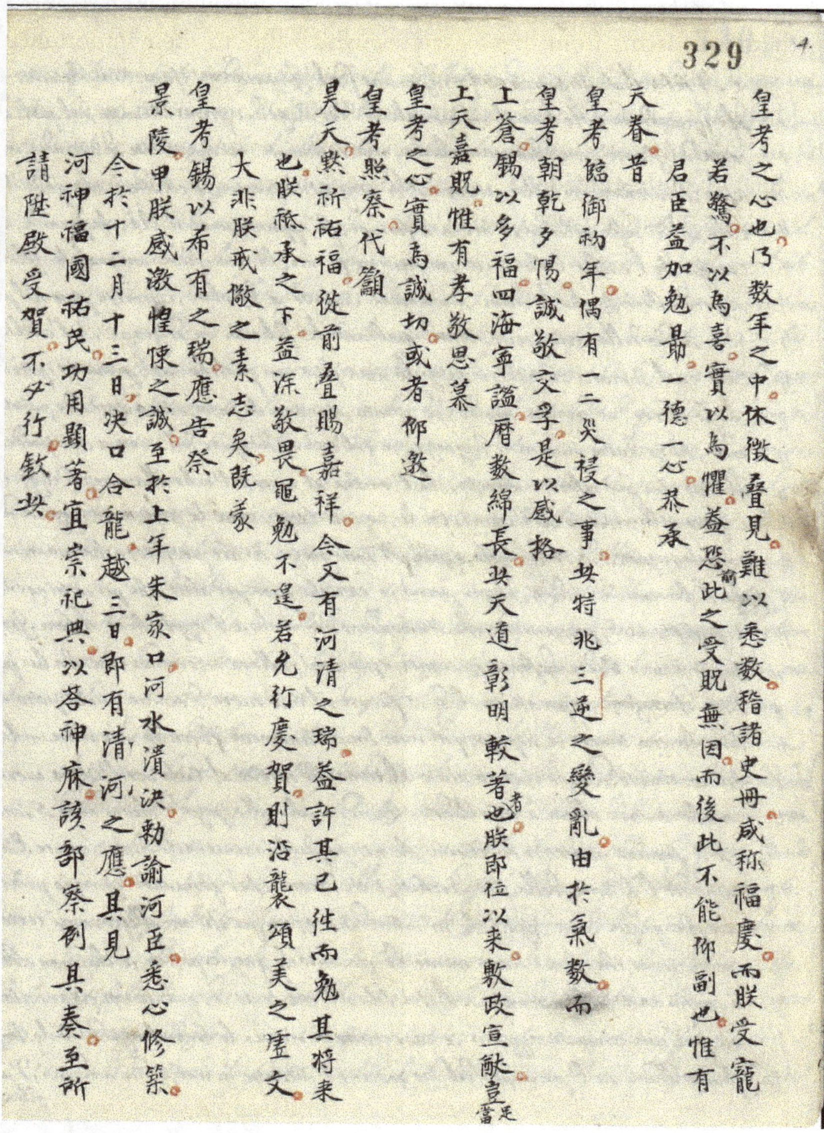

329

皇考之心也乃數年之中休徵疊見難以悉數稽諸史冊咸稱福慶而朕受寵
若驚不以為喜實以為懼益恐前此之受既無因而後此不能仰副也惟有
君臣益加勉勗一德一心恭承
天眷昔
皇考臨御初年偶有一二災祲之事此特兆三逆之變亂由於氣數而
皇考朝乾夕惕誠敬交孚是以感格
上蒼錫以多福四海寧謐曆數綿長此天道彰明較著者也朕即位以來敷政宣猷豈足當
上天嘉貺惟有孝敬思慕
皇考之心實為誠切或者仰邀
皇考照察代籲
昊天默祈祐福從前疊賜嘉祥今又有河清之瑞益許其已往而勉其將來
也朕祗承之下益深敬畏黽勉不遑若先行慶賀則沿襲頌美之虛文
大非朕戒儆之素志矣既蒙
皇考錫以希有之瑞應告祭
景陵申朕感激惶悚之誠至於上年朱家口河水潰決勅諭河臣悉心修築
今於十二月十三日決口合龍越三日即有清河之應其見
河神福國祐民功用顯著宜崇祀典以答神庥該部察例具奏至所
請陞殿受賀不必行欽此

literal and *ad verbum* translation (*interpretazione*); this will be implemented with other news items from these gazettes, which due to their importance deserve such diligence."[72] As an example, the beginning of this edict is transcribed here: the Chinese texts with the punctuation as provided by Perroni, his Italian translation, and an English translation of this Italian translation. As an examination of the provided Chinese text demonstrates, Perroni did indeed make a very literal and precise translation.

雍正五年。正月初六日。奉
旨。覽諸王大臣所奏。以黄河澄清。恭請陞殿。
行慶賀禮。朕思
上天之錫福降災。即如人君之賞罰也。若
上天嘉佑。示以休徵。而承之者。驕矜縱肆。怠
惰前修。則將轉福為災矣。若
上天譴責。示以咎徵。而承之者。戒慎恐懼。
省改前愆。則將化災為福矣。
天人感應。捷於影響。視其人之自取。
而
天心仁愛。雷霆雨露。均屬成就之恩。一
如君臣上下之間。用賞用罰。無非曲成之。
使其遷善改過也。朕事
皇考四十餘年。當時凡遇
聖諭訓責。嘉奬恩寵。此心皆以恐懼
儆惕處之。一念愚誠。深蒙
皇考垂鑒。御極以後。事
天之心。即當日事
皇考之心也。乃數年之中。休徵疊見。難以悉數。稽諸史冊。咸稱福慶。而朕受寵
若驚。不以為喜。實以為懼。蓋恐前此之受貺無因。而後此不能仰副也。惟有
君臣益加勉勗。一德一心。恭承
天眷。[73]

72 APF, SOCP, vol. 33 (dall'Anno 1727 al 1728), fol. 328v.

73 Lay-out and punctuation following APF, SOCP, vol. 33 (dall'Anno 1727 al 1728), fols. 328v–329r; see also *Qing shilu*, vol. 7, pp. 779–781 (*juan* 52) (YZ5/1/癸巳 [= 6] = 27 Jan. 1727); *Shizong xianhuangdi shangyu neige, juan* 52, pp. 2a–4a (*SKQS*, vol. 414, pp. 522–523) (YZ5/1/6 = 27 Jan. 1727); *Yongzheng chao qijuzhu ce*, vol. 2, pp. 918–920 (YZ5/1/5 = 26 Jan. 1727).

Anno 5. Luna 1. giorno 6. [27.Gennario] del'Imperadore Yum-cim. Rescritto del'Imperadore. Hò letto il memoriale di Voi Regoli, e primi Ministri, nel quale à causa del fiume croceo divenuto chiaro, riverentemente mi supplicate, d'ascender in trono, ed ammettervi alla ceremonia di congratulazione. Io considero, che qu[an]do il cielo ci dà delle felicità, ò invia infortuni, fa appunto come il Rè, che premia, e castiga. Se l'eccelso Cielo vuol compartirci favori, lo manifesta con qualche felice augurio: Però se chi lo riceve, ne diviene superbo, e dissoluto, e rendesi pigro nel pristino studio della virtù; certamente cambiara le felicità in disgrazie. Se l'eccelso Cielo vuol inviarci castighi, innanzi lo manifesta con qualche mal pronostico; però se chi lo riceve, ne diviene timido, ed attento, esamina se stesso, e si corregge de passati eccessi; senza dubio mutarà le disgrazie in felicità. Q[ue]st'operar dell'uomo, e corrisponder del Cielo son più veloci, e connessi, che l'ombra al corpo, e l'echo alla voce: L'elegger è posto nell'arbitrio dell'uomo. Cosi li strepitosi tuoni, come le pioggie, e ruggiade dell amoroso, e pietoso cuor del Cielo, egualm[en]te sono grazie à n[ost]ro profitto; nella maniera che il Rè con suoi sudditi, adopta premi, e castighi, non per altro, che per costringerli à perfettionarsl; procurando, che s'emendino dal male, e s'applichino al bene. Io hò servito à mio Padre defonto quaranta, e più anni; allora occorrendo tener da lui qualsisia esortazione, riprensione, lode, ò favore, il mio cuore diveniva più disposto à servirlo con timore, e rispetto; q[ue]sti miei sinceri sentimenti furon da mio Padre molto ben conosciuti. Doppo esser io asceso al trono, hò servito al Cielo con l'istesso cuore con che servivo allora à mio Padre. Quindi è, che nello spazio d'alcuni anni si sono vissi si frequenti pronostici di felicità, che non è facile numerarli distintamente. Esa minando l'historie della Monarchia, tutte dicono esser fortunati segni; io però ricevo q[ue]ste grazie come segni, che m'intimidiscono; né per essi mi allegro, anzi certamente temo, che forse senza merito hò ricevuto le grazie passate, e che non abbian à continuarsi nell'avvenire. Resta solam[en]te, che tanto io, quanto voi ci animiamo vie più con virtuose azzioni, e cuor unito à ricever le benivolenze del Cielo.[74]

{English translation of the Italian text}

Year 5. Moon 1. day 6. [27th January] of the Emperor Yum-cim. Rescript of the Emperor. I have read the memorial of You *Regoli*, [=Princes] and Prime Ministers, in which, because of the river that has become clear,

74 APF, SOCP, vol. 33 (dall'Anno 1727 al 1728), fol. 329v.

> you reverently beg me to ascend the throne and to admit you to the congratulatory ceremony. I reckon that when Heaven gives us happiness, or sends misfortunes, it acts just like the King, who rewards and punishes. If the sublime Heaven wants to share favours with us, it manifests it with some happy wishes: But if the one who receives it becomes proud and idle, and makes himself lazy in the pristine study of virtue; it will certainly turn happiness into misfortune. If the lofty heaven wants to send us punishments, it first manifests it with some bad prediction; however, if whoever receives it becomes timid and attentive, examines himself, and corrects himself for the past excesses; no doubt it will turn misfortunes into happiness. The work of man, and the reciprocation of Heaven are faster and more connected than the shadow to the body, and the echo to the voice: The choice is placed in the will of man. So the resounding thunder, like the rains, and roaring with the loving, pitiful heart of Heaven, are likewise thanks to our profit; in the way that the King, with his subjects, uses rewards and punishments, for no other reason than to force them to perfection; ensuring that they correct themselves from evil, and apply themselves to good. I have served my Father for forty or more years; at that time when it happened to receive from him any exhortation, reproof, praise, or favour, my heart became more disposed to serve him with fear and respect; these sincere sentiments of mine were very well known to my Father. After having ascended the throne, I served Heaven with the same heart with which I then served my Father. So it is that in the space of a few years there have been such frequent predictions of happiness, that it is not easy to enumerate distinctly. Examining the histories of the Monarchy, they all say that they are lucky signs; however, I receive such graces as signs, that intimidate me, and nor I feel joy for them, in fact I certainly fear that maybe without merit I received past graces, and that [they] do not have to continue in the future. It remains only, that both I and you animate ourselves more and more with virtuous actions, and with a united heart to receive the benevolence of Heaven.

In the following part of his edict, the emperor states that he is not worthy of this praise. Instead, he insists that the clearing of the Yellow River is a sign by his father, the Kangxi emperor, of the blessings granted by Heaven, the happiness of the country, and the protection of the people by the Spirit of the River. Therefore, he is of the opinion that the proposed ceremony of congratulations "certainly would cause me to be carried away by the vanity of praise; which would be more than a little contrary to my sincere intention to mortify myself."[75] He deems that he should make a sacrifice of gratitude at the tomb of his father, and that sacrifices should be made to the Spirit of the River, for which he asks the Ministry of Rites to examine the proper ways. Perroni explains that, in spite of the emperor's refusal, the grand secretaries and high officials replied with a second memorial a few days later, still pleading to be admitted to a congratulatory ceremony. On the one hand, "all busy praising the virtues and great gifts of their Prince,"[76] they enumerate the various signs of happiness given by Heaven after he had ascended to the throne. These included the conjunction of the planets in heaven, nine ears of wheat from the same stem in the fields, extraordinary precious stones in rivers and in the sea, trees blooming out of season in woods, extraordinary snows in multiple provinces, and, most recently, the crystalline appearance of the Yellow River. On the other hand, the officials point out that "those wishes of happiness had been sent by his deceased Father for the merit of his great virtues: now if he received happiness from his Father, the peoples were made happy by him."[77] They once more insist on having a congratulatory ceremony and are of the opinion that "in this way the spirit [or soul] of the Emperor His Father, who is in Heaven, would certainly be happy with it."[78] Here, again, Perroni quotes the original Chinese phrase: 聖祖在天之靈必忻喜嘉悅.[79] The memorial in which this sentence originally appeared has not yet been found.

This description of the process through which the emperor communicated with his officials is followed by the second edict of the emperor, first in Chinese and then in its Italian translation. The edict builds on the idea that the benefits come from Heaven and from the late Kangxi emperor. The Yongzheng emperor is of the opinion that prosperity is not the result of one person, but of the common effort of the emperor and the officials, in the capital and in the provinces. He firmly refuses any congratulatory ceremony. At the same time, he considers the sovereign and his ministers to constitute one and the same body (*istesso corpo* 一体). Therefore, in the same way as he usually passed the instructions which he received from Heaven and his father on to the officials, the felicity which he received from Heaven and his father should also be passed on to them. Consequently, he decided to remunerate them by elevating them all by

75 APF, SOCP, vol. 33 (dall'Anno 1727 al 1728), fol. 330r.
76 APF, SOCP, vol. 33 (dall'Anno 1727 al 1728), fol. 330v.
77 APF, SOCP, vol. 33 (dall'Anno 1727 al 1728), fol. 330v.
78 APF, SOCP, vol. 33 (dall'Anno 1727 al 1728), fol. 330v.
79 APF, SOCP, vol. 33 (dall'Anno 1727 al 1728), fol. 330v.

one grade above their original rank. He ends the edict by asking them to find the proper ways to express their gratitude to Heaven and his father.[80]

What follows in Perroni's report after this edict is a description of the subsequent steps. In execution of the orders by the emperor, the Ministry of Rites, together with the high officials, discussed the sacrificial ceremonies to the Kangxi emperor and to the Spirit of the River, and concluded that "it did not seem appropriate for those sacrifices to be made according to the customary ceremonies prescribed by the Ritual; but that a new and extraordinary rite was needed to pass on to posterity the memory of that clearing."[81] The emperor conceded to their plea, and the grand counsellors made decisions regarding details such as the date, the place, and the prayers. These were presented in a memorial on the sixth of the second month (26 February 1727) in which again the officials "exalted the great humility"[82] of the emperor. "They added that his Father's soul, who is in Heaven, will undoubtedly be pleased by the news, which they want to give him through that Sacrifice, of the clearing of the river."[83] Perroni seems to have been so impressed by this statement that he again quotes the Chinese text: 今以黃河澄清。上告聖祖。聖祖在天之靈。亦必懽忻喜嘉悅. He finishes his narration by mentioning that the emperor approved the proposals, and that "in the following gazettes we read [about] the expedition of not one, but two high officials to sacrifice to the said spirit of the river, one to the Province of Ho-nan, and the other to that of Nankino; and the third was sent to the tomb of his father in order to sacrifice in the manner prescribed by the consultation."[84]

Perroni's conclusion is a kind of counterpoint. In it, he establishes a sharp contrast between the flattery and adulation of the officials, and the blindness of the emperor. He makes this judgment on the basis of what he deems to be the state of the country:

> From what has been said so far in the present section, the unhappy condition of this Emperor can easily be concluded, blinded (*acciecato*) by the flattery (*adulazioni*) of His Ministers who do not let him know about the bad state in which China finds itself in these few years of his government. The sea, passing beyond the shore, invaded a large region in the province of Ce-Kiang; the rivers have inundated almost everywhere,

80 APF, SOCP, vol. 33 (dall'Anno 1727 al 1728), fols. 330v–331v (Chinese); fols. 332r–333r (Italian).
81 APF, SOCP, vol. 33 (dall'Anno 1727 al 1728), fol. 333r.
82 APF, SOCP, vol. 33 (dall'Anno 1727 al 1728), fol. 333v.
83 APF, SOCP, vol. 33 (dall'Anno 1727 al 1728), fol. 333v.
84 APF, SOCP, vol. 33 (dall'Anno 1727 al 1728), fols. 333v–334r.

> [resulting in] great ruins; there have been famines without interruption, continuing either in one or in another province with the death of innumerable people; There was no shortage of fires, and among these that of the famous Confucius temple in the Province of Sian-tum: His Generals, who he most favoured, were unfaithful to him: he was forced to shed much blood of Mandarins, and to get rid of some of His brothers with other various misfortunes. And at the sight of so many calamities, flattery (*adulazione*) gives him to believe that Heaven favours him with prodigies and that China enjoys the times of a golden century.[85]

As appears from this case, Perroni was a careful reader of the gazettes. He refers to gazettes published over a longer period of time, quoting from some of them, and brings the material together in one narrative. The whole report is constructed around two edicts of which the Chinese text and the precise translation are presented. In the entire collection of available pre-1800 European texts about the gazettes, this is the only case in which both the Chinese version and the translation appear together in the same text.

2.1.3 *Vision on the Emperor and the Bureaucracy*

The vision on the emperor and the bureaucracy that emerges from Perroni's concluding reflections is confirmed by the other cases that he presents in the "Ristretto" of both 1727 and 1728. Basing himself on the information provided by the gazettes, he offers an outsider's view on both the emperor and the bureaucratic system. From this perspective, he seems to see what others do not: that the officials constantly flatter and misinform an emperor who is blind to the troubles that plague his country. Perroni's vision, however, is multidimensional and at times even contradictory. At first sight, Perroni offers a very positive image of the Yongzheng emperor and his bureaucracy. Yongzheng himself seems to possess qualities for good rulership that allow him to surpass his predecessors. His style is characterized by strict governance and meticulous vigilance over the officials' performance. At the end of an overview of the different topics that are included in the gazettes in the "Ristretto" of 1728, Perroni exclaims: "The application of this Monarch to the government of his peoples is incredible, as well as the extreme vigilance he keeps so that the Magistrates fulfil their duties."[86] He concludes:

---

85 APF, SOCP, vol. 33 (dall'Anno 1727 al 1728), fols. 333r–v.

86 APF, SC, Indie orientali e Cina, vol. 19 (dal 1727 al 1728), fol. 722r.

> [It is unconceivable to us] that a monarch of an empire so vast and expansive has time to examine as much as he can, even the smallest detail, and to give to everything the praise or blame it deserves, with such a fine criticism, which would be astonishing even for the most impertinent critics of our Europe.[87]

Perroni depicts the emperor as someone who is good at lecturing and who holds speeches to reproach his officials, for instance expressing his aversion to superfluous and extravagant spending, in particular on the occasion of the celebration of his fifty-sixth anniversary.[88] Yet he is also very benevolent towards them, as in the case of those who did not succeed in the metropolitan examination. He appointed some as officials in the provinces and gave to others a viaticum of five taels to return home, contrary to the custom that those who failed should return at their own expense.[89] The emperor is portrayed as a humble person when he refuses congratulations and superfluous celebrations: "On various other occasions during his government, the Emperor gave a display of the aversion he takes to expenses that are made at whim and for mere pomp without utility or necessity," such as the luxurious presents he received at the occasion of the Dragon Boat Festival (5th day of the 5th month).[90] Rejecting the praise for successes that the officials attribute to his virtue and wisdom, he ascribes everything to the mercies of Heaven and to the secret help of his father, as in the case of the Yellow River or the victory over rebels in Tibet.[91] The Yongzheng emperor is also depicted as someone who highly respects the ancient teachings. For instance, regarding the two principles of respect for Master Confucius and the obedience to one's parents, "which the Chinese policy regards among others as the basis of good governance of the state,"[92] Perroni is of the opinion that "for the present emperor, who in political government either surpasses, or does not yield to any of his predecessors, everything is in the practice of these maxims."[93] Finally, the emperor is attentive to the needs of his people during critical times. For instance, he promulgated a new law to relieve local people after a bad harvest. It was "received with extreme joy and is of great advantage to [the affected] peoples."[94] In short, Perroni appears

87 APF, SC, Indie orientali e Cina, vol. 19 (dal 1727 al 1728), fol. 722v.
88 APF, SOCP, vol. 33 (dall'Anno 1727 al 1728), fols. 340v ff.
89 APF, SOCP, vol. 33 (dall'Anno 1727 al 1728), fol. 340v.
90 APF, SOCP, vol. 33 (dall'Anno 1727 al 1728), fols. 344r ff.
91 APF, SC, Indie orientali e Cina, vol. 19 (dal 1727 al 1728), fol. 720r.
92 APF, SOCP, vol. 33 (dall'Anno 1727 al 1728), fol. 334v.
93 APF, SOCP, vol. 33 (dall'Anno 1727 al 1728), fol. 333r.
94 APF, SC, Indie orientali e Cina, vol. 19 (dal 1727 al 1728), fol. 722r.

to be of the opinion that the Yongzheng emperor really is worthy of praise, his only limitation being that he should have more consideration for "the things of Heaven":

> Whatever the judgment that will be made of such a custom [of presenting gifts to the emperor] elsewhere, it cannot be denied that the two speeches [against useless spending and encouraging parsimony] referred to above show that the Emperor holds maxims worthy of praise and useful for the good governance of his peoples: so that if beautiful words correspond to the facts, and if what he says does not arise from a hypocritical and simulated heart, China has so far kept few emperors who can be compared to him, and he would be incomparable, if to the beautiful lights he has for [the things] on earth, some lights were joined to the things of Heaven.[95]

Perroni's view on the functioning of the bureaucracy appears equally positive at first sight. Cases like the one of the Yellow River illustrate the constant interaction and communication between the emperor and the different councils and ministries in the decision-making process. Officials were always involved when dealing with issues, and they would work together as a consultation team to formulate the most appropriate advice, which would in turn be confirmed by the emperor. Officials took initiatives to avoid abuses and correct mistakes. For instance, Perroni makes reference to officials of "the sect of the literati" who made use of the emperor's zeal for Confucius to make proposals to reform some abuse, which over time had introduced itself into the ceremonies towards their Master;[96] others questioned the emperor's prohibition of sea trade and pleaded to reopen the foreign trade for Chinese merchants for the sake of the economy.[97]

Yet, this positive vision on the emperor and the bureaucracy is contrasted with another vision. The central topic in Perroni's narrative is that of the emperor's blindness. In the first place, the emperor is blinded (*acciecato*) by the adulation of the officials, as appears from Perroni's conclusion of the Yellow River case. Commenting on another case – the tillage rite (*gengji li* 耕耤禮) which was extended from Beijing to the other provinces – Perroni similarly remarks that "the adulations that are read in the Chinese gazettes on the occasion of this new law are unbelievable, which every day blinds (*acceccano*) this poor

95 APF, SOCP, vol. 33 (dall'Anno 1727 al 1728), fol. 347r.
96 APF, SOCP, vol. 33 (dall'Anno 1727 al 1728), fol. 336v.
97 APF, SOCP, vol. 33 (dall'Anno 1727 al 1728), fol. 337r.

(*povero*) Emperor more and more."[98] In the conclusion of his description of this case, Perroni points to the disconnect between the emperor's words, and what is really happening in the country: "the Emperor makes pompous speeches, and the peoples everywhere experience nothing but misery and famine."[99] One year later, when the emperor attributes the fertility of the harvest to the fact that the officials put the tillage rite into practice throughout the empire, and the officials confirm him in this view, Perroni holds a different opinion:

> In this we see the deception in which they keep him even if he does not pretend to ignore the famine, which every year has afflicted one or another province of China since the time he ascended the Throne.[100]

Thus, the negative vision of the emperor is accompanied by a negative depiction of the bureaucratic system. Officials seem often to be fearful of the emperor and his power, and are perpetually flattering, praising, or exalting the emperor (*adulare, loddare, esaltare*). They are apt to make sumptuous manifestations of respect and gratitude, and they imitate and pander to the preferences of the emperor. They ascribe any possible "auspicious" event to the emperor's merits, whilst keeping silence about the real external circumstances. As a result, the emperor is described as a blind person who is left oblivious to the terrible famines and problems afflicting the country: he is a poor emperor (*povero Imperadore*) in an unhappy condition (*infelice condizione*).[101]

Yet, as suggested above, there is a second reason as to why the emperor is blind in Perroni's eyes, and this is related to Christianity. Yongzheng is blind to "Heavenly things" and impeded by the "blindness of his heart." This appeared clearly in the speech he gave at the occasion of the audience of the Portuguese Ambassador Alexandre Metelo, which coincided with the birthday of the Buddha (YZ5/4/8 = 28 May 1727). This speech was printed "in the Gazettes of Beijing (*Gazette di Pekino*), and went all over China under the eyes of an infinite number of people, who take delight in this kind of reading."[102] In this discourse "the Emperor revealed the blindness of his heart (*la cecità del Suo cuore*), and the disadvantageous idea that he nourished of Our Holy Religion, indeed of all the Religions of the world, not sparing even that of His

98 APF, SOCP, vol. 33 (dall'Anno 1727 al 1728), fol. 349v.

99 APF, SOCP, vol. 33 (dall'Anno 1727 al 1728), fol. 350r.

100 APF, SC, Indie orientali e Cina, vol. 19 (dal 1727 al 1728), fol. 723r.

101 APF, SOCP, vol. 33 (dall'Anno 1727 al 1728), fol. 333r.

102 APF, SOCP, vol. 33 (dall'Anno 1727 al 1728), fol. 351v. It was probably printed on YZ5/4/22 (= 11 June 1727), the date which is mentioned on the transcript of the Chinese text in APF, SOCP, vol. 33 (dall'Anno 1727 al 1728), fol. 418.

Confucius."[103] In Perroni's opinion, the emperor's blindness results in the persecution of Christianity. In the case of the Christian Sunu family, which was loved and held in high esteem by the Kangxi emperor, Yongzheng is vindictive (*fa vendetta*) and holds a grudge. He applies punishments cruelly (*crudeltà*), including to other political enemies, such as his two brothers.[104] He eliminates all his opponents, who are put on trial and eliminated under various pretexts, "and in a short time no one will remain who can make this emperor jealous, grand master of state government, according to the blind maxim of the world (*la cieca massima del mondo*)."[105]

> But in these [=the things of Heaven] he is completely blind (*cieco*): as he has clearly revealed it, and reveals by rejecting the Christian Religion, and with growing every day more in the fatal commitment of not wanting it to be preached in the Provinces so that after so many attempts, which were useless, to make him favourable to it, there is nothing left but to offer fervent prayers to the Lord God, so that he may limit the heart, and make him understand that the true policy to make oneself and one's peoples truly happy is to know and subject oneself to Jesus Christ.[106]

This contrastive vision of the emperor and the bureaucracy makes Perroni's texts distinctive from other contemporary interpretations.

2.1.4 *Other Documents*

Aside from the two versions of the "Ristretto" discussed above, the Archivio Storico "de Propaganda Fide" also contains some Chinese documents that are related to the persecution of Christians and missionaries and that were apparently copied from the relevant publications in the gazettes. For example, the Archivio holds two documents related to the execution of João Mourão (Mu Jingyuan 穆經遠, 1681–1726),[107] who had sided with one of the Yongzheng emperor's brothers who had competed for the throne. His case also involved high-ranking Christians from the Sunu 蘇努 family (mentioned

103 APF, SOCP, vol. 33 (dall'Anno 1727 al 1728), fol. 351v.
104 APF, SOCP, vol. 33 (dall'Anno 1727 al 1728), fol. 356r.
105 APF, SC, Indie orientali e Cina, vol. 19 (dal 1727 al 1728), fol. 721v.
106 APF, SOCP, vol. 33 (dall'Anno 1727 al 1728), fols. 347r–v.
107 *HCC*, p. 317; Huang Pei (1974), pp. 48–50; on this case, see the extensive study: Pasquale M. d'Elia, *Il lontano confino e la tragica morte del p. Joâo mourâo S. I. Missionario in Cina (1681–1726): Nella storia e nella leggenda, secondo documenti in gran parte inediti*, Lisboa: Agencia-geral do ultrama, 1963.

above in Perroni's "Ristretto" of 1727). Members of this family who had become Christians were allies of the competitors for the throne:

- deposition and condemnation of João Mourão by the Ministry of Justice (Xingbu 刑部) on 21 July 1726 (YZ4/6/22), which "was promulgated in the whole of China in the public gazettes published in Beijing"[108]
- passages from a lengthy imperial edict of 2 July 1726 (YZ4/6/3) about the crimes of the Emperor's brothers Yinsi 胤禩 (Yunsi 允禩) (1681–1726) and Yintang 胤禟 (Yuntang 允禟) (1683–1726),[109] including Mourão's role in the twenty-eight crimes of Prince Yintang, also promulgated in the whole empire[110]

In addition, there are also a few scattered references to the persecution of Christians in individual letters preserved in the Archivio Storico. These letters include transcripts of Chinese texts, some of which may have been copied from gazettes.

- Three texts are added to a letter dated 18 October 1729 by the Carmelite Rinaldo Maria Romei da San Giuseppe O.C.D. (1685–1760), who came to Beijing as a member of the papal legation (1720–1721), led by Carlo Ambrogio Mezzabarba (c. 1685–1741), and stayed there until 1732. These include an excerpt of an edict of the Yongzheng emperor, which discusses the tolerant attitude of the Kangxi emperor towards Lamas, Westerners, Buddhists,

---

108 APF, SC, Indie orientali e Cina, vol. 18 (anno 1726): Confessio P. Ioan. Moraon, et sententia in eundem lata a Tribunali Criminum pervulgata per totam Sinam in Gazulis publicis Pekini impressis (Confession of Fr. J. Mourão, and sentence issued against the same by the Tribunal of Crimes, and proclaimed all over China in the public Gazettes printed in Peking); Chinese: fols. 532v–533v; transl.: fols. 534r–536r (Latin); (YZ4/6/22 = 21 July 1726). Mokros (2016), p. 213; Mokros (2021), p. 119 mentions how London papers printed Mourão's confession to conspiracy with the note, "This confession has been inserted in all the Gazettes of China, which are never published but by the Emperor's Command ..." ("Extract of a Letter from Canton, dated the 2d of January, 1727," *Daily Post*, December 28, 1728).

109 *ECCP*, vol. 2, pp. 927–929.

110 APF, SC, Indie orientali e Cina, vol. 18 (anno 1726): Excerpta ex prolixo Imperatoris edicto per totum Imperium promulgato, quae concernunt eandem causam P. Ioan. Moraon (Excerpts from the long edict of the Emperor, proclaimed in the whole empire, which concern the same case of Fr. J. Mourão); Chinese: fols. 536r–v; transl.: fols. 536v–537v (Latin). For more information see Dudink (2022). First text: also transcript in Yan Zonglin (2007), pp. 112–113 (with reference to BAV, Borgia Cinese 439), appendix 4.2; see also Han Qi & Wu Min (2008), doc. no. 17 (pp. 41–43), based on AMEP (Archives des Missions Étrangères de Paris), vol. 432, fols. 430–436. Second text: see also transcript in Yan Zonglin (2007), pp. 111–112, appendix 4.1 (reference to Archivio Storico "de Propaganda Fide," T. 18, p. 36).

and Taoists (edict of YZ6/12/10 = 9 January 1729; gazette of YZ7/1/17 = 14 February 1729)[111]

- Two texts are added to a letter dated 5 August 1733 by the Italian Franciscan Francesco Iovino da Ottaviano O.F.M. It concerns two edicts by the Yongzheng emperor (YZ11/3/14 = 14 April 1733; YZ10/4/24 = 17 May 1732), which are referred to in order to evidence the emperor's protection and high opinion of Buddhism and Taoism. This is cited as the probable reason for the persecution of Christianity in Canton (and the banishment of the missionaries there to Macau in September 1732)[112]

Unique for the documents in the Archives of Propaganda Fide is that Chinese transcripts of original gazettes have been preserved, such as in the example of Perroni's "Ristretto." They demonstrate how the gazettes were used by the administrators of the Propaganda Fide to inform Rome on the basis of concrete proofs. Their main interest was the state of the Catholic Church in China, and they were especially interested in material related to this topic in the gazettes. Yet, their interest was broader and included, as Perroni's texts show, critical descriptions of the Chinese political system.

2.2 Letters by Contancin in *Lettres édifiantes et curieuses*

While the letters about the gazettes sent to the Propaganda Fide remained closed in the archives, other letters were printed and reached a wide audience. An important informant whose letters about the Chinese gazette were published, was the Jesuit Cyr Contancin (1670–1732). He is not a well-known missionary: for instance, he never occupied a position at the court nor published a book in Chinese. In fact, his letters on the gazette are among the few textual traces left by him. He arrived in China in 1701 and spent some years in the Zhejiang province before moving to Beijing in 1711, where he was superior of the residence of the French Jesuits for a few years (1716–1718). After some years in Shanxi and Jiangxi, he was exiled to Canton in 1725. Several years later, he

111 APF, SOCP, vol. 34 (dall'Anno 1729 al 1730), fols. 606–608: Chinese: fol. 608r; APF, SOCP, vol. 35: duplicate; Chinese: fol. 266.

112 APF, SOCP, vol. 39 (15 Luglio-18 Sept. 1736), fols. 336r–v (Italian translation fol. 337): Chinese: fol. 336r. Condemnation of Zhao Gao 趙杲, magistrate of Tangshan District 唐山縣 (Shunde Prefecture 順德府, Zhili), who demolished Buddhist and Taoist temples in his district (YZ10/4/24 = 18 May 1732).

was sent back to France to inform the Jesuits about the needs of the mission, arriving there in 1731. He died on his return to China in November 1732.[113]

During his short stay in France, Contancin participated in the revision of Jean-Baptiste Du Halde's (1674–1743) *Description géographique, historique, chronologique, politique, et physique de l'empire de la Chine et de la Tartarie chinoise*, published for the first time in 1735 (Paris: P.G. Le Mercier; 4 vols.).[114] This was one of the first major collections informing Europe about China. It was based on the correspondence that Du Halde had established with his fellow French Jesuit missionaries in China. Some of the letters of this correspondence had previously been published in *Lettres édifiantes et curieuses*, a series originally started by the Jesuit Charles Le Gobien (1652–1708) and continued by Du Halde after the death of the former. These letters followed the tradition of the Jesuit information network, by which the Jesuits communicated different types of information through correspondence. This included not only (personnel) matters internal to the order and therefore kept within the order; but also political, social, and cultural matters of interest to a wider public and therefore often published. The entire collection of *Lettres édifiantes et curieuses* was published in 34 volumes between 1702 and 1776 and became an important source of information about the Americas, the Middle East, India, and China in the eighteenth century.[115] In the first edition of this collection, 98 letters by missionaries from China are reproduced (on a total of 259).[116]

Du Halde published three of Contancin's letters in *Lettres édifiantes et curieuses*: Contancin's letter from 2 December 1725 in the volume published in 1728, 15 December 1727 in the volume of 1729, and 19 October 1730 a few years later in the volume of 1736.[117] The first two letters were addressed to the Jesuit Etienne Souciet (1671–1744), who was one of the editors of *Mémoires de Trévoux*, a journal founded by the Jesuits, which published critical reviews of contemporary books on literary, scientific, historical, and religious subjects; the last letter was addressed to Du Halde himself. In total they cover 320 pages in the original edition (159 pages in the reprint). They explicitly refer to and quote the Chinese gazette.[118]

113 See Dehergne (1973), no. 192; Pfister (1932–1934), no. 256.
114 For Contancin's role in this revision, see Landry-Deron (2002), p. 126ff; p. 368.
115 For an introduction, see Vissière & Vissière (1979), p. 11ff.; Dehergne (1977).
116 Barthélemy (2019), p. 229.
117 Landry-Deron (2002), p. 127 n. 64: the third letter was published much later because of lack of space in earlier volumes.
118 Unfortunately, the original texts seem not to have been preserved (the letters are not in the Archives jésuites de la Compagnie de Jésus en France (personal communication by the archivists)). They are not included in the list of manuscript letters that have been identified by Barthélemy (2019), pp. 262–264.

"Lettre du Père Contancin, missionnaire de la Compagnie de Jésus, au Père Etienne Souciet, de la même Compagnie" (2 December 1725 in Canton, Guangzhou 廣州), in *Lettres édifiantes et curieuses, écrites des missions étrangères par quelques missionnaires de la Compagnie de Jésus* (1703–1776), vol. 18 (= 1728), pp. 428–463 (also in *Lettres édifiantes et curieuses, écrites des missions étrangères* (1810–1811), vol. 20, pp. 298–316).

"Lettre du Père Contancin, missionnaire de la Compagnie de Jésus, au Père Etienne Souciet, de la même Compagnie" (15 December 1727 in Canton, Guangzhou 廣州), in *Lettres édifiantes et curieuses, écrites des missions étrangères par quelques missionnaires de la Compagnie de Jésus* (1703–1776), vol. 19 (= 1729), pp. 265–404 (also in *Lettres édifiantes et curieuses, écrites des missions étrangères* (1810–1811), vol. 21, pp. 75–144).

"Lettre du Père Contancin, missionnaire de la Compagnie de Jésus, au Père Duhalde, de la même Compagnie" (19 October 1730 in Canton, Guangzhou 廣州), in *Lettres édifiantes et curieuses, écrites des missions étrangères par quelques missionnaires de la Compagnie de Jésus* (1703–1776), vol. 22 (= 1736), pp. 189–325 (also *Lettres édifiantes et curieuses, écrites des missions étrangères* (1810–1811), vol. 21, pp. 235–304).

The three letters by Contancin were originally written in Canton. These letters were also translated into German (published in 1729 and 1755) and Spanish (1756).[119]

2.2.1 *First Letter*

Contancin's first description of the Chinese gazette appears in his first letter. The central theme of this letter is a portrayal of the Yongzheng emperor. For this depiction, Contancin uses gazettes as his primary source, which leads him to include an explanation of some characteristics of the Chinese gazette. Despite the "sad state to which the Mission is reduced" – Contancin himself being exiled to Canton – he intends to entertain his addressee Etienne Souciet about the new emperor "who occupies the Throne since three years." The "sad state" refers to the proscription of Christianity by the Yongzheng emperor shortly

119 For the references of these publications, see CCT-database. There is also a 19th century translation into Italian. The modern Japanese translation was made by Yazawa Toshihiko 矢澤利彥, who also added notes to his translation, identifying some texts with *Qing shilu*; see Yazawa Toshihiko (1973). The modern Chinese translation dates from 2001–2005. For a first description of Contancin's letters in Chinese, see Wu Boya (2015).

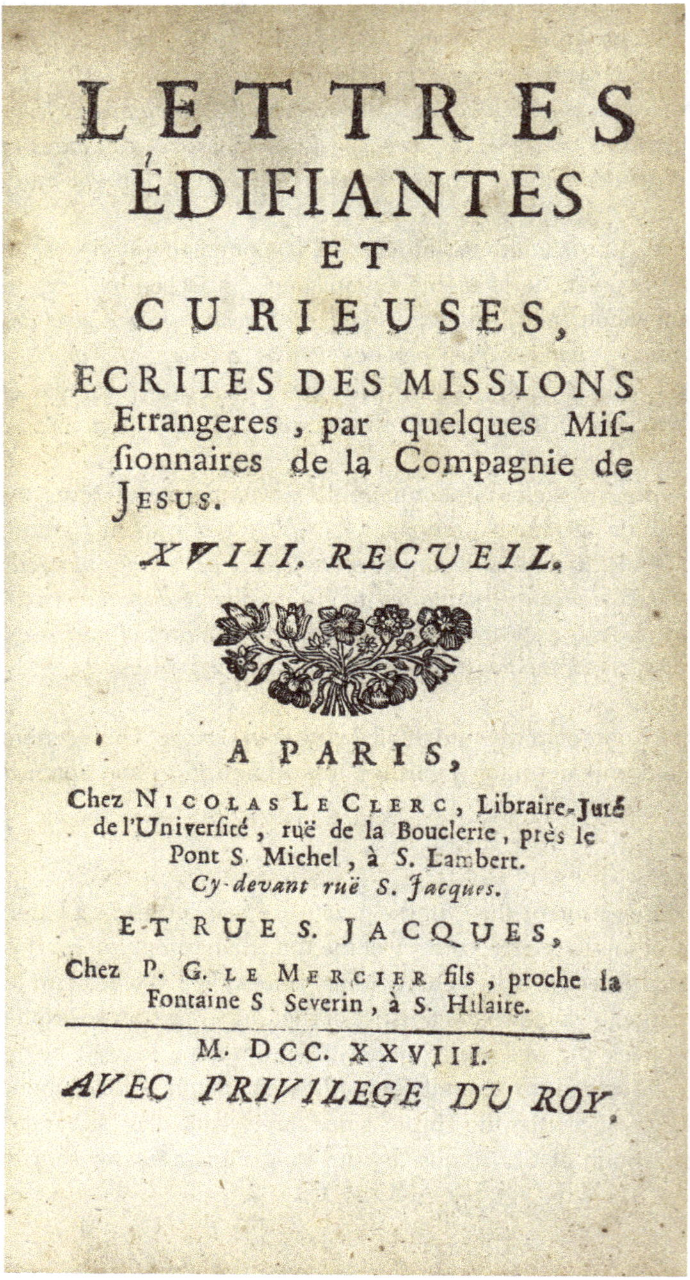

LETTRES
ÉDIFIANTES
ET
CURIEUSES,
ECRITES DES MISSIONS
Etrangeres, par quelques Missionnaires de la Compagnie de Jesus.

XVIII. RECUEIL.

A PARIS,
Chez Nicolas Le Clerc, Libraire-Juré de l'Université, ruë de la Bouclerie, près le Pont S. Michel, à S. Lambert.
Cy-devant ruë S. Jacques.

ET RUE S. JACQUES,
Chez P. G. le Mercier fils, proche la Fontaine S. Severin, à S. Hilaire.

M. DCC. XXVIII.
AVEC PRIVILEGE DU ROY.

ILLUSTRATION 6 The first letter by Cyr Contancin (Canton, 2 December 1725): *Lettres édifiantes et curieuses*, vol. 18 (1728), title page and p. 428

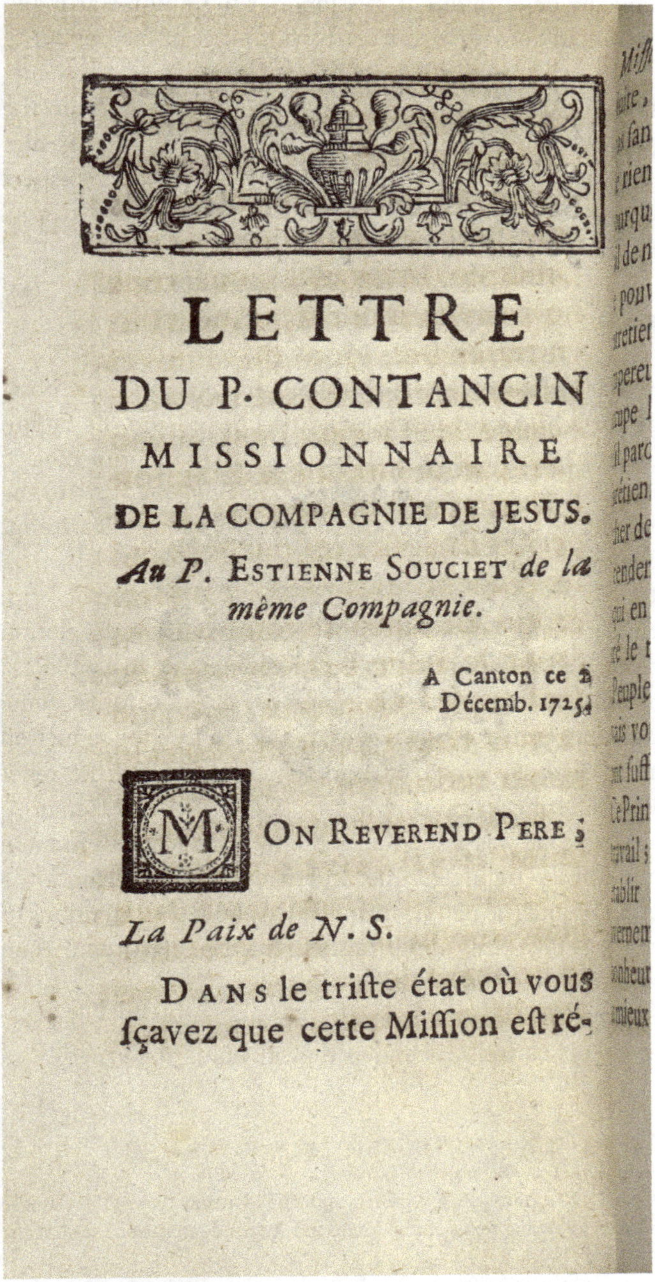

LETTRE
DU P. CONTANCIN
MISSIONNAIRE
DE LA COMPAGNIE DE JESUS.
Au P. ESTIENNE SOUCIET *de la même Compagnie.*

A Canton ce 2
Décemb. 1725.

MON REVEREND PERE;

La Paix de N. S.

DANS le triſte état où vous ſçavez que cette Miſſion eſt ré-

after his accession and the deportation of missionaries to Canton starting in October 1724. Yet, Contancin does not dwell on the sufferings of the mission:

> As alienated as he [= the Yongzheng emperor] appears to be from the Christian religion, one cannot help but praise the qualities that make him worthy of the Empire, and that in such a short time attracted the respect and love of his peoples for him. Some features that I will report to you, will make this sufficiently known to you.[120]

In the eyes of Contancin,

> This Prince is indefatigable in work; he thinks night and day [about how] to establish the form of a wise government, and to procure the happiness of his subjects. He cannot be better courted than by proposing to him some design that tends to public utility (*utilité publique*), and to the relief of the people; he adopts it with pleasure and executes it without any regard to the expense.[121]

Central in Contancin's laudatory description of the emperor are the notion of a "wise government" and an attention to the "happiness of his subjects." Substantiating his opinion of the emperor, Contancin goes on to list some examples of the Yongzheng emperor's service to "public utility": the reduction of taxes expected from Suzhou, Songjiang, and Nanchang;[122] and the relief offered by the emperor after heavy rains in Beijing, Shandong, and Henan.[123] The imperial instruction that was issued at the latter occasion, Contancin explains, "was included in the public gazette, and distributed throughout the empire so that the officials and the people be informed about the intentions of His Majesty."[124] Contancin takes this opportunity to make a "digression"[125] on the characteristics and contents of the gazette.

Contancin starts by making a comparison with Europe, similar to what was mentioned by other Jesuits as well. He shows that in China the gazette is a

---

120 *LEC* (1728), vol. 18, p. 429; *LEC* (1810–1811), vol. 20, pp. 298–299.

121 *LEC* (1728), vol. 18, pp. 429–430; *LEC* (1810–1811), vol. 20, pp. 298–299.

122 *LEC* (1728), vol. 18, p. 430; *LEC* (1810–1811), vol. 20, p. 299. The identification of the Chinese sources of this text and following texts can be found in the "Guide to the sources" at the end of this book.

123 *LEC* (1728), vol. 18, pp. 431–434; *LEC* (1810–1811), vol. 20, pp. 299–301; the letter of Contancin mentions Canton, but more likely this is Shandong.

124 *LEC* (1728), vol. 18, p. 434; *LEC* (1810–1811), vol. 20, p. 301.

125 *LEC* (1728), vol. 18, p. 441; *LEC* (1810–1811), vol. 20, p. 305.

centralised communication system with the emperor as central figure, with an instructive purpose:

> What makes the Gazette of China very useful for the government is that, instead of filling it, as is done in certain parts of Europe, with useless things and often with slanders and calumny, it only mentions what relates to the Emperor; and as the Chinese government is perfectly monarchical, and all the small and important affairs of the Empire are reported to him, this Gazette contains nothing that cannot be very useful in directing the Mandarins in the exercise of their office, and in instructing the Literati and the People.[126]

Next, Contancin provides a detailed overview of topics that are included in the gazette (here only presented in summary), a description that quite closely resembles the contents in scholarly descriptions today:[127]

- The names of officials who have been demoted or punished and the reasons why, as well as the names of those who have been promoted
- Criminal cases that received capital punishment
- Disasters that occurred in the provinces, and the relief offered by the officials or by order of the emperor
- Expenses made for the subsistence of the soldiers, the people, public works, and the benefit of the Prince
- Admonitions by high officials towards the emperor regarding his conduct or decisions
- Rituals performed by the emperor, such as ploughing the fields or instructing the officials on subjects taken from the canonical books
- The laws and new customs
- Praise and blame from the emperor for his officials[128]

These subjects correspond to the different roles of the sovereign, "since, as the Chinese say, he is emperor to govern, pontiff to sacrifice, master to teach."[129] Concerning the instructive role of the gazette, Contancin points out that it helps in a very practical way in directing the behaviour of the officials:

> Finally, as I have already said, the Chinese gazette is such that it is very useful in teaching the Mandarins how to govern the Peoples well. So they

126 *LEC* (1728), vol. 18, pp. 434–435; *LEC* (1810–1811), vol. 20, pp. 301–302.
127 Mittler (2004), p. 187ff.; Fang Hanqi (2013), pp. 36–37; Mokros (2016), p. 32ff.
128 *LEC* (1728), vol. 18, pp. 435–440; *LEC* (1810–1811), vol. 20, pp. 302–304.
129 *LEC* (1728), vol. 18, p. 440; *LEC* (1810–1811), vol. 20, p. 304.

> read it exactly; most even write down observations on the things that can direct their conduct.[130]

In the subsequent section of his letter, Contancin gives numerous examples taken from the gazettes that display the actions of the Yongzheng emperor. In addition to the aforementioned reduction in taxes and relief provided after heavy rains, Contancin included the following cases, which appear successively without subtitle:

- Imperial edict on the reciprocation between Heaven and the human being (*jianren jiaogan* 天人交感), in response to a memorial of Li Weijun 李維鈞 (?–1727), Governor-General of Zhili; written after having fasted because of drought[131]
- Imperial instruction that the Yellow River floods should not be blamed on the officials[132]
- Measures taken regarding prisoners because of excessive heat in Beijing[133]
- Encouragement to fulfil one's duties, as well as critique by the Emperor on prayers addressed to him in temples in gratitude for the tax exemption in Songjiang and Suzhou[134]
- On the attention the Emperor pays to the just treatment and fair condemnation of criminals (to capital punishment)[135]

Contancin also cites several new rules that the Yongzheng emperor installed:

- To inspire peasants to work (harder) and to lead a regular life: in each district select one exemplary peasant to be honoured with the symbols of the eighth rank (*ba pin* 八品) in the official hierarchy[136]
- To encourage female chastity: erect monuments in their honour (*jingbiao jianfang* 旌表建坊)[137]
- To promote filial piety: allow the transferring of official titles to deceased parents[138]

---

130 *LEC* (1728), vol. 18, pp. 440–441; *LEC* (1810–1811), vol. 20, pp. 304–305.
131 *LEC* (1728), vol. 18, pp. 442–443; *LEC* (1810–1811), vol. 20, pp. 305–306.
132 *LEC* (1728), vol. 18, p. 443; *LEC* (1810–1811), vol. 20, p. 306.
133 *LEC* (1728), vol. 18, pp. 444–445; *LEC* (1810–1811), vol. 20, pp. 306–307.
134 *LEC* (1728), vol. 18, pp. 455–458; *LEC* (1810–1811), vol. 20, pp. 312–314.
135 *LEC* (1728), vol. 18, pp. 459–460; *LEC* (1810–1811), vol. 20, pp. 314–315.
136 *LEC* (1728), vol. 18, pp. 446–448; *LEC* (1810–1811), vol. 20, p. 308.
137 *LEC* (1728), vol. 18, pp. 448–449; *LEC* (1810–1811), vol. 20, pp. 308–309.
138 *LEC* (1728), vol. 18, pp. 449–450; *LEC* (1810–1811), vol. 20, pp. 309–310; *LEC* (1728), vol. 18, pp. 450–451; *LEC* (1810–1811), vol. 20, p. 310.

- To increase the oversight of the officials: conduct the three-yearly evaluation (*daji* 大計)[139]

These examples included in the first letter by Contancin function as an illustration of the emperor and his government. They mainly consist of descriptions of the cases and translations (or paraphrases) of passages taken from the gazettes. Contancin's short personal comments, in which he indicates why he has chosen these specific examples, are relatively scarce. In his eyes, the incidents he describes illustrate how much the emperor "was touched by the miseries of his people,"[140] as in the case of the relief he provided for bad harvests, or how his "attention and clemency is generally extended to all his subjects," showing a "fatherly tenderness (*une tendresse de père*),"[141] as in the case of the relaxation of the treatment of prisoners during the extreme summer heats. According to Contancin, the new rules installed by the emperor "prove his vigilance and his application to govern his peoples well."[142] In addition, Contancin highlights how the emperor takes initiatives to carry "filial piety to the highest points it can reach"[143] by allowing officials to transfer their honorific titles to their parents, and he organises the three-yearly evaluation in order "to know well all the officials of the empire."[144] Finally, in the eyes of Contancin, "this new monarch has the good of the empire so deeply at heart" that he inaugurated a system of secret memorials, which can "contribute to good government."[145]

In conclusion, Contancin is of the opinion that all these characteristics show "the application of this Prince. His continual study is to learn to govern his people well, and to procure their happiness."[146] With this statement, Contancin again underlines the exemplary role of the emperor that he depicted at the beginning of his letter. He sketches a picture of an emperor who should be praised as administrator, educator, and caretaker of his people. In fact, the emperor's main shortcoming is his attitude towards Christianity: "May God inspire him with sentiments more favourable to our holy Religion, so that the pastors torn by his orders from their dear flock, may some day be reunited with them."[147]

139 *LEC* (1728), vol. 18, pp. 452–455; *LEC* (1810–1811), vol. 20, pp. 310–312. The highest degree of excellence: *Tcho-y* = *zhuoyi* 卓異.
140 *LEC* (1728), vol. 18, p. 441; *LEC* (1810–1811), vol. 20, p. 305.
141 *LEC* (1728), vol. 18, p. 446; *LEC* (1810–1811), vol. 20, p. 307.
142 *LEC* (1728), vol. 18, p. 446; *LEC* (1810–1811), vol. 20, p. 307.
143 *LEC* (1728), vol. 18, p. 450; *LEC* (1810–1811), vol. 20, p. 310.
144 *LEC* (1728), vol. 18, p. 452; *LEC* (1810–1811), vol. 20, p. 310.
145 *LEC* (1728), vol. 18, pp. 462–463; *LEC* (1810–1811), vol. 20, p. 316.
146 *LEC* (1728), vol. 18, p. 463; *LEC* (1810–1811), vol. 20, p. 316.
147 *LEC* (1728), vol. 18, p. 463; *LEC* (1810–1811), vol. 20, p. 316.

2.2.2 *Second Letter*

Written two years after the first letter, the attention in Contancin's second letter shifts from the emperor to the gazettes themselves. Like the previous letter, it was addressed to Souciet, who had stated that he had read with pleasure the pieces concerning "the government of China" that were taken from the "public gazette."[148] To be sure, the emperor and his governance remain an important topic, but the gazette as a means to channel information to a wider public comes to the forefront. The beginning of this letter not only contains evidence of Contancin's own reading practices, but also a precise description of the contents of the gazette that helps to identify which type of gazette he might have been reading. In length, this letter is two and a half times longer than the previous one (in the original version: 140 pages compared to 40; in the reprint: 70 pages compared to 20). Unfortunately, Contancin does not explicitly explain how he made the selection of the specific cases taken from the gazettes.

The letter starts with a note on Contancin's personal use of the gazettes. This reads as a personal reflection. He relates how he discovered the gazettes at the occasion of the events that resulted in the proscription of Christianity in January 1724 and the deportation of missionaries to Canton in October of the same year:

> I confess that I would never have imagined that the reading of this gazette could be as useful to a Missionary as it really is: and I regret having spent more than twenty years in China without having read it. A reason which interested the Religion and its Ministers, encouraged me to read it, for the first time, in the year 1723. You know that then a Superintendent [=Governor] of two Provinces sent an accusation to the Court both against the Christian law and against the Europeans who preached it. The Emperor exiled us all, with the exception of the Missionaries of Peking, first to Macao, then to Canton, where we still are. Everything that happened regarding such an important matter for us was published in the gazette. That's what gave me the curiosity to read it.[149]

---

148 *LEC* (1729), vol. 19, pp. 265–266; *LEC* (1810–1811), vol. 21, pp. 75–76.

149 *LEC* (1729), vol. 19, pp. 266–267; *LEC* (1810–1811), vol. 21, p. 76. The accusation against Christianity by the Governor of two provinces refers to Gioroi Mamboo 覺羅滿保 (1673–1725), Governor-General of Fujian and Zhejiang. The Ministry of Rites responded to his memorial on YZ1/2/17 (= 12 January 1724). For the Chinese texts, see also Han Qi & Wu Min (2008), doc. no. 4 (pp. 26–27), based on ARSI (Archivum Romanum Societatis Iesu), Jap. Sin. 179, fols. 304–305.

This is a rare insight in the reading practice of the gazette by missionaries in China. In Contancin's eyes, the gazettes had a wider significance, also for Europeans:

> I learned from reading it that it was very instructive, not only for the Chinese, but especially for a European. It is there that one learns the Religion, the doctrine, the Laws, the customs, the morals of the Chinese, and consequently the manner of conversing with and treating them. One also learns the most appropriate expressions, which one must use to speak well and to write well on all sorts of subjects.[150]

This description underscores the role of the gazette as a source of information, also for non-Chinese. Again, Contancin makes a comparison with the European gazettes, stressing that the difference between the two is situated in the fact that the Chinese gazettes are not only about the emperor but emanate from the emperor:

> Yet the European Missionaries have always neglected this reading; some because they do not know the language enough; others because they have to make expenses which they consider much more necessary. Most do not even know about it; and at the mere word of gazette they hear, they imagine that it resembles certain gazettes of Europe, in which one puts or has put everything one wants, good and bad, without any distinction. Now, by reasoning thus on the gazette of China, they are strongly mistaken; for nothing is printed here which has not been presented to the Emperor, or which does not come from the Emperor himself. Those who take care of it, would not dare to add anything to it, not even their own reflections, under the penalty of corporal punishment. Last year the Writer of a Tribunal, and another Writer, who was employed in the Bureau of the Post, were sentenced to death for having inserted in the Gazette some circumstances which were false. The reason on which the Criminal Court of Justice based its judgment is that in that they had disrespected His Majesty; and that the law holds that whoever lacks the respect he owes to the Emperor, deserves death.[151]

150 *LEC* (1729), vol. 19, pp. 267–268; *LEC* (1810–1811), vol. 21, pp. 76–77.

151 *LEC* (1729), vol. 19, pp. 267–269; *LEC* (1810–1811), vol. 21, pp. 76–77. Condemnation of two officials for having put false information in the gazette; *Qing shilu*, vol. 7, pp. 646–647 (*juan* 44); vol. 7, pp. 660–661 (*juan* 44) (YZ4/5/庚子 [= 9]; YZ4/5/庚戌 [= 19] = 8 June 1726; 18 June 1726); *Shizong xianhuangdi shangyu neige, juan* 44, pp. 10a–12a; *juan*

The case of the two officials condemned to death for publishing false news seems to correspond with the case of a capital punishment mentioned by Perroni. It refers to the consequences of a report that appeared in the *xiaochao* 小抄 (also called *xiaobao* 小報) which was, as mentioned earlier, a newspaper sometimes produced by agents of the postal office in charge of compiling the gazette (*titang* 提塘) or, as in this case, of the reporting offices (*baofang* 報房), which printed and disseminated the gazettes. In addition to collecting the official news, these agents also independently gathered information that was published separately. The purpose of this separate publication was to provide officials in the provinces with extra information about the court.[152]

The case reported by Contancin concerns an event that took place on 4 June 1726 (YZ4/5/5) when a few princes and high officials went to the Yuanmingyuan 圓明園 to pay respects to the emperor. In the *xiaochao*, two commoners, He Yu'en 何遇恩 and Shao Nanshan 邵南山, reported that after the meeting the emperor had ordered the officials to join him on the dragon boats. They alleged that the emperor and high officials had had a good time together, accompanied by music and wine, and that they had made a tour from the East to the West Lake, returning to the palace quite late in the afternoon (皇上出宮。登龍舟。命王大臣等登舟。共數十隻。俱作樂。上賜蒲酒。由東海至西海。駕於申時回宮等語). This description, according to the emperor, did not correspond to the ordinary meal (*jiachang shizhuan* 家常食饌) that was offered in one of the halls, while they were merely enjoying the flowers (*kanhua* 看花), not taking a boat ride at all, and the whole event lasting less than one hour. The report published in the *xiaochao* was considered "untrue and abominable" (以無為有, 甚屬可惡). The story was perceived as damaging the emperor's reputation, painting a picture of a frivolous ruler drinking wine every day (日日飲酒). Both He Yu'en and Shao Nanshan were condemned to decapitation and were executed after an initial delay.[153]

44, pp. 20a–22a; *SKQS*, vol. 414, pp. 390–391; vol. 414, pp. 395–396 (YZ4/5/9; YZ4/5/19 = 8 June 1726; 18 June 1726).

152 Fang Hanqi (1992–1999), vol. 1, p. 202; Fang Hanqi (2013), pp. 34–35.

153 See *Qing shilu*, vol. 7, pp. 646–647 (*juan* 44), YZ4/5/庚子 [= 9] (= 8 June 1726); vol. 7, pp. 660–661 (*juan* 44), YZ4/5/庚戌 [= 19] (= 18 June 1726); *Shizong xianhuangdi shangyu neige, juan* 44, pp. 10a–12a; *juan* 44, pp. 20a–22a; *SKQS*, vol. 414, pp. 390–391; vol. 414, pp. 395–396, YZ4/5/9; YZ4/5/19 (= 8 June 1726; 18 June 1726) (the *Qijuzhu* of that month is missing). Modern authors consider this the earliest case of execution with full identification of names in the Chinese history of newspapers: see Fang Hanqi (1992–1999), vol. 1, pp. 203–204; Fang Hanqi (2000), vol. 1, pp. 15–16. Mokros (2021), p. 56 refers to this case in the discussion of Yongzheng's actions against document leaks and trivial talk. The case is also reported in the private jottings by Xiao Shi 蕭奭, *Yong xianlu* 永憲錄 (1997),

The emperor's violent reaction to the "news" of his so-called boat trip can be attributed to the context in which the affair took place. At that time, the emperor was engaged in a campaign of merciless repression against his political opponents, several of the victims of which were his own brothers (including the aforementioned Yintang (Yuntang) and Yinti 胤禵 (Yunti 允禵) (1688–1755)), who had been accused of forming a "clique" with the goal of denigrating the emperor and challenging his legitimacy. The first imperial edict related to the boat trip begins by evoking the evils of this clique, which had been formed at the end of the Kangxi reign and joined by all kinds of disreputable people, "including Buddhist monks, Taoist priests, Lamas, healers, diviners, astrologers, physiognomists, and even actors, low servants, as well as Westerners (*xiyangren* 西洋人) and the slaves of high ministers."[154] After the Yongzheng emperor's accession to the throne, these plotters were said to have spread rumours essentially accusing him of being a drunkard, while "in reality by nature he is unable to drink a single drop of alcohol" (然朕實天性素不能飲).[155] This context puts Contancin's brief reference to the death penalty in a different light. Whether the omission of this additional information was on purpose or not is unclear, as it is uncertain what sources Contancin used for this reference, either personal information or a gazette. If it was a gazette, he may have only seen the one with the memorial of the Ministry of Justice (Xingbu 刑部) proposing the death penalty and the subsequent imperial rescript, which did not make reference to the larger context. Contancin may thus have prudently decided to refrain from alluding to the punishment's circumstances, or he may simply have been unaware of them.

In addition to describing the gazette's role in the centralised circulation of information, Contancin also gives more insight into its content, length, and frequency of appearance. He especially stresses the centrality of "public affairs":

> But what does this Gazette contain that is so important? I have already pointed out something in my letter of December 13, 1725. And to give you

p. 280 (*juan* 4). This unofficial historical treatise is based on various sources, presumably also gazettes, and records events from 1722 (KX61) to 1728 (YZ6) (with an original preface dated 1752 (QL17)). In this jotting, Xiao Shi states that the Yongzheng emperor had already decreed the prohibition of small gazettes in 1723, and that after the execution of the two individuals in 1726 they definitively disappeared (*sihou xiaochao yong jue yi* 嗣後小抄永絕矣) (other contemporary sources indicate that the small gazette continued to circulate in spite of this prohibition).

154 See *Qing shilu*, vol. 7, p. 646; this passage is also translated in Fu Lo-shu (1966), p. 145.

155 See *Qing shilu*, vol. 7, p. 646.

> a clearer idea, I will tell you that the Chinese Gazette contains almost all the public affairs that take place in this vast empire. It is a collection, containing the Memorials and the Petitions presented to the Emperor, the answers this Prince has given, the instructions he has given, and the graces he has granted to the Mandarins or the people. This collection is printed daily and is in the form of a brochure that contains 60 to 70 pages.[156]

Next, he gives an example of the content and structure of the gazette:

> Here is a model.
>
> On the 15th of December, which will be the third of the second month,
>
> First, one puts the titles of the memorials that arrived at the court on the third of the eleventh moon, with the subject in question, but in a few words.[157] For example, Memorial of the Viceroy of Canton on the rice stores that must be filled … Memorial of the General of the Chinese Troops of the Province of Tche-Kiang, in which he accuses Mandarin so and so of having demanded money from his subordinate officers, & c. At the beginning of such a collection, one usually announces in the same way twenty or thirty memorials.
>
> Second, one puts the answers that the Emperor has given to several other memorials or placets that day. If the Emperor has not given any, it is stated: that day there was no response from his Majesty.
>
> Third, one puts the instructions & orders given by the Emperor, either on his own or in response to the points proposed to him.
>
> Fourth, one sees the deliberations that the courts have presented, to receive the confirmation of his Majesty.
>
> At the end come several of the memorials that were sent to the Emperor by the great Mandarins of the Provinces, such as the Viceroys, the Generals of the Troops either Chinese or Tartars, & the other Officers of the First Order.

156 *LEC* (1729), vol. 19, pp. 269–270; *LEC* (1810–1811), vol. 21, pp. 77–78.

157 Notice that there is a problem with the date: 15 December 1727 is the third of the eleventh month [of the fifth year of the Yongzheng era] (as correctly mentioned in the second sentence), not of the second month (as mentioned in the first sentence). This may be a problem that occurred in the process of transcription. The editors of the 1810–1811 edition noticed the anomaly and corrected (erroneously) the second sentence by also using second month.

> This is how the Gazette is laid out, which is produced in over three hundred small collections per year.[158]

This detailed information is helpful to identify, at least partly, the type of gazette used by Contancin. The problem in this search is that hardly any gazette of the Yongzheng period has been preserved, and if any is preserved, very limited information about the content or format is publicly available. Still, existing texts that could be considered to be associated with the gazette can be divided in two categories.

First, there are at least four documents, each bound as a booklet, which carry on their covers an etiquette with the title *dibao* 邸報, which is commonly considered the printed version of the official gazette.[159] These could seem to contradict certain statements that in 1723, during the reign of the Yongzheng emperor, "*jingbao*" 京報 was prescribed as the official term for the printed version of the official gazette.[160] References to these booklets can be found on the internet, but unfortunately the location where they are preserved is usually not disclosed. As a result, they could not be consulted for further investigation. The length of each booklet is unknown, except for one that counts 52 pages, which at first sight seems comparatively close to Contancin's statement that the gazette is "in the form of a brochure that contains 60 to 70 pages." A closer examination indicates that these booklets appear to be distinct issues of what became known as (*Yongzheng*) *Shangyu neige* (雍正) 上諭內閣 (Edicts of the Yongzheng reign issued through the Grand Secretariat), first published in 1731

158 *LEC* (1729), vol. 19, pp. 269–272; *LEC* (1810–1811), vol. 21, pp. 78–79.

159 YZ2/12/? (Jan.-Febr. 1725): illustration in Wu Boya (2015), p. 369.
YZ3/3/3 (15 April 1725): auctioned at Diandi paimai 点滴拍卖 LOT02 (2017-04-01), web.archive.org/web/20210421090120/http://www.qudiandi.com/auction/item/aid/1.html; mainly related to Nian Gengyao 年羹堯 (with illustrations).
YZ7/10/1 (21 November 1729): auctioned at ePailive.com 易拍全球 Lot1398 (2020-07-26), web.archive.org/web/20210527123035/https://www.epailive.com/goods/13447060 (with illustrations).
YZ7/11/3-30 (22 December 1729–18 January 1730): illustration and description in *Zhongguo jibao jingpin* 中国集报精品 (2013), pp. 8–9. This copy, which is in the hands of Miao Shiming 苗世明, counts 52 pages.
YZ7/11/3 (22 December 1729): illustration in general article about dibao "Liaoliao Zhongguo gudai zuizao de baozhi – dibao" 聊聊中国古代最早的报纸 – 邸报 on website Meiri toutiao 每日头条 (2018-08-26), web.archive.org/web/20210527123637/https://kknews.cc/zh-sg/history/vea2k9l.html (with illustrations). This appears to be the same copy as the previous one.

160 Kong Zhengyi & Chen Chen (2012), p. 123; Mittler (2004), p. 179.

and then in 1741.[161] This work has no division in *juan*, but brings together in each issue the edicts proclaimed during one month. These issues usually consist of 15 to 25 folios (equivalent to 30 to 50 pages), with some containing only 4 folios (8 pages), and others as many as 32 folios (64 pages) (11 columns, 1+ 20 characters).[162] Each issue starts with the same formulaic introduction: first the year and month covered in the issue, next the number of edicts included in it (with *dao* 道 as measure word for edicts), and then the date of the first date of issue. E.g.:

> 雍正七年十一月
> 上諭三十一道
> 初三日

The precise nature of *Shangyu neige* is as of yet unclear. It may have been an entirely free-standing work compiling (only) edicts issued through the Grand Secretariat, which may or may not have been published in a gazette first. Alternatively, it may have been a compilation of an existing monthly publication of edicts, with the original title *dibao*, such as the four existing documents under investigation. Even if the latter is the case, it is unlikely that Contancin's detailed description refers to this gazette, since these booklets with the title *dibao* only contain the edicts issued through the Grand Secretariat (and e.g. no responses to memorials by the Governors) and cover a whole month (instead of only one day). Still, they are an important source, since nearly all the edicts reported on by Contancin and Perroni and preserved in the Archives of Propaganda Fide are also mentioned in *Shangyu neige*.

The second existing text that could be considered to be the gazette is entitled *tizou quanlu* 題奏全錄 (complete record of memorials). So far only one copy of *tizou quanlu* has been identified.[163] The cover mentions the title *Tizou quanlu* as well as a date: 題奏全錄雍正九年八月十八日 (YZ9/8/18 =

---

161 It was published in *Siku quanshu* under the title *Shizong xianhuangdi shangyu neige* 世宗憲皇帝上諭内閣 (159 *juan*). *Yongzheng chao hanwen yuzhi huibian*, vols. 6–8. According to the explanation in *Qinding Siku quanshu zongmu* (1997), vol. 1, pp. 765–766, originally the work had no title, but it was added at the moment of compilation for the *Siku quanshu*.

162 On the basis of *Yongżheng chao hanwen yuzhi huibian*, vol. 8 (p. 88: 32 fols.; p. 221: 4 fols.).

163 Preserved in the Österreichische Nationalbibliothek, Vienna: Sin. 251; see Fang (1992), p. 52: "Tí Tsou Ch'üan Lu: Sammlung von Eingaben an Kaiser Yung Cheng (1723–35) in Staatsangelegenheiten Peking. 1731."; see also https://digital.onb.ac.at/RepViewer/viewer.faces?doc=DTL_8800128&order=1&view=SINGLE. This was also identified as one of the earliest preserved wax-plate printings; discovered by Han Qi 韩琦 in 2002; Zhang Xiumin (2006), vol. 2, p. 410; Zhang Xiumin (2009), p. 215 (with illustration). See also next chapter.

18 September 1731). The text is folded like a memorial and consists of c. forty-two "pages" of c. five columns of 1 + 14 characters each. At the same time, there are also five folio numbers (two to six, the first and seventh seem to be missing) in the text, with each number apparently covering more or less six "pages" (though this is not clear how many "pages" belong to the first (absent) folio number). This high number of pages seems to align with the number of pages reported by Contancin. The text is structured in a way that matches Contancin's description much more closely than the aforementioned *dibao* did. The one preserved copy of the *tizou quanlu* starts with the title *Lunyin* 綸音("silk sounds"): imperial pronouncements ("utterances"). Following this title, there are ten memorials with the imperial rescripts (*zhi* 旨). These are presented in summary (normally not more than one line for the memorial and one for the rescript), and several of them appear in full further in the gazette. This corresponds to Contancin's description that at the beginning of the gazette there are the titles of the memorials "with the subject in question, but in a few words." Next, there is a long edict, which had been channelled through the Grand Secretariat (introduced by *Neige feng shangyu* 内閣奉上諭). This is followed by five memorials by provincial officials, three of which appeared in summary at the beginning. At the end there is still one more short edict (again introduced by *Neige feng shangyu* 内閣奉上諭) and three very short imperial rescripts (two to three lines), mainly concerning appointments in the ministries and the provinces. Most of these texts were published in the *tizou quanlu* fairly quickly after the imperial decision (a consultation of other sources reveals that most decisions were taken on YZ9/8/13 and 14 = 13 and 14 September 1731).[164] The content is not entirely the same as the categories indicated by Contancin for the issue of YZ5/12/3, but the basic structure is.

The Muséum national d'histoire naturelle in Paris contains a Chinese mineral collection that was sent from Canton by Jacques-François Vandermonde, medical doctor from the Compagnie française des Indes orientales (who left Macau in 1731). One sample of this collection indicates how the glass jars containing the minerals must have been packaged to survive the sea journey: a stack of paper is squeezed into the jar to immobilise the samples inside. Based on the characters that are visible through the glass, this paper could possibly be a (local) Chinese gazette. Personal communication by Wu Huiyi (unpublished paper). Mentioned by Mokros (2021), p. 118.

164 *Qing shilu*, vol. 8, pp. 449–451 (*juan* 109) (YZ9/8/13–14 = 13–14 Sept. 1731); *Yongzheng chao hanwen yuzhi huibian*, vol. 4, p. 70 n. 74; vol. 5, pp. 254–255 n. 336–338; vol. 8, pp. 217–218; *Shizong xianhuangdi shangyu neige, juan* 109, pp. 3a–5a (*SKQS*, vol. 415, pp. 571–572) (YZ9/8/13–14); *Qingdai qijuzhu ce: Guoli Gugong bowuyuan zhencang. Yongzheng chao*, vol. 5, pp. 2323–2327 (YZ9/8/13), pp. 2234–2235; 2238–2240 (YZ9/8/14), pp. 2345–2346 (YZ9/8/16).

In Chinese databases of primary and secondary sources, so far no references to *tizou quanlu* could be found.[165] The only record that could be discovered is again of non-Chinese origin: it concerns a travelogue composed by the Korean scholar-official Hwang Ja 黃梓 (1689–c. 1756). While he was visiting Beijing as secretary of the Joseon embassy in 1734 (*jiayin* 甲寅) (*Gabin yeonhaengnok* 甲寅燕行錄 and *Gabin yeonhaeng byeollok* 甲寅燕行別錄), he consulted the gazette to gather information.[166] His travelogue includes two explicit references to *tizou quanlu*. On the seventeenth of the ninth month (= 13 October 1734), Hwang Ja writes that he "managed to see the *tizou quanlu*: On the first of the tenth month [27 October 1734], at the *meng* sacrifices (*mengdong ji* 孟冬祭) in the Taimiao 太廟 (Temple of Ancestors) the emperor will go in person to perform the rituals."[167] In an additional note on *tizou quanlu* Hwang explicitly explains that "this is similar to the court gazette (*chaobao* 朝報) of our country." In another (undated) discussion about Buddhism, he again briefly refers to the gazette, saying that he "happened to see in the *tizou quanlu* that the Yongzheng emperor conferred posthumous titles on some monks."[168]

The description by Contancin and the reference in Hwang Ja's travelogue lead to several conclusions: first, it seems very likely that the main source used by Contancin was the *tizou quanlu*; second, the *tizou quanlu* appears to have been a common official gazette during the Yongzheng reign; third, as will be shown in the next chapter, given the many similarities in structure, the *tizou quanlu* can be considered the forerunner of the *tizou shijian* 題奏事件, which was an important gazette during the later Qianlong reign.

After his formal description of the gazette, Contancin moves on to the content. His argumentation makes it clear that in his second letter his aim has become to present the wide range of topics to be found in a Chinese gazette:

> It is easy to see that when you read it carefully, you are informed of an infinity of different and curious things: & in order to make it better

165 Besides databases, also no record in *Zhongguo guji zongmu: Shibu* (2009).

166 In an overview article on the experiences of the Joseon envoys with the Catholic church in Beijing, Pierre-Emmanuel Roux already pointed out that the reports they made for the king on their return to Korea comprised a description of the mission, the main events, and all the information gleaned from the capital gazette (*dichao* 邸鈔) and other records; see Roux (2016), p. 15. For an overview of these tributary relations and the cultural transfers to Korea, including the transfer of Western learning, see Lim Jongtae (2016).

167 Huang Ja, *Gabin yeonhaengnok* 甲寅燕行錄, *juan* 3 [p. 40a] (2015), p. 60 (trans. p. 222): 十七日己丑陰得見題奏全錄如我國朝報十月初一日太廟孟冬祭皇帝將親詣行禮云矣.

168 Huang Ja, *Gabin yeonhaeng byeollok* 甲寅燕行別錄, *juan* 2 [p. 37a] (2015), p. 42 (trans. p. 131): 適見題奏全錄雍正之追贈僧師凡幾人矣.

> known to you, I am going to report to you some extracts that I have taken from it, & which may perhaps satisfy your curiosity.[169]

This letter by Contancin covers seventeen different topics, combining translations, summaries, and paraphrases of documents taken from the gazette. Either Contancin himself or the editor of *Lettres édifiantes* provided each of these topics with a subtitle. The names, places, and characters that appear in the following list of the seventeen topics have been identified on the basis of the same preserved Chinese (official) sources as used for the texts used by Perroni. For a detailed overview with reference to Chinese primary sources, see the "Guide to the sources" at the end of this book.

Complimens de toute la Cour sur le choix & la déclaration de l'Impératrice (Compliments of the whole Court on the choice and the declaration of the Empress)
- After the end of the three-year mourning period for the Kangxi emperor (1654–1722) and for the Yongzheng emperor's mother, Xiaogong ren huanghou 孝恭仁皇后 (1660–1723), the court announced the installation of the empress Xiaojing xian huanghou 孝敬憲皇后 (1681–1731); with a detailed description of the congratulatory rite *qinghe celi huanghou li* 慶賀冊立皇后禮 on YZ3/10/6 (10 November 1725)[170]

Libéralité de l'Impératrice en faveur des femmes avancées en âge (Generosity of the Empress in favour of women of advanced age)
- Generous gifts of the empress to women older than 70 years (in three groups: 70–80, 80–90, and more than 90 years old)[171]

Grace accordée à un homme condamné à mort / Ordre de l'Empereur (Grace granted to a man condemned to death / Order of the Emperor)
- A commoner called Tçao-chin from Tchang-chou (= Changshu 常熟), who was condemned to strangulation for causing his wife's death,

169 *LEC* (1729), vol. 19, p. 272; *LEC* (1810–1811), vol. 21, p. 79.

170 *LEC* (1729), vol. 19, pp. 273–275; *LEC* (1810–1811), vol. 21, pp. 79–80.
LEC (1729), vol. 19, pp. 275–281; *LEC* (1810–1811), vol. 21, pp. 80–83: Ceremony of installation (but only very brief mention in Chinese sources).
LEC (1729), vol. 19, pp. 282–288; *LEC* (1810–1811), vol. 21, pp. 84–87: Ceremony with court women, concubines (Quei-fei).

171 *LEC* (1729), vol. 19, pp. 288–296; *LEC* (1810–1811), vol. 21, pp. 87–91.

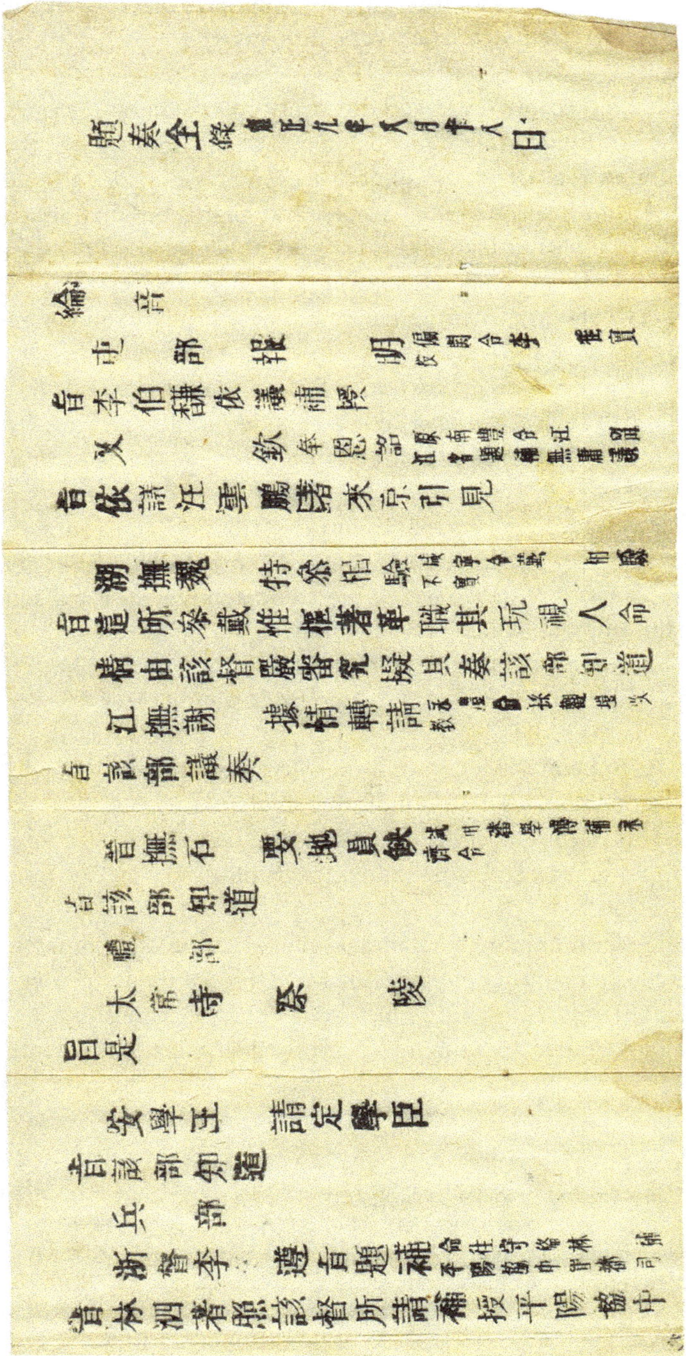

ILLUSTRATION 7 First pages of a *tizou quanlu* 題奏全錄 (YZ9/8/18 = 18 September 1731): Österreichische Nationalbibliothek, Vienna: Sin. 251

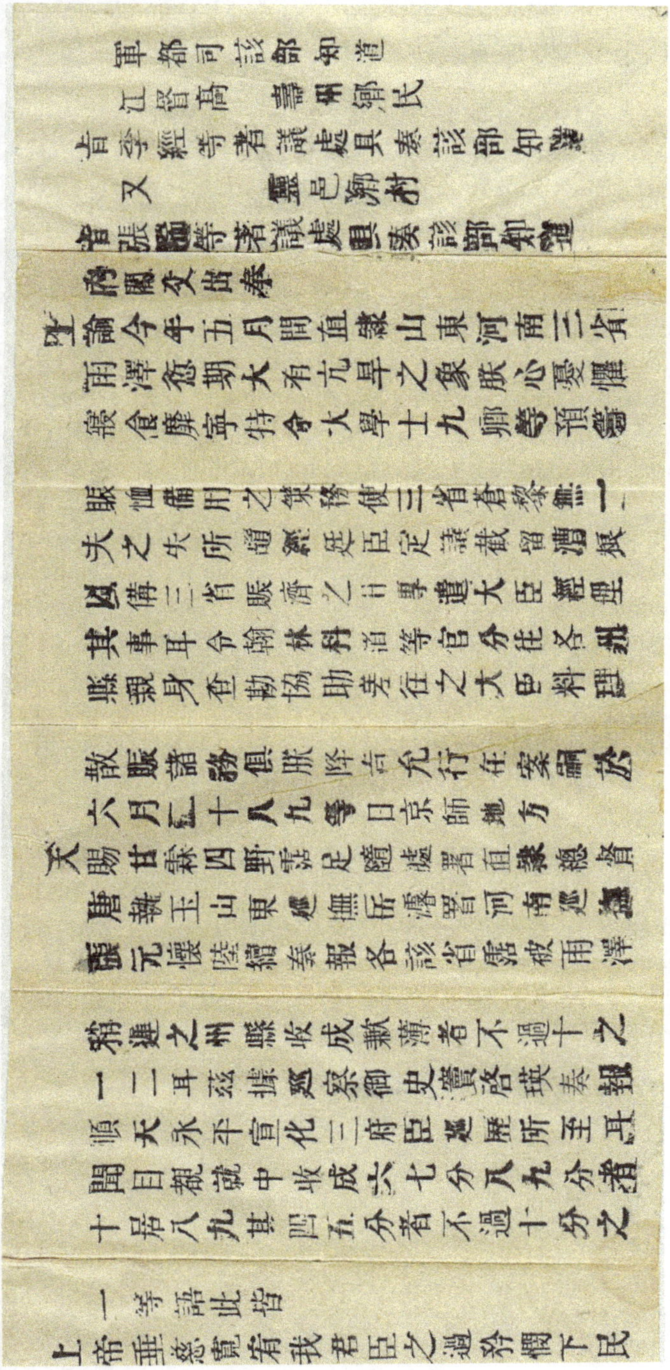

receives a reduced punishment (beating) so that he can continue to take care of his elderly parents[172]

Exemple d'un fils qui demande la grace de mourir à la place de sa mere (Example of a son who asks for the grace to die in place of his mother)
– A son asks to receive punishment in place of his mother after a conflict between two women in Y-hoang (= Yihuang 宜黄, Jiangxi), as a result of which one of them died[173]

Ordre qui prouve l'attention de l'Empereur à soulager son Peuple (Order that proves the attention of the Emperor to relieving his People)
– Edict of November 1725 ordering the supplement of rice (130.000 measures) kept in Tien-tçing (= Tianjin 天津) to be distributed in the villages that suffered from the excessive rain in Zhili[174]

Mémorial d'un Surintendant de deux Provinces qui parle à l'Empereur avec une noble hardiesse / Réponse de ce Mandarin à l'Empereur (Memorial of a Superintendent of two Provinces, who speaks to the Emperor with noble boldness / Response of this Mandarin to the Emperor)
– Memorial by Zha Bina 查弼納 (1683–1731), Governor-General of Jiangnan and Jiangsu, concerning the accusation and condemnation of Nian Gengyao 年羹堯 (?–1726)[175] and Long-ke-duo 隆科多 (?–1728),[176] asking for a stronger prosecution of the latter[177]

Festin pour honorer dans chaque Ville les personnes distinguées par leur probité & leur bon exemple (Feast to honour in each City the people distinguished by their integrity and their good example)
– Memorial, most probably by Zhang Linghuang 張令璜 (*jinshi* 1709), Metropolitan Governor, concerning the local banquets honouring those who were promoted to official duties (*xiangyin jiuli* 鄉飲酒禮)[178]

---

172 *LEC* (1729), vol. 19, pp. 297–304; *LEC* (1810–1811), vol. 21, pp. 91–95.
173 *LEC* (1729), vol. 19, pp. 304–307; *LEC* (1810–1811), vol. 21, pp. 95–96.
174 *LEC* (1729), vol. 19, pp. 307–315; *LEC* (1810–1811), vol. 21, pp. 97–100.
175 *ECCP*, vol. 1, pp. 587–590; Huang Pei (1974), p. 102ff.
176 *ECCP*, vol. 1, pp. 552–554; Huang Pei (1974), p. 107ff.
177 *LEC* (1729), vol. 19, pp. 315–324; *LEC* (1810–1811), vol. 21, pp. 100–105.
178 *LEC* (1729), vol. 19, pp. 325–329; *LEC* (1810–1811), vol. 21, pp. 105–107.

Autre Reglement pour honorer le mérite (Other Regulation to honour merit)
– Order of the Emperor to honour the deceased, including chaste women.[179] The next two items are examples.

Déliberation du Souverain Tribunal des Rites en faveur d'une fille qui a estimé la chasteté plus que sa propre vie / Ordre de l'Empereur (Deliberation of the Sovereign Tribunal of Rites in favour of a girl who valued chastity more than her own life / Order of the Emperor)
– Memorial by the Ministry of Rites concerning the construction of a memorial archway (*jianfang* 建坊) in Xinhui 新會 (Guangdong) for a girl with family name Liang 梁[180]

Autre déliberation du même Tribunal des Rites touchant une femme qui a donné des marques d'amour tendre pour son mari (Another deliberation of the same Tribunal of Rites concerning a woman who gave evidence of tender love for her husband)
– Other memorial by the Ministry of Rites concerning a woman with the family name Shao 邵, wife of Xu Wenyuan 徐文源 in Wuyi 武義 (Zhejiang), who committed suicide after the death of her husband (*liefu* 烈婦)[181]

Mémorial présenté contre un ordre de l'Empereur (Memorial presented against an order of the Emperor)
– Memorial by Tian Wenjing 田文鏡 (1662–1732),[182] Governor of Henan, in refute of an earlier order by the Emperor concerning the prosecution of robbers; in his response the emperor praises Tian and asks to investigate his proposal[183]

Mémorial dans lequel on propose à l'Empereur un moyen de secourir le peuple dans les années stériles / Réponse de l'Empereur (Memorial in which the Emperor is offered a means of helping the people in barren years / Response of the Emperor)

179 *LEC* (1729), vol. 19, pp. 329–331; *LEC* (1810–1811), vol. 21, pp. 108–109.
180 *LEC* (1729), vol. 19, pp. 331–334; *LEC* (1810–1811), vol. 21, pp. 109–110.
181 *LEC* (1729), vol. 19, pp. 334–337; *LEC* (1810–1811), vol. 21, pp. 110–112.
182 *ECCP*, vol. 2, pp. 719–721; Huang Pei (1974), p. 234.
183 *LEC* (1729), vol. 19, pp. 338–345; *LEC* (1810–1811), vol. 21, pp. 112–116r.

- Memorial by Liu Yuyi 劉於義 (1675–1748), Provincial Education Commissioner of Shanxi 提督山西學政, proposing a method to rescue the people in years with bad harvests; the proposals are approved by the emperor[184]

Pesche des perles tirée d'un Mémorial (Pearl fishing; taken from a Memorial)

- Short report on the yearly fishing of pearls by Manchus from the eight banners in a river in Manchuria, to the east of Liaodong; in 1725 more than 600 men participated in it, but with little result[185]

Anciens Ordres renouvellez en faveur des parens infirmes ou fort âgez (Old Orders renewed in favour of infirm or very old parents)

- In order to avoid that provincial officials would leave their position under the pretext of needing to go home to take care for their infirm or aged parents, more precise rules were stipulated for the possibility of *zhongyang* 終養 (care for parents until the end)[186]

Tendresse paternelle de l'Empereur pour les pauvres (Paternal tenderness of the Emperor for the poor)

- Orders by the Emperor to relieve the poor who had fled to Beijing and Shandong after heavy rains[187]

L'Empereur offre un sacrifice au commencement du Printems & va labourer la terre, pour obtenir une année abondante (The Emperor offers a sacrifice at the beginning of Spring and goes to plough the land in order to obtain a bountiful year)

- Description of a ceremony at the start of spring (YZ4/2/24 = 27 March 1726) during which the emperor personally ploughs the land and offers at the Xiannong 先農 altar, and a memorial by the Ministry of Rites determining the details of this ritual[188]

184 *LEC* (1729), vol. 19, pp. 345–364; *LEC* (1810–1811), vol. 21, pp. 116–125.

185 *LEC* (1729), vol. 19, pp. 364–366; *LEC* (1810–1811), vol. 21, pp. 125–126.

186 *LEC* (1729), vol. 19, pp. 366–379; *LEC* (1810–1811), vol. 21, pp. 127–133.

187 *LEC* (1729), vol. 19, pp. 379–384; *LEC* (1810–1811), vol. 21, pp. 133–135.

188 *LEC* (1729), vol. 19, pp. 384–392; *LEC* (1810–1811), vol. 21, pp. 135–139.

Instruction par laquelle l'Empereur déclare quel est l'objet de son culte (Instruction by which the Emperor declares what is the goal of his worship)
– Li Weijun 李維鈞, Governor-General of Zhili, had sent a memorial mentioning the prayers of common people in the temples of General Liu Meng 劉猛 at the occasion of the damage caused by locusts. In response, the emperor discusses the utmost principle of reciprocation between Heaven and the human being (*tianren ganying zhi li* 天人感應之至理).[189]

Contancin concludes his letter by again emphasizing how suitable the gazettes are for getting an exact knowledge of the customs of the Chinese, and of the form of their government, as he had experienced in his own reading practice. They are based on facts and used to instruct the public:

> I believe, my Reverend Father, that you will think like me, that they [the gazettes] are very apt to provide an exact knowledge of the manners of the Chinese, and of the form of their government: at least one cannot doubt about the truth of these facts, which are derived from the Memorials, Petitions, Instructions, and Orders of the Emperor, about which the public is instructed, and which are spread throughout the empire.[190]

The image that appears from Contancin's reading of the Chinese gazette in this second letter confirms his laudatory portrayal of the emperor as administrator, educator, and caretaker of the people as it appeared in his first letter. This vision is constructed indirectly through the selection of the cases he took from the gazettes, but also directly when he occasionally uses evaluative language, such as "Paternal tenderness (*tendresse paternelle*) of the Emperor towards the poor."[191] In certain cases, the imperial decision is explicitly presented as evidence of his good governance, as is the case for "the order which proves the attention of the emperor to relieving his people."[192] Even if this title was added by the editor in France, it reflects Contancin's own vision, which is made clear at the end of the translation of this edict. The vocabulary he uses in doing so is telling: in addition to words such as "tenderness" and "attention," he also uses

189 *LEC* (1729), vol. 19, pp. 393–402; *LEC* (1810–1811), vol. 21, pp. 139–144.
190 *LEC* (1729), vol. 19, pp. 402–403; *LEC* (1810–1811), vol. 21, pp. 139–144.
191 *LEC* (1729), vol. 19, p. 379; *LEC* (1810–1811), vol. 21, p. 133.
192 *LEC* (1729), vol. 19, p. 307; *LEC* (1810–1811), vol. 21, p. 133.

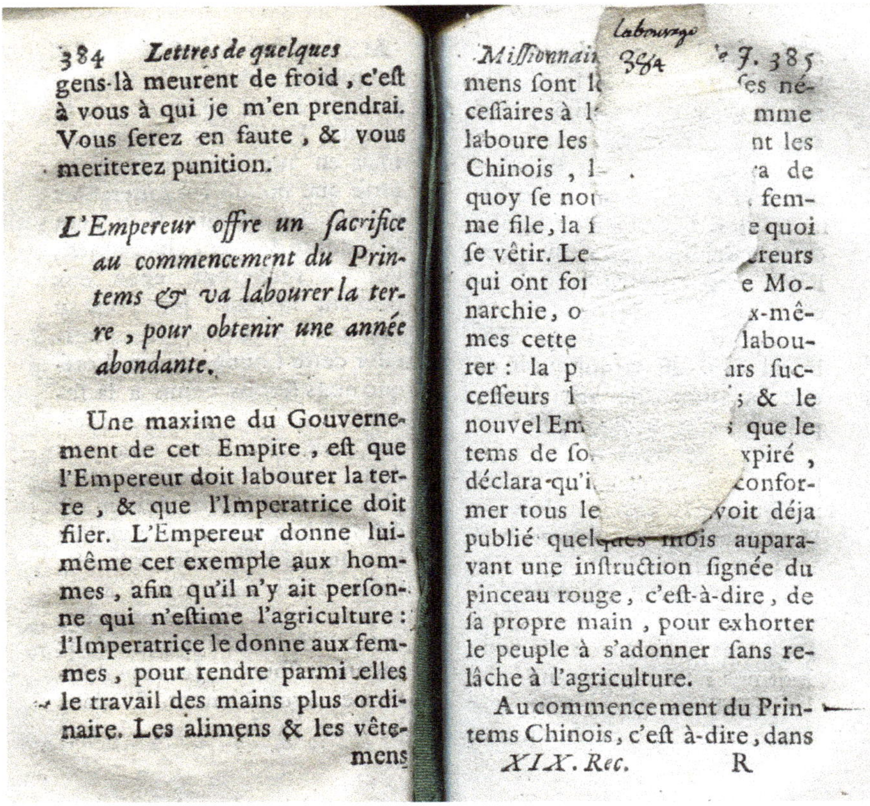
384 *Lettres de quelques*

gens-là meurent de froid, c'eſt à vous à qui je m'en prendrai. Vous ſerez en faute, & vous meriterez punition.

L'Empereur offre un ſacrifice au commencement du Printems & va labourer la terre, pour obtenir une année abondante.

Une maxime du Gouvernement de cet Empire, eſt que l'Empereur doit labourer la terre, & que l'Imperatrice doit filer. L'Empereur donne lui-même cet exemple aux hommes, afin qu'il n'y ait perſonne qui n'eſtime l'agriculture: l'Imperatrice le donne aux femmes, pour rendre parmi elles le travail des mains plus ordinaire. Les alimens & les vêtemens

Miſſionnai[...] 385

mens ſont l[...] [...]es né-
ceſſaires à l[...] [...]mme
laboure les [...] [...]nt les
Chinois, l[...] [...]a de
quoy ſe no[...] [...] fem-
me file, la [...] [...]e quoi
ſe vêtir. Le[...] [...]reurs
qui ont fo[...] [...]e Mo-
narchie, o[...] [...]x-mê-
mes cette [...] [...]labou-
rer: la p[...] [...]rs ſuc-
ceſſeurs [...] [...]; & le
nouvel Em[...] [...]; que le
tems de ſo[...] [...]xpiré,
déclara qu'i[...] [...]confor-
mer tous le[...] [...]voit déja
publié quel[...] mois aupara-
vant une inſtruction ſignée du pinceau rouge, c'eſt-à-dire, de ſa propre main, pour exhorter le peuple à s'adonner ſans relâche à l'agriculture.

Au commencement du Printems Chinois, c'eſt à-dire, dans

XIX. Rec. R

ILLUSTRATION 8 The ceremony of the emperor ploughing the land in the second letter by Cyr Contancin (Canton, 15 December 1727): *Lettres édifiantes et curieuses*, vol. 19 (1729), pp. 384–385, with Voltaire's bookmark "labourage"

expressions which had already been present in the first letter, such as "application" and "vigilance."

> We see from this order, that the smallest affairs go to the Emperor. He is informed of everything: he enters into the greatest detail; he governs & decides everything by himself. This is what makes the Chinese government so good. An Emperor does not have time to entertain himself. He must use his entertainment to fulfil the duty of the Emperor, and to make sure by his application, by his vigilance, by his tenderness for his Subjects, that one can truthfully say of him that he is the Father & Mother

> of the People. It is the Chinese expression. Without that he falls into a sovereign contempt.[193]

Just like in the first letter, emperors "inspire virtue" through "very sage laws, and very pure maxims of morality" and even by "organising certain exterior customs," such as the *xiangyin* banquets organised by local officials in the name of the emperor to honour people with exemplary virtuous conduct.[194] Other rules, such as being allowed to leave office to take care of one's sick parents, have been installed to inspire "respect, love and tenderness for one's parents," which form "the basis and foundation on which the beauty and solidity of the Chinese government rest."[195] Contancin adds that "we can say without exaggeration that to undermine this foundation would be absolutely to overthrow the empire of this nation so wise and so polite."[196]

Contancin's letters also contain a depiction of an active bureaucracy: central institutions, such as the Ministry of Rites, suggest names of people to be honoured, while officials, such as Liu Yuyi, proactively make proposals to rescue the people at times of bad harvests. In some cases officials, such as Zha Bina, even question decisions "with noble boldness (*avec une noble hardiesse*),"[197] by which the emperor "does not appear to be irritated at all."[198] Some, like Tian Wenjing, even refute earlier decisions by the emperor, who accepts their alternatives. There are all kind of regulations to avoid solicitations by family and friends, such as the rule of avoidance of serving in the same province as one's own family (i.e. *huibi* 迴避), "because an official should only think of the public good (*bien public*)."[199] In short, though the focus shifted to the gazettes, the second letter still conveys a portrayal of the emperor and the government that is very similar to the depiction that emerged from Contancin's first letter.

2.2.3 *Third Letter*

The third letter was written nearly three years later. It was ready to be sent in November 1730, when unexpectedly Contancin was sent back to France as a delegate and carried the letter with him. By that time Contancin had already

---

193 LEC (1729), vol. 19, pp. 313–315; LEC (1810–1811), vol. 21, p. 100. Another reference to "father of the people": LEC (1729), vol. 19, p. 349; LEC (1810–1811), vol. 21, p. 118.

194 LEC (1729), vol. 19, pp. 325–326; LEC (1810–1811), vol. 21, pp. 105–106.

195 LEC (1729), vol. 19, p. 379; LEC (1810–1811), vol. 21, pp. 132–133.

196 LEC (1729), vol. 19, p. 379; LEC (1810–1811), vol. 21, p. 133.

197 LEC (1729), vol. 19, p. 315; LEC (1810–1811), vol. 21, p. 100.

198 LEC (1729), vol. 19, p. 323; LEC (1810–1811), vol. 21, p. 104.

199 LEC (1729), vol. 19, p. 369; LEC (1810–1811), vol. 21, p. 128.

received volume 19 of *Lettres édifiantes et curieuses* in which his second letter was published. His correspondent, this time Du Halde himself, reports that the previous letter was much appreciated and read with great pleasure, and therefore he wishes that Contancin continues to write on the same subject. In response, Contancin makes his purpose clear at the beginning of this third letter:

> This one will only keep you informed about the orders, instructions, regulations, examples of virtue that have been made public throughout the Empire.[200]

In this third letter the attention has fully shifted to the content of the gazettes. Contancin discusses fifteen topics. Besides one eyewitness account and one explanation of the bureaucratic reward and punishment system, the thirteen others are based on official documents published in the gazettes. They have been selected over a long period of time, the oldest dating to YZ3/10/9 (13 November 1725) and the youngest to YZ6/7/5 (10 August 1728). This indicates that, in one way or another, Contancin must have archived the gazettes. Just like the second letter, the third one is quite long (more than 139 pages in the original edition, 70 pages in the reprint) and the topics again cover a wide variety of themes. For a detailed overview with reference to Chinese primary sources, see the "Guide to the sources" at the end of this book.

> [Without title]
> – Death sentence of Long-ke-duo 隆科多 (?–1728) turned into imprisonment in a house at Tchang-thcun-yuen (= Changchunyuan 暢春園)[201]
>
> L'Empereur déclare que lorsqu'il va passer quelque tems à sa maison de plaisance, c'est pour jouir d'un meilleur air, & non pas pour chercher du repos (The Emperor declares that when he goes to spend some time at his country house, it is to enjoy better air, and not to seek rest)
> – After an audience at which no officials appeared, declaration by the Emperor explaining that when he goes to Yuanmingyuan 圓明園 it is for better air, not for rest, and he continues to work[202]
>
> L'Empereur voyant son Peuple menacé de la disette, en est si sensiblement touché, qu'il prie les principaux Officiers de lui déclarer ses fautes,

200 *LEC* (1729), vol. 22, p. 190; *LEC* (1810–1811), vol. 21, pp. 235–236.
201 *LEC* (1736), vol. 22, pp. 191–196; *LEC* (1810–1811), vol. 21, pp. 236–239.
202 *LEC* (1736), vol. 22, pp. 196–202; *LEC* (1810–1811), vol. 21, pp. 239–241.

sans aucun déguisement (The Emperor, seeing his people threatened with famine, was so sensibly affected that he begged the principal officials to report his faults to him without any disguise)

- Long edict by the Emperor concerning the suffering of people because of drought and his request to criticize him because of his failures (YZ4/6/1 = 30 June 1726)[203]

Expédiens Pour faire défricher les terres incultes, & par-là procurer l'abondance (Expedients to clear wasteland, and thereby provide abundance)

- Memorial by E-er-tai 鄂爾泰 (1680–1745),[204] Governor-General of Yunnan and Guizhou, with six proposals for land reclamation measures, with the approval by the emperor (except for one proposal)[205]

Explication Des Notes honorables, & de quelques autres legeres recompenses & punitions (Explanations of honourable grades, and some other minor rewards and punishments)

- Explanation (without memorial or edict) of the *Ki-lu* (= *jilu* 紀錄), i.e. registration of an official's deeds and accomplishments in a book for the government's record, and the related system of rewards and punishments, namely *kia-kie* (= *jiaji* 加級), i.e. the raising of rank, or *kiang-kie* (*jiangji* 降級), i.e. the lowering of rank[206]

Mémorial du Viceroi de la province de Chan tong, qui avertit l'Empereur d'une inondation & du secours qu'il a donné au Peuple (Memorial of the Viceroy of Chan-tong Province, who notifies the Emperor of a flood and the relief he has given to the People)

- Memorial of the Governor of Shandong concerning floods; this may instead have been a memorial by Yang Wenqian 楊文乾 (1682–1728), Governor of Guangdong[207]

[Without title]

- Rescript of the Emperor to the reports by Kong Yuxun 孔毓珣 (?–1730), Governor-General of Guangdong, on the floods in Jiangnan[208]

---

203 LEC (1736), vol. 22, pp. 202–209; LEC (1810–1811), vol. 21, pp. 242–246: the French text mentions YZ4/6/5 (= 4 July 1727).

204 ECCP, vol. 1, pp. 601–603; Huang Pei (1974), pp. 235, 244, 289–295, 300.

205 LEC (1736), vol. 22, pp. 210–223; LEC (1810–1811), vol. 21, pp. 246–253.

206 LEC (1736), vol. 22, pp. 223–239; LEC (1810–1811), vol. 21, pp. 253–261.

207 LEC (1736), vol. 22, pp. 239–243; LEC (1810–1811), vol. 21, pp. 261–263; Cf. Yazawa (1973), p. 244 n. 27.

208 LEC (1736), vol. 22, pp. 244–246; LEC (1810–1811), vol. 21, pp. 263–265.

[Without title]

– Rescript of the Emperor to the memorial by E-er-tai 鄂爾泰, Governor-General of Yunnan and Guizhou, and his exhortation to go beyond one's task in presenting memorials (*yuezhi chenzou* 越職陳奏)[209]

[Without title]

– Memorial of Sai-leng-e 塞楞額 (1686–1748), Governor of Shandong, to allow people to build housing on the riverbanks in order to earn a living through fishing[210]

Cérémonie qui s'est observée l'année 1725, lorsqu'on a présenté à l'Empereur le Livre de la Généalogie Impériale, ou l'Histoire de la Dynastie Tartare (Ceremony observed in the year 1725, when the Emperor was presented with the book of Imperial Genealogy, or the history of the Tartar dynasty)

– Detailed description of the ceremony for the presentation of the imperial genealogy (*yudie* 玉牒) to the Emperor that took place on YZ3/10/9 (= 13 November 1725) (possibly based on an eyewitness account, since details seem to be absent in the available official sources)[211]

L'Empereur Fait l'éloge de son Précepteur, & l'honore après sa mort (The Emperor praises his Tutor, and honours him after his death)

– Eulogy of Gu-ba-dai 顧八代 (?–1709),[212] who was removed as Minister of Rites in 1693, but continued his services in the palace school for princes, also instructing the Yongzheng emperor; the latter ordered that Gu-ba-dai be posthumously restored to his former ranks and canonized as Wenduan 文端[213]

Ordre admirable qu'on garda à Peking, lorsqu'il fallut renvoyer plus de quarante mille Pauvres, chacun dans son pays (Admirable order that was issued in Peking, when it was necessary to send back more than forty thousand poor, each to their own Region)

– The Emperor approves financial support for forty thousand people who had to be sent back to the provinces in the beginning of YZ4/2

209 *LEC* (1736), vol. 22, pp. 246–248; *LEC* (1810–1811), vol. 21, pp. 265–266.
210 *LEC* (1736), vol. 22, pp. 248–249; *LEC* (1810–1811), vol. 21, p. 266.
211 *LEC* (1736), vol. 22, pp. 249–262; *LEC* (1810–1811), vol. 21, pp. 266–273.
212 *ECCP*, vol. 1, p. 271.
213 *LEC* (1736), vol. 22, pp. 263–270; *LEC* (1810–1811), vol. 21, pp. 273–277.

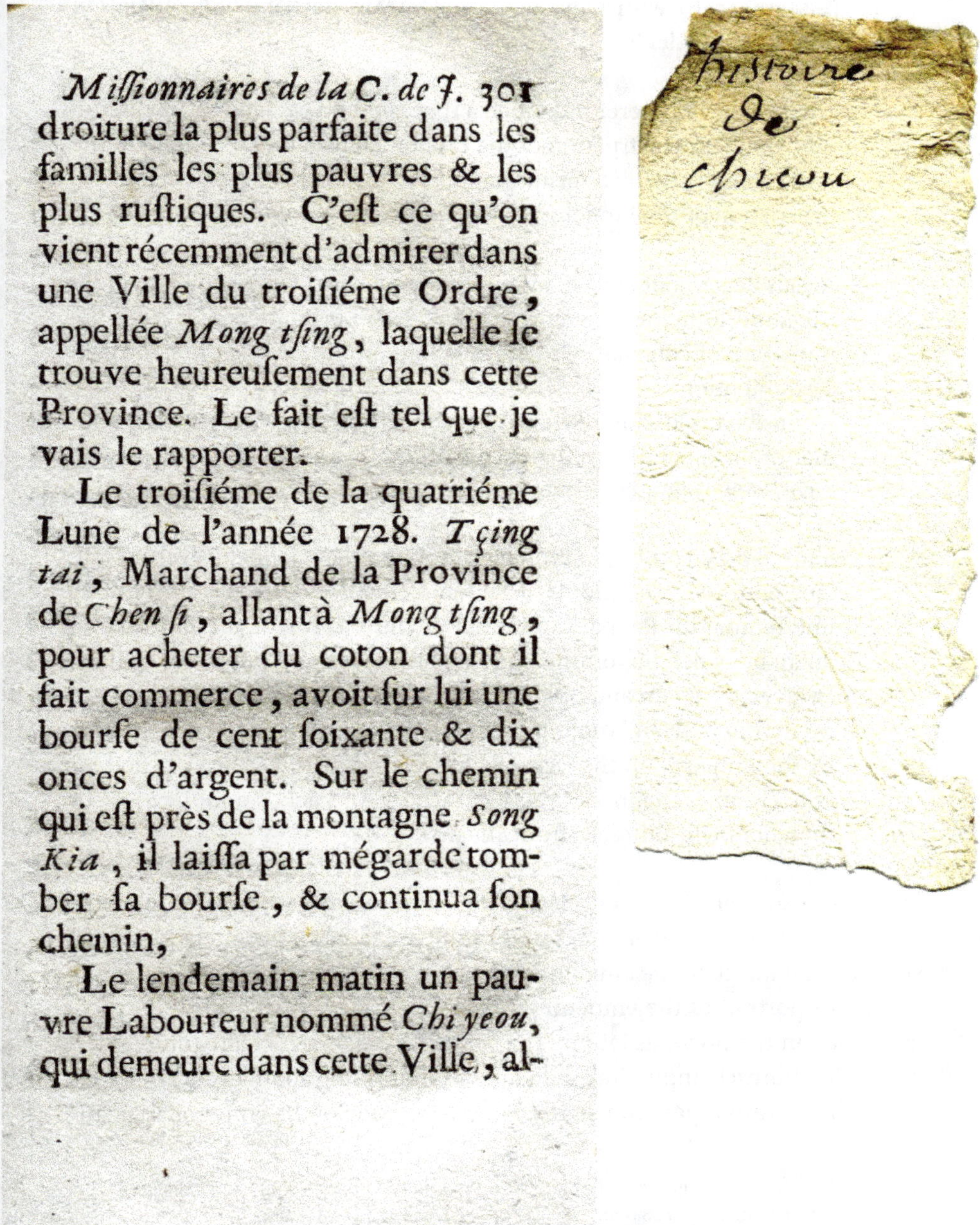

Miſſionnaires de la C. de J. 301

droiture la plus parfaite dans les familles les plus pauvres & les plus ruſtiques. C'eſt ce qu'on vient récemment d'admirer dans une Ville du troiſiéme Ordre, appellée *Mong tſing*, laquelle ſe trouve heureuſement dans cette Province. Le fait eſt tel que je vais le rapporter.

Le troiſiéme de la quatriéme Lune de l'année 1728. *Tçing tai*, Marchand de la Province de *Chen ſi*, allant à *Mong tſing*, pour acheter du coton dont il fait commerce, avoit ſur lui une bourſe de cent ſoixante & dix onces d'argent. Sur le chemin qui eſt près de la montagne *Song Kia*, il laiſſa par mégarde tomber ſa bourſe, & continua ſon chemin,

Le lendemain matin un pauvre Laboureur nommé *Chi yeou*, qui demeure dans cette Ville, al-

ILLUSTRATION 9 Voltaire's bookmark to the third letter by Cyr Contancin (Canton, 19 October 1730): *Lettres édifiantes et curieuses*, vol. 22 (1736), pp. 301–302 (added to the previous page), "histoire de chieou" (the case of Chi yeou = Cui Shiyou)

(= March 1726), with a long memorial by Ministers and high officials to execute the order[214]

Instruction de l'Empereur, Donnée à l'occasion du caractere Chinois, qui signifie bonheur (Instruction of the Emperor, given in the context of the Chinese character which means happiness)

– Instruction of the Emperor related to the character *fu* 福[215]

Nouveau Règlement sur l'examen des Mandarins / Ordre de l'Empereur qui regarde le même Examen général (New Regulation regarding the examination of Officials / Order of the Emperor regarding the same general examination)

– Extensive discussion of new rules concerning the three-yearly examination of officials, among others on the examination of those who have been evaluated as excellent (*zhuoyi* 卓異)[216]

Mémorial du Viceroi de la Province de Ho-nan, par lequel il avertit l'Empereur d'un bel exemple de désintéressement, donné par un homme & une femme du Peuple (Memorial of the Viceroy of the province of Ho-nan, by which he informs the Emperor of a fine example of selflessness, given by a man and a woman of the People)

– Memorial by Tian Wenjing 田文鏡, Governor of Henan, and reaction by the Emperor on the case of Chi yeou = Cui Shiyou 翟世有 and his wife (from Mengjin xian 孟津縣) who gave back the money lost by merchant Qin Tai 秦泰 (from Shaanxi)[217]

Even more so than the second letter, the third letter intends to provide the reader with an overview of topics that are included in the gazette, rather than sketching an image of the emperor. To be sure, the content of the gazettes still suggests a portrait of the emperor and his government. Yet this is less articulated than in the previous letters. The style of this letter is clearly different. It resembles more a compilation of documents informing about events that took place, than an attempt to transmit a consistent vision of the emperor. In nearly

214 *LEC* (1736), vol. 22, pp. 270–284; *LEC* (1810–1811), vol. 21, pp. 278–284.

215 *LEC* (1736), vol. 22, pp. 284–287; *LEC* (1810–1811), vol. 21, pp. 284–286.

216 *LEC* (1736), vol. 22, pp. 288–299; *LEC* (1810–1811), vol. 21, pp. 286–292.

217 *LEC* (1736), vol. 22, pp. 299–324; *LEC* (1810–1811), vol. 21, pp. 292–304; the texts translated by Contancin are much more extensive than the official texts that have been preserved. This is the same case as the one mentioned by Perroni: APF, SC, Indie orientali e Cina, vol. 19 (dal 1727 al 1728), fol. 718v.

each section, Contancin immediately enters into the subject of the excerpt of the gazette, often even without further introduction or context. Translations become more important than paraphrases or summaries. They include, as mentioned earlier, more material than the surviving official sources, such as *Qing shilu* or *Qijuzhu*. In addition to information taken from the gazettes, the letter also includes two extensive explanations of the evaluation system of the officials (one of which does not include a translation of a memorial or edict) and a detailed description of the submission of the imperial genealogy, of which the origin is unclear (possibly based on an eyewitness account, since details seem to be absent from available official sources). Contancin's personal comments about why he made a selection or what a case might prove are limited, though occasionally still present. For instance, in the case of the posthumous honour to Gu Badai, Contancin remarks: "We see from this example of the Emperor, what is the intention of the Chinese, when they honour their masters after death."[218] The result of Contancin's selective overview is a wealth of information, which is both extensive in scope and rich in detail. This third letter reveals a fairly thorough knowledge of the institutions and legislation of the empire, but leaves it up to the reader to construct an image of the Chinese government on the basis of these documents.

2.2.4 *Evaluating Contancin's Letters as a Source*

Contancin's letters constitute a valuable source on the Chinese gazette of the Yongzheng reign. In certain cases, his translations include much more information than preserved in the surviving Chinese official sources. This concerns especially memorials by officials, such as the one by Liu Yuyi 劉於義 mentioned in the second letter, which were often published *in extenso* in the gazettes but not included in later sources that contain the imperial voice, such as the *Qing shilu*. As such, Contancin's translations contain texts that are presumably no longer available in Chinese sources.

At the same time, it is prudent to remain aware that Contancin offers a particular lens on the Chinese gazette. Quite evidently, Contancin has translated only a selection of the edicts or memorials that appeared in the gazettes, which in themselves were already a selection of the documents that passed through the hands of the emperor. Aside from focusing on government affairs and customs, Contancin's selection seems to reveal an interest in certain topics that reflect the Chinese way of thinking, such as the "reciprocation between Heaven and the human being" (*tianren ganying* 天人感應), which is mentioned in the last text of the second letter, as well as in the first edict quoted in his first letter.

218 *LEC* (1736), vol. 22, p. 267; *LEC* (1810–1811), vol. 21, p. 275.

Moreover, Contancin intermingles his translation with general comments and various explanations, sometimes paraphrasing or summarizing information. In certain cases, such as the pearl fishing in Manchuria, he does not provide any translation, but only a description "taken from a memorial."

In general, the translations Contancin does provide are faithful to the original. An example can be given from the imperial edict in response to the memorial by the aforementioned Liu Yuyi.

> 得旨、劉於義所奏常平積貯事宜。甚為有益。著交與山西總督伊都立、就近酌量。一面定數具奏。一面舉行。從來積貯米穀。自督撫以及州縣。皆躭延瞻顧。苟且塞責。此弊務須痛革。實心奉行。[219]
>
> Réponse de l'Empereur.
>
> Ce que Lieou yu-y m'expose dans son Mémorial touchant les Magazins & les provisions de ris, est très-avantageux pour le peuple. J'ordonne au Vice-Roi de la Province de Chansi de délibérer au plutôt sur la manière de l'exécuter: Que d'une part il détermine la somme qu'on doit employer, & qu'en même-tems on mette la main à l'oeuvre. Pour ce qui regarde le passé: les provisions ne se sont pas faites, & c'est la faute des principaux Mandarins & de leurs subalternes qui ont été négligents, qui ont cherché leurs propres intérêts, & ont fui le travail. Dans l'affaire dont il s'agit, j'attends un zèle & une vigilance particulière, autrement il n'y aura point de pardon. Qu'on envoie promptement cet Ordre.[220]
>
> {English translation of the French text}
>
> What Lieou yu-y puts forward to me in his Memorial concerning the Stores & Provisions of Rice is very advantageous for the people. I order the Viceroy of the Province of Chansi to deliberate as soon as possible on the way to carry it out: That on the one hand he determine the amount that must be used, & that at the same time we put our hand at work. As for the past: provisions were not made, & it is the fault of the main Mandarins & their subordinates who were negligent, who sought their own interests, & fled work. In the business in question, I expect special zeal and vigilance, otherwise there will be no forgiveness. Let this Order be sent promptly.

---

219 Punctuation following *Qing shilu*, vol. 7, p. 583 (*juan* 39) (YZ3/12/辛卯 [= 28] = 30 Jan. 1726).

220 *LEC* (1729), vol. 19, pp. 363–364; *LEC* (1810–1811), vol. 21, p. 136.

Quotations from two additional passages (both from the third letter) can provide further insight into the quality of Contancin's translations, as they represent two different styles. The first is written in more of a narrative style, in which the emperor gives an account of what happened when no official appeared at the audience in the Yuanmingyuan. The second passage represents a more philosophical style, as the emperor reflects on how the cultivation of virtues contributes to prosperity. One may notice that especially in the latter example the very condensed style of classical Chinese is translated in a more fluid French style.

> 諭大學士等。今日朕坐勤政殿。以待諸臣奏事。乃部院八旗、竟無奏事之人。想諸臣以朕駐 圓明園 、欲圖安逸、故將所奏之事。有意簡省耶。朕因郊外水土氣味、較城內稍清。故駐蹕於此。而每日辦理政事、與宮中無異。未嘗一刻肯自暇逸。已曾屢降諭旨、切告廷臣。令其照常奏事。若朕偶欲靜息、自當曉諭諸臣知之。儻廷臣不知仰體朕心、將陳奏事件、有意簡省。是不欲朕駐蹕圓明園矣。[221]

> Aujourd'hui je suis allé, selon ma coûtume, m'asseoir dans la salle *King tching tien*, pour recevoir les Placets & donner audience, mais nul Officier ni des Tribunaux, ni des huit Bannieres ne s'est présenté pour me parler d'affaire. Je fais réflexion qu'on s'imagine peut-être que je viens ici, pour me divertir, & pour éviter le travail: sur cette fausse idée ne prétendroit-on point suspendre les affaires publiques? Si cela est, on se trompe, je viens ici, parce que l'air de la campagne est un peu meilleur que celui qu'on respire dans l'enceinte des murs; mais pendant le tems que j'y séjourne, mon intention est que les affaires du Gouvernement n'en souffrent point: je veux m'appliquer chaque jour au bien de l'Empire, comme je fais à *Peking*, sans aucune différence, je ne prétends pas me donner aucun moment de repos ni de divertissement; il y a eu plusieurs occasions où j'en ai déjà averti les principaux Mandarins des Tribunaux, afin qu'à l'ordinaire ils me fissent leur rapport sur les affaires de la Cour & des Provinces. Pourquoi ne sont-ils pas venus? Si par hazard il me survenoit quelque raison d'interrompre ces occupations, je les en ferai avertir. Que si après cet ordre, ils ne se conforment pas à mes intentions, j'aurai sujet de croire qu'ils n'agréent pas le séjour que je fais dans cette maison de plaisance.[222]

---

221 Punctuation following *Qing shilu*, vol. 7, pp. 596–597 (*juan* 40) (YZ4/1/癸丑 [= 20] = 21 Febr. 1726).

222 *LEC* (1736), vol. 22, pp. 197–199; *LEC* (1810–1811), vol. 21, pp. 239–240.

{English translation of the French text}

Today I went, according to my custom, to sit down in the *King tching tien* room, to receive the memorials and give an audience, but no Officer neither of the Courts, nor of the eight Banners came to speak to me about cases. I made the reflection that people may imagine that I come here, to entertain myself, and to avoid work: on this false idea, would one not pretend to suspend public affairs? If so, one is wrong, I am coming here, because the country air is a little better than the one we breathe inside the walls; but during the time that I stay there, my intention is that the business of the Government does not suffer: I want to apply myself every day to the good of the Empire, as I do in *Beijing*, without any difference, I do not pretend to give myself any moment of rest or entertainment; there have been several occasions when I have already informed the principal Mandarins of the Courts of this, so that they usually report back to me on the affairs of the Court and the Provinces. Why have they not come? If by any chance I should have any reason to interrupt these occupations, I will let them know. That if after this order, they do not comply with my intentions, I will have reason to believe that they do not agree with my stay in this country house.

奉
上諭。天下之治平。在乎端風俗。而風俗之整理。在乎正人心。若人之存心。果能守法奉公。安分知足。則不貪苟得之財。不為非理之事。衾影無愧。俯仰寬舒。而和氣致祥。自然災害潛消。諸福畢至。子孫竝獲安享。所謂積善之家。[223]

La tranquillité & la beauté du Gouvernement consiste à établir de sages coûtumes; & la meilleure manière d'y réussir, c'est de rectifier le cœur de l'homme. Car si l'homme sçait garder son cœur, s'il en est le maître, il se conforme à l'Ordre, il remplit ses devoirs, il cherche le bien public, il borne ses desirs, il ne veut point d'argent injustement acquis. La raison est sa régle, il ne fait rien qui lui soit contraire. La nuit il peut voir des Spectres, des esprits sans rien craindre; soit qu'il léve la tête, soit qu'il la baisse, il est content, la joye paroît peinte sur son visage, la calamité le fuit, le bonheur l'accompagne par tout, & passe jusqu'à ses enfans & à ses petits fils, qui jouissent tranquillement de la prospérité, comme d'un

223 Punctuation following *Qing shilu*, vol. 7, pp. 1060–1061 (*juan* 71) (YZ6/7/甲寅 [= 5] = 10 Aug. 1728).

> héritage que la vertu de leurs peres leur auroit procuré. Et n'est-ce pas ce que signifie cet ancien proverbe? La famille qui s'applique à amasser un trésor de vertus, ne manquera de rien: elle jouira d'un bonheur qui ira même au-delà de ses desirs.[224]
>
> {English translation of the French text}
>
> The tranquillity & beauty of government consists in establishing wise customs; & the best way to do so is to rectify the heart of man. For if man knows how to keep his heart, if he is its master, he conforms to the Order, he fulfils his duties, he seeks the public good, he limits his desires, he does not want money unfairly acquired. The reason is his rule, he does nothing that is contrary to it. At night he can see Spectres, and spirits without fearing anything; either he raises his head or lowers it, he is happy, joy seems painted on his face, calamity shuns him, happiness accompanies him everywhere, & passes to his children & his grand-sons, who quietly enjoy prosperity, like an inheritance which the virtue of their fathers would have procured for them. And is that not what this ancient proverb means? The family that strives to amass a treasure of virtues will lack nothing: it will enjoy a happiness that will go even beyond its desires.

In evaluating these translations, however, some caution is needed because the printed version of these letters could not be compared with the original manuscripts, which have apparently been lost. Such comparison would be necessary to make a definitive evaluation, since it is well known that Jean-Baptiste Du Halde rewrote texts and made changes to the letters of the Jesuit missionaries in China – to the extent that he was criticised by them when they saw the results in the *Lettres édifiantes et curieuses*.[225] Besides embellishing the style, Du Halde's changes could also affect the letters' content. This may have been the case for Contancin's description of the spring sacrifice at the occasion of the ploughing of the land at the Xiannong 先農 altar. The French text mentions that the emperor, "like a grand Pontiff, offers to Chang-ti (= Shangdi 上帝) to ask him for abundance in favour of his people."[226] This would have been unlikely and was certainly not recorded in the Chinese text. From other cases, it is known that Du Halde did not like the elements that might suggest that the (ancient) Chinese believed in spirits, and that he wanted to stress that they

224 *LEC* (1736), vol. 22, pp. 308–310; *LEC* (1810–1811), vol. 21, p. 297.
225 For a review of these criticisms, see Landry-Deron (2002), p. 109ff.
226 *LEC* (1729), vol. 19, p. 387; *LEC* (1810–1811), vol. 21, p. 136.

believed in a unique and personal God.[227] As of yet, it is impossible to determine to what extent Du Halde also intervened in Contancin's texts.

Finally, a brief comparison of Contancin's letters with Perroni's two "Ristretto" can help further clarify the specific characteristics of each of these documents. Such a comparison is facilitated by the fact that their respective selections overlap for a few cases. For instance, in "a succinct collection of news that occupies the Gazettes of China," Perroni briefly mentions the case of the peasant who gave back the lost money to the merchant. Contancin's third letter, for its part, develops this same case to a far larger extent, including not only the imperial edict but also the long memorial, which is much more than is preserved in the surviving official sources. It bears pointing out that it is unclear whether Contancin and Perroni, who were both in Canton during the same years, ever communicated on their work on the gazettes.

On the whole, the formal differences between the two resources are obvious: Contancin's letters are much more extensive and much more detailed than Perroni's texts, while the latter include the Chinese texts for the imperial edicts, something that is unique for the documents discussed in this reader. In Perroni's "Ristretto" the different parts – his own description and comments, the Chinese texts, and the translation – are relatively clearly distinguished, while in the texts of Contancin, the comments and translation intertwine more easily and are interspersed with paraphrases.

Content-wise, there are further points of comparison. Despite the fact that Christianity is persecuted and that they themselves are in exile, both are very laudatory about the Yongzheng emperor and the functioning of the Chinese bureaucracy. Yet in Perroni's texts this praise is countered with a negative view of a blind emperor and constantly adulating officials, while in Contancin's letters the portrait remains continuously positive, highlighting an attentive and dedicated emperor and a pro-active bureaucracy.

That Contancin's consistently positive view was not shared by all Jesuits is evident from the introduction to the volume of *Lettres édifiantes et curieuses* in which the first letter of Contancin appeared. In it, the Jesuit Jean-Baptiste Du Halde, editor of the volume, gave the following brief description of the Yongzheng emperor – possibly also using information provided by other Jesuits, such as Antoine Gaubil:[228]

227 See on these differences, Pinot (1932), p. 132ff; Standaert (2016), pp. 121–123.

228 Compare for instance the information provided by Gaubil in a letter to the Jesuit Louis Gaillard (1676–1740) (27 October 1725). After his first encounter with the emperor, Gaubil

> This new Emperor is about fifty years old: he is of an advantageous size and his air inspires respect. He seems to have wit; he speaks well, but quickly, and without giving time to respond to him. Perhaps it is an affectation on his part, in order not to listen to reasons which should make him change resolutions already taken, and which he does not want to give up. Besides this, he is attentive to everything, applied to the affairs of the State, firm & decisive, always ready to receive memorials & to respond to them, governing entirely by himself; so that in a government as despotic as that of China, it is not possible to see a more absolute & more feared Master.[229]

Du Halde clearly balances the praise with a critical description of a sovereign whom he considers despotic.

2.3 Reception

How was the information about the Chinese gazettes spread and received in Europe? Some answers to this question can be found in the reception history of Contancin's letters. A first type of reception are the contemporary periodicals (*journaux*) and pamphlets in which the letters were reviewed. This made it possible for their content to reach a much wider audience. Second, a special case of reception history is the collection *Description … de la Chine* in which Contancin's information about the Chinese gazette was incorporated. Third, both the letters and the collection *Description … de la Chine* were extensively quoted in works on Chinese and world history. They both also inspired Enlightenment scholars such as Voltaire, Montesquieu, and Quesnay. These thinkers discussed the characteristics of the Chinese gazette and developed their own ideas on the basis of examples taken from them. Finally, Contancin's discussions of the Chinese gazette also played a role in the writing of the *Swedish Freedom of Writing and the Press Act*.

---

writes that "He is tall, stout, 49 years old, speaks well but quickly, appears to have wit, and looks fairly good"; Gaubil (1970), p. 92.

229 *LEC* (1728), vol. 18, pp. vii–viii (Epistre aux Jesuites de France).

2.3.1 *Academic Journals and Pamphlets:* Journal des sçavans, Mémoires de Trévoux, *and the* Bee

The seventeenth- and eighteenth-century French world of savants had access to a large number of various kinds of periodicals, including academic journals.[230] Characteristic of some of these academic journals is that they offered extensive and detailed reviews of recent publications. Rather than providing comments, these reviews tended to consist chiefly of long excerpts from the original publication, allowing the reader to trace to a certain extent what was considered "curious" – in the eighteenth-century usage of the word – in the eyes of the reviewer. In the course of the eighteenth century, such periodicals published an increasing number of reviews of books on China, including the different volumes of *Lettres édifiantes et curieuses*.[231]

One well-known example is the *Journal des sçavans* (established in 1665; renamed *Journal des savans* in 1791 and *Journal des savants* in 1831), which is considered one of the earliest academic journals published in Europe, primarily devoted to discoveries in the arts and sciences.[232] Among the contemporary French journals, it is the most official and academic, and also the journal that contained the most reviews on China.[233] The three volumes of *Lettres édifiantes et curieuses* that contain Contancin's letters were reviewed in the *Journal des sçavans* of 1728, 1730, and 1737.[234] In comparison with the other letters included in the same volumes of *Lettres édifiantes et curieuses*, these articles pay considerable attention to the letters by Contancin.

The review of the first letter refers to it as a letter on the new emperor of China, "whose main care is to watch over the happiness of his subjects. He cannot be better courted than by proposing to him some design that tends to

230 The website "Le gazetier universel: Liste des titres de périodiques" (http://gazetier-universel.gazettes18e.fr/) includes more than 800 titles in French for the seventeenth and eighteenth centuries. Besides expanding the scope to include more French periodicals, further study could also include the reception of information about the Chinese gazette in different other European journals, such as the Dutch, German, and English journals.

231 See on this topic Milsky (1977), chap. x "La Chine dans les journaux," vol. 1, pp. 437–464; see also Ma Li (2019), "Introduction" to her study on Chinese governance in French periodicals between 1750 and 1789.

232 See Milsky (1977), vol. 1, p. 438ff.; Touboul Bouyeure (1993), pp. 237–255; Pettegree (2014), p. 270.

233 Milsky (1977), vol. 1, p. 445: *Journal des sçavans* published 91 articles on China between 1701 and 1780, *Mémoires de Trévoux* published 74 articles in the same period. On this journal, see also Censer (1994), p. 144ff.

234 Volume 18 of *Lettres édifiantes et curieuses* in *Journal des sçavans* (juin 1728), pp. 361–373 and (octobre 1728), pp. 626–634 (letter of Contancin: pp. 630–634); volume 19 in *Journal des sçavans* (février 1730), pp. 88–92 (letter of Contancin: pp. 89–90); volume 22 in *Journal des sçavans* (janvier 1737), pp. 3–16 (fully devoted to the letter of Contancin).

public utility (*utilité publique*), and to the relief of those who are suffering; he adopts it with pleasure, and executes it without any regard to the expense."[235] This quasi-literal quote from Contancin's letter is followed by a selection of examples taken from that same text. The review also faithfully adopts Contancin's description of the utility of the gazette, including his comparison with its European equivalent, but leaves out the overview of the gazette's contents: "One has to look in the letter of Fr. Contancin itself [for a description of] the way in which these Gazettes have been conceived, and which subjects they treat; the passage is curious to read, we skip it with regret."[236]

As in the letters themselves, the focus in the second review shifts from the emperor more fully to the gazette, which is said to "contain nearly all public affairs of the Chinese Empire."[237] Again, a description is given that closely follows Contancin's original wording, including the reference to two authors condemned to death in 1726, followed by further examples of the content. The review of volume 22 of *Lettres édifiantes et curieuses* is devoted entirely to Contancin's third letter, "which appeared to us the most interesting and the most curious."[238] This review is based on the content of the gazettes, but little reference is made to the gazette itself. The framing topic is entirely shifted back to the emperor, who is praised for his multiple qualities, despite his attitude towards Christianity:

> With admiration we see in [this letter] the extraordinary application of the Emperor of China to the government of his states; his constant vigilance over the conduct of the high [officials] and of the people, his sensitivity to public miseries, his attention and his activity to prevent and relieve them, his singular inclination for virtue and for those who practice it. Reading what Father Contancin tells about all these topics, one cannot help but moan that such a great Prince has not inherited the affection that his father had for the Christian Religion and for the Workers of the Gospel.[239]

This is followed by twelve double-column pages with detailed examples, such as the land reclamation measures, the system of promotion in grade for officials, and a nearly complete reproduction of the case of the ordinary man who

235 *Journal des sçavans* (octobre 1728), p. 630. The first part of the review starts with Du Halde's description of the emperor (*Journal des sçavans* (juin 1728), p. 361).

236 *Journal des sçavans* (octobre 1728), p. 631.

237 *Journal des sçavans* (février 1730), p. 89.

238 *Journal des sçavans* (janvier 1737), p. 3.

239 *Journal des sçavans* (janvier 1737), pp. 3–4.

gave back the lost money to the merchant, which, just like other examples that have been omitted, are said to be a "testimony of the great virtues of the Emperor."[240]

Another academic journal was the *Mémoires pour l'Histoire des Sciences & des beaux-Arts*, often called the *Mémoires de Trévoux* or *Journal de Trévoux*. It appeared monthly in France between January 1701 and December 1782. Most of the critical reviews in it were written by Jesuits.[241] Composed in a style very similar to the *Journal des sçavans*, the *Mémoires de Trévoux* of 1728, 1730, and 1737 contain reviews of the three volumes of *Lettres édifiantes et curieuses* which contain Contancin's letters.[242]

The first review describes the letter of Contancin, "which is not the least curious [of the collection]" as follows:

> It paints a complete portrait of the Emperor now reigning: although he is an enemy of the Christian Religion, one cannot help rendering him the justice which is due to him elsewhere, and praising the qualities which make him worthy of the Empire.[243]

After quoting Du Halde's aforementioned short description of the emperor, the review cites several examples illustrating the emperor's concern for his empire, again directly copying Contancin's wording. At the end, mention is made of the Chinese gazette:

> This is because, far from being filled with futilities like some of the Gazettes of Europe, it is a daily History of State and Court, the most useful Code for those who govern, and the key to Government. For as all matters of some importance go to the Emperor, and it is willed only with his Decrees, one finds there without fear of error, all that concerns the vast Empire of China.[244]

The review of Contancin's second letter in *Mémoires de Trévoux* again takes up the theme of the gazette. In this context, the review notes that Contancin "just

---

240 *Journal des sçavans* (janvier 1737), p. 10.

241 Milsky (1977), vol. 1, p. 445ff. On this journal, see also Censer (1994), p. 110ff.

242 Volume 18 of *Lettres édifiantes et curieuses* in *Mémoires de Trévoux* (mai 1728), article 52, pp. 872–891 (letter of Contancin: pp. 885–891); volume 19 in *Mémoires de Trévoux* (février 1730), article 11, pp. 220–240 (letter of Contancin: pp. 228–235); volume 22 in *Mémoires de Trévoux* (février 1737), article 17, pp. 278–295 (letter of Contancin: pp. 280–282).

243 *Mémoires de Trévoux* (mai 1728), p. 885.

244 *Mémoires de Trévoux* (mai 1728), pp. 890–891.

like the other missionaries, had not taken it upon himself to read [the gazette], since he judged the Chinese gazette by those of Europe."[245] This remark is followed by the description of the characteristics of the gazette, taken directly from the original letter, as well as some examples of the gazette's content. Finally, the reader is told that further "curious particularities" can be found in the letter itself.[246]

The review of Contancin's last letter is, by comparison, much shorter, containing hardly any direct quotes. It focuses on the emperor, who had passed away in the meantime, sketching an extremely laudatory portrayal. He is considered

> one of those rare men whom Providence intended for the Sceptre for the happiness of the nations. Just, wise, vigilant, hard-working, all he needed was to be more favourable to the Christian Religion: which did not prevent the Missionaries from rendering justice to his eminent qualities.[247]

As pointed out by Milsky, these journals, which are essentially composed of book reviews, were intended to inform rather than to criticize. In the eighteenth century, their purpose was to make known the merits of certain books and to inform the readers of what they could learn from them, without direct criticism.[248] The reviews published in *Journal des sçavans*, as well as those in *Mémoires de Trévoux*, provide an angle on the interest in China among the narrow circle of the learned elite.[249] As is evident from their reviews of Contancin's letters, both journals offer first-hand documentation on the most diverse subjects, including the Chinese gazette. From these articles, one can understand the multifaceted and diverse curiosity of the scholarly world of the time for all that was related to China. In addition, neither journal hides their praise of the Yongzheng emperor – despite his attitude towards

---

245 *Mémoires de Trévoux* (février 1730), p. 228.

246 *Mémoires de Trévoux* (février 1730), p. 235.

247 *Mémoires de Trévoux* (février 1737), pp. 280–281.

248 Milsky (1977), vol. 1, p. 437.

249 Another journal is *Mercure de France*. It reached a broader, less erudite audience and presented itself as a journal intended not only for instruction, but also for the amusement of its readers. The articles (Milsky (1977), pp. 450–451) on China are less numerous. The fact that *Mercure de France* was interested in the most important publications and those most accessible to a broad audience, explains why reports on *Lettres édifiantes et curieuses* are very limited. Volume 18 of *Lettres édifiantes et curieuses* in *Mercure de France* (mars 1728), pp. 521–523 (very short and mentioning only a few of the topics discussed in the volume); volume 19: not included; volume 22: *Mercure de France* (Janvier 1737), pp. 85–86 (only announcement); *Mercure de France* (avril 1733), p. 751 mentions Contancin as collaborator of *Description ... de la Chine*.

Christianity – and both commend the Chinese gazette. The *Mémoires de Trévoux*, representing the engaged Jesuit point of view, is even more laudatory than the *Journal des sçavans*. These journals contributed to the spread of knowledge about the Chinese gazette and further disseminated the vision of the emperor and his government that emerged from Contancin's translations – even to those who had no direct access to his letters in *Lettres édifiantes et curieuses*.

That the reception of Contancin's letters was not limited to France or to French (academic) journals, can be observed from an English pamphlet periodical titled *Bee, or the universal weekly pamphlet* (February 1733–May 1735). It was published by English politician and writer Eustace Budgell (1686–1737), who is known for the passionate journals and pamphlets of his later years, chiefly directed against the then leading Whig administration in Great Britain. His *Bee* contained a lot of news about China,[250] and most of the extracts on the topic can be traced to Contancin's first and second letters, which had only recently been published at the time. As T.C. Fan has shown, Budgell had an eye on contemporary British politics while translating and transposing almost verbatim the French sources. In doing so, he presented an idealised view of China, which was to him an ideal commonwealth.[251]

The "Publick Gazettes" of China, Budgell paraphrases from Contancin, "are the Reverse of our European News-Papers, which are a Medley of Truth and Falshood [sic]," whereas the Chinese ones are "so strictly tied done to Truth and Fact, that to deviate from them is a capital Crime." He gives the example used by Contancin of two writers "who were sentenced to die for having inserted

---

250 *Bee*, vol. 2, no. 18 (23 June 1733), pp. 798–802 = *LEC* (1729), vol. 19, pp. 267–272; pp. 315–324; vol. 2, no. 19 (30 June 1733), pp. 848–849 = *LEC* (1729), vol. 19, pp. 297–304; vol. 2, no. 23 (28 July 1733), pp. 1015–1020 = *LEC* (1729), vol. 19, pp. 307–315; pp. 379–384;
Bee, vol. 3, no. 28 (1 Sept. 1733), pp. 1224–1229 = *LEC* (1729), vol. 19, pp. 325–329; pp. 338–345; vol. 3, no. 35 (20 Oct. 1733), pp. 1546–1551 = *LEC* (1729), vol. 19, pp. 288–296; pp. 331–334; pp. 334–337;
Bee, vol. 8, no. 97 (28 Dec. 1734), pp. 197–201 = *LEC* (1729), vol. 19, pp. 393–402; vol. 8, no. 102 (1 Febr. 1735), pp. 396–400 = *LEC* (1729), vol. 19, pp. 273–288;
Bee, vol. 2, no. 24 (4 Aug. 1733), pp. 1058–1063: reference to the publicity of Du Halde's *Description ... de la Chine* (two sheets in folio) with reference to the role of Contancin (Contencin); vol. 4, no. 49 (26 Jan. 1734), pp. 423–434 = *Description ... de la Chine*; vol. 4, no. 50 (2 Febr. 1734), pp. 468–476 = *Description ... de la Chine*;
Bee, vol. 6, no. 66 (25 May 1734), pp. 34–38: on the earthquake in Beijing (30 Sept. 1730) (not in Contancin).

251 This case is discussed by Fan (1949), pp. 142–143 and referred to by Mokros (2021), p. 209 n. 36.

some Circumstances in the Gazette, which, upon Examination, appeared to be False."[252] Elaborating on the concrete content of the gazettes, he proceeds to present an account "of the Publick Spirit, with which a Chinese Mandarin [i.e. Zha Bina] accused one of the Emperor's chief Favourites, a Prince of the Blood, and his Prime Minister, of several Malversations, and Oppressions of the Subject."[253] Budgell is of the opinion that in such examples translated from the gazette, "is to be seen a noble Spirit of Liberty in a Subject, and the Wisdom of the Government of China in the impartial Administration of Publick Justice."[254] They show "the Emperor's Justice, and, at the same Time, his Tenderness and Compassion for his Subjects."[255] In a later issue, Budgell cites the "instance of a Chinese Manderin [sic], who dared to oppose an Order of the Emperor, and the Grand Council, which he conceived tended to the Prejudice of the Subject."[256] This particular example seems to echo Budgell's own experiences: in 1730, he had kneeled at Court and had petitioned George II (1683–1760) about the injustice done to him by prime minister Robert Walpole (1676–1742).[257] Budgell gives other examples of how in China "Liberality, and a noble publick Spirit" is not confined to men alone, but is also exhibited by several women, such as the empress.[258] These translations clearly both informed the British public about China and suited Budgell's own political standpoints.[259]

2.3.2 *The Collection* Description … de la Chine

Contancin was also involved in another work edited by Jean-Baptiste Du Halde, a brief discussion of which can give an indication of how the information about

252 *Bee*, vol. 2, no. 18 (23 June 1733), p. 798. In the eyes of Budgell, these gazettes, which are published daily, "are properly a Sort of Pamphlets."

253 *Bee*, vol. 2, no. 18 (23 June 1733), p. 799.

254 *Bee*, vol. 2, no. 19 (30 June 1733), p. 848.

255 *Bee*, vol. 2, no. 23 (28 July 1733), p. 1015; see also vol. 8, no. 97 (28 Dec. 1734), p. 197: "Generosity, Justice and paternal Care."

256 *Bee*, vol. 3, no. 28 (1 Sept. 1733), p. 1227.

257 Fan (1949), p. 143.

258 *Bee*, vol. 3, no. 35 (20 Oct. 1733), pp. 1546.

259 Another example of the reception of the *Lettres édifiantes et curieuses* can be found with bishop and author Thomas Percy (1729–1811). In the notes to *Hau Kiou Choaan, or The Pleasing History* (1761), a heavily revised version of the translation of *Haoqiu zhuan* 好逑傳, he refers to the three letters of Contancin on the gazettes and to the passage in *Description … de la Chine*. He also translates the detailed description of the content of one gazette and the case of the two officials sentenced to death, as can be found in the second letter (*LEC* (1729), vol. 19, pp. 267–272). See *Hau Kiou Choaan* (1761), vol. 3, pp. 12–16; Porter (2010), p. 162; Mokros (2021), p. 122.

and from the Chinese gazettes was incorporated into different European publications. It concerns a very extensive collection (in four volumes) that systematically brought together the information gathered by the French Jesuits and that was intended for a European audience: *Description géographique, historique, chronologique, politique, et physique de l'empire de la Chine et de la Tartarie chinoise* (usually abbreviated as *Description ... de la Chine*).[260] It was published in Paris in 1735, with a reprint in The Hague in 1736 and an English translation in the same year with reprints in 1738, 1739, and 1741 (*The General History of China. Containing a Geographical, Historical, Chronological, Political and Physical Description of the Empire of China, Chinese-Tartary, Corea and Thibet. Including an Exact and Particular Account of Their Customs, Manners, Ceremonies, Religion, Arts and Sciences*). The work was also translated into German (1747–1756) and Russian (1774, 1777; partial translation).[261] Jean-Baptiste Du Halde himself never went to China, but for the finalisation of *Description ... de la Chine* he partially relied on the help of Contancin when the latter returned to France. As reported in the sales prospectus and introduction to the book, one of the final stages in the development of the book was its careful rereading by Contancin, who "after thirty-two years" in China had just returned to France in 1731. Du Halde presents this as an advantage that has greatly enriched his work.[262] According to Landry-Deron, Contancin's contribution may have been even more important than the simple editorial revision.[263]

There are some sporadic references to gazettes in *Description ... de la Chine*, especially in allusion to the years immediately before the collection's publication. For instance, at the end of the general overview of Chinese history from the early times until the Qing dynasty, reference is made to the dismissal of Yinreng 胤礽 (Yunreng 允礽) (1674–1725) as Crown Prince by the Kangxi emperor in 1707: "The public Gazettes (*Gazettes publiques*) were filled with manifestoes and invectives against the Prince's conduct, whose life had been examined since his childhood."[264] In another passage discussing the topic of the authority of the emperor, it is mentioned that at this occasion "the public gazettes (*Gazettes publiques*) were immediately filled with manifestoes, by which the Emperor informed his subjects of the reasons he had had for coming

260 Notice that in the abbreviation "et de la Tartarie chinoise" is omitted.
261 For further details, see CCT-database.
262 Landry-Deron (2002), pp. 126–131, 367–368.
263 This is the opinion voiced by Landry-Deron (2002), p. 128.
264 *Description ... de la Chine* (1735), vol. 1, p. 547 (under "Fastes de la monarchie chinoise"); *General History of China* (1736), vol. 1, p. 497 (publick New-Papers).

to such a brilliant state of affairs."[265] A few years later, when the Kangxi emperor's ninth son, the above-mentioned Yintang 胤禟 (1683–1726), died shortly after being exiled by the new emperor, it is reported that "The Gazettes published that he was dead of the dysentery."[266] There are also two references to the gazettes in relation to Christianity: both the favourable statement by the Kangxi emperor concerning the Chinese rites (*Brevis relatio*, 1700)[267] and the proscription of Christianity by the Yongzheng emperor (in January 1724) were included in the gazettes.[268] Some of these references may have been introduced by Contancin; others are from earlier years and indicate that the (anonymous) missionaries who wrote the reports read and consulted gazettes.

The most interesting reference, however, is a description of gazettes in the section on the "form of government," which includes an overview of the institutional structure of the government (including the Ministries) as well as the function, powers, and honours attributed to the officials (Mandarins). Herein the significance and utility of gazettes is reframed in the context of the fight against misbehaviour by officials. The anonymous author enumerates and describes six measures that should remedy possible "disorder" so as to "retain the Mandarins in duty and protect the people from vexations."[269] These measures include:

> 1) The fact that officials are almost sure to lose their position when they are not able to appease protests by people who are suffering under oppression, because such uprisings are imputed to them; 2) The rule of avoidance for officials to serve in their native province and the limited number of years for an official duty;[270] 3) The three-yearly review of all the officials in the country;[271] 4) the fact that from time to time the

265 *Description … de la Chine* (1735), vol. 2, p. 11 (under "De l'ancienneté & de l'étendue de la monarchie Chinoise: De l'autorité de l'empereur …"); *General History of China* (1736), vol. 2, p. 16 (publick Gazettes).

266 *Description … de la Chine* (1735), vol. 1, p. 550 (under "Fastes de la monarchie chinoise"); *General History of China* (1736), vol. 1, p. 502 (the reference to the gazettes is not translated).

267 *Description … de la Chine* (1735), vol. 3, p. 33 (under "De la religion des Chinois"); not translated in *General History of China* (1736).

268 *Description … de la Chine* (1735), vol. 3, p. 127 (under "De l'établissement & du progrés de la religion Chrètienne dans l'empire de la Chine"); not translated in *General History of China* (1736).

269 *Description … de la Chine* (1735), vol. 2, p. 38 (under "De la forme du gouvernement de la Chine …"); *General History of China* (1736), vol. 2, p. 62.

270 Mentioned by Contancin in *LEC* (1729), vol. 19, p. 369; *LEC* (1810–1811), vol. 21, p. 128.

271 Mentioned by Contancin in *LEC* (1728), vol. 18, pp. 454–455; *LEC* (1810–1811), vol. 20, pp. 311–312.

> emperor secretly sends inspectors to the provinces; 5) the fact that he sometimes decides to visit some provinces in person, in order to listen for the just complaints that the people have to make against those who govern them.[272]

The sixth and final measure concerns the gazette:

> In a word nothing can be more instructive, and more capable of keeping the Mandarins in order, and prevent the Faults they might be guilty of, than the Gazette which is printed every Day at Peking (*la Gazette qui s'imprime chaque jour à Peking*), and dispersed from thence into all the Provinces.[273]

The description of the characteristics of the gazette that follows this enumeration was taken directly from Contancin's first and second letter, including an explicit reference to the capital punishment of the two lower officials who reported about an imperial meeting in the Yuanmingyuan. This passage is worth quoting in full since it reads as a summary of Contancin's letters. Moreover, it provides a clear idea of what was transmitted to the large readership of *Description ... de la Chine*, including the Enlightenment thinkers:

> There is nothing inserted in [the Gazette] but what has reference to the Government; and as the Chinese Government is absolute Monarchy, and the most trifling Affairs are brought before the Emperor, it contains nothing but what may be very serviceable to direct the Mandarins in the Exercise of the Office, and instruct the Learned as well as the Vulgar.
>
> It contains, for instance, the Names of the Mandarins that have been deprived of their Offices, and for what Reason: One for being negligent in gathering the Emperor's Tribute, or for squandering it away; another because he was too indulgent or too severe in his Punishments; this for his Oppression, that for want of Talents to govern as he ought. If any Mandarin has been raised to a considerable Office or been depressed; or if he has been deprived, for any Fault, of the Annual Pension that he ought to receive of the Emperor, it is immediately put into the Gazette.

272 *Description ... de la Chine* (1735), vol. 2, pp. 38–42 (under "De la forme du gouvernement de la Chine ..."); *General History of China* (1736), vol. 2, pp. 62–68.

273 *Description ... de la Chine* (1735), vol. 2, p. 42 (under "De la forme du gouvernement de la Chine ..."); *General History of China* (1736), vol. 2, pp. 69–70.

It speaks likewise of all Criminal Affairs for which Persons are capitally condemned, and likewise the Names of the Officers who fill the Places of the Mandarins that were removed, and also the Calamities that happened in such and such a Province, and the Assistance given by the Mandarins of the Place in pursuance of the Emperor's Order; it likewise contains the Expenses disbursed for the Subsistence of the Soldiers, the Necessities of the People, the Publick Works, and the Benefactions of the Prince; there are also the Remonstrances of the Supreme Tribunals, which have been made to the Emperor concerning his own Conduct, or his Decisions.

They therein mention the Day that the Emperor tilled the Earth, that they may excite Emulation in the Minds of the People, and inspire those who govern them with a Love of Labour and Application for the Culture of the Fields; they mention likewise the Time of the Convention of the Grandees at *Peking*, and all the Chief Mandarins of the Tribunals, that they may be instructed in their Duty. There you may find the Laws and new Customs that have been established, the Praises and Reprimands given by the Emperor to a Mandarin: For instance, such a Mandarin has not a very good Reputation, and if he does not amend he will be punished.

In short the *Chinese* Gazette is made in such a manner that it is very useful to instruct the Mandarins how to govern the People as they ought, for which reason they read it constantly; and as it gives an account of all the Publick Affairs that are transacted in this vast Empire, the greatest part commit to writing their Observations upon the things that it contains, which may direct them in their Conduct.

Nothing is printed in the Gazette but what has been presented to the Emperor, or comes from the Emperor himself; those who have the care of it dare not add a Tittle thereto, nor even their own Reflections, upon pain of Corporal Punishments.

In 1726 a Writer of a Tribunal, and another Writer, who was employed at the Board of the Post-Office, were condemned to Death for having inserted Circumstances in the Gazette that were found to be false; The Reason upon which the Tribunal of Criminal Affairs founded their Judgment, was, that he had failed in Respect to his Majesty, and the Law declares whoever fails in Respect to his Majesty deserves Death.[274]

274 *Description … de la Chine* (1735), vol. 2, pp. 42–43 (under "De la forme du gouvernement de la Chine …"); *General History of China* (1736), vol. 2, pp. 70–71; *LEC* (1728), vol. 18, pp. 434–441; *LEC* (1810–1811), vol. 20, pp. 301–305; *LEC* (1729), vol. 19, pp. 268–269; *LEC* (1810–1811), vol. 21, p. 77.

This section of *Description … de la Chine* is important because it shows how the information about gazettes from Contancin's letters is used in a more systematic way to explain, probably with the help of Contancin himself, characteristics of Chinese governance. In this section, the gazettes are notably interpreted as a means to discipline the officials.

Description … de la Chine became an important source of information about China, and as such it also shaped the European perception of China. For instance, the largely optimistic view on the Chinese bureaucracy presented in Du Halde's *Description … de la Chine* became a point of reference on the empire and determined to a large extent the opinion of the general public in the eighteenth century and beyond. This view contrasted with Perroni's depiction of a blind emperor and adulating officials. It also contrasted with an earlier and very negative notion of a corrupt bureaucracy, which could be found for instance in Gabriel de Magalhães' (1609–1677) *Nouvelle relation de la Chine* (1688),[275] which traces the history of the first twenty-five years of the Qing dynasty.[276]

2.3.3 *Works on Chinese and World History*

Contancin's texts in both *Lettres édifiantes et curieuses* and *Description … de la Chine* became important sources for works on Chinese history in the eighteenth century. A clear example is the major work by Joseph-Anne-Marie de Moyriac de Mailla: *Histoire générale de la Chine, ou Annales de cet Empire, traduites du Tong-kien-kang-mou* (1777–1785), which was also translated into Italian. With its thirteen volumes and more than 7.000 pages of text, it is still the most extensive work on Chinese history, based on Chinese and Manchu primary sources and basically compiled by one author, in any European language.[277] It covers the history from the earliest times until the Qianlong era. Joseph de Mailla arrived in China in 1703 and died in 1748. His work was published thirty years later, carefully edited by l'abbé Grosier (i.e. Jean-Baptiste Grosier, 1743–1823), who was aided by Michel-Ange-André Le Roux Deshauterayes (1724–1795), professor of Arabic at the Royal College of France, who also knew some Chinese. The latter edited volume 11, which included a year-by-year chronology of events that happened during the Yongzheng reign. Especially for the years 1725–1727, the annals quote quasi literally the gazettes translated by Contancin, a fact that is also explicitly acknowledged in the notes.[278] The result is that

275 Gabriel De Magalhães, *Nouvelle relation de la Chine*, Paris: C. Barbin, 1688; English translation *A New History of China*, London: T. Newborough, 1688.

276 For a detailed comparison, see Will (2015), pp. 157, 162–177.

277 On this work, see Standaert (2016), pp. 133–139.

278 de Mailla, *Histoire générale*, vol. 11 (1780), p. 369 n.1: the editor explains that he used *Lettres édifiantes et curieuses*, since de Mailla himself was not able to finish the section on the

very large sections of his letters are reprinted in a slightly edited form.[279] Not the gazette as such, but its historical content is the focus of attention. In an introductory note, Deshauterayes admits to a degree of apprehension in compiling the chapters on the reigns of the Yongzheng and Qianlong emperors, pointing out that certain sections of the *Lettres édifiantes* – one of his main sources of information – need to be read "with the greatest caution" (*avec la plus grande circonspection*). His sense of responsibility towards his readership eventually led him to continue with the project in spite of the shortcomings of his source materials, basing himself on the information that had managed to reach Europe.[280]

Around the time of publication of *Histoire générale de la Chine*, scholars with an interest in world history also more frequently based themselves on *Description … de la Chine*. One example is François-Marie de Marsy (1714–1763), a former Jesuit who wrote several books on history. His *Histoire moderne des Chinois, des Japonnois, des Indiens, des Persans, des Turcs, des Russiens, &c.* (1755–1771; 30 vols. of which the first eleven were edited by de Marsy; the others by Adrien Richer (1720–1798)) starts with a volume on China. Besides an overview of Chinese history, it contains chapters on geography, government, economy, sciences, and religion. The chapter on government includes a passage on the gazettes. Like other sections, this appears to have been based on *Description … de la Chine* and adopts the same vision on the government's continuous effort of illuminating the conduct of officials through the gazettes.[281] Though it is only a short reference, this example is another

---

Yongzheng and Qianlong emperors; p. 408 n. 2: reference to Contancin's letters in *LEC*, vol. 18 and 19; see also note p. 523 n. 1 with explicit reference to *LEC*, vol. 19. In fact, the editor also used LEC, vol. 22 and rearranged the content of the volumes chronologically.

279 1725: vol. 11, pp. 408–409 = *LEC* (1728), vol. 18, p. 430; pp. 409–410 = *LEC* (1728), vol. 18, pp. 455–458; pp. 410–411 = *LEC* (1728), vol. 18, pp. 431–434; pp. 411–413 = *LEC* (1729), vol. 19, pp. 379–384; pp. 413–415 = *LEC* (1729), vol. 19, pp. 307–315; pp. 415–419 = *LEC* (1729), vol. 19, pp. 345–364; pp. 419–420 = *LEC* (1728), vol. 18, pp. 444–445; pp. 420–421 = [*LEC* (1729), vol. 19, pp. 325–329]; pp. 421–422 = *LEC* (1728), vol. 18, pp. 448–449; pp. 422–423 = *LEC* (1728), vol. 18, pp. 449–450; pp. 423–424 = *LEC* (1728), vol. 18, pp. 452–455; pp. 424–425 = *LEC* (1728), vol. 18, pp. 446–448; pp. 432–435 = *LEC* (1729), vol. 19, pp. 315–324; pp. 435–438 = *LEC* (1736), vol. 22, pp. 249–262.

1726: vol. 11, pp. 438–441 = *LEC* (1736), vol. 22, pp. 202–209; pp. 441–443 = *LEC* (1729), vol. 19, pp. 384–392; pp. 443–446 = *LEC* (1729), vol. 19, pp. 366–379; [the Sunu story is taken from other letters].

1727: vol. 11, pp. 473–474 = *LEC* (1729), vol. 19, pp. 338–345; pp. 474–478 = *LEC* (1736), vol. 22, pp. 210–223; pp. 478–479 = *LEC* (1736), vol. 22, pp. 244–245; pp. 481–483 = *LEC* (1736), vol. 22, pp. 191–196; pp. 483–491 = *LEC* (1736), vol. 22, pp. 299–324.

280 de Mailla, *Histoire générale*, vol. 11 (1780), p. 369 n.1.

281 Marsy (1755), vol. 1, pp. 201–202; he reformulated certain sentences; compare with *Description … de la Chine* (1735), vol. 2, pp. 42–43.

illustration of how Contancin's information ended up in early modern books on world history.

2.3.4 *Enlightenment Thinkers: Voltaire, Montesquieu, Quesnay*

Striking examples of the reception history of Contancin's letters on the Chinese gazette and of *Description ... de la Chine* can also be found in the way they inspired Enlightenment scholars such as Voltaire, Montesquieu, and Quesnay. This is not the place to discuss in detail Voltaire's, Montesquieu's, or Quesnay's vision of the Chinese government and imperial system, or to determine to what extent their vision of China was constructed and used to advance their own ideas – topics which have already been the subject of many studies.[282] Instead, the goal of this next section will be to trace how these Enlightenment thinkers received information on or excerpts from the Chinese gazette, and how they in turn used and interpreted this information in their own writing. As will be observed, their vision on the Chinese gazette often coincided with their vision on China.

2.3.4.1 Voltaire

It is well known that Voltaire (François-Marie Arouet; 1694–1778) took China as a mirror and example to develop his ideas about history, religion, and government.[283] It is less known that, in developing these ideas, Voltaire drew on the translation and description of the Chinese gazette provided by Contancin. Information about Voltaire's reading practices are ample because his library is preserved, and the marginal notes or bookmarks he added to the texts he read have been compiled and edited in a special collection. As a result, it is easy to prove that Voltaire read Contancin's letters. This can be shown, for example, by referring to his bookmarks on Contancin's letters of 15 December 1727 (second letter)[284] and 19 October 1730 (third letter).[285] He also read *Description ... de la Chine*, edited by Du Halde.[286]

---

282 Besides the references in the notes below, see also CCT-database for further bibliography.

283 For a quick overview of his ideas concerning China, see Meng Hua (2003), pp. 198–203.

284 Voltaire, *Corpus des notes marginales de Voltaire: Tome V* (OCV 140a) (2012), pp. 345–346: *LEC* (1729), vol. 19, pp. 292–293: "faits singuliers / dans la gazette / 40000 vieilles / etc" on the bookmark (pp. 268/269); *LEC* (1729), vol. 19, pp. 384–386: "labourage" on the bookmark (pp. 384/285); *LEC* (1729), vol. 19, pp. 389–391: "la main à la Charruë" underlined and line in the margin (pp. 240/241).

285 Voltaire, *Corpus des notes marginales de Voltaire: Tome V* (OCV 140a) (2012), pp. 348–349: *LEC* (1736), vol. 22, pp. 217–218: "defricheurs / mandarns [sic]" on the bookmark; *LEC* (1736), vol. 22, pp. 270–271: 40000 / pauvres / secourus" on the bookmark (pp. 270/271); *LEC* (1736), vol. 22, pp. 301–302: "histoire / de / chieou" on the bookmark (pp. 298/299).

286 Voltaire, *Corpus des notes marginales de Voltaire: Tome III: Dale-Frisi* (OCV 138) (2010), p. 263: "Yong tching. Troisiéme Empereur."

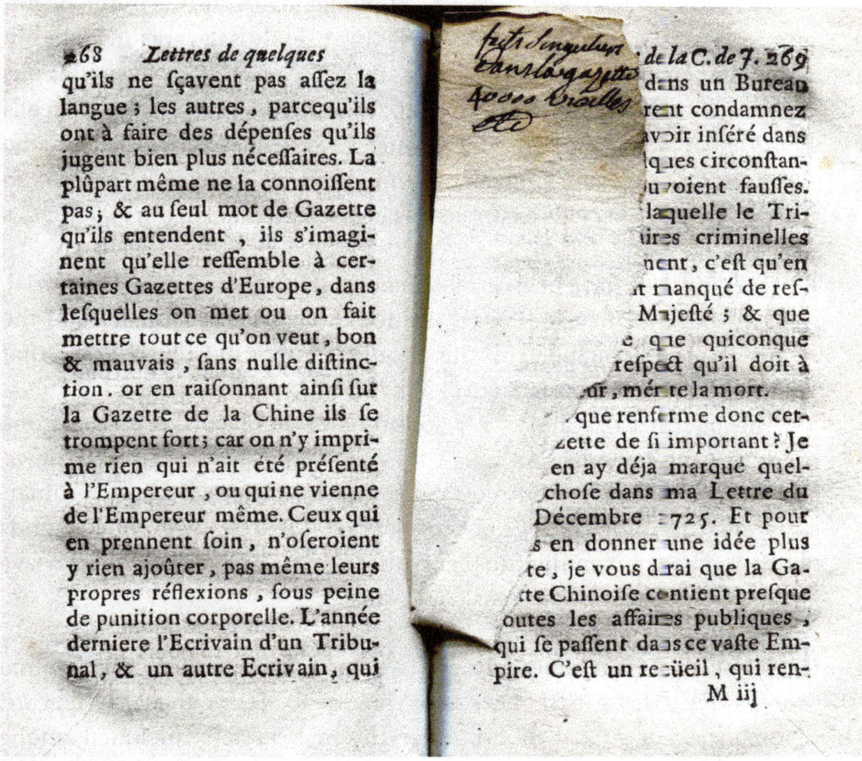

268 *Lettres de quelques*

qu'ils ne ſçavent pas aſſez la langue ; les autres, parcequ'ils ont à faire des dépenſes qu'ils jugent bien plus néceſſaires. La plûpart même ne la connoiſſent pas ; & au ſeul mot de Gazette qu'ils entendent, ils s'imaginent qu'elle reſſemble à certaines Gazettes d'Europe, dans leſquelles on met ou on fait mettre tout ce qu'on veut, bon & mauvais, ſans nulle diſtinction. or en raiſonnant ainſi ſur la Gazette de la Chine ils ſe trompent fort; car on n'y imprime rien qui n'ait été préſenté à l'Empereur, ou qui ne vienne de l'Empereur même. Ceux qui en prennent ſoin, n'oſeroient y rien ajoûter, pas même leurs propres réflexions, ſous peine de punition corporelle. L'année derniere l'Ecrivain d'un Tribunal, & un autre Ecrivain, qui

de la C. de J. 269

dans un Bureau
rent condamnez
avoir inſéré dans
lques circonſtan-
uvoient fauſſes.
laquelle le Tri-
ires criminelles
nent, c'eſt qu'en
t manqué de reſ-
Majeſté ; & que
e que quiconque
reſpect qu'il doit à
ur, mérite la mort.
. que renferme donc cet-
zette de ſi important ? Je
en ay déja marqué quel-
choſe dans ma Lettre du
Décembre 1725. Et pour
s en donner une idée plus
te, je vous dirai que la Ga-
zette Chinoiſe contient preſque
outes les affaires publiques,
qui ſe paſſent dans ce vaſte Empire. C'eſt un recüeil, qui ren-

M iij

ILLUSTRATION 10 Voltaire's bookmark to the second letter by Cyr Contancin: *Lettres édifiantes et curieuses*, vol. 19 (1729), pp. 268–269, "faits singuliers / dans la gazette / 40000 vieilles / etc" (refers to pp. 292–293)

Voltaire not only read these texts but also used them in his own writings. He referred to gazettes in his most famous book *Essai sur les mœurs et l'esprit des nations* (1756), which starts with a chapter on China, as well as in several other texts. All of these discuss both the gazette as a topic and the contents of gazettes as presented through Contancin's translations.

First, Voltaire was well aware of the existence of gazettes in China and used this knowledge when he treated the subject of newspapers. He was the author of the lemma "Gazette" in the *Encyclopédie, ou dictionnaire raisonné des sciences, des arts et des métiers* (better known as *Encyclopédie*), edited by Denis Diderot (1713–1784) and Jean Le Rond d'Alembert (1717–1783) and published between 1751 and 1772. In this lemma, the Chinese gazette is used to provide a different perspective on the European concept of gazettes. In addition, Voltaire situates its history much earlier than the European one.

> GAZETTE, s. f. (*Mod. hist.*) account of public affairs. It was at the beginning of the seventeenth century that this useful usage was invented in Venice, at the time when Italy was still the centre of the negotiations of Europe, and when Venice was still the sanctuary of liberty. One calls these sheets which were produced once a week, *gazettes*, from the name of *gazetta*, a small coin equivalent to one of our half-sous, which was then common in Venice. This example was next imitated in all the major cities of Europe.
>
> Such journals have been established in China from time immemorial, and the *gazette* of the empire is printed there every day by order of the court. If [what is included in] this gazette is true, it must be believed that not all truths are there. Moreover, they should not all be there.
>
> The *gazettes* of China only look at this empire; those of Europe embrace the universe. Although they are often filled with false news, they can, however, provide good materials for history; because, ordinarily, the errors of one *gazette* are corrected by the following, and one finds in them almost all authentic pieces that the sovereigns themselves have inserted therein.[287]

The topic of the Chinese gazettes is also touched upon in the lemma "Historiographe" (Historiographer) that Voltaire wrote for the *Encyclopédie*. This lemma was not published in the *Encyclopédie*, but later included among other articles in *Nouveaux mélanges* (1765) and published with Voltaire's support.[288] In this article, Voltaire describes how the Chinese historiographers compose what he calls an "authentic history" (*une histoire authentique*) of the previous dynasty. The Chinese gazettes also have a role to play in the composition of this history. In this context, Voltaire holds them to be superior to the European ones:

287 The article was published in *Encyclopédie*, vol. VII (1757), pp. 534–535; see (annotated) online edition: Édition Numérique Collaborative et CRitique de l'Encyclopédie, http://enccre.academie-sciences.fr/. See also: Voltaire, *Œuvres alphabétiques I* (OCV 33) (1987), pp. 113–114; for a (slightly different) English translation, see: Voltaire, "Gazette." *The Encyclopedia of Diderot & d'Alembert Collaborative Translation Project.* Translated by Kenneth Garner. Ann Arbor: Michigan Publishing, University of Michigan Library, 2016, web.archive.org/web/20210528213132/https://quod.lib.umich.edu/d/did/did2222.0001.107?view=text;rgn=main. Trans. of "Gazette," *Supplément à l'Encyclopédie ou Dictionnaire raisonné des sciences, des arts et des métiers*, vol. 7 (Amsterdam, 1776–77), pp. 534–535.

288 *Nouveaux mélanges* (1765), vol. 2, pp. 381–384. See on this issue Voltaire, *Œuvres alphabétiques I* (OCV 33) (1987), pp. 215–216.

> The general newspaper of the empire also serves to form the body of history; this newspaper is superior to our gazettes, in that it is made under the supervision of the mandarins of each province, reviewed by a supreme tribunal, and that each piece bears with it a genuine authenticity (*authenticité*) which is decisive in contentious matters.[289]

In *Essai sur les mœurs et l'esprit des nations*, Voltaire gives a similar positive appreciation of the Chinese gazette, stressing its authentic character and the aspect of "public needs."

> The journal of the Chinese empire, the most authentic (*authentique*) and useful newspaper in the world, since it contains the details of all the public needs, resources, and interests of all the orders of the State.[290]

Voltaire not only describes the Chinese gazettes, but he also uses the information transmitted in the gazettes translated by Contancin to use the Chinese government and imperial system as sources for his argumentation. For instance, the reference to the Chinese gazette cited above is immediately followed by the example of generosity (*libéralité*) of the new Chinese empress, who distributed gifts to poor elderly women all over China.[291] The same first chapter of *Essai sur les mœurs et l'esprit des nations* argues that "in other countries the laws punish crimes; in China, they do more; they reward virtue," which is followed by the example of the poor peasant being rewarded after giving back the money lost by a merchant.[292] Both examples are taken from Contancin's second letter. Other examples appear in *Siècle de Louis XIV*, which contains a chapter on the Chinese Rites Controversy. In it, Voltaire adopts a very positive view of the Yongzheng emperor, partly inspired by Contancin's stress on "public utility," but also by his own stress on respect for the law:

---

289 Voltaire, *Œuvres alphabétiques I* (OCV 33) (1987), p. 217.

290 Voltaire, *Essai sur les mœurs et l'esprit des nations: Tome 2: Avant-propos et chapitres 1–37* (OCV 22) (2009), p. 31.

291 Voltaire, *Essai sur les mœurs et l'esprit des nations: Tome 2: Avant-propos et chapitres 1–37* (OCV 22) (2009), p. 31; Voltaire, *Corpus des notes marginales de Voltaire: Tome V* (OCV 140a) (2012), p. 345. Voltaire is referring here to the case mentioned in LEC (1729), vol. 19, pp. 292–293; LEC (1811), vol. 21, p. 89. He tries to calculate how much this generosity would have cost.

292 Voltaire, *Essai sur les mœurs et l'esprit des nations: Tome 2: Avant-propos et chapitres 1–37* (OCV 22) (2009), pp. 48–49; Voltaire, *Corpus des notes marginales de Voltaire: Tome V* (OCV 140a) (2012), p. 349 ("histoire de chieou"). Voltaire is referring here to the case mentioned in LEC (1736), vol. 22, p. 303ff; LEC (1811), vol. 21, p. 294ff.

> The new emperor Yontching [= Yongzheng] surpassed his father in the love of laws and the public good. No emperor encouraged agriculture more.[293]

Voltaire corroborates this assertion with examples taken directly from Contancin's first letter, such as the elevation of exemplary peasants to the rank of mandarin of the eighth degree,[294] the rule that any capital punishment should be submitted for approval to the emperor,[295] and the emperor's critique on the prayers offered in the temple in gratitude for his tax exemption.[296] One can notice that Voltaire not only copied these examples, but interpreted and reframed them within the structure of his own argument. Thus, while some of these cases were only briefly mentioned in Contancin's original letter, Voltaire incorporated them into a wider argumentation.

Voltaire pays much attention to the role of the emperor and explicitly refers to the Jesuits when he describes him in a chapter on "China in the seventeenth and early eighteenth centuries" in *Essai sur les mœurs et l'esprit des nations*.

> The same Jesuits (…) confess with all the others that this emperor was one of the wisest of the most generous princes who ever reigned.[297]

In the descriptions of China offered by the gazettes, Voltaire discovers the image of an ideal government: with a monarch who governs relying on subordinated administrative boards or courts (*tribunaux* in Contancin) and officials who were selected through exams.[298] In the eyes of Voltaire, such a formula would permit the keeping of the monarchical form while eliminating the abuses to liberty which marred the system in France.[299] Since "everything in China is arranged by these courts," it is impossible that "in such an

293 Voltaire, *Siècle de Louis XIV: Tome 6: chapitres 31–39* (OCV 13D) (2016), p. 158.

294 Voltaire, *Siècle de Louis XIV: Tome 6: chapitres 31–39* (OCV 13D) (2016), p. 158; Voltaire, *Corpus des notes marginales de Voltaire: Tome V* (OCV 140a) (2012), p. 349. This refers to the case mentioned in LEC (1728), vol. 18, pp. 446–447; LEC (1811), vol. 20, p. 308.

295 Voltaire, *Siècle de Louis XIV: Tome 6: chapitres 31–39* (OCV 13D) (2016), p. 158. This refers to the case mentioned in LEC (1728), vol. 18, p. 459; LEC (1811), vol. 20, p. 314.

296 Voltaire, *Siècle de Louis XIV: Tome 6: chapitres 31–39* (OCV 13D) (2016), pp. 158–159. This refers to the case mentioned in LEC (1728), vol. 18, pp. 455–458; LEC (1811), vol. 20, pp. 312–314.

297 Voltaire, *Essai sur les mœurs et l'esprit des nations: Tome 8: Chapitres 177–197* (OCV 26C) (2015), p. 298.

298 See also Vissière & Vissière (1979), p. 34.

299 See Rowbotham (1932), p. 1053.

administration the emperor exercises an arbitrary power."[300] These statements are made in a context of a debate, among others with Montesquieu (see below) about whether or not the Chinese government could be said to be despotic in nature.[301] In the eyes of Voltaire, "the travellers and especially the missionaries saw despotism everywhere,"[302] but for him there is no evidence of a despotic or arbitrary government. Though Voltaire draws on information provided by Contancin in constructing his argument, he goes further than Contancin, since Contancin himself never actually used the term "despotic." In fact, it was Du Halde who first connected Contancin's letters to this debate, using the word in above-mentioned description of the Yongzheng emperor in the volume of *Lettres édifiantes et curieuses* in which the first letter appeared. Voltaire rejects this framing:

> The despotic government would be the one where the prince could, without breaking the law, deprive a citizen of property or life, without form and for no other reason than his will. But if there ever was a state in which the life, honour, and property of men were protected by law, it is the Empire of China.[303]

The Yongzheng emperor also appears in the philosophical tale *La Princesse de Babylone*, which focuses on an unknown shepherd and the Princess of Babylon, whose mutual love drives them to travel across Europe and Asia. When the Princess is presented to the Chinese emperor, Voltaire sketches the following (idealized) image of the emperor, with elements that also appear in the gazettes quoted by Contancin:

> He was the most righteous, polite, and wise monarch of the earth. It was he who first ploughed a small field with his imperial hands, to make agriculture respectable to his people. He was the first to establish prizes for virtue.[304]

---

300 Voltaire, *Essai sur les mœurs et l'esprit des nations: Tome 8: Chapitres 177–197* (OCV 26C) (2015), p. 287.

301 See also Ma Li (2019), pp. 80–81.

302 Voltaire, *Essai sur les mœurs et l'esprit des nations: Tome 2: Avant-propos et chapitres 1–37* (OCV 22) (2009), p. 45.

303 Voltaire, *Essai sur les mœurs et l'esprit des nations: Tome 8: Chapitres 177–197* (OCV 26C) (2015), pp. 287–288.

304 Voltaire, *Œuvres de 1768 (II)* (OCV 66) (1999), p. 129; For the case of the emperor ploughing the land, see: Voltaire, *Corpus des notes marginales de Voltaire: Tome V* (OCV 140a) (2012), p. 346 ("labourage"). This refers to LEC (1729), vol. 19, pp. 384–492; LEC (1811), vol. 21, pp. 135–139. On this topic, see also a short passage in the chapter on China in

This quotation illustrates what many authors have called Voltaire's sinophily and sinomania.[305]

Concerning the descriptions of the governmental system under the Yongzheng emperor, Isabelle and Jean-Louis Vissière point out how the meaning of the texts changed from Contancin to Voltaire. While regretting the Yongzheng emperor's attitude towards Christianity, Contancin still saw China as a state which ultimately would be open to evangelisation. Voltaire, by contrast, discovered in the China case the object of his hopes: a lay state based on justice and merit in which virtue is independent from religion, in which personal value was more important than hereditary privileges, and in which a simple peasant could accede to the dignities of the mandarins.[306] This interpretation, in turn, leads Voltaire to be more positive about the Yongzheng emperor than Contancin: not in spite, but *because* of the emperor's negative attitude towards Christianity. In this regard, Voltaire quotes the emperor: "What would you say if I sent a troop of monks and lamas to your country? How would you receive them? If you knew how to deceive my father, do not hope to deceive me in the same way."[307] In Voltaire's opinion, the Yongzheng emperor is a wise monarch who is striving to protect his empire from the evils of Christian fanatism.[308] As such, Voltaire recasts that which was still negative in Contancin's interpretation of the emperor, and keeps only the positive image that was ultimately based on information that was contained in the Chinese gazettes as transmitted by Contancin.

2.3.4.2 Montesquieu

A second well-known Enlightenment thinker who referred to the gazettes is Charles Louis de Secondat, baron de la Brède et de Montesquieu (1689–1755). He often had a more critical view of China than Voltaire. Montesquieu's own readings are also well documented. Manuscripts, such as *Geographica*, contain extensive extracts and notes from the texts he read, and have been recently edited. Though Montesquieu read the volumes on China of the *Lettres édifiantes et curieuses*, no notes were taken on the letters by Contancin. By contrast, his notes on a passage on the gazette from Du Halde's *Description ... de la Chine*

Voltaire, *La Philosophie de l'histoire* (OCV 59) (1969), p. 155. On the prizes for virtue, see the above-mentioned cases of promotion of peasants.

305 E.g. an early article with many references is Rowbotham (1932).

306 Vissière & Vissière (1979), p. 302.

307 Voltaire, *Essai sur les mœurs et l'esprit des nations: Tome 8: Chapitres 177–197* (OCV 26C) (2015), p. 297; see also note 42 on the same page: Voltaire quotes from the letter of 16 October 1724 by Joseph Marie Anne de Moyriac de Mailla (1669–1748).

308 Rowbotham (1932), pp. 1063–1064.

have been preserved.[309] Montesquieu does not discuss the gazette as such, but refers to the case (mentioned in Contancin's second letter) of the capital punishment imposed on the two officials who published an article in the *xiaobao* reporting on a supposed feast in the Yuanmingyuan, which was considered false information by the emperor. Montesquieu adds his personal comments to it:

> The author [i.e. Contancin] praises the gazette of Peking printed every day, being very apt, he says, to direct the conduct of mandarins. Nothing is put into it that has not been presented to the Emperor. Two writers were punished with death for putting false circumstances. The judgment of the tribunal was founded on the fact that they had disrespected the Emperor, which is a capital crime. *Nothing so dangerous as these vague laws, the disrespect is an arbitrary thing.[310]

This passage is also referred to in Montesquieu's *L'Esprit des lois* (1748) in a section of the chapter on "the crime of high-treason." In it, he develops his disdain for vague laws:

> It is determined, by the laws of China, that whosoever shows any disrespect to the emperor is to be punished with death. As they do not mention in what this disrespect consists, everything may furnish a pretext to take away a man's life, and to exterminate any family whatsoever.
>
> Two persons of that country, who were employed to write the court gazette (*la gazette de la court*), having inserted some circumstances relating to a certain fact that were not true, it was pretended that to tell a lie in the court gazette was a disrespect shown to the court; in consequence of which they were put to death. (…)
>
> If the crime of high treason be indeterminate, this alone is sufficient to make the government degenerate into arbitrary power. I shall descant more largely on this subject when I come to treat the composition of laws.[311]

---

309 For an overview of the references to *Description … de la Chine* in Montesquieu's works, see Cartier (1997), pp. 20–23. On Montesquieu's reading of *Description … de la Chine*, see also Pereira (2008), p. 317ff.

310 Montesquieu, *Geographica* (2007), p. 214; it refers to *Description … de la Chine* (1735), vol. 2, p. 43; which was based on *LEC* (1729), vol. 19, pp. 268–269; *LEC* (1810–1811), vol. 21, p. 77. See also Pereira (2008), p. 376 n. 1.

311 Montesquieu, *Esprit des lois* (1849), pp. 160–161 (Livre XII: Des lois qui forment la liberté politique dans son rapport avec le citoyen, Chapitre VII: Du crime de lèse-majesté); Montesquieu, *The Spirit of Laws* (1777), vol. 1, pp. 249–250.

This reference again shows how the information contained in gazettes translated by Contancin was incorporated into a broader argument, this time concerning "laws that form political liberty." In this case, information transmitted by Contancin is used to substantiate the need for a carefully structured juridical system.[312] In terms of ways of transmission, it is noteworthy that this case drew the attention of Enlightenment thinkers despite the fact that it represented not more than one sentence in Contancin's letter. Other references taken from the gazettes in *Esprit des lois* are rather limited. In a short chapter on the "good custom" of China, Montesquieu makes a brief reference to the ceremony of the emperor ploughing the land (also in *Description … de la Chine*) and to the yearly elevation of exemplary peasants to the rank of mandarin of the eighth degree (both in Contancin's first letter), which were also quoted by Voltaire.[313]

In using phrases like "arbitrary thing" and "arbitrary power" for the case of the two officials sentenced to death, Montesquieu signals his participation in the debate about despotism.[314] In *Esprit des lois*, he had developed his theory of the three types of government: the republican government, "in which the body, or only a part of the people, is possessed of the supreme power," is led by the principle of virtue; monarchy, "in which a single person governs by fixed and established laws," implements sentiments of honour; a despotic government, "in which a single person directs everything by his own will and caprice," is founded on fear.[315] Montesquieu acknowledges that some might have trouble classifying the Chinese empire according to his typology. Various institutions would evoke, if not the monarchical government, in the acceptance of an aristocratic state founded on the sense of honour, a regime attaching great importance to virtue, with an emperor who is not a tyrant, but a sovereign who must recognize the authority of the sacred books, and legislation that gives preference to prevention over repression. An analysis of the different characteristics of the Chinese government, which Montesquieu based primarily on *Description … de la Chine*, would seem to suggest that China does not entirely fit within his framework – potentially undermining his theory altogether:

---

312 For a discussion of Montesquieu's understanding of Chinese law on the basis of *Description … de la Chine*, see Pereira (2008), p. 396.

313 Montesquieu, *Esprit des lois* (1849), p. 106 (Livre XIV: Des lois dans le rapport qu'elles ont avec la nature du climat, Chapitre VIII: Bonne coutume de la Chine); Montesquieu, *The Spirit of Laws* (1777), vol. 1, pp. 300–301.

314 For a broader discussion, see also Osterhammel (2018), p. 340ff.

315 Montesquieu, *Esprit des lois* (1849), p. 9 (Livre II: Des lois qui dérivent directement de la nature du gouvernement, Chapitre I: De la nature des trois divers gouvernements); p. 24 (Livre III: Des principes des trois gouvernements, Chapitre IX: Du principe du gouvernement despotique); Montesquieu, *The Spirit of Laws* (1777), vol. 1, pp. 9, 33. On this topic, see: Cartier (1997), pp. 25–26; Pereira (2008), p. 11; Ma Li (2019), pp. 79–80.

> Our missionaries inform us that the government of the vast empire of China is admirable, and that it has a proper mixture of fear, honour, and virtue. Consequently I must have given an idle distinction in establishing the principles of the three governments.[316]

In response to this potential objection, Montesquieu raises the following question: "Might not our missionaries have been deceived by an appearance of order?"[317] He goes on to make a list of defects in the Chinese system that contrast with the view of the missionaries. His final conclusion is:

> China is therefore a despotic state, whose principle is fear. Perhaps, in the earliest dynasties, when the empire had not so large an extent, the government might have deviated a little from this spirit; but the case is otherwise at present.[318]

The capital punishment attributed to two persons who had inserted false information in a gazette only occupies a very marginal place in Contancin's letter, but it gave rise to a much broader reflection on the functioning of a legal system and the types of government, with the negative view of China as a despotic state in Montesquieu. The interaction between the gazettes, Contancin's letters and Montesquieu's reception of them shows how much effect some key figures could have on the image of China in Europe – even seemingly small choices by Contancin could have a significant impact on this image.

2.3.4.3 Quesnay

A third author who was drawn to China was the physiocrat François Quesnay (1694–1774). He used descriptions of the Chinese imperial system to detail his own political thought and to propose reforms in France. Quesnay's work was published twenty years later than Montesquieu's work. While Montesquieu had sparked in France the conversation around what he viewed as "*despotisme chinois*," Quesnay continued the debate. Both authors refer to Du Halde's *Description … de la Chine*, but the viewpoints they adopt are in diametrical opposition to one another: where Montesquieu criticizes the favourable view

---

316 Montesquieu, *Esprit des lois* (1849), p. 106 (Livre VIII De la corruption des principes des trois gouvernements, Chapitre XXI: De l'empire de la Chine); Montesquieu, *The Spirit of Laws* (1777), vol. 1, p. 161.

317 Montesquieu, *Esprit des lois* (1849), p. 106 (Livre VIII, Chapitre XXI: De l'empire de la Chine); Montesquieu, *The Spirit of Laws* (1777), vol. 1, p. 162.

318 Montesquieu, *Esprit des lois* (1849), p. 108 (Livre VIII, Chapitre XXI: De l'empire de la Chine); Montesquieu, *The Spirit of Laws* (1777), vol. 1, p. 164.

of the Jesuit texts, Quesnay positions himself as a defender of China.[319] His long article "Despotisme de la Chine" was originally published anonymously in four issues of another important monthly periodical, *Éphémérides du citoyen, ou Chronique de l'esprit national* (1767). In this text, "despotic" has lost the negative connotations Montesquieu had originally attached to it, and China appears as the prototype of what later came to be called "legal despotism" or even "enlightened despotism."[320] In Quesnay's eyes, China is a country governed by legitimate despots, whose legitimacy is manifested both in the moral and economic laws of the empire and in their control of absolute power. Quesnay advocated the Chinese meritocratic selection of officials instead of the French aristocratic system and underscored the importance of agriculture to the welfare of a nation. In his second chapter on the fundamental laws of the empire, Quesnay has a section on "Instruction," ranging from the early instruction of children to the instruction of high officials by the emperor himself. The section ends with a description of the gazettes, of which the instructive value is put to the forefront:

> The gazette of the interior government of the empire is still, for the public, a daily historical instruction, which presents it with examples of all kinds which inspire veneration for virtue, love for the sovereign, and the horror for vice; it expands the knowledge of the people on the order, on the acts of justice, on the vigilance of the government.[321]

Next, in correspondence with the lists made by Contancin in his letters,[322] Quesnay lists the topics that are included in the gazettes. Within his argumentation, they are framed as ideals for governance in Europe:

> This gazette also mentions pensions granted or withdrawn, etc. It reports, with the greatest truth, the judgments of the Courts; the calamities in the Provinces, the help given by the local Mandarins by order of the Emperor. The extract from the ordinary and extraordinary expenses of the Prince; the remonstrances which the higher courts give him on his conduct and on his decisions; the praises which the Emperor gives to his Ministers or

319 Cartier (1998), p. 17; and pp. 27–29 for the references to China in Quesnay's work; Ma Li (2019), chap. 9.

320 Cartier (1998), p. 32; Ma Li (2019), pp. 12, 48–49, 85–86, 184.

321 Quesnay, "Despotisme de la Chine," *Éphémérides du citoyen, ou Chronique de l'esprit national* (1767): Tome IV.1, pp. 20–21; "Despotisme de la Chine" (1965), p. 597.

322 At the end of the paragraph, Quesnay refers to "(*Mélanges intéressants et curieux*)"; see *LEC* (1728), vol. 18, pp. 435–440; *LEC* (1810–1811), vol. 20, pp. 302–304.

> the reprimands he gives them are included therein. In a word, it contains a faithful and contextualized detail of all the affairs of the empire.[323]

Quesnay also directly adopts other information concerning the gazette from Contancin, such as the comment that a gazette contains 70 pages.[324] He points out that those who are in charge of composing the gazette must always present it to the Emperor before making it public, and that it is severely forbidden to them to add on their own account the least equivocal circumstance or the slightest reflections. As an example, he refers again to the capital punishment of two officials that was mentioned earlier (from Contancin's second letter): "In 1726, two writers were sentenced to death for having inserted facts which were false."[325] Finally, from this overview of different ways of instruction, including by means of the gazette, Quesnay concludes: "This is how in China the books that contain the basic laws of the state are in everyone's hands; the emperor must comply. In vain did an emperor want to abolish them, they triumphed over tyranny."[326]

Quesnay also quotes examples taken from the gazettes in Contancin's letters to provide insight in the functioning of the government in China. For instance, in chapter three he discusses positive legislation:

> The laws of China are all founded on the principles of morality, for, as has already been said, morality and politics form to China only one science; and in this empire all positive laws tend only to maintain the form of government (*Mélanges intéressants et curieux*).[327]

In this context he underscores that the law in China permits the practice of remonstration of the emperor: "There is perhaps no country where the sovereign can be remonstrated with more liberty than in China."[328] As an example, Quesnay gives the case of an official (i.e. Zha Bina 查弼納) insisting "with boldness" (*hardiesse*) on the condemnation of a general despite the fact that the latter rendered considerable services to the State. It concerns the case of

323 Quesnay, "Despotisme de la Chine," *Éphémérides du citoyen, ou Chronique de l'esprit national* (1767): Tome IV.1, pp. 21–22; "Despotisme de la Chine" (1965), p. 597.

324 *LEC* (1729), vol. 19, p. 270; *LEC* (1810–1811), vol. 21, p. 78.

325 Quesnay, "Despotisme de la Chine," *Éphémérides du citoyen, ou Chronique de l'esprit national* (1767): Tome IV.1, p. 22; "Despotisme de la Chine" (1965), p. 598.

326 Quesnay, "Despotisme de la Chine," *Éphémérides du citoyen, ou Chronique de l'esprit national* (1767): Tome IV.1, p. 22; "Despotisme de la Chine" (1965), p. 598.

327 Quesnay, "Despotisme de la Chine," *Éphémérides du citoyen, ou Chronique de l'esprit national* (1767): Tome IV.1, pp. 43–44; "Despotisme de la Chine" (1965), p. 605.

328 Quesnay, "Despotisme de la Chine," *Éphémérides du citoyen, ou Chronique de l'esprit national* (1767): Tome IV.1, pp. 51–52; "Despotisme de la Chine" (1965), p. 608.

Long-ke-duo 隆科多, which is taken directly from a gazette translated in the second letter by Contancin and titled "Memorial of a Superintendent of Two Provinces, who speaks to the Emperor with a noble boldness / Answer of this Mandarin to the Emperor."[329] These examples served to underscore Quesnay's vision of the Chinese government: "This is not a barbarian government; its fundamental Constitution was entirely independent from the emperor."[330] It can be pointed out that Quesnay clearly idealises this possibility of criticizing an emperor. Under the Qing, criticizing emperors on their personal conduct was out of the question and no one dared to do so; at most, one could very respectfully discuss a decision or a policy.

Voltaire, Montesquieu, and Quesnay all based themselves on the same sources. They arrived, however, at very different visions on China: Voltaire and Quesnay were positive, and Montesquieu negative. In this regard, Jürgen Osterhammel points out that the objection that China was idealised in the "Sinophile" texts such as those written by these Enlightenment thinkers, who drew their information mainly from *Description … de la Chine*, may be correct, but it misses the point. "On the one hand, the Chinese bureaucracy in the first half of the eighteenth century was indeed perhaps the best functioning in the world; its idealisation was therefore not a flight of fancy, merely an extrapolation from reality. On the other hand, reports from the Middle Kingdom summarised by Du Halde gave European theorists the first opportunity to come to grips in a detailed way with the problems of administration and governance."[331] Regardless of the specific conclusions drawn from them, Contancin's letters and the Chinese gazettes which they introduced reveal themselves as a significant source for the development of their ideas.

2.3.5 *The Swedish Freedom of Writing and the Press Act of 1766*

The information about the Chinese gazette in Contancin's letters and in *Description … de la Chine* was not only received by savants in France, but also by politicians in other European countries. This is apparent from the role these texts and their ideas played in the writing of what is considered the world's first freedom of information act: *Konglige Majestäts Nådige Förordning, Angående Skrif- och Tryck-friheten* (His Majesty's Gracious Ordinance Relating to Freedom of Writing and of the Press), which was passed in the Swedish Diet

329 Quesnay, "Despotisme de la Chine," *Éphémérides du citoyen, ou Chronique de l'esprit national* (1767): Tome IV.1, pp. 52–54; "Despotisme de la Chine" (1965), pp. 608–609: = LEC (1729), vol. 19, pp. 315–324.

330 Quesnay, "Despotisme de la Chine," *Éphémérides du citoyen, ou Chronique de l'esprit national* (1767): Tome IV.1, p. 49; "Despotisme de la Chine" (1965), p. 607.

331 Osterhammel (2018), p. 407.

on 2 December 1766. Through an examination of their political pamphlets, Lena Rydholm has shown in detail how Swedish politicians such as Anders Nordencrantz and Anders Chydenius used China as an example to strengthen the arguments for a Freedom of the Press Act in Sweden.[332] Basing themselves on Du Halde's descriptions, these politicians claimed that the freedom of writing, of the press, and of information had been in existence in China since ancient times, and had contributed substantially to the wealth and stability of China.

Anders Nordencrantz (1697–1772) was a successful self-made businessman, who after studying trade and commerce in London, returned to Sweden with radical ideas about society and economy. He became a member of the Diet in 1729. After several rejections by the official censor, his 1756 political pamphlet *Oförgripeliga tankar om Frihet i bruk af Förnuft, Pennor och Tryck* (Thoughts about the Freedom to use Reason, Pens and Printing) was finally approved for publication. In it, Nordencrantz argued that the freedom of writing and of the press could provide the most efficient means for a free people to ensure government by reason and righteousness and to prevent corruption. He used China as a major example of the freedom of the press and of information. To corroborate this, he quoted in French a long passage on the Chinese gazette from *Description … de la Chine*, which was based on Contancin's description (the same passage was cited above).[333] Nordencrantz saw the gazette as an effective means for the people to access information, and to monitor the authorities, as well as for the state to control government officials' behaviour. However, when he quoted the abovementioned passage on the Chinese gazette, he omitted the final two paragraphs, which started with "Nothing is printed in the Gazette but what has been presented to the Emperor, or comes from the Emperor himself" and finished with the death sentence passed on two writers for disrespecting the emperor in 1726. These aspects obviously did not suit his political agenda and by omitting them he presented an idealised view of the gazette.[334]

The person who played a crucial role in the development of the Swedish Act was Anders Chydenius (1729–1793), a Finnish priest (Sweden included

---

332 Rydholm (2013); the following summary is entirely based on this article. See on this topic also Mokros (2021), p. 124.

333 Rydholm (2013), pp. 50–51. The quotation appears in the longer 1756 version (pp. 15–16), not in the shorter 1761 version.

334 Rydholm (2013), pp. 49–52. The quotation appears in the longer 1756 version, not in the shorter 1761 version. Rydholm also points out that in 1759, Nordencrantz published a memorandum about the freedom of the press of over seven hundred pages addressed to the Estates of the Swedish Diet, in which he again used the Chinese gazette as an example in the political debate. About a thousand copies were distributed among the Estates, thus making the Chinese gazette known to all members of the Estates.

Finland at that time) who was also a farmer. In his memoirs, Chydenius wrote about the insights he gained from reading Nordencrantz's pamphlet. However, Chydenius was more radical than Nordencrantz, and he argued for the complete abolition of pre-printing censorship (with the exception of religious texts). He published *Berätt else om Chinesiska Skrif-friheten* (An Account of the Chinese Freedom of Writing) in April 1766, arguing that the Chinese freedom of writing was the cause of the country's wealth and the happiness of its people.

The second part of Chydenius' pamphlet was a translation from Danish into Swedish by Chydenius of the entry "Om Frihed at skrive" (About the Freedom of Writing) by the Danish author Friderich C. Lütken (1698–1784), which deals with China and is based on Du Halde's work.[335] When Rydholm compared the passages in Du Halde's original French text with Lütken's translations of these passages into Danish and next with Chydenius' translation into Swedish, she observed that both Lütken and Chydenius used their source in a way that suited their political agenda. In doing so, they "help[ed] to shape a certain image of the freedom of writing in China in Denmark and in Sweden."[336]

To revisit, Lütken regularly omits the context of the dynamics he is discussing. As such, he does not mention that the "freedom of expression" he describes concerned only the writing of memoranda. These documents were not intended to be printed or made public, and were only meant to be read by the Emperor himself. Even when the emperor was asking all his subjects for advice, this was essentially an instruction to officials to write memoranda and thus not an endorsement of a general freedom of the press as envisioned by Lütken.

In translating Lütken's already distorted version of Du Halde's work, Chydenius further shaped an image of China that fitted his own political agenda, the Swedish debate at the time, and the intended readers by adding, omitting, or substituting words.[337] After intense debates in the Swedish Diet of 1765–66, Chydenius' hard work paid off: on 2 December 1766, Sweden's first Freedom of Writing, of the Press Act was passed in the Diet, based on the ideas

---

335 Rydholm (2013), p. 54: Friderich C. Lütken, *Oeconomiske Tanker till hoiere Eftertanke* [Economic Ideas for Deeper Reflection], Vol 6. Kiöbenhavn: Nicolaus Möller, 1749, pp. 8–21: Chapter 1, "Nogle Chinesiske Stats- Regler og Oeconomiske Maximer eller Skikke: Uddragne af le Pere du Halde" [Some Chinese Rules of State and Economic Maxims or Customs: Extracts from Father Du Halde].

336 Rydholm (2013), p. 55.

337 Rydholm (2013), pp. 54–60.

and formulations by Chydenius in his memorial.[338] It is a striking example of the intercultural use of texts and arguments.

Conclusion

The presence of texts about the Chinese gazettes in both archives and published documents leads to various conclusions about the Chinese gazette during the Yongzheng period.

The documents preserved in the Archives of Propaganda Fide draw their value from the fact that they include transcripts from the Chinese originals, some of which are no longer in existence. As such, they provide faithful information on selections from original gazettes. These texts concern issues related to Christianity, but also include more general topics. They also inform us about the use of the Chinese gazette by missionaries. In these cases, the missionaries were not Jesuits but missionaries from other congregations, who were usually administrators of the Propaganda Fide. Their reports based on the gazette are part of the bureaucratic communication with Rome, providing information about the Chinese government and issues related to Christianity. These were not intended to be published but were for internal use, and their veracity was supported by the transcription of the original Chinese texts. On the other hand, the letters on the Chinese gazette by Contancin draw their value not only from their length and the extent of the details included in them, but also from the fact that they were published. As such, they made knowledge of the Chinese gazette enter into the Republic of Letters, promoting the further spread of this knowledge within the rich culture of academic journals and political pamphlets, and stimulating the production of new ideas by Enlightenment thinkers and European politicians.

During the Yongzheng period, one also finds the first systematic descriptions of the gazette. These were not only sent to Europe as manuscripts, but were also published there. Contancin's depiction of the Chinese gazette provides insight into the form and contents of the gazette in general, but also into characteristics that may well be typical for the Yongzheng period. His description of the formal features of the gazettes he consulted helps us to identify *tizou quanlu* 題奏全錄 as the gazette during the Yongzheng period, which was also used as primary source by the missionaries. In Contancin's transmission, the contents of the Chinese gazettes are reframed to support certain perspectives. As such, his first letter uses the gazettes to underscore the role of the emperor

338 Rydholm (2013), p. 53.

and his efforts regarding the public good. His second letter is oriented towards the multiple roles of the gazettes, while the third merely focuses on various cases. Throughout his letters, Contancin presents a clear description of the gazette and includes his own interpretation, at times by making the comparison with Europe. A primary focus of these comparisons were the sources and nature of the information included in the gazettes. The image that Contancin and also Perroni depict of European newspapers, which in their own words are often filled "with useless things and with slanders and calumny"[339] and with "all sorts of successes, whether they are true or false,"[340] echoes the characteristics of European political newspapers of the early eighteenth century. In this context, Jack Censer has pointed at the distance between the readers and even editors of a newspaper, and the reported events in Europe: "Differences of fact or interpretation emerged from one issue of a paper to the next or even in different parts of a single issue."[341] In his view, "these contradictions reinforced a perception of the newspaper as an accumulation of many biases alien to the reader."[342] Even a newspaper such as *Gazette de France*, which was a government organ, treated events in largely the same way as the other gazettes: "Information was well presented but was of little use. Readers surely sensed this was not taking them close to events."[343] Against this background, Contancin in particular stressed the Chinese gazette's public character, the link with the central government and the emperor, and its role in the circulation of information and the instruction of officials. The disciplinary and instructive character was also stressed in *Description ... de la Chine* and adopted by Quesnay.

These aspects correspond to what Emily Mokros has called the gazette's role in effectuating the "curated transparency" of the imperial system.[344] This refers to the idea that selective transparency through widespread circulation of the gazettes could improve the administrative efficiency and discipline the bureaucracy. The documents discussed in this chapter illustrate how the gazettes were part of a larger "information order," in which both the emperor and the central bureaucracy played an active role. In this "information order," the dissemination of state news was bound to rules and restrictions in order to protect the central authority, even when officials occasionally proposed alternatives to imperial decisions with "noble boldness." As the content of the gazettes translated by Contancin indicated, the imperial control and surveillance went beyond the question of what information could be released in gazettes. It also

339 *LEC* (1728), vol. 18, pp. 434–435; *LEC* (1810–1811), vol. 20, pp. 301–302.
340 APF, SOCP, vol. 33 (dall'Anno 1727 al 1728), fol. 326r.
341 Censer (1994), p. 18.
342 Censer (1994), pp. 18–20.
343 Censer (1994), pp. 24–25.
344 See on these notions Mokros (2021), esp. pp. 14–17.

included other information systems, such as the three-yearly evaluation (*daji* 大計), which could increase the supervision of officials. Taken together, these aspects drew increased attention to the Chinese information order, not only on the part of the missionaries, but also for the European savants.

The letters discussed in this chapter also function as sources of information on the reading practices of the missionaries. Contancin points out that many missionaries neglected its reading because of its language, because they were too expensive, or simply because of their ignorance about its existence. While Contancin also overlooked the usefulness of the gazette for a long time, he ultimately discovered how useful it could be for understanding the Chinese government. He actively took the initiative to report about it to Europe. Perroni likewise became a careful reader of the Chinese gazette, in the first place in search of information related to the state of the Church in China. By extension, however, he also reported to his superiors in Rome about the emperor and the Chinese government.

In addition to evidence about the distribution of information about the gazettes, we are also well informed about the reception history of these letters. Pamphlets such as the *Bee* and various academic journals such as *Journal des sçavans* and *Mémoires de Trévoux* made the information embedded in Contancin's letters available to a wider public. However tendentious and incomplete the information transmitted by missionaries may have been, this reception history shows that their letters revealed to Europe large parts of an institutional mechanism and a mode of governance with which it had previously been unfamiliar. The cases of the three Enlightenment thinkers and the two Swedish politicians discussed above further show that their ideas were inspired by the information about the gazettes as translated by Contancin. It is striking that, despite being a relatively unknown figure, Contancin's decision to read the Chinese gazette after more than twenty years in China and to translate some of its sections made it possible for the gazette to address a more global public. If he had not done so, the European view on the functioning of the Chinese government may well have been different.

In interpreting the perceptions of China that European thinkers constructed on the basis of Contancin's letters, it is important to remember that these letters are part of a continuous chain of selection: the selection first happened when official documents were released for publication in the gazettes by the emperor and Grand Council, and next when they were actually selected by the agents producing the gazette. A simple comparison with the *Qijuzhu* reveals that only a minority of the documents that passed through the hands of the emperor were published in the gazettes, and the reasons for this selection are not very clear. At the same time, gazettes seem also to have contained much more information than has ultimately been preserved in (later) official sources, such as *Qijuzhu* and *Qing shilu*. The latter sources contain mainly the emperor's voice, whereas the gazettes also contained the voice of officials. In the gazettes, memorials by officials seem to have been quoted in full, and not only summarized as was the case in the emperor's rescript. These full memorials most often did not survive, except in translations by the missionaries. For these translations, missionaries such as Perroni and Contancin in turn made a new selection. Sometimes they gave an explicit reason for this selection, but most often they did not. Their selection balances between the wish to inform Europe about China, its government, and its customs, and the wish to transmit an explicit vision about the emperor and his governance, which could significantly differ from one translator to the other. This tension between information and interpretation is also present in the above-mentioned reviews published in French academic journals. Particularly in argumentative texts, this balance tends to lean more towards the interpretative side, as seen in the discussed English translation in British political pamphlets, the quotations in Swedish political journals, some of which were based on Danish translations of Du Halde's texts, and the relevant work of the Enlightenment thinkers. Throughout the chain of selection, what had been only a marginal detail in one document could enter into the main text of another, and what had originally belonged to the main text might disappear in the background.

The difference in opinion between the Enlightenment thinkers underlines how the intention of a message and the impact of its reception do not necessarily coincide. From the same texts, these savants drew drastically different conclusions – influenced by their own values and the argument they were building. In this sense, the outlined conversations about "Chinese despotism" and about the Chinese "freedom of writing and the press" are perhaps less about China than about what a good government (in Europe) should look like. This reinterpretation can be considered a limitation, yet it also points to the fact that despite the chain of multiple selections, the information included in the Chinese gazettes entered into a global conversation and contributed to the creation of new ideas.

CHAPTER 3

The Qianlong Period (1736–1795)

Like the Kangxi reign, the Qianlong reign was again very long.[1] The situation of Christianity, with a decreased number of foreign missionaries, had stabilised since the late Yongzheng years. Occasionally there were persecutions, with large scale persecutions in the late 1740s and around 1785.[2] During the entire period, however, missionaries continued to serve in various positions at the court in the capital. They were important interlocutors for the transmission of knowledge about the Qing to Europe.

European sources concerning the gazettes belong to two different periods of the Qianlong reign. For the early years of the Qianlong era, there are a few scattered references from the 1740s, mainly preserved in the Archivio Storico "de Propaganda Fide"; for the later years of the Qianlong period, there are many references to the gazette in the French manuscript and printed documents from the 1770s and 1780s.

The documents in the Archivio Storico "de Propaganda Fide" include seven texts related to the anti-Christian movement of 1746, which resulted in the execution of seven missionaries in Fujian and Jiangsu. These include memorials by provincial governors, of which at least one was approved by the emperor and published in the gazette ("Edictum Imp.ris publicatum in gazetis publicis"); as well as the imperial edict of 12 August 1746 (QL11/6/26), ordering all provincial authorities to search for Europeans hiding in the provinces, to arrest them and deport them to Canton.[3] In addition, there is also a reference to the

1 For a general overview of the Qianlong reign in English, see Kahn (1971), Woodside (2002), and Elliott (2009).

2 See Ad Dudink, "Opponents," in *HCC*, p. 522ff.

3 See Dudink (2022): APF, SOCP, vol. 47 (dall'Anno 1748 al 1750), tomo primo, Chinese: fols. 102r–107r (duplicate fols. 995r–996r; 924r–927v): transl.: fols. 66r–79r (Latin); APF, SOCP, vol. 47: Edictum Imp.ris publicatum in Gazetis publicis (Edict of the emperor published in the public gazettes); Chinese: fol. 102r; transl.: fols. 66r–68r (Latin); undated anti-Christian memorial (1746) of Ma-er-tai 馬爾泰 (?–1748), Governor-General of Zhejiang-Fujian, and Zhou Xuejian 周學健 (?–1748), Governor of Fujian (QL11 = 1746); APF, SOCP, vol. 47: duplicate; Chinese: fol. 996r (QL11 = 1746); APF, SOCP, vol. 47: Sententia prolata à Prorege Scian si in P. Ioannem a Bormio (Sentence issued by the Governer on Scian si against Fr. Johannes a Bormio); Chinese: fol. 103r; transl.: fols. 68r–69r (Latin); Chinese text of the Shanxi Governor's sentence of the (on 10 April 1746) arrested Giambattista Pedracini da Bormio O.F.M. (in China since 1740) (QL11 = 1746); APF, SOCP, vol. 47: duplicate; Chinese: fol. 995r (QL11 = 1746); APF, SOCP, vol. 47: Libellus supplex Praefecti Yung chang ad Proregem Xan Xi / Proregis declaratio

 | DOI:10.1163/9789004505001_005

persecution of Christians added to an individual letter preserved in the same archives.[4] Though limited in number, these clearly illustrate how some imperial decisions directly affecting Christians appeared in the gazettes.

In contrast, the sources for the later Qianlong period are much more numerous. As such, they are the main subject of this chapter. They are introduced and compared in order to illuminate the text management in terms of selection and translation that took place from the publication of the gazette in China to the final publication in Europe. The availability of these sources allows us to trace in a unique way how exactly the extracts from the gazette were selected, presented, translated, and interpreted. It turns out that despite their particular frame of interpretation, the European documents are remarkably exhaustive and precise translations of Chinese documents. The act of selecting material

seu mandatum (Petition by prefect Yung chang to the Governor of Xan Xi / Declaration or mandate by the Governor); Chinese: fols. 104r–103v; transl.: fols. 71v–73r (Latin); Chinese text of undated report of Shen Rongchang 沈榮昌, magistrate of Huozhou 霍州, to the Governor of Shanxi about the arrest, on 10 April 1746 (QL11/3/20) of Pedracini (QL11 = 1746); APF, SOCP, vol. 47: duplicate; Chinese: fols. 924r–925v (QL11 = 1746); APF, SOCP, vol. 47: Accusationes factae ad praefectos provinciae Fo Kien (Accusations made against the prefects of the province Fo Kien); Chinese: fols. 105r–104v; transl.: fols. 73r–75r (Latin); Chinese text of the anti-Christian accusations in the report of Dong Qizuo 董啓祚, Prefect of Funing (Fujian) (QL11 = 1746); APF, SOCP, vol. 47: duplicate; Chinese: fols. 924v–925r (QL11 = 1746); APF, SOCP, vol. 47: Edictum prolatum Macai contra Christianos Sinenses (Edict issued in Macau against Chinese Christians); Chinese: fol. 106r; transl.: fols. 75r–76r (Latin); Chinese text of the edict, dated 24 August 1746 (QL11/7/8), issued by Gu Song 顧嵩, who from 1732 until 1750 was District Vice Magistrate 縣丞 of Xiangshan 香山 and one of the officials responsible for Macao (QL11 = 1746); APF, SOCP, vol. 47: duplicate; Chinese: fols. 926r–927v (QL11 = 1746); APF, SOCP, vol. 47: Edictum emanatum in Provincia Fuo Kien contra S. Religionem (Edict issued in the Fuo Kien province against the Sacred Religion), dated QL11/5/10 = 28 June 1746 (Edict issued in the Fuo Kien province against the Sacred Religion); Chinese: fols. 107r–106v; transl.: fols. 76r–77v (Latin); Chinese text of the edict issued by the Prefect of Xinghua 興化 (Fujian) (QL11 = 1746); APF, SOCP, vol. 47: duplicate; Chinese: fols. 927r–926v (QL11 = 1746); APF, SOCP, vol. 47: Mandatum Imp.ris contra S. Religionem (Mandate of the emperor against the Sacred Religion); Chinese: fol. 107v; transl.: fols. 77v–79r (Latin); Chinese text of the Imperial edict of QL11/6/26 (= 12 August 1746) ordering "all provincial authorities to conduct a rigorous search for Europeans hiding in the provinces and to arrest them and deport them to Canton" (in response to memorial of Zhang Ne 張訥) (QL11 = 1746); APF, SOCP, vol. 47: duplicate; Chinese: fol. 927v (QL11 = 1746).

4 One text is added to a letter dated "Macao, 20 February 1741" by Arcangelo Miralta C.R.M. (1682–1751), who was the Propaganda Fide procurator in 1729–1750. It concerns the imperial edict (QL5/9/24 = 13 November 1740) condemning Yang Congqing 楊從清 for spreading a prophecy that an earthquake would occur in Beijing on QL6/10/30 (18 December 1740) because of the restauration of the Nantang 南堂 (Southern Church). APF, SC, Indie orientali e Cina, vol. 23 (dal 1741 al 1743), fol. 38; Chinese: fol. 38.

on the Chinese side actually contributed as much to shaping the information as the missionaries' inherent biases.

3.1 European and Chinese Sources

There are two major European sources: the multi-volume collection *Mémoires concernant les Chinois* and one extensive manuscript preserved in Bibliothèque nationale de France (BnF), Bréquigny 10. Moreover, there is an additional corpus of manuscript letters, which missionaries and European savants exchanged with each other. The main Chinese source is the *tizou shijian* 題奏事件, which is the most important type of gazette that has been preserved from the time before 1800.

3.1.1 *European Sources: A Collection, a Manuscript, and Letters*

The first major European source on the Chinese gazette for the Qianlong period is the monumental collection *Mémoires concernant l'histoire, les sciences, les arts, les moeurs, les usages, &c. des Chinois, par les missionnaires de Pékin* (17 vols.). When the first volume appeared in 1776, the *Journal des sçavans* devoted ten pages to it. It aptly described the *Mémoires'* purpose as follows:

> This collection (…) is the result of a correspondence that has been maintained for ten years with the missionaries who are in this empire [of China] and with two Chinese who once lived in France where they learned the sciences of Europe. They returned to China in 1765, with Memoirs and questions on all the objects on which one wished to have clarifications. These are the answers to these Memoirs that we intend to publish every year, and the volume we are announcing now is the first in this collection.[5]

Of the *Mémoires concernant les Chinois*, as the work is usually abbreviated, fifteen volumes appeared between 1776 and 1791; two extra volumes were published in 1814. Most texts included in it were originally sent to Henri Bertin (1720–1792), French statesman and general controller of finances of Louis XV (1759–1763), who was one of the strongest promotors of the collection.[6] His

5 *Journal des Sçavans* (février 1777), p. 75; quoted at the beginning of the overview article by Dehergne (1983), p. 267; the review of the first volume appeared in *Journal des Sçavans* (février 1777), pp. 75–80 and (mars 1777), pp. 159–164.

6 Sacy & Antoine (1970), p. 157ff.

ILLUSTRATION 11 Engraving of Henri Bertin, made by René Gaillard (1719–1790) after a portrait by Alexandre Roslin (1718–1793)

interest in China was increased by the presence of two young Chinese who spent more than a decade in France. Louis Ko (Aloys; Gao Ren 高仁; 1732–after 1795) and Etienne Yang (Yang Zhide 楊執德; 1733–1798) both left Beijing in 1751 to study in France.[7] They entered the Society of Jesus in 1759 and were ordained priests in 1763, when the Society of Jesus was being suppressed in France. Before returning to China in 1765, they conducted a one-year survey in France, which was organized by Bertin and which allowed them to visit various (industrial) places in order to be better acquainted with science, technology, and agriculture. When leaving France, they received a pension from the French king on the understanding that they would send from China memoirs and reports that would contribute to the knowledge of China in France.[8] The *Mémoires concernant les Chinois* can be considered an outcome of these exchanges. Several texts in the first volumes were written by or with the help of these two Chinese. Bertin also established an intensive direct correspondence with French missionaries in Beijing, whose texts were also published in the *Mémoires concernant les Chinois*. The two most important correspondents-authors were Jean-Joseph-Marie Amiot, usually called Joseph-Marie Amiot (1718–1793)[9] and Pierre-Martial Cibot (1727–1780), followed by François Bourgeois (1723–1792) and Louis Collas (1735–1781). These correspondents somehow specialized in certain topics, such as literature, Chinese script, natural sciences, etc.[10]

Both the form and content of the texts in the *Mémoires concernant les Chinois* are diverse: there are short reports of a few pages and longer treatises devoted to one specific topic, one of which even spans over 400 pages. These thematic articles respond to some of the major questions raised by the world of the savants in the late eighteenth century, including questions concerning the origin of the Chinese, their chronology, and their script. There is also a wide variety of other topics, such as music, filial piety, (natural) sciences, medicine, and literature. In the later volumes (starting with volume 9) there are, besides reports, also extracts of letters that discuss various topics, including descriptions of events that happened in China in the year preceding the correspondence. In general, the collection depended on the somewhat random questions raised in France as well as on the interests and circumstances of the missionaries in China. As Joseph Dehergne pointed out, the result is that no

7 For basic biographical references of these and other Jesuits mentioned in this chapter, see Dehergne (1973) and Pfister (1932–1934).

8 Dehergne (1965); Huard & Wong (1966); Burson (2013); Finlay (2020), chap. 1.

9 For a biography of Amiot, see Hermans (2005) and (2019). For a *nianpu* 年譜, see Long Yun 龍云 (2015), pp. 235–268.

10 A portion of the original incoming and outgoing letters between Bertin and these Jesuits has also been preserved in the Institut de France in Paris.

method guided the publication, which makes the contributions rather unequal and sometimes incomplete.[11]

Quotations from the Chinese gazettes, which are particularly relevant for this study, mainly appear in the later letters, which discuss recent events in China. Altogether, these texts amount to over 440 pages, the most prominent author on this topic being Joseph-Marie Amiot. Amiot had arrived in China in 1750 and spent forty-two years in Beijing. He was a scholar with very wide scientific and literary interests who wrote texts on Chinese music and dances, edited a biography of Confucius, translated ancient military texts such as *Sunzi bingfa* 孫子兵法, and compiled a *Dictionnaire Tartare-Mandchou-François* (3 vols., Paris: 1789–1790). He had an extensive correspondence with Henri Bertin: between 1766 and 1793, Amiot wrote at least 172 letters to Bertin, some of which were fifty or sixty pages long.[12] Many of these texts and letters can be found in *Mémoires concernant les Chinois*. Compared to his texts on specific topics, such as the life of Confucius and his disciples or the overview of Chinese history, which cover several hundred pages each, the letters on the basis of the gazettes only occupy a limited space in the respective volumes.

The collection contains also an extensive report based on the Chinese gazette written by François Bourgeois, the second most prominent author on this topic, in 1778. Bourgeois arrived in China in 1767 and spent twenty-four years in Beijing. After the suppression of the Society of Jesus, he was appointed by the French king Louis XVI to be the religious superior in Beijing and the administrator of the French mission in 1776.[13] While fulfilling these duties, he tried to solve the inner-church conflicts in the aftermath of the suppression. He also was in regular epistolary correspondence with Bertin.

In addition to Amiot and Bourgeois, there were Chinese collaborators who helped them in their research and translation. What is unique about Amiot is that his texts provide some explicit insight into the collaboration that existed between Jesuits and Chinese scholars. In a letter to Bertin dated 2 October 1784, he reports that Yang-ya-ko-pe (Yang 楊 Ya-ge-bo 雅各伯 = Jacobus), his collaborator for thirty years, had died one year earlier.[14] Amiot describes Yang-ya-ko-pe's education and training and the way they worked together:

> Yang-ya-ko-pe, who for more than thirty years was the faithful companion of all my literary works, died last autumn in the fifty-second year of

11 Dehergne (1983), p. 268.

12 Milsky (1977), vol. 1, p. 350; Hermans (2005), p. 63.

13 See Dehergne (1973), no. 104; Pfister (1932–1934), no. 430.

14 See letter of Amiot to Bertin (2 October 1784), *MCC*, vol. 11, pp. 520–522.

ILLUSTRATION 12 Engraving of Joseph-Marie Amiot, made by Isidore-Stanislas Helman after a portrait by Giuseppe Panzi (1789): *Mémoires concernant les Chinois*, vol. 15 (1791), opposite the frontispiece

> his age. I had trained him myself in our way of studying, I had inspired him with the taste for the ancients, I had taught him the art of reasonable criticism; he was such, in a word, that I could ask him to make the best possible use of the documents of his Nation. More universally and more solidly educated than ordinary Literati are, he made a point of consulting them, whenever I required him, when it came to some point of contention on which the sentiments were divided. He told me faithfully the reasons pro and contra, he discussed them impartially and if I decided in favour of the opinion contrary to his, he settled for telling me that it was not possible for him to think like me, that however, he would not forget to find anything to support with new proof what I thought was a truth. What he said, he executed it to the letter, and I can say to his glory that it has not once occurred to him to want to mislead me because of laziness or want of good will.[15]

Amiot also gives insight into the daily routine of Jacobus Yang:

> Every day, after devoting part of his time to the exercises of piety, and to the care which he owed to his family, he went to our house in the room which was for his use, shut himself in, took a brush or a book, read or wrote. And when I was at leisure, or when my occupations of state did not call me elsewhere, we worked together with the same exactness and the same care with which we had become accustomed for a long-time.[16]

Finally, he also expresses his hopes for a replacement:

> I am currently investigating to find someone who can replace him, at least partly, in his duties to me. If I met by chance one of those first-rate Literati, who, unoccupied in the literary tribunals, are none the less skilful, I would certainly not let him escape. He would help me in my research to compare the ancient documents of China with those of other nations.[17]

---

15 MCC, vol. 11, pp. 520–521 (Extrait d'une autre lettre de M. Amiot, Ecrite de Pé-king le 2 Octobre 1784) (Extract from another letter by Mr. Amiot, Written from Peking on 2 October 1784).

16 *MCC*, vol. 11, p. 522 (Extrait d'une autre lettre de M. Amiot, Ecrite de Pé-king le 2 Octobre 1784).

17 *MCC*, vol. 11, p. 521 (Extrait d'une autre lettre de M. Amiot, Ecrite de Pé-king le 2 Octobre 1784).

Hardly anything more is known about Jacobus Yang.[18] Still, these references show how the reports sent to Europe, most probably also those on the gazettes, were prepared in a collaborative effort and were the result of close interaction. In this regard, Jacobus Yang can be considered a co-author of Amiot's texts.

The second major European source about the gazette is an extensive manuscript preserved in BnF, Bréquigny 10, named after Louis-Georges de Bréquigny (1714–1795). He was one of the scholars invited by Bertin to edit the *Mémoires concernant les Chinois* and the author of several historical works. He developed a very wide correspondence within the Republic of Letters of his time. The Bibliothèque nationale de France contains 165 volumes of documents classified under his name, including volumes about China. One of them is a volume of 214 numbered pages entirely devoted to gazettes, with the following bibliographical address at the beginning of the text (written by the person who catalogued the manuscript):

> Bréquigny 10 / Manuscrits d'Amiot / VI / Gazettes chinoises / Kien Long 53 / 1788 / no. 23

The title on the first page is "Gazettes de l'Empire."[19] It contains the French translation of *all* gazettes from QL53/1/21 (27 February 1788) to QL53/3/16 (1 May 1788).[20] In contrast with the *Mémoires concernant les Chinois*, it is not an excerpt but a full translation. Although it is attributed to Amiot, it is in fact François Bourgeois who should be considered its author, as Emily Mokros has pointed out.[21] This can be confirmed not only by the handwriting, which appears to be Bourgeois' handwriting, but also on the basis of three letters that Bourgeois addressed to Bertin. In one of them, which describes the documents that were sent to Paris, Bourgeois states that "I have translated two hundred

18 Inst. 1517, fols. 174r–175v: copy of Amiot's testament (confirmed 15 November 1791, but written many years earlier; apparently before the death of Jacobus Yang). In it one finds reference to three persons to whom he wishes to donate the money that is left over after his death: Yang Ya-ko-pe (Ya-ge-bo 雅各伯 = Jacobus), first servant; Yang Mo-Eulh-kio-eulh (Mo-er-jue-er 默尔覺尔 = Melchior), his cousin, second servant; and Yang Lei-see (Lei-si 類斯 = Ludovicus), orphan of his former servant Yang.

19 BnF, Bréquigny 10, p. 1. The first line refers to "Les Gazettes de Chine"; in the text they are usually referred to as "Gazette."

20 Except for the gazette of QL53/1/24 (= 1 March 1788), which is reported to be lost, and there is no record for QL53/1/30.

21 Mokros (2021), pp. 126, 210 n. 50. The reasons for the attribution to Amiot are not clear, but texts by Bourgeois and Amiot were sent in the same envoy.

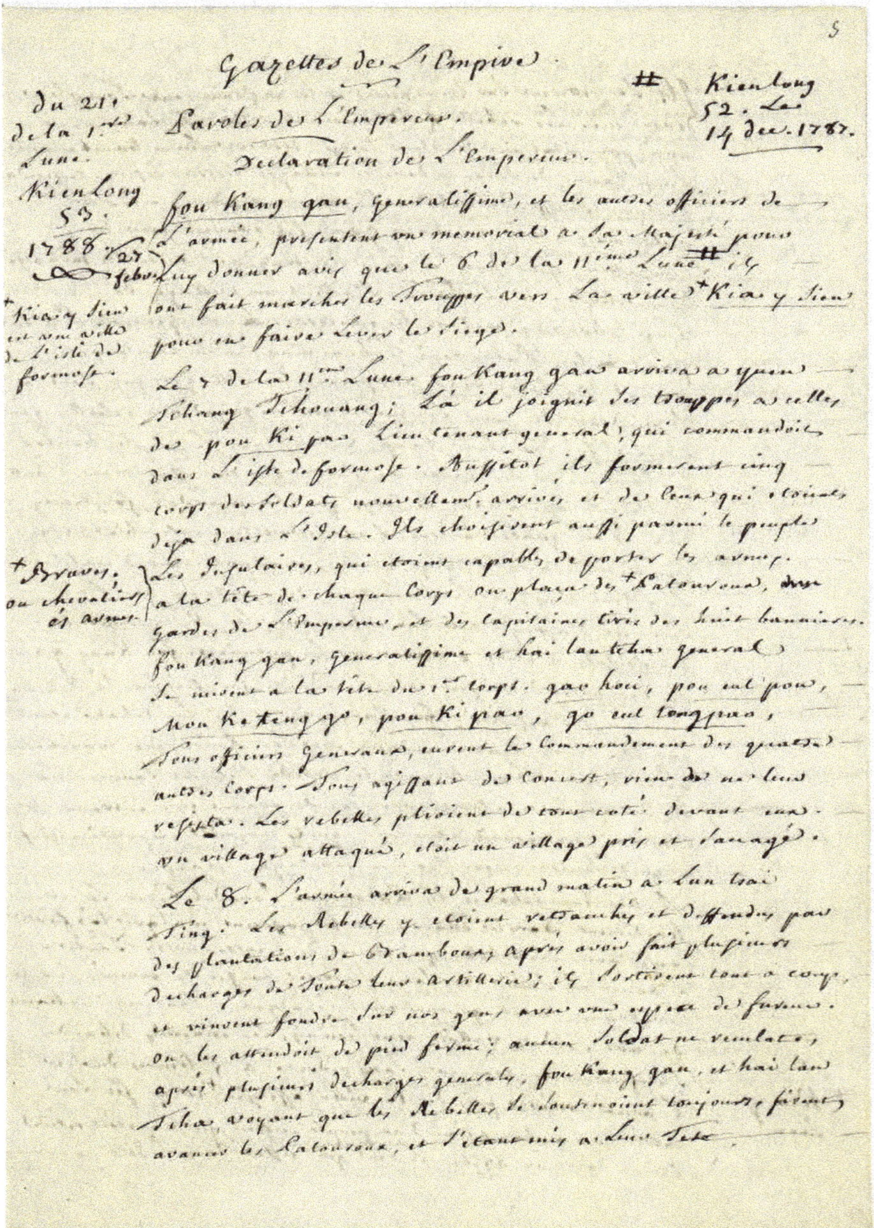

5

Gazettes de l'Empire.

Du 21e de la 1re Lune. Kienlong 53. 1788 le 27 febr.

Kienlong 52. Le 14 dec. 1787.

Paroles de l'Empereur.

Declaration de l'Empereur.

fou Kang gan, generalissime, et les autres officiers de l'armée, presentent un memorial a Sa Majesté pour luy donner avis que le 6 de la 11me Lune # ils ont fait marcher les Trouppes vers La ville +Kia y Sien pour en faire Lever le siege.

+Kia y Sien est une ville de l'isle de formose.

Le 7 de la 11me Lune fou Kang gan arriva a yuen tchang Tchouang; La il joignit les trouppes a celles de pou Ki pao Lieutenant general, qui commandoit dans L'isle de formose. Aussitot ils formerent cinq corps des soldats nouvellement arrivés et de ceux qui etoient deja dans l'Isle. Ils choisirent aussi parmi le peuple les Insulaires, qui etoient capables de porter les armes. a la tete de chaque Corps on placa des +Batourou, des gardes de l'Empereur, et des capitaines tirés des huit bannieres.

+Braves, ou chevaliers és armes.

fou Kang gan, generalissime et hai lan tcha general se mirent a la tete du 1er corps. gao houi, pou ul pou, Mou Ke teng ye, pou Ki pao, yo eul tong pao, tous officiers Generaux, eurent le commandement des quatre autres corps. Tous agissant de concert, rien ne leur resista. Les rebelles plioient de tout coté devant eux. un village attaqué, etoit un village pris et saccagé.

Le 8. l'armée arriva de grand matin a Lun tsai Ting. Les Rebelles y etoient retranchés et deffendus par des plantations de Bambous; apres avoir fait plusieurs decharges de toute leur artillerie; ils sortirent tout a coup, et vinrent fondre sur nos gens avec une espece de fureur. On les attendoit de pied ferme; aucun soldat ne recula; apres plusieurs decharges generales, fou Kang gan, et hai lan Tcha, voyant que les Rebelles se soutenoient toujours fermes, avancer les Batourou, et s'etant mis a leur Tete

ILLUSTRATION 13 Beginning of the translation by François Bourgeois of the Chinese gazette of QL53/1/21 (27 February 1788): BnF, Brequigny 10, p. 5

pages of Chinese gazettes."[22] In another letter he writes the following about his work:

> I have spent some time translating the gazettes of the empire each day. It is the Chinese gazettes that I translated and not the Tartar ones, because these are only for the banners, and besides, they contain only the few articles from the Chinese gazettes that interest them more particularly; your greatness will see in the Chinese gazettes that the emperor sometimes orders that an article be translated into Tartar, and that it is published for all the banners.[23]

Noteworthy in this statement is that the missionaries not only were aware of the Manchu gazettes, but also seem to have had some access to them. From Bourgeois' letters, which were written in the fall of 1788, it is also apparent that the translation was meant to be published, since Bourgeois gave instructions for the editor in Paris.[24]

This manuscript has so far hardly been investigated. As it remained a manuscript, its content was barely disseminated. Yet, it is a unique testament to the tremendous efforts that not only Amiot but also Bourgeois made to make the Chinese gazette and the news it contained known in Europe.

The third source about the gazettes, which is in fact at the basis of the previous two sources, is the corpus of letters that Amiot and Bourgeois exchanged with Bertin. A closer look at their epistolary exchange can help illustrate how information on and excerpts from the gazette were sent to Europe. The correspondence between Amiot and Bertin started in the mid-1760s, and Amiot wrote his first extensive reports based on the gazettes in the years 1778–1779. In a letter to Bertin dated 16 September 1779, he points out that the contents of these gazettes are of "interest for a statesman and an enlightened amateur of letters" (*un homme d'état et un amateur éclairé des lettres*) as Bertin was in his eyes. The same letter also indicates that he sent some original copies of the gazettes to Europe:

> I dare to flatter myself that you will be grateful to me for having reported to you those of our public newsletters of which the content has something

22 Letter of Bourgeois to Bertin (Beijing, 9 November 1788): BnF, Bréquigny 2, fols. 221r–223r: fol. 222r; also in Walter (2008), p. 330.

23 Letter of Bourgeois to Bertin (Beijing, 10 October 1788): BnF, Bréquigny 2, fols. 209r–212r: fol. 209r.

24 E.g. Letter of Bourgeois to Bertin (Beijing, 10 October 1788): BnF, Bréquigny 2, fol. 210v.

> of interest for a statesman and an enlightened amateur of letters. I will put in the same envelope as this letter, the Chinese gazettes from which I drew what I report. These gazettes should have been with my second letter, as I told you when writing it, but I forgot them on my table when I closed the letter.[25]

Given the dates of this correspondence, the gazettes that he sent to Bertin can be identified as those now preserved in the Bibliothèque nationale de France (BnF), as will be shown in the next section.

Bertin appears to have been interested in receiving more information of this kind.[26] Amiot's envoy of the next year, 1779, took more time to arrive than usual[27] and we do not have Bertin's immediate reaction to it. Yet, in response to the envoys of the 1780s, Bertin expresses his gratitude to Amiot for having sent him such material. He promises to publish it in the *Mémoires concernant les Chinois,* as it will confirm the image of the Emperor of China as both absolute (despotic) and paternal sovereign:

> I am obliged to you for the very interesting details that you gave me about what happened in the course of last year at the Peking Court. These relations and the translations of the Emperor's decrees that accompany them will be inserted in our *Mémoires sur les Chinois* and will contribute to spreading variety and to inciting curiosity. One shall see above all with pleasure a sovereign as powerful and as ~~despotic~~ absolute[28] as the Emperor of China, ~~to undertake~~ himself ~~to~~ narrating to his subjects in a public decree the last illness and the death of one of his ministers, and lowering himself to give them an account, with the tone and expressions of a father to his children, of the motives which had determined him to raise him by degrees to the ministry.[29]

Ten years later Amiot was still sending reports based on the Chinese gazette to Bertin, and Bertin continued to ask for more, suggesting that other missionaries could become involved in the project. In a letter by Bertin to Amiot, dated

---

25 Letter of Amiot to Bertin (Beijing, 16 September 1779): Inst. 1516, p. 236, fol. 1v.

26 In the margin Bertin seems to have written: "[lu]y demander [a] continuer."

27 The letter had not yet arrived in December 1780: see letter of Bertin to Amiot (Paris, 31 December 1780): Inst. 1523, fol. 68r.

28 'Despot' is replaced by 'absolute' in the original manuscript.

29 Letter of Bertin to Amiot (Paris, 16 November 1781): Inst. 1523, fols. 126r–135v: fol. 127r–v. Strikethrough in original text.

22 November 1787, Bertin expresses his concern about Amiot's health due to the burden of his work related to the translation of gazettes:

> This work seems to me so immense for you that I would desire and urge you at any moment that you allow yourself to be helped for the copies and the translation of the gazettes and all things of this kind; it would be enough for you to supervise and read these objects for correctness and accuracy, it will leave you at least a few moments of rest that your health requires,...[30]

In a letter to Bertin, dated 10 November 1789, Amiot responds to the suggestion:

> You advise to transfer the translation of gazettes and other public papers to someone else; I followed your advice, and I begged M. Bourgeois to take upon himself this task; he willingly took charge of it; and helped by one of our Chinese priests, he put into French all that he thought that could prick your curiosity among the events of this year, you will judge yourself of his talent by the choice he made of the objects he puts under your eyes. As he has not communicated to me the fruit of his labours, I can only speak to you of his diligence and his application to endeavour to make it worthy of being offered to you.[31]

Noteworthy is the reference to the help of "one of the Chinese priests," which is most likely the above mentioned Etienne Yang, who at that time belonged to the Beijing house of mostly French missionaries.[32] It is known that Bourgeois translated various sorts of (civil and military) almanacs,[33] but it is not clear

30 Letter of Bertin to Amiot (Paris, 22 November 1787): Inst. 1524: fols. 90r–99v: fol. 90r.

31 Letter of Amiot to Bertin (10 November 1789): Inst. 1517, fols. 65r–86v: fol. 66r; also in Walter (2008), p. 365.

32 Letter of Bourgeois to Bertin (Beijing, 9 November 1788): BnF, Bréquigny 2, fols. 213r–214r: fol. 214r; Letter of Yang to Bertin (31 August 1788), BnF, Bréquigny 2, fols. 201r–203v. Letter of the lazarist Nicolas Raux (1754–1801) to Bertin (6 September 1788), BnF, Bréquigny 2, fols. 215r–218v: fol. 217r: after his arrest in Jiangxi in May 1787, Yang arrived in the French house in Beijing in January 1788, where he regained the freedom to move.

33 Letter of Bourgeois to Bertin (23 June 1789): Inst. 1519, fols. 281r–284v; also in Walter (2008), pp. 351–352. Bourgeois reports that he decided to translate the Chinese almanac, "because it contains an infinity of things that one does not see elsewhere, or that one hardly sees." It concerns an almanac that is corrected every three months with the changes of officials. Bourgeois mentions that he had to rush because he absolutely wanted the shipment to leave that year. See also Letter of Bourgeois to Bertin (16 October 1790): Inst. 1519, fol. 286r: Bourgeois announces that he intends to translate the military almanac (in addition to the

whether the report by Bourgeois mentioned in this letter of Amiot, which was sent one year after the letter with the translation of the two hundred pages of Chinese gazette, ever arrived in France. With the French revolution in 1789, the exchange of correspondence took a new turn and was soon interrupted by the deaths of Bertin and Bourgeois in 1792 and Amiot's death in 1793.

3.1.2 *Chinese Source:* tizou shijian 題奏事件

In addition to the above-mentioned European sources, valuable Chinese sources have also been preserved for the Qianlong period. In particular, shelf number Chinois 2216 in the Bibliothèque nationale de France contains a volume of 10 Chinese gazettes, bound together in the European way.[34] It concerns a set of *tizou shijian*, which Amiot thematically arranged in four bundles of one to four gazettes, with short handwritten notices containing the topic of the case he selected from the gazette and the Chinese date converted into the European calendar. They can without any doubt be identified as the source of the translations included in Amiot's letter to Bertin of 25 July 1779 and published in *Mémoires concernant les Chinois*.[35] Moreover, Amiot clearly used the *tizou shijian* as his main source for his other quotations of the gazettes, and Bourgeois did the same for his translation preserved in Bréquigny 10. *Tizou shijian* was the name of the Chinese gazette published by the accredited bookseller Gongshen tang 公慎堂 during the later Qianlong and early Jiaqing reigns.[36] The importance of the *tizou shijian* has already been underscored in the bibliographical overview in the introduction to this book.[37] Since this type

civil almanac, which he sent one year earlier). This refers probably to the lists of officeholders entitled *DaQing jinshen quanshu* 大清搢紳全書 (List of officeholders) or *Juezhi quanlan* 爵秩全覽 (Guides to ranks and emoluments) and the equivalent list for military officials *Zhongshu beilan* 中樞備覽 (Guide to the Ministry of War) (see Wilkinson (2018), 66.4.4. p. 936). BnF, Chinois 2238, 2239–2240 contains issues for the year 1789.

34 This volume is classified under "Fonctionnaires civils" in the catalogue of Maurice Courant (1902–1912), p. 130. It is given the title " 京報 *King pao* Gazette de la Capitale." In fact, two front pages of these *tizou shijian* were already reproduced in Britton (1976; originally 1933), plates 2–3: BnF, Chinois 2216, 3.1. (QL43/4/7 = 3 May 1778) and 4.1. (QL44/4/1 = 16 May 1779).

35 *MCC*, vol. 15, pp. 292–346: Extrait d'une lettre de M. Amiot, Ecrite de Péking, le 25 Juillet 1779 (Extract from a letter by Mr. Amiot, Written from Peking, 25 July 1779); Bréquigny 5, fols. 26r–58v; Bréquigny 3, fols. 59r–89v.

36 On the Gongshen tang, see Mokros (2021), pp. 42–43 and pp. 78–81. It operated for about sixty years, between 1760 and at least 1820.

37 I thank Martin Heijdra (Princeton) for pointing out this importance and for sharing his material. For the different libraries with the corresponding dates, see table in the "Guide to the sources" at the end of this book. The table is based on Pan Tianzhen (1992), p. 85; Ma Ting (1993), p. 118; Kong Zhengyi & Zhang Lu (2014), pp. 171–172; Yin Qing (2018), p. 1811; *Zhongguo guji zongmu: Shibu* (2009), vol. 6, p. 3558, no. *shi* 61247900.

of gazette is relatively unknown, the following section first describes it in more detail, relying partly on the resources provided by Amiot and Bourgeois.

The gazette under investigation is known under the name *tizou shijian* 題奏事件. *Tizou* 題奏 is a generic term for "memorials." It refers to the two major types of memorials: *tiben* 題本, which are memorials chiefly concerning routine local civil affairs (they bore the seal of the memorialists); and *zouben* 奏本 or *zouzhe* 奏摺, which are memorials mainly concerning important matters of state or the personal affairs of the memorialist (they did not bear the seal).[38] *Shijian* 事件 is sometimes translated in the modern sense of the word as "matters." Combined, *tizou shijian* could be translated to "matters that have been memorialised" or "memorialised matters."[39] However, based on Ming and early Qing references, Pan Tianzhen pointed out that *shijian* can be more accurately interpreted as "(official) document" (*wenjian* 文件 or *wen'an* 文案).[40] Thus, the combination means "memorialised documents."[41]

The copies are preserved in:

- China: Nanjing Library 南京图书馆, Capital Library of China 首都图书馆, Historical Museum of China 中国历史博物馆 (renamed 中国国家博物馆), National Library of China 中国国家图书馆 (= former Beijing Library 北京图书馆); several of these sources (Pan Tianzhen (1992), Kong Zhengyi & Zhang Lu (2014), and *Zhongguo guji zongmu: Shibu* (2009)) also mention Beijing Cultural Relics Bureau 北京文物局. After an inquiry, however, this Bureau could not locate the copies (personal communication); in fact, Pan Tianzhen (1992), p. 91 n. 3 already mentions that "according to data from 1980, they have been returned to their original location, but one does not know where they are located now." Maybe they have been stored in the Historical Museum of China 中国历史博物馆, which was unsuccessfully contacted for inquiry.
- Japan: National Diet Library, 国立国会図書館; Institute of Advanced Studies on Asia, Tokyo University 東京大学東洋文化研究所; private collector Tian Tao 田 濤.
- USA: Princeton University Library: "Ti zou shi jian" (https://catalog.princeton.edu/catalog/4093844), last accessed 14 October 2020; see also Yale Project: "Exploring the Peking Gazette (*jingbao* 京報)," ed. Michael Hunter (https://tenthousandrooms.yale.edu/project/exploring-peking-gazette-jingbao-jing-bao/ti-zou-shi-jian), last accessed 14 October 2020.
- Europe: Bibliothèque nationale de France (BnF).

38 Fairbank & Têng (1940), pp. 6–7. Fairbank points out that the historical difference between them is not always very distinct.

39 Ma Ting (1993), p. 121, referring to modern Chinese and Japanese; Mokros (2016), p. 135; Mokros (2021), pp. 81, 174.

40 Pan Tianzhen (1992), pp. 84–85.

41 In the Scripta Sinica database, *tizou shijian* as an expression starts to appear during the Yongzheng period (*Qing shilu* 清實錄 and *DaQing huidian* 大清會典 from the Yongzheng period).

Tizou shijian has the following formal characteristics.[42] Each issue contains on average 3 folios (6 pages), sometimes 4 folios (7–8 pages), and exceptionally 5–6 or 1–2 folios (respectively 9–12 or 2–4 pages).[43] The text is printed with black ink on bamboo paper of poor quality. Different dimensions of the format are reported.[44] There is no title on the cover (no mention of *bao* 報), but there is a fore-edge margin with the four characters *tizou shijian* 題奏事件. Immediately under these characters there is one black fishtail (there is no second fishtail).[45] The page numbers are printed on the lower half of the page.

There are no frames for the characters and no separating lines for the columns. The pages are usually full, with few empty spaces. There is an enormous variation in the number of columns and the number of characters between the issues and even within the same issue. The issues preserved at the Bibliothèque nationale de France have between 13 and 15 lines per page, but the number of lines on the two pages of one folio is not necessarily the same (a folio can have two pages with 15 lines each, but also one page with 15 lines and one with 14 lines). Moreover, one issue can combine folios with different number of lines per page (e.g. one folio with 14 lines per page, and the next folio with 13 lines per page). A variation exists in the number of characters per line: 19 characters + 1 or 2 elevated characters; 20 + 1 characters; 21 + 1 characters. This can also vary within one issue, in one case even within the same page: 20 + 1 characters and 19 + 1 characters, which is usually an indication of movable type print.[46]

Most scholars believe that the text was printed with movable type, using either wooden or clay movable characters.[47] However, print historians Zhang Xiumin 张秀民 and Han Qi 韩琦 have argued that the *tizou shijian* was printed

42 Based on the BnF copies (1 vol.), Princeton copies (5 vols.) (https://catalog.princeton.edu/catalog/4093844) and the descriptions by Pan Tianzhen (1992), p. 83 and Ma Ting (2004), p. 145, which include copies in China (Nanjing tushuguan) and Japan.

43 Pan Tianzhen (1992), p. 83; Ma Ting (2004), p. 145; of the 10 *tizou shijian* in Paris there are 7 with 6 pages (1a–3b, 1 with 5 pages (1a–3a), 1 with 7 pages (1a–4a), one with 9 pages (1a–5a); nearly all Princeton copies have 6 pages (1a–3b), with around 3 with 7 pages (1a–4a), 1 with 8 pages (1a–4b) and a few damaged copies.

44 Pan Tianzhen (1992), p. 83: 17.4 × 24.1 cm (line to line); Ma Ting (1993), p. 118: 20 × 26 (bound volumes 21 × 28 and 22.5 × 33.5); Ma Ting (2004), p. 145: the size of the half-leaf is about 20 × 28 cm, and in the 1800s it was 17 × 24 cm. Princeton: 27 cm (online catalogue); Paris: 28 cm (online catalogue). Britton (1976), plates 2–3 give as format 26x20 cm for the Paris copies.

45 Pan Tianzhen (1992), p. 82 mentions that the fishtail is not yet present in the issues of QL35 kept in Nanjing tushuguan but they are present in those of QL38.

46 BnF Chinois 2216, 4. 1 (QL44/4/1), p. 1a.

47 Pan Tianzhen (1992), p. 83; Ma Ting (2004), p. 142; see also discussion in Mokros (2021), pp. 79–80.

with wax (covered) plate instead.[48] Their hypothesis is based on information about wax plates in the Qing found only in Western sources, including Du Halde's *Description ... de la Chine*. This source mentions the usage of wax plates when documents needed to be printed urgently:

> In urgent affairs, as when an order comes from Court which contains multiple articles, and which must be printed in one night, they have another method of engraving: They cover a plate with yellow wax, and trace out the characters with a surprising quickness.[49]

One of the earliest extant wax plate prints that these historians identified is the aforementioned *tizou quanlu* 題奏全錄 of YZ9/8/18 (18 September 1731).[50] However, Ai Junchuan 艾俊川 has contested the existence of wax printed *tizou shijian*, arguing that this hypothesis lacks enough evidence and that even the Western sources are unclear and contradictory. He is of the opinion that the *tizou shijian* are movable type prints.[51] Evidence in *Mémoires concernant les Chinois* supports this opinion. For example, gazettes are mentioned in a discussion of the invention of printing in China, which is part of a critical review of Cornelius de Pauw's (1739–1799) *Recherches philosophiques sur les Egyptiens et les Chinois* (1773).[52] De Pauw's work refuted the at the time fashionable thesis that the Chinese originated from the Egyptians. This refutation also criticized China and the Chinese. In response to his claim that movable type printing was invented in Europe, Ko and Cibot refer to the fact that "the Gazette is printed in movable type like those in Europe" (1775).[53] Similar information is also mentioned in a letter by Bourgeois, sent on 19 November 1784.[54] Whether

48 Zhang Xiumin (2006), vol. 2, pp. 407–412; Zhang Xiumin (2009), pp. 212–217. For an early reference to wax plate printing, see Britton (1976), pp. 4 and 139.

49 *Description ... de la Chine* (1735), vol. 2, p. 250; *General History of China* (1741), vol. 2, p. 436 (wrongly printed as p. 536).

50 Zhang Xiumin (2006), vol. 2, p. 410; Zhang Xiumin (2009), p. 215. See also previous chapter.

51 Ai Junchuan (2009), pp. 11–13.

52 Cornelius de Pauw, *Recherches philosophiques sur les Egyptiens et les Chinois*, 2 vols., Amsterdam/Leiden: Barth. Vlam. & J. Murray, 1773.

53 MCC, vol. 2, p. 454 [Peking, 27 juillet 1775] ("Remarques sur un écrit de M. Pxxx de Pauw intitulé: Recherches sur les Égyptiens et les Chinois"). In this review, in total 105 statements about Chinese and Manchu history, architecture, customs or habits (including infanticide and footbinding) are discussed.

54 MCC, vol. 11, p. 579 (Extrait d'une lettre de M. Bourgeois, missionnaire, Ecrite de Pé-king le 19 Novembre 1784) (Extract from a letter by Mr. Bourgeois, missionary, Written from Peking on 19 November 1784); see also the introduction to the same volume (p. ix).

or not the movable type and wax theory are entirely mutually exclusive, is still a matter of investigation.[55]

The investigation on wax plate printing leads to another conclusion. As mentioned in the previous chapter, the *tizou quanlu* 題奏全錄 from the Yongzheng period may well be the forerunner of *tizou shijian*. In addition, the *tizou quangao* 題奏全稿 (complete copy of memorials) from the Daoguang and Xianfeng periods may be a successor, though in both cases it is not clear whether they were printed by the reporting office (*baofang*) or one of the specialized private publishers. So far only one *tizou quanlu*, dated YZ9/8/18 (18 September 1731), has been identified.[56] Of the successor *tizou quangao* more copies remain: DG10 (late 1830 and early 1831), DG17 (1837), DG18 (1838), DG22 (1842), XF5 (early 1856).[57]

In principle, the *tizou shijian* appeared every day. So far, the oldest preserved copy dates to QL35/3/4 (30 March 1770) and the most recent to JQ6/11/27 (1 January 1802), covering a period of 30 years, 9 months, and 3 days. Bourgeois adds important new information concerning the dates of publication, since during some periods of the year, it did not appear:

> The whole empire is on holidays from the 20th of the last month of the Chinese year until the 20th of the first month of the next year. Even the gazettes are not printed during that time. This is why I only started my gazettes on the 21st of the first month; this year 1788 it was on 7 February.[58]

This information seems to be confirmed by the fact that of all the *tizou shijian* that so far have been identified, only one is dated within that timeframe of holidays.[59]

Unlike the *jingbao* from the nineteenth century, there is no separate table of contents in the *tizou shijian*. Every issue starts with the date (e.g. 乾隆四十四年五月十九日 (QL44/5/19 = 2 July 1779)) followed by the name of the accredited publishing house Gongshen tang, which daily received documents from

55 Information provided by Martin Heijdra.

56 Preserved in the Österreichische Nationalbibliothek, Vienna: Sin. 251. See previous chapter.

57 Preserved in the Österreichische Nationalbibliothek, Vienna: Sin 221.B.1856; see Fang (1992), p. 46: "Tizou quangao Sammlung von Throneingaben." See also http://digital.onb.ac.at/OnbViewer/viewer.faces?doc=ABO_%2BZ43282909. There is a cover page with the title 題奏全稿, a table of contents, followed by the memorials and edicts. For other references see Kong Zhengyi and Zhang Lu (2014), pp. 172–173; *Zhongguo guji zongmu: Shibu* (2009), vol. 6, p. 3560, no. *shi* 61247925 (DG); still other references can be found on the internet.

58 BnF, Bréquigny 10, p. 2; also in Walter (2008), p. 331.

59 Princeton, vol. 4: QL37/12/22 (14 January 1773).

the Grand Secretariat to be disseminated. As the title *tizou shijian* suggests, the imperial decisions that are included in it are usually given in response to memorials submitted by high officials from the central or provincial governmental institutions. An average *tizou shijian* usually includes (some of) the following sections:

Lunyin 綸音 ("silk sounds"): imperial pronouncements ("utterances"), usually rescripts (*zhi* 旨) concerning appointments: they are short and normally appear on the first page. It is the only section introduced by a "subtitle."[60]

Shangyu 上諭: imperial edicts, usually introduced by the expression *Neige feng shangyu* 內閣奉上諭: the approved imperial decrees received by the Grand Secretariat (even though the Grand Councillors drafted the actual documents themselves).

Tizou 題奏: memorials, usually introduced by the function and the family name of the (first) memorialist followed by *jinzou* 謹奏 (or *juzou* 具奏) or *jinti* 謹題: "respectfully submits a memorial of important matter" or "routine memorial" respectively. The memorialists were officials from the offices (ministries) in the capital and from the offices in the provinces. The text includes the imperial decision in various forms (endorsement *zhidaoliao* 知道了 or rescript *zhi* 旨), closed with the expression *qinci* 欽此 "respect this." One of the often-mentioned types of memorials are those including a *yinjian* 引見, i.e. the names of officials due for promotion or appointment to be presented for imperial audience by the Ministry of Personnel (Libu 吏部).

Not all these sections are present in each issue of the gazette, and one issue can even contain only one single text (for instance a long edict or memorial). Moreover, a text can be spread over two issues, which is indicated by the expression *cigao weiwan* 此稿未完 at the end of the first issue in which the

60 Pan Tianzhen (1992), p. 82; Fairbank & Têng (1940), p. 60: also called *silun* 絲綸 (imperial utterances), literally silken cords (from *Liji* 禮記, 30 "Ziyi" 緇衣: 王言如絲，其出如綸 "the prince's words are like silk threads, they issue forth like cords." It is a general term for decrees, proclamations, ordinances, and commands emanating from the Emperor. The title also appears as first section in the above mentioned *tizou quanlu* 題奏全錄 (Yongzheng); also as first section in *Tizou quangao* 題奏全稿 (Beijing, 1830). Britton (1976), plate 4 reproduces the BnF manuscript gazette *jingchao* 京抄) (DG3/2/18-19 = 30–31 March 1823), which also starts with *Shiyin*. The later *jingbao* 京報 starts with *gongmen chao* 宮門抄, which also includes court news on the activities of the emperor including audiences and rituals.

text appears.[61] In addition, two of the identified gazettes only carry the lists of selected candidates for martial and civic appointments *wu/wen xuandan* 武選單 and 文選單 (without a precise date).[62]

This information about the *tizou shijian* can be complemented by contemporary Korean sources. Just as they had done with the *tizou quanlu* for the Yongzheng period, the Korean delegations to China during the Qianlong period actively used the Chinese gazette as a source of information for their reports to the Korean king. Like their precursors during the Yongzheng era, they compared these Chinese gazettes with their own court gazette (*chaobao* 朝報).[63]

A unique source confirming the existence of the *tizou shijian* is *Hwanbo sanjeol* 環報刪節, an anonymous and undated manuscript in 3 *juan* kept at the Kyujanggak Institute of Korean Studies Collection, Seoul National University,[64] which was recently described and studied by Ding Chennan 丁晨楠.[65] It was probably compiled by someone in the delegation of envoy Hong Gye-hee 洪啓禧 (1703–1771), who went to Beijing in 1760.[66] The compiler explains in his introduction that while residing in Beijing, he received "one year of the *tangbao* 塘報, which is also called *xunhuanbao* 循環報 (serial gazette), and also called *tizou shijian* 題奏事件" from the translation office.[67] *Tangbao*, sometimes even called *tangbao* 堂報, was originally the term for the military post courier gazette, but in Korean sources of the mid-Qing it had become interchangeable with the gazettes dispatched from the capital to local governments. *Xunhuanbao*, sometimes rendered as *xunbu* 循簿 or *huanbu* 環簿, is a term that is only used in Korean sources. It is from this term that *Hwanbo sanjeol*'s title was derived.[68] The manuscript's mention of *tizou shijian* is important because it indicates that this gazette existed already in 1760, i.e. ten years before the earliest extant copy of *tizou shijian*.

What makes *Hwanbo sanjeol* even more unique and, in terms of importance, as valuable as Bourgeois' manuscript Bréquigny 10 is that it contains

61 BnF, Chinois 2216, 1.1. p. 3b (QL44/5/19); see Pan Tianzhen (1992), p. 83.

62 Nanjing: QL42/2/? (see Pan Tianzhen (1992), pp. 82, 84); Princeton: 乾隆三十七年十二月分武選單, 乾隆三十七年十二月分文選單 (follows after the gazette of QL37/12/17 = 9 January 1773).

63 E.g. Ding Chennan (2018), pp. 112, 117.

64 Shelf number: 奎 4553-v.1–3.

65 Ding Chennan (2018), pp. 144–154. The envoys' use of the gazette during the Qianlong reign will be the subject of her forthcoming article.

66 Ding Chennan (2018), p. 146.

67 *Hwanbo Sanjeol* 環報刪節, *juan* 1, p. 1; photoreproduction and transcript in Ding Chennan (2018), p. 147.

68 Ding Chennan (2018), p. 148.

a selective transcript of the Chinese gazette of nearly one year: from Joseon Yeongjo 朝鮮英祖 (Qianlong 25) 36/1/27 till 36/12/26 (= 14 March 1760 to 31 January 1761). This transcript was most probably based on copies of the *tizou shijian*. The compiler explains in his introduction that he merely made a selection of imperial decisions and added his own opinion (thus leaving out the appointments, as well as memorials without response). In total there are 201 excerpts, from 181 different days, of which 90 excerpts can be neatly matched with the *Qing shilu*.[69] Each entry is followed by a short comment. The compiler's intention was to understand the durability of the one-hundred-year rule of the Qing. His affirmative comments on Qing government and administration indicate that he joined other Joseon scholars in breaking away from the stereotypical interpretation that the regime of "barbarians" could not last for more than a hundred years.[70] Besides this manuscript, there are also other indications that the Korean envoys contacted the private publishing house Gongshen tang and purchased the *tizou shijian*.[71]

3.2 Text Management in Terms of Selection and Translation

The availability of both European and Chinese sources helps to trace how the extracts from the gazette were selected, presented, translated, and interpreted. In this process both European and Chinese agents were at work. Using Amiot as a primary example, an investigation into this text management helps to explain why gazettes were used as source to inform Europe about events happening in China. Amiot's reports, and to a lesser extent Bourgeois' reports, were also supplemented by information they obtained through personal contacts.

3.2.1 *Selection Process*

The bundle of ten gazettes of *tizou shijian* in the Bibliothèque nationale de France and the translation by Amiot in manuscript and printed form allow us to compare them in order to get an insight into his selection and translation process. In addition, the comparison of these *tizou shijian* with other Chinese sources also give a more precise insight into the documents selected for inclusion in the gazette by the Chinese publishers.

The *tizou shijian* preserved in the Bibliothèque nationale de France (BnF) with shelf number Chinois 2216 can be briefly described in the following table:

69 For an overview, see Ding Chennan (2018), pp. 175–186.

70 Ding Chennan (2018), pp. 150ff., 188.

71 Ding Chennan (2018), p. 134: poem by Lee Chaehag 李在學, member of the embassy of 1793.

TABLE 1 The *tizou shijian* in the Bibliothèque nationale de France (BnF, Chinois 2216)

BnF, Chinois 2216		**Topic**	**Date of original record**	**Date of appearance in gazette** **Days after original**	**Structure of documents in gazette** ***Italics: translated by Amiot***
1. Gazettes qui ont rapport au medecin qui lui fit presenter le livre dans lequel il supposoit la duree de la dynastie	1. pp. 1a–3b	On the condemnation of the book *DaQing tianding yunshu* 大清天定運數 by Zhi Tianbao 智天豹	QL44/4/29 = 13 June 1779	QL44/5/19 = 2 July 1779 (20 days)	– *One memorial*
	2. pp. 1a–3b	Idem	Idem	QL44/5/20 = 3 July 1779 (21 days)	– Two appointments – *Continuation of memorial + edict by emperor*
2. Gazettes qui concernent le lettré qui fit ses representations	1. pp. 1a–4a	Answer of the Emperor to the request of Jin Congshan 金從善	QL43/9/9 = 28 Oct. 1778	QL43/9/29 = 17 Nov. 1778 (21 days)	– *Edict by emperor*
	2. pp. 1a–5a	On the case of Jin Congshan 金從善	QL43/9/21 = 9 Nov. 1778	QL43/10/8 = 26 Nov. 1778 (18 days)	– *Edict by emperor*
	3. pp. 1a–3b	Condemnation of Jin Congshan	QL43/9/12 = 31 Oct. 1778	QL43/10/10 = 28 Nov. 1778 (29 days)	– Edict by emperor – *Memorial + decision by emperor* – Memorial by Astronomical bureau

TABLE 1 The *tizou shijian* in the Bibliothèque nationale de France (BnF, Chinois 2216) (*cont.*)

BnF, Chinois 2216		Topic	Date of original record	Date of appearance in gazette Days after original	Structure of documents in gazette *Italics: translated by Amiot*
3. Gazettes qui regardent la grande collection See-[kou]-tsiuen-[chou]	1. pp. 1a–3b	On the *Siku quanshu* 四庫全書 project	QL43/3/27 = 27 March 1778	QL43/4/7 = 3 May 1778 (38 days)	– One appointment – *Edict by emperor* – Edict by emperor – Memorial
	2. pp. 1a–3b	On the *Siku quanshu* 四庫全書 project	QL43/4/8 = 4 May 1778	QL43/4/29 = 25 May 1778 (22 days)	– *Lunyin*: Three appointments – One appointment – Edict by emperor – *Memorial* – Six presentations (*yinjian*)
	3. pp. 1a–3a	On the *Siku quanshu* 四庫全書 project	QL43/5/26 = 20 June 1778	QL43/6/10 = 3 July 1778 (14 days)	– *Lunyin*: Two appointments – One appointment – *Edict by emperor* – Four presentations (*yinjian*) – Two memorials
	4. pp. 1a–3b	On the *Siku quanshu* 四庫全書 project	QL44/2/1 = 18 March 1779	QL44/2/10 = 27 March 1779 (9 days)	– Four appointments – *Edict by emperor* – One presentation (*yinjian*) – Three memorials
4. Gazette au sujet du livre des 99 moyens de detruire les mantchoux	1. pp. 1a–3b	On the anti-Manchu text *Jiushijiu chou* 九十九籌 (The ninety-nine ways to destroy the Manchus)	QL44/2/26 = 12 April 1779	QL44/4/1 16 May 1779 (34 days)	– One presentation (*yinjian*) – *Memorial + decision by emperor*

This compilation provides an understanding of Amiot's text management. The process involves various combinations of four crucial operations, which Ann Blair has called the four S's of text management: storing, sorting, selecting, and summarizing.[72] In the case of intercultural texts, translating could be added as a fifth operation. Amiot and his collaborator Jacobus Yang seem to have carefully stored the gazettes over a long period of time. Except for the first two, the issues preserved by Amiot did not appear on consecutive days. Instead, they are spread over a period of one year and two months: the first on 3 May 1778 (QL43/4/7) and the last on 3 July 1779 (QL44/5/20). After storing the gazettes for this long period, Amiot and Jacobus Yang sorted them according to four themes. They then selected the relevant extracts related to these themes and summarized them in French. These summaries can be found at the beginning of each theme in *Mémoires concernant les Chinois*. Finally, they translated the selected extracts and sent them to Europe, together with the originals.

In Europe, a new phase of text management began, during which the manuscript text was selected and sometimes amended before publication. In this case, there are two manuscript versions: Bréquigny 5, fols. 26r–58v contains the original letter by Amiot on which an anonymous editor made some redactional comments; Bréquigny 3, fols. 59r–89v is a complete transcript of this letter ready for publication, with some comments by Bertin.

Similar processes of text management also happened on the Chinese side before the texts appeared in the gazette. From the various Chinese records that were consulted, it is easy to notice that the documents that ended up in the gazettes are just a small minority of the many memorials and edicts that passed through the hands of the Emperor and the Grand Council on any given day. Records that allow for an insight into this extensive circulation of official texts include: *Qijuzhu* 起居注 (Court diaries or Records of activity and repose), which not only contain records on the daily activities taking place at the inner court, but also records of imperial decrees and memorials; *Qing shilu* 清實錄 (Qing veritable records), which are partly based on the *Qijuzhu* and perforce are a selection of it;[73] *Shangyu dang* 上諭檔 (Record book of imperial edicts), a record book of the Grand Council in which imperial edicts were copied and which contains often full edicts and memorials that are only summarized in the *Qing shilu*; and *Junjichu suishou dengji dang* 軍機處隨手登記檔 (Record

72 Blair (2010), p. 3.

73 Ocko (1973), pp. 41–42, already made some general remarks on the differences between *shilu* and the *Peking Gazette*: "I not unexpectedly found that the gazettes duplicated only ten percent of the Shih-lu' s entries. But surprisingly for a 'veritable record' the Shih-lu contained less than twenty percent of the gazettes' documents …" Now many more sources for comparison are available.

registers of the Grand Council), which lists all memorials received and edicts or orders sent out, usually with a brief summary of the contents. It should be emphasized that some of these records, such as *Junjichu suishou dengji dang*, contain the original texts of the day when the official document was treated and recorded. Yet, for most of the other records, especially *Qing shilu*, the texts were edited at a later stage, often later than the publication of the text in the gazette. At that stage they could still be selected and summarized. This explains why the gazettes also contain records that do not appear in the above list of sources, especially in the case of memorials rather than edicts. The *Qing shilu*, for instance, represents the imperial voice and usually integrates the memorials of officials within the imperial edicts, while in the gazette they appeared separately, a fact which is underscored by the presence of the word "memorial" (*tizou*) in the title of *tizou shijian*. This also explains why in some instances, in the search for the original of a memorial mentioned in a French translation, this memorial could not be found: though it had evidently been published in the gazette, it was not recorded in the surviving sources. The same applies to appointments. The gazettes include many references to appointments of officials, which were proposed by the Ministry of Personnel (Libu 吏部), which sources mentioned above often fail to include. These are rather unique to the gazettes.

In order to illustrate the selection process, both on the Chinese and the European side, two cases are presented here. They are the two first topics in of Amiot's letter to Bertin of 25 July 1779 published in volume 15 of *Mémoires concernant les Chinois*.[74] An illustration of the selection on the Chinese side is followed by the translation by Amiot, and finally the editorial selection before the publication in Paris.

The first case concerns the provincial student (*xiucai* 秀才), Jin Congshan 金從善 from Jinxian 錦縣, who accosted the Qianlong emperor during his October 1778 eastern tour through Liaoning 遼寧, in order to petition him to proclaim a successor, since the emperor had not yet done so.[75] It was a dangerous exploit, since Jin's status as a scholar-commoner was hardly commensurate with the act of submitting even routine memorials through regular channels. The emperor was furious and termed the suggestions "unprecedently wild and rebellious" 狂誕悖逆，為從來所未. Jin Congshan was arrested on the spot,

---

74 *MCC*, vol. 15, pp. 292–346: Extrait d'une lettre de M. Amiot, Ecrite de Péking, le 25 Juillet 1779; Bréquigny 5, fols. 26r–58v; Bréquigny 3, fols. 59r–89v.

75 This was the third eastern tour of the Qianlong emperor to Mukden in order to pay his respects to the tombs of his ancestors. The emperor left Beijing on 10 September 1778 (QL43/7/20) and returned on 14 November 1778 (QL43/9/26). He was accosted on his return from Mukden on 28 October 1778 (QL43/9/9).

condemned, and executed.[76] Because of this event, the emperor wrote two memorials in which he made explicit his position regarding the appointment of an heir apparent.[77]

The second case concerns Zhi Tianbao 智天豹, a lower literatus who did not succeed in the exams, but who was acquainted with medicine and horoscopes. He compiled a book, *DaQing tianding yunshu* 大清天定運數 (Heaven's Determinations on the Great Qing Dynasty), in which he predicted that the dynasty would last longer than the Zhou dynasty (which lasted 800 years) but that the Qianlong emperor's reign would be shorter than 60 years. Zhi Tianbao was also condemned and executed.

A comparison with other Chinese primary sources can perhaps illustrate the selection that was made on the Chinese side before the inclusion of a particular text in the gazettes.

3.2.1.1 The Case of Jin Congshan 金從善

The original official documents on this case include in chronological order: a first edict by the emperor on 28 October 1778, in which he explained what happened during his tour, expressed his fury against Jin, and gave an initial explanation for not appointing a successor; next a memorial by Grand Secretary (*daxueshi* 大學士) Yu Minzhong 于敏中 (1714–1779) and others on the condemnation of Jin, followed by a decision by the emperor on 31 October; and finally on 9 November an additional long edict by the emperor clarifying in more detail why he had not yet chosen an heir apparent. However, the three gazettes about this case deviate from this order, which reflects a different sorting of the documents. In the following overview the selection of the gazette is compared with the records in the other sources.

The first gazette QL43/9/29 = 17 November 1778 (BnF, Chinois 2216, 2.1. pp. 1a–4a) is completely devoted to the first edict of the emperor (pp. 1a–4a). It appeared twenty-one days after the issuing of the edict.

---

76 *MCC*, vol. 15, pp. 297–335: Bréquigny 5, fols. 29r–51r; Bréquigny 3, fols. 61v–83v. This is followed by another case on the condemnation of the book *DaQing tianding yunshu* 大清天定運數 by Zhi Tianbao 智天豹: *MCC*, vol. 15, pp. 336–344; BnF, Bréquigny 5, fols. 52r–57r; Bréquigny 3, fols. 83v–88v; BnF, Chinois 2216, 1.1. pp. 1a–3b (QL44/5/19 = 2 July 1779); 1.2. pp. 1a–3b (QL44/5/20 = 3 July 1779).

77 The case was notorious enough to have been known over a decade later by members of the mission led by Lord George Macartney (1737–1806) in 1793. See Staunton (1797), vol. 2, p. 223; cf. Kahn (1971), p. 244 note 35.

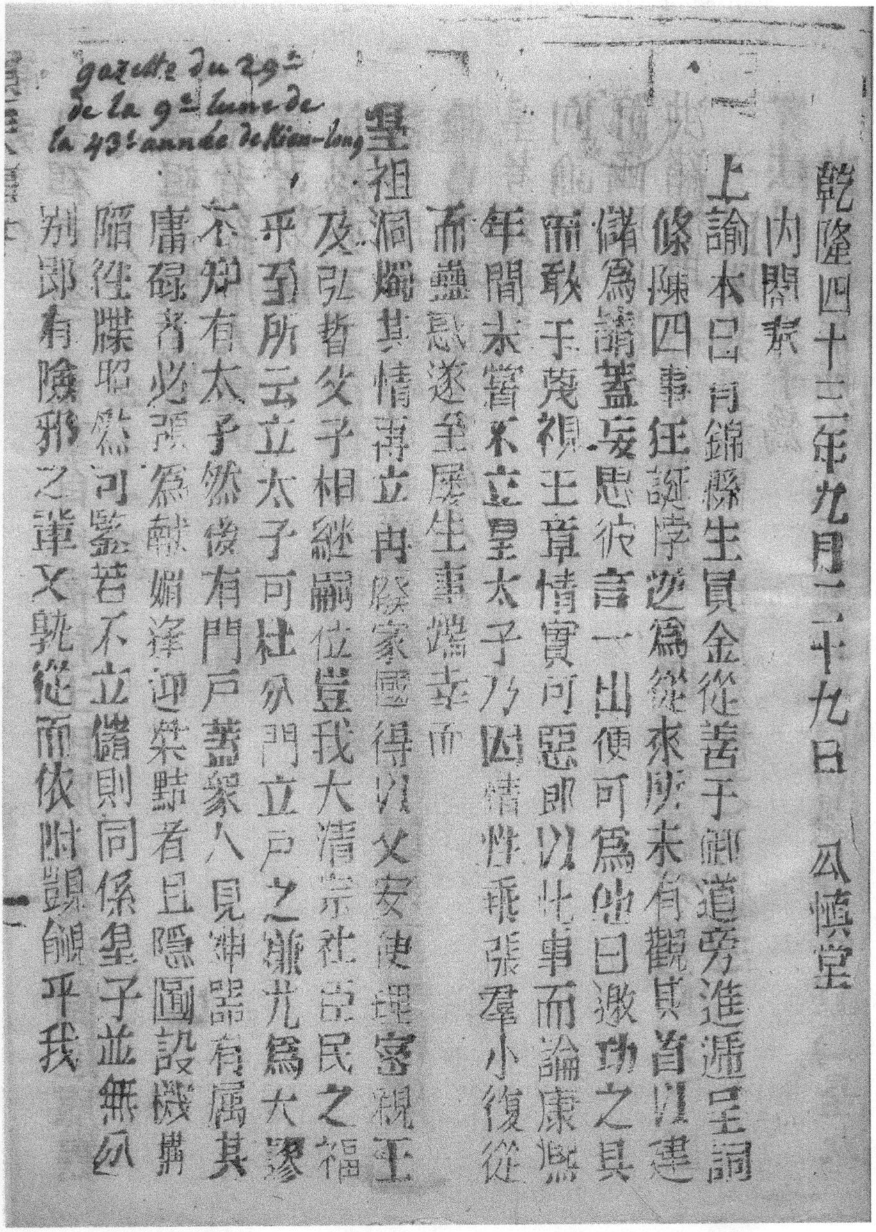

乾隆四十三年九月二十九日 公慎堂

內閣抄

上諭本日有錦縣生員金從善于御道旁進遞呈詞

條陳四事狂誕悖逆爲從來所未有觀其首以建

儲爲請蓋妄思彼言一出便可爲他日邀功之具

而歌于堯視王章情實可惡即以此事而論康熙

年間未嘗不立皇太子乃因情性乖張群小復從

而蠱惑遂至屢生事端去而

聖祖洞燭其情再立再廢家國得以乂安使理密親王

及弘皙父子相繼嗣位豈我大清宗社臣民之福

乎至所云立太子可杜外門立戶之漸尤爲大謬

不知有太子然後有門戶蓋眾人見神器有屬其

庸碌者必預爲獻媚逢迎桀黠者且隱圖設機構

陷從牒昭然可鑒若不立儲則同係皇子並無所

別即有險邪之輩又孰從而依附覬覦乎我

ILLUSTRATION 14 First page of the gazette (*tizou shijian* 題奏事件) containing the answer of the emperor to the request of Jin Congshan 金從善 (QL43/9/29 = 17 Nov. 1778): BnF, Chinois 2216, 2.1. p. 1a

Qing shilu, vol. 22, pp. 259–262 (*juan* 1066) (QL43/9/乙未[= 9] = 28 October 1778) contains the full text of the edict, together with three edicts on other topics and one appointment.

Qianlong chao shangyu dang, vol. 9, pp. 299–301 n. 743 (QL43/9/9 = 28 October 1778) contains the full text of the edict, together with two other edicts and two memorials with corresponding edict.

No *Qijuzhu* has been preserved for the year QL43, so this could not be verified.

Junjichu suishou dengji dang, vol. 30, p. 474 (QL43/9/9 = 28 October 1778) contains a reference to the edict on Jin Congshan, as well as three edicts, three memorials, and vermilion endorsements of memorials of six officials, another three edicts, and vermilion endorsements of memorials of one official.

The second gazette QL43/10/8 = 26 November 1778 (BnF, Chinois 2216, 2.2. pp. 1a–5a) (published eighteen days after the issuing of the edict) is also entirely devoted to a long edict by the emperor, in which he further justifies why he had not yet chosen a successor.

Qing shilu, vol. 22, pp. 275–280 (*juan* 1067) (QL43/9/丁未 [= 21] = 9 November 1778) contains the full text of the edict, together with two other edicts and one appointment.

Qianlong chao shangyu dang, vol. 9, pp. 325–328 n. 793 (QL43/9/21 = 9 November 1778) contains the full text of the edict, together with three other memorials and edicts.

Junjichu suishou dengji dang, vol. 30, p. 495 (QL43/9/21 = 9 November 1778); reference to edict, as well as vermilion endorsement of memorials of four officials, and three edicts.

The third gazette QL43/10/10 = 28 November 1778 (BnF, Chinois 2216, 2.3. pp. 1a–3b) (published twenty-nine days after the relevant original text) contains first another memorial, then a memorial by Grand Secretary Yu Minzhong and others with a proposal for condemnation of Jin Congshan followed by the decision by the emperor (pp. 1a–3b), and at the end another memorial by the *Qintianjian* 欽天監 (Astronomical bureau).

Qing shilu, vol. 22, p. 265 (*juan* 1066) (QL43/9/戊戌[= 12] = 31 October 1778) contains only a very brief reference to the memorial and the decision by the emperor, together with two other brief edicts and one other memorial.

Qianlong chao shangyu dang, vol. 9, pp. 303–304 n.749 and 750 (QL43/9/12 (both) = 31 October 1778) contains the full text of the memorial, including the twelve names of the memorialists, and the full text of the edict (*zhi* 旨).

Junjichu suishou dengji dang, vol. 30, p. 479 (QL43/9/12 = 31 October 1778); reference to edict, as well as three edicts, and vermilion endorsement of memorials of five scholars.

In short: the gazette published the first edict (of 28 October) on 17 November; it published the additional long edict (of 9 November) on 26 November, and finally the earlier condemnation memorial and imperial decision (of 31 October) appeared on 28 November. The texts published in the gazettes are only a selection of the text production on the original date. For the last memorial, *Qing shilu* has significantly less than what appeared in the gazette. The version in *Qianlong chao shangyu dang*, however, has the full list of memorialists, which are normally not recorded in the gazette.

In his translation, Amiot also changed the order. He puts first the edict published on 26 November in which the emperor explained why he did not yet choose a successor.[78] Amiot adds that this was published "a few days after the arrival of the Emperor in Beijing."[79] Next, he puts the first edict that was published in the gazette "nine days before the previous one"[80] and finally the condemnation memorial and imperial decision which appeared on 28 November.[81] Given the fact that Amiot was only interested in the case of Jin Congshan, he merely selected these texts from the gazettes.

3.2.1.2 The Case of Zhi Tianbao 智天豹

The gazettes which include records of Zhi Tianbao's case were published twenty and twenty-one days after the dates of those records in other official texts. The first gazette QL44/5/19 = 2 July 1779 (BnF, Chinois 2216, 1.1. pp. 1a–3b) is completely devoted to a memorial by Yu Minzhong and others; the second

---

78 *MCC*, vol. 15, pp. 297–315: 3. Ecrit de l'Empereur pour se justifier de ne pas déclarer le nom de son successeur (QL43/10/8 = 26 Nov. 1778); Bréquigny 5, fols. 29r–40r; Bréquigny 3, fols. 61v–72v.

79 *MCC*, vol. 15, p. 297. The Emperor returned to Beijing on QL43/9/壬子[= 26] = 14 November 1778 (*Qing shilu*, vol. 22, p. 283 (*juan* 1617)).

80 *MCC*, vol. 15, pp. 315–327: 4. Réponse de l'Empereur à la requête de Kin-Tsoung-chao (QL43/9/29 = 17 November 1778); Bréquigny 5, fols. 40r–47r; Bréquigny 3, fols. 72v–79v; quotation: *MCC*, vol. 15, p. 315.

81 *MCC*, vol. 15, pp. 328–335: Tché-y: 5. Condamnation de cet Auteur & de son livre (QL43/10/10 = 28 November 1778).

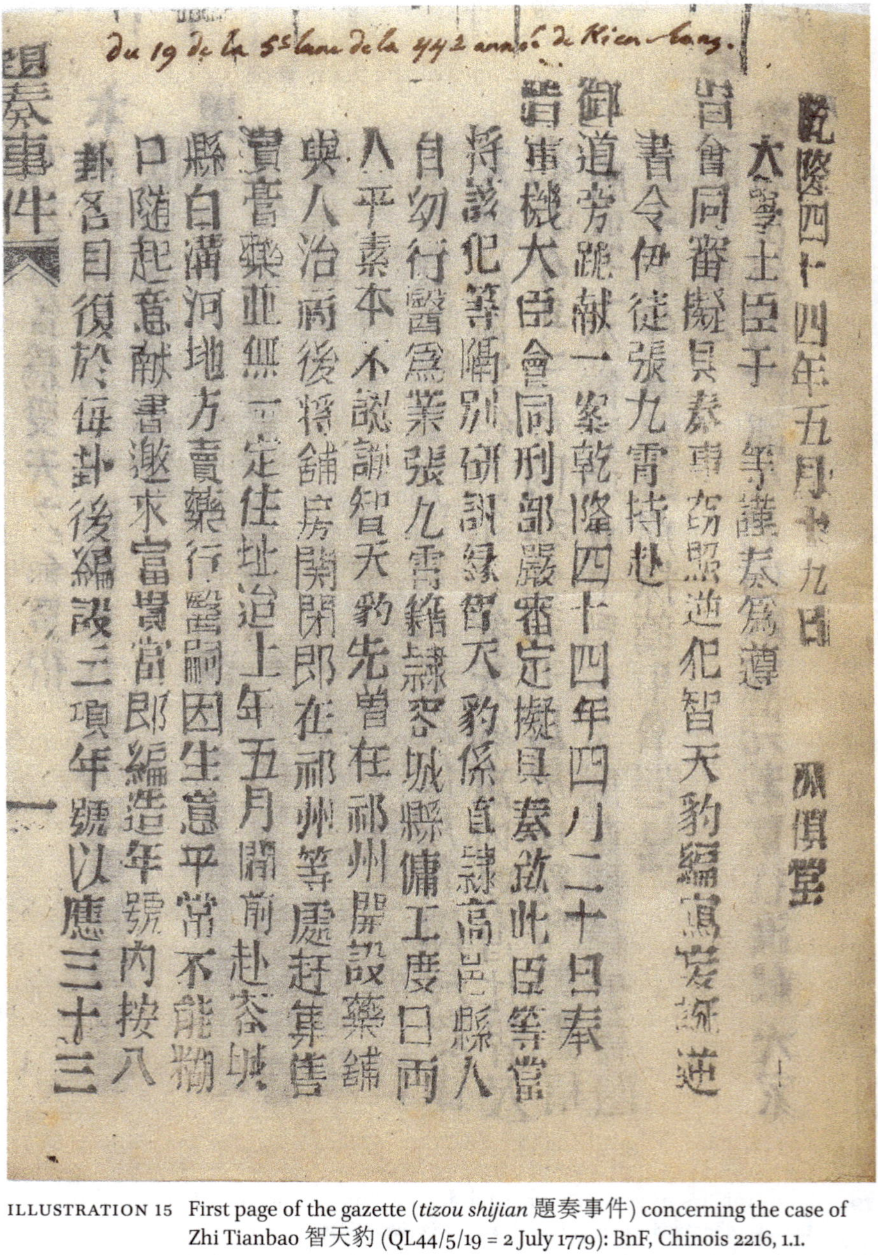

du 19 de la 5e lune de la 44e année de Kien-long.

乾隆四十四年五月十九日　聚[illegible]堂
大學士臣于　等謹奏爲遵
旨會同審擬具奏事　竊照逆犯智天豹編寫妄誕逆
書令伊徒張九霄持赴
御道旁跪獻一案乾隆四十四年四月二十日奉
旨軍機大臣會同刑部嚴審定擬具奏欽此臣等當
將該犯等隔別研訊緣智天豹係直隸高邑縣人
自幼行醫爲業張九霄籍隸容城縣傭工度日兩
人平素本不認識智天豹先曾在祁州開設藥鋪
與人治病後將鋪房關閉即在祁州等處趕集售
賣膏藥並無一定住址迨上年五月間前赴容城
縣白溝河地方賣藥行醫嗣因生意平常不能糊
口隨起意獻書邀求富貴當即編造年號內按八
卦名目復於每卦後編設三項年號以應三十三

題奏事件　一

ILLUSTRATION 15 First page of the gazette (*tizou shijian* 題奏事件) concerning the case of Zhi Tianbao 智天豹 (QL44/5/19 = 2 July 1779): BnF, Chinois 2216, 1.1. p. 1a gazette QL44/5/20 = 3 July 1779 (BnF, Chinois 2216, 1.2. pp. 1a–3b) starts with two nominations on vacant positions (*bushou* 補授), followed by the second part of the memorial by Yu (pp. 1a–2a) and the related imperial edict (*zhi* 旨, pp. 2a–3b).

> *Qing shilu*, vol. 22, pp. 532–534 (*juan* 1081) contains only the edict (*yu* 諭) of the emperor (QL44/4/癸未 [=29] = 13 June 1779); together with around four other memorials and the related imperial decisions.
>
> *Qianlong chao shangyu dang*, vol. 9, pp. 680–681 n. 1618 contains only the edict (*zhi* 旨) of the emperor (QL44/4/29 = 13 June 1779); on the same day there is no other record.
>
> *Qianlong di qijuzhu*, vol. 29, pp. 140–142 (QL44/4/29 = 13 June 1779); after one of the two appointments also to be found in the gazette, it contains the edict of the emperor (*yuzhi* 諭旨), followed by 10 edicts of appointment.
>
> *Junjichu suishou dengji dang*, vol. 31, p. 208 (QL44/4/29 = 13 June 1779); reference to edict, as well as two other edicts, and vermilion endorsement of memorials of six officials.

In this case, the gazette is the only record of the full memorial by Yu Minzhong and others, containing the results of their investigation, since it has not been preserved in any other record. Amiot translated the memorial together with the edict by the emperor.[82]

The comparison of the various Chinese texts included in these sources reveals that the gazette contains only a very limited selection of the documents that were treated by the emperor and the Grand Council. Yet, in certain cases, the documents that appeared in the gazette are the only ones that have been preserved. This is not only the case for the numerous appointments, but also for some memorials. This selection made on the Chinese side in turn determined partially the selection made by Amiot. At least in the two cases described above, he and his collaborator appear to have brought together all the essential documents available through the gazette.

3.2.2 *Translation into French*

As an example of how Amiot translated the gazette into French, two passages have been chosen from the aforementioned case studies. They concern in both cases the condemnation of the offenders.

82 MCC, vol. 15, pp. 336–344 (edict of emperor pp. 340–344): 6. Condamnation du livre intitulé: Destinée de la Dynastie de Tai-Tsong & de son regne (QL44/5/19 = 2 July 1779).

For the case of Jin Congshan, the passage is taken from the end of the memorial by Yu Minzhong, followed by the imperial decree. First the passage of the original Chinese version from the gazette (in original layout) is reproduced, followed by the printed French version (with original spelling and layout) and the modern English translation of the French version.

　。。。乃敢呈遞逆詞狂悖不法已屬罪不
　容誅至所稱豈以不正之運自待一語胆敢詆斥
　本朝尤為罪大惡極非碎磔不足以蔽辜金從善應
　照律凌遲處死以伸
國法而快人心所有應行緣坐之胞兄金從辛及脆侄
　金德昌並擬斬立決其子金德盛雖年僅十三俱金
　從善情罪重大非尋常逆犯可比金德盛應一併擬
　斬立決其妻女財產俱交刑部按律辦理至該管之
　教職及兼管學政之奉天府丞並交吏部查取職名
　分別嚴加議處謹將臣等公同審訊緣由理合恭摺
　具奏伏乞
皇上聖鑒謹奏奉
旨金從善著從寬改爲斬決其緣坐之金從辛金德昌
　金德盛俱著改為應斬監侯秋後處決依議餘欽此[83]

Comment a-t-il pu tomber dans la tête d'un tel homme, de composer un Ecrit aussi calomnieux que celui qu'il a eu l'insolence de présenter à Votre Majesté? Son crime ne mérite aucun pardon; il faut qu'il soit puni, suivant la Loi, dans toute sa rigueur. *Pour ce qu'il a dit que la glorieuse Dynastie ne possédoit pas légitimement le Trône, il mérite d'être coupé en pieces. Nous le condamnons à ce supplice, qui est celui que les Chinois eux-mêmes ont etabli. Nous sommes sûrs qu'il ne s'en trouvera aucun parmi eux qui n'approuve notre jugement. Nous condamnons* Kin-tſoung-ſin, *frere aîné du criminel, &* Kin-tê-tchang, *son neveu, à être décapités, sans attendre le tems prescrit pour les exécutions; nous nous conformons en cela à la Loi Chinoise, Suivant la même Loi,* Kin-tê-yng, *propre fils du criminel, ne devroit pas mourir, parce qu'il n'est âgé que de treize ans; mais comme le crime du pere est au premier chef, il faut eteindre la race, & faire mourir le fils avec le pere. Pour ce qui est des femmes & des filles, il faut qu'elles soient livrées au Tribunal des crimes, qui les jugera suivant les Loix. Nous jugeons aussi que le* Hio-yuen (c'est-à-dire, le grand Mandarin qui préside à l'examen des Lettrés), *le* Tché-fou (le Gouverneur pour le peuple) *de la ville*

---

83 BnF, Chinois 2216, 2.3. pp. 3a–b (QL43/10/10).

de Foung-tien-fou, *& le* Kiao-koan (c'est-à-dire, le grand Mandarin qui a l'inspection immédiate des Lettrés du lieu), *doivent comparoître devant le Tribunal des rites, qui leur imposera la peine qu'ils méritent, s'ils sont trouvés coupables. Tel est le jugement que nous avons cru devoir porter, après avoir examiné l'affaire avec toute l'attention dont nous sommes capables; nous soumettons le tout aux lumieres de Votre Majesté*

TCHE-Y, (c'est-à-dire ordre de l'Empereur)

Votre jugement, conforme aux Loix, condamne le criminel Kin-tſoung-chao *à être coupé en pièces; j'en adoucis la rigueur. Qu'on se contente de lui trancher la tête sans délai. Comme il paroît que son frere, son fils & son neveu n'ont point trempé dans son crime, qu'on attende l'automne pour décider de leur sort. Qu'on suive par-tout le reste votre jugement, parce qu'il suivant la Loi.*[84]

{English translation of the French text}

How could it have fallen into the mind of such a man to compose such a slanderous writing as the one he had the insolence to present to Your Majesty? His crime does not deserve forgiveness; he must be punished, according to the law, in all its rigour. For what he said that the Glorious Dynasty did not rightfully own the Throne, he deserves to be cut to pieces. We condemn him to this torture, which is that which the Chinese themselves have established. We are sure that there will be none among them who will not approve of our judgment. We condemn Kin-tſoung-ſin, elder brother of the criminal, & Kin-tê-tchang, his nephew, to be beheaded, without waiting for the time prescribed for the executions; in this we comply with Chinese Law, According to the same Law, Kin-tê-yng, the criminal's own son, should not die, because he is only thirteen years old; but as the father's crime is of the first order, the race must be extinguished, and the son must be killed with the father. As for women & daughters, they must be delivered to the Criminal Court, which will judge them according to the Laws. We also judge that the Hio-yuen (that is to say, the great Mandarin who presides over the examination of the Scholars), the Tché-fou (the Governor for the people) of the city of Foung-tien-fou, & the Kiao-koan (that is to say, the great Mandarin who has the immediate inspection of the Literati of the place), must appear before the Tribunal

84 MCC, vol. 15, pp. 334–335. Italics in original printed text.

of rites, which will impose on them the punishment they deserve, if they are found guilty. Such is the judgment which we felt it necessary to pass, after having examined the affair with all the attention of which we are capable; we submit everything to the insight of your majesty

TCHE-Y, (i.e. order of the Emperor)

Your judgment, in accordance with the Laws, condemns the criminal Kin-tfoung-chao to be cut to pieces; I soften the rigour. Just chop off his head without delay. As it appears that his brother, his son and his nephew were not involved in his crime, that one waits until autumn to decide their fate. Let us follow your judgment everywhere else, because it is according to the Law.

The example for the case of Zhi Tianbao is taken from the end of the imperial edict:

。。。且設果如逆犯智天豹所云乾隆五十七
年之言朕其時壽躋八十有二即歸政亦不為早
况歷代帝王在位五十餘年而歸政者實所罕覯
朕尚有何不足乎是該犯此條不得謂之呪詛不
必執此以定爰書也惟該犯敢於妄編年號三十
餘條且于
皇祖廟諱直書不澼並謊稱
世祖章皇帝顯聖於彼希冀惑眾動聽此則喪心病狂
身蹈大逆不可不按律懲治然究與誹謗毀斥者
稍為有間智天豹著從寬改為斬決至張九霄拜
逆犯為師代其呈獻逆書亦應按律處斬姑念其
人本属鄉愚無知且不識字情尚可憫張九霄著
從寬改為應斬監候秋後處決餘依議並將此通
諭中外知之欽此[85]

L'Auteur du Livre limite à cinquante-sept ans la durée de mon regne. Supposons que la chose arrive ainsi, j'aurai atteint la quatre-vingt-deuxième année de mon âge: n'aurai-je pas assez vécu? un regne de cinquante-sept ans n'est-il pas assez long? Dans la liste des Empereurs, s'en trouve-t-il beaucoup qui aient régné cinquante ans? Je ne regarde pas ce, que dit l'auteur sur cela, comme une offense qu'il m'ait faite; ainsi je l'absous de toute

85 BnF, Chinois 2216, 1.2. pp. 3a–b (QL44/5/20).

punition, quant à cet article. De quoi il mérite d'être exemplairement puni, c'est de ce qu'il a osé dire dans une trentaine d'articles, où, en parlant de mes Ancêtres & de moi, il nous appelle de notre petit nom: insulte qui n'est pas faite impunément aux personnes les moins qualifiées, & qui, à plus forte raison, ne doit pas rester impunie, quand elle est faite à des Souverains. Il mérite encore d'être puni, pour avoir voulu m'en imposer, ainsi qu'à tous ceux qui auroient pu lire son Livre, en assurant que mon Aïeul lui avoit apparu, & lui avoit donné lui-même ce Livre. Suivant les Loix Chinoises, auxquelles vous vous êtes conformés dans le jugement que vous avez porté contre lui, il devroit être coupé en pièces: cependant, comme il y a moins de malice dans son crime, que si, de dessein formé, il eût médit & de moi & de ma Dynastie, il suffit qu'on lui tranche la tête, sans attendre le temps des exécutions ordinaires. En vous conformant aux mêmes Loix Chinoises, vous avez condamné Tchang-kieou-hiao, Disciple de Tché-tien-pao, à avoir la tête tranchée. Comme ce malheureux n'a eu aucune mauvaise intention, en se prêtant au dessein de son maître, & qu'il n'a eu part à la confection du Livre qu'il m'a présenté de sa part, il faut avoir compassion de lui. Ainsi qu'on attende à l'automne pour décider de son sort. Qu'on se conforme pour tout le reste à votre jugement. Je veux que dans toute l'étendue de l'Empire le public soit instruit de cette affaire, & de la maniere dont je l'ai terminée.[86]

{English translation of the French text}

The Author of the Book limits the duration of my reign to fifty-seven years. Suppose it happens like this, I will have reached the eighty-second year of my age: will I not have lived enough? Isn't a reign of fifty-seven years long enough? In the list of Emperors are there many who have reigned for fifty years? I don't look at what the author says about it as an offense to me; thus I absolve him of any punishment, as for this article. For what he deserves to be punished exemplarily, it is for what he dared to say in about thirty articles, where, speaking of my Ancestors and of me, he calls us by our name: this is an insult which is not done with impunity to the least qualified people, & which, with all the more reason, should not go unpunished, when it is done to Sovereigns. He also deserves to be punished, for having wanted to impose on me, as well as on all those who could have read his Book, the assurance that my Grandfather had appeared to him, & had given him this Book himself.

86 *MCC*, vol 15, pp. 343–344.

> According to the Chinese Laws, to which you conformed in the judgment you brought against him, he should be cut to pieces: however, as there is less malice in his crime, than if, by formed design, he had slandered me & my Dynasty, it suffices that his head be cut off, without waiting for the time of ordinary executions. By conforming to the same Chinese Laws, you condemned Tchang-kieou-hiao, Disciple of Tché-tien-pao, to have his head cut off. As this unfortunate man had no bad intentions, in lending himself to his master's plan, and as he did not take part in the making of the Book which he presented to me on his behalf, we must have compassion on him. Therefore that one waits until the fall to decide its fate. That one abides by your judgment for everything else. I want the public throughout the Empire to be informed about this affair, and the way I concluded it.

In general, Amiot makes a fairly precise translation. His style endeavours to reflect in French the official administrative style that is characteristic of the Chinese documents, using equivalent (honorific) expressions from official French correspondence (e.g. in French the honorific "His Majesty" is "Sa Majesté" followed by sentences in the feminine). At times the style looks a bit baroque (the English translation of the French is usually shorter), but it does not appear significantly different from the style in which he addresses Henri Bertin, who as a French statesman was his superior. Though Amiot rarely omits passages of the original text, as he attempts to translate the whole memorial or edict, he occasionally summarizes certain passages. For instance, details about Zhi Tianbao's past as keeper of a medical drugstore in Qizhou 祁州 and next as an itinerant salesman, which were included at the beginning of the memorial by Yu Minzhong and others, were summarized as; "[he] was a man of low standing, who knew a bit of medicine, and knew medicinal drugs, and made a retail business out of them ..."[87] The Chinese administrative style is often very concise and therefore needs more explanation in modern translation, both in Chinese and European languages. This is also the case in Amiot's translations, which sometimes add some explanation of specific terms or explicitly repeat content that is implied in the Chinese terms. He usually also provides the full name of the memorialist, though the gazette generally gives only the family name. This indicates that he and his collaborator were well informed about the key figures in the central government bodies.

87 BnF, Chinois 2216, 1.1. p. 1a (QL44/5/19); *MCC*, vol. 15, p. 337.

大學士臣于 等謹奏。。。

Nous, Grands de l'Empire, Maîtres de la Doctrine, &c. &c. Yu-ming-tchoung & les autres[88]

Nous Grands de l'Empire, grands Maîtres de la Doctrine, Présidens & Conseillers des neuf grands Tribunaux, Yu-ming-tchoung, & les autres ...[89]

Additional observations need to be made for Bourgeois' selection process in the translation of the gazettes in Bréquigny 10, which in principle contains the French translation of all gazettes from QL53/1/21 (27 February 1788) to QL53/3/16 (1 May 1788). Exceptions are the gazette of QL53/1/24 (1 March 1788), which is reported to be lost, and QL53/1/30, for which there is no record. Bourgeois avowedly gives a *full* translation of each issue.

I rendered the gazettes as they are; I did not skip anything, so that one can better understand their genius, and that one see what their goal is.[90]

In practice this is also the case, and the abundance of translated information from one gazette after another gives a concrete idea of what these documents contained. His arrangement of the contents confirms the structure of *tizou shijian*. Bourgeois' most frequently used subtitles distinguish the following sections:

Paroles de l'Empereur = *lunyin* 綸音
Declaration imperial = *shangyu* 上諭; *ordre de l' empereur* = *zhi* 旨
Memorial or *representation* = *tizou* 題奏; sometimes with more specifications: *memorial d'accusation* = *canzou* 參奏 (memorial of impeachment); (*placet en forme de*) *remerciement* = 謹奏為恭謝...; *In kien ou presentation des Mandarins* = *yinjian* 引見
They are usually concluded by the formal: *qu'on respecte cecy, qu'on respecte cet ordre, qu'on respecte ces paroles, qu'on observe cecy* = *qinci* 欽此; once it is concluded with *Je le sais* (*c'est a dire J'approuve tout ce que vous proposez*) = *zhidaoliao* 知道了

88 MCC, vol. 15, pp. 336–337.
89 MCC, vol. 15, p. 328.
90 BnF, Bréquigny 10, p. 2: see also similar statement in the Letter of Bourgeois to Bertin (Beijing, 10 October 1788): BnF, Bréquigny 2, fols. 209r–212r: fol. 209v: "The Gazettes of the Empire are made with art. I have not put anything aside, so that your greatness will know its genius better."

There are, however, two exceptions to Bourgeois' commitment to translate everything, which involves a certain selection. Bourgeois makes a short summary for a total of nine gazettes, when he is of the opinion that the gazette is a (kind of) repetition or rather continuation of the preceding gazette or a previous issue.[91] This does not mean that continuation is always avoided: certain topics, such as the examination of the literati, are discussed at length.[92] The second exception is the section on *yinjian* 引見, concerning the appointment or promotion of officials. At about one fourth of his translation, Bourgeois adds the following note:

> Almost every day the gazette includes *in Kien* [*yinjian*]. As we do not know the subjects who were promoted, and as their advancement does not interest Europe at all; because the formula is always the same anyway; which would become boring in the long run; we will skip them from now on, but only put those which will have something special.[93]

Bourgeois indeed occasionally includes some *yinjian*.[94] The criterium of whether it is interesting for Europe is also the reason that is ultimately given in the last two days of gazette in his manuscript for the discontinuation of his project.

> [...] Nothing interesting in the rest of the gazette[95]

> In this gazette and in the following ones, it is only a question of the *in kien*, of the mandarins to be replaced; mandarins to be promoted & Nothing of interest for Europe[96]

Unique for Bourgeois is that the letters to Bertin which accompany the mailing of the manuscript include a reflection on his own translation:

> My translation of the gazettes needs leniency, and a lot of care from the editor. I realized that the proper word did not come back to me at the

91 BnF, Bréquigny 10, p. 79 (QL53/2/10), p. 113 (QL53/2/21), p.126 (QL53/2/25), p. 144 (QL53/2/28), p. 157 (QL53/3/3), p. 161 (QL53/3/6), p. 163 (QL53/3/9), p. 177 (QL53/3/15), p. 187 (QL53/3/18).

92 The rules for the examination are treated in four issues: BnF, Bréquigny 10, pp. 79–81, pp. 81–86 (QL53/2/11–14).

93 BnF, Bréquigny 10, p. 43 (QL52/2/2).

94 BnF, Bréquigny 10, p. 72 (QL52/2/8), p. 100 (QL52/2/18).

95 BnF, Bréquigny 10, p. 43 (QL52/3/25).

96 BnF, Bréquigny 10, p. 43 (QL52/3/26).

> moment; I had to put an equivalent. I have used the same expression several times in a row; no others came to me to vary. We haven't spoken our mother tongue for so long that it's no wonder words escape us, especially as we approach our seventieth year.[97]

In this context he refers to the editorial work that was accomplished by Jean-Baptiste Du Halde for the *Lettres édifiantes et curieuses* regarding the letters by Dominique Parrenin (1665–1741) fifty years earlier. Bourgeois clearly had a different opinion than his predecessors, who had criticized Du Halde for his extensive interventions in their texts:

> Father Parrennin [sic] wrote well; however, Father du Halde rendered him great services. I compared the manuscripts of his texts that were sent to France, with the *Lettres édifiantes*, in which they came back to us printed: a word appropriately replaced, an expression added, a little turn of the sentence gives it an entirely other grace.[98]

In another letter, Bourgeois points out additional shortcomings of his translation and emphasized the need for editorial improvements:

> I notify to your greatness that there are a few places in the two hundred folio pages, translated from Chinese gazettes, which require special attention. There are more specifically one or two *changyu* (*déclaration impériale* = imperial declaration) word for word (*paroles d'en haut* = words from above) where I was not aware when the Emperor began to speak. I only saw this afterwards but too late to fix things properly. There are also three or four obscure places, for lack of the proper expression in our language to render exactly the Chinese. I rely on the editor for everything. He will see roughly the meaning. I did my best to do so.[99]

3.2.3 *Editorial Work in Paris*

As indicated by Bourgeois' comments, once the letters arrived in Paris, there was still some editorial work before publication. Unfortunately, Bourgeois' manuscript was never printed, and therefore editorial changes could not be verified in his case.

---

97 Letter of Bourgeois to Bertin (Beijing, 10 October 1788): BnF, Bréquigny 2, fols. 209r–212r: fol. 211v.

98 Letter of Bourgeois to Bertin (Beijing, 10 October 1788): BnF, Bréquigny 2, fol. 211v.

99 Letter of Bourgeois to Bertin (Beijing, 9 November 1788): BnF, Bréquigny 2, fol. 214r.

Regarding Amiot's letters, the existence of two manuscript versions (Bréquigny 5 with the original letter and Bréquigny 3 with a transcript of the letter ready for publication) makes it possible to trace the selection process that preceded the final publication. Overall, the end result in the published version is very faithful to the original letter. The structure has generally remained the same: first an introduction, next the translation of the documents (sometimes with a short transition if there are several documents), and at the end a short conclusion with personal comments by Amiot.[100] The most obvious change is the addition of a table of contents to the letters with corresponding numbers added in the text, which facilitates the reading-experience of the longer letters (some counting over fifty pages).[101]

Amiot's letters in *Mémoires concernant les Chinois* did not undergo the radical rewriting and changes that Du Halde made in the letters and reports by the Jesuit missionaries in China and for which, as mentioned above, they criticised Du Halde when they saw the results in the *Lettres édifiantes et curieuses* or in *Description de la Chine*.[102] In Amiot's case the changes are minimal, a fact that one should keep in mind while examining the following examples from the letter of 25 July 1779. If changes occur, they pertain to Amiot's own comments or remarks, and only occasionally – but not for this letter – to Amiot's translations of the Chinese texts. The changes normally occur in the transition from Amiot's original letter (Bréquigny 5) to the transcript of this letter (Bréquigny 3).

A first type of change made by the editors is stylistic. The honorific style that Amiot uses in his letters to address the statesman Bertin is changed to a more neutral style for the reader of the *Mémoires concernant les Chinois*. Thus, the vocative "your highness" (*votre grandeur*) is changed to "Sir" (*Monsieur*).

For instance, Amiot starts his letter of 25 July 1779 with:

> L'année dernière, *si je m'en souviens bien*, j'ay fait part *à votre grandeur* du voyage qu'avoit fait l'Empereur dans la capitale de ses anciens états, ...[103]

100 The order of the gazettes in BnF, Chinois 2216 (first the case of Zhi Tianbao, next of Jin Congshan) is different in the letter that Amiot sent to Bertin and that was ultimately published in *Mémoires concernant les Chinois*. This reversal, however, was not necessarily Amiot's choice, since the numbering of the texts and the binding of Chinois 2216 was done in Paris.

101 *MCC*, vol 15, p. 292; this index is not yet present in Bréquigny 3; in *MCC*, the text runs from p. 292 to 346.

102 For a review of these criticisms, see Landry-Deron (2002), p. 109ff.

103 BnF, Bréquigny 5, fol. 26r. The text in italics appears in the manuscript surrounded by a circle (added by an editor).

> Last year, *if I remember correctly*, I shared *with your highness* the journey which the Emperor undertook to the capital of his former states, …

Two parts of the sentence have been circled (here put in italics) by the anonymous editor. In the version ready for publication (Bréquigny 3) these have been either deleted or changed, and this is also how they appear in the printed version.

> L'année dernière, je vous ai fait part, Monsieur, du voyage qu'avoit fait l'Empereur dans la Capitale de ses anciens-Etats,…

> Last year, I shared with you, Sir, the journey which the Emperor undertook to the capital of his former states,…[104]

The text that is transcribed in Bréquigny 3 (a copy version of the original letter) was not amended before publication. There are, however, some editorial remarks by Bertin, easily recognisable by his (large) handwriting. In this passage, Bertin gives a suggestion for the place of the letter in volume 15 of *Mémoires concernant les Chinois*.

> I believe that this long Letter can come after that of M. Bourgeois and another of M. Amyot on the persecutions and the indulgent treatment of the Emperor[105]

A second type of change is when some parts of the letter are deleted. This does not occur with the translation of the gazette, but with the introduction, transition sentences, or conclusion of Amiot. These deletions are acknowledged by the fact that in *Mémoires concernant les Chinois* the letters are referred to as "extracts" (*extrait*) of Amiot's letters.

In certain cases, portions of the text were possibly deleted because of Amiot's baroque style in addressing Bertin. In the text where Amiot makes the transition from the first case on Jin Congshan to the second case on Zhi Tianbao, the following passage was deleted.

> Here, sir, are all the details of a case of which, at the start of this letter, I only intended to give you the summary. What has happened to me is what happens to those who willingly talk to someone else; they extend

104 BnF, Bréquigny 3, fol. 59r; *MCC*, vol. 15, p. 292.

105 BnF, Bréquigny 3, fol. 59r.

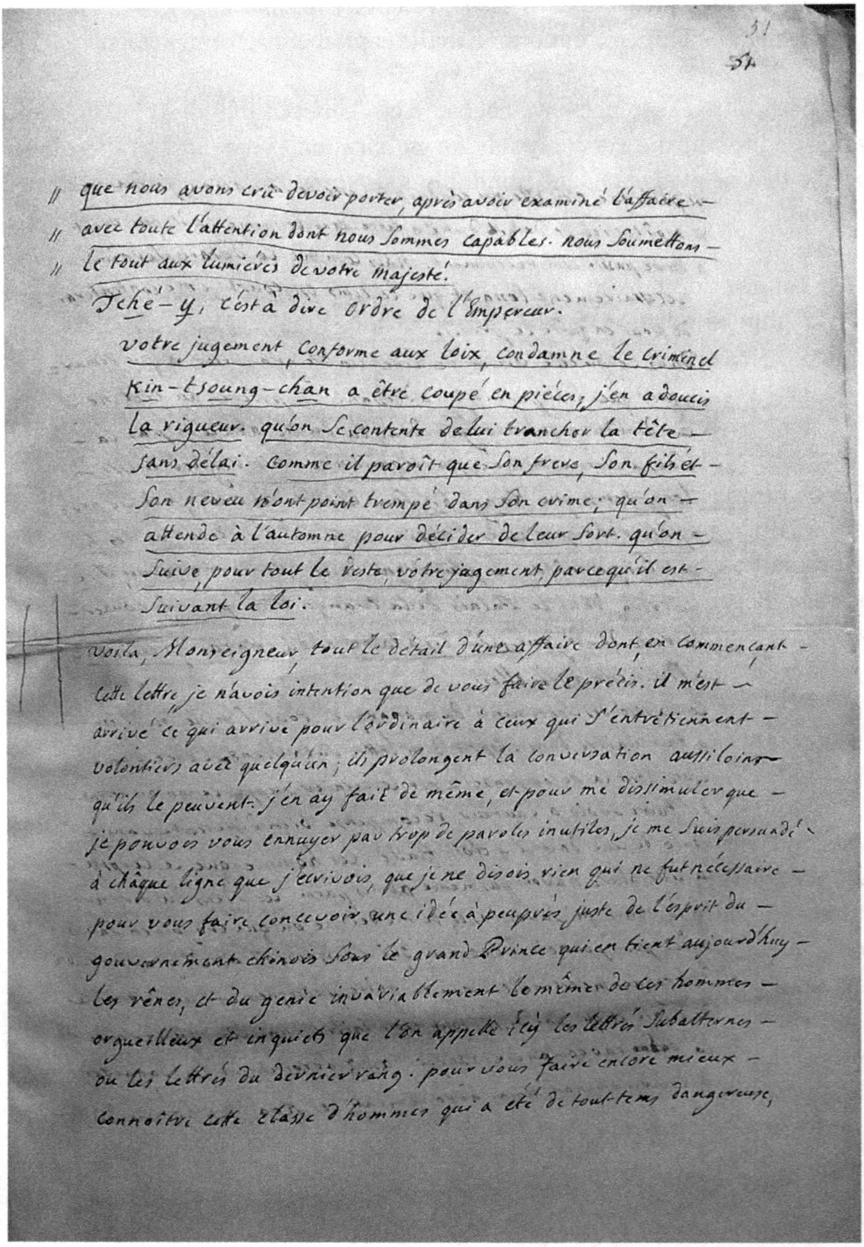

51

// que nous avons crû devoir porter, après avoir examiné l'affaire –
// avec toute l'attention dont nous Sommes capables. nous Soumettons –
// le tout aux lumières de votre majesté.

Tché-y, c'est à dire Ordre de l'Empereur.

votre jugement, conforme aux loix, condamne le criminel
Kin-tsoung-chan a être coupé en pièces; j'en adoucis
la rigueur. qu'on se contente de lui trancher la tête –
sans délai. comme il paroît que son frere, son fils et –
son neveu n'ont point trempé dans son crime; qu'on –
attende à l'automne pour décider de leur sort. qu'on –
suive pour tout le reste, votre jugement, parcequ'il est –
suivant la loi.

voila, Monseigneur, tout le détail d'une affaire dont, en commençant –
cette lettre je n'avois intention que de vous faire le précis. il m'est –
arrivé ce qui arrive pour l'ordinaire à ceux qui s'entretiennent –
volontiers avec quelqu'un; ils prolongent la conversation aussi loin –
qu'ils le peuvent. j'en ay fait de même, et pour me dissimuler que –
je pouvois vous ennuyer par trop de paroles inutiles, je me suis persuadé –
à chaque ligne que j'écrivois, que je ne disois rien qui ne fut nécessaire –
pour vous faire concevoir une idée à peu près juste de l'esprit du –
gouvernement chinois sous le grand Prince qui en tient aujourd'huy –
les rênes, et du genie invariablement le même de ces hommes –
orgueilleux et inquiets que l'on appelle icy les lettrés Subalternes –
ou les lettrés du dernier rang. pour vous faire encore mieux –
connoître cette classe d'hommes qui a été de tout tems dangereuse,

ILLUSTRATION 16 Original letter of Joseph-Marie Amiot to Henri Bertin (Beijing, 25 July 1779) with the translation of the imperial order to execute Jin Congshan 金從善, and the passage with Amiot's conclusions that was deleted in the printed version: BnF, Bréquigny 5, fols. 51r (absent in Bréquigny 3, fol. 83v and in *MCC*, vol. 15, p. 335)

> the conversation as far as they can. I did the same, and in order to hide from myself that I could bore you with too many unnecessary words, I persuaded myself with each line that I wrote, that I did not say anything that was not necessary to make you conceive a more or less true idea of the spirit of the Chinese government under the great Prince who now holds the reins, and of the genius invariably the same of those arrogant and anxious men who are called here the subaltern literati or the literati of the last rank. To make you even better acquainted with this class of men who have always been dangerous, because it is they who lead the rest of the nation, I should add here the details of an affair in the same flavour which has taken place just recently,...[106]

The baroque style of this passage may have been a reason for deletion. Still, this transition clarifies that Amiot establishes a contrast between the "more or less true idea of the spirit of the Chinese government under the great Prince" and the "arrogant subaltern literati," who in his eyes are dangerous to the nation. This is reminiscent of some of the remarks made by Perroni during the Yongzheng period.

In other cases the deletion is more striking because it concerns more explicitly personal comments by Amiot on the interpretation of China's political structure. This happens when he enters into discussion with Enlightenment philosophers from the middle and the late eighteenth century to show that the Chinese emperor is not a "despot":

> What I just said is hardly interesting for your highness; what I am going to add will interest him perhaps in that it will make him know the current spirit of the Chinese government, and that he will be able to conclude that the monarch who holds the reins is anything but a despot, as certain authors boldly assert who believe they can decide everything, because they have given themselves the title of philosophers.[107]

In this passage, which appears in the introduction preceding the Jin Congshan case in his letter, Amiot clearly states his objectives. Besides the fact that he wants to show Bertin what gazettes look like, he intends to make clear "the current spirit of the Chinese government" by proving that it is not despotic. The scholars who according to Amiot claim the title of "philosophe" are the Enlightenment thinkers, such as Montesquieu and Quesnay who discussed

---

106 BnF, Bréquigny 5, fols. 51r–v; absent in Bréquigny 3, fol. 83v; *MCC*, vol. 15, p. 335.

107 BnF, Bréquigny 5, fol. 28v; absent in Bréquigny 3, fol. 61r; *MCC*, vol. 15, p. 295.

China's despotism.[108] But it also refers to the work of Cornelius de Pauw, whose book was mentioned earlier and whose work was criticised in *Mémoires concernant les Chinois* volumes 2 and 6. This is made explicit in the final sentence of this letter discussing the two cases of Jin Congshan and Zhi Tianbao, which in both manuscript versions makes an explicit reference to the work of Cornelius de Pauw.

> From those I have just reported, your highness will judge for himself whether the maker of *réflexions philosophiques sur les Egyptiens et les Chinois* reflected philosophically when he said that the latter were ruled arbitrarily by the will of a despot.[109]

It is noteworthy that this final sentence was still present in the version ready for printing, and that it was only deleted in the final stage. In the printed version of *Mémoires concernant les Chinois*, this letter ends with the sentence:

> It is by facts analogous to the way in which a nation governs itself, that one can judge the vices or the goodness of its government.[110]

In the debates about the question whether Chinese rulers were despotic, Amiot was of the opinion that a despot is a ruler who exercises power in an arbitrary manner by creating the law according to his own will. However, in his opinion, the emperor of China follows the law. He certainly possesses absolute power, but mandarins and censors can warn him in case his actions do not conform to the principles that govern Chinese society as a whole. Moreover, among the Chinese emperors, few are those who arbitrarily exercised their power. Therefore, Amiot does not consider the Chinese government despotic.[111]

> A Despot has only to say: *I want it*, and everything is done. Let an Emperor of China say the same: *I want it*; if what he wants is not just or does not comply with the law, or is contrary to some accepted custom, nothing is done, unless violence gets involved, & in this case he is regarded as a tyrant.[112]

---

108 See Cartier (1998); Ma Li (2019), chapter 3 (with other examples).

109 BnF, Bréquigny 5, fol. 58r–v; Bréquigny 3, fol. 89v: only changed the addressee: "vous jugerez, Monsieur" instead of "votre grandeur jugera elle même."

110 *MCC*, vol. 15, p. 346.

111 *MCC*, vol. 6, pp. 333–336: "Le gouvernement Chinois n'est point despotique." Cf. Ma Li (2019), pp. 82–83.

112 *MCC*, vol. 6, p. 334.

Apparently, the anonymous editor or Bertin wanted to avoid remarks that were too apologetic or too repetitive with what Amiot had already explained concerning this topic in volume 6 of *Mémoires concernant les Chinois*. As a result, in this case the printed version of the letter represents less the personal interpretation by Amiot than the manuscript version.

Amiot's and Bourgeois' translations of Chinese gazettes are the result of a subtle interplay of successive text management by both Chinese and European actors. They were dependent on the selection that the emperor and higher officials had made of texts to be made public and that ultimately ended up in a gazette. Though these gazettes only represent a minority of the official documents that were produced daily, they regularly contain texts that cannot be found elsewhere in the still extant Chinese sources. Amiot made his own selection in terms of what he considered of interest to Europeans in general, and to a European statesman such as Bertin in particular. He was also involved in discussions concerning European interpretations of the Chinese way of governing and wanted to voice an opinion based on Chinese sources. This explains why his letters contain so many translations directly taken from the gazettes. Another example of this approach can be found in Bourgeois' translation of more than two months of gazettes in Bréquigny 10. In a style that is characteristic of their time, both Amiot's and Bourgeois' translations are faithful to the source and contain few changes. This is also the case for Bourgeois' and especially Amiot's other translations on music, ancient dances, military strategy, history, and sciences. The attempt to let the Chinese (and also Manchu) sources speak for themselves is indeed characteristic of the work of Amiot, Bourgeois, and other Jesuits. As a result, many sources about Chinese culture were available in translation at the end of the eighteenth century.

3.2.4 *Reasons for the Use of Gazettes as Source*

There were various reasons as to why missionaries used gazettes for their reports about the contemporary situation in China at their time. In fact, Amiot, for his part, uses two kinds of sources for his letters: written texts, usually published in the gazette, and first-hand information, usually based on personal contacts or experiences by others or himself.

Amiot insists on the textual sources as his primary reference: "the documents, the petitions of the high officials in place or the Tribunals, the public writings, the Emperor himself, are the guarantees of what I say: because I never say anything, except according to them."[113] Important in this quote is that

113 *MCC*, vol. 9, p. 7; see same page: "according to the emperor himself"; *MCC*, vol. 9, p. 25: "according to Akoui himself in his letters to the emperor, and according to the emperor."

Amiot aims to give voice to the emperor or officials by translating their texts directly, and that the documents he uses for this are usually "public writings" (*écrits publics*). In another phrasing he writes: "I cannot say anything better than what His Majesty himself said in a public writing which he provided on this occasion."[114] Among these texts the most important source is the Chinese gazette, to which Amiot refers many times: in addition to referring to it explicitly as the text he translates,[115] or the texts he has read,[116] he regularly alludes to a connection to the gazette by pointing out that the emperor or an official "has ordered" the publication of a particular text.[117] He mentions on several occasions that these gazettes are meant for the instruction of the mandarins[118] and of the people. In the latter case, he makes the distinction between two types of gazette: "Here is [the discourse of the emperor] as it was inserted in the Gazette of the Court, so that by this way it can be passed on to the one that is intended for the instruction of the people."[119] In rare instances, Amiot used official texts before they appeared in the gazettes. For instance, he "secretly" (*secretement*) translated the letter of the emperor to the Dalai Lama (Jampäl Gyatso, 1758–1804) (at the occasion of the death of sixth Panchen Lama Erdeni (Lobsang Palden Yeshe, 1738–1780)), the original of which he received from the mandarin who translated the text into Mongol.[120]

Compared with the letters by Contancin, Amiot's letters do not constitute the same systematic presentation of the gazette or of the rule and governance of the emperor, though by their nature they do represent a view of the Qing government. They appear in the first place as annual reports, in the words of Amiot, "of the main events which have taken place in the course of this year [= 1779–1780], chosen from among those which I believe deserve some attention, or which may help to bring to the fore what is happening in our Tartaro-Chinese Court."[121] As already appeared from the analysis above, his selection was determined by multiple factors: events reported in the gazettes in the months preceding the letter, follow-ups of certain events that were reported in a previous letter, questions raised by Bertin, personal interests of

114 *MCC*, vol. 11, p. 502.

115 E.g. *MCC*, vol. 11, pp. 512, 514; vol. 13, p. 418; vol. 14, p. 560; vol. 15, p. 328.

116 E.g. *MCC*, vol. 11, p. 559 (gazettes of the past year); p. 609 (list of criminals in the gazette of this year); vol. 13, p. 454 (edicts of the past month).

117 E.g. *MCC*, vol. 11, pp. 559, 594, 601; vol. 15, p. 297 (emperor); *MCC*, vol. 11, p. 585 (A-gui).

118 *MCC*, vol. 11, p. 559; vol. 13, p. 429.

119 *MCC*, vol. 14, p. 536.

120 *MCC*, vol. 9, pp. 446–447.

121 *MCC*, vol. 9, p. 6. Notice also *MCC*, vol. 9, pp. 441–454, which is an example of a letter that intends to report on recent developments, without any indication of specific other purpose.

Amiot, etc. Amiot is of the opinion that the reader of these texts "will be able to form an almost fair idea of the Government of this great Prince in particular & of the nature of the Government in general."[122] Further clarifying his selection, Amiot explains that he tries to present topics that he deems to be of some interest to his correspondent, as in the case when he introduces the new topic of literature and the way "this important subject" is managed.[123] He also edited the texts in accordance with his purpose: "I only took what is essential in [the emperor's] writing: what I extracted is more than enough to give you an idea of how he governs."[124] At times, Amiot even tries to imagine what Bertin would feel about the topics, as in the instance of a report on the problems caused by successive years of drought: "It is time that I turn your eyes away from [such] spectacle that cannot fail to provoke your sensitivity and sadden your heart."[125]

By contrast, the more personal interaction with Bertin is absent from the manuscript of Bréquigny 10, only being preserved in the introduction. In this translation of two months of the gazette, Bourgeois' main objective appears to be to present the gazette itself in the most comprehensive way possible, with a strict and full report of events that took place during that period. In this way, Bourgeois also stated that he wanted to substantiate the instructive role of the gazette, and how officials might find rules of conduct in them. The Bréquigny 10 manuscript, however, does not include insertions with personal comments on the emperor and his government.[126]

In addition to Amiot's and Bourgeois' own objectives one can keep in mind that Bertin himself also had a purpose in publishing their letters. In an anonymous introduction to the five letters included in volume 15 of *Mémoires concernant les Chinois*, the publication's purpose is made explicit: the various letters could be used "to make the Chinese more and more known & to give exact notions about their government, their habits and their customs."[127]

For Amiot, his insistence on the use of documents such as gazettes in the analysis of the Chinese way of governing is also a reaction to a perceived problem of what he describes as "popular rumours," which were in his eyes a source for European publications about China:

> ... I avoid with great care to speak of things which are based only on popular rumours. It would be hoped that all those who write from distant

122 *MCC*, vol. 15, p. 315.
123 *MCC*, vol. 9, p. 60.
124 *MCC*, vol. 9, p. 41.
125 Letter by Amiot (20 May 1786), *MCC*, vol 13, p. 428.
126 BnF, Bréquigny 10, p. 1; also in Walter (2008), p. 330; on the instructive role, see also below.
127 *MCC*, vol 15, p. 28; the introduction does not appear in Bréquigny 3, fol. 34v.

> countries would do the same; they would not expose themselves to the drawbacks of giving for certain facts the fantasies which only existed in the imagination of a few idlers who do not even know to maintain likelihood.[128]

Related to this, Amiot is very critical of the derogatory description of China that Pierre Sonnerat (1748–1814)[129] published in his *Voyage aux Indes orientales et a la Chine*. Sonnerat was a French explorer and naturalist, whose works are known for the description of numerous species of plants and animals.[130] On his travels between 1774 and 1781 by order of King Louis XV, he stayed for some months in Canton in 1776–1777. But China, which had been his long-sought goal, turned out to be a total disappointment for Sonnerat. He was confined to a place on the outskirts of Canton, his freedom of movement restricted by constant surveillance, and his explorations and studies rendered sterile.[131] As a result, his frustration turned into spite. This is clearly reflected in the report of his sojourn, which contains many candid judgmental statements regarding the Chinese and the perception of China communicated by the Jesuits. His account concludes with the remark that "the Chinese form a nation as contemptible in its character as in its ignorance,"[132] which is also quoted by Amiot.[133] Echoing the exasperation of the disillusioned European traders and voicing the bitterness of his personal disappointment, Sonnerat presents a view on China that clearly differs from the one proposed by the Jesuit missionaries. In his reaction, Amiot is in turn outspoken about Sonnerat's depiction of China:

> Every impartial and enlightened reader will not allow to be imposed upon him the accounts of a Traveller who describes a country he has neither seen nor been able to see, who defines a nation he does not know and which he has not been able to know, and who characterizes a government of which he does not have even the slightest idea.[134]

---

128 *MCC*, vol. 9, p. 7.

129 For an account of his life and work, see Ly-Tio-Fane (1976).

130 Sonnerat (1782), vol. 2, first chapter "De la Chine" pp. 1–37; there is also an English translation: Pierre Sonnerat, *A Voyage to the East-Indies and China, Performed by Order of Lewis XV, Between the Years 1774 and 1781*, 3 vols., Calcutta: Stuart and Cooper, 1788, vol. 2, pp. 178–235: "Of China."

131 Ly-Tio-Fane (1976), pp. 18–19.

132 Sonnerat (1782), vol. 2, p. 37.

133 *MCC*, vol. 11, p. 559.

134 Ibidem.

Amiot's reaction to Sonnerat underscores that his own account is largely based on the perspective of a high cultural elite and how – in Amiot's descriptions – an informant's trustworthiness depended on his social status:

> Let's tell the truth, Mr. Sonnerat neither had nor could have conversations with educated Chinese. The Chinese with whom it has been possible for him to talk & converse are Boatmen, Porters, *Compradors*, *Hanists* & a few Merchants or Negotiators. You will readily agree that what such characters *have told themselves* about the great objects of the customs of the Government, of politics, of Religion, of the Sciences and of the Arts of the Chinese Nation could not counterbalance the testimony of so many Missionaries who have lived in China for twenty, thirty & even forty years, who have known the language of the country, read the Books, frequented the Greats, the Sçavans, the Literati & men of all classes.[135]

Sonnerat criticized the Jesuits because they "represented the Chinese in the most favourable light, & painted them with the brightest colours,"[136] and thus disguised their "sacred despotism":[137]

> Since the Chinese had to serve as the basis of their system, they had to represent the despot who governed them, as a prince enjoying a sacred & absolute authority over innumerable peoples, & hiding his policy & his decrees under an impenetrable veil for the vulgar. They were to present at the same time the Chinese as a gentle, humane, happy & satisfied people under the guidance of such a father, skilled in agriculture, commerce & the arts, governed by wise laws, & in the moral & civil position that all men must aspire to.[138]

In Sonnerat's eyes, the French "economists" (i.e. the physiocrats) revived in their agronomical lectures "the fables which the Jesuits had reported of the commerce and the government of China":

> The day when the Emperor descends from his throne to the plough has been celebrated in all their writings; they recommended this vain

135 *MCC*, vol. 11, p. 545; italics in original. '*Hanists*' refers to the Cohong (*gonghang* 公行), the guild of Chinese merchants or *hongs* who operated the import-export monopoly in Canton; see also note in Sonnerat (1782), vol. 2, p. 10.

136 Sonnerat (1782), vol. 2, p. 2.

137 Sonnerat (1782), vol. 2, p. 3.

138 Sonnerat (1782), vol. 2, p. 3.

> ceremony, which is as frivolous as the worship rendered by the Greeks to Ceres, & which does not prevent thousands of Chinese from starving to death, or exposing their children, by the inability to provide in their livelihood.[139]

Sonnerat himself is of the opinion that the Chinese are a "people of slaves."[140] Amiot, for his part, hopes that the edicts of the emperor taken from the gazette will prevent Bertin from believing such statements:

> Of this swarm of Travellers who boldly decide on the Religion, Laws, Mores and Usages, & c. of Peoples of which they hardly know the name & of which they have not even seen the first surface, [I hope] you will not believe them, I say, on their word, when they say that the Chinese Monarch is a despot, in all the extent of the odious meaning that one attaches to this word, and that the People over whom he reigns is only a people of slaves, which only fear contains within the outer limits of duty. For this is what one dares to print every day, even in France, where one has so much information to know China as it was in its primitive constitution, as it was preserved for thirty centuries despite so many revolutions that agitated it, & as it is still today under the domination of the Tartars-Manchus.[141]

The example of his refutation of Sonnerat shows how Amiot consciously used the information contained in the gazettes to transmit a certain image of the emperor and his government.

Earlier, in the comparison between the printed and manuscript versions of the case of Jin Congshan and Amiot's reaction to the vision of Cornelius de Pauw, it was already pointed out that Amiot did not consider the Qianlong emperor to be a despot. Besides the idea that the emperor of China follows the law, another argument used to support this vision is that the emperor acts in consultation with his officials. In the discussion with Sonnerat, Amiot writes: "This is how business both large and small is handled here. It is always the Sovereign who concludes them; but he only concludes them after having taken the advice of his Council, or his Ministries."[142] Amiot's letters can be read from this perspective: there is a continuous interaction between proposals and actions by high officials, and the response of the emperor. The gazettes,

139 Sonnerat (1782), vol. 2, p. 4.
140 Sonnerat (1782), vol. 2, p. 5.
141 *MCC*, vol. 13, pp. 499–500.
142 *MCC*, vol. 13, p. 499.

specifically in the genre of *tizou shijian*, which focuses on memorialised (*tizou*) documents, contributed to this interplay between different actors in Amiot's letters.

3.2.5 *Supplement through Personal Contacts*

Besides the gazette, Amiot could also avail himself of first-hand information. Compared to Perroni and Contancin who lived in Canton, Amiot was in a unique position: not only was he located in Beijing, but his frequent contacts with the court allowed him to have access to information that the others did not have. This can be observed from brief remarks such as "through an important person (*Grand*) from the Emperor's suite, I could get details of what would have taken place in Gêhol [= Rehe]"[143] or "I was told that when [A-gui] was in the presence of His Majesty, he laid down a large topographical map of the places ..."[144] The descriptions of several happenings are indeed not only based on texts but also on the testimony of eyewitnesses. Examples of this include the events related to the prompt action by Chief Grand Councillor A-gui 阿桂 when a lightning strike caused a fire near Xizhimen 西直門 and burned down a pavilion in June 1783;[145] a ceremony performed by actors in the palace for those who were condemned to death in the same year;[146] the fact that A-gui was secretly informed by eunuchs that the Emperor was far from cured and in fact was hiding his illness in early 1784;[147] and the spring colloquium on the classics (*jingyan* 經筵) in March 1786.[148] In certain cases, Amiot refers to his own presence at ceremonies, such as the celebration of the emperor's 70th birthday (*wan shou* 萬壽) in 1780 (QL45), where the French missionaries offered some gifts to the emperor (porcelains of the Royal Manufacture of France, and in particular two small cups with their saucers and a sugar bowl).[149] At one occasion in 1777, a eunuch informs Amiot about the imperial decisions concerning memorials about an anti-Christian incident in Shaanxi. These memorials, Amiot notes, did not appear in the gazettes.[150] Amiot uses such first-hand information to provide context for the official texts. Conversely, these events may have been what prompted him to select the corresponding documents in the first place.

143 *MCC*, vol. 9, p. 7.
144 *MCC*, vol. 9, p. 27.
145 *MCC*, vol. 11, pp. 509–512.
146 *MCC*, vol. 11, pp. 555–558; A-gui attended the ceremony.
147 *MCC*, vol. 11, p. 581.
148 *MCC*, vol. 13, pp. 487–489.
149 *MCC*, vol. 9, p. 11. Amiot was also present at the ceremony for the emperor's 75th anniversary in 1785 (wrongly mentioned as 85th anniversary) and hopes to be present at the 76th anniversary (*MCC*, vol. 13, p. 505).
150 *MCC*, vol. 15, p. 285.

Amiot's letters are thus marked by an interaction between written sources and personal contacts. It is striking that, among the high officials mentioned by Amiot, three appear more frequently than others: A-gui 阿桂 (1717–1797), Manchu General and Chief Grand Councillor, Yu Minzhong 于敏中 (1714–1779), Qing official and writer, and Li Shiyao 李侍堯 (?–1788), high official with several positions as Governor-General. The most important among them is certainly A-gui, and Amiot does not hide his admiration for him: "You will undoubtedly say that Akoui is my Hero," Amiot writes to Bertin, "I do not deny it. I see in him a host of precious qualities which make me esteem & love him; but I do not blind myself on his account, I do him justice."[151] It appears that some other Jesuits had personal contacts with these three officials as well, and that Bertin closely followed reports about them. The exchange of letters between Peking and Paris confirms these contacts.

Unique documents in this regard are two drawings of A-gui and Yu Minzhong made by the Jesuit painter Giuseppe Panzi (1734-before 1812). Panzi arrived in China in 1771 and had a long, seemingly unremarkable career as a painter at the Qing court. Only a handful of works can be attributed to him, some of which were sent to Henri Bertin and served as basis for engravings that were inserted in *Mémoires concernant les Chinois*. These include an engraving of a portrait of the Qianlong emperor made by François Nicholas Martinet (1731–1804) after a portrait by Panzi (1773) in volume 1 (1776),[152] and an engraving of a portrait of Joseph-Marie Amiot made by Isidore-Stanislas Helman (1743–1806) after a portrait by Giuseppe Panzi (1789) in volume 15 (1791).[153] The portraits of A-gui and Yu Minzhong also seem to have been drawn at the initiative of Bertin. In the draft for an answer to the letter that Panzi sent to Bertin (Peking, 10 November 1779), Bertin writes that he is interested in paintings of officials, and that he "will not be angry to receive a portrait of A-gui,

---

151 MCC, vol. 11, p. 514; see also *MCC*, vol. 9, p. 26: "[The emperor] cast his eyes on Akoui, his Prime Minister, and believed that nothing would be impossible for a man of such genius as his and of an active nature that no obstacle was capable of repelling."; *MCC*, vol. 13, p. 458: "The reputation of the great General is in all respects so well established here that from the Emperor down to the least of his subjects, both Manchus and Chinese, no one has tried to disapprove of him in anything."

152 See Cordier (1913), p. 442; Walravens & Steinicke (2014), p. 63; Choi (2015), pp. 53–55; Lee Chao Ying (2016), p. 150; the portrait was also translated into a freestanding figure in Sèvres biscuit porcelain and a porcelain plaque.

153 The portrait of Amiot was sent to Bertin in 1789. It is kept in Bibliothèque Nationale de France (BnF), Départment des estampes et photographies, N-4. An engraving appeared opposite the frontispiece in *MCC*, vol. 15. See Cordier (1913), p. 442; Walravens & Steinicke (2014), p. 59; Choi (2015), pp. 56–57 (note 33); Lee Chao Ying (2016), p. 156. The portrait reproduced in Beurdeley (1997), p. 186 (Inst. 1515, fol. Iii) and Lee Chao Ying (2016), p. 153 is a later watercolour (1820).

ILLUSTRATION 17 Drawing of Yu Minzhong 于敏中 by Giuseppe Panzi (c. 1780): BnF, Bréquigny 114, fol. 175r

in case [Panzi] made one, and one of Li Shiyao, if the latter however, knows to appreciate what [Bertin] has done for him."[154] From a letter of Panzi in the following year (Peking, 5 August 1780) we know that he has started to make

154 Letter from Panzi to Bertin (Peking, 10 November 1779), in Cordier (1913), p. 435.

ILLUSTRATION 18 Drawing of A-gui 阿桂 by Giuseppe Panzi (c. 1780): BnF, Bréquigny 114, fol. 177r

portraits (*Ritratti*) of Amiot and A-gui and that he hopes to transmit them to Bertin at the occasion of the next envoy.[155] It is unclear how far the portraits were advanced, but in an episode told in a letter of Amiot at the end of the

155 Letter from Panzi to Bertin (Peking, 5 August 1780), in Cordier (1913), p. 436.

year (Peking, 4 November 1780), Amiot explains how he finally managed to obtain some portraits. Amiot had just received some bottles of "vin de grave" (Bordeaux wine) from Bertin. They arrived without any damage in Beijing. Amiot opened the first bottle with Panzi, when he was for a few days of rest at the graveyard of Zhengfusi 正福寺. Amiot notices that "two or three shots of this excellent Bordeaux wine, in a country where we are so little accustomed to drink good wine, revive numb spirits and give diligence to the laziest." He adds that he had the proof of this effect on Panzi, by demanding from him the portraits of A-gui and Yu Minzhong, at least by pencil, to be sent to Bertin. Panzi added a few verses to the portraits, which incited Amiot to do the same in order to add them below the portraits.[156] It should be noticed that earlier in that year Yu Minzhong, whom Amiot considered "one of the greatest lights of Chinese literature,"[157] had died (14 January 1780 (QL44/12/8)).[158] Thus Panzi may have made these drawings on the basis of a drawing or painting made before his death. From a letter of Bertin to Panzi, dated 16 November 1781, we know that Bertin received the portraits sent by Amiot.[159] These portraits, which to our knowledge have never been reproduced, are now preserved in BnF, Bréquigny 114, together with the laudatory verses by Panzi (in Italian) and by Amiot (in French).[160] In the same letter Bertin also mentions that he did not receive the portraits of Cibot [= Pierre-Martial Cibot (1727–1780)] and Delcon [= Nathanael Burger OFM (1733–1780), bishop of Shanxi-Shaanxi (1777–1780),

156 Letter of Amiot to Bertin (Peking, 4 November 1780), Inst. 1516, pp. 261–264 = 4 unnumbered fols = [3v–4r]; this final part is not included in the reproduction of the letter in *MCC*, vol. 9, pp. 60–64.

157 *MCC*, vol. 9, p. 45.

158 Letter of Amiot to Bertin (Peking, 26 September 1780), Inst. 1516, p. 245 (p. 1); *MCC*, vol. 9, pp. 45–46: "He died near the end of the twelfth month of the forty-fourth year of Qianlong." According to the Baidu record it was on 12/8: web.archive.org/web/20210528214331/https://baike.baidu.com/item/%E4%BA%8E%E6%95%8F%E4%B8%AD.

159 Letter of Bertin to Panzi (Paris, 16 November 1781); Cordier (2013), pp. 437–438; Inst. 1523, fol. 118r. Bertin acknowledges the receipt of the letter of 5 Aug. 1780, as well as the receipt of the portraits of A-gui and Yu Minzhong, sent by Amiot.

160 BnF, Bréquigny 114, fol. 171r: verses in Italian [by Panzi] about A-gui and Yu Minzhong; fol. 1[74r]: verses in French [by Amiot] to be put below the portrait of Yu Minzhong; fol. 175r: "Portrait du célébre yu-ming-tchoung par le Signor Panzi. Peintre italien au service de l'Empereur de la Chine pour la mission françoise"; fol. 176r: portrait; fol. 177r: verses in French [by Amiot] to be put below the portrait of A-gui; fol. 178r: "Portrait du général Akoui par le Signor Panzi. Peintre italien au service de l'Empereur de la Chine pour la mission françoise"; fol. 179r: portrait. Walravens & Steinicke (2014) write (without further reference), p. 68 n. 53 that the portraits of the two statesmen produced as part of the documentation of the colonial campaigns for the Hall of Purple Shining have been preserved (in private collections); and that these could be copies by Panzi.

titular bishop of Delcon], which Panzi announced, and Bertin does not know whether they were added to the envoy. He particularly regrets not having received the portrait of Cibot (who had died), and hopes that Panzi can repair the loss in case he made a copy of it.[161] It likely arrived later, since a portrait of Cibot by Panzi (probably made in 1780) can be found in the collection of Bertin's correspondence in the Institut de France.[162]

In addition to A-gui and Yu Minzhong, there is also Li Shiyao, whose portrait was also requested by Bertin in the above-mentioned letter, and about whom one finds regular reports based on the gazettes in *Mémoires concernant les Chinois*. Before becoming Governor-General of Guizhou-Yunnan in 1777, he had been acting Governor-General of Guangdong-Guangxi in 1757 and 1759, and Governor-General of the same provinces in 1759–1761 and 1767–1777. In this function he had to deal with foreigners arriving in Canton, including French missionaries who intended to serve at the court in Beijing.[163] From a list of "*bagatelles*" (trivia) sent by Amiot to Bertin and added to the letter requesting the portraits, it appears that Amiot had (in)direct contact with Li Shiyao. Among the trivial gifts accompanying this letter, there are nine small balls of *Pou-eulh-tcha* (= Pu'er cha 普洱茶), which Li Shiyao (or the official who had gone – as will be explained below – to judge him) brought back from Yunnan and offered to Amiot to be sent, as he said, "to his friends from Europe."[164]

In a letter to Amiot sent on 16 November 1781 (same date as the letter to Panzi), it becomes clear that there had been longer contacts even between Bertin and Li Shiyao, probably via the missionaries.

> I sent a few years ago gifts to Li Shiyao, then Viceroy of Canton, whom I knew to have treated the French well on more than one occasion, and of whom I wished that he would be even better in their favour (even to engage, if it had been possible and if his master allowed him, a direct

161 Letter of Bertin to Panzi (Paris, 16 November 1781); Cordier (2013), pp. 437–438; Inst. 1523, fol. 118r.

162 Inst. 1519, fol. 92v. It is put together with the last letter of Cibot to Bertin, dated 3 August 1780 (Cibot died 8 August 1780). It is a drawing with black and red pencil. A reproduction can be found in Huard, Sonolet & Wong (1959), p. 19; Picard (1973), ill. 12; Beurdeley (1997), p. 187 (where is it wrongly mentioned as a print (gravure) on the basis of a drawing by Panzi); Walravens & Steinicke (2014), p. 58, ill. 1. Online reproduction: https://photo.rmn.fr/ark:/36255/14-535066?posInSet=2&queryId=059aff69-ab29-4484-8f54-1bf536c02312.

163 *ECCP*, vol. 1, p. 480; see examples in Fu Lo-shu (1966), vol. 1, pp. 217–219 (a case involving English merchants in 1759), pp. 251–252 (two French missionaries in March 1769), p. 273 (regulations stipulating that only those Westerners who wish to live in China permanently are allowed in Beijing in Aug. 1774).

164 BnF, Bréquigny 114, fol. 172r–173v: fol. 172r.

> correspondence between him and me); I attached a short note to these presents which was to be handed over to him with them. When they arrived in Guangzhou, Li Shiyao was removed from office, and Mr. Bourgeois having noticed this to me, I wrote him to try to send to him, despite his disgrace, what I had destined to him.[165]

The arrest and condemnation of Li Shiyao, as well as the confiscation of his property, were reported in the letter of Amiot to Bertin (10 September 1780) and published in volume 9 of *Mémoires concernant les Chinois*.[166] In 1781 Bertin is informed that his presents are not among the confiscated goods.

> I see from Mr. Bourgeois' reply of January 4th, 1781, and from other letters, that these presents are in the hands of Mr. Bourgeois, who has them reserved to be handed over to Li Shiyao in a happier time. As the main motive for my action still remains, I learned with pleasure, despite Li Shiyao's faults, that this shipment did not reach him soon enough to have been included in the confiscation of his property.[167]

Unlike Amiot, Bourgeois himself was not a court Jesuit but the superior and administrator of the French mission, and it is not clear how far his personal contacts reached. Yet, even at the moment of translating the gazettes in 1788, he could avail of the information transmitted by his fellow missionaries who had direct contact with the court.[168] Occasionally he himself also attended ceremonies at the court. For instance, he reports that during the ceremony in the palace on New Year's Day of the fifty-second year of the Qianlong reign (18 February 1787), which he attended, the missionaries were informed about the unrest in Taiwan and told that the emperor would not be notified about it until the next day.[169]

These personal contacts shed a different light on the criteria that were used in the selection of certain topics to be communicated to Europe. They were at least partially determined by direct and indirect relationships between the missionaries and the officials. Moreover, as in the case of Li Shiyao, there were even some connections with European officials such as Bertin.

---

165 Letter of Bertin to Amiot (Paris, 16 November 1781); Inst. 1523, fol. 127v.

166 *MCC*, vol. 9, pp. 41–44.

167 Letter of Bertin to Amiot (Paris, 16 November 1781); Inst. 1523, fols. 127v–128r.

168 See for example the Letter of Bourgeois to Bertin (Beijing, 10 October 1788): BnF, Bréquigny 2, fols. 211v–212r, in which he reports that they were informed about the danger the Emperor encountered during his recent hunt.

169 BnF, Bréquigny 10, p. 4.

3.3 Presence of the Gazettes in *Mémoires concernant les Chinois*

Unlike the translated gazettes of Bréquigny 10 which remained manuscript, those that were published in *Mémoires concernant les Chinois* reached a wide audience. They give an idea about how the European readership of the late eighteenth century was informed about the Chinese gazette and about China. After a general overview of the topics that were reported, the case of the *Siku quanshu* is taken as a specific example. This highlights some prominent characteristics of the presentation of the gazette in *Mémoires concernant les Chinois*.

3.3.1 *References to the Gazettes*

References to the gazettes can be found in certain thematic articles in volumes 1–8 of *Mémoires concernant les Chinois* but are more explicit in the letters in the later volumes 9–15. Before focussing on these later volumes, the following section gives a short overview of those earlier references to the gazettes in the collection.

The earliest references appear in volume 1 (the report by Ko and Yang, see below). In the subsequent volumes there are only a few marginal direct references to the gazettes. For instance, in Cibot's treatise on filial piety it is mentioned that "Soldiers & Officers are named in the gazettes, and their name resounds throughout the Empire."[170] There is also an anonymous text "on the general idea of China and its relations with Europe," not written by missionaries but by the unidentified Mxxx. It includes a short description of the gazettes, which in perspective is very similar to the one by Contancin and the one found in Du Halde's *Description*, insisting on the instructive value of the gazettes:

> Lastly, nothing is more instructive for the Mandarins, & more capable of containing them in the same order as the Gazette, which is printed in Peking, and which is spread in the Provinces …[171]

As discussed before, the gazettes are mentioned in a debate about the invention of printing in China, which is part of a critical review of the aforementioned *Recherches philosophiques sur les Egyptiens et les Chinois* by Cornelius de Pauw in the second volume of *Mémoires concernant les Chinois*. Gazettes

---

170 MCC, vol. 4, p. 155 ("Doctrine ancienne et nouvelle des Chinois sur la piété filiale"). On the military rewards or call for them published in the gazettes, see also a note in *MCC*, vol. 7, p. 292 (Amiot, "L'Art militaire des Chinois").

171 *MCC*, vol. 5, p. 39 ("Idée générale de la Chine et de ses relations avec l'Europe [de Mxxx et non des missionnaires]").

also appear directly or indirectly in other treatises. Particularly Amiot drew information from gazettes. Sometimes he mentioned his dependence on them explicitly, as is the case with his treatise on the subjugation of the 'Miaozi' 苗子 (= 'Miaozu' 苗族):

> The report which I have the honour to send to you today, was drawn only from the Gazettes which the Court sends to the Banners, or from what is published by order of the Sovereign.[172]

Noteworthy in this quotation is the reference to the gazettes designated to the banners. Elsewhere in volume 15, a similar reference is made to the "gazette of the Tartar banners" ("gazette des bannières tartares"), clearly distinguished from the one of the Empire.[173] Other documents by Amiot in these volumes also quote imperial edicts or memorials that may have been taken from gazettes.[174]

Extensive quotations from the gazettes in *Mémoires concernant les Chinois* appear in about eighteen letters which were published in volumes 9 and 11–15 (not in volume 10). They were all written by Amiot, except one by Bourgeois. These letters, however, do not necessarily appear in chronological order. Due to problems in the mailing of 1779, the letters of that year arrived much later than those of the following years. The result is that the letters of the 1779 envoy were only published in volume 15 (published in 1791),[175] whereas the letters from 1780 to 1787 appeared more or less in chronological order in volumes 9 to 14 (published between 1783 and 1789). In an introduction to the letter section of volume 15, the editors point out another reason for this late publication: despite the numerous extracts from letters that had already been published from a correspondence that lasted twenty years, there were still some letters that had been left aside:

172 MCC, vol. 3, p. 387 ("Lettre sur la réduction des Miao-tsée en 1775").

173 MCC, vol. 15, p. 122 (Cibot, "Suite du Parallèle des Mœurs et Usages des Chinois, avec les Mœurs et Usages décrits dans le livre d'Esther" (Sequel to the Parallel between the manners and customs of the Chinese, and the manners and customs described in the book of Esther); in the same text (pp. 133, 135) there are two other brief references to the gazette.

174 See for instance in Amiot, "Observations sur le livre de M. Pxx, intitulé: 'Recherches philosophiques sur les Égyptiens et les Chinois'. Extrait d'une lettre de M. Amiot à Mxxx, du 28 septembre 1777" (Observations on the book of M. Pxx, entitled Philosophical Research on the Egyptians and the Chinese. Extract from a letter of M. Amiot to Mxxx, 28 September 1777), MCC, vol. 6, pp. 275–345: p. 293ff.

175 Inst. 1524, fols. 16r–23r: Letter of Bertin to Amiot (31 December 1784): fol. 16r: the letters of 25 July, 5 and 16 September 1779, and 22 November 1783 have arrived; they were planned to be published in MCC, vol. 11, but in fact were only published in MCC, vol. 15.

> We realized that we had not made use of various Letters that could be used to make the Chinese more and more known, and to give exact notions of their Government, their usages, and their customs.[176]

In order to "repair this omission," the editors published some (older) letters, most of which are based on material from the gazettes.

Rearranged in order by date of sending, the resulting collection of published letters is as follows: 31 July 1778 (= Bourgeois); 25 July 1779, 5 September 1779 (in vol. 15); 13 August 1780, 10 September 1780, 26 September 1780, 4 November 1780, 17 August 1781 (in vol. 9); 22 November 1783, 2 October 1784, 19 November 1784, 29 November 1784 (in vol. 11); 15 October 1785 (in vol. 12); 20 November 1785 (in vol. 15); 20 May 1786, 14 September 1786 (in vol. 13); 25 January 1787, 19 November 1787 (in vol. 14).[177]

Usually there is an interval of more or less one year between the date of sending (related to the annual envoy and reception of letters), but in certain cases a series of successive letters was sent (e.g. 13 August, 10 September, 26 September and 4 November 1780; or 2 October, 19 November, 29 November 1784). The letters are also of various length, ranging from a few to over forty pages in the printed format.

The difference is obvious between these printed letters and the manuscript in BnF, Bréquigny 10, which is a translation of all gazettes from 27 February 1788 to 1 May 1788, more recent than the last printed letter on the gazettes. Herein the topics are not selected by Bourgeois, but by the gazettes themselves. The theme that dominates the gazettes in Bréquigny 10 is the "rebellion" in Taiwan. There is also a manuscript letter by Amiot to Bertin, dated 1 July 1788, that can be read as a summary of the first three months of QL53 contained in Bréquigny 10, similar to the ones that were published in *Mémoires concernant les Chinois*.[178]

3.3.2 *Topics Reported on the Basis of the Chinese Gazette*

Though most topics for which Amiot used the gazettes appear without a title (except for the topics in volume 15), one can tentatively delineate certain categories under which his descriptions could be classified in order to give an idea

176 *MCC*, vol. 15, p. 281.

177 There are also brief references in the letter by Raux (17 Nov. 1786) and Grammont (21 March 1789) (in vol. 15).

178 Inst. 1517, fols. 34r–41v: Letter of Amiot to Bertin (1 July 1788). At the start of his letter, Amiot states that he cannot but say anything about "our august old man, the oldest as well as the longest [in reign] of all the known sovereigns, since he counts the seventy-seventh year of his age and the fifty-third of his glorious reign." Amiot depicts the image of an emperor who has a good health and who is still in full control.

of what he reported on in *Mémoires concernant les Chinois*. These categories correspond to those described by Contancin, by Amiot himself, but also by modern accounts of mid-Qing gazettes. A detailed overview with identification of the Chinese primary sources can be found in the "Guide to the sources" at the end of this book.

- Rituals: Feast and celebrations for the 70th birthday (*wanshou* 萬壽) of the Qianlong emperor, with reference to the visit of the sixth Panchen Lama Erdeni 班禪額爾德尼 (Lobsang Palden Yeshe,1738–1780) (QL44/8/18 = 27 September 1779);[179] letter of the Emperor to the Dalai Lama 達賴喇嘛 (Jampäl Gyatso, 1758–1804) at the occasion of the death of this Panchen Lama Erdeni;[180] feast for elderly (*qiansouyan* 千叟宴) (QL50/1/6 = 14 February 1785);[181]
- Major actions by high officials:
  - A-gui 阿桂 (1717–1797),[182] Manchu General and Chief Grand Councillor: his initiatives for flood control of the Huanghe;[183] A-gui and He-shen

179 *MCC*, vol. 9, pp. 1–64: Extraits de diverses lettres écrites par M. Amiot, missionnaire en Chine, en 1780, de Pékin (Extracts from various letters written by M. Amiot, missionary in China, in 1780, from Peking).

MCC, vol. 9, pp. 6–24: La seconde, du 13 Août, sur la fête de *Ouan-cheou* de l'Empereur (The second, 13 August, on the feast of *Ouan-cheou* of the Emperor); Inst. 1516, pp. 238–244: pp. 1–14: Feast of the 70th birthday of the Qianlong emperor, including the translation of an imperial edict, dated Qianlong 44/8/19. *MCC*, vol. 9, pp. 7–11: (QL44/8/19 = 28 Sept. 1779); Inst. 1516, pp. 239–240: pp. 3–5: Edict of the Emperor of QL44/8/19 [>18] concerning the tour he will undertake and the (minor) ceremonies because of the death of his mother. *MCC*, vol. 9, pp. 11–17: (QL45/1/1 = 5 Febr. 1780); Inst. 1516, pp. 240–242: pp. 5–10: Edict of Emperor QL45/1/1 concerning various benefits at the occasion of the celebration; Edict of Emperor QL44/11/13 [>6] concerning the incomplete execution of the rites by the Emperor. *MCC*, vol. 9, pp. 21–24: (QL44/11/19 = 26 Dec. 1779); Inst. 1516, pp. 243–244: pp. 12–14: Response by Taichangsi 太常寺 (QL44/11/19) and reaction of the Emperor.

180 *MCC*, vol. 9, pp. 446–453: 2°. Une lettre de l'Empereur au Talaï-lama (2nd, A letter from the Emperor to the Talaï-lama); Inst. 1516, pp. 278–280: pp. 15–20.

181 *MCC*, vol. 12, pp. 509–530: Extrait d'une lettre de M. Amiot, Ecrite de Péking le 15 Octobre 1785 (Extract from a letter by Mr. Amiot, Written from Peking on 15 October 1785).

MCC, vol. 12, p. 515: Confirmation of successor in Korea. *MCC*, vol. 12, pp. 515–516: Invitation to reception. *MCC*, vol. 12, p. 516: Offering of gifts. *MCC*, vol. 12, pp. 517, 527–528: Feast for elderly *qiansouyan* 千叟宴.

182 *ECCP*, vol. 1, pp. 6–8.

183 *MCC*, vol. 9, pp. 25–45: La troisieme, du 10 septembre 1780, sur les travaux d'Akoui pour prévenir le débordement du Hoang-ho, & sur Ly-che-yao, Gouverneur de Canton. Letter of 10 September 1780 (The third, 10 September 1780, on Akoui's works to prevent the overflowing of the Hoang-ho, & on Ly-che-yao, Governor of Canton); Inst. 1516, pp. 253–260: pp. 1–16.

MCC, vol. 9, pp. 27–28: Inst. 1516, p. 254: pp. 3–4: Early request by A-gui and the costs it will take. *MCC*, vol. 9, pp. 28–30: (QL44/12/13 = 19 Jan. 1780); Inst. 1516, pp. 254–255: pp. 4–5: Memorial by A-gui requesting grace for Li Yongji 李永吉. *MCC*, vol. 9, p. 30: Inst. 1516,

和珅 (1750–1799) are sent to Lanzhou 蘭州, which is under siege after a Muslim attack from Hezhou 河州;[184] various other activities, such as demanding the delay of the departure for the southern tour because of the emperor's illness, or writing a letter on the Hui (*huimin* 回民)[185]

- Li Shiyao 李侍堯 (?–1788):[186] his condemnation and dismissal as Governor-General of Guizhou-Yunnan (1777–1780);[187] his appointment as the new Governor-General of Shaanxi and Gansu;[188] new condemnation to exile[189]
- Yu Minzhong 于敏中 (1714–1779),[190] Qing official and writer: historical elegy; the family dispute regarding the division of his heritage[191]

---

p. 255: p. 5: De-cheng 德成 is sent to Henan. *MCC*, vol. 9, p. 30: Inst. 1516, p. 255: pp. 5–6: Subsidies for reparation works. *MCC*, vol. 9, p. 31: Inst. 1516, p. 255: p. 6: Answer of A-gui to De-cheng. *MCC*, vol. 9, pp. 32–34: Inst. 1516, pp. 255–256: pp. 6–8: Report by A-gui, Chen Huizu 陳輝祖 (1732–1783), Li Fenghan 李奉翰 (?–1799) and others on the achievement of the works and response by the Emperor. *MCC*, vol. 9, pp. 35–41: Inst. 1516, pp. 256–259: pp. 8–13: Further edict by the Emperor.

184 *MCC*, vol. 9, pp. 441–454: Extrait d'une lettre ecrite de Pé-king le 17 Août, par M. Amiot, Missionnaire, sur les services d'Akoui; & sur la mort du Pan-tchan Lama (Extract from a letter written from Peking on 17 August [1781], by Mr. Amiot, Missionary, on Akoui's services; & on the death of Pan-tchan Lama); Inst. 1516, pp. 271–280: pp. 1–20.
MCC, vol. 9, pp. 441–446: Extrait d'une lettre ecrite par M. Amiot, Missionnaire, contenant, 1°. Les services rendus par Akoui (Extract from a letter written by Mr. Amiot, Missionary, containing, 1st, the services rendered by Akoui); Inst. 1516, pp. 276–278: pp. 11–15.

185 *MCC*, vol. 11, pp. 580–609: Extrait d'une lettre de M. Amiot, Missionnaire, Ecrite de Péking, le 29 Novembre 1784 (Extract from a letter by Mr. Amiot, Missionary, Written from Peking, 29 November 1784); Inst. 1516: pp. 333–344: pp. 1–24.
MCC, vol. 11, pp. 580–585: Inst. 1516: pp. 333–335: pp. 1–5: A-gui demanding the delay of the departure. *MCC*, vol. 11, pp. 593–601: Inst. 1516: pp. 338–342: pp. 12–20: On the rebellious Huizu in Gansu. *MCC*, vol. 11, pp. 601–604: Inst. 1516: pp. 342–343: pp. 20–21: Letter on the Huizu by A-gui and answer of the Emperor. *MCC*, vol. 11, pp. 605–606: Inst. 1516: p. 343: p. 21: Rewards for the suppression of the rebellion.

186 *ECCP*, vol. 1, pp. 480–482.

187 *MCC*, vol. 9, pp. 41–44: (QL45/4/5 = 8 May 1780); Inst. 1516, pp. 259–260: pp. 13–15: Edict by the Emperor concerning the complot by Li Shiyao 李侍堯 et al. *MCC*, vol. 9, p. 44: Inst. 1516, p. 260: pp. 15–16: Condemnation of Li Shiyao.

188 On his appointment as new Governor, see previous note on A-gui. See also *MCC*, vol. 11, pp. 591–593: Inst. 1516: p. 338: pp. 11–12.

189 *MCC*, vol. 14, pp. 544–545: Inst. 1516, pp. 429–430: pp. 8–9: Summary of several events related to Li Shiyao: audiences with emperor; activities in Huang'an 黃安 (Hubei); condemnation to Yili 伊犁.

190 *ECCP*, vol. 2, pp. 942–944.

191 *MCC*, vol. 9, pp. 45–60: La quatrieme, du 26 septembre 1780, Éloge historique du Yu-ming-tchoung; Letter of 26 September 1780 (The fourth, 26 September 26, 1780, historical Elegy of Yu-ming-tchoung); Inst. 1516, pp. 245–252: pp. 1–15.

- Various cases of misbehaviour and punishment/demotion of officials or acquaintances: condemnation of former Governor Le-er-jin 勒爾謹 (?–1781); condemnation of a family member of Fu-long-an 福隆安 (1743 (1746?)-1784), who was in charge of the matters related to missionaries at the court,[192] for killing a mason;[193] dismissal of Fu-le-hun 富勒渾 (?–1790), Governor-General of Guangdong-Guangxi;[194] dismissal of Ya-de 雅德 (?–1801), Governor of Zhejiang,[195] etc.[196]
- Various rewards: edict on granting honorific titles to the Mongol members of the imperial family;[197] imperial visit to the Confucius temple (*xianshi*

MCC, vol. 9, pp. 47–53: Inst. 1516, pp. 246–248: pp. 3–8; Text by Yu Minzhong. *MCC*, vol. 9, pp. 53–56: (QL44/12/15 = 22 Dec. 1780); Inst. 1516, pp. 249–250: pp. 9–11: Elegy by the Emperor. *MCC*, vol. 9, pp. 56–60: Inst. 1516, pp. 250–251: pp. 11–14: Family dispute regarding the division of the heritage of Yu Minzhong.

192 *ECCP*, vol. 1, pp. 259–260.

193 *MCC*, vol. 9, p. 45: Inst. 1516, p. 260: p. 16: Demand to alleviate capital punishment by Fu-long-an.
MCC, vol. 11, pp. 515–568: Extrait d'une autre lettre de M. Amiot, Ecrite de Pé-king le 2 Octobre 1784 (Extract from another letter by Mr. Amiot, Written from Peking on 2 October 1784); Inst. 1516, pp. 308–332: pp. 1–50.
MCC, vol. 11, pp. 553–559; Inst. 1516, pp. 327–329: pp. 39–43: Family member of Fu-long-an killed a mason; case was investigated further. *MCC*, vol. 11, pp. 553–559; Inst. 1516, pp. 327–329: pp. 39–43: Condemnation of family member of Fu-long-an to be included in the gazette; easily 20 similar condemnations in the gazettes of the same year.

194 *MCC*, vol. 13, pp. 429–430: (QL51/4/28 = 25 May 1786); Inst. 1516, p. 357: pp. 17–18: Edict in response to Fu-le-hun.
MCC, vol. 13, pp. 437–440: (QL51/5/26 = 21 June 1786); Inst. 1516, pp. 360–364: pp. 24–28: Edict concerning the case of Fu-le-hun in response to Sun Shiyi 孫士毅 (1720–1796), Governor of Guangdong.
MCC, vol. 13, pp. 441–443: (QL51/6/1 = 26 June 1786); Inst. 1516, pp. 364–366: pp. 29–31: Edict concerning Yin Shijun 殷士俊, domestic worker of the demoted Fu-le-hun. *MCC*, vol. 13, pp. 443–448: (QL51/6/18 = 13 July 1786); Inst. 1516, pp. 366–368: pp. 31–37; same subject.

195 *MCC*, vol. 13, p. 458; Inst. 1516, p. 373: p. 48.

196 *MCC*, vol. 11, pp. 586–587; Inst. 1516: p. 336: pp. 7–8: Punishment of high officials.
MCC, vol. 13, pp. 449–450: (QL51/6/1 = /); Inst. 1516, pp. 368–369: pp. 37–39: Edict concerning misuse in distribution of money and rice in response to a report of the censorate (Duchayuan 都察院) on the basis of the information by Jiang Luyu 蔣魯玉, commoner from Hubei.

197 *MCC*, vol. 11, pp. 501–515: Extrait d'une lettre de M. Amiot, Ecrite de Pé-king le 22 Novembre 1783 (Extract from a letter by Mr Amiot, Written from Peking on 22 November 1783); Inst. 1516: pp. 287–294: fols [1r–8v].

miao 先師廟) with rewards for scholars and students;[198] at the occasion of the birth of the Emperor's first great-great-grandson (fifth generation) Zai-xi 載錫 (1784–1821), restauration of the titles to the child's father;[199] rewards to elderly people;[200] honorific title of Fengfu 奉福 to Xi-xian 希賢 and of Fengshou 奉壽 to Jue-long-a 覺隆阿,[201] etc.[202]

- Instruction: Examination of the officials on the *jing* 經 and *sishu* 四書;[203] edict on the monthly instruction of the people by the officials in response to the Censorate[204]
- Natural disasters in the provinces and relief offered by the officials or by order of the emperor: thunderstorm in Beijing and the burning down of one of the court's pavilions, and reaction of the emperor in response to A-gui's report about it;[205] edicts (with monetary subvention or tax reductions) concerning a drought in Jiangnan, Jiangxi, and Hubei;[206] earthquake in Sichuan;[207]

MCC, vol. 11, pp. 502–508: Chang-yu (QL47/10/4 = 8 Nov. 1783); Inst. 1516: pp. 288–290: fols. [2v–4v]: Edict on granting honorific titles to the Mongol members of the imperial family. *MCC*, vol. 11, p. 509: (QL48/1/10 = 11 Febr. 1783); Inst. 1516: p. 291: fol. [5r]: Ceremony.

198 *MCC*, vol. 11, pp. 587–589; Inst. 1516: pp. 336–337: pp. 8–9.

199 *MCC*, vol. 11, pp. 608–609; Inst. 1516: p. 344: pp. 23–24.

200 *MCC*, vol. 12, pp. 511–512.

201 *MCC*, vol. 12, pp. 513–515.

202 *MCC*, vol. 12, pp. 512–513: Call for promotion of unknown officials.

203 *MCC*, vol. 13, pp. 487–489: (QL51/2/6 = 5 March 1786); Inst. 1516, pp. 390–391: pp. 33–36.

204 *MCC*, vol, 13, pp. 494–499: (QL51/1/20 = 18 Febr. 1786); Inst. 1516, pp. 394–397: pp. 41–47.

205 *MCC*, vol. 11, pp. 509–514: (QL48/6/3 = 2 July 1783); Inst. 1516: pp. 291–293: fols [5r–7v].

206 *MCC*, vol. 13, pp. 421–422: (QL50/12/21 = 20 Jan. 1786); Inst. 1516, p. 352: pp. 7–8: Edict concerning drought in Jiangnan at the occasion of the audience with Li Feng 李封.
MCC, vol. 13, pp. 422–424: Autre Chang-yu (QL51/2/20 = 19 March 1786); Inst. 1516, pp. 352–353: pp. 8–10: Edict regarding grain prices in response to He Yucheng 何裕城 (1726–1790), Governor of Jiangxi.
MCC, vol. 13, pp. 424–426: (QL51/2/10 [= 20] = 19 March 1786); Inst. 1516, pp. 353–354: pp. 10–12: Edict regarding monetary subvention for drought in response to Wu Yuan 吳垣, Governor of Hubei.
MCC, vol. 13, pp. 427–428: (QL51/3/1 = 30 March 1786); Inst. 1516, pp. 355–356: pp. 14–15: Edict on tax reduction because of drought.
MCC, vol. 13, pp. 428–429: (QL51/3/28 = 26 April 1786); Inst. 1516, p. 356: pp. 15–16: Memorial by Bi Yuan 畢沅 (1730–1797), Governor of Henan concerning help because of drought.
MCC, vol. 13, pp. 454–457: (QL51/7/2 = 26 July 1786); Inst. 1516, pp. 371–373: pp. 43–47: Edict on paternal governance in response to Biyuan 畢沅, Governor of Henan.

207 *MCC*, vol. 13, pp. 453–454: Inst. 1516, pp. 370–371: pp. 42–43: Edict on earthquake in Sichuan, reported by Bao-ning 保寧 (?–1808), Governor of Sichuan.

floods in Hubei and Hunan;[208] state of the channels, related to the drought in Jiangnan, Henan, Shandong;[209] a solar eclipse,[210] etc.[211]

- Human conflicts: in Gansu between the red-headed and white-headed Muslims (*hongmao* 紅帽, *baimao* 白帽);[212] the White Lotus Sect (*Bailianjiao* 白蓮教) in Bazhou 霸州[213]
- Particular cases: the case of a living Buddha (*huofo* 活佛);[214] the case of the provincial student (*xiucai* 秀才), Jin Congshan 金從善 from Jinxian 錦縣, who accosted the Qianlong emperor during his October 1778 tour through Liaoning in order to petition him to proclaim a successor. Jin Congshan was condemned and executed[215]

---

208 MCC, vol. 13, pp. 451–453: (QL51/6/7 = 31 July 1786); Inst. 1516, pp. 369–370: pp. 40–42: Edict concerning floods in response to Yu Jin'ao 俞金鰲 (?–1793), Governor-General of Hubei and Hunan.

209 MCC, vol. 13, pp. 460–463; Inst. 1516, pp. 375–376: pp. 3–6.

210 MCC, vol. 13, pp. 478–485: (QL50/12/19 = 18 Jan. 1786); Inst. 1516, pp. 384–388: pp. 22–30.

211 MCC, vol. 13, pp. 433–435; Inst. 1516, pp. 359–360: pp. 21–23: Edict in response to an anonymous censor concerning famine.
MCC, vol. 13, pp. 429–430: (QL51/4/28 = 25 May 1786); Inst. 1516, p. 357: pp. 17–18: Edict concerning support in case of drought in response to Fu-le-hun 富勒渾 (?–1790), Governor-General of Guangdong-Guangxi.
MCC, vol. 13, p. 432; Inst. 1516, p. 358: pp. 19–20: Edict concerning gifts by foreign merchants, related to previous case.
MCC, vol. 14, pp. 536–561: Extrait d'une lettre de M. Amiot, Missionnaire, Ecrite de Péking, le 19 Novembre 1787 (Extract from a letter by Mr. Amiot, Missionary, Written from Peking, 19 November 1787); Inst. 1516, pp. 426–435: pp. 1–20.
MCC, vol. 14, pp. 536–541; Inst. 1516, pp. 426–428: pp. 2–6: Speech at the moment of the winter solstice (*dongzhi* 冬至).
MCC, vol. 14, pp. 545–546; Inst. 1516, p. 430: pp. 9–10: Memorial by Ji Huang 嵇璜 (?).
MCC, vol. 14, pp. 549–550; Inst. 1516, p. 431: pp. 11–12: On the harvest in Henan.

212 MCC, vol. 11, pp. 590–591; Inst. 1516: pp. 337–339: pp. 9–11.

213 MCC, vol. 15, pp. 282–283 (memorial); p. 283 (edict): 1. Rebellion des Sectaires à Pa-tcheou en 1777 (1. Rebellion of the Sectarians in Pa-tcheou in 1777); BnF, Bréquigny 3, fols. 34v–35v.

214 MCC, vol. 14, pp. 553–560; Inst. 1516, pp. 432–435: pp. 14–20.
MCC, vol. 14, pp. 553–557, 559; Inst. 1516, pp. 432–434: pp. 14–18: Case and edict. MCC, vol. 14, p. 558; Inst. 1516, p. 434: p. 17: Condemnation. MCC, vol. 14, pp. 559–560; Inst. 1516, pp. 434–435: pp. 18–19: Edict.

215 MCC, vol. 15, pp. 292–346: Extrait d'une lettre de M. Amiot, Ecrite de Péking, le 25 Juillet 1779 (Extract from a letter by Mr. Amiot, Written from Peking, 25 July 1779); BnF, Bréquigny 5, fols. 26r–58v; BnF, Bréquigny 3, fols. 59r–89v: MCC, vol. 15, pp. 297–315: 3. Ecrit de l'Empereur pour se justifier de ne pas déclarer le nom de son successeur (3. Writing by the Emperor to justify not declaring the name of his successor) (QL43/10/8 = 26 Nov. 1778); BnF, Bréquigny 5, fols. 29r–40r; BnF, Bréquigny 3, fols. 61v–72v: Edict by Emperor to justify himself.

- Christianity: the end of the persecution of the missionaries[216]
- Publication of books: on a book about distinguished military men presented to the emperor (*Zhaozhongci lie zhuan* 昭忠祠列傳, remained manuscript);[217] a new *huidian* 會典 (digest of statutes);[218] on the punishment of Wang Xihou 王錫侯 (1713–1777) for his criticism of the *Kangxi zidian* 康熙字典;[219] on the condemnation of the book *DaQing tianding yunshu* 大清天定運數 by Zhi Tianbao 智天豹;[220] poem of the emperor;[221] on the *Siku quanshu* 四庫全書 project.

This overview illustrates the wide variety of topics that were reported to Europe. Some of them are discussed in one letter, others in two or more. The

---

MCC, vol. 15, pp. 315–327: 4. Réponse de l'Empereur à la requête de Kin-Tsoung-chao (4. Response of the Emperor to the request of Kin-Tsoung-chao) (QL43/9/29 = 17 Nov. 1778); BnF, Bréquigny 5, fols. 40r–47r; BnF, Bréquigny 3, fols. 72v–79v: Answer of the Emperor.

MCC, vol. 15, pp. 328–335: Tché-y: 5. Condamnation de cet Auteur & de son livre (Tché-y: 5. Condemnation of this Author & his book) (QL43/10/10 = 28 Nov. 1778); BnF, Bréquigny 5, fols. 47r–51r; BnF, Bréquigny 3, fols. 79v–83v: Condemnation of Jin Congshan.

216 *MCC*, vol. 15, pp. 373–381: Extrait d'une lettre de M. Amiot, Ecrite de Péking, le 20 Novembre 1785: Fin de la persécution contre les Missionaires en Chine (Extract from a letter by Mr. Amiot, Written from Peking, 20 November 1785, End of the persecution of Missionaries in China); BnF, Bréquigny 3, fols. 105r–109v; Inst. 1516, pp. 345–348: fols. [1r–4r]: On the end of the persecution of the missionaries (see also the next text).

MCC, vol. 15, pp. 382–383: Extrait d'une lettre de M. Raux, Ecrite de Péking, le 17 Novembre 1786. Chang-yu ou Edit de l'Empereur de Chine, par lequel il délivre les Missionnaires Européens arrêtés dans son Empire, traduit du Chinois (Extract from a letter by Mr. Raux, Written from Peking, 17 November 1786. Chang-yu or Edict from the Emperor of China, by which he sets free the European Missionaries arrested in his Empire, translated from Chinese) (QL50/10/8 = 9 Nov. 1785); BnF, Bréquigny 3, fols. 110r–111v: Idem on the liberation of the missionaries who were arrested.

217 *MCC*, vol. 9, pp. 60–63: La cinquieme, du 4 Novembre 1780, sur un livre ordonné par l'Empereur à l'honneur des guerriers qui se sont distingués (The fifth, 4 November 4, 1780, on a book ordered by the Emperor in honour of military men who distinguished themselves) (QL45/1/28 = 3 March 1780); Inst. 1516, pp. 261–264, fols. [1r–3r]: The initiative goes back to Shu-he-de 舒赫德 (1710–1777) and Yu Minzhong 于敏中 (1714–1779).

218 *MCC*, vol. 13, pp. 500–505: (QL51/2/16 = 15 March 1786); Inst. 1516, pp. 399–402: pp. 51–57.

219 *MCC*, vol. 15, pp. 286–289 (memorial); p. 289 (edict): 3. Sévérité contre un Lettré (3. Severity against a Scholar); BnF, Bréquigny 3, fols. 37r–39r.

220 *MCC*, vol. 15, pp. 336–344 (edict of emperor pp. 340–344): 6. Condamnation du livre intitulé: Destinée de la Dynastie de Tai-Tsong & de son regne (6. Condemnation of the book entitled: Destiny of the Dynasty of Tai-Tsong & his reign) (QL44/5/19 = 2 July 1779); BnF, Bréquigny 5, fols. 52r–57r; BnF, Bréquigny 3, fols. 83v–88v.

221 *MCC*, vol. 13, pp. 417–458: Extrait d'une lettre de M. Amiot, Missionnaire, Ecrite de Peking, le 20 Mai 1786 (Extract from a letter by Mr. Amiot, Missionary, Written from Peking, 20 May 1786); Inst. 1516, pp. 349–373: pp. 1–48.

MCC, vol. 13, pp. 419–420: Traduction des Vers de l'Empereur (Translation of Verses by the Emperor); Inst. 1516, pp. 350–351: pp. 4–6; Poem by the emperor.

content is quite obviously limited by the specific genre of the gazettes and reflects the issues that the court considered important to be spread to the officials, and that Amiot subsequently deemed of value to transmit to a statesman such as Bertin and other Europeans. Noteworthy is that issues related to (the end of the persecution of) Christianity are only mentioned once by Amiot.[222] Missionaries such as Amiot are known for their translation of "traditional" Chinese sources. The amount of translated contemporary sources such as the gazettes shows that he was also very actively engaged in "China news analysis" destined for Europe.

3.3.3 *The Case of the* Siku quanshu 四庫全書

In order to get a deeper insight into how *Mémoires concernant les Chinois* drew on gazettes to report on certain events, the *Siku quanshu* 四庫全書 (Complete Books in the Four Treasuries), the major book project initiated by the Qianlong emperor in 1773, can function as a case study. It illustrates to what extent and depth Europe was informed about this major project.

The first reference to this project appears in volume 11 of *Mémoires concernant les Chinois* (published in 1786). It is a short notice in a letter by Bourgeois dated 19 November 1784.

> I have already told you about the Encyclopaedia made by the Emperor. It is an immense collection of good Chinese books. It is said that it is the matter of six hundred thousand volumes. They work on it energetically. The two Princes, eldest sons of the Emperor, the sixth & eighth (Ago [= son of emperor]), are at the head of this amazing enterprise. The work goes on, and was to be finished in three years, but it looks as though it will not be done so soon. They have already asked the Emperor for extra time. He only granted it with regret.[223]

In this short quotation there is no specific reference to a gazette, but the general information was most probably obtained from gazettes,[224] as appears from

222 There is also a "Extrait d'une lettre de M. Raux, Ecrite de Péking, le 17 Novembre 1786. Chang-yu ou Edit de l'Empereur de Chine, par lequel il délivre les Missionnaires" on the liberation of missionaries who were arrested: *MCC*, vol. 15, pp. 382–383.

223 *MCC*, vol. 11, p. 579: Extrait d'une lettre de M. Bourgeois, missionnaire, Ecrite de Pé-king le 19 Novembre 1784 (Extract from a letter by Mr. Bourgeois, missionary, Written from Peking on 19 November 1784); Inst. 1520, fol. 260r.

224 There were several memorials in 1784 concerning this issue, e.g. *Qing shilu*, vol. 24, pp. 20–21 (*juan* 1198) (QL49/2/丁巳 [= 1] = 21 Febr. 1784) and vol. 24, p. 104 (*juan* 1204) (QL49/4/己丑 [= 5] = 23 May 1784).

the reports included below. These references do not rule out that information was also gathered from personal court contacts.

The above quote, however, is not the earliest reference to the *Siku quanshu* sent from China, as can be observed from the remark "I have already told you …" Due to the aforementioned delay in communication, some earlier letters (of the years 1778–1779) had arrived only after the publication of the quote above. In the chronological order of the day of sending, the oldest reference to the *Siku quanshu* appears in an extract from a letter dated six years earlier, 31 July 1778, also written by Bourgeois and included in volume 15 of *Mémoires concernant les Chinois*.[225] The extract discusses four numbered topics: the White Lotus Sect (*Bailianjiao* 白蓮教) in Bazhou 霸州,[226] the persecution of Christians,[227] the punishment of Wang Xihou 王錫侯 (1713–1777) for his criticism of the *Kangxi zidian* 康熙字典,[228] and the *Siku quanshu* project. The latter is a relatively short text of 1,5 pages that partly reads like a modern encyclopaedic reference.

> The Emperor is now busy with a major project. A few years ago, he published throughout the Empire [this refers to an edict in QL38/2 = 1773] that he wanted to make a collection of all excellent books that China had. He ordered that all those who would have valuable books or manuscripts should send them to the Court, declaring that after making the choice they would be returned faithfully. The Emperor received books to infinity; he determined that the collection would be six hundred thousand volumes. He invited to Peking the greatest Literati of the Empire, called Han-Lin [= the Hanlin academy 翰林院], and the most skilful printers; he gave them an infinite number of Assessors whom he lodged in large palaces. He put at the head of the undertaking high officials & even his sixth son. They report the smallest mistakes. A single point missing in the most complicated characters costs them part of their income. The books that come out of the Imperial Printing House must be without fault.[229]

225 MCC, vol. 15, pp. 281–346: Extrait d'une lettre, Ecrite de Péking, le 31 Juillet 1778 (Extract from a letter, Written from Peking, 13 July 1778); Bréquigny 3, fols. 34v–40r; the manuscript mentions M. Bourgeois.

226 *MCC*, vol. 15, pp. 282–283 (memorial); p. 283 (edict): 1. Rebellion des Sectaires à Pa-tcheou en 1777 (1. Rebellion of the Sectarians in Pa-tcheou in 1777).

227 *MCC*, vol. 15, pp. 283–285: 2°. Persécutions contre les Chrétiens (2. Persecutions against the Christians).

228 *MCC*, vol. 15, pp. 286–289 (memorial); p. 289 (edict): 3. Sévérité contre un Lettré (3. Severity against a Scholar).

229 *MCC*, vol. 15, pp. 289–291 (Extrait d'une lettre, Ecrite de Péking, le 31 Juillet 1778: 4. Projet de l'Empereur de faire un Recueil général des meilleurs Ecrits) (4. The Emperor's plan to

Next Bourgeois points out that the collection would include three Christian texts: Matteo Ricci's *Tianzhu shiyi* 天主實義 (The solid meaning of the Lord of Heaven, 1603), Diego de Pantoja's *Qike* 七克 (Seven victories, ca. 1610–1615), and Ferdinand Verbiest's *Jiaoyao xulun* 教要序論 (Introductory discussion of the essentials of the teaching,). Ultimately, they were not included but the first two received a mention among the books only listed by title (*cunmu* 存目) in the *Qinding Siku quanshu zongmu tiyao* 欽定四庫全書總目提要 (Imperially Commissioned Annotated Catalogue of the Complete Books in the Four Treasuries; 1798).[230] Bourgeois gives no direct reference to a specific gazette, only a very general statement that "in the gazettes of the past month, the Emperor declared that there were already two hundred printed volumes."[231]

Following the chronological order, the next reference appears in an extract from a letter by Amiot dated 5 September 1779,[232] also in volume 15 of *Mémoires concernant les Chinois*. It discusses the *Siku quanshu*, the anti-Manchu text *Jiushijiu chou* 九十九籌 (The ninety-nine ways [to destroy the Manchus]) examined by Yu Minzhong 于敏中,[233] and very briefly (not from the gazette but from personal observation) a natural phenomenon that happened in Beijing the night of 5 to 6 August 1779.[234]

The description of the *Siku quanshu* covers seventeen pages[235] and is the most detailed of the European texts reporting about the work at that time. Amiot first sketches the origin of the work, the procedure to gather the books,

---

produce a general Collection of the best Writings); BnF, Bréquigny 3, fols. 39r–40r; *Qing shilu*, vol. 22 (*juan* 1057), pp. 131–132 (QL43/5/乙酉 [= 26] = 20 June 1778); *Qianlong chao shangyu dang*, vol. 9, pp. 103–104 n. 295 (QL43/5/26 = 20 June 1778).

230 *Qinding Siku quanshu zongmu tiyao* (1997), vol. 2, p. 2: 1672–1674 (*zibu* 子部 35, *zajialei cunmu* 雜家類存目 2).

231 *MCC*, vol. 15, p. 290.

232 *MCC*, vol. 15, pp. 347–372: Extrait d'une lettre de M. Amiot, Ecrite de Péking, le 5 Septembre 1779 (Extract from a letter by Mr. Amiot, Written from Peking, 5 September 1779); BnF, Bréquigny 5, fols. 12r–25v; BnF, Bréquigny 3, fols. 90r–105r.

233 *MCC*, vol. 15, pp. 363–372: 2. Ouvrage contre les Mant-choux (2. Work against the Mant-choux) Précis de la Gazette du premier de la quatrieme Lune de la quarante-quatrieme année du regne de Kien-long (c'est-a-dire, du 16 Mai 1779) (Concise overview of the Gazette of the 10th of the sixth Month of the forty-fourth year of the reign of Kien-long (that is to say, of 16 May 1779)) (QL44/4/1 = 16 May 1779).

234 This text refers to temperature measurements with "Réaumur's alcohol thermometer"; for the meteorological observations between 1 June 1789 (QL54) and 26 Sept 1789, see Inst. 1519, fols. 271r–276v.; for earlier observations by Jesuit missionaries in Beijing in 1743, see Zhang & Demarée (2004).

235 *MCC*, vol. 15, pp. 347–363 (Extrait d'une lettre de M. Amiot, Ecrite de Péking, le 5 Septembre 1779: 1. Collection générale des meilleurs Ecrits, ordonnée par l'Empereur) (1. General collection of the best Writings, ordered by the Emperor); BnF, Bréquigny 5, fols. 12r–25v; BnF, Bréquigny 3, fols. 90r–105r.

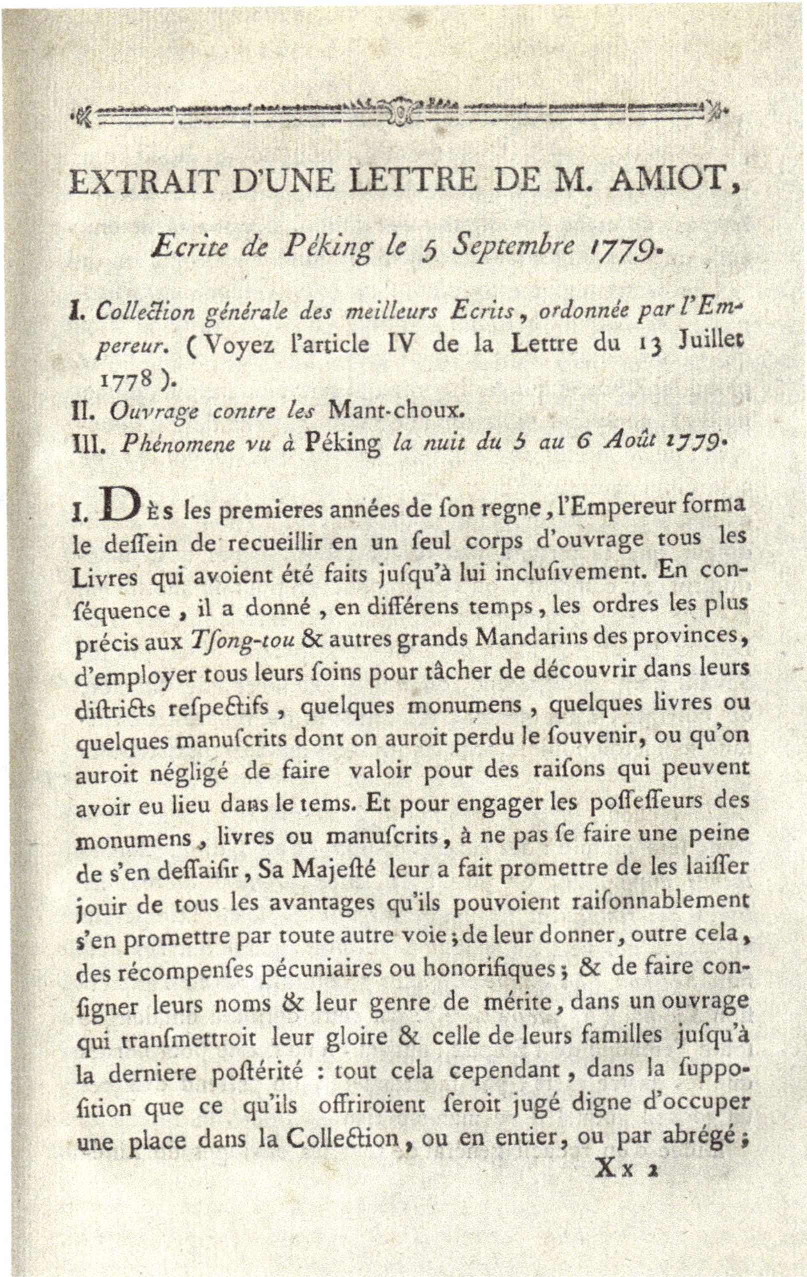

EXTRAIT D'UNE LETTRE DE M. AMIOT,

Ecrite de Péking le 5 Septembre 1779.

I. *Collection générale des meilleurs Ecrits, ordonnée par l'Empereur.* (Voyez l'article IV de la Lettre du 13 Juillet 1778).

II. *Ouvrage contre les* Mant-choux.

III. *Phénomene vu à* Péking *la nuit du 5 au 6 Août 1779.*

I. DÈS les premieres années de ſon regne, l'Empereur forma le deſſein de recueillir en un ſeul corps d'ouvrage tous les Livres qui avoient été faits juſqu'à lui incluſivement. En conſéquence, il a donné, en différens temps, les ordres les plus précis aux *Tſong-tou* & autres grands Mandarins des provinces, d'employer tous leurs ſoins pour tâcher de découvrir dans leurs diſtricts reſpectifs, quelques monumens, quelques livres ou quelques manuſcrits dont on auroit perdu le ſouvenir, ou qu'on auroit négligé de faire valoir pour des raiſons qui peuvent avoir eu lieu dans le tems. Et pour engager les poſſeſſeurs des monumens, livres ou manuſcrits, à ne pas ſe faire une peine de s'en deſſaiſir, Sa Majeſté leur a fait promettre de les laiſſer jouir de tous les avantages qu'ils pouvoient raiſonnablement s'en promettre par toute autre voie; de leur donner, outre cela, des récompenſes pécuniaires ou honorifiques; & de faire conſigner leurs noms & leur genre de mérite, dans un ouvrage qui tranſmettroit leur gloire & celle de leurs familles juſqu'à la derniere poſtérité : tout cela cependant, dans la ſuppoſition que ce qu'ils offriroient ſeroit jugé digne d'occuper une place dans la Collection, ou en entier, ou par abrégé;

Xx 2

ILLUSTRATION 19 Beginning of the letter by Joseph-Marie Amiot concerning the *Siku quanshu* 四庫全書 project (5 September 1779): *Mémoires concernant les Chinois*, vol. 15 (1791), pp. 347–348

ce qui se détermineroit par les Tribunaux littéraires de la Capitale, lesquels n'ayant d'autre intérêt que celui des Lettres mêmes, & etant des Juges très-eclairés, ne pouvoient être aussi que des Juges très-integres.

Ces ordres ont eté exécutés dans toute l'etendue de l'Empire. Les Grands Mandarins des Provinces, ceux sur-tout qui sont Chinois, & par conséquent Lettrés (car il n'y a parmi les Chinois que les Lettrés qui parviennent aux grands postes), ne se sont pas moins fait un plaisir qu'un devoir rigoureux, de se prêter aux vues de leur Maître. Ils ont envoyé à la Cour tout ce qu'ils ont pu déterrer, & ils ont pris cette occasion pour placer quantité de Gens de Lettres qui attendoient que la fortune vînt les chercher, parce qu'ils manquoient ou d'argent, ou de protecteurs pour se mettre en etat de l'aller chercher eux-mêmes. De leur côté, les Tribunaux Littéraires n'ont cessé de s'occuper, & d'occuper les Savans dont ils disposent, du soin d'examiner, de discuter, de corriger, d'augmenter, d'abréger & de rendre aussi parfaits qu'il seroit possible, tous les ouvrages qui doivent composer le recueil.

Ce recueil, le plus complet qui ait eté fait jusqu'à présent, sera intitulé : *Sée-kou-tsiuen-chou* (c'est-à-dire, *Bibliotheque universelle*, ou plus à la lettre, *Recueil de tous les livres qui remplissent les quatre magasins*). C'est l'Empereur lui-même qui veut qu'on le nomme ainsi, parce que l'expression *Sée-kou* (*les quatre magasins*) contraste avec l'expression *Sée-hai* (*les quatre mers*) : par cette derniere on désigne toute l'étendue de l'Empire, auquel on ne donne pour bornes que les quatre mers ; par la premiere, on prétend désigner un recueil auquel il ne manque rien.

L'idée d'un recueil général de tous les ouvrages de Litté-

the name of the *Recueil*, and the reasons why throughout Chinese tradition such collections were compiled: to conserve the literary productions and avoid that the names of the authors be forgotten. In addition, he points out that it is not simply a matter of printing books, "but of printing good books, that is to say, books corrected, increased, or abridged according to the need of books which have been marked with the seal of public approval."[236] In this regard, Amiot depicts the moral role that the emperors play regarding the book collections that are compiled under their auspices and orders. They are "fathers"[237] and "masters":

> The Sovereigns have always prided themselves here on being reputed at the same time for being the fathers and the masters in the doctrine and manners of all the men whose government has been entrusted to them by Heaven: this is the pivot around which their politics has always revolved.[238]

In order to prove his case, Amiot extensively quotes gazettes. The extract from the gazette of QL43/6/10 (3 July 1778) contains various topics: a general state of the art of the project after five years of operation; a description of the incident when the Emperor found mistakes in a volume selected at random and consequently the need for careful inspection; the fact that the collection will contain 168.000 volumes (*ce* 冊); the good treatment and encouragement of the collaborators by the Emperor; the new decision that revisers should inspect all volumes (and not only one or two out of ten); the fact that the emperor will follow the progress closely and give rewards.[239]

The extract from the gazette of QL43/4/29 (25 May 1778) includes the following themes: the memorial by A-gui suggesting that more severe norms need to be applied for the punishment of inspectors: punishment should apply not just in the case of three mistakes in three months, but already in the case of one mistake in three months; mistakes by princes are to be punished in the same

236 MCC, vol. 15, p. 349.

237 On Amiot's presentation of the Qianlong emperor as a "father" (*un pere tendre, le pere commun*), see MCC, vol. 6, pp. 333–335; Nii Yōko (2017), pp. 185–188; Ma Li (2019), pp. 82–83.

238 MCC, vol. 15, p. 350.

239 MCC, vol. 15, pp. 351–356: (QL43/6/10 = 3 July 1778); (Extrait de la Gazette du 10 de la sixieme Lune de la quarante-troisieme année du regne de Kien-long) BnF, Bréquigny 5, fols. 14v–17r; BnF, Bréquigny 3, fols. 92r–94v; BnF, Chinois 2216, 3.3. pp. 1a–2a (QL43/6/10 = 3 July 1778); *Qing shilu*, vol. 22, p. 131 (*juan* 1057) (QL43/5/乙酉 [= 26] = 20 June 1778); *Qianlong chao shangyu dang*, vol. 9, pp. 103–104 n. 295 (QL43/5/26 = 20 June 1778); *Qianlong chao junjichu suishou dengji*, vol. 30, p. 258 (QL43/5/26 = 20 June 1778).

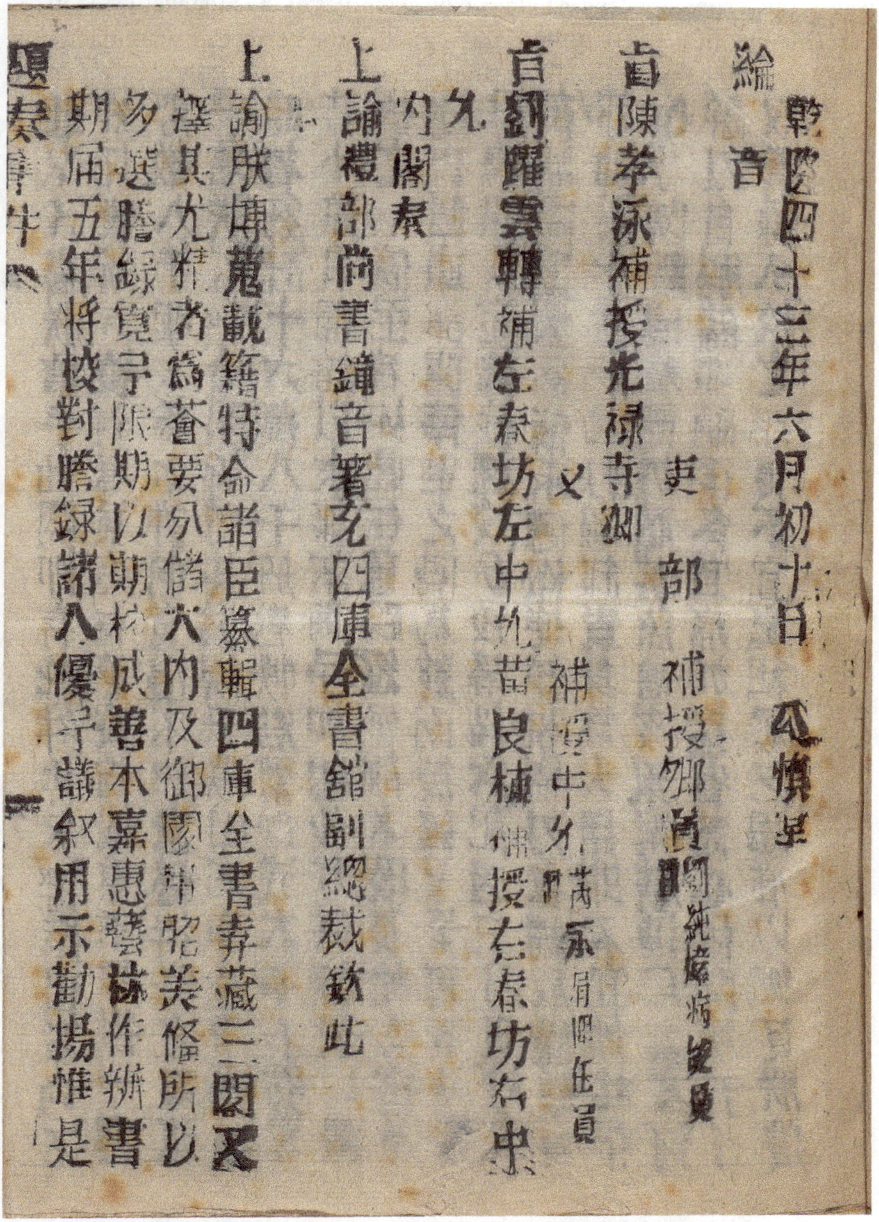
乾隆四十三年六月初十日 [illegible]
綸音
旨陳孝泳補授光祿寺卿 吏部 補授[illegible]
旨劉躍雲轉補左春坊左中允 昔良棟補授右春坊右中允
又 補授中允 [illegible]
允
內閣奏
上諭禮部尚書鍾音著充四庫全書館副總裁欽此
上諭朕博覽載籍特命諸臣纂輯四庫全書弆藏三閣又
擇其尤精者為薈要分儲大內及御園第昭美備所以
多選謄錄寬予限期以期[illegible]成善本嘉惠藝林作辦書
期屆五年將校對謄錄諸人優予議敘用示勸揚惟是
題奏事件

ILLUSTRATION 20 First page of a gazette (*tizou shijian* 題奏事件) concerning the *Siku quanshu* 四庫全書 project (QL43/6/10 = 3 July 1778): BnF, Chinois 2216, 3.3. p. 1a

way as the inspectors. This is followed by examples of the mistakes listed in the first three months of QL43, with the names of the correctors who made mistakes, including the eighth and eleventh son of the emperor, Princes Yongxuan 永璇 (1746–1832) and Yongxing 永瑆 (1752–1823).[240]

The summary (*précis*) of the gazette of QL44/2/10 (27 March 1779) mentions the following topics: the eighth prince and the eleventh prince are appointed as general presidents of the office of the *Siku quanshu*; there is also the appointment of thirteen new examiners; these are added to the names that were mentioned in an earlier gazette (QL43/4/7 = 3 May 1778).[241] Characteristic for the last text is that Amiot cites the names of the newly appointed collaborators:

> Although it does not matter to you very much, Sir, to know their names, here they are anyway arranged by order: Sié-young, Tcheou-hoang, Ta-tchun, Ouang-ting-yu, Tfien-tfai, Hou-keo-ouang, Teou-koang-nai, Tfao-ouen-tché, Kin-ché-foung, Ly-ouang-tou, Tchou-kouei, Ny-tcheng-Koan, & Ki-mong-hioung. All these names, which, as we see, are purely Chinese names, will be attached in the printed form …[242]

These names can easily be identified on the basis of Chinese primary sources: Xie Yong 謝墉, Zhou Huang 周煌, Da Chun 達椿, Wang Tingyu 汪廷璵, Qian Zai 錢載, Hu Gaowang 胡高望, Dou Guangnai 竇光鼐, Cao Wenzhi 曹文埴, Jin Shisong 金士松, Li Wangdu 李汪度, Zhu Gui 朱珪, Ni Chengkuan 倪承寬, Ji Mengxiong 吉夢熊.[243]

---

240 *MCC*, vol. 15, pp. 356–359: (QL43/4/29 = 25 May 1778); (Extrait de la Gazette du 29 de la quatrieme Lune de la quarante-troisieme année de Kien-long) (Extract from the Gazette of the 39th of the fourth Month of the forty-third year of the reign of Kien-long); BnF, Bréquigny 5, fols. 17r–18v; BnF, Bréquigny 3, fols. 94v–96v; BnF, Chinois 2216, 3.2. pp. 1b–2b (QL43/4/29 = 25 May 1778); *Qianlong chao shangyu dang*, vol. 9, p. 29 n. 84 (QL43/4/8 = 4 May 1778); *Qianlong chao junjichu suishou dengji*, vol. 30, p. 397 (QL43/4/8 = 4 May 1778).

241 *MCC*, vol. 15, p. 363; BnF, Chinois 2216, 3.1. p. 1a (QL43/4/7 = 3 May 1778); *Qing shilu*, vol. 22, p. 73 (*juan* 1053) (QL43/3/丁亥[= 27] = 23 April 1778); *Qianlong chao shangyu dang*, vol. 9, p. 14 n. 40 (QL43/3/27 = 23 April 1778); *Qianlong chao junjichu suishou dengji*, vol. 30, p. 145 (QL43/3/28 = 24 April 1778).

242 *MCC*, vol. 15, p. 363; (QL43/4/7 = 3 May 1778); BnF, Bréquigny 5, fol. 20v; BnF, Bréquigny 3, fol. 98r.

243 BnF, Chinois 2216, 3.4. p. 1b (QL44/2/10 = 27 March 1779); *Qing shilu*, vol. 22, p. 437 (*juan* 1076) (QL44/2/丙辰朔 [= 1] = 18 March 1779); *Qianlong chao shangyu dang*, vol. 9, p. 556 n. 1305 (QL44/2/1 = 18 March 1779); *Qianlong di qijuzhu*, vol. 29, p. 12 (QL44/2/1 = 18 March 1779); *Qianlong chao junjichu suishou dengji*, vol. 31, p. 53 (QL44/2/2 = 19 March 1779).

Such enumerations are often left out in other European publications, but here they confirm the detailed information that Amiot transmitted from the gazettes. From Amiot's small commentaries and remarks made to his correspondent, it is clear that he intended not only to inform Bertin about the book collection itself, but also to convey an image of the emperor and those who contributed to the project. After quoting the gazette of QL43/4/29 (25 May 1778) on the more severe rules regarding possible mistakes, which ends with the Emperor's simple endorsement of having been informed "*zhidaoliao* 知道了,"[244] Amiot writes in this regard:

> From the content of this supplication and from the tone which reigns in it, it is easy to perceive that there is no greater concern than the perfection of a work which the Emperor regards as having to become, in the eyes of Posterity, the main part of the glory of his reign.[245]

In this letter, Amiot informs Europe about a topic by quoting not one single gazette but a series of gazettes, which were published over a long time. Amiot and his Chinese collaborator compiled data from gazettes that range from 3 May 1778 to 27 March 1779, which also seems to indicate that they kept the gazettes over such a long period.

The next reference to the *Siku quanshu* in chronological order of sending appears in volume 13 of *Mémoires concernant les Chinois* in a very long letter (forty-five printed pages) by Amiot dated 14 September 1786.[246] The letter contains a variety of subjects, such as reports by the Ministry of Works (Gongbu 工部) on the state of the channels related to the drought in Jiangnan, Henan, Shandong;[247] a report by the Governor of Henan, Bi Yuan 畢沅 (1730–1797), on the public works at the Jialu 賈魯 river;[248] an edict on a solar eclipse;[249]

---

244 L'Empereur répondit: *Tchi-tao-leao* (c'est-à-dire *je suis au fait*). The Emperor answered: *Tchi-tao-leao* (i.e. *I am aware*).

245 MCC, vol. 15, p. 359.

246 MCC, vol. 13, pp. 459–506: Extrait d'une lettre de M. Amiot, Missionnaire, Ecrite de Peking, le 14 Septembre 1786 (Extract from a letter by Mr. Amiot, Missionary, Written from Peking, September 14, 1786); Inst. 1516, pp. 374–403: pp. 1–59.

247 MCC, vol. 13, pp. 460–463; Inst. 1516, pp. 375–376: pp. 3–6; *Qing shilu*, not yet found.

248 MCC, vol. 13, pp. 463–465: Inst. 1516, pp. 376–377: pp. 6–8; *Qing shilu*, possibly vol. 24, p. 946 (*juan* 1260) (QL51/run 7/丙子 [= 5] = 28 Aug. 1786); MCC, vol. 13, pp. 465–466: Inst. 1516, pp. 377–378: pp. 8–9; *Qing shilu*, vol. 24, p. 946 (*juan* 1260) (QL51/run 7/丙子 [= 5] = 29 Aug. 1786).

249 MCC, vol. 13, pp. 478–485: (QL50/12/19 = 18 Jan. 1786); Inst. 1516, pp. 384–388: pp. 22–30; *Qing shilu*, vol. 24, pp. 718–719 (*juan* 1243) (QL50/11/乙亥 [= 29] = 30 Dec. 1786); *Qianlong chao shangyu dang*, vol. 12, p. 937 n. 2430 and pp. 937–938 n. 2431 (QL50/11/29 = 30 Dec. 1786).

the examination of the officials on the classics and Four Books;[250] an edict on the monthly instruction of the people by the officials in response to the Censorate;[251] and an edict on a new *huidian* 會典 (digest of statutes).[252] Eight pages are devoted to the *Siku quanshu*, of which most consist of the translation of an edict (Chang-yu (discours d'en haut) = *shangyu* 上諭).[253]

This is an example of a text that appears not to have been preserved in the original Chinese form, but only in the translation by Amiot. Thus, the translation informs us about the content of the initial gazette. The text can be qualified as authentic since its beginning has also been preserved, repeating the initial memorial in the usual way within the edict.[254]

The topic of the edict is related to the apparent contradiction concerning the number of volumes that the collection will contain. Amiot points at the difference between the 168.000 volumes that he reports, and the 600.000 volumes reported earlier by Bourgeois.

> It could be that I confuse the whole collection with the number of the volumes that had not yet been delivered to the printing, or the latter with the total number. I have not yet found the opportunity to inquire with someone who is fully instructed to tell on which side is the error. You will be able to conclude it for yourself if you want to take the trouble to combine the different articles of the accounts of a new kind [of calculation] which were given to the Emperor, & and that His Majesty has made public in a *Chang-yu* fallen from his brush on the 14th of the Third Moon in the fifty-first year of his glorious reign.[255]

---

250 MCC, vol. 13, pp. 487–489: (QL51/2/6 = 5 March 1786); Inst. 1516, pp. 390–391: pp. 33–36; *Qing shilu*, vol. 24, pp. 767–769 (*juan* 1248) (QL51/2/庚辰 [= 6] = 5 March 1786); *Qianlong di qijuzhu*, absent.

251 MCC, vol, 13, pp. 494–499: (QL51/1/20 = 18 Febr. 1786); Inst. 1516, pp. 394–397: pp. 41–47; *Qing shilu*, not yet found.

252 MCC, vol. 13, pp. 500–505: (QL51/2/16 = 15 March 1786); Inst. 1516, pp. 399–402: pp. 51–57; *Qing shilu*, vol. 24, pp. 773–774 (*juan* 1248) (QL51/2/甲申 [= 10] = 9 March 1786); *Qianlong chao shangyu dang*, vol. 13, p. 33 n. 88 (QL51/2/10 = 9 March 1786).

253 MCC, vol. 13, pp. 470–477; pp. 471–476: "Chang-yu (discours d'en haut)" (QL51/3/14 = 12 April 1786); Inst. 1516, pp. 380–383: pp. 14–20; *Qing shilu*, reference but not the full text: vol. 24, p. 723 (*juan* 1244) (QL50/12/丁丑 [= 2] = 1 Jan. 1786).

254 Memorial from censor Zuo Zhou 左周: *Qing shilu*, vol. 24, p. 723 (*juan* 1244) (QL50/12/丁丑 [= 2]) (1 Jan. 1786).

255 MCC, vol. 13, p. 470. Bertin in a letter to Amiot had asked further explanation about the difference in the number of volumes: Letter of Bertin to Amiot (Paris, 31 December 1784): Inst. 1524, fols. 16r–23r: fol. 16v.

This new kind of calculation was initiated by a request from a censor named Zuo Zhou 左周 who asked to calculate the exact number of characters included in the collection and confront this number with the total payment so as to evaluate the equity in the remuneration of the scribes. The edict discusses this issue in detail.[256] This quote also illustrates that Amiot seeks personal information in addition to the gazettes. At the end, Amiot shares his personal comments with Bertin:

> If this report to His Imperial Majesty does not entirely satisfy your question on the total number of volumes contained in the general collection, it will serve at least to inform you of the manner in which people proceed here for great as well as for little things. You will without doubt regard it as a function unworthy of a Minister of State and of the first Mandarins of the Empire, that which has just been fulfilled by Lieou-young [= Liu Yong 劉墉 (1720–1805)], Fou-tchang-ngan [= Fu-chang-an 福長安 (?–1817)], and the others who are named above. I will not undertake to dissuade you.[257]

In this subtle critique on micromanagement Amiot takes into account his correspondent's position, as Bertin himself was Minister of State.

A final reference to the *Siku quanshu* appears in the translations of gazettes by Bourgeois preserved in the manuscript BnF, Bréquigny 10. It occurs in the gazette of QL53/1/28 (5 March 1788)[258] together with an edict concerning Fu-kang-an's 福康安 (?–1796)[259] demand for rewards for troops in Taiwan after a battle at Douliumen 斗六門,[260] Xu Siceng's 徐嗣曾 (?–1790) report on the arrest of five thieves in Fujian,[261] and Li Shiyao's 李侍堯 request to fill a post in Taiwan.[262] The memorial about the *Siku quanshu* concerns the appointment of two new officials, Wu Yude 吳裕德 and Peng Yuanchong 彭元珫, to the *Siku quanshu* project, in replacement of two officials who had retired earlier.[263]

256 The edict also makes reference to the (*Siku*) *Quanshu huiyao* (四庫) 全書薈要, an extract collection of volumes selected during the compilation process (*MCC*, vol. 13, p. 474).

257 *MCC*, vol. 13, pp. 476–477. For Liu Yong see: *ECCP*, vol. 1, pp. 536–537; Fu-chang-an: *ECCP*, vol. 1, p. 249.

258 BnF, Bréquigny 10, pp. 33–38.

259 *ECCP*, vol. 1, pp. 253–255.

260 BnF, Bréquigny 10, p. 33: Paroles de l'empereur: Declaration impériale.

261 BnF, Bréquigny 10, pp. 34–35: Declaration impériale.

262 BnF, Bréquigny 10, pp. 36–37: Placet presenté à l'Empereur.

263 The original text is not yet found, but their names can be identified partly because of the reference to another edict earlier in the month. BnF, Bréquigny 10, p. 36; *Qing shilu*, vol. 25, pp. 363–364 (*juan* 1294) (QL52/12/乙未 [= 2] = 9 Jan. 1788); *Qianlong chao shangyu dang*,

This is an example of the appearance of the *Siku quanshu* in a completely translated gazette. It illustrates how the topic is one among others, in this case not selected by a European intermediary but originally by the editors of the gazette. It also illustrates the detail with which information was transmitted to Europe.

3.4 Vision on the Gazette and the Emperor

On the basis of the gazettes, Amiot presented in his yearly correspondence with Bertin a chronology of events that happened in China. A detailed overview of a shorter period was provided in Bourgeois' translation of more than two months of gazettes. At the same time, their presentations also transmitted a vision on the public function of the Chinese gazette and on the information that was contained in it. Moreover, Amiot's letters reveal a certain image of the emperor and his art of governing that partly emanates from the gazettes.

3.4.1 *Public Good, Imperial Truth, and Critical Views*

The *Mémoires concernant les Chinois* contain not only selective translations of gazettes, but also descriptions of their characteristics, as could already be observed from the above quotations. The very first references to the gazettes in *Mémoires concernant les Chinois* appear at the beginning of the first volume. These are two short and even indirect references but the context in which they occur illustrates well that the question of the public good is one of the major frames of interpretation in *Mémoires concernant les Chinois*. At the beginning of their essay on the antiquity of the Chinese, Ko and Yang, the Chinese who had spent several years in France, clarify the position of the Chinese literati regarding high antiquity, first explaining their own relative disinterest in this topic. This is an occasion to elucidate the reasons for their disinterest, which according to Ko and Yang can be found in the types of knowledge and sciences that are practiced in China:

> Our government has always wanted to have savants and scientists for more than thirty centuries, but in its own way and according to the views of its policy; that is to say, to preserve in the Empire the purity of public education, to maintain the rules of morality, to fix the discoveries of

---

vol. 14, p. 90 n. 258 (QL52/12/2 = 9 Jan. 1788); *Qianlong di qijuzhu*, vol. 36, pp. 360–361 (QL52/12/2 = 9 Jan. 1788); see also *Qinding Siku quanshu zongmu* (1997), vol. 1, p. 22.

> the arts of need or usefulness, to elevate youth in the knowledge and the practice of its tasks,...[264]

This emphasis on utility is reflected in the actions of the Ministries, including in what is mentioned in the gazettes:

> Our Ministry has no other cry than *the public good*; it wants only the men of letters whom it needs for public affairs, and the most beautiful geniuses only attract its attention, as far as they are useful: it is so singular in this respect that, while a simple soldier who has received wounds in war is mentioned in all the gazettes, it would not allow to say a word in a hundred years about a thousand system-makers. Knowledge and talent are nothing but words (in the eyes of the Ministry), when the state derives no real utility from it.[265]

As Chinese with European experience and returned to China, Ko and Yang also explain the general attitude towards the sciences and how this is reflected in a difference between European and Chinese publications, including the gazettes:

> The sciences here have a much narrower atmosphere than in Europe, and the Nation in general has little interest in what goes on there. There are no literary journals, no public papers announcing the works of scholars and their successes. The gazette of the Empire speaks only of the great compilations, editions, or new books which the Court has entrusted to the Literati of the Imperial College.[266]

Similar reflections on the contribution of the gazettes to the public good and public utility have also appeared in the texts by Contancin fifty years earlier.

A more ample description of the gazettes or 'public documents' can be found in a letter by Amiot, dated 25 January 1787, which is included in volume 14 of *Mémoires concernant les Chinois*. In it, Amiot first distinguishes Chinese gazettes from the public writings in Europe. Unlike some scholars who tend to see the gazettes as a precursor of the modern newspaper, these descriptions

264 "Essai sur l'antiquité des Chinois": "Articles premier: Position des Lettres Chinois d'aujourd'hui par rapport à la connoissance de la haute antiquité," *MCC*, vol. 1, p. 10.

265 "Essai sur l'antiquité des Chinois": "Articles premier: Position des Lettres Chinois d'aujourd'hui par rapport à la connoissance de la haute antiquité," *MCC*, vol. 1, p. 11.

266 "Essai sur l'antiquité des Chinois": "Articles premier: Position des Lettres Chinois d'aujourd'hui par rapport à la connoissance de la haute antiquité," *MCC*, vol. 1, p. 11.

highlight certain characteristics of the Chinese gazette through a comparison with European gazettes. Especially the official character and "certainty of facts" are stressed. Chinese gazettes originate from the central political power, in which a significant number of officials are involved, and are a precise reflection of governmental decisions:

> It is here not the same as with public writings in Europe. Not one appears without the approval of the Government, and without being extracted from the registers of the different Courts; as a result, one can count on the certainty of the facts they tell. These excerpts from the registers of the different Courts are made by the Officers themselves of the Courts to which the cases referred to belong; they are delivered to men in place who cannot alter them or allow them to be altered in the least, without exposing themselves to the penalties imposed by law against counterfeiters & prevaricators & who consequently read them carefully, and examine them with the greatest care before passing them to the post office, which alone has the privilege of having them printed to be sent as they were received, to the principal Mandarins of the Capital & Provinces & to all those who in the Capital, or elsewhere, subscribe to receive them.[267]

The "certainty of facts" is further developed in a closer comparison with the European gazettes: the Chinese gazettes are much more trustworthy than the European ones, as was also noted by earlier Jesuit reports about the Chinese gazettes.

> The name of Gazettes, which we are accustomed to give them, might make you believe that they are almost similar to the Gazettes of Europe, in which the Composers bring pell-mell all that they think about to insert: truth beside lies, the reality of events dressed up with circumstances which disfigure the frivolity of the conjectures, false reasonings, and the absurdity of popular noises in the wake of the political presentations. It is not in these features that one can recognize the daily announcements which are in use among the Chinese.[268]

---

267 *MCC*, vol. 14, pp. 523–524: Extrait d'une lettre de M. Amiot, Missionnaire, Ecrite de Péking, le 25 Janvier 1787 (Extract from a letter by Mr. Amiot, Missionary, Written from Peking, 25 January 25, 1787).

268 *MCC*, vol. 14, p. 524: Extrait d'une lettre de M. Amiot, Missionnaire, Ecrite de Péking, le 25 Janvier 1787.

In Amiot's opinion, the gazettes have a public role since they contain information that the public should know – especially concerning the efficient bureaucratic administration. Gazettes make it possible to circulate this information within society:

> I have just insinuated it: these announcements are merely a summary of what is going on throughout the whole Empire, in good and evil, and that the Government itself makes known to all the Orders of the state, not in order to satisfy a vain curiosity, but to manifest the intentions, instructions, ordinances, and in general all that emanates from the supreme authority; promotions to the Dignities, Charges & Jobs throughout the Empire, the writings of Mandarins in the form of supplications, requests, information, warnings, indictments or prayers in favour of the people or against those who offend them; the answers of the Sovereign to these writings, and his conduct accordingly; Decisions, Sentences & Judgments of the Courts; in a word, all the physical and moral events which deserve some attention on the part of the public, or about which the public ought not to be ignorant. I leave it to you to judge if, when I share with you in our language some articles that I draw from these Writings, I can mislead you in error, by telling you the facts that have been proven ...[269]

These reports emerge in a French descriptive context in which public good (*bien public*) is considered an important political value. The notion also appears in other essays in volume 14 of *Mémoires concernant les Chinois*. Within the political context of the authors, public good is considered "the first and most essential of all the laws of the State."[270] This explains why the gazettes are framed in this public discourse as well.[271]

A similar description of the characteristics of the Chinese gazette can also be found in Bourgeois' translation in BnF, Brequigny 10. In the eyes of Bourgeois,

---

269 *MCC*, vol. 14, pp. 524–525: Extrait d'une lettre de M. Amiot, Missionnaire, Ecrite de Péking, le 25 Janvier 1787.

270 These ideas appear in the text by Cibot, "Parallèle des mœurs et usages des Chinois, avec les Mœurs et usages décrits dans le livre d'Esther," MCC, vol. 14, p. 393; other similar references: p. 411: "Chinese philosophy sees in it a compassion of wisdom, and a true love of the Emperor and of the public good"; vol. 14, p. 445: "the Ministry policy must take charge of the public good"; vol. 14, p. 447: "your zeal & your love for the public good"; see also letter of Amiot (19 November 1787), vol. 14, p. 543: "he goes to their representations when they have the public good for object."

271 On this topic, see especially Nii Yōko (2017), pp. 195–198. Notice that in the dictionaries of the eighteenth century 'public' is not yet opposed to 'private' but to 'particular'; see Ozouf (1997), p. 351.

the gazettes play an informative role for the public, and an instructive role for the officials. In one of the letters to Bertin that accompanied the sending of this manuscript translation, Bourgeois writes the following concise description:

> The Gazettes of the Empire are made with art. I have not put anything aside, so that your greatness will know its genius better. By their means one turns the mandarins and the people where one wants; one suppresses the rumours, which circulate, and the fears, which spread; one pushes the great towards their duties; one is especially careful to provide the highest idea of the Emperor by reporting all that he says, and all that he does for his good people.[272]

In the short introduction to the manuscript itself, Bourgeois equally stresses this instructive role. Gazettes enable the encouragement of a uniform conduct in the bureaucracy:

> The Gazettes of China are not only to amuse ~~the people~~; their purpose is to instruct. Mandarins find rules of conduct in them; they see the pitfalls they must avoid, and the road by which they can reach the highest honours. The sample of these gazettes that I give here, is enough to know what their goal is, and by which means they obtain what one wants.[273]

Bourgeois then goes on to explain the entire administrative procedure of documents that ultimately results in the production of a gazette: officials sending memorials, the deliberation of two Manchu and two Chinese Ministers with the emperor at four o'clock in the morning during summer and five o'clock during winter, and the final decision-making by the emperor. Bourgeois insists again on the involvement of the emperor in the composition of the gazette. Not only does he control the content, but "he almost always speaks in the gazette":

> The gazette is only printed in Peking, from where it is spread throughout the Empire. (...) It is printed every day; and says nothing that has not passed under the eyes of the Emperor; there is more, it is almost always the Emperor who speaks in it. These are his replies to various placets or memorials that are presented to him at the Court, or by the mandarins of the Provinces.[274]

---

272 Letter of Bourgeois to Bertin (Beijing, 10 October 1788): BnF, Bréquigny 2, fol. 209v.
273 BnF, Bréquigny 10, p. 1; also in Walter (2008), p. 330. Strikethrough in original text.
274 BnF, Bréquigny 10, p. 1; also in Walter (2008), p. 330.

This raises the question of truth. The above-mentioned quotations may give the impression that these missionaries are only submissive admirers of the Chinese emperor and that they believe that the gazettes are fully trustworthy, precisely because the documents that are printed have passed "under the eyes of the emperor" and received governmental approval before being printed. Yet, in the context of the translated gazettes preserved in Bréquigny 10, Bourgeois displays a more critical engagement with the information published in the gazettes. He takes as an example the 1787–1788 "rebellion" in Taiwan, to which a large portion of the gazettes translated in Bréquigny 10 are devoted. The main figure is Lin Shuangwen 林爽文 (1756–1788), said to be a leader of the sworn brotherhood Heaven and Earth Society (*Tiandihui* 天地會), who was able to mobilise a force of some 100,000 men against the Qing administration and to control most of the island's territory. The Qianlong emperor first called upon the recently disgraced Li Shiyao to oppress the rebels, but after six months of useless exertions, he turned to the trusted Manchu commander Fu-kang-an. Arriving in late 1787 with a fresh force of several 10,000 troops, together with the experienced general Hai-lan-cha 海蘭察 (?–1793), they subdued the main rebel forces in a short time. Lin Shuangwen first escaped, but was subsequently arrested and transported to Beijing for trial, where he was executed in April 1788.[275] This campaign was considered very significant by the emperor and has even been the subject of a suite of twelve copperplate engravings produced by Chinese court artists. This suite belongs to a series of c. nine suites of the Qianlong emperor's successful military victories, of which the first two (concerning the campaigns in East Turkistan) were collaboratively produced by European and Chinese artists.[276] The large format prints (50.5cm x 87.4cm) of the campaign in Taiwan (*Pingding Taiwan zhantu* 平定台灣戰圖 or *Pingding Taiwan deshengtu* 平定台灣得勝圖) were produced at Wuyingdian 武英殿 within the imperial palace (1788–1790), and included poems by the Qianlong emperor. Among the twelve scenes, the second and third depict the conquest of Douliumen 斗六門, and the seventh depicts Lin Shuangwen being captured alive.[277]

---

275 For a short description of this "rebellion," see Elliott (2009), pp. 158–159; Shepherd (2016), pp. 105–108.

276 On these prints, see Reed (2017).

277 Zhang Xiaoguang (2003), pp. 39–52; Douliumen: pp. 42–43; Lin Shuangwen: p. 47. For online versions: web.archive.org/web/20210528214526/https://www.dpm.org.cn/ancient/yuanmingqing/163517.html (The Palaces Museum); web.archive.org/web/20210528214802/http://www.battle-of-qurman.com.cn/e/hist.htm (list of different versions).

ILLUSTRATION 21 Seventh scene of the copperplate engravings of the campaign in Taiwan that were produced at Wuyingdian 武英殿 within the imperial palace (*Pingding Taiwan zhantu* 平定台灣戰圖, 1788–1790): Staatsbibliothek zu Berlin, Preußischer Kulturbesitz, Libri sin. 1603–39

ILLUSTRATION 22 Detail of the seventh scene: depiction of Lin Shuangwen 林爽文 being captured alive (1788): Staatsbibliothek zu Berlin, Preußischer Kulturbesitz, Libri sin. 1603–39

Bourgeois, however, presents an alternative view. In his opinion, the information on the rebellion comes from the generals, who appear to have deceived the emperor. What they reported is contradicted by Bourgeois' own information.

> I rendered the gazettes as they are; I have not deleted anything, in order to better understand their genius, and so that one can see what their purpose is. They talk a lot about the revolt of the island of Formosa. I had to follow them. I followed them; a good Literatus assured me of their meaning; but nothing could assure their veracity. I must even warn that the generals of Formosa have turned things in their own way, and presented them to the Emperor in the most favourable light for them; and as they are the only ones who can describe to the Emperor the state of affairs, and as moreover they know how to handle the necessary contacts at the court, one can only count poorly on what they say, at least in the details. The Emperor is deceived, and in spite of his vigilance, his application to

> affairs, and his great genius for the government, it is impossible for him to know things as they are. Here is the true story of the island of Formosa. We know it for certain from individuals who were on the scene and had no interest in disguising the truth.[278]

In this comment one can see a reaction similar to the one reflected in Perroni's comments on the Yongzheng emperor. Despite his vigilance, the Qianlong emperor is deceived by officials. In spite of his doubts, Bourgeois himself tries to convey the content of the gazette as faithfully as possible. At the same time, he provides his own version of events that diverges from the official account. He first describes how Lin Shuangwen originated from Fujian, "from a large and honest family; several branches of this family have been Christians for a long time."[279] He went to Formosa to trade and was especially successful in sugar. "Because he had funds and talent, he became the richest merchant on the whole island. He was loved and respected as a good man."[280] Next, Bourgeois recounts how Lin Shuangwen became victim to his own goodness, "since he was not able to get out of the mess he had been thrown into by fate." There was in the island a gang of thieves who harassed the people, and Qing officials were not capable of capturing them. At the end of 1786 (QL51) five or six of them came to see Lin Shuangwen. He asked them how much they needed to engage in trade, without having to steal and therefore leaving the people in peace. Since they promised no longer to harass people, he paid fifty taels to sixty of them and peace was installed. When a Qing official got to know the story, in the hope of extorting money from a man who could offer such generous gifts, he arrested Lin under the pretext that he was connected to the thieves. Subsequently the thieves attacked the office of the official, killed him, and liberated Lin Shuangwen "Since this is a crime without grace, they stood up to raise the standard of rebellion. They led the unfortunate Lin Shuangwen [into their action] and declared him emperor. Since he was beloved, he soon united around him a crowd of battered people."[281] The leader of the thieves trained them as soldiers and appointed Lin as their head. They started to attack cities and conquered them. This was unexpected in the peaceful isle of Formosa, where officials had discharged their soldiers. The news about these events reached Beijing on New Year's Day of the fifty-first year of the Qianlong period (18 February 1787).

---

278 BnF, Bréquigny 10, pp. 2–3; also in Walter (2008), p. 331.
279 BnF, Bréquigny 10, p. 3.
280 Ibidem.
281 BnF, Bréquigny 10, p. 4.

It is difficult to assess the version reported by Bourgeois, since the modern accounts base themselves on official sources such as memorials and decrees preserved in the *Qing shilu*. Yet the fact that Bourgeois proposed another reading is significant, since his purpose is precisely to contest these sources, as in his opinion the generals misled the emperor.

In one of his letters to Bertin, Bourgeois further reflects on what is disguised in the gazettes, and how he himself erroneously believed in the information they presented. He starts with the observation that since only high officials have the right to write to the emperor, "news only comes out as much and as the court wants." He continues with a reflection on the events in Formosa:

> This obliges me to mitigate a little of what I had the honour to write to your greatness about the Formosa earthquake. I believed the gazettes to be truer than they are. It is certain that one disguises many facts therein, and that from a small thing one knows how to make a big one. For example, it seems that in Formosa there was only the first action that was a bit considerable; the others, which are mentioned in the gazettes, are so embellished for the honour of the general and the officers that those who have been there do not recognize them. Woe to the general and the great officers, if they were accused of having disguised [the matter]; but this accusation is not easy to make; and it would be very risky to embark on such a business. It is believed that the loss of the brave officer Tchaye ta ki [= Chai Daji 柴大紀 (1732–1788)] stems from an accusation he made against Heng joüi [= Heng-rui 恒瑞 (1744–1801)], who was a generalissimo in Formosa, when the rebellion began there.[282]

In another letter to Bertin, Amiot provides additional explanation about the behaviour of officials. Some information is concealed from the emperor, and this is explained by an attitude of filial piety on the part of the officials.

> … the Princes, the ministers, and the grandees are in agreement with each other to conceal from the sovereign all the affairs which, from near or far, could in the least alter his good humour. It is, they say, one of the essential articles of filial piety; we would be guilty, if, being able to observe what is prescribed, we failed to do so.[283]

---

282 Letter of Bourgeois to Bertin (Beijing, 10 October 1788): BnF, Bréquigny 2, fol. 209v. One finds references to Heng-rui and Chai Daji in the following passages in BnF, Bréquigny 10, pp. 56–57, 61–70, 113–121, 178–182.

283 Letter of Amiot to Bertin (4 October 1790): Inst. 1517, fols. 104r–136v: fol. 119r.

Sometimes bad news has to be reported, such as in the case of drought or floods, in particular when a request for help is made. But the officials who report about it primarily stress their own efforts in relieving the people. In the opinion of Amiot,

> To hide the truth, or to tell it in such a way as to make it unrecognizable in the eyes of the one who has the right to know it, is to deceive in all the rigor of the term.[284]

As is evident from these remarks, reporting about the gazettes did not prevent Amiot and Bourgeois from making their own judgments. In their representation, the gazettes combine both transparency and secrecy, public good and internal control.

3.4.2 *A Certain Image of the Emperor*

Amiot's vision of the emperor and his government has recently been the object of studies by Nii Yōko[285] and Ma Li.[286] Since in this instance the gazettes are the main focus of investigation, it will suffice to outline some general characteristics. This section thus intends to explore Amiot's presentation of the emperor in three roles, his identification of the emperor as both a Manchu and Chinese Monarch, and his praise for the emperor. Since these aspects are not explicitly treated in Bourgeois' translation, his vision is not included here.

Just like his predecessors and other Europeans (including Contancin), Amiot attributes three roles to the emperor: the equitable sovereign, the high priest, and the master of the doctrine.[287] He not only deduces these roles on the basis of the gazettes, but he also uses them as an interpretative frame and searches for examples in the gazettes to present the emperor in accordance with them.[288]

As equitable sovereign (*Souverain équitable*), the emperor "punishes faults at the same time as he rewards good deeds."[289] In this role, he is most often identified as a "father" (*père*): "a beneficial sovereign, who is less the sovereign than the father of his peoples."[290] Amiot develops the idea of a "paternal gov-

---

284 Letter of Amiot to Bertin (4 October 1790): Inst. 1517, fols. 104r–136v: fol. 119v.
285 Nii Yōko (2017), esp. chapter 6.
286 Ma Li (2019), pp. 197ff.
287 The three roles mentioned together in *MCC*, vol. 9, p. 24; vol. 13, p. 487.
288 See e.g. his explanation on *MCC*, vol. 9, pp. 18 and 21.
289 *MCC*, vol. 9, p. 24.
290 *MCC*, vol. 9, p. 18; see also *MCC*, vol. 13, p. 460: "father of the people."

ILLUSTRATION 23 Engraving of the Qianlong emperor, made by François Nicholas Martinet after a portrait by Giuseppe Panzi (1773): *Mémoires concernant les Chinois*, vol. 1 (1776), opposite the frontispiece

ernment"[291] by applying the metaphor of "family father" (*père de famille*) to the relationship between the sovereign and his subject: "The Emperor always shows himself as a family father who listens kindly to the representations of his children, for family matters which are within their competence; & the Subjects, represented by the Great, the Mandarins & all the men in place always show themselves before the Emperor, like obedient & respectful children …"[292] In another instance he writes that the emperor is "a family father who talks to his children to urge them to do well."[293] This paternal attitude also concerns women, as is evidenced by the case of the woman who pretended to be a living Buddha: "His paternal solicitude extends even to persons of the other sex, to instruct them in their duties when they think of failing to do so, and to submit them to punishment, if they reoffend after having been instructed."[294]

As high priest of the nation and highest sacrificer (*Grand-Prêtre & le Souverain-Sacrificateur*), he is the chief of religion in his empire.[295] In this role, he fulfils the obligations of offering sacrifices at different occasions, such as those at the temple of Heaven at winter solstice.[296] Whatever the weather is like, Amiot states, he attends to the functions of his priesthood precisely and diligently.[297]

As a master of doctrine (*Maître de la Doctrine*), he is a master who instructs.[298] He is a "a Sovereign who instructs his subjects about what may be useful to them or about some event which is important for them not to ignore."[299]

Another characteristic of Amiot's approach is that he describes the emperor as both a Manchu and Chinese sovereign. This was a common perspective among eighteenth-century missionaries in China. As such, in his discussion of the way of dealing with the cases of Jin Congshan and Zhi Tianbao, Amiot made the distinction between the Chinese and Manchu way of governing.[300] The final condemnation of these offenders by the emperor was more lenient than the condemnation (execution or way of execution) proposed by the officials. Amiot insists that his evaluation concerns the Chinese way of governing

291 *MCC*, vol. 13, p. 454.
292 *MCC*, vol. 11, p. 584.
293 *MCC*, vol. 13, p. 417.
294 *MCC*, vol. 14, p. 553.
295 *MCC*, vol. 9, pp. 18, 21.
296 *MCC*, vol. 14, pp. 536, 542.
297 *MCC*, vol. 14, pp. 542–543.
298 *MCC*, vol. 9, p. 25; vol. 13, p. 487.
299 *MCC*, vol. 13, p. 417.
300 See also the remark in the example of the punishment of Wang Xihou 王錫侯 that follows these cases. Amiot is of the opinion that this severity "is not quite in our customs," but he presents it "as it makes known those of the Tartars & Chinese people" (*MCC*, vol. 15, p. 286).

and not the Manchu way. This appears clearly from an observation at the beginning of his concluding remarks that is mentioned both in the manuscript and the printed versions.

> It is not necessary to point out to you, Sir, that the two cases which I have just described to you were treated in a purely Chinese manner. The tone in which the Emperor speaks is by no means the Tartar tone. He talks to Chinese people, & he tells them what needs to be said to make an impression on their minds. He judges them only according to their own laws, the severity of which he moderates, and of which the Chinese themselves are the interpreters. What more can he do to please them?[301]

More generally speaking, he describes the Qianlong emperor quite systematically as a "Tartaro-Chinese Monarch" (*Monarque Tartaro-Chinois*).[302] Moreover, Amiot discerns distinct Manchu and Chinese styles in the emperor's ways of exercising his various roles. Regarding the execution of rituals, for instance, Amiot insists on a Manchu style:

> Rain, snow, wind are never a sufficient reason for [the Qianlong emperor] to dispense with attending certain etiquette exercises, however little important they appear to be. He acts thus to give a good example & to prevent *his Manchus from becoming Chinese. I want to do even the smallest things*, he says, *that can help make me look like my Ancestors. It was by leading a hard life that they set themselves up to conquer the Empire; it will only be by imitating them at this point that their descendants will keep it*.[303]

On the other hand, Amiot goes on to explain how the Qianlong emperor at the same time adopts a Chinese style regarding governance, especially regarding the contacts with the officials:

> If he imitates his Ancestors in the austerity of Tartar manners, for the conduct of his own people and for his own conduct, he likewise imitates the wisest of the Chinese Emperors for the general government of the Empire, and for his manner to act towards Magistrates & Greats. He deliberates with them, he encourages them to express their opinion with

---

301 BnF, Bréquigny 5, p. 57r; Bréquigny 3, fols. 88v–89r; *MCC*, vol. 15, pp. 344–345: "vous … Monsieur" instead of "à votre grandeur."

302 *MCC*, vol. 9, p. 53; vol. 13, p. 420; "Cour Tartaro-Chinoise": *MCC*, vol. 9, p. 6; "Sa Majesté Tartaro-chinoise": *MCC*, vol. 13, pp. 417, 454, 472.

303 *MCC*, vol. 14, p. 543; italics in original text.

> freedom, he goes to their representations when they have the public good as an object, he admits them in his presence whenever the case requires it, & in particular when they take charge.[304]

As a court missionary, Amiot certainly had encounters with the Qianlong emperor at various occasions, but it is unclear how personal these contacts were. The letters under investigation do not reveal much about their relationship. What is clear is that Amiot is full of praise for the emperor. One can follow his admiration over the course of the years, during which both the emperor and he himself advanced in age. The emperor was born in 1711, and as such was only seven years older than Amiot, who was born in 1718. Here are some examples of his praise in chronological order.

In a letter dated 26 September 1780, Amiot makes a general judgement: "If these Historians [who will write the history of his reign] are fair, they will put Kien-long among the greatest Princes who have ruled their Empire."[305] Three years later, in November 1783, Amiot includes the following self-reflection on his opinion of the emperor, by claiming that what he says is "truth" (*vérité*):

> [Kien-long] enjoys perfect health, & governs his vast Empire with the same vigour & care as he did thirty years ago. He sees everything & does everything by himself. His vigilance extends to all branches of Government & there is none of which he does not want to know even the smallest twigs. It is not his eulogy that I am making here; it is the truth that I am telling by doing him justice.[306]

Another three years later, in May 1786, Amiot compares Qianlong's poetic qualities to Voltaire:

> Since your Voltaire died, there is not, I imagine, an older Poet, of those Poets, I mean, who enjoy a somewhat widespread fame, than our Emperor Kien-long.[307]

And in September of the same year, Amiot writes the following about "our august old man" (*notre auguste Vieillard*):[308]

---

304 *MCC*, vol. 14, p. 543.
305 *MCC*, vol. 9, p. 56.
306 *MCC*, vol. 11, p. 501.
307 *MCC*, vol. 13, p. 417.
308 *MCC*, vol. 13, p. 505; see also vol. 14, p. 542.

> The lifestyle which the Emperor led when he was at the height of his strength, he still leads today with the same assiduity, same work, same exercises, same trips, same recreations.[309]

One year later, in November 1787, Amiot notes his admiration for the Qianlong emperor's physical health, which allows him to continue governing at full capacity:

> By reading what I have just reported about our old August elderly, you will undoubtedly regard him as a virtuous and even devout Prince; you will not be mistaken: he is both. (…) We are astonished to see him, especially at his age, attend exactly to the functions of the Priesthood & deal by himself with all the affairs of his vast empire with a confidence and an assiduity which have no example. (…) It looks as if he has a different constitution than other men. He fears neither the cold nor the heat.[310]

And a bit further in the same letter:

> You see, Monsieur, that our old Auguste does not slow down in his course even though he is nearing the end of his career. He is not afraid to enter into the most minute details, when their object is the advantage of his subjects.[311]

Finally in a letter to Bertin dated 1 July 1788, Amiot states that he cannot but say anything about "our august old man, the oldest as well as the longest [in reign] of all the known sovereigns, since he counts the seventy-seventh year of his age and the fifty-third of his glorious reign." Subsequently, Amiot depicts the image of an emperor who has a good health and who is still in full control.[312]

This overview illustrates how the image Amiot constructs of the Qianlong emperor and, more generally speaking, the Manchu-Chinese monarch is the result of an interaction of different factors. These include the presentation of the emperor in the gazettes, the personal contacts Amiot had with the court, and the frames of interpretation and the debates that existed in Europe. Still, one should keep in mind that Amiot's main purpose, unlike Contancin's, was not to provide detailed information on the emperor or the gazette as such, but rather to communicate the chronology of events that took place. This does not

309 *MCC*, vol. 13, p. 487.
310 *MCC*, vol. 14, pp. 542–543.
311 *MCC*, vol. 14, p. 553.
312 Inst. 1517, fols. 34r–v: Letter of Amiot to Bertin (1 July 1788).

mean that missionaries such as Bourgeois were not interested in presenting the Chinese gazette as such. This is clearly the case with the manuscript of Bréquigny 10, which includes a complete chronology of events and decisions in two months. Yet, it is not intended to praise the emperor or to illustrate his government, rather to present the gazette as a means to instruct the officials.[313]

3.5 Reception History

To what extent the information about the gazettes contained in the *Mémoires concernant les Chinois* was adopted by European scholars, still needs to be investigated. After 1790 and well into the nineteenth century, Europe was less oriented towards China, and the new encounter after the Opium War no longer produced scholars such as Voltaire who saw China as a political model. Still, some indications of the early reception history can be found both in academic journals and in the manuscript letters of Bertin.

3.5.1 *Academic Journals*

Some academic journals provide a glimpse of the reception history of the information that Amiot sent to Europe. One example is *Journal des sçavans*, already mentioned in the reception history of *Lettres édifiantes et curieuses*. At the end of the century, *Journal des sçavans* still contained reviews of publications on China, including the different volumes of *Mémoires concernant les Chinois*.[314] The reviews of volumes 9 to 15, which included Amiot's letters analysed in this chapter, were published between 1783 and 1791.[315] The reviews were written by Joseph de Guignes (1721–1800), French scholar and orientalist, who had studied Chinese under Étienne Fourmont (1683–1745). De Guignes was a long time correspondent of Amiot and had published, among others, Amiot's *Art militaire des Chinois* (1772).[316] In his articles on *Mémoires concernant les Chinois*, de Guignes underscores repeatedly that the specific volume under review is not

313 BnF, Bréquigny 10, p. 1; see also below.

314 For a general overview of China in French journals in the second part of the 18th century, see the sources mentioned earlier: Milsky (1977), chap. x and Ma Li (2019), chap. 2.

315 MCC, vol. 9: *Journal des sçavans* (Juin 1783), p. 444; (Octobre 1783), pp. 659–665. MCC, vol. 10: *Journal des sçavans* (Janvier 1785), pp. 7–11. MCC, vol. 11: *Journal des sçavans* (Octobre 1786), pp. 650–656; (Decembre 1786), pp. 785–790. MCC, vol. 12: *Journal des sçavans* (Aoust 1787), pp. 532–537. MCC, vol. 13: *Journal des sçavans* (Juin 1788), pp. 395–401. MCC, vol. 14: *Journal des sçavans* (Fevrier 1789), pp. 87–91; (Septembre 1789), pp. 577–584. MCC, vol. 15: *Journal des savans* (Mai 1791), pp. 251–257; (Septembre 1791), pp. 507–512.

316 Hermans (2005), p. 38ff.

less "curious" or "interesting" than the previous volumes,[317] "which makes one wish for the continuation of this collection, much more useful than all that the Missionaries published formerly, because their own feelings are neither disguised nor altered by the editors."[318] The latter remark clearly refers to the criticism against Du Halde, about whom missionaries complained "that they no longer recognised their work"[319] after Du Halde's editorial work.

Amiot's letters only occupy a peripheral place in de Guignes' reviews, since his attention goes to the main articles on "the arts, the sciences, the government and religion of the Chinese,"[320] with topics such as Chinese characters, the life of important Chinese, astronomical and zoologic subjects, treatment of meat and money, the life of Confucius and his disciples, and Chinese history. These articles could occupy up to several hundred pages in the volumes of *Mémoires concernant les Chinois*, in comparison with which the topic of gazettes appears rather marginal. When de Guignes discusses the letters Amiot based on the gazettes, he usually limits himself to the enumeration of some "events" (*événemens*),[321] such as A-gui's actions regarding the floods (brief mention),[322] the exile of princes to Tartary, the fire in one of the court's pavilions, the death of Amiot's Chinese collaborator, the Muslim conflicts in Shaanxi,[323] the feast for the elderly in 1785,[324] and the question of the nomination of a successor.[325] In these descriptions no attention is paid to the Chinese gazettes. De Guignes clearly considers these letters primarily as annual reports "on what happens in China at this moment,"[326] an approach also proposed by Amiot himself.[327] Consequently, for a reader such as de Guignes, Amiot's occasional short personal remarks on the emperor appear insignificant. Only once did he quote Amiot's characterisation of the emperor as "a family father who talks to his children to urge them to do well, who praises a good action, &c."[328] By contrast, the literary enterprise of the *Siku quanshu* draws the attention of de Guignes as a savant. In September 1791, in one of the last issues before the

317 *Curieux: Journal des sçavans* (Octobre 1783), pp. 659, 665; (Octobre 1786), p. 650; *intéressant: Journal des sçavans* (Janvier 1785), p. 7; (Octobre 1786), p. 650; (Septembre 1791), p. 507; *intéresser: Journal des sçavans* (Juin 1788), p. 395.

318 *Journal des sçavans* (Octobre 1783), p. 665.

319 *Journal des sçavans* (Janvier 1785), p. 11.

320 *Journal des sçavans* (Octobre 1783), p. 664.

321 *Journal des sçavans* (Decembre 1786), p. 789; see also MCC, vol. 14, p. 525.

322 *Journal des sçavans* (Octobre 1783), p. 659.

323 *Journal des sçavans* (Decembre 1786), pp. 787–790.

324 *Journal des sçavans* (Aoust 1787), pp. 536–538.

325 *Journal des sçavans* (Decembre 1786), p. 787; (Septembre 1791), p. 508.

326 *Journal des sçavans* (Decembre 1786), p. 787.

327 Cf. for instance MCC, vol. 9, p. 6 quoted earlier.

328 MCC, vol. 13, p. 417 quoted in *Journal des sçavans* (Juin 1788), pp. 399–400.

Journal des sçavans' publication was temporarily discontinued (1792–1815) in the aftermath of the French Revolution, de Guignes' review of volume 15 of *Mémoires concernant les Chinois* contained a lengthy description of the *Siku quanshu* project, with references to the imperial edicts quoted in Amiot's letters, thus making the project known to a wide academic and learned public.[329]

De Guignes appreciated the information sent by the missionaries. At the end of his review of volume 14 he writes the following comment:

> Elsewhere, Mr. Amiot notes that the Chinese pay little attention to trade with foreign nations, that they only receive embassies as far as they can be seen as a mark of submission, that such ambassadors are so observed, that they cannot say a word that is not reported to the Minister, that they cannot leave the hotel assigned to them without permission, likewise, to make or receive visits, to give parties. He adds that on the supposition that an English or Russian embassy came to China, the Savants who would join it could in no way satisfy their curiosity, because they would be constantly spied on. Thus, he said, the plan to send Savants and Artists other than those who would be in the service of the Emperor, to learn in the workshops, in the factories, to travel the countryside, and to make observations of natural history; such a project can only be carried out when the Chinese have changed the form of their government. Therefore, one must be absolutely Missionary and Artist of the Emperor to enter China, that is to say, one must devote oneself to eternal slavery.[330]

This statement underscores the difficulty Europeans experienced in attempting to gain direct access to information about China. Though solely based on printed sources such as books and gazettes, the *Mémoires concernant les Chinois* were a welcome supplement to remediate this deficiency.

3.5.2 *Bertin and the French King*

Another example of reception history, more on an interpersonal level, is the correspondence between Amiot and Bertin, which is a unique, though very limited, lens. As could be observed from an earlier quotation, Bertin was enthusiastic about the information presented to him and asked more about the gazettes. This does not mean that he has accepted all of Amiot's interpretations:

---

329 *Journal des Savans* (Septembre 1791), pp. 507–512: on the *Siku quanshu*, pp. 508–510. The review was written by Joseph de Guignes (1721–1800, French scholar and orientalist, who had studied Chinese).

330 *Journal des sçavans* (Septembre 1789), p. 584.

> Your reports that are singularly interesting familiarize us with a country that was so little known to the Europeans a few years ago, and diminish, so to speak, the interval which separates us from it. But if I am sure that you will be read by everyone with equal pleasure, I would not be surprised, however, that people do not adopt universally and entirely the inductions that you draw on the advantages of the Chinese Government ~~and the real qualities of the present sovereign of the Emperor~~[331]

Bertin criticises the severe punishment for relatively small delicts as in the earlier case of Jin Congshan 金從善:

> People shall be more struck by the injustice and barbarity of such penal laws, which obviously were originally made to flatter the pride of a despot and to place him at a greater distance from his subjects.[332]

Bertin was also in regular contact with the French king Louis XVI (1754–r.1774–1793), and at times he indirectly refers to the reaction of the king, including on the *Siku quanshu*:

> I thank you for the details you give me about the large collection that the Emperor has printed (). +++ (note by Bertin in the margins:) The King has read everything, and the extracts from the gazettes with pleasure[333]

A similar reaction is given to other letters that report on the *Siku quanshu*, among other topics:

> ... they [=the documents] arrived in time to be put under the eyes of the King who charged me to testify his satisfaction to you, and to be inserted in and complete the 13th volume of our memoirs, which you will receive I hope for this monsoon.[334]

---

331 Letter of Bertin to Amiot (Paris, 31 December 1784): Inst. 1524, fols. 16r–23r: fol. 16r. Strikethrough in original text.

332 Letter of Bertin to Amiot (Paris, 31 December 1784): Inst. 1524, fols. 16r–23r: fol. 16v.

333 Letter of Bertin to Amiot (Paris, 31 December 1784): Inst. 1524, fols. 16r–23r: fol. 16v.

334 Letter of Bertin to Amiot (Paris, 22 November 1787), in response to the letters of 26 May, 14 September, and 1 October 1786: Inst. 1524: fols. 90r–99v: fol. 90r. For other examples: Inst. 1524, fols. 27r–34v: Letter of Bertin to Amiot (19 October 1785; in fact later): fol. 27r (among others in response to the ceremony for old people, reported in Letter of 15 October 1785): "I hope that the King will read it with pleasure, and that it will have the same success in our memories." Inst. 1524, fols. 36r–51r: Letter of Bertin to Amiot (21 December 1785): "I have at this moment extracted your three letters of October 2, November 15 and 29, and I propose still to put them under the eyes of the King, who, I am sure, will read them with

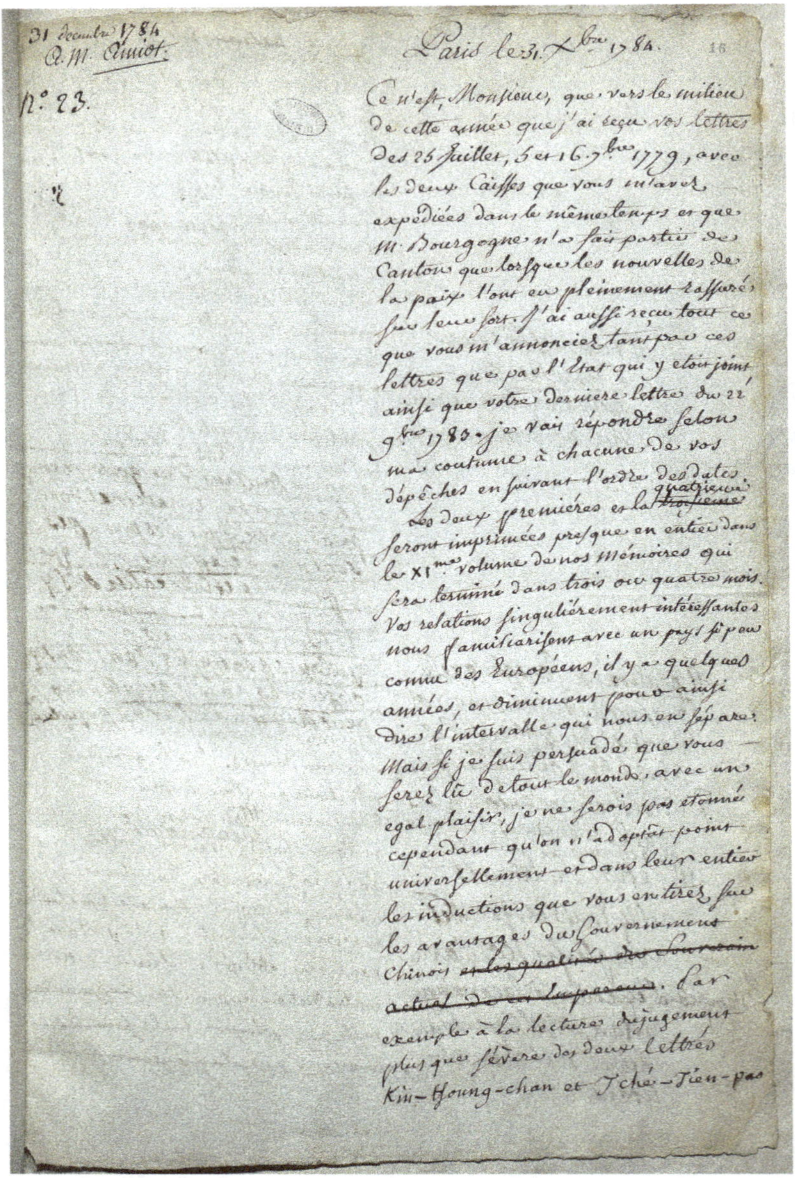

31 decembre 1784
a M. Amiot

No. 23.

Paris le 31. Xbre 1784. 16

Ce n'est, Monsieur, que vers le milieu de cette année que j'ai reçu vos lettres des 25 Juillet, 5 et 16. 7bre 1779, avec les deux Caisses que vous m'avez expédiées dans le même temps et que M. Bourgogne n'a fait partir de Canton que lorsque les nouvelles de la paix l'ont eu pleinement rassuré sur leur sort. J'ai aussi reçu tout ce que vous m'annonciez tant par ces lettres que par l'Etat qui y étoit joint ainsi que votre derniere lettre du 22 9bre 1780. je vais répondre selon ma coutume à chacune de vos dépêches en suivant l'ordre des dates.

Les deux premières et la ~~troisieme~~ quatrieme seront imprimées presque en entier dans le XIme volume de nos Mémoires qui sera terminé dans trois ou quatre mois. Vos relations singulierement intéressantes nous familiarisent avec un pays si peu connu des Européens, il y a quelques années, et diminuent pour ainsi dire l'intervalle qui nous en sépare. Mais si je suis persuadé que vous serez lû de tout le monde, avec un egal plaisir, je ne serois pas étonné cependant qu'on n'adoptât point universellement et dans leur entier les inductions que vous en tirez, sur les avantages du Gouvernement Chinois ~~et les qualités du Souverain actuel de cet Empire~~. Par exemple à la lecture du jugement plus que sévère des deux lettrés Kin-Houng-chan et Tché-Tien-pao

ILLUSTRATION 24 Letter of Bertin to Amiot (Paris, 31 December 1784): "*Je vous remercie des details que vous me donnez sur la grande collection que fait imprimer l'Empereur*" ("I thank you for the details you give me about the large collection that the Emperor has printed"). +++ (note by Bertin to be added) "*Le Roy a lu le tout, et les extraits des gazettes avec plaisir*" ("The King has read everything, and the extracts from the gazettes with pleasure"): Institut de France, 1524, fol. 16v

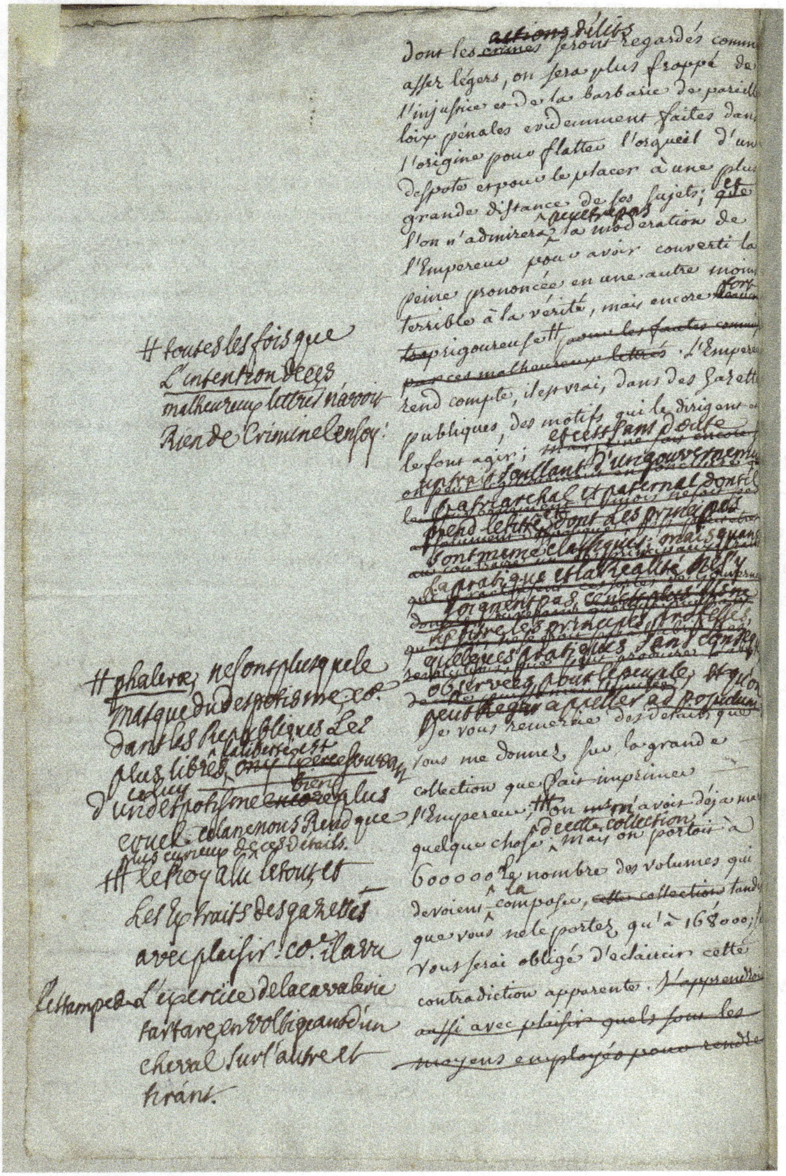

dont les ~~crimes~~ délits seront regardés comme
assez légers, on sera plus frappé de
l'injustice et de la barbarie de pareilles
loix pénales evidemment faites dans
l'origine pour flatter l'orgueil d'un
despote et pour le placer à une plus
grande distance de ses sujets; et que
l'on n'admirera peut-être pas la modération de
l'Empereur pour avoir converti la
peine prononcée en une autre moins
terrible à la vérité, mais encore fort
rigoureuse [illegible]. L'Empereur
rend compte, il est vrai, dans des Gazettes
publiques, des motifs qui le dirigent et
le font agir; [illegible]
Je vous remercie des détails que
vous me donnez sur la grande
collection que fait imprimer
l'Empereur; on m'avoit déja mandé
quelque chose de cette collection, mais on portoit à
600000 le nombre des volumes qui
devoient la composer, tandis
que vous ne le portez qu'à 168000; je
vous serai obligé d'eclaircir cette
contradiction apparente. ~~J'apprendrois aussi avec plaisir quels sont les moyens employés pour rendre~~

toutes les fois que L'intention de ces malheureux lettrés n'avoit rien de criminel en soy.

phaleræ, ne sont plus que le masque du despotisme etc. dans les Républiques les plus libres [illegible] d'un despotisme [illegible] plus cruel. cela ne nous rend que plus curieux de ces détails.

le Roy a lu le tout, et les extraits des gazettes avec plaisir. co. il a vu l'estampe de l'exercice de la cavalerie tartare en voltigeant d'un cheval sur l'autre et tirant.

Bertin himself was very excited about the *Siku quanshu* and even dreamt of having a copy of it so as to better spread Chinese knowledge in Europe.

> But there is, moreover, a real magnificence in the project which the Emperor has conceived to assemble into an immense collection of 600 thousand volumes all that China contains of good books. This collection would be a superb present to make to our Europe which could thus enjoy all the Chinese literature. Please let me know if it would be possible to acquire it, transmitted and packaged at Canton, for example, by making some gifts of price to the Emperor, which may be agreeable to him, for example, tapestries, goblins, mirrors,...[335]

This ambitious project shows the open attitude of a French statesman towards one of the highlights of cultural productions in the mid-Qing dynasty. Even if he himself did not master the Chinese language, he at least was aware that Europe could learn from it. All this was made possible through the communication about the *Siku quanshu*, originally based on the gazettes.

Conclusion

The reports sent to Europe and published in *Mémoires concernant les Chinois* give a very ample insight into the gazettes of the late Qianlong reign. In addition, the Bréquigny 10 document presents their content in the most systematic way. Being a quasi-full translation, it reflects the structure of the Chinese gazette of that period – the *tizou shijian*. The information that these documents provide about the content of the gazettes is considerably more extensive than the information that is available for the Kangxi and Yongzheng periods: many topics were discussed and some in great detail, as was shown by the example of the *Siku quanshu*. Alongside these descriptions, one can also observe the interpretations made by the translators.

In these interpretative comments, the documents presented above echo some of the themes that had already been present in earlier texts on the gazette. One hundred years after the first reports on the topic, they still emphasized a

---

as much pleasure as those that have already received from His Majesty the most flattering approval."

335 Letter of Bertin to Bourgeois (Paris, 15 December 1779): Inst. 1523, fols. 43r–50v: fol. 45r–v. In response, among others, to the letters of 1778 (on the punishment of Wang Xihou 王錫侯 (1713–1777) and the *Siku quanshu* project).

comparison with the European gazette, and continued to reflect on the related questions of trustworthiness and truth. They also underscored various aspects that were already remarked upon in the discussion of the letters of Contancin: the importance of the public good, the instructive nature of the gazette for officials, its role in efficient administration, and its function as representation of imperial truth. Amiot's and Bourgeois' presentations align with the idea that both secrecy and transparency were integral to the Qing information order. They indicate that the court authorised the circulation of selected official documents, not only to instruct and discipline the bureaucracy, but also to inform the larger public.

Unlike the European authors during the two previous reigns who were most often located in Canton, Amiot and Bourgeois resided in Beijing, were in close contact with the court and could benefit from first-hand information. Therefore, they represent a courtly rather than a provincial view. Their documents thus present slightly different reading practices by the Jesuits who were involved. One may assume that Amiot, Bourgeois, and others were regular readers of the gazette, and certainly that Amiot was helped in this regard by a Chinese collaborator. Their reports were primarily made to inform Europeans such as Bertin about China and its government. Given the regular exchange of letters between Bertin and the missionaries, the reports also responded to requests and questions by Bertin. Moreover, the letters were addressed to a statesman, who is clearly interested in the state affairs reported in the letters. The interest of the primary audience framed what was subsequently published for the European audience. The letters provide a wealth of information not only about the emperor, but also about actions by high officials, and governance in general. Indeed, it was decided at a relatively early stage of the exchange of letters that some of them would be published, thus reaching a much wider public.

ILLUSTRATION 25 Painting of Joseph-Marie Amiot, gouache (?) on paper, anonymous, undated (possibly c. 1780)
@TONG BINGXUE 仝冰雪, PRIVATE COLLECTOR

General Conclusion

Enlightenment thinkers such as Voltaire, French statesmen such as Bertin, and European scholars such as the readers of *Journal des sçavans* got access to information about China through translated versions of the Chinese gazette, a unique medium that made intercultural communication possible in the seventeenth and eighteenth centuries. This book intends to be a guide or source reader to these European sources about the Chinese gazette of the pre-1800 period, mostly compiled by missionaries who lived in China in the early and mid-Qing. By presenting these documents as extensively as possible, this book aims to show how they shed light on the early existence, form, structure, content, and the intercultural use of the Chinese gazette.

Looking at China from the Periphery

The approach that is used here is one of "looking at China from the periphery" (从周边看中国) and "interconnected cultural history" (交错的文化史), which are also research lines pursued by academic centres such as the National Institute for Advanced Humanistic Studies at Fudan University 复旦大学文史研究院. The notions refer to the practice of observing and studying Chinese traditions and culture through written materials preserved in various cultural areas around China and in the West. This facilitates a closer look at how Chinese culture is interconnected with the cultural history of other regions, such as Europe or Korea. The investigation into both Chinese and foreign documents on the Chinese gazette preserved outside of China shows that these not only confirm the established knowledge on the gazette in the early and mid-Qing, but that they also significantly expand the knowledge about it.

European sources are not the only way of look at the Chinese gazette from the periphery. While this book is focused specifically on Sino-European contacts, intercultural communication at that time was thus broader in scope. This can be illustrated through a brief look at Korean envoys in the early and mid-Qing, who have been the subject of investigation in Ding Chennan's research on intelligence gathering by these envoys. She first investigated how during the Ming, Korean emissaries collected information on the basis of military post courier gazettes (*tangbao* 塘報) and other official reports, which they managed to obtain in a context of severe restrictions concerning the divulgence of intelligence. In the early and mid-Qing, as the *tangbao*'s role as a form of military communication began to fade, the official Chinese gazette, for which

© NICOLAS STANDAERT, 2022 | DOI:10.1163/9789004505001_006

the emissaries often continued to use the term *tangbao*, became an important source of information for the reports that they submitted to the Joseon court. They sometimes received copies from the Qing translation office, or bought them directly from the publishing houses in Beijing.

There are of course differences between the Joseon envoys and the missionaries, such as the fact that the former stayed only briefly in the capital and were used to communicating in the same script as the Chinese, whereas the missionaries remained on a long-term basis and communicated with Europe in different languages, thus being obligated to translate. In addition, there were also differences with regards to the audiences who might have access to certain information: while the Korean reports originally remained confined to the Joseon court, in the European case, information could circulate more widely. While some documents remained confined to the administrators of Propaganda Fide in Rome or to the royal advisor Bertin, most of the information was made public through publications in collections such as *Lettres édifiantes et curieuses* or *Mémoires concernant les Chinois*, which reached a large European audience. Yet there are also several striking similarities. In both the European and the Korean case, information was not only transmitted through personal observation and data provided by eyewitnesses, but also on the basis of the gazettes. In other words, even if they unavoidably looked at the Qing from their own perspective and with their own frames of interpretation, they also employed an indigenous medium that informed them about the government's decisions and that considerably and independently supplemented their knowledge – something that was rather unique in cultural exchanges at that time, especially in the exchange with Europe. In both cases, the gazettes were used as an account of events happening in China, but also as a way to get insight into the functioning of the Qing government. Concerning the topic of governance, the documents served also to inform local debates: in Europe, about whether or not the Manchu-Chinese emperor was a despot; in Korea, on whether a foreign government would be able to sustain their rule for more than one hundred years. Finally, in both cases the view from the periphery not only provides insight into the global dispersion of the gazette, but into the gazette itself as well.

Form, Structure, Content

The reports that have been analysed in this book inform us in the first place about the form, structure, and content of the Chinese gazettes. Regarding the form and structure, important resources are systematic descriptions of the gazette such as those provided by Contancin or Bourgeois, which are in fact very similar to modern descriptions of the Chinese gazette. There are also the few remaining copies of the gazette sent to Europe by Amiot and preserved in the Bibliothèque nationale de France, and the transcripts of the Chinese excerpts Perroni added to the translations he sent to Rome and which are preserved in the Archives of the Propaganda Fide. Another important source is the full translation of more than two months of the gazette made by Bourgeois in the manuscript of BnF, Bréquigny 10. All these sources taken together give more insight into the existence and form of the gazette, and led to the identification of *tizou quanlu* 題奏全錄 as the gazette for the Yongzheng period and confirmation of *tizou shijian* 題奏事件 as the gazette of the Qianlong period. These identifications were further confirmed by the above-mentioned travel accounts of the Korean envoys to China, which further underscores the potential role of sources from the periphery. In addition, the sources reviewed in this book provide detailed information about the formal aspects of the gazettes. This includes the printing of the gazette with movable characters, the page structure and length of an average gazette during the Yongzheng period, and the one-month break of publishing around the Chinese New Year period during the Qianlong reign. Some questions, however, remain unsolved, especially regarding the direct or indirect (re)production and use of the gazette in the provinces or the Manchu banners.

Concerning the content, the European sources provide a broad scope of information, which is also instructive for the study of the gazette as such. This is especially so because the Chinese originals for these reigns have almost all disappeared and the information can no longer be found in the surviving official Chinese sources, such as *Qing shilu*. In other words, European sources on the gazette regularly provide additional information to the official sources concerning state affairs on which historians base themselves today. The European sources transmit this information, sometimes in a fragmented way, such as the scattered references about the Tancheng earthquake, including the ominous events that accompanied it. Other times, information was transmitted in a more structured way, as with the letters by Contancin and Perroni, as well as Amiot. Finally, Bourgeois' translations in the manuscript Bréquigny 10 represent a very systematic transmission of information to Europe. It should be noted that Christianity was only rarely the subject of the reports on the gazettes, even when the missionaries were eager to search for news related to this issue. This also seemingly indicates that there was generally little information about this subject in the gazettes. By contrast, the selection made by the missionaries covers a wide range of topics related to the art of governing: rituals, relief for disasters, the demotion and punishment of officials, rewards for virtuous commoners, and imperial speeches. In short, the translated reports regularly underscore the instructive value of the "acta, verba et gesta" of the emperor and his officials for China itself.[1] Given the nature of this "China news analysis," the missionaries' reports quite naturally became points of reference for European considerations of Chinese governmental structures. They touched upon themes such as the role of the emperor, the selection of officials, the efficacy of the bureaucracy, and even the *bien public*.

Participants in the Local Information System

European sources afford insight not only into the gazette itself, but also into how contemporary Europeans read the gazette within China, and how they, as global agents, became writers and interpreters who informed Europe about China. They made the Chinese gazette part of a global information network. Before looking at the global aspect, it is worthwhile to take a closer look at their agency within the context of changes in the local information system within China of the late Ming and early Qing times.

Wang Hung-tai has argued that, especially during the late Ming, the Chinese gazette evolved from a relatively limited system intended to convey information from the court to the civil service, to a system that became more open and expansive and that entered into the daily lives of many more people. The gazette turned into a means of broadcasting information and became a must-read for people taking an interest in the matters of the court. Moreover, gazettes helped set up what might be simply called a "public sphere" in which the individual could participate in and scrutinize matters of the state. The readers, though separated by distance, could form a shared view of current events and the functioning of the state through a reading of the same gazettes and by openly discussing state matters. In the eyes of Wang, in this "public sphere," the readers not only played the role of observer, but made a step towards becoming actual participants. He also shows how drama, novels, and personal interactions likewise made it possible for information to be circulated and public opinion to be formed. As media offered an avenue to view, judge, and affect society, it allowed individuals to participate in what could be collectively called a "public society."[2]

1 Wagner (2007), p. 3.

2 Wang Hung-tai (2010), pp. 169, 172, 177, 187, 210–211. This is the translated version of Wang Hung-tai (2009). Similar ideas concerning the development of a public opinion are expressed by Wang Fan-sen (2018), pp. 5–6.

It should be noted that Wang Hung-tai's study sketches the society of the Ming and the beginning of the Qing, which was much less politically controlled than that of the Yongzheng or Qianlong era under discussion here. Still, this book extended Wang's interpretation of the circulation of information to the early and mid-Qing at two levels. First, the scope of the "public sphere" is expanded to include foreigners such as missionaries in China. Second, the circulation of information that makes this "public sphere" possible is extended outwards, toward Europe.

In order to investigate the use of gazettes by foreigners, it is useful to remind oneself that the European missionaries in China constituted only a small group of people, which in the course of the eighteenth century declined considerably in number: from a climax of 144 European missionaries in 1701, their number had declined to 86 around 1724, after the expulsions by the Kangxi emperor and just before the new wave of expulsions under the Yongzheng emperor. In the middle of the century under the Qianlong reign, in 1765, there were 57 missionaries, and in 1775 this number had already been reduced to 43 missionaries. At the end of the century in 1800, there were only 26 European missionaries left in China.[3] Thus, within China at least, this analysis concerns only a very small number of potential foreign readers.

Rudolf Wagner points out that the most important factor in the operations of a medium such as the gazette in the public sphere is its acceptance by a reader. "It is the pull rather than the push."[4] However, a lack of available sources about readership often leads studies to take the gazette itself (the "push side") as basis in order to imagine the reader (the "pull side"). By contrast, in using the European sources that were analysed in this book, one gets direct access to the reader, in the same way (but more extensively) as jottings (*biji*) by Chinese scholars can give access to the Chinese readership. Seen from the point of view of the producers, though, one may assume that in the mid-Qing the missionaries were not (yet) the envisaged readers of the gazette, since its imagined readers were officials (i.e. the bureaucratic community), who through this medium could be informed and instructed about state affairs.[5] Yet, the European sources have shown that the gazettes also circulated beyond the bureaucracy: by the early and mid-Qing they had reached a wider public, beyond the strict

3 Nicolas Standaert, "Number of missionaries," in *HCC*, pp. 300–308.

4 Wagner (2020), p. 421; in this article as well as his introduction to Wagner (2009), Wagner discusses Jürgen Habermas' ideas about 'public sphere,' and Benedict Anderson's concept of 'imagined communities.'

5 This context changed in the mid-nineteenth century when the Qing government was well aware that the *jingbao* was read by foreigners, and this seems to have made it wary about what to release for publication. See Harris (2018), p. 13; Mokros (2012), pp. 114, 170.

literati network. This broader audience included Europeans in China, some of whom actively read the gazettes. Just like for other readers, reading the gazettes enabled individual missionaries to exceed the normal range of daily life experience. It allowed them to share news – at a distance – among themselves and with Chinese collaborators, thus facilitating shared participation in a wider public society in the Chinese context in which they were living. They discussed state affairs and even expressed their opinion about them independently of the state.

These European sources also reveal some characteristics of the reading practices of the missionaries. The missionaries discussed in this book evidently represent only a small portion of the potential readers among missionaries, since, as attested by the letters, only a small number among them actually read the gazette. Some among them did so very intensively, often with the help of Chinese scholars or Chinese priests. They read the gazettes to be kept informed not only about issues related to Christianity, but also about broader administrative, political, and governmental concerns. At times, this common sharing of information on the basis of the gazette created a network among the missionaries in Beijing and Canton, or other places such as Raozhou. They shared information about new appointments or demotions of officials who were favourable to them. The agency of the European reader within China went beyond their own circle. On the basis of the information gathered from the gazettes, they could interact with Qing officials. Occasionally their participation could even extend to (attempted) involvement in the shaping of the information circulated in this public sphere, as when missionaries attempted to get particular texts published, or when they published certain favourable decrees towards Christianity separately in different provinces.

Writers and Translators in a Global Information Network

Missionaries were not only readers, they also became writers. They were not only agents in the domestic public sphere within China but also extended this communication network outwards, namely through the transmission of information about and from the gazettes to Europe. Thereto they also became translators.

Compared to the reading of the gazettes, this intercultural circulation of information involved an even smaller number of missionaries. Aside from the missionaries during the Kangxi period who made some scattered references to the gazette in their writings, the most substantial resources about the gazettes were produced by only two to four individuals: Contancin and Amiot, whose works were published; and Perroni and Bourgeois, whose works remained as manuscripts and thus reached a far smaller audience. On their own initiative, they became aware of the importance of the Chinese gazette, felt it important to communicate its existence to Europe, and started to report about it and translate selections from it. In Europe as well, the dissemination relied on the initiative of only a few individuals, such as Du Halde or Bertin. Yet, despite being few in numbers, they realised an enormous impact, as their efforts contributed to the wide cultural communication between China and Europe that was built through the gazettes.

At least two factors enabled this communication: the existence of a relatively advanced print culture, and translation practices by the missionaries. The fact that both China and Europe had a firmly established print culture significantly facilitated this intercultural communication. Since the early Qing, the gazette was printed (with movable type) and spread over the country, so that even foreigners in China, such as European missionaries both in Beijing and Canton, had easy access to it. The missionaries' own communication with Europe was handwritten, but their reports on the gazettes were ultimately published in various printed collections in Europe and thus reached a wide audience. This connection to print technology is underscored by the missionaries' adoption of the European term 'gazette,' the existence of which was closely linked to the development of print culture in Europe. The circulation of news by means of gazettes was one of the aspects that contributed to the developments that took place regarding the production, distribution, and consumption of information in Europe that have collectively been labelled the 'information revolution.' The existence of a gazette in China and the transmission of its contents to Europe by the missionaries helped expand the existing information networks and contributed to the opening up of global perspectives in this circulation of information.[6]

The other main characteristic is that most missionaries chose to translate primary sources. In this regard, the texts about the Chinese gazette are representative of the European knowledge production about Asia in the late eighteenth century. A significant aspect in the production of this knowledge is the importance of local textual sources. As Jürgen Osterhammel pointed out in a comparative perspective, one of the characteristics of late eighteenth-century authors writing about the East is that they increasingly drew on local scholarship, expressed in Asian works and documents, for which Europeans needed to know the local languages. "Pushed a little further, the high esteem in which the native texts were held could give rise to the view that it was not the task of

6 See on this topic Blair & Fitzgerald (2015).

European Orientalists to discourse *on* Asiatic cultures but rather, through translation, to allow these cultures speak for themselves to a European readership."[7] Several of the treatises discussed in this book are an excellent example of this phenomenon, with the manuscript of Bréquigny 10 as the clearest example of allowing Chinese gazettes to speak for themselves. With their texts, the missionaries tried to contribute to the growth of European knowledge about Chinese gazettes "by presenting as much information as systematically as possible, without overly subjective impressions getting in the way."[8]

This is not to say that there were no subjective elements involved in the process by which information on the Chinese gazette was transmitted to Europe. One such element is the way of translating itself, which Osterhammel summarized as follows for the eighteenth century: "The translator saw his relationship to the translated text as one of mastery, not servitude."[9] What is true for eighteenth-century translators in general is true for the translators of Chinese texts that were included in *Description ... de la Chine* and *Mémoires concernant les Chinois*, namely that very few of them "felt duty-bound to cling slavishly to the text."[10] In certain cases, they dealt with the translation by providing extensive details; in other cases, they tampered with the original texts to make them more accessible for Europeans, which sometimes made the identification of the sources difficult. This also happened in the case of the translation of the Chinese gazettes. Still, it is noteworthy that in the instances where the French and Italian texts could be confronted with the original Chinese text, it appears that Perroni, Contancin, Amiot and Bourgeois made very precise translations, which were faithful to the original text, rather than interpretative paraphrases. Another subjective element concerns the selection of the texts: first by the missionaries and their Chinese collaborators, and then by the editors who prepared the missionaries' manuscripts for publication. It was pointed out that this selection was preceded by another selective process on the Chinese side, since the Chinese gazettes themselves were composed of texts that the emperor and higher officials had selected to be made public. What the European readers got to see was thus the result of a process of selection on both the Chinese and European sides.

Still, the choice for extensive translations by the missionaries ensured that the discourse *by* Chinese gazettes was still primary to the discourse *on* Chinese gazettes. This aspect needs to be underscored since modern scholarship tends

7 Osterhammel (2018), pp. 203–204.
8 Cf. Osterhammel (2018), p. 215.
9 Osterhammel (2018), p. 232.
10 Ibidem.

to focus on the (mis)interpretation of China by Europeans in the eighteenth century, while it underestimates the amount and quality of the translations of which the works by Perroni, Contancin, Amiot, and Bourgeois are examples and which made the rather unique cultural communication with Europe possible. In this respect, Osterhammel points out on the basis of contemporary evidence that "around the mid-eighteenth century, the public in France and Germany was better informed about China than about many countries on Europe's periphery."[11] This was made possible, on the one hand, because there was something like the gazette in China, and, on the other hand, because these missionaries "embodied a distinctively modern type of European living abroad."[12] They were not private travellers who happened to pass through a culture, but experts who learned the language and translated texts with the help of Chinese collaborators. In addition, they were members of a large supranational organisation that was willing to inform Europe about China. Through their translations of the Chinese gazette, they gave European readers access to knowledge about the Qing art of governing they would otherwise have been denied.[13]

Interpreters and Commentators

Europeans not only read or translated the Chinese gazette, but also provided an interpretation of the gazettes themselves and commented on its content. In doing so, they extended the local discussions they had on Chinese state affairs and enabled potential discussions in Europe. In the introduction to this book it was pointed out that there are at least three frames along which modern historians study the Chinese gazette: the history of the press, the history of the state, and the history of information in society.[14] Applying these to the ways in which the missionaries interpreted the gazette, it becomes clear that they framed the gazette primarily as an instrument of bureaucratic administration, and less as a premodern government newspaper or as a medium for the circulation of information in society, though the latter two approaches are not entirely absent. Thus, the missionaries saw and presented the Chinese gazette as a means to instruct the officials and form an empire-wide bureaucracy, as an effective means to communicate imperial decisions within a large bureaucratic

11 Osterhammel (2018), pp. 115–116.
12 Osterhammel (2018), p. 131.
13 Cf. Osterhammel (2018), p. 231.
14 Cf. Mokros (2016), pp. 14–20.

system and to the population, and as a concrete proof of administrative efficiency. This also explains why the emperor and his way of governing are so often at the centre of their interpretation. Thus relying on a different vocabulary the missionaries' presentation and interpretation of the gazettes echo in a striking way the notions of "curated transparency," "information order," and "documentary authority" used by Emily Mokros in her interpretation of the Qing gazettes. The court and the central bureaucracy were depicted as sharing the notion that the transparent and widespread circulation of imperial documents could discipline the bureaucracy and improve administrative efficiency. Moreover, their depictions illustrated how the communication systems which established an information order enabled strong-willed emperors to consolidate their power and authority vis-à-vis the bureaucracy, as was the case with the Kangxi, Yongzheng, and Qianlong emperors.[15]

The fact that gazettes mainly addressed a literati audience, and presented a literati view on China and its government, also coloured the view of China that was presented to Europe. Though one does find traces of the "common people" in some of the articles published in the gazettes, such as commoners who got honoured or people who suffered from natural disasters, the representation of them is still made through the perspective of this high cultural elite. The reports on the gazettes by the missionaries are an echo of this viewpoint, with a literati perspective on the populace rather than an active involvement of the "common people" in the construction of their (own) image.

In this context, it is useful to be reminded that, besides personal contacts, the gazette was more or less the only way to have access to (official) news at the time. In other words, despite the fact that information spread via drama performances and novels, there were basically no newspapers that distributed news that had not been sanctioned by the court, no politically-oriented pamphlets that antagonised rivals, and there were no periodicals that shared reviews of recent publications. In this sense, it is no surprise that the missionaries spontaneously made a comparison with the European context, where such media did exist. Such comparisons can already be found in the earliest reports about the gazette and still existed one hundred years later. Yet what is most striking in these comparisons, is that the authors linked the gazette and the state news they included to questions of trustworthiness, authenticity, and truth.

In order to illustrate this point, one can bring together some of the quotes that were already cited in this book. Already during the Kangxi reign, one finds remarks such as: "The public newsletters in China, however, are not like the ones in Europe, where accounts of different nature are brought together. In those of

15 Mokros (2021).

China, which come forth from the Court, one can hardly read anything else than the deeds and the decrees of the Emperor."[16] More than twenty-five years later, Perroni remarks upon the following difference with European gazettes: "In the gazettes of China we do not encounter that license, which we see in ours, to tell without examination all sorts of successes, whether they are true or false; nor is there any danger that the story will be altered by the passion of the writer … As a result, what is written in the [Chinese gazettes] is equipped with all the authenticity necessary to deserve faith and to exclude any reasonable suspicion that passion, ignorance, and particular interest may have changed or altered the truth."[17] Around the same time, Contancin expresses a similar view: "What makes the Gazette of China very useful for the government is that, instead of filling it, as is done in certain parts of Europe, with useless things and often with slanders and calumny, it only mentions what relates to the Emperor."[18] He also explains that one of the reasons why European missionaries do not read the gazette is that "at the mere word of gazette they hear, they imagine that it resembles certain gazettes of Europe, in which one puts or has put everything one wants, good and bad, without any distinction."[19] More than fifty years later, Amiot comes up with similar arguments, even pointing out that the name 'gazette' leads the Europeans in a certain direction of interpretation: "The name of Gazettes, which we are accustomed to give them, might make you believe that they are almost similar to the Gazettes of Europe, in which the Composers bring pell-mell all that they think about to insert: truth beside lies, the reality of events dressed up with circumstances which disfigure the frivolity of the conjectures, false reasonings, and the absurdity of popular noises in the wake of the political presentations."[20]

These citations have three traits in common: they establish a contrast between the European and Chinese gazettes; this difference is linked to the question of truth, authenticity, and trustworthiness; and this in turn is linked to the official validation of the information contained in the gazettes. The European gazettes are not only depicted as being filled "with useless things and often with slanders and calumny," but in them "true and false," "good and bad," and "truth and lies" are mixed together. Chinese gazettes, by contrast, are "equipped with all the authenticity necessary to deserve faith." They come forth from the court "for nothing is printed here which has not been presented to

16 *Brevis relatio* (1701), p. 14b, in Standaert (2012), p. 429.
17 APF, SOCP: vol. 33 (dall'Anno 1727 al 1728), fol. 326r.
18 *LEC* (1728), vol. 18, pp. 434–435; *LEC* (1810–1811), vol. 20, pp. 301–302.
19 *LEC* (1729), vol. 19, pp. 267–269; *LEC* (1810–1811), vol. 21, pp. 76–77.
20 *MCC*, vol. 14, p. 524: Extrait d'une lettre de M. Amiot, Missionnaire, Ecrite de Péking, le 25 Janvier 1787.

the Emperor, or which does not come from the Emperor himself."[21] Moreover, authors such as Intorcetta and Contancin insist that those who are in charge of publishing the gazette, "would not dare to add anything to it, not even their own reflections, under the penalty of corporal punishment,"[22] referring to the case of the two persons condemned to capital punishment because they spread false information about the Yongzheng emperor's trip in the Yuanmingyuan. Even Voltaire, in his *Essai sur les mœurs et l'esprit des nations*, wrote that "the journal of the Chinese empire, [is] the most authentic and useful newspaper in the world, since it contains the details of all the public needs, resources and interests of all the orders of the State."[23] And elsewhere he stresses, in the same vein as Perroni, the gazette's "authentic" character by stating that it "is superior to our gazettes, in that it is made under the supervision of the mandarins of each province, reviewed by a supreme tribunal, and that each piece bears with it a genuine authenticity which is decisive in contentious matters."[24]

The questions of trustworthiness, authenticity, and truth, which can be distinguished but which also overlap each other, contain different aspects. The gazettes are considered trustworthy because they are officially approved. The fact that the private printing houses had to reproduce the approved information without changes or additions of other texts made that the gazette contained reliable information about decisions by the court. In this sense the information is also "authentic." But it was not only considered reliable regarding its source and processing, it was usually also considered true regarding its content. This is largely due to the style and format of the gazette, which represents the literal transcription of memorials and imperial decisions without alteration. Such kind of appreciation towards the Chinese gazette, when read altogether with opinions expressed by some of the Jesuits regarding bureaucracy, civil examination, and women, implies that there was a rather strong inclination towards the more "ordered" or "rigid" social structure present in China. The expression of such an inclination could be understood as a critique towards Europe.

Yet, as Voltaire pointed out, without further explanation, "if [what is included in] this gazette is true, it must be believed that not all truths are there. Moreover, they should not all be there."[25] There have been various indi-

21 *LEC* (1729), vol. 19, pp. 267–269; *LEC* (1810–1811), vol. 21, pp. 76–77.

22 *LEC* (1729), vol. 19, pp. 267–269; *LEC* (1810–1811), vol. 21, pp. 76–77.

23 Voltaire, *Essai sur les mœurs et l'esprit des nations: Tome 2: Avant-propos et chapitres 1–37* (*OCV* 22) (2009), p. 31.

24 Voltaire, *Œuvres alphabétiques I* (*OCV* 33) (1987), p. 217.

25 *Encyclopédie*, vol. VII (1757), pp. 534–535; see also: Voltaire, *Œuvres alphabétiques I* (*OCV* 33) (1987), pp. 113–114. It is not entirely clear what he means by this statement.

cations about such truth with lacunes within the missionary documents. One significant but also unresolved example is the Tancheng earthquake. The missionary sources reveal an enormous wealth of detailed information about this earthquake. In one such missionary letter, de Rougemont affirms that there is nothing that is narrated by him, that he did not take "from the public letters published at the Court itself, which the royal postmen commonly brought" to Canton,[26] which indicates that the gazettes were his main source of information. Yet, how can it then be explained that the surviving contemporary official sources do not contain this information? Was the information still present in the gazettes but left out from inclusion in the *Qing shilu*? Or did de Rougemont mistakenly associate other types of sources with the gazette published at the court? Other examples of truth not included in the gazettes are referred to in comments made by Perroni. He established a sharp contrast between the blindness of the emperor and the flattery and adulation of the officials, which resulted in the fact that large floods, famines, and fires were not reported in the gazette. Amiot, from his side, pointed out how the generals and officials deceived the emperor in hiding the truth about such incidents, and when they ultimately had no other option but to report them, they "tell it in such a way as to make it unrecognizable in the eyes of the one who has the right to know it."[27] Finally, Bourgeois admitted that he had once believed the gazettes to be truer than they actually were, and that he discovered that "one disguises many facts in them."[28] What is noteworthy in these statements is that neither of them interprets the absence of such information as a strategy towards the population (although that may have been a consideration in practice – e.g. with the Tancheng earthquake, which could raise concerns about the dynasty), but as a strategy against the emperor. Even though the gazette's information comes from the court, it is the emperor – the very centre of the court – who is being blinded. Still another example of lacunes is the anti-Christian incident in Shaanxi that Amiot heard about via a eunuch, while noting that this information did not appear in the gazettes themselves. This offers a counterpoint to where it is not only the emperor being blinded to certain information in the context of the gazette, but also the wider readership.[29]

The fact that these missionaries' discussions of state affairs were expressed in a language to which the court did not have access, made it so that the contents of the gazette could also be questioned without provoking direct

26 de Rougemont, *Historia Tartaro-Sinica Nova* (1673), p. 316. See Golvers (2016), p. 326.
27 Letter of Amiot to Bertin (4 October 1790): Inst. 1517, fol. 119v.
28 Letter of Bourgeois to Bertin (Beijing, 10 October 1788): BnF, Bréquigny 2, fol. 209v.
29 *MCC*, vol. 15, p. 285.

criticism from the court. Moreover, this use of foreign language facilitated the dissemination of the gazette to Europe and created a much wider network of communication.

The missionaries' comparisons with Europe and their comments on the trustworthiness and truthfulness of officially sanctioned state news in China should be understood within the context of their expectations in relation to the circulation of information. These expectations in general would change in the course of the nineteenth century, both in Europe and in China. For the missionaries, gazettes were intended to inform their public of officials about the general course for the empire and the behaviour expected of its civil servants. As such, they were not expected to be sources of objective and extensive information, nor were they expected to express diverse or varying opinions. In the eighteenth century, debates on the freedom of press (i.e. the right to report news or circulate opinion without censorship from the government) were taking place, and some laws were even installed to protect it. However, the common practice in most European countries was still to seek the government's approval for a publication. For instance, the volumes of the *Mémoires concernant les Chinois* as well as the well-known Enlightenment *Encyclopédie* were published "avec approbation, et privilege du Roi." This King's Privilege, while granting protection against counterfeiting, allowed the ruler a measure of control over the text since it required approval from the royal censors (religious or lay depending on the text) to be protected. It was inevitably considered as a proof of "approved truth."

Keeping this context in mind, the praise for the Chinese gazette by the missionaries and the Enlightenment thinkers, could instead be read as an indirect criticism of the European gazette: in their eyes the Chinese gazette was superior precisely because all information came from the court. This stood in contrast with Europe, where all kinds of different information could be collected in the gazettes. Since most of the European readership would never see the Chinese gazette itself, they would not be able to judge for themselves whether the praise for the Chinese gazette was indeed correct, but it could make them question the quality of the European gazette. This usage of the Chinese gazette to criticize European practices was clearly in evidence in Budgell's use of the Chinese gazette against his rivals in his weekly *the Bee, or the universal weekly pamphlet*, and in how Nordencrantz and Chydenius claimed that the freedom of writing, of the press, and of information had been in existence in China since ancient times, which suited a political agenda that resulted in the *Swedish Freedom of Writing and the Press Act of 1766*. This context would definitively change with the *Human Civil Rights Declaration of the French Revolution* (1789) and the *First Amendment to the Constitution of the United States* (1791), which explicitly protect the freedom of speech and of press. The difference appears clearly in the late nineteenth century in China. When Chinese newspapers emerged and the "free press" was held up, the gazettes were no longer considered superior in the way they had been in the eyes of the missionaries and Enlightenment thinkers in the eighteenth century.[30]

Interconnected Cultural History

Looking at China from the periphery also implies looking at the periphery, in this case Europe, from China – and thus searching for the ways in which particular Chinese media, such as the Chinese gazette, shaped the European intellectual world. Indeed, the entire process of text management of the Chinese gazettes facilitated communication not only in China but also its extension to Europe: from the selection by the emperor and the high officials, over the transcription and publication by printing offices, to the selection by European missionaries, their effort of writing, translating, and interpreting and finally the republication and reinterpretation in Europe. There, the translations of and reports about the Chinese gazette reached a more global public, consisting of both the individual readers of the missionaries' letters and the wider public that had access to the printed version in various collections. Though the reception history remains limited, it has been noticed that important aspects of the Enlightenment view on the Chinese imperial system and government were based on texts that were directly related to the gazettes. They are the concrete proofs that the Chinese gazettes and the ideas expressed in them joined a global public much earlier than so far assumed. As such, the practices surrounding the reading and (re)publication of the Chinese gazette form an example of interconnected cultural history that is worthy of attention.

30 It is noteworthy that John Barrow (1764–1848) who accompanied the Macartney expedition to China (1792–1794) was of the opinion that "The press in China is as free as in England, and the profession of printing open to every one, which is a singular circumstance, and perhaps the only instance of the kind, in a despotic government." Barrow (1806), pp. 392–393; see also Osterhammel (2018), p. 375.

Guide to the Sources

This guide to the sources contains the references of the European primary sources used in this book, together with the identification of Chinese sources to the extent that they could be found. Note that, as explained in the introduction to this book, these sources are not the gazettes themselves (except for ten issues), but edicts or memorials that can be found in other Chinese official sources and that are linked to the texts or events reported in the gazettes. In certain cases, the exact text that was translated into French or Italian could be found, in other cases the sources referenced here provide the context in which the events that are reported took place.

1 Archivio Storico "de Propaganda Fide" (APF), Rome[1]

1.1 *Scritture Originali delle Congregazioni Particolari dell'Indie orientali e Cina* (SOCP)

SOCP, vol. 33 (dall'Anno 1727 al 1728), fols. 326r–327r: [Domenico Perroni] Ristretto de varie notizie cavate dalle Gazzette impresse in Pekino nel 1727 (Selection of various news extracted from the Gazettes imprinted in Pekin in 1727): Introduction

SOCP, vol. 33 (dall'Anno 1727 al 1728), fols. 327r–333r: 1. L'acque del fiume croceo di gialle divengono cristalline, e chiare (The waters of the Yellow River become crystalline and clear):

Chinese: fols. 328v–329r (edict); fols. 330v–331v (imperial rescript); transl.: fols. 329v–330r; 332r–333r (Italian)

Officials want a ceremony of congratulations for the emperor because the water of the Yellow River has become clear; two rescripts of the emperor rejecting the proposals and ordering a ceremony for his father, the Kangxi emperor, and for the Spirit of the Yellow River (*heshen* 河神) (YZ5/1/6 = 27 January 1727; YZ5/1/17 = 6 February 1727); *Qing shilu*, vol. 7, pp. 779–781 (*juan* 52) (YZ5/1/癸巳 [= 6] = 27 Jan. 1727); *Shizong xianhuangdi shangyu neige, juan* 52, pp. 2a–4a (*SKQS*, vol. 414, pp. 522–523) (YZ5/1/6 = 27 Jan. 1727); *Yongzheng chao qijuzhu ce*, vol. 2, pp. 918–920 (YZ5/1/5 = 26 Jan. 1727)

1 For additional information, see Ad Dudink, *Catalogue of Chinese Documents in the "Propaganda Fide" Historical Archives (1622–1830)*, Rome: Urbaniana Univ. Press, 2022.

 | DOI:10.1163/9789004505001_007

Qing shilu, vol. 7, pp. 784–786 (*juan* 52) (YZ5/1/甲辰 [= 17] = 7 Febr. 1727); *Shizong xianhuangdi shangyu neige*, *juan* 52, pp. 7a–9b (*SKQS*, vol. 414, pp. 524–525) (YZ5/1/13 = 3 Febr. 1727); *Yongzheng chao qijuzhu ce*, vol. 2, pp. 931–932 (YZ5/1/17 = 7 Febr. 1727)

SOCP, vol. 33 (dall'Anno 1727 al 1728), fols. 334v–336r: 2. Nuova legge di celebrarsi il giorno natale a Kam-hi, e a Confusio (New laws to celebrate the birthdays of Kangxi and Confucius):

Chinese: fols. 335r–v; transl.: fols. 335v–336r (Italian)

A proposal from the Ministry of Rites about the way to celebrate the birthdays of the Kangxi emperor ([YZ5/]3/18 = 9 April 1727) and of Confucius ([YZ5/]8/27 = 11 Oct. 1727); *Qing shilu*, vol. 7, p. 800 (*juan* 53) (YZ5/2/甲子 [= 7] = 27 Febr. 1727); *Shizong xianhuangdi shangyu neige*, *juan* 53, p. 13a (*SKQS*, vol. 414, p. 540) (YZ5/2/7 = 27 Febr. 1727); *Yongzheng chao qijuzhu ce*, vol. 2, p. 974 (YZ5/2/18 = 28 Febr. 1727)

SOCP, vol. 33 (dall'Anno 1727 al 1728), fols. 336v–340r: 3. Navigazione e commercio a Regni forastieri riaperto a Cinesi (Navigation and trade in foreign kingdoms reopened to Chinese):

Chinese: fols. 339r–340r; transl. / summary: fols. 337r–339r (Italian)

The imperial approval of the deliberations of the Ministry of War on YZ5/3/10 (1 April 1727) about the memorial of Gao Qizhuo 高其倬 (1676–1738), Governor of Fujian, asking for the reopening of foreign trade for Chinese merchants; *Qing shilu*, vol. 7, p. 822 (*juan* 54) (YZ5/3/辛丑 [= 14] = 5 April 1727); English transl. in Fu Lo-shu (1966), vol. 1, p. 157

SOCP, vol. 33 (dall'Anno 1727 al 1728), fols. 340v–343v: 4. Spese superflue vietate dal Imperadore a suoi popoli, e sue Massime concernenti tal materia (Superfluous expenses forbidden by the Emperor to his peoples, and his Maxims concerning this matter):

Chinese: fols. 342v–343v; transl.: fols. 341r–342v (Italian)

The emperor's admonition addressed to the new *jinshi* 進士 of that year showing his aversion of superfluous, extravagant, and useless spending (YZ5/4/5 = 22 June 1727); *Shizong xianhuangdi shangyu neige*, *juan* 55, pp. 29a–33b (*SKQS*, vol. 414, pp. 585–587) (YZ5/4/29 = 18 June 1727)

SOCP, vol. 33 (dall'Anno 1727 al 1728), fols. 344r–347v: Spese superflue vietate dal Imperadore a suoi popoli, e sue Massime concernenti tal materia (continued):

Chinese: fols. 346 r–v; transl.: fols. 344r–346r (Italian)
Similar admonitions the emperor gave on other days (e.g. YZ5/5/7 = 25 June 1727); *Qing shilu*, vol. 7, pp. 866–867 (*juan* 57) (YZ5/5/己未 [= 4] = 22 June 1727); *Shizong xianhuangdi shangyu neige, juan* 57, pp. 1a–4a (SKQS, vol. 414, pp. 613–615) (YZ5/5/4 = 22 June 1727); *Yongzheng chao qijuzhu ce*, vol. 2, pp. 1232–1234 (YZ5/5/4 = 22 June 1727)

SOCP, vol. 33 (dall'Anno 1727 al 1728), fols. 347v–351r: 5. Ceremonie di arar la terra, costumata dal sol'Imperadore in Pekino, deve farsi in tutte le Città di Cina da Mandarini che in esse presiedono (Ceremonies of ploughing the land, performed by only the Emperor in Pekino, must be executed in all the cities of China by Mandarins who preside in them):

Chinese: fols. 350r–351r; transl.: fols. 348v–349v (Italian)
Memorial of the Ministry of Rites concerning the rite of ploughing the land at the Xiannong 先農 altar (also called 'tillage rite' (*gengji li* 耕耤禮), to be practised by officials in the provinces (YZ5/7/3 = 19 Aug. 1727); not yet found

SOCP, vol. 33 (dall'Anno 1727 al 1728), fols. 351r–356r: 6. Discorso dell' Imper.e ingiurioso alla Religione Cristiana impresso nelle Gazzette (Speech of the emperor, which was insulting the Christian Religion, imprinted in the Gazettes):

Chinese: fols. 355r–356r; transl.: fols. 351v–354v (Latin)
Anti-Christian sermon of the emperor given to the head of the Portuguese Embassy to China (Alexandre Metelo de Sousa e Meneses (1687–1766)), which happened to take place on the birthday of the Buddha (*fodan* 佛誕) (YZ5/4/8 = 28 May 1727); *Shizong xianhuangdi shangyu neige, juan* 56, pp. 17a–20a (SKQS, vol. 414, pp. 596–598) (YZ5/4/8 = 28 May 1727); *Yongzheng chao qijuzhu ce*, vol. 2, pp. 1175–1177 (YZ5/4/8 = 28 May 1727); English transl. in Fu Lo-shu (1966), vol. 1, pp. 155–156
SOCP, vol. 33 (dall'Anno 1727 al 1728), fol. 418: other copy
SOCP, vol. 33 (dall'Anno 1727 al 1728), fol. 422: other copy

SOCP, vol. 33 (dall'Anno 1727 al 1728), fols. 356r–357r: 7. Principi del sangue perseguitati dall'Imperadore, tra gli parecchi sono Christiani: & alcuni d'essi condennati a morte per non voler renunciare alla Religione (Blood princes persecuted by the Emperor, among whom many are Christians: & some of them sentenced to death for not wanting to renounce the Religion):

Chinese: fols. 356v–357r; transl.: fols. 356r–356v (Italian)

Persecution of imperial family members including Christians of the family of Sunu 蘇努 (1648?–1725), a fourth cousin of the Yongzheng emperor. In this case: Sunu's third son Su-er-jin 蘇爾金, his eleventh son Ku-er-cheng 庫爾成, and others (YZ5/3/5 = 27 March 1727; YZ5/3/- = ? March-April 1727; YZ5/6/21 = 8 August 1727); in total three Chinese texts.

SOCP, vol. 33 (dall'Anno 1727 al 1728), fol. 357v: L'imperadore non approvò la sud.a sentenza, benche à seconda del suo gusto, e ordinò la gita d'un Regolo a quei Prencipi Xrani per esortarli ad abbandonar la Relig.e che se non si arrendepero, erano degni di morte. Il decreto Imp.le secondo fu sparso fuora, è come segue (The emperor did not approve the aforementioned sentence, although it was according to his taste, and ordered the visit of a Regulus to those Christian princes to exhort them to abandon the Religion; that if they did not surrender, they were worthy of death. The second imperial decree was spread outside, it is as follows):

Chinese: fol. 357v

Christians of the family of Sunu (YZ5/3/- = ? March-April 1727)

SOCP, vol. 33 (dall'Anno 1727 al 1728), fols. 358r–v: Supplica fatta all'Imp.re dal Tribunale soprastante à Regoli, e Prencipi del sangue acciò totalm.te estingua la famiglia de soprad.i Prencipi senza distinzione de Xr.ani, e gentili, che sono in essa (A petition made to the Emperor by the aforementioned Tribunal for the Regoli, and Blood Princes so that the family of the aforementioned Princes be completely extinguished, without distinction between Christians and gentiles, who are among them):

Chinese: fols. 358r–v

Christians of the family of Sunu (YZ5/6/21 = 8 Aug. 1727); *Qing shilu*, vol. 7, pp. 889–890 (*juan* 58) (YZ5/6/辛丑 [= 16] = 3 Aug. 1727); *Shizong xianhuangdi shangyu neige, juan* 58, pp. 30b–32b (SKQS, vol. 414, pp. 642–643) (YZ5/6/16 = 3 Aug. 1727)

SOCP, vol. 34 (dall'Anno 1729 al 1730):

Chinese: fol. 606r

Memorial by Kong Yuxun 孔毓珣 (?–1730), Governor-General of Guangxi and Guangdong, concerning the arrival of Alexandre de La Charme 孫璋 (1695–1767) and Valentin Chalier 沙如玉 (1693–1747) and request for permission to go to Beijing (YZ6/12/21 = 20 Jan. 1729)

SOCP, vol. 35: duplicate; Chinese: fol. 263

SOCP, vol. 34 (dall'Anno 1729 al 1730):

Chinese: fol. 607r

Answer to previous memorial: permission granted (YZ7/2/4 = 3 March 1729)

SOCP, vol. 35: duplicate; Chinese: fol. 264

SOCP, vol. 34 (dall'Anno 1729 al 1730):

Chinese: fol. 608r

Edict from the Yongzheng emperor on tolerance (YZ7/1/17 = 14 Febr. 1729); *Shizong xianhuangdi shangyu neige, juan* 76, pp. 3a–7b (*SKQS*, vol. 415, pp. 166–168) (YZ6/12/10 = 9 Jan. 1729); *Yongzheng chao qijuzhu ce*, vol. 3, pp. 2466–2467 (YZ6/12/10 = 9 Jan. 1729)

SOCP, vol. 35: duplicate; Chinese: fol. 266

SOCP, vol. 39 (15 Luglio–18 Sept. 1736):

Chinese: fol. 336r

The emperor's protection of Buddhism and his high opinion of Buddhism and Taoism, as the probable reason for the persecution of Christianity in Canton (YZ11/3/- = April-May 1733); *Shizong xianhuangdi shangyu neige, juan* 129, pp. 2a–5a (*SKQS*, vol. 415, pp. 652–654) (YZ11/3/14 = 27 April 1733); *Yongzheng chao hanwen yuzhi huibian*, vol. 2, pp. 183–184 n. 302 (YZ11/3/14 = 27 April 1733)

SOCP, vol. 39 (15 Luglio–18 Sept. 1736):

Chinese: fol. 336v

Condemnation of Zhao Gao 趙杲, magistrate of Tangshan District 唐山縣 (Shunde Prefecture 順德府, Zhili), who demolished Buddhist and Taoist temples in his district (YZ10/4/24 = 18 May 1732); *Yongzheng chao hanwen yuzhi huibian*, vol. 2, pp. 118–119 n. 181 (YZ10/4/20 = 14 May 1732)

SOCP, vol. 47 (dall'Anno 1748 al 1750): Edictum Imp.ris publicatum in Gazetis publicis (Edict of the emperor published in the public gazettes):

Chinese: fol. 102r; transl.: fols. 66r–68r (Latin)

Undated anti-Christian memorial (1746) of Ma-er-tai 馬爾泰 (?–1748), Governor-General of Zhejiang-Fujian, and Zhou Xuejian 周學健 (?–1748), Governor of Fujian (QL11 = 1746)

SOCP, vol. 47: duplicate; Chinese: fol. 996r (QL11 = 1746)

SOCP, vol. 47 (dall'Anno 1748 al 1750): Sententia prolata à Prorege Scian si in P. Ioannem a Bormio (Sentence issued by the Governor of Scian si against Fr. Johannes a Bormio):

Chinese: fol. 103r; transl.: fols. 68r–69r (Latin)

Chinese text of the Shanxi Governor's sentence issued against the (on 10 April 1746) arrested Giambattista Pedracini da Bormio O.F.M. (in China since 1740) (QL11 = 1746)

SOCP, vol. 47: duplicate; Chinese: fol. 995r (QL11 = 1746)

SOCP, vol. 47 (dall'Anno 1748 al 1750): Libellus supplex Praefecti Yung chang ad Proregem Xan Xi / Proregis declaratio seu mandatum (Petition by prefect Yung chang to the Governor of Xan Xi / Declaration or mandate by the Governor):

Chinese: fols. 104r–103v; transl.: fols. 71v–73r (Latin)

Chinese text of undated report of Shen Rongchang 沈榮昌, magistrate of Huozhou 霍州, to the Governor of Shanxi about the arrest on 10 April 1746 (QL11/3/20) of Pedracini (QL11 = 1746)

SOCP, vol. 47: duplicate; Chinese: fols. 924r–925v (QL11 = 1746)

SOCP, vol. 47 (dall'Anno 1748 al 1750): Accusationes factae ad praefectos provinciae Fo Kien (Accusations made against the prefects of the province Fo Kien):

Chinese: fols. 105r–104v; transl.: fols. 73r–75r (Latin)

Chinese text of the anti-Christian accusations in the report of Dong Qizuo 董啓祚, Prefect of Funing 福寧 (Fujian) (QL11 = 1746)

SOCP, vol. 47: duplicate; Chinese: fols. 924v–925r (QL11 = 1746)

SOCP, vol. 47 (dall'Anno 1748 al 1750): Edictum prolatum Macai contra Christianos Sinenses (Edict issued in Macau against Chinese Christians):

Chinese: fol. 106r; transl.: fols. 75r–76r (Latin)

Chinese text of the edict, dated 24 August 1746 (QL11/7/8), issued by Gu Song 顧嵩, who from 1732 until 1750 was District Vice Magistrate 縣丞 of Xiangshan 香山 and one of the officials responsible for Macao (QL11 = 1746)

SOCP, vol. 47 (dall'Anno 1748 al 1750): duplicate; Chinese: fols. 926r–927v (QL11 = 1746)

SOCP, vol. 47 (dall'Anno 1748 al 1750): Edictum emanatum in Provincia Fuo Kien contra S. Religionem (Edict issued in the Fuo Kien province against the Sacred Religion) (dated QL11/5/10 = 28 June 1746):

Chinese: fols. 107r–106v; transl.: fols. 76r–77v (Latin)

Chinese text of the edict issued by the Prefect of Xinghua 興化 (Fujian) (QL11 = 1746)

SOCP, vol. 47 (dall'Anno 1748 al 1750): duplicate; Chinese: fols. 927r–926v (QL11 = 1746)

SOCP, vol. 47 (dall'Anno 1748 al 1750): Mandatum Imp.ris contra S. Religionem (Mandate of the emperor against the Sacred Religion):

Chinese: fol. 107v; transl.: fols. 77v–79r (Latin)

Chinese text of the Imperial edict of QL11/6/26 (= 12 Aug. 1746) ordering "all provincial authorities to conduct a rigorous search for Europeans hiding in the provinces and to arrest them and deport them to Canton" (in response to a memorial of Zhang Ne 張訥) (QL11 = 1746); *Qing shilu*, vol. 12, p. 502 (*juan* 69) (QL11/6/庚寅 [= 26] = 12 Aug. 1746); *Xiangshan xianzhi* 香山縣志 (8 + 1 *juan*) (QL15 = 1750), ed. by Bao Yu 暴煜, *juan* 8, *haojing'ao* 濠鏡嶴, pp. 26b–27b; *Guangzhou dadian* 廣州大典, vol. 296, Guangzhou: Guangzhou chubanshe, 2015, pp. 235–236

SOCP, vol. 47 (dall'Anno 1748 al 1750): duplicate; Chinese: fol. 927v (QL11 = 1746)

1.2 *Scritture riferite nei Congressi (SC), Indie orientali e Cina*

SC, Indie orientali e Cina, vol. 18 (anno 1726): Confessio P. Ioan. Moraon, et sententia in eundem lata a Tribunali Criminum pervulgata per totam Sinam in Gazulis publicis Pekini impressis (Confession of Fr. J. Mourão, and sentence issued against the same by the Tribunal of Crimes, and proclaimed all over China in the public Gazettes printed in Peking):

Chinese: fols. 532v–533v; transl.: fols. 534r–536r (Latin)

Chinese text of deposition and condemnation of the Jesuit João Mourão 穆經遠 (1681–1726) by the Ministry of Justice on 21 July 1726 (YZ4/6/22)

SC, Indie orientali e Cina, vol. 18 (anno 1726): Excerpta ex prolixo Imperatoris edicto per totum Imperium promulgato, quae concernunt eandem causam P. Ioan. Moraon (Excerpts from the long edict of the Emperor, proclaimed in the whole empire, which concern the same case of Fr. J. Mourão):

Chinese: fols. 536r–v; transl.: fols. 536v–537v (Latin)

Quoting several passages (concerning the role of Mourão in the twenty-eight crimes of Prince Yintang 胤禟 (1683–1726)) from a lengthy imperial edict of 2 July 1726 (YZ4/6/3) about the crimes of the Emperor's brothers Yinsi 胤禩 (1681–1726) and Yintang; *Qing shilu*, vol. 7, pp. 669–680 (*juan* 45) (YZ4/6/甲子 [= 3] = 2 July 1726)

SC, Indie orientali e Cina, vol. 19 (dal 1727 al 1728): fols. 717r–v: [Domenico Perroni] Ristretto de varie notizie cavate dalle Gazzette impresse in Pekino nel 1728 (Selection of various news extracted from the Gazettes printed in Pekin in 1728): Introduction

SC, Indie orientali e Cina, vol. 19 (dal 1727 al 1728): fols. 718r–722v: 1. Succinta Raccolta di nuove che occupano le Gazzette di Cina (Concise summary of news that occupies the Gazettes of China): Summary:

SC, Indie orientali e Cina, vol. 19 (dal 1727 al 1728), fols. 718r–v:

In Shandong: after verification, Ran Tianlin 冉天琳, a descendant in the sixty-seventh generation of Confucius' disciple ?Jen-zu (= Ranzi 冉子 = Ran Yong 冉雍) is conferred the title *Wujing boshi* 五經博士, which is the same title as the one granted to four other families of descendants of Confucius (since 1724); *Qing shilu*, vol. 7, p. 1051 (*juan* 70) (YZ6/6/癸未 [= 4] = 10 July 1728). This title for descendants was introduced in 1724: *Qing shilu*, vol. 7, p. 327 (*juan* 20) (YZ2/5/辛酉 [= 19] = 9 July 1724)

SC, Indie orientali e Cina, vol. 19 (dal 1727 al 1728), fol. 718v:

In Henan: a peasant, Cui Shiyou 翟世有 from the Mengjin district 孟津縣, is commended because he gave back a large amount of money lost by merchant Qin Tai 秦泰 (from Shaanxi); *Qing shilu*, vol. 7, pp. 1060–1061 (*juan* 71) (YZ6/7/甲寅 [= 5] = 10 Aug. 1728); *Shizong xianhuangdi shangyu neige, juan* 71, pp. 6a–10a; *SKQS*, vol. 415, pp. 94–96 (YZ6/7/5 = 10 Aug. 1728); *Yongzheng chao qijuzhu ce*, vol. 3, pp. 2107–2109 (YZ6/7/5 = 10 Aug. 1728)

SC, Indie orientali e Cina, vol. 19 (dal 1727 al 1728), fols. 718v–719r:
In Nanjing: as a wind, which used to blow and impede boat traffic on the rivers that converged into the lake of Hum-ze (= Hongzi hu 洪澤湖), had ceased blowing for four years, an honorary title is asked and sacrifices are made to thank the Spirit of this Wind (*fengshen* 風神); *Qing shilu*, vol. 7, p. 1068 (*juan* 71) (YZ6/7/庚午 [= 21] = 26 Aug. 1728)

SC, Indie orientali e Cina, vol. 19 (dal 1727 al 1728), fol. 719r:
In Shaanxi: Shuo-se 碩色, Surveillance Commissioner and Salt Supervisor, had written a memorial reporting that a large amount of high-quality salt had formed by itself during the winter. In response, a temple is built to the Spirit of Salt (= *yanshen* 鹽神) to make sacrifices twice a year; *Qing shilu*, vol. 7, p. 990 (*juan* 64) (YZ5/12/乙巳 [= 24] = 3 Febr. 1728); *Yongzheng chao qijuzhu ce*, vol. 2, p. 1706 (YZ5/12/24 = 3 Febr. 1728)

SC, Indie orientali e Cina, vol. 19 (dal 1727 al 1728), fols. 719r–v:
Memorials reporting on elderly people who reach a very high age (60, 70, 80, 90, or 100 years) and presents that are given (30 taels) and celebrations that are organised on such an occasion; there are many such examples, e.g. a man of 118 years old who received the 30 taels: *Qing shilu*, vol. 7, p. 703 (*juan* 46) (YZ4/7/己未 [= 29] = 26 Aug. 1726)

SC, Indie orientali e Cina, vol. 19 (dal 1727 al 1728), fols. 719v–720r:
Reward (5 *shi* 石 of rice and 10 *pi* 疋 of cloth) for the birth of male triplets (*yichan sannan* 一產三男); not yet found

SC, Indie orientali e Cina, vol. 19 (dal 1727 al 1728), fol. 720r:
In Tibet: suppression of a rebellion (led by A-er-bu-ba 阿爾布巴, i.e. Ngaphöpa Dorje Gyalpo (?–1728), one of the Tibetan ministers) after the king asks the emperor for help; at the sight of the Chinese troops, the rebels immediately surrendered without any fight; the emperor attributes the success to his father; *Qing shilu*, vol. 7, pp. 1066–1067 (*juan* 71) (YZ6/7/乙丑 [= 16] = 21 Aug. 1728); *Yongzheng chao qijuzhu ce*, vol. 3, p. 2132 (YZ6/7/16 = 21 Aug. 1728)

SC, Indie orientali e Cina, vol. 19 (dal 1727 al 1728), fol. 720r:
In order to stimulate agriculture, the emperor orders a reward for old peasants who have spent their lives cultivating the land; 559 are rewarded; no reference found to the 559 who were rewarded; edict to reward old peasants: *Qing shilu*, vol. 8, pp. 7–8 (*juan* 77) (YZ7/1/壬申 [= 27] = 24 Febr. 1729); *Shizong xianhuangdi shangyu neige, juan* 77, pp. 12a–13b (*SKQS*, vol. 415, pp. 184–185) (YZ7/1/27 = 24 Febr. 1729); *Yongzheng chao qijuzhu ce*, vol. 4, pp. 2562–2563 (YZ7/1/27 = 24 Febr. 1729)

SC, Indie orientali e Cina, vol. 19 (dal 1727 al 1728), fols. 720r–v:
Instruction to collect objects made of brass, in order to limit the use of such metals to the production of money, and to control its distribution; *Qing shilu*, vol. 7, pp. 927–928 (*juan* 61) (YZ5/9/乙卯 [= 2] = 16 Oct. 1728); *Shizong xianhuangdi shangyu neige, juan* 61, pp. 1a–3a (*SKQS*, vol. 414, pp. 688–689) (YZ5/9/2 = 16 Oct. 1728); *Yongzheng chao qijuzhu ce*, vol. 3, pp. 1449–1450 (YZ5/9/2 = 16 Oct. 1728)

SC, Indie orientali e Cina, vol. 19 (dal 1727 al 1728), fols. 720v–721r:
Condemnation of Muslims and butchers who secretly slaughter cows or buffalo, which should only be used for the cultivation of the fields; stronger punishment for Muslims in Beijing where the rules are stricter; *Qing shilu*, vol. 8, pp. 47–49 (*juan* 80) (YZ7/4/辛巳 [= 7] = 4 May 1728); *Shizong xianhuangdi shangyu neige, juan* 80, pp. 4a–6a (*SKQS*, vol. 415, pp. 225–226) (YZ7/4/7 = 4 May 1728); *Yongzheng chao qijuzhu ce*, vol. 4, pp. 2718–2720 (YZ7/4/7 = 4 May 1728)

SC, Indie orientali e Cina, vol. 19 (dal 1727 al 1728), fols. 721r–v:
Condemnation of Yan-xin 延信 (1673–1728), General in Shaanxi, who thought of usurpation, following the prognostication of an old witch; also accused of association with the party of Sunu 蘇努 and Yinsi 胤禩 (1681–1726), brother of the emperor; *Qing shilu*, vol. 7, pp. 980–981 (*juan* 64) (YZ5/12/丁亥 [= 6] = 16 Jan. 1728); *Shizong xianhuangdi shangyu neige, juan* 64, pp. 8b–9a (*SKQS*, vol. 414, pp. 746–747) (YZ5/12/丁亥 [= 6] = 16 Jan. 1728) (only edict); *Yongzheng chao qijuzhu ce*, vol. 2, p. 1642 (YZ5/12/丁亥 [= 6] = 16 Jan. 1728) (only edict); his association with the Taoist nun by the name of Wang 道姑王氏 and the spreading of *yaoyan* 妖言 is mentioned in *Qing shilu*, vol. 8, p. 212 (*juan* 90) (YZ8/1/壬午 [= 13] = 1 March 1730) and *Qing shilu*, vol. 8, p. 391 (*juan* 105) (YZ9/4/庚子 [= 8] = 13 May 1731)

SC, Indie orientali e Cina, vol. 19 (dal 1727 al 1728), fol. 721v:
Imperial measures to reduce personal interventions in the judicial courts when treating conflicts between officials; not yet found

SC, Indie orientali e Cina, vol. 19 (dal 1727 al 1728), fols. 721v–722r:
A new law passed by the emperor to relieve the people suffering as a result of bad harvests; not yet found

SC, Indie orientali e Cina, vol. 19 (dal 1727 al 1728), fols. 722r–v:
Other topics that are mentioned in the gazettes: homicides, adulteries, thefts, and other offenses and how they were handled; punishments of gamblers and merchants engaged in gambling, and of the officials of the regions where the incidents occurred; inundations; …

SC, Indie orientali e Cina, vol. 19 (dal 1727 al 1728): 2. L'Imperadore attribuisce la fertilità della raccolta, alla cerimonia da lui istituita d'arar la terra (The Emperor attributes the fertility of the harvest to the ceremony he instituted to work the land):

Chinese: fols. 724v–725r; transl.: fols. 723r–724v (partial Italian)
Edict about the ceremony of ploughing land (*gengji li* 耕耤禮) by officials of rank 1–3 in imitation of the Emperor in Beijing (YZ5/8/16 = 30 Sept. 1727); *Qing shilu*, vol. 7, pp. 909–910 (*juan* 57) (YZ5/7/丁亥 [= 29] = 14 Sept. 1727); *Shizong xianhuangdi shangyu neige*, *juan* 59, pp. 34b–36a (*SKQS*, vol. 414, pp. 672–673) (YZ5/7/29 = 14 Sept. 1727); *Yongzheng chao qijuzhu ce*, vol. 2, pp. 1391–1392 (YZ5/7/29 = 14 Sept. 1727)

SC, Indie orientali e Cina, vol. 19 (dal 1727 al 1728): 3. Sacrificii ordinati in ringraziamento per essersi ritirate l'acque del fiume croceo da un gran tratto di paese, che folevano inondare e render inutile alla coltura (Sacrifices ordered in thanksgiving for the withdrawal of the waters of the Yellow River from a large stretch of land, which used to become flooded and rendered useless for cultivation):

Chinese: fols. 727r–v; transl.: fols. 725v–727r (partial Italian)
Edict about sacrifices to be made in gratitude for the fact that an impending inundation did not take place (YZ5/11/9 = 21 Dec. 1727)

SC, Indie orientali e Cina, vol. 19 (dal 1727 al 1728): 4. L'amore de figli à loro Genitori e della Moglie al Marito deve avere i suoi limiti (The love of children for their Parents and of the Wife for the Husband must have its limits):

Chinese: fols. 730r–731r; transl.: fols. 728r–730r (partial Italian)

Edict about the limits that there should be in the expression of love of children towards their parents [xiao 孝] and of wives towards their husbands. For instance, the rejection of *gegan* 割肝 ("cutting the liver") (YZ6/3/12 = 20 April 1728); *Qing shilu*, vol. 7, pp. 1017–1019 (*juan* 67) (YZ6/3/壬子 [= 2] = 10 April 1728); *Shizong xianhuangdi shangyu neige*, *juan* 67, pp. 2a–6a (*SKQS*, vol. 415, pp. 23–25) (YZ6/3/2 = 10 April 1728)

SC, Indie orientali e Cina, vol. 23 (dal 1741 al 1743):

Chinese: fol. 38

Imperial decree that condemns Yang Congqing 楊從清 for spreading a prophecy that, because of the restauration of the Nantang 南堂 (Southern Church) (damaged because of the earthquake of 30 Sept. 1730), an earthquake would occur in Beijing on QL5/10/30 (18 Dec. 1740) (QL5/9/24 = 13 Nov. 1740); *Qing shilu*, vol. 10, pp. 856–857 (*juan* 127) (QL5/9/壬辰 [= 24] = 13 Nov. 1740)

2 *Lettres édifiantes et curieuses* (*LEC*)[2]

2.1 "Lettre du Père Contancin, missionnaire de la Compagnie de Jésus, au Père Etienne Souciet, de la même Compagnie" (2 December 1725 in Canton), in *Lettres édifiantes et curieuses, écrites des missions étrangères par quelques missionnaires de la Compagnie de Jésus* (1703–1776), vol. 18 (= 1728), pp. 428–463 (*also in Lettres édifiantes et curieuses, écrites des missions étrangères* (1810–1811), vol. 20, pp. 298–316)

LEC (1728), vol. 18, p. 430; *LEC* (1810–1811), vol. 20, p. 299:

Reduction of taxes expected from Suzhou and Songjiang; *Qing shilu*, vol. 7, p. 460 (*juan* 30) (YZ3/3/丁巳 [= 19] = 1 May 1725); *Shizong xianhuangdi shangyu neige*, *juan* 30, pp. 20a–21b; *SKQS*, vol. 414, p. 265 (YZ3/3/19 = 1 May 1725)

LEC (1728), vol. 18, p. 430; *LEC* (1810–1811), vol. 20, p. 299:

Similar reduction for Nanchang not found in same context, but both mentioned in other reference; *Qing shilu*, vol. 7, pp. 478–479 (*juan* 31)

2 For electronic versions, see archive.org.

(YZ3/4/戊子 [= 21] = 1 June 1725); *Shizong xianhuangdi shengxun, juan* 18, pp. 5a–6b; *SKQS*, vol. 412, pp. 246–247 (YZ3/4/戊子 [= 21] = 1 June 1725)

LEC (1728), vol. 18, pp. 431–434; *LEC* (1810–1811), vol. 20, pp. 300–301:

Imperial instruction on the heavy rains in the provinces of Beijing, Shandong, and Henan; *Qing shilu*, vol. 7, p. 522 (*juan* 34) (YZ3/7/辛酉 [= 26] = 30 Aug. 1725); *Shizong xianhuangdi shangyu neige, juan* 34, pp. 20a–21a; *SKQS*, vol. 414, p. 309 (YZ3/7/26 = 30 Aug. 1725)

LEC (1728), vol. 18, pp. 442–443; *LEC* (1810–1811), vol. 20, pp. 305–306:

Imperial edict on the reciprocation between Heaven and the human being (*tianren jiaogan* 天人交感), in response to a memorial of Li Weijun 李維鈞 (?–1727), Governor-General of Zhili; written after having fasted because of drought; *Qing shilu*, vol. 7, pp. 483–484 (*juan* 32) (YZ3/5/戊戌 [= 1] = 11 June 1725); *Shizong xianhuangdi zhupi yuzhi, juan* 10 下, pp. 55a–57a; *SKQS*, vol. 416, pp. 581–582 (YZ3/5/1 = 11 June 1725)

LEC (1728), vol. 18, p. 443; *LEC* (1810–1811), vol. 20, p. 306:

Yellow River floods should not be blamed on the officials; not yet found

LEC (1728), vol. 18, pp. 444–445; *LEC* (1810–1811), vol. 20, pp. 306–307:

Measures taken regarding prisoners because of excessive heat in Beijing; *Qing shilu*, vol. 7, pp. 499–500 (*juan* 32) (YZ3/6/壬申 [= 6]; YZ3/6/癸酉 [= 7] = 15–16 July 1725); *Shizong xianhuangdi shangyu neige, juan* 33, pp. 12a–12b; *SKQS*, vol. 414, p. 290 (YZ3/6/7 = 16 July 1725)

LEC (1728), vol. 18, pp. 446–448; *LEC* (1810–1811), vol. 20, p. 308:

[Rules for better government of the people:] To encourage peasants to work; *Qing shilu*, vol. 7, pp. 277–278 (*juan* 16) (YZ2/2/甲子 [= 20] = 14 March 1724); *Shizong xianhuangdi shangyu neige, juan* 16, pp. 8a–b; *SKQS*, vol. 414, p. 143 (YZ2/2/20 = 14 March 1724)

LEC (1728), vol. 18, pp. 448–449; *LEC* (1810–1811), vol. 20, pp. 308–309:

[Rules for better government of the people:] To encourage widows to keep chastity: erect monuments in their honour (*jingbiao jianfang* 旌表建坊);

Qing shilu, vol. 7, pp. 219–220 (*juan* 12) (YZ1/10/甲寅 [= 8] = 5 Nov. 1723); more rules in *DaQing huidian* (*Yongzheng chao*) 大清會典 (雍正朝), *juan* 68, fols. 19ff. (*guanmin jingbiao* 官民旌表), see *DaQing wuchao huidian*, vol. 5 (*Yongzheng huidian* 雍正會典), p. 1079.

LEC (1728), vol. 18, pp. 449–450; LEC (1810–1811), vol. 20, pp. 309–310:

[Rules for better government of the people:] To increase children's filial piety towards their parents; not yet found

LEC (1728), vol. 18, pp. 450–451; LEC (1810–1811), vol. 20, p. 310:

[Rules for better government of the people:] To promote filial piety: allow the transferring of official titles to deceased parents; *Qing shilu*, vol. 7, p. 528 (*juan* 35) (YZ3/8/辛未 [= 6] = 12 Sept. 1724)

LEC (1728), vol. 18, pp. 452–455; LEC (1810–1811), vol. 20, pp. 310–312:

[Rules for better government of the people:] To increase the oversight of the officials: conduct the three-yearly examination (*daji* 大計); *Qing shilu*, vol. 7, p. 160 (*juan* 8) (YZ1/6/乙亥 [= 28] = 29 July 1723); *Shizong xianhuangdi shangyu neige, juan* 8, pp. 10a–b; SKQS, vol. 414, p. 86 (YZ1/6/28 = 29 July 1723). See also the statistics in *Qing shilu*, vol. 7, p. 160 (*juan* 29) (YZ3/2/乙亥 [= 7] = 20 March 1725).

LEC (1728), vol. 18, pp. 455–458; LEC (1810–1811), vol. 20, pp. 312–314:

Encouragement to fulfil one's duties and critique by the Emperor on prayers addressed to him in temples because of tax exemption in Songjiang and Suzhou; *Qing shilu*, vol. 7, pp. 487–488 (*juan* 32) (YZ3/5/癸丑 [= 16] = 26 June 1725); *Shizong xianhuangdi shangyu neige, juan* 32, pp. 3a–4a; *Shizong xianhuangdi zhupi yuzhi, juan* 32, pp. 14a–16a; SKQS, vol. 414, pp. 279–280; vol. 418, pp. 65–66 (YZ3/5/16; YZ3/7/8 = 26 June 1725; 15 Aug. 1725)

LEC (1728), vol. 18, pp. 459–460; LEC (1810–1811), vol. 20, pp. 314–315:

On the attention the Emperor pays to the just treatment and fair condemnation of criminals (to capital punishment); not yet found

2.2 "Lettre du Père Contancin, missionnaire de la Compagnie de Jésus, au Père Etienne Souciet, de la même Compagnie" (15 December 1727 in Canton), in *Lettres édifiantes et curieuses, écrites des missions étrangères par quelques missionnaires de la Compagnie de Jésus* (1703–1776), vol. 19 (= 1729), pp. 265–404 (also in *Lettres édifiantes et curieuses, écrites des missions étrangères* (1810–1811), vol. 21, pp. 75–144)

LEC (1729), vol. 19, p. 266; *LEC* (1810–1811), vol. 21, p. 76:

Accusation against Christianity; *Qing shilu*, vol. 7, pp. 251 (*juan* 14) (YZ1/12/壬戌 [= 17] = 12 Jan. 1724); *Shizong xianhuangdi shangyu neige, juan* 14, p. 6a; *SKQS*, vol. 414, p. 133 (YZ1/2/17 = 12 Jan. 1724)

LEC (1729), vol. 19, p. 267; *LEC* (1810–1811), vol. 21, p. 76:

Condemnation of missionaries to exile; *Qing shilu*, vol. 7, p. 419 (*juan* 27) (YZ2/12/庚寅 [= 21] = 3 Febr. 1725); *Shizong xianhuangdi zhupi yuzhi, juan* 7/1, pp. 68a–70b; *SKQS*, vol. 421, pp. 270–271 (YZ2/10/29 = 14 Dec. 1724)

LEC (1729), vol. 19, pp. 268–269; *LEC* (1810–1811), vol. 21, p. 77:

Condemnation of two officials for having put false information in the gazette; *Qing shilu*, vol. 7, pp. 646–647 (*juan* 44); vol. 7, pp. 660–661 (*juan* 44) (YZ4/5/庚子 [= 9]; YZ4/5/庚戌 [= 19] = 8 June 1726; 18 June 1726); *Shizong xianhuangdi shangyu neige, juan* 44, pp. 10a–12a; *juan* 44, pp. 20a–22a; *SKQS*, vol. 414, pp. 390–391; vol. 414, pp. 395–396 (YZ4/5/9; YZ4/5/19 = 8 June 1726; 18 June 1726)

LEC (1729), vol. 19, pp. 270–272; *LEC* (1810–1811), vol. 21, pp. 78–79:

Short description of structure of gazette of 15 December 1727

LEC (1729), vol. 19, pp. 273–275; *LEC* (1810–1811), vol. 21, pp. 79–80: Complimens de toute la Cour sur le choix & la déclaration de l'Impératrice (Compliments of the whole Court on the choice and the declaration of the Empress)

After the end of the three-year mourning period for the Kangxi emperor and for the Yongzheng emperor's mother, Xiaogong ren huanghou 孝恭仁皇后 (1660–1723), the court announced the installation of the empress

Xiaojing xian huanghou 孝敬憲皇后 (1681–1731); with a detailed description of the congratulatory rite *qinghe celi huanghou li* 慶賀冊立皇后禮 on YZ3/10/6 (10 Nov. 1725); *Qing shilu*, vol. 7, p. 51 (*juan* 34) (YZ3/7/己酉 [= 14] = 21 Aug. 1725); *Shizong xianhuangdi shangyu neige*, *juan* 34, pp. 9b–10a; *SKQS*, vol. 414, pp. 303–304 (YZ3/7/14 = 21 Aug. 1725)

LEC (1729), vol. 19, pp. 275–281; *LEC* (1810–1811), vol. 21, pp. 80–83:

Ceremony of the installation of the new empress (but only very brief mention in Chinese sources); *Qing shilu*, vol. 7, p. 548 (*juan* 37) (YZ3/10/庚午 [= 6] = 10 Nov. 1725); *Yongzheng chao qijuzhu ce*, vol. 1, p. 593 (YZ3/10/6 = 10 Nov. 1725)

LEC (1729), vol. 19, pp. 282–288; *LEC* (1810–1811), vol. 21, pp. 84–87:

Ceremony with court women, concubines (Quei-fei); not yet found

LEC (1729), vol. 19, pp. 288–296; *LEC* (1810–1811), vol. 21, pp. 87–91: Libéralité de l'Impératrice en faveur des femmes avancées en âge (Generosity of the Empress in favour of women of advanced age):

Gifts of the empress to women older than 70 years (in three groups: 70–80, 80–90, and more than 90 years old); not yet found)

LEC (1729), vol. 19, pp. 297–304; *LEC* (1810–1811), vol. 21, pp. 91–95: Grace accordée à un homme condamné à mort / Ordre de l'Empereur (Grace granted to a man condemned to death / Order of the Emperor):

Grace given to Tçao-chin from Tchang-chou (= Changshu 常熟), who was condemned to strangulation for causing his wife's death, receives a reduced punishment (beating) so that he can continue to take care of his elderly parents; not yet found

LEC (1729), vol. 19, pp. 304–307; *LEC* (1810–1811), vol. 21, pp. 95–96: Exemple d'un fils qui demande la grace de mourir à la place de sa mere (Example of a son who asks for the grace to die in place of his mother):

A son asks to receive punishment in place of his mother after a conflict between two women in Y-hoang (= Yihuang 宜黄, Jiangxi), as a result of which one of them died; not yet found

LEC (1729), vol. 19, pp. 307–315; *LEC* (1810–1811), vol. 21, pp. 97–100: Ordre qui prouve l'attention de l'Empereur à soulager son Peuple (Order that proves the attention of the Emperor to relieving his People):

> Supplement of rice (130.000 measures) kept in Tien-tçing (= Tianjin 天津) to be distributed in the villages that suffered from the excessive rain in Zhili; mentioned in *Qing shilu*, vol. 7, pp. 554–555 (*juan* 38) (YZ3/11/乙未 [= 1] = 5 Dec. 1725); *Shizong xianhuangdi shangyu neige*, *juan* 38, pp. 1a–2a; *SKQS*, vol. 414, pp. 330–331 (YZ3/11/1 = 5 Dec. 1725); *Yongzheng chao qijuzhu ce*, vol. 1, pp. 605–607 (YZ3/11/1 = 5 Dec. 1725)

LEC (1729), vol. 19, pp. 315–324; *LEC* (1810–1811), vol. 21, pp. 100–105: Mémorial d'un Surintendant de deux Provinces qui parle à l'Empereur avec une noble hardiesse / Réponse de ce Mandarin à l'Empereur (Memorial of a Superintendent of two Provinces, who speaks to the Emperor with noble boldness / Response of this Mandarin to the Emperor):

> Memorial by Zha Bina 查弼納 (1683–1731), Governor-General of Jiangnan and Jiangsu, concerning the accusation and condemnation of Nian Gengyao 年羹堯 (?–1726) and Long-ke-duo 隆科多 (?–1728), asking for a stronger prosecution of the latter; *Qing shilu*, exact passage not yet found, but the case starts vol. 7, p. 514 (*juan* 34) (YZ3/7/癸卯 [= 8] = 15 Aug. 1725)

LEC (1729), vol. 19, pp. 325–329; *LEC* (1810–1811), vol. 21, pp. 105–107: Festin pour honorer dans chaque Ville les personnes distinguées par leur probité & leur bon exemple (Feast to honour in each City the people distinguished by their integrity and their good example):

> Memorial, most probably by Zhang Linghuang 張令璜 (*jinshi* 1709), Metropolitan Governor, concerning the local banquets honouring those who were promoted to official duties (*xiangyin jiuli* 鄉飲酒禮); not yet found for YZ3 (= 1725)

LEC (1729), vol. 19, pp. 329–331; *LEC* (1810–1811), vol. 21, pp. 108–109: Autre Reglement pour honorer le mérite (Other Regulation to honour merit):

> Order of the Emperor to honour the deceased, including chaste women; *Qing shilu*, vol. 7, p. 458 (*juan* 30) (for women) (YZ3/3/乙卯 [= 17] = 29 April 1725); *Shizong xianhuangdi shangyu neige*, *juan* 30, pp. 18a–19a

(more complete); *SKQS*, vol. 414, p. 264 (YZ3/3/17 = 29 April 1725); *Yongzheng chao qijuzhu ce*, vol. 1, p. 459 (more complete) (YZ3/3/17 = 29 April 1725)

LEC (1729), vol. 19, pp. 331–334; *LEC* (1810–1811), vol. 21, pp. 109–110: Déliberation du Souverain Tribunal des Rites en faveur d'une fille qui a estimé la chasteté plus que sa propre vie / Ordre de l'Empereur (Deliberation of the Sovereign Tribunal of Rites in favour of a girl who valued chastity more than her own life / Order of the Emperor):

> Memorial by the Ministry of Rites concerning the construction of a memorial archway (*jianfang* 建坊) in Xinhui 新會 for a girl with family name Liang 梁; *Qing shilu*, vol. 7, p. 576 (*juan* 39) (YZ3/12/壬午 [= 19] = 21 Jan. 1726)

LEC (1729), vol. 19, pp. 334–337; *LEC* (1810–1811), vol. 21, pp. 110–112: Autre délib-eration du même Tribunal des Rites touchant une femme qui a donné des marques d'amour tendre pour son mari (Another deliberation of the same Tribunal of Rites concerning a woman who gave evidence of tender love for her husband):

> Other memorial by the Ministry of Rites concerning a girl with the family name Shao 邵, wife of Xu Wenyuan 徐文源 in Wuyi 武義 (Zhejiang), who committed suicide after the death of her husband (*liefu* 烈婦); *Qing shilu*, vol. 7, p. 652 (*juan* 44) (YZ4/5/丁未 [= 16] = 15 June 1726)

LEC (1729), vol. 19, pp. 338–345; *LEC* (1810–1811), vol. 21, pp. 112–116: Mémorial présenté contre un ordre de l'Empereur (Memorial presented against an order of the Emperor):

> Memorial by Tian Wenjing 田文鏡 (1662–1732), Governor of Henan, in refute of an earlier order by the Emperor, with approval by the Emperor concerning the prosecution of robbers; in his response the emperor praises Tian and asks to investigate his proposal; *Shizong xianhuangdi shangyu neige*, *juan* 58, pp. 18b–20a; *SKQS*, vol. 414, pp. 636–637 (YZ5/6/12 = 30 July 1727); *Yongzheng chao qijuzhu ce*, vol. 2, pp. 1304–1305 (YZ5/6/12 = 30 July 1727)

LEC (1729), vol. 19, pp. 345–364; *LEC* (1810–1811), vol. 21, pp. 116–125: Mémorial dans lequel on propose à l'Empereur un moyen de secourir le peuple dans les années stériles (Memorial in which the Emperor is offered a means of helping the people in barren years / Response of the Emperor):

> Memorial by Liu Yuyi 劉於義 (1675–1748), Provincial Education Commissioner of Shanxi 提督山西學政, proposing a method to rescue the people in years with bad harvests; the proposals are approved by the emperor; *Qing shilu*, vol. 7, p. 583 (*juan* 39) (YZ3/12/辛卯 [= 28] = 30 Jan. 1726)

LEC (1729), vol. 19, pp. 364–366; LEC (1810–1811), vol. 21, pp. 125–126: Pesche des perles tirée d'un Mémorial (Pearl fishing; taken from a Memorial):

> Short report on the yearly fishing of pearls by Manchus from the eight banners in a river in Manchuria, to the east of Liaodong; in 1725 more than 600 men participated in it, but with little result; not yet found

LEC (1729), vol. 19, pp. 366–379; LEC (1810–1811), vol. 21, pp. 127–133: Anciens Ordres renouvellez en faveur des parens infirmes ou fort âgez (Old Orders renewed in favour of infirm or very old parents):

> In order to avoid that provincial officials would leave their position under the pretext of needing to go home to take care for their infirm or aged parents, more precise rules were stipulated for the possibility of *zhongyang* 終養 (care for parents until the end); *Qing shilu*, vol. 7, p. 916 (*juan* 60) (YZ5/8/丙申 [= 13] = 27 Sept. 1727)

LEC (1729), vol. 19, pp. 379–384; LEC (1810–1811), vol. 21, pp. 133–135: Tendresse paternelle de l'Empereur pour les pauvres (Paternal tenderness of the Emperor for the poor):

> Orders by the Emperor to relieve the poor in Beijing who had fled to Beijing and Shandong after heavy rains; *Qing shilu*, vol. 7, p. 576 (*juan* 39) (YZ3/12/壬午 [= 19] = 21 Jan. 1726); *Shizong xianhuangdi shangyu neige*, *juan* 39, pp. 11a–12a; SKQS, vol. 414, pp. 341–342 (YZ3/12/19 = 21 Jan. 1726); *Yongzheng chao qijuzhu ce*, vol. 1, p. 632 (YZ3/12/19 = 21 Jan. 1726)

LEC (1729), vol. 19, pp. 384–392; LEC (1810–1811), vol. 21, pp. 135–139: L'Empereur offre un sacrifice au commencement du Printems & va labourer la terre, pour obtenir une année abondante (The Emperor offers a sacrifice at the beginning of Spring, and goes to plough the land, in order to obtain a bountiful year):

Description of a ceremony at the start of spring (YZ4/2/24 = 27 March 1726) during which the emperor personally ploughs the land and offers at the Xiannong 先農 altar, and a memorial by the Ministry of Rites determining the details of this ritual; *Qing shilu*, vol. 7, p. 613 (*juan* 41) = ceremony; memorial not yet found (YZ4/2/丁亥 [= 24] = 27 March 1726)

LEC (1729), vol. 19, pp. 393–402; *LEC* (1810–1811), vol. 21, pp. 139–144: Instruction par laquelle l'Empereur déclare quel est l'objet de son culte (Instruction by which the Emperor declares what is the goal of his worship):

Li Weijun 李維鈞, Governor-General of Zhili, had sent a memorial mentioning the prayers of common people in the temples of General Liu Meng 劉猛 at the occasion of the damage caused by locusts. In response, the emperor discusses the utmost principle of reciprocation between Heaven and the human being (*tianren ganying zhi li* 天人感應之至理); *Qing shilu*, vol. 7, pp. 515–516 (*juan* 34) (YZ3/7/丙午 [= 11] = 18 Aug. 1725); *Shizong xianhuangdi shangyu neige*, *juan* 34, pp. 5b–7a; *SKQS*, vol. 414, pp. 301–302 (YZ3/7/11 = 18 Aug. 1725); *Yongzheng chao qijuzhu ce*, vol. 1, pp. 530–531 (YZ3/7/11 = 18 Aug. 1725)

2.3 "Lettre du Père Contancin, missionnaire de la Compagnie de Jésus, au Père Duhalde, de la même Compagnie" (19 October 1730 in Canton), in *Lettres édifiantes et curieuses, écrites des missions étrangères par quelques missionnaires de la Compagnie de Jésus* (1703–1776), vol. 22 (= 1736), pp. 189–325 (also *Lettres édifiantes et curieuses, écrites des missions étrangères* (1810–1811), vol. 21, pp. 235–304)

LEC (1736), vol. 22, pp. 191–196; *LEC* (1810–1811), vol. 21, pp. 236–239:

Death sentence of Long-ke-duo 隆科多 (?–1728) turned into imprisonment in a house at Changchunyuan 暢春園; *Qing shilu*, vol. 7, p. 949 (*juan* 62) (YZ5/10/丁亥 [= 5] = 17 Nov. 1727); *Shizong xianhuangdi shangyu neige*, *juan* 62, pp. 3a–4a; *SKQS*, vol. 414, pp. 705–706 (YZ5/10/5 = 17 Nov. 1727); *Yongzheng chao hanwen yuzhi huibian*, vol. 1, pp. 282–283 n. 401 (YZ5/10/5 = 17 Nov. 1727); *Yongzheng chao qijuzhu ce*, vol. 2, p. 1518 (YZ5/10/5 = 17 Nov. 1727)

LEC (1736), vol. 22, pp. 196–202; *LEC* (1810–1811), vol. 21, pp. 239–241: L'Empereur déclare que lorsqu'il va passer quelque tems à sa maison de plaisance, c'est pour jouir d'un meilleur air, & non pas pour chercher du repos (The Emperor

declares that when he goes to spend some time at his country house, it is to enjoy better air, and not to seek rest):

> Declaration by the Emperor explaining that when he goes to Yuanmingyuan 圓明園 it is for better air, not for rest; *Qing shilu*, vol. 7, pp. 596–597 (*juan* 40) (YZ4/1/癸丑 [= 20] = 21 Febr. 1726); *Shizong xianhuangdi shangyu neige, juan* 40, pp. 20b–22a; *SKQS*, vol. 414, pp. 358–359 (YZ4/1/20 = 21 Febr. 1726); *Yongzheng chao qijuzhu ce*, vol. 1, p. 676 (YZ4/1/20 = 21 Febr. 1726)

LEC (1736), vol. 22, pp. 202–209; *LEC* (1810–1811), vol. 21, pp. 242–246: L'Empereur voyant son Peuple menacé de la disette, en est si sensiblement touché, qu'il prie les principaux Officiers de lui déclarer ses fautes sans aucun déguisement (The Emperor, seeing his people threatened with famine, was so sensibly affected that he begged the principal officials to report his faults to him without any disguise):

> Declaration by the Emperor concerning the suffering of people because of drought and his request to criticize him because of his failures; *Qing shilu*, vol. 7, pp. 666–668 (*juan* 45) (YZ4/6/壬戌 [= 1] = 30 June 1726); *Shizong xianhuangdi shangyu neige, juan* 45, pp. 1a–2b; *SKQS*, vol. 414, pp. 397–398 (YZ4/6/1 = 30 June 1726); *Yongzheng chao hanwen yuzhi huibian*, vol. 1, pp. 183–184 n. 292 (YZ4/6/1 = 30 June 1726)

LEC (1736), vol. 22, pp. 210–223; *LEC* (1810–1811), vol. 21, pp. 246–253: Expédiens Pour faire défricher les terres incultes, & par-là procurer l'abondance (Expedients to clear wasteland, and thereby provide abundance):

> Memorial by E-er-tai 鄂爾泰 (1680–1745), Governor-General of Yunnan and Guizhou, with six proposals for land reclamation measures, with the approval by the emperor (except for one proposal); *Shizong xianhuangdi shangyu neige, juan* 58, pp. 3b–25a; *SKQS*, vol. 414, pp. 638–639 (YZ5/6/14 = 1 Aug. 1727); *Yongzheng chao hanwen yuzhi huibian*, vol. 7, p. 107 (YZ5/6/14 = 1 Aug. 1727); *Yongzheng chao qijuzhu ce*, vol. 2, pp. 1309–1310 (YZ5/6/14 = 1 Aug. 1727)

LEC (1736), vol. 22, pp. 223–239; *LEC* (1810–1811), vol. 21, pp. 253–261: Explication Des Notes honorables, & de quelques autres legeres recompenses & punitions (Explanations of honourable grades, and some other minor rewards and punishments):

Explanation (without memorial or edict) of the *Ki-lu* (= *jilu* 紀錄), i.e. registration of an official's deeds and accomplishments in a book for the government's record, and the related system of rewards and punishments, namely *kia-kie* (= *jiaji* 加級), i.e. the raising of rank, or *kiang-kie* (*jiangji* 降級), i.e. the lowering of rank; no record of this explanation

LEC (1736), vol. 22, pp. 239–243; LEC (1810–1811), vol. 21, pp. 261–263: Mémorial du Viceroi de la province de Chan tong, qui avertit l'Empereur d'une inondation & du secours qu'il a donné au Peuple (Memorial of the Viceroy of Chantong Province, who notifies the Emperor of a flood and the relief he has given to the People):

Memorial of the Governor of Shandong concerning floods; not yet found. May instead have been a memorial by Yang Wenqian 楊文乾, Governor of Guangdong; *Qing shilu*, vol. 7, p. 753 (*juan* 50) (YZ4/11/己亥 [= 11] = 4 Dec. 1726); *Shizong xianhuangdi shangyu neige, juan* 50, pp. 7b–8a; SKQS, vol. 414, pp. 489–490 (YZ4/11/11 = 4 Dec. 1726); *Yongzheng chao qijuzhu ce*, vol. 1, pp. 852–853 (YZ4/11/11 = 4 Dec. 1726)

LEC (1736), vol. 22, pp. 244–246; LEC (1810–1811), vol. 21, pp. 263–265:

Rescript of the Emperor to the reports by Kong Yuxun 孔毓珣 (?–1730), Governor-General of Guangdong, on the floods in Jiangnan; *Qing shilu*, vol. 7, p. 917 (*juan* 60) (YZ5/8/己亥 [= 16] = 30 Sept. 1727); *Shizong xianhuangdi shangyu neige, juan* 60, pp. 11a–12a; SKQS, vol. 414, pp. 678–679 (YZ5/8/16 = 30 Sept. 1727); *Yongzheng chao qijuzhu ce*, vol. 2, pp. 1419–1420 (YZ5/8/16 = 30 Sept. 1727)

LEC (1736), vol. 22, pp. 246–248; LEC (1810–1811), vol. 21, pp. 265–266:

Rescript of the Emperor to the memorial by E-er-tai 鄂爾泰, Governor-General of Yunnan and Guizhou, and his exhortation to go beyond one's task in presenting memorials (*yuezhi chenzou* 越職陳奏); *Qing shilu*, vol. 7, pp. 936–937 (*juan* 61) (YZ5/9/己巳 [= 16] = 30 Oct. 1727); *Shizong xianhuangdi shangyu neige, juan* 61, pp. 21b–22a; SKQS, vol. 414, pp. 698–699 (YZ5/9/16 = 30 Oct. 1727); *Yongzheng chao qijuzhu ce*, vol. 2, pp. 1480–1481 (YZ5/9/16 = 30 Oct. 1727)

LEC (1736), vol. 22, pp. 248–249; LEC (1810–1811), vol. 21, p. 266:

Memorial of Sai-leng-e 塞楞額 (1686–1748), Governor of Shandong, to allow people to build housing on the riverbanks in order to earn a living through fishing; *Qing shilu*, vol. 7, p. 938 (*juan* 61) (YZ5/9/辛未 [= 18] = 1 Nov. 1727); *Shizong xianhuangdi shangyu neige, juan* 61, pp. 22b–23a; *SKQS*, vol. 414, p. 699 (YZ5/9/18 = 1 Nov. 1727); *Yongzheng chao qijuzhu ce*, vol. 2, p. 1483 (YZ5/9/18 = 1 Nov. 1727)

LEC (1736), vol. 22, pp. 249–262; *LEC* (1810–1811), vol. 21, pp. 266–273: Cérémonie qui s'est observée l'année 1725, lorsqu'on a présenté à l'Empereur le Livre de la Généalogie Impériale, ou l'Histoire de la Dynastie Tartare (Ceremony observed in the year 1725, when the Emperor was presented with the book of Imperial Genealogy, or the history of the Tartar dynasty):

Detailed description of the ceremony for the presentation of the imperial genealogy (*yudie* 玉牒) to the Emperor that took place on YZ3/10/9 (= 13 November 1725) (possibly based on an eyewitness account, since details seem to be absent in the available official sources); *Qing shilu*, vol. 7, p. 548 (*juan* 37) (YZ3/10/癸酉 [= 9] = 13 Nov. 1725); *Yongzheng chao qijuzhu ce*, vol. 1, pp. 596–597 (YZ3/10/9 = 13 Nov. 1725)

LEC (1736), vol. 22, pp. 263–270; *LEC* (1810–1811), vol. 21, pp. 273–277: L'Empereur Fait l'éloge de son Précepteur, & l'honore après sa mort (The Emperor praises his Tutor, and honours him after his death):

Eulogy of Gu-ba-dai 顧八代 (?–1709), who was removed as Minister of Rites in 1693, but continued his services in the palace school for princes, also instructing the Yongzheng emperor; the latter ordered that Gu-ba-dai be posthumously restored to his former ranks and canonized as Wenduan 文端; *Qing shilu*, vol. 7, pp. 597–598 (*juan* 40) (YZ4/1/乙卯 [= 22] = 23 Febr. 1726); *Shizong xianhuangdi shangyu neige, juan* 40, pp. 23a–25a; *SKQS*, vol. 414, pp. 359–360 (YZ4/1/22 = 23 Febr. 1726); *Yongzheng chao qijuzhu ce*, vol. 1, p. 679 (YZ4/1/22 = 23 Febr. 1726)

LEC (1736), vol. 22, pp. 270–284; *LEC* (1810–1811), vol. 21, pp. 278–284: Ordre admirable qu'on garda à Peking, lorsqu'il fallut renvoyer plus de quarante mille Pauvres, chacun dans son pays (Admirable order that was issued in Peking, when it was necessary to send back more than forty thousand poor, each to their own Region):

The Emperor approves financial support for forty thousand people who had to be sent back to the provinces in the beginning of YZ4/2

(= March 1726), with a long memorial by Ministers and high officials to execute the order; *Qing shilu*, vol. 7, pp. 604–605 (*juan* 41) (YZ4/2/庚午 [= 7] = 10 March 1726); *Shizong xianhuangdi shangyu neige*, *juan* 41, pp. 2a–2b; SKQS, vol. 414, p. 363 (YZ4/2/7 = 10 March 1726)

LEC (1736), vol. 22, pp. 284–287; LEC (1810–1811), vol. 21, pp. 284–286: Instruction de l'Empereur, Donnée à l'occasion du caractere Chinois, qui signifie bonheur (Instruction of the Emperor, given in the context of the Chinese character which means happiness):

Instruction of the Emperor related to the character *fu* 福; not yet found; similar content vol. 7, pp. 773–774 (*juan* 51) (YZ4/12/庚辰 [= 23] = 14 Jan. 1726); *Shizong xianhuangdi shangyu neige*, *juan* 51, pp. 41a–42a; SKQS, vol. 414, pp. 515–516 (YZ4/12/23 = 14 Jan. 1726)

LEC (1736), vol. 22, pp. 288–299; LEC (1810–1811), vol. 21, pp. 286–292: Nouveau Règlement sur l'examen des Mandarins / Ordre de l'Empereur qui regarde le même Examen général (New Regulation regarding the examination of Officials / Order of the Emperor regarding the same general examination):

Extensive discussion of new rules concerning the three-yearly examination of officials, among others on the examination of those who have been evaluated as excellent (*zhuoyi* 卓異); only partially: *Qing shilu*, vol. 7, pp. 1045–1046 (*juan* 69) (YZ6/5/己巳 [= 19] = 26 June 1728); *Shizong xianhuangdi shangyu neige*, *juan* 69, pp. 13a–14a; SKQS, vol. 415, pp. 62–63 (YZ6/5/19 = 26 June 1728); *Yongzheng chao qijuzhu ce*, vol. 3, p. 2001 (YZ6/5/己巳 [= 19] = 26 June 1728); see also earlier instruction: *Qing shilu*, vol. 7, p. 681 (*juan* 45) (YZ4/6/丙寅 [= 5] = 4 July 1726); *Shizong xianhuangdi shangyu neige*, *juan* 45, p. 3a; SKQS, vol. 414, p. 398 (YZ4/6/5 = 4 July 1726)

LEC (1736), vol. 22, pp. 299–324; LEC (1810–1811), vol. 21, pp. 292–304: Mémorial du Viceroi de la Province de Ho-nan, par lequel il avertit l'Empereur d'un bel exemple de désintéressement, donné par un homme & une femme du Peuple (Memorial of the Viceroy of the province of Ho-nan, by which he informs the Emperor of a fine example of selflessness, given by a man and a woman of the People):

Memorial by Tian Wenjing 田文鏡, Governor of Henan, and reaction by the Emperor on the case of Chi yeou (= Cui Shiyou 翟世有) and his wife (from Mengjin fu 孟津縣) who gave back the money lost by merchant Qin Tai 秦泰 (from Shaanxi); *Qing shilu*, vol. 7, pp. 1060–1061 (*juan* 71)

(YZ6/7/甲寅 [= 5] = 10 Aug. 1728); *Shizong xianhuangdi shangyu neige*, *juan* 71, pp. 6a–10a; *SKQS*, vol. 415, pp. 94–96 (YZ6/7/5 = 10 Aug. 1728); *Yongzheng chao qijuzhu ce*, vol. 3, pp. 2107–2109 (YZ6/7/5 = 10 Aug. 1728)

3 *Mémoires concernant l'histoire, les sciences, les arts, les mœurs, les usages, &c. des Chinois, par les missionnaires de Pékin*, 17 vols., Paris: Nyon Libraire – Treuttel et Würtz, 1776–1814. (*MCC*)[3]

3.1 *Mémoires concernant ... les Chinois* (*MCC*), Vol. 9 (1783)

MCC, vol. 9, pp. 1–64: Extraits de diverses lettres écrites par M. Amiot, missionnaire en Chine, en 1780, de Pékin (Extracts from various letters written by M. Amiot, missionary in China, in 1780, from Peking)

MCC, vol. 9, pp. 6–24: La seconde, du 13 Août, sur la fête de *Ouan-cheou* de l'Empereur (The second, 13 August, on the feast of *Ouan-cheou* of the Emperor) (13 Aug. 1780):

Inst. 1516, pp. 238–244: pp. 1–14:
Feast for the 70th birthday (*wanshou* 萬壽) of the Qianlong emperor, with reference to the visit of the 6th Panchen Lama Erdeni 班禪額爾德尼 (Lobsang Palden Yeshe, 1738–1780) and including the translation of an imperial edict, dated QL44/8/19 (= 28 Sept. 1779)

MCC, vol. 9, pp. 7–11 (QL44/8/19 = 28 Sept. 1779):
Inst. 1516, pp. 239–240: pp. 3–5
Edict of the Emperor of QL44/8/19 [>18] concerning the tour he will undertake and the (minor) ceremonies because of the death of his mother; *Qing shilu*, vol. 22, pp. 624–625 (*juan* 1089) (QL44/8/己巳 [18] = 27 Sept. 1779); *Qianlong chao shangyu dang*, vol. 9, p. 788 n. 1915 (QL44/8/18 = 27 Sept. 1779); *Qianlong di qijuzhu*, vol. 29, pp. 239–240 (QL44/8/18 = 27 Sept. 1779)

MCC, vol. 9, pp. 11–17 (QL45/1/1 = 5 Febr. 1780):
Inst. 1516, pp. 240–242: pp. 5–10
Edict of the Emperor of QL45/1/1 concerning various benefits at the occasion of the celebration; *Qing shilu*, vol. 22, pp. 712–714 (*juan* 1098) (QL45/1/庚辰 [1] = 5 Febr. 1780); *Qianlong di qijuzhu*, vol. 30, pp. 1–3 (QL45/1/1 = 5 Febr. 1780)

3 For electronic versions, see Gallica (Bibliothèque nationale de France, Paris).

MCC, vol. 9, pp. 18–21 (QL44/11/13 = 20 Dec. 1779):
Inst. 1516, pp. 242–243: pp. 10–12
Edict of Emperor QL44/11/13 [>6] concerning the incomplete execution of the rites by the Emperor; *Qing shilu*, vol. 22, pp. 677–679 (*juan* 1094) (QL44/11/丙戌 [6] = 13 Dec. 1779); *Qianlong chao shangyu dang*, vol. 9, pp. 861–862 n. 2109 (QL44/11/6 = 13 Dec. 1779); *Qianlong di qijuzhu*, vol. 29, pp. 334–336 (QL44/11/6 = 13 Dec. 1779)

MCC, vol. 9, pp. 21–24 (QL44/11/19 = 26 Dec. 1779):
Inst. 1516, pp. 243–244: pp. 12–14
Response by Taichangsi 太常寺 (QL44/11/19) and reaction of the Emperor; not yet found

MCC, vol. 9, pp. 25–44: La troisieme, du 10 septembre 1780, sur les travaux d'Akoui pour prévenir le débordement du Hoang-ho, & sur Ly-che-yao, Gouverneur de Canton (The third, 10 September 1780, on Akoui's works to prevent the overflowing of the Hoang-ho, & on Ly-che-yao, Governor of Canton) (10 Sept. 1780):
Inst. 1516, pp. 253–260: pp. 1–16
On the initiatives by A-gui 阿桂 (1717–1797), Manchu general, to prevent the overflowing of the Yellow River, and on Li Shiyao 李侍堯 (?–1788), Governor of Guizhou-Yunnan (1777–1780)

MCC, vol. 9, pp. 27–28:
Inst. 1516, p. 254: pp. 3–4
Early request by A-gui and the costs it will take; not yet found

MCC, vol. 9, pp. 28–30 (QL44/12/13 = 19 Jan. 1780):
Inst. 1516, pp. 254–255: pp. 4–5
Memorial by A-gui requesting grace for Li Yongji 李永吉; *Qing shilu*, vol. 22, pp. 694–696 (*juan* 1096) (QL44/12/辛亥 [1] = 7 Jan. 1780); *Qianlong chao shangyu dang*, vol. 9, pp. 890–891 n. 2176 (QL44/12/1 = 7 Jan. 1780); *Qianlong di qijuzhu*, vol. 29, p. 375 (QL44/12/1 = 7 Jan. 1780)

MCC, vol. 9, p. 30:
Inst. 1516, p. 255: p. 5
De-cheng 德成 is sent to Henan; *Qing shilu*, vol. 22, p. 696 (*juan* 1096) (QL44/12/癸丑 [3] = 9 Jan. 1780); *Qianlong chao shangyu dang*, vol. 9, p. 892 n. 2183 (QL44/12/3 = 9 Jan. 1780); *Qianlong di qijuzhu*, vol. 29, p. 377 (QL44/12/3 = 9 Jan. 1780)

MCC, vol. 9, p. 30:

Inst. 1516, p. 255: pp. 5–6

Subsidies for reparation works; *Qing shilu*, vol. 22, p. 697 (*juan* 1096) (QL44/12/甲寅 [4] = 10 Jan. 1780); *Qianlong chao shangyu dang*, vol. 9, p. 892 n. 2185 (QL44/12/4 = 10 Jan. 1780); *Qianlong di qijuzhu*, vol. 29, p. 378 (QL44/12/4 = 10 Jan. 1780)

MCC, vol. 9, p. 31:

Inst. 1516, p. 255: p. 6

Answer of A-gui to De-cheng; *Qing shilu*, vol. 22, p. 697 (*juan* 1096) (QL44/12/乙丑 [15] = 21 Jan. 1780); *Qianlong chao shangyu dang*, vol. 9, pp. 902–903 n. 2236 (QL44/12/15 = 21 Jan. 1780); *Qianlong di qijuzhu*, vol. 29, p. 378 (QL44/12/15 = 21 Jan. 1780)

MCC, vol. 9, pp. 32–34:

Inst. 1516, pp. 255–256: pp. 6–8

Report by A-gui, Chen Huizu 陳輝祖 (1732–1783), Li Fenghan 李奉翰 (?–1799) and others on the achievement of the works and response by the Emperor; *Qing shilu*, exact text not yet found

MCC, vol. 9, pp. 35–41:

Inst. 1516, pp. 256–259: pp. 8–13

Further edict by the Emperor; *Qing shilu*, vol. 22, pp. 738–740 (*juan* 1101) (QL45/2/壬申 [23] = 28 March 1780); *Qianlong chao shangyu dang*, vol. 9, pp. 975–976 n. 2450 (QL45/2/23 = 28 March 1780); *Qianlong di qijuzhu*, vol. 29, p. 378 (QL45/2/23 = 28 March 1780)

MCC, vol. 9, pp. 41–44 (QL45/4/5 = 8 May 1780):

Inst. 1516, pp. 259–260: pp. 13–15

Edict by the Emperor concerning the complot by Li Shiyao 李侍堯 et al.; *Qing shilu*, vol. 22, pp. 761–764 (*juan* 1103) (QL45/3/丁酉 [18] = 22 April 1780); *Qianlong chao shangyu dang*, vol. 10, pp. 39–40 n. 105 and 106 (QL45/3/18 = 22 April 1780); *Qianlong di qijuzhu*, vol. 30, pp. 42–44 (QL45/3/18 = 22 April 1780)

MCC, vol. 9, p. 44:

Inst. 1516, p. 260: pp. 15–16

Condemnation of Li Shiyao; *Qing shilu*, vol. 22, pp. 799–800 (*juan* 1106) (QL45/5/乙酉 [7] = 10 June 1780); *Qianlong chao shangyu dang*, vol. 10,

p. 119 n. 301 (QL45/5/7 = 10 June 1780); *Qianlong di qijuzhu*, vol. 30, p. 88 (QL45/5/7 = 10 June 1780)

MCC, vol. 9, p. 45:
Inst. 1516, p. 260: p. 16
Demand to alleviate capital punishment by Fu-long-an 福隆安 (1743 (1746?)-1784); not yet found

MCC, vol. 9, pp. 45–60: La quatrieme, du 26 septembre 1780, Éloge historique du Yu-ming-tchoung (The fourth, 26 September 1780, historical Elegy of Yu-ming-tchoung) (26 Sept. 1780):

Inst. 1516, pp. 245–252: pp. 1–15
Historical elegy on the Qing official and writer Yu Minzhong 于敏中 (1714–1779); *Qing shilu*, vol. 22, pp. 647–648 (*juan* 1091) (QL44/9/丁酉 [16] = 25 Oct. 1780); *Qianlong chao shangyu dang*, vol. 9, p. 819 n. 1982 (QL44/9/16 = 25 Oct. 1780); *Qianlong di qijuzhu*, vol. 29, pp. 266–267 (QL44/9/16 = 25 Oct. 1780)

MCC, vol. 9, pp. 47–53:
Inst. 1516, pp. 246–248: pp. 3–8
Text by Yu Minzhong; full text not yet found

MCC, vol. 9, pp. 53–56 (QL44/12/15 = 22 Dec. 1780):
Inst. 1516, pp. 249–250: pp. 9–11
Elegy by the Emperor; *Qing shilu*, vol. 22, pp. 698–699 (*juan* 1096) (QL44/12/戊午 [8] = 14 Jan. 1780); *Qianlong chao shangyu dang*, vol. 9, p. 895 n. 2205 (QL44/12/8 = 14 Jan. 1780); *Qianlong di qijuzhu*, vol. 29, p. 394 (QL44/12/8 = 14 Jan. 1780)

MCC, vol. 9, pp. 56–60:
Inst. 1516, pp. 250–251: pp. 11–14
Family dispute regarding the division of the heritage of Yu Minzhong; *Qing shilu*, vol. 22, p. 829 (*juan* 1109 (QL45/6/戊辰 [21] = 22 July 1780); *Qianlong chao shangyu dang*, vol. 10, pp. 151–152 n. 418 (QL45/6/21 = 22 July 1780)
Family dispute regarding the division of the heritage of Yu Minzhong; *Qing shilu*, vol. 22, pp. 839–840 (*juan* 1110) (QL45/7/戊寅 [2] = 1 Aug. 1780)
Family dispute regarding the division of the heritage of Yu Minzhong; *Qing shilu*, vol. 22, pp. 847–848 (*juan* 1110) (QL45/7/戊子 [12] = 11 Aug. 1780);

Qianlong chao shangyu dang, vol. 10, pp. 171–172 n. 473 (QL45/7/12 = 11 Aug. 1780); *Qianlong chao junjichu suishou dengji*, vol. 32, pp. 372–373 (QL45/7/12 = 11 Aug. 1780)

Family dispute regarding the division of the heritage of Yu Minzhong; *Qing shilu*, vol. 22, pp. 853–854 (*juan* 1111) (QL45/7/己亥 [23] = 22 Aug. 1780); *Qianlong chao shangyu dang*, vol. 10, p. 177 n. 491 (QL45/7/23 = 22 Aug. 1780); *Qianlong chao junjichu suishou dengji*, vol. 32, p. 388 (QL45/7/23 = 22 Aug. 1780)

MCC, vol. 9, pp. 60–64: La cinquieme, du 4 Novembre 1780, sur un livre ordonné par l'Empereur à l'honneur des guerriers qui se sont distingués (QL45/1/28 = 3 March 1780) (The fifth, 4 November 1780, on a book ordered by the Emperor in honour of military men who distinguished themselves) (4 Nov. 1780):

Inst. 1516, pp. 261–264, fols. [1r–3r]

On a book about distinguished military men presented to the emperor (*Zhaozhongci lie zhuan* 昭忠祠列傳, remained manuscript). The initiative goes back to Shu-he-de 舒赫德 (1710–1777) and Yu Minzhong 于敏中 (1714–1779); not yet found

MCC, vol. 9, pp. 441–454: Extrait d'une lettre ecrite de Pé-king le 17 Août, par M. Amiot, Missionnaire, sur les services d'Akoui; & sur la mort du Pan-tchan Lama (Extract from a letter written from Peking on 17 August, by Mr. Amiot, Missionary, on Akoui's services; & on the death of Pan-tchan Lama) (17 Aug. 1781):

Inst. 1516, pp. 271–280: pp. 1–20

MCC, vol. 9, pp. 441–446: Extrait d'une lettre ecrite par M. Amiot, Missionnaire, contenant, 1º. Les services rendus par Akoui (Extract from a letter written by Mr. Amiot, Missionary, containing, 1st, the services rendered by Akoui):

Inst. 1516, pp. 276–278: pp. 11–15

A-gui 阿桂 and He-shen 和珅 (1750–1799) are sent to Lanzhou 蘭州 that is under siege after a Muslim attack of Hezhou 河州; *Qing shilu*, vol. 23, pp. 66–67 (*juan* 1127) (QL46/3/壬寅 [29] = 22 April 1781)

[A-gui is sent]; *Qing shilu*, vol. 23, p. 71 (*juan* 1128) (QL46/4/甲辰 [1] = 24 April 1781); *Qianlong chao shangyu dang*, absent; *Qianlong di qijuzhu*, vol. 31, p. 131; *Qianlong chao junjichu suishou dengji*, vol. 33, p. 185 (QL46/4/1 = 24 April 1781)

[He-shen will arrive first]; *Qing shilu*, vol. 23, pp. 73–74 (*juan* 1128) (QL46/4/丁未 [4] = 27 April 1781); *Qianlong chao shangyu dang*, absent; *Qianlong chao junjichu suishou dengji*, vol. 33, p. 194 (QL46/4/4 = 27 April 1781)

[He-shen arrives in Lanzhou]; *Qing shilu*, vol. 23, pp. 93–94 (*juan* 1129) (QL46/4/己巳 [26] = 19 May 1781); *Qianlong chao junjichu suishou dengji*, vol. 33, pp. 249–250 (QL46/4/26 = 19 May 1781)

[A-gui is in Lanzhou and has matters under control]; *Qing shilu*, vol. 23, pp. 94–95 (*juan* 1129) (QL46/4/庚午 [27] = 20 May 1781); *Qianlong chao junjichu suishou dengji*, vol. 33, pp. 252–253 (QL46/4/27 = 20 May 1781)

[Report on the first days]; *Qing shilu*, vol. 23, pp. 95–98 (*juan* 1129) (QL46/4/壬申 [29] = 22 May 1781); *Qianlong di qijuzhu*, vol. 31, pp. 178–181; *Qianlong chao junjichu suishou dengji*, vol. 33, pp. 255–259 (QL46/4/29 = 22 May 1781)

[Precise days of arrival]; *Qing shilu*, vol. 23, pp. 100–102 (*juan* 1130) (QL46/5/甲戌 [2] = 24 May 1781); *Qianlong di qijuzhu*, vol. 31, pp. 184–185 (QL46/5/2 = 24 May 1781)

[Appointment of Li Shiyao 李侍堯 as new Governor]; *Qing shilu*, vol. 23, pp. 115–116 (*juan* 1131) (QL46/5/戊子 [16] = 7 June 1781); *Qianlong chao shangyu dang*, vol. 10, p. 479 n. 1389 (QL45/5/16 = 7 June 1781)

[Condemnation of former Governor Le-er-jin 勒爾謹 (?–1781)]; *Qing shilu*, vol. 23, pp. 128–129 (*juan* 1132) (QL46/run5/癸卯 [1] = 22 June 1781)

MCC, vol. 9, pp. 446–453: 2°. Une lettre de l'Empereur au Talaï-lama (2nd, A letter from the Emperor to the Talaï-lama):

Inst. 1516, pp. 278–280: pp. 15–20

Letter of the Emperor to the Dalai Lama 達賴喇嘛 (Jampäl Gyatso, 1758–1804) at the occasion of the death of Pan-tchan Lama Erdeni 班禪額爾德尼; *Qing shilu*, vol. 23, p. 5 (*juan* 1122) (QL46/1/癸未 [10] = 2 Febr. 1781)

3.2 *Mémoires concernant … les Chinois* (MCC), Vol. 11 (1786)

MCC, vol. 11, pp. 501–515: Extrait d'une lettre de M. Amiot, Ecrite de Pé-king le 22 Novembre 1783 (Extract from a letter by Mr Amiot, Written from Peking on 22 November 1783):

Inst. 1516: pp. 287–294: fols. [1r–8v]

MCC, vol. 11, pp. 502–508: Chang-yu (QL47/10/4 = 8 Nov. 1783):

Inst. 1516: pp. 288–290: fols. [2v–4v]

Edict on granting honorific titles to the Mongol members of the imperial family (with the nobility titles: *wang* 王, *beile* 貝勒, *beizi* 貝子, *gongzi* 公子); *Qing shilu*, vol. 23, pp. 609–610 (*juan* 1164) (QL47/9/己酉 [15] = 21 Oct. 1782); *Qianlong di qijuzhu*, vol. 32, pp. 287–288 (QL47/9/15 = 21 Oct. 1782)

MCC, vol. 11, p. 509 (QL48/1/10 = 11 Febr. 1783):

Inst. 1516: p. 291: fol. [5r]

Ceremony; *Qing shilu*, vol. 23, p. 720 (*juan* 1172) (QL48/1/壬寅 [10] = 11 Febr. 1783); *Qianlong di qijuzhu*, vol. 33, p. 9 (QL48/1/10 = 11 Febr. 1783)

MCC, vol. 11, pp. 509–514 (QL48/6/3 = 2 July 1783):

Inst. 1516: pp. 291–293: fols. [5r–7v]

Lightening causes fire near Xishimen 西直門 and burns down a pavilion; reaction of the Emperor in response to A-gui's report about it; *Qing shilu*, vol. 23, p. 830 (*juan* 1182) (QL48/6/乙丑 [5] = 4 July 1783); *Qianlong chao shangyu dang*, vol. 11, p. 698 n. 1790 (QL48/6/5 = 4 July 1783)

MCC, vol. 11, pp. 515–568: Extrait d'une autre lettre de M. Amiot, Ecrite de Pé-king le 2 Octobre 1784 (Extract from another letter by Mr. Amiot, Written from Peking on 2 October 1784):

Inst. 1516, pp. 308–332: pp. 1–50

MCC, vol. 11, pp. 553–559:

Inst. 1516, pp. 327–329: pp. 39–43

Family member of Fu-long-an 福隆安, who was in charge of the matters related to missionaries at the Court, killed a mason; case was investigated further; *Qing shilu*, vol. 23, pp. 952–953 (*juan* 1093) (QL48/11/丙午 [19] = 12 Dec. 1783); *Qianlong chao shangyu dang*, vol. 11, p. 890 n. 2376 (QL48/11/19 = 12 Dec. 1783); *Qianlong di qijuzhu*, vol. 33, pp. 472–474 (QL48/11/19 = 12 Dec. 1783)

MCC, vol. 11, pp. 553–559:

Inst. 1516, pp. 327–329: pp. 39–43

Condemnation of family member of Fu-long-an 福隆安 to be included in the gazette; easily 20 similar condemnations in the gazettes of the same year; *Qing shilu*, vol. 23, pp. 954–955 (*juan* 1193) (QL48/11/庚戌

[23] = 16 Dec. 1783); *Qianlong chao shangyu dang*, vol. 11, p. 897 n. 2395 (QL48/11/23 = 16 Dec. 1783); *Qianlong di qijuzhu*, vol. 33, pp. 480–481 (QL48/11/23 = 16 Dec. 1783)

MCC, vol. 11, pp. 577–579: Extrait d'une lettre de M. Bourgeois, missionnaire, Ecrite de Pé-king le 19 Novembre 1784 (Extract from a letter by Mr. Bourgeois, missionary, Written from Peking on 19 November 1784):

Inst. 1520, fols. 258–260: fol. 260r

MCC, vol. 11, p. 579: Mobile characters used for gazette; same page also contains a reference to *Siku quanshu*

MCC, vol. 11, pp. 580–609: Extrait d'une lettre de M. Amiot, Missionnaire, Ecrite de Péking, le 29 Novembre 1784 (Extract from a letter by Mr. Amiot, Missionary, Written from Peking, 29 November 1784):

Inst. 1516: pp. 333–344: pp. 1–24

MCC, vol. 11, pp. 580–585:
Inst. 1516: pp. 333–335: pp. 1–5
Illness of the Emperor before leaving on Southern Tour and A-gui demanding the delay of the departure; not yet found despite various small references in the early days of QL49/1 (original departure QL49/1/5 = 26 Jan. 1784)

MCC, vol. 11, pp. 586–587:
Inst. 1516: p. 336: pp. 7–8
Punishment of high officials; not yet found

MCC, vol. 11, pp. 587–589:
Inst. 1516: pp. 336–337: pp. 8–9
Visit to Confucius temple (*xianshi miao* 先師廟) with rewards for scholars and students; *Qing shilu*, vol. 24, p. 27 (*juan* 1198) [only mentions the visit to Confucius temple] (QL49/2/丙寅 [10] = 1 March 1784)

MCC, vol. 11, pp. 590–591:
Inst. 1516: pp. 337–339: pp. 9–11
Conflict in Gansu between the red-headed and white-headed Muslims (*hongmao* 紅帽, *baimao* 白帽); *Qing shilu*, vol. 24, pp. 178–179 (*juan* 1208)

(QL49/6/甲申 [1] = 17 July 1784); *Qianlong di qijuzhu*, vol. 34, pp. 264–265 (QL49/6/1 = 17 July 1784)

MCC, vol. 11, pp. 591–593:
Inst. 1516: p. 338: pp. 11–12
Li Shiyao 李侍堯 becomes the new Governor; *Qing shilu*, vol. 24, pp. 210–211 (*juan* 1209) (QL49/6/庚戌 [27] = 12 Aug. 1784); *Qianlong di qijuzhu*, vol. 34, pp. 306–308 (QL49/6/27 = 12 Aug. 1784)

MCC, vol. 11, pp. 593–601:
Inst. 1516: pp. 338–342: pp. 12–20
On the rebellious Huizu in Gansu; not yet found

MCC, vol. 11, pp. 601–604:
Inst. 1516: pp. 342–343: pp. 20–21
Letter on the Hui (*huimin* 回民) by A-gui and answer of the Emperor; *Qing shilu*, vol. 24, pp. 224–225 (*juan* 1210) (QL49/7/辛酉 [8] = 23 Aug. 1784)

MCC, vol. 11, pp. 605–606:
Inst. 1516: p. 343: p. 21
Rewards for the suppression of the rebellion, including the title of Commandant of Light Chariots (*qingche duwei* 輕車都尉) for He-shen 和珅; *Qing shilu*, vol. 24, pp. 225–229 (*juan* 1210) (QL49/7/甲子 [11] = 26 Aug. 1784)

MCC, vol. 11, pp. 607–608:
Inst. 1516: p. 343: p. 22
The Emperor taking care of the elderly because of the extreme cold; not yet found

MCC, vol. 11, pp. 608–609:
Inst. 1516: p. 344: pp. 23–24
At the occasion of the birth of the Emperor's first great-great-grandson (fifth generation), Zai-xi 載錫 (1784–1821), restauration of the titles to the child's father; *Qing shilu*, vol. 24, p. 306 (*juan* 1216) (QL49/10/丙戌 [= 4] = 16 Nov. 1784); *Qianlong chao shangyu dang*, vol. 12, p. 308 n. 859 (QL49/10/4 = 16 Nov. 1784); *Qianlong di qijuzhu*, vol. 34, p. 466 (QL49/10/4 = 16 Nov. 1784) (giving of name)

3.3 *Mémoires concernant … les Chinois* (MCC), Vol. 12 (1786)

MCC, vol. 12, pp. 509–530: Extrait d'une lettre de M. Amiot, Ecrite de Péking le 15 Octobre 1785 (Extract from a letter by Mr. Amiot, Written from Peking on 15 October 1785); On the celebration of old people:

MCC, vol. 12, pp. 509–510 (QL49/10/25 = 7 Dec. 1784):
Grace extended to Li Shiyao 李侍堯; *Qing shilu*, vol. 24, pp. 247–248 (*juan* 1211) (QL49/10/癸巳 [11] = 23 Nov. 1784); *Qianlong chao shangyu dang*, vol. 12, p. 324 n. 896 (QL49/10/11 = 23 Nov. 1784)

MCC, vol. 12, pp. 511–512:
Rewards to elderly people; *Qing shilu*, e.g. vol. 24, pp. 385–387 (*juan* 1222) (QL50/1/辛亥 [1] = 9 Febr. 1785); *Qianlong di qijuzhu*, vol. 35, pp. 1–4 (QL50/1/1 = 9 Febr. 1785)

MCC, vol. 12, pp. 512–513:
Call for promotion of unknown officials; not yet found

MCC, vol. 12, pp. 513–515:
Honorific title of Fengfu 奉福 to Xi-xian 希賢 and of Fengshou 奉壽 to Jue-long-a 覺隆阿; *Qing shilu*, vol. 24, p. 306 (*juan* 1216) (QL49/10/丙戌 [= 4] = 16 Nov. 1784); *Qianlong chao shangyu dang*, vol. 12, p. 308 n. 859 (QL49/10/4 = 16 Nov. 1784); *Qianlong di qijuzhu*, vol. 34, p. 466 (QL49/10/4 = 16 Nov. 1784)

MCC, vol. 12, p. 515:
The Korean King Yi San 李祘 (1752–1800) confirms his son Yi Sun 李賰 (1782–1786) as crown prince; *Qing shilu*, vol. 24, pp. 277–278 (*juan* 1082) (QL49/9/乙卯 [3] = 16 Oct. 1784); *Qianlong di qijuzhu*, vol. 34, p. 403 (QL49/9/3 = 16 Oct. 1784)

MCC, vol. 12, pp. 515–516:
Invitation to reception; *Qing shilu*, vol. 24, pp. 297–298 (*juan* 1215) (QL49/9/庚辰 [28] = 10 Nov. 1784); *Qianlong chao shangyu dang*, vol. 12, p. 293 n. 822 and p. 294 n. 823 (QL49/9/28 = 10 Nov. 1784); *Qianlong di qijuzhu*, vol. 34, p. 454 (QL49/9/28 = 10 Nov. 1784)

MCC, vol. 12, p. 516:
Offering of gifts; *Qing shilu*, vol. 24, p. 339 (*juan* 1218) (QL49/11/壬戌 [11] = 12 Dec. 1784); *Qianlong chao shangyu dang*, vol. 12, p. 364 n. 1005

(QL49/11/11 = 12 Dec. 1784); *Qianlong di qijuzhu*, vol. 34, p. 521 (QL49/11/11 = 12 Dec. 1784)

MCC, vol. 12, pp. 517, 527–528:

Feast for elderly (*qian sou yan* 千叟宴); *Qing shilu*, vol. 24, p. 388 (*juan* 1222) (QL50/1/丙辰 [6] = 14 Febr. 1785); *Qianlong chao shangyu dang*, vol. 12, p. 428 n. 1196 and p. 429 n. 1197, 1198 (QL50/1/6 = 14 Febr. 1785); for longer version *Qinding qiansouyan shi* 欽定千叟宴詩, SKQS, vol. 1452, p. 6 (*juan* 1, p. 1)

3.4 *Mémoires concernant ... les Chinois* (MCC), Vol. 13 (1788)

MCC, vol. 13, pp. 417–458: Extrait d'une lettre de M. Amiot, Missionnaire, Ecrite de Peking, le 20 Mai 1786 (Extract from a letter by Mr. Amiot, Missionary, Written from Peking, 20 May 1786):

Inst. 1516, pp. 349–373: pp. 1–48

MCC, vol. 13, pp. 419–420: Traduction des Vers de l'Empereur (Translation of Verses by the Emperor):

Inst. 1516, pp. 350–351: pp. 4–6

Poem by the emperor; *Qing shilu*, vol. 24, pp. 801–802 (*juan* 1250) (QL51/3/壬子 [= 8] = 6 April 1786); *Qianlong chao shangyu dang*, vol. 13, p. 72 n. 194 (only a brief mention, text not included) (QL51/3/8 = 6 April 1786); *Qianlong di qijuzhu*, absent

MCC, vol. 13, pp. 421–422 (QL50/12/21 = 20 Jan. 1786):

Inst. 1516, p. 352: pp. 7–8

Edict concerning a drought in Jiangnan at the occasion of the audience with Li Feng 李封 (1723–1796), Provincial Administration Commissioner in Suzhou 蘇州布政使; *Qing shilu*, vol. 24, p. 728 (*juan* 1244) (QL50/12/丁亥 [= 12] instead of 21 = 11 Jan. 1786); *Qianlong chao shangyu dang*, vol. 12, p. 956 n. 2474 (QL50/12/12 = 11 Jan. 1786); *Qianlong di qijuzhu*, vol. 35, pp. 518–519 (QL50/12/12 = 11 Jan. 1786)

MCC, vol. 13, pp. 422–424: Autre Chang-yu (Another Chang-yu) (QL51/2/20 = 19 March 1786):

Inst. 1516, pp. 352–353: pp. 8–10

Edict regarding grain prices in response to He Yucheng 何裕城 (1726–1790), Governor of Jiangxi; *Qing shilu*, vol. 24, pp. 756–757 (*juan* 1247) (QL51/1/庚午 [= 25] = 23 Febr. 1786); *Qianlong chao shangyu dang*, vol. 13, p. 15 n. 43 (QL51/1/25 = 23 Febr. 1786)

MCC, vol. 13, pp. 424–426 (QL51/2/10 [= 20] = 19 March 1786):
Inst. 1516, pp. 353–354: pp. 10–12
Edict regarding monetary subvention for drought in response to Wu Yuan 吳垣 (?–1786), Governor of Hubei; *Qing shilu*, vol. 24, p. 738 (*juan* 1245) (QL50/12/癸卯 [= 28] = 27 Jan. 1786); *Qianlong chao shangyu dang*, vol. 12, p. 970 n. 2521, 2522 (QL50/12/27; QL50/12/28 = 26, 27 Jan. 1786)

MCC, vol. 13, pp. 427–428 (QL51/3/1 = 30 March 1786):
Inst. 1516, pp. 355–356: pp. 14–15
Edict on tax reduction because of drought; *Qing shilu*, vol. 24, p. 785 (*juan* 1249) (QL51/2/丁酉 [= 23] = 22 March 1786); *Qianlong chao shangyu dang*, vol. 13, p. 50 n. 135 (QL51/2/23 = 22 March 1786)

MCC, vol. 13, pp. 428–429 (QL51/3/28 = 26 April 1786):
Inst. 1516, p. 356: pp. 15–16
Memorial by Bi Yuan 畢沅 (1730–1797), Governor of Henan, concerning help because of drought; not yet found, but similar record in vol. 24, p. 790 (*juan* 1249) (QL51/2/辛丑 [= 27] = 26 March 1786); *Qianlong chao shangyu dang*, vol. 13, pp. 56–57 n. 156 (QL51/2/27 = 26 March 1786)

MCC, vol. 13, pp. 429–430 (QL51/4/28 = 25 May 1786):
Inst. 1516, p. 357: pp. 17–18
Edict concerning support in case of drought in response to Fu-le-hun 富勒渾 (?–1790), Governor-General of Guangdong-Guangxi; *Qing shilu*, vol. 24, p. 830 (*juan* 1252) (QL51/4/癸未 [= 10] = 7 May 1786); *Qianlong chao shangyu dang*, vol. 13, p. 111 n. 304 (QL51/4/10 = 7 May 1786)

MCC, vol. 13, p. 432:
Inst. 1516, p. 358: pp. 19–20
Edict concerning gifts by foreign merchants, related to previous case; not yet found

MCC, vol. 13, pp. 433–435:
Inst. 1516, pp. 359–360: pp. 21–23
Edict in response to an anonymous censor concerning famine; not yet found

MCC, vol. 13, pp. 437–440 (QL51/5/26 = 21 June 1786):
Inst. 1516, pp. 360–364: pp. 24–28
Edict concerning the case of Fu-le-hun in response to Sun Shiyi 孫士毅 (1720–1796), Governor of Guangdong; *Qing shilu*, vol. 24, pp. 852–854

(*juan* 1254) (QL51/5/丙辰 [= 14] = 9 June 1786); *Qianlong chao shangyu dang*, vol. 13, pp. 158–159 n. 423 (QL51/5/14 = 9 June 1786)

MCC, vol. 13, pp. 441–443 (QL51/6/1 = 26 June 1786):
Inst. 1516, pp. 364–366: pp. 29–31
Edict concerning Yin Shijun 殷士俊, domestic worker of the demoted Fu-le-hun; *Qing shilu*, possibly vol. 24, pp. 855–856 (*juan* 1254) (QL51/5/丁巳 [= 15] = 10 June 1786); *Qianlong chao shangyu dang*, vol. 13, pp. 161–162 n. 429 (QL51/5/15 = 10 June 1786)

MCC, vol. 13, pp. 443–448 (QL51/6/18 = 13 July 1786):
Inst. 1516, pp. 366–368: pp. 31–37
Same subject; *Qing shilu*, possibly vol. 24, pp. 866–868 (*juan* 1255) (QL51/5/庚午 [= 28] = 23 June 1786); *Qianlong chao shangyu dang*, vol. 13, pp. 188–189 n. 482 (QL51/5/28 = 23 June 1786)

MCC, vol. 13, pp. 449–450 (QL51/6/1 = 26 June 1786):
Inst. 1516, pp. 368–369: pp. 37–39
Edict concerning misuse in distribution of money and rice in response to a report of the Censorate (Duchayuan 都察院) on the basis of the information by Jiang Luyu 蔣魯玉, commoner from Hubei; *Qing shilu*, vol. 24, pp. 857–858 (*juan* 1255) (QL51/5/己未 [= 17] = 12 June 1786); *Qianlong chao shangyu dang*, vol. 13, p. 164 n. 438 (QL51/5/17 = 12 June 1786)

MCC, vol. 13, pp. 451–453 (QL51/6/7 = 31 July 1786):
Inst. 1516, pp. 369–370: pp. 40–42
Edict concerning floods in response to Yu Jin'ao 俞金鰲 (?–1793), Governor-General of Hubei and Hunan; *Qing shilu*, possibly vol. 24, pp. 884–885 (*juan* 1256) (QL51/6/丁亥 [= 15] = 10 July 1786); *Qianlong chao shangyu dang*, vol. 13, p. 222 n. 546 (QL51/6/15 = 10 July 1786)

MCC, vol. 13, pp. 453–454:
Inst. 1516, pp. 370–371: pp. 42–43
Edict on earthquake in Sichuan, reported by Bao-ning 保寧 (?–1808), Governor of Sichuan; *Qing shilu*, vol. 24, p. 868 (*juan* 1255) (QL51/5/辛未 [= 29] = 24 June 1786); *Qianlong chao shangyu dang*, vol. 13, p. 192 n. 487 (QL51/5/29 = 24 June 1786)

MCC, vol. 13, pp. 454–457 (QL51/7/2 = 26 July 1786):
Inst. 1516, pp. 371–373: pp. 43–47

Edict on paternal governance in response to Bi Yuan 畢沅, Governor of Henan; *Qing shilu*, vol. 24, pp. 870–871 (*juan* 1255) (QL51/5/壬申 [= 30] = 25 June 1786); *Qianlong chao shangyu dang*, vol. 13, p. 195 n. 491 (QL51/5/30 = 25 June 1786)

MCC, vol. 13, p. 458:
Inst. 1516, p. 373: p. 48
Dismissal of Ya-de 雅德 (?–1801), Governor of Zhejiang; *Qing shilu*, Vol. 24, pp. 898–900 (*juan* 1257) (QL51/6/辛丑 [= 29] = 24 July 1786); *Qianlong chao shangyu dang*, vol. 13, pp. 241–242 n. 597 (QL51/6/29 = 24 July 1786)

MCC, vol. 13, pp. 459–506: Extrait d'une lettre de M. Amiot, Missionnaire, Ecrite de Peking, le 14 Septembre 1786 (Extract from a letter by Mr. Amiot, Missionary, Written from Peking, September 14, 1786):

Inst. 1516, pp. 374–403: pp. 1–59

MCC, vol. 13, pp. 460–463:
Inst. 1516, pp. 375–376: pp. 3–6
Reports by the Ministry of Works (Gongbu 工部) on the state of the channels, related to the drought in Jiangnan, Henan, Shandong; not yet found

MCC, vol. 13, p. 463:
Inst. 1516, p. 376: p. 6
Response by the Emperor; not yet found

MCC, vol. 13, pp. 463–465:
Inst. 1516, pp. 376–377: pp. 6–8
Governor of Henan, Bi Yuan 畢沅, on the public works at the Gulu 賈魯 river, which has its source in the Dazhou mountain 大周山 in Rongyang 滎陽; *Qing shilu*, possibly vol. 24, p. 946 (*juan* 1260) (QL51/run 7/丙子 [= 5] = 28 Aug. 1786)

MCC, vol. 13, pp. 465–466:
Inst. 1516, pp. 377–378: pp. 8–9
More extensive report on the same subject; *Qing shilu*, vol. 24, p. 946 (*juan* 1260) (QL51/run 7/丙子 [= 5] = 29 Aug. 1786)

MCC, vol. 13, pp. 471–476: Chang-yu (discours d'en haut) (Chang-yu (speech from above)) (QL51/3/14 = 12 April 1786):
Inst. 1516, pp. 380–383: pp. 14–20
Edict on the response of Liu Yong 劉墉 (1720–1805) and others to the memorial by censor Zuo Zhou 左周 on the counting of the number of characters in the *Siku quanshu* 四庫全書; *Qing shilu*, vol. 24, p. 723 (*juan* 1244) (QL50/12/丁丑 [= 2] = 1 Jan. 1786) (reference but not full text)

MCC, vol. 13, pp. 478–485 (QL50/12/19 = 18 Jan. 1786):
Inst. 1516, pp. 384–388: pp. 22–30
Edict on a solar eclipse that was to take place on New Year 元旦日食 (QL51/1/1 = 18 Febr. 1787); *Qing shilu*, vol. 24, pp. 718–719 (*juan* 1243) (QL50/11/乙亥 [= 29] = 30 Dec. 1786); *Qianlong chao shangyu dang*, vol. 12, p. 937 n. 2430 and pp. 937–938 n. 2431 (QL50/11/29 = 30 Dec. 1786)

MCC, vol. 13, pp. 487–489 (QL51/2/6 = 5 March 1786):
Inst. 1516, pp. 390–391: pp. 33–36
Examination of the officials on the *jing* 經 and *sishu* 四書, i.e. the *jingyan* 經筵, in spring; *Qing shilu*, vol. 24, pp. 767–769 (*juan* 1248) (QL51/2/庚辰 [= 6] = 5 March 1786); *Qianlong di qijuzhu*, absent

MCC, vol. 13, pp.494–499 (QL51/1/20 = 18 Febr. 1786):
Inst. 1516, pp. 394–397: pp. 41–47
Edict on the monthly instruction of the people by the officials in response to the Censorate; not yet found

MCC, vol. 13, pp. 500–505 (QL51/2/16 = 15 March 1786):
Inst. 1516, pp. 399–402: pp. 51–57
Edict on a revised version of the *huidian* 會典 (digest of statutes); *Qing shilu*, vol. 24, pp. 773–774 (*juan* 1248) (QL51/2/甲申 [= 10] = 9 March 1786); *Qianlong chao shangyu dang*, vol. 13, p. 33 n. 88 (QL51/2/10 = 9 March 1786)

3.5 *Mémoires concernant … les Chinois* (MCC), Vol. 14 (1789)

MCC, vol. 14, pp. 523–535: Extrait d'une lettre de M. Amiot, Missionnaire, Ecrite de Péking, le 25 Janvier 1787 (Extract from a letter by Mr. Amiot, Missionary, Written from Peking, 25 January 1787):

Inst. 1516, pp. 408–425: pp. 1–36

MCC, vol. 14, pp. 523–525:

Inst. 1516, pp. 408–409: pp. 2–3
Description of gazettes

MCC, vol. 14, pp. 536–561: Extrait d'une lettre de M. Amiot, Missionnaire, Ecrite de Péking, le 19 Novembre 1787 (Extract from a letter by Mr. Amiot, Missionary, Written from Peking, 19 November 1787):

Inst. 1516, pp. 426–435: pp. 1–20

MCC, vol. 14, pp. 536–541:
Inst. 1516, pp. 426–428: pp. 2–6
Speech at the moment of the winter solstice (*dongzhi* 冬至); *Qing shilu*, vol. 24, pp. 1096–1098 (*juan* 1268) (QL51/11/壬申 [= 2] = 22 Dec. 1786); *Qianlong chao shangyu dang*, vol. 13, pp. 561–563 n. 1369; p. 571 n. 1393, 1394 (QL51/11/2 and 3 = 22 and 23 Dec. 1786)

MCC, vol. 14, pp. 544–545:
Inst. 1516, pp. 429–430: pp. 8–9
Summary of several events related to Li Shiyao 李侍堯: Audiences with emperor; *Qing shilu*, vol. 24, p. 1067 (*juan* 1266) (QL51/10/壬寅 [= 2] = 22 Nov. 1786); *Qianlong chao shangyu dang*, vol. 13, pp. 494–495 n. 1203 (QL51/10/2 = 22 Nov. 1786); activities in Huang'an 黃安 (Hubei); *Qing shilu*, vol. 24, pp. 1094–1095 (*juan* 1267) (QL51/10/庚午 [= 30] = 20 Dec. 1786); *Qianlong chao shangyu dang*, vol. 13, p. 560 n. 1367 (QL51/10/30 = 20 Dec. 1786); condemnation to Yili 伊犁; *Qing shilu*, vol. 24, pp. 1123–1124 (*juan* 1270) (QL51/12/戊申 [= 9] = 27 Jan. 1787)

MCC, vol. 14, pp. 545–546:
Inst. 1516, p. 430: pp. 9–10
Memorial by Ji Huang 嵇璜 (1711–1794); not yet found

MCC, vol. 14, pp. 549–550:
Inst. 1516, p. 431: pp. 11–12
On the harvest in Henan; not yet found

MCC, vol. 14, pp. 553–560:
Inst. 1516, pp. 432–435: pp. 14–20
On the case of a woman declaring herself to be a living Buddha (*huofo* 活佛); *Qing shilu*, vol. 25, p. 196 (*juan* 1283) (QL52/6/庚申 [= 24] = 7 Aug. 1787); *Qianlong chao shangyu dang*, vol. 13, p. 889 n. 2173; *Qianlong di qijuzhu*, vol. 36, pp. 167–168 (QL52/6/24 = 7 Aug. 1787)

MCC, vol. 14, pp. 553–557, 559:

Inst. 1516, pp. 432–434: pp. 14–18

Case and edict; *Qing shilu*, vol. 25, p. 196 (*juan* 1283) (QL52/6/庚申 [= 24] = 7 Aug. 1787); *Qianlong chao shangyu dang*, vol. 13, p. 889 n. 2173 (QL52/6/24 = 7 Aug. 1787); *Qianlong di qijuzhu*, vol. 36, pp. 167–168 (QL52/6/24 = 7 Aug. 1787)

MCC, vol. 14, p. 558:

Inst. 1516, p. 434: p. 17

Condemnation; *Qing shilu*, vol. 25, pp. 207–208 (*juan* 1284) (QL52/7/乙亥 [= 10] = 22 Aug. 1787); *Qianlong chao shangyu dang*, vol. 13, p. 913 n. 2225 (QL52/7/10 = 22 Aug. 1787); *Qianlong di qijuzhu*, vol. 36, p. 185 (QL52/7/10 = 22 Aug. 1787)

MCC, vol. 14, pp. 559–560:

Inst. 1516, pp. 434–435: pp. 18–19

Edict; *Qing shilu*, see previous reference (QL52/6/庚申 [= 24] = 7 Aug. 1787) and vol. 25, p. 203 (*juan* 1284) (QL52/7/丁卯 [= 2] = 14 Aug. 1787)

3.6 *Mémoires concernant … les Chinois* (MCC), Vol. 15 (1791)

MCC, vol. 15, pp. 281–291: Extrait d'une lettre, Ecrite de Péking, le 13 Juillet 1778 (Extract from a letter, Written from Peking, 13 July 1778):

Bréquigny 3, fols. 34v–40r according to the manuscript: "du M. Bourgeois" (from Mr. Bourgeois)

MCC, vol. 15, pp. 282–283 (memorial); p. 283 (edict): 1. Rebellion des Sectaires à Pa-tcheou en 1777 (1. Rebellion of the Sectarians in Pa-tcheou in 1777):

Bréquigny 3, fols. 34v–35v

On the White Lotus Sect (*Bailianjiao* 白蓮教) in Bazhou 霸州; *Qing shilu*, vol. 21, pp. 994–995 (*juan* 1045) (QL42/2/癸未 [= 21] = 20 Dec. 1777); vol. 21, pp. 998–999 (*juan* 1045) (QL42/11/乙酉 [= 23] = 20 and 2 Dec. 1777); *Qianlong chao shangyu dang*, vol. 8, pp. 830–831 n. 2214, pp. 831–832 n. 2215, p. 832 n. 2217, and p. 833 n. 2218 (QL42/11/21, QL42/11/22, QL42/11/23 = 20, 21, 22 Dec. 1777)

MCC, vol. 15, pp. 286–289 (memorial); p. 289 (edict): 3. Sévérité contre un Lettré (3. Severity against a Scholar):

Bréquigny 3, fols. 37r–39r

On the punishment of Wang Xihou 王錫侯 (1713–1777), for his criticism of the *Kangxi zidian* 康熙字典; *Qing shilu*, Decision of emperor not included; see a.o. vol. 21, pp. 982–983 (*juan* 1044) (QL42/11/甲戌 [= 12] = 11 Dec. 1777); decision by the emperor in *Qianlong chao shangyu dang*, vol. 8, p. 819 n. 2182, p. 820 n. 2183, pp. 835–836 n. 2224, pp. 842–843 n. 2243, p. 843 n. 2244 (QL42/11/12, QL42/11/24, QL42/11/28 = 11, 23, 27 Dec. 1777)

MCC, vol. 15, pp. 289–291: 4. Projet de l'Empereur de faire un Recueil général des meilleurs Ecrits (4. The Emperor's plan to produce a general Collection of the best Writings):

Bréquigny 3, fols. 39r–40r

On the *Siku quanshu* 四庫全書 project; *Qing shilu*, vol. 22, pp. 131–132 (*juan* 1057) (QL43/5/乙酉 [= 26] = 20 June 1778); *Qianlong chao shangyu dang*, vol. 9, pp. 103–104 n. 295 (QL43/5/26 = 20 June 1778)

MCC, vol. 15, pp. 292–346: Extrait d'une lettre de M. Amiot, Ecrite de Péking, le 25 Juillet 1779 (Extract from a letter by Mr. Amiot, Written from Peking, 25 July 1779):

Bréquigny 5, fols. 26r–58v; Bréquigny 3, fols. 59r–89v

MCC, vol. 15, pp. 297–315: 3. Ecrit de l'Empereur pour se justifier de ne pas déclarer le nom de son successeur (3. Text by the Emperor to justify not declaring the name of his successor) (QL43/10/8 = 26 Nov. 1778):

Bréquigny 5, fols. 29r–40r; Bréquigny 3, fols. 61v–72v

On the case of the provincial student (*xiu cai* 秀才), Jin Congshan 金從善 from Jinxian 錦縣, who accosted the Qianlong emperor during his October 1778 tour through Liaoning 遼寧 in order to petition him to proclaim a successor. Jin Congshan was condemned and executed. Edict by Emperor to justify himself; BnF, Chinois 2216, 2.2. pp. 1a–5a (QL43/10/8 = 26 Nov. 1778); *Qing shilu*, vol. 22, pp. 275–280 (*juan* 1067) (QL43/9/丁未 [= 21] = 9 Nov. 1778); *Qianlong chao shangyu dang*, vol. 9, pp. 325–328 n. 793 (QL43/9/21 = 9 Nov. 1778)

MCC, vol. 15, pp. 315–327: 4. Réponse de l'Empereur à la requête de Kin-Tsoung-chao (4. Response of the Emperor to the request of Kin-Tsoung-chao) (QL43/9/29 = 17 Nov. 1778):

Bréquigny 5, fols. 40r–47r; Bréquigny 3, fols. 72v–79v

Answer of the Emperor; BnF, Chinois 2216, 2.1. pp. 1a–4a (QL43/10/8 = 26 Nov. 1778); *Qing shilu*, vol. 22, pp. 259–262 (*juan* 1066) (QL43/9/乙未

[= 9] = 28 Oct. 1778); *Qianlong chao shangyu dang*, vol. 9, pp. 299–301 n. 743 (QL43/9/9 = 28 Oct. 1778)

MCC, vol. 15, pp. 328–335: Tché-y: 5. Condamnation de cet Auteur & de son livre (Tché-y: 5. Condemnation of this Author & his book) (QL43/10/10 = 28 Nov. 1778):

Bréquigny 5, fols. 47r–51r; Bréquigny 3, fols. 79v–83v

Condemnation of Jin Congshan; BnF, Chinois 2216, 2.3. pp. 1a–3b (QL43/10/10 = 28 Nov. 1778); *Qianlong chao shangyu dang*, vol. 9, pp. 303–304 n. 749 and 750 (QL43/9/12 (both) = 31 Oct. 1778)

MCC, vol. 15, pp. 336–344 (edict of the emperor, pp. 340–344): 6. Condamnation du livre intitulé: Destinée de la Dynastie de Tai-Tsong & de son regne (6. Condemnation of the book entitled: Destiny of the Dynasty of Tai-Tsong & his reign) (QL44/5/19 = 2 July 1779):

Bréquigny 5, fols. 52r–57r; Bréquigny 3, fols. 83v–88v

On the condemnation of the book *DaQing tianding yunshu* 大清天定運數 by Zhi Tianbao 智天豹; BnF, Chinois 2216, 1.1. pp. 1a–3b; 1.2. pp. 1a–2a; *Qing shilu*, vol. 22, pp. 532–534 (*juan* 1081) only edict of the emperor (QL44/4/癸未 [= 29] = 13 June 1779); *Qianlong chao shangyu dang*, vol. 9, pp. 680–681 n. 1618 only edict of the emperor (QL44/4/29 = 13 June 1779); *Qianlong di qijuzhu*, vol. 29, pp. 140–142 (QL44/4/29 = 13 June 1779)

MCC, vol. 15, pp. 347–372: Extrait d'une lettre de M. Amiot, Ecrite de Péking, le 5 Septembre 1779 (Extract from a letter by Mr. Amiot, Written from Peking, 5 September 1779):

Bréquigny 5, fols. 12r–25v; Bréquigny 3, fols. 90r–105r
On the *Siku quanshu* 四庫全書 project

MCC, vol. 15, pp. 351–356: 1. Collection générale des meilleurs Ecrits, ordonnée par l'Empereur (1. General collection of the best Writings, ordered by the Emperor): Extrait de la Gazette du 10 de la sixieme Lune de la quarante-troisieme année du regne de Kien-long (Extract from the Gazette of the 10th of the sixth Month of the forty-third year of the reign of Kien-long) (QL43/6/10 = 3 July 1778):

Bréquigny 5, fols. 14v–17r; Bréquigny 3, fols. 92r–94v

On the *Siku quanshu* 四庫全書 project; BnF, Chinois 2216, 3.3. pp. 1a–2a (QL43/6/10 = 3 July 1778); *Qing shilu*, vol. 22, p. 131 (*juan* 1057) (QL43/5/乙酉 [= 26] = 20 June 1778); *Qianlong chao shangyu dang*, vol. 9, pp. 103–104 n. 295 (QL43/5/26 = 20 June 1778)

MCC, vol. 15, pp. 356–359: Extrait de la Gazette du 29 de la quatrieme Lune de la quarante-troisieme année du regne de Kien-long (Extract from the Gazette of the 39th of the fourth Month of the forty-third year of the reign of Kien-long) (QL43/4/29 = 25 May 1778):
Bréquigny 5, fols. 17r–18v; Bréquigny 3, fols. 94v–96v
On the *Siku quanshu* 四庫全書 project; BnF, Chinois 2216, 3.2. pp. 1b–2b (QL43/4/29 = 25 May 1778); *Qianlong chao shangyu dang*, vol. 9, p. 29 n. 84 (QL43/4/8 = 4 May 1778)

MCC, vol. 15, pp. 362–363: Other Gazette (QL44/2/10 = 27 March 1779):
Bréquigny 5, fol. 20r; Bréquigny 3, fol. 98r
On the *Siku quanshu* 四庫全書 project; BnF, Chinois 2216, 3.4. p. 1b (QL44/2/10 = 27 March 1779); *Qing shilu*, vol. 22, p. 437 (*juan* 1076) (QL44/2/丙辰朔 [= 1] = 18 March 1779); *Qianlong chao shangyu dang*, vol. 9, p. 556 n. 1305 (QL44/2/1 = 18 March 1779); *Qianlong di qijuzhu*, vol. 29, p. 12 (QL44/2/1 = 18 March 1779)

MCC, vol. 15, p. 363: Other Gazette (QL43/4/7 = 3 May 1778):
Bréquigny 5, fol. 20v; Bréquigny 3, fol. 98r
On the *Siku quanshu* 四庫全書 project; BnF, Chinois 2216, 3.1. p. 1a (QL43/4/7 = 3 May 1778); *Qing shilu*, vol. 22, p. 54 (*juan* 1051) (QL43/2/庚申 [= 29] = 27 March 1779)

MCC, vol. 15, pp. 363–372: 2. Ouvrage contre les Mant-choux (2. Work against the Mant-choux) Précis de la Gazette du premier de la quatrieme Lune de la quarante-quatrieme année du regne de Kien-long (c'est-a-dire, du 16 Mai 1779) (Concise overview of the Gazette of the 10th of the sixth Month of the forty-fourth year of the reign of Kien-long (that is to say, of 16 May 1779)) (QL44/4/1 = 16 May 1779):
Bréquigny 5, fols. 20v–24r; Bréquigny 3, fols. 98r–103r
On the anti-Manchu text *Jiushijiu chou* 九十九籌 (The ninety-nine ways to destroy the Manchus), examined by Yu Minzhong 于敏中; BnF, Chinois 2216, 4.1. pp. 1a–3b (QL44/4/1 = 16 May 1779); *Qing shilu*, vol. 22, p. 473, (*juan* 1077) (QL44/2/辛巳 [= 26] = 12 April 1779); *Qianlong chao shangyu dang*, vol. 9, pp. 590–592 n. 1391 (QL44/2/26 = 12 April 1779)

MCC, vol. 15, pp. 373–381: Extrait d'une lettre de M. Amiot, Ecrite de Péking, le 20 Novembre 1785: Fin de la persécution contre les Missionaires en Chine (Extract from a letter by Mr. Amiot, Written from Peking, 20 November 1785, End of the persecution of Missionaries in China):

Bréquigny 3, fols. 105r–109v; Inst. 1516, pp. 345–348: fols. [1r–4r]
On the end of the persecution of the missionaries (see also the next text); *Qing shilu*, vol. 24, p. 684 (*juan* 1240) (QL50/10/甲申 [= 8] = 9 Nov. 1785); *Qianlong chao shangyu dang*, vol. 12, p. 868 n. 2258 (QL50/10/8 = 9 Nov. 1785); *Qianlong di qijuzhu*, vol. 35, pp. 414–415 (QL50/10/甲申 [= 8] = 9 Nov. 1785)

MCC, vol. 15, pp. 382–383: Extrait d'une lettre de M. Raux, Ecrite de Péking, le 17 Novembre 1786. Chang-yu ou Edit de l'Empereur de Chine, par lequel il délivre les Missionnaires Européens arrêtés dans son Empire, traduit du Chinois (Extract from a letter by Mr. Raux, Written from Peking, 17 November 1786. Chang-yu or Edict from the Emperor of China, by which he sets free the European Missionaries arrested in his Empire, translated from Chinese) (QL50/10/8 = 9 Nov. 1785):

Bréquigny 3, fols. 110r–111v
On the liberation of the missionaries who were arrested; *Qing shilu*, vol. 24, p. 684 (*juan* 1240) (QL50/10/甲申 [= 8] = 9 Nov. 1785); *Qianlong chao shangyu dang*, vol. 12, p. 868 n. 2259 (QL50/10/8 = 9 Nov. 1785); *Qianlong di qijuzhu*, vol. 35, pp. 414–415 (QL50/10/甲申 [= 8] = 9 Nov. 1785)

4 Bibliothèque nationale de France (BnF), Paris, Département des manuscrits: Bréquigny 10: Manuscrits d'Amiot [should be Bourgeois] / VI / Gazettes chinoises / Kien Long 53 / 1788 / no. 23

QL53/1/21 = 27 Febr. 1788

pp. 5–8: Paroles de l'empereur / Declaration impériale (Words from the emperor/ Imperial declaration): Fu-kang-an 福康安 (?–1796) leads troops to Jiayi 嘉義, Taiwan, in the fight against the rebel (*nifei* 逆匪) Lin Shuangwen 林爽文 (1756–1788):
Qing shilu, vol. 25, pp. 373–374 (*juan* 1294) (QL52/12/丁未 [= 14] = 21 Jan. 1788); *Qianlong di qijuzhu*, vol. 36, pp. 396–397 (QL52/12/14 = 21 Jan. 1788)

pp. 8–9: Declaration impériale (Imperial declaration): Emperor plans to travel to Tianjin 天津 to inspect the construction of the dikes:
Qing shilu, vol. 25, p. 379 (*juan* 1295) (QL52/12/己酉 [= 16] = 23 Jan. 1788); *Qianlong chao shangyu dang*, vol. 14, p. 109 n. 324 (QL52/12/16 = 23 Jan. 1788)

p. 9: Declaration impériale (Imperial declaration): Two appointments: Han Rong 韓鑅 (1729–1804) as Right Vice-Minister of Works and Zhu Gui 朱珪 (1731–1806) as Right Vice-Minister of Rites.

Qing shilu, vol. 25, p. 384 (*juan* 1295) (QL52/12/庚戌 [= 17] = 24 Jan. 1788); *Qianlong chao shangyu dang*, vol. 14, p. 109 n. 326 (QL52/12/16 = 23 Jan. 1788); *Qianlong di qijuzhu*, vol. 36, p. 406 (QL52/12/17 = 24 Jan. 1788)

p. 9: Possible conflict of interest of Shu-lin 書麟 (?–1801), Governor-General of the two Jiang provinces (Liang Jiang 兩江 = Jiangnan and Jianxi), and his younger brother:
Qianlong chao shangyu dang, vol. 14, p. 121 n. 363 and 364 (QL52/12/23 = 30 Jan. 1788); *Qianlong di qijuzhu*, vol. 36, p. 415 (QL52/12/乙卯 [= 22] = 29 Jan. 1788)

p. 9: Declaration impériale (Imperial declaration): Examinator Zhang Tao 張燾 in Huguang 湖廣 leaves post to mourn a parent (*dingyou* 丁憂):
Qianlong chao shangyu dang, vol. 14, p. 121 n. 365 (QL52/12/23 = 30 Jan. 1788)

pp. 9–10: Declaration impériale (Imperial declaration): Extra money for restauration of damages in Taiwan:
Qing shilu, vol. 25, p. 384 (*juan* 1295) (QL52/12/庚戌 [= 17] = 24 Jan. 1788); *Qianlong chao shangyu dang*, vol. 14, p. 109 n. 327 (QL52/12/17 = 24 Jan. 1788); *Qianlong di qijuzhu*, vol. 36, p. 404 (QL52/12/17 = 24 Jan. 1788)

p. 10: Ministry of Rites asks to replace the position of censor in Zhejiang by appointing Ge (Mingyang) 葛 (鳴陽) (1736–?):
Qianlong di qijuzhu, vol. 36, p. 409 (QL52/12/18 = 25 Jan. 1788)

p. 10: Nota (Note): On parlera souvent de In kien [= *yinjian* 引見] (We will often speak of In-kien)

QL53/1/22 = 28 Febr. 1788

p. 11: Paroles de l'empereur (Words from the emperor): Sacrifice at Taidongling 泰東陵, tomb of empress Xiaoshengxian 孝聖憲皇后 (1693–1777), mother of the Qianlong emperor, in Yixan 易縣 (Hebei):
Qing shilu, vol. 25, p. 429 (*juan* 1297) (QL53/1/丙戌 [= 23] = 29 Febr. 1788); *Qianlong di qijuzhu*, vol. 37, first month of QL53 is absent

p. 11: Declaration impériale (Imperial declaration): Response to memorial of Min Eyuan 閔鶚元 (1720–1797) regarding the tax deficit of the customs in Yangguan 揚關 and Youzha 由閘:
Qing shilu, vol. 25, p. 372 (*juan* 1294) (QL52/12/丙午 [= 13] = 20 Jan. 1788); *Qianlong chao shangyu dang*, vol. 14, p. 106 n. 313 (QL52/12/13 = 20 Jan. 1788); *Qianlong di qijuzhu*, vol. 36, pp. 395–396 (QL52/12/13 = 20 Jan. 1788)

p. 12: Declaration impériale (Imperial declaration): Response to memorial of Xu Siceng 徐嗣曾 (?–1790) on customs in Fujian:
Qing shilu, vol. 25, p. 385 (*juan* 1295) (QL52/12/辛亥 [= 18] = 25 Jan. 1788); *Qianlong chao shangyu dang*, vol. 14, p. 112 n. 336 (QL52/12/18 = 25 Jan. 1788); *Qianlong di qijuzhu*, vol. 36, p. 408 (QL52/12/18 = 25 Jan. 1788)

pp. 12–13: Declaration impériale (Imperial declaration): Response to memorial of Li Shiyao 李侍堯 (?–1788) on taxes in Taiwan:
Qing shilu, vol. 25, pp. 376–377 (*juan* 1294) (QL52/12/戊申 [= 15] = 22 Jan. 1788); *Qianlong chao shangyu dang*, vol. 14, p. 107 n. 320 (QL52/12/15 = 22 Jan. 1788); *Qianlong di qijuzhu*, vol. 36, p. 399 (QL52/12/15 = 22 Jan. 1788)

pp. 13–14: Declaration impériale (Imperial declaration): Report on the nearby end of the war in Taiwan:
Qing shilu, vol. 25, p. 400 (*juan* 1295) (QL52/12/庚申 [= 27] = 3 Febr. 1788); *Qianlong di qijuzhu*, vol. 36, p. 404 (QL52/12/27 = 3 Febr. 1788)

pp. 14–15: Appointments: not yet found; *Qianlong di qijuzhu*, vol. 37, first month of QL53 is absent

QL53/1/23 = 29 Febr. 1788

p. 15: Paroles de l'empereur (Words from the emperor): Sacrifice to the dragon spirit (*longwang zhi shen* 龍王之神):
Qing shilu, vol. 25, p. 441 (*juan* 1298) (QL53/2/甲午 [= 1] = 8 March 1788)

pp. 15–17: Declaration impériale (Imperial declaration): on the Taiwan prefecture 臺灣府, capital of the Formosa Island:
Qing shilu, vol. 25, pp. 383–384 (*juan* 1295) (QL52/12/庚戌 [= 17] = 24 Jan. 1788); *Qianlong chao shangyu dang*, vol. 14, pp. 110–111 n. 333 (QL52/12/17 = 24 Jan. 1788); *Qianlong di qijuzhu*, vol. 36, pp. 404–406 (QL52/12/17 = 24 Jan. 1788)

p. 18: Appointments: not yet found

pp. 18–19: Capture of thieves in another district: not yet found

QL53/1/24 = 1 March 1788, lost

QL53/1/25 = 2 March 1788

pp. 19–20: Paroles de l'empereur (Words from the emperor): Appointments: not yet found

p. 20: Declaration impériale (Imperial declaration): Appointment: not yet found

pp. 20–22: Declaration impériale (Imperial declaration): update from Fu-kang-an 福康安 (?–1796) in Taiwan: Douliumen 斗六門 has been conquered
Qing shilu, vol. 25, pp. 391–392 (*juan* 1295); vol. 25, pp. 397–398 (*juan* 1295) (QL52/12/丁巳 [= 24], QL52/12/丁巳 [= 26] = 31 Jan., 2 Febr. 1788)
pp. 22–24: On the Emperor's sacrifice in the Kunning palace 坤寧宮 (Palace of Earthly Tranquillity):
Qing shilu, vol. 25, pp. 367–368 (*juan* 1294) (QL52/12/庚戌 [= 6] = 13 Jan. 1788); *Qianlong chao shangyu dang*, vol. 14, p. 96 n. 277 (QL52/12/6 = 13 Jan. 1788); *Qianlong di qijuzhu*, vol. 36, pp. 367–368 (QL52/12/6 = 13 Jan. 1788)
p. 24: Two appointments: not yet found

QL53/1/26 = 3 March 1788
pp. 24–25: Declaration impériale (Imperial declaration): Several cases of honours awarded to people of one hundred years old:
Qing shilu, vol. 25, p. 409 (*juan* 1296); vol. 25, p. 436 (*juan* 1297) (QL53/1/戊辰 [= 5], QL53/1/己丑 [= 26] = 11 Febr., 3 March 1788); *Qianlong chao shangyu dang*, vol. 14, p. 127 n. 381, p. 128 n. 382, p. 130 n. 389, p. 131 n. 391, p. 131 n. 392 and 393, p. 133 n. 397, p. 139 n. 419 (QL53/1/4, QL53/1/5, QL53/1/7, QL53/1/8, QL53/1/9, QL53/1/11, QL53/1/26 = 10, 11, 13, 14, 15, 17 Febr., 3 March); *Qianlong di qijuzhu*, first month is absent
p. 25: Declaration impériale (Imperial declaration): De-cheng 德成 is put in charge of the reconstruction of towns in Taiwan:
Qing shilu, vol. 25, p. 408 (*juan* 1296) (QL53/1/丁卯 [= 4] = 10 Febr. 1788)
pp. 25–26: Declaration impériale (Imperial declaration): Changes of personnel: Bao-ning 保寧 (?–1808) becomes General of Yili 伊犁, Li Shijie 李世傑 (1716–1794) replaces him as Governor-General of Sichuan, assisted by the Mongol Suo-no-mu Zha-mu-chu 索諾木扎木楚
Qing shilu, vol. 25, pp. 387–388 (*juan* 1295) (QL52/12/乙卯 [= 22] = 29 Febr. 1788); *Qianlong chao shangyu dang*, vol. 14, p. 119 n. 358 (QL52/12/22 = 29 Febr. 1788); *Qianlong di qijuzhu*, vol. 36, pp. 414–415 (QL52/12/22 = 29 Febr. 1788)
p. 26: Two appointments: not yet found
pp. 27–29: Memorial de Fou Kang gan, generalissime des troupes dans l'isle de Formose (Memorial of Fou Kang gan, generalissimo of the troops on the island of Formose): Fu-kang-an 福康安 asks for rewards for troops in Taiwan: not yet found

QL53/1/27 = 4 March 1788

p. 29: Paroles de l'empereur (Words from the emperor): Sacrifices, a.o. to loyal generals honoured in Zhaozong si 昭忠祠 (Shrine of Loyalty): *Qing shilu*, vol. 25, p. 445 (*juan* 1298) (QL53/2/乙未 [= 2] = 9 March 1788)

pp. 29–30: Declaration impériale (Imperial declaration): Case of a corrupt magistrate: not yet found

pp. 30–32: Memorial (Memorial): Su-ling-a 蘇凌阿 (?–1799) and Liu Bingtian 劉秉恬 (?–1800) on the restoration of granaries in Beijing: *MingQing dang'an*, A25177 (QL52/12/26 = 2 Febr. 1788)

QL53/1/28 = 5 March 1788

p. 33: Paroles de l'empereur / Declaration impériale (Words from the emperor/ Imperial declaration): Fu-kang-an 福康安 requests rewards for troops in Taiwan after battle at Douliumen 斗六門:
Qing shilu, vol. 25, pp. 423–424 (*juan* 1297) (QL53/1/己卯 [= 16] = 22 Febr. 1788)

pp. 34–35: Declaration impériale (Imperial declaration): Xu Siceng 徐嗣曾 reports the arrest of five criminals in Fujian:
Qing shilu, vol. 25, p. 425 (*juan* 1297) (QL53/1/庚辰 [= 17] = 23 Febr. 1788); *Qianlong chao shangyu dang*, vol. 14, p. 116 n. 353, pp. 135–136 n. 406 (QL52/12/21, QL53/1/17 = 28 Jan. 1788, 23 Febr. 1788); *Qianlong di qijuzhu*, vol. 36, p. 413 (QL52/12/21 = 28 Jan. 1788)

p. 36: Memorial (Memorial): On the appointment of two new officials to the *Siku quanshu* project in replacement of two who had retired:
Not yet found [but reference to vol. 25, pp. 363–364 (*juan* 1294) (QL52/12/乙未 [= 2] = 9 Jan. 1788)]; *Qianlong chao shangyu dang*, vol. 14, p. 90 n. 258 (QL52/12/2 = 9 Jan. 1788); *Qianlong di qijuzhu*, vol. 36, pp. 360–361 (QL52/12/2 = 9 Jan. 1788)

pp. 36–37: Placet presenté à l'Empereur (Memorial presented to the Emperor): Li Shiyao 李侍堯 requests to fill a post in Taiwan: not yet found

QL53/1/29 = 6 March 1788

p. 38: Ordre de l'Empereur (Order of the Emperor): Decision by the Ministry of Justice on three criminals: not yet found

p. 38: Ordre de l'Empereur (Order of the Emperor): The commoner Meng Hanting 孟捍廷 accuses the Governor of Shandong, Chang-lin 長麟 (1758–?; *jinshi* 1775):
Qing shilu, vol. 25, p. 385 (*juan* 1295) (QL52/12/壬子 [= 19] = 26 Jan. 1788); *Qianlong chao shangyu dang*, vol. 14, p. 114 n. (344 and) 345 (QL52/12/19

= 26 Jan. 1788); *Qianlong di qijuzhu*, vol. 36, p. 410 (QL52/12/19 = 26 Jan. 1788)

pp. 38–39: Declaration impériale (Imperial declaration): Chang-lin 長麟, Governor of Shandong, reports the arrest of three thieves:
Qianlong chao shangyu dang, vol. 14, p. 115 n. 346 (QL52/12/19 = 26 Jan. 1788); *Qianlong di qijuzhu*, vol. 36, p. 410 (QL52/12/19 = 26 Jan. 1788)

p. 39: Ordre de l'Empereur (Order of the Emperor): He Yucheng 何裕城 (?–1790), Governor of Jiangxi, proposes to award a distinction to a man who has turned a hundred years old:
Qianlong chao shangyu dang, vol. 14, p. 127 n. 380 (QL53/1/4 = 10 Febr. 1788)

p. 39: Ordre de l'Empereur (Order of the Emperor): Announcement of colloquium on the classics (*jingyan* 經筵):
Qing shilu, vol. 25, pp. 451–452 (*juan* 1298) (QL53/2/己亥 [= 6] = 13 March 1788); *Qianlong chao shangyu dang*, vol. 14, p. 133 n. 398 (QL53/1/13 = 19 Febr. 1788)

p. 40: Declaration impériale (Imperial declaration): Li Shiyao 李侍堯 and the delayed payment of taxes:
Qing shilu, vol. 25, p. 384 (*juan* 1295) (QL52/12/庚戌 [= 17] = 24 Jan. 1788); *Qianlong chao shangyu dang*, vol. 14, p. 110 n. 332 (QL52/12/17 = 24 Jan. 1788); *Qianlong di qijuzhu*, vol. 36, p. 404 (QL52/12/17 = 24 Jan. 1788)

QL53/1/30 = 7 March 1788: no reference

QL53/2/1 = 8 March 1788

p. 41: Paroles de l'empereur (Words from the emperor): Liu Yong 劉墉 (1719–1805) will perform the sacrifice to Confucius:
Qing shilu, vol. 25, p. 446 (*juan* 1298) (QL52/2/丁酉 [= 4] = 11 Febr. 1788)

pp. 41–42: Declaration impériale (Imperial declaration): Salt merchants offer money to end the rebellion in Taiwan:
Qing shilu, vol. 25, p. 410 (*juan* 1296) (QL53/1/己巳 [= 6] = 12 Jan. 1788); *Qianlong chao shangyu dang*, vol. 14, pp. 128–129 n. 384 (QL53/1/6 = 12 Jan. 1788)

QL53/2/2 = 9 March 1788

p. 42: Paroles de l'empereur / Declaration impériale (Words from the emperor/ Imperial declaration): Measure regarding drought in Gansu (especially the districts Gaolan 皐蘭, Jinxian 金縣, and Jin'an 金安):

Qing shilu, vol. 25, p. 407 (*juan* 1296) (QL53/1/丙寅 [= 3] = 9 Febr. 1788); *Qianlong chao shangyu dang*, vol. 14, pp. 126–127 n. 378 (QL53/1/3 = 9 Jan. 1788)

p. 43: In kien ou presentation des mandarins (In kien or presentation of the mandarins), followed by Nota (note): Presentation of new officials (*yinjian* 引見): not yet found

pp. 43–46: Placet en forme de remerciement (Memorial for thanksgiving): Thanksgiving for edict of the Emperor:
Edict; *Qing shilu*, vol. 25, p. 408 (*juan* 1296) (QL53/1/丁卯 [= 4] = 10 Jan. 1788)

QL53/2/3 = 10 March 1788

pp. 46–47: Declaration impériale (Imperial declaration): Floods in Guide fu 歸德府 in Henan:
Qing shilu, vol. 25, p. 407 (*juan* 1296) (QL53/1/丙寅 [= 3] = 9 Jan. 1788); *Qianlong chao shangyu dang*, vol. 14, p. 126 n. 376 (QL53/1/3 = 9 Jan. 1788)

p. 47: Declaration impériale (Imperial declaration): Drought in Datong fu 大同府 in Shanxi:
Qing shilu, vol. 25, p. 412 (*juan* 1296) (QL53/1/庚午 [= 7] = 13 Febr. 1788); *Qianlong chao shangyu dang*, vol. 14, p. 129 n. 387 (QL53/1/7 = 13 Febr. 1788)

pp. 47–48: Declaration impériale (Imperial declaration): Drought in Xuanhua fu 宣化府 in Beizhili:
Qing shilu, vol. 25, pp. 411–412 (*juan* 1296) (QL53/1/庚午 [= 7] = 13 Febr. 1788); *Qianlong chao shangyu dang*, vol. 14, p. 129 n. 386 (QL53/1/7 = 13 Febr. 1788)

pp. 48–50: Placet en forme de remerciement (Memorial for thanksgiving): Thanksgiving by Shu-lin 書麟:
Qing shilu, vol. 25, pp. 355, 360 (*juan* 1293) (QL52/11/丙戌 [= 23], QL52/11/丙戌 [= 27] = 30 Jan. 1788, 3 Febr. 1788); *Qianlong chao shangyu dang*, vol. 14, p. 73 n. 214, pp. 82–83 n. 237 (QL52/11/22, QL52/11/27 = 29 Jan. 1788, 3 Febr. 1788); *Qianlong di qijuzhu*, vol. 36, p. 349 (QL52/11/22 = 29 Jan. 1788)

QL53/2/4 = 11 March 1788

pp. 51–52: Declaration impériale (Imperial declaration): On granaries in Xuanhua fu 宣化府: not yet found

pp. 52–53: Declaration impériale (Imperial declaration): Relief efforts for floods in Huazhou 華州, Huayin 華陰, and Tongguan 潼關 in Shaanxi:

Qing shilu, vol. 25, p. 408 (*juan* 1296) (QL53/1/丁卯 [= 4] = 10 Febr. 1788); *Qianlong chao shangyu dang*, vol. 14, p. 127 n. 379 (QL53/1/4 = 10 Febr. 1788)

pp. 53–54: Memorial (Memorial): Memorial by Bao-ning 保寧, Governor of Sichuan, about the filling of the position of *zhifu* 知府 in the capital: not yet found

QL53/2/5 = 12 March 1788

pp. 54–55: Declaration impériale (Imperial declaration): Fu-kang-an 福康安 on people who secretly tried to escape by boat from Taiwan: *Qing shilu*, vol. 25, p. 416 (*juan* 1296) (QL53/1/甲戌 [= 11] = 17 Febr. 1788)

p. 56: Declaration impériale (Imperial declaration): Vacancy of the position of *zhifu* 知府 in Nanchang 南昌: *Qianlong chao shangyu dang*, vol. 14, p. 137 n. 412 (QL53/1/22 = 28 Febr. 1788)

pp. 56–57: Memorial (Memorial): Memorial by Heng-rui 恒瑞 (1744–1801), General in Yanshuigang 鹽水港 (Taiwan), asking for more troops: not yet found

QL53/2/6 = 13 March 1788

p. 58: Declaration impériale (Imperial declaration): He Yucheng 何裕城 reports about a salt official who died and his merits during his illness: *Qianlong chao shangyu dang*, vol. 14, p. 137 n. 410 (QL53/1/21 = 27 Febr. 1788)

p. 58: Declaration impériale (Imperial declaration): Bao-ning 保寧 about the honours for a man who is one hundred years old: *Qing shilu*, vol. 25, p. 436 (*juan* 1297) (QL53/1/己丑 [= 26] = 3 March 1788); *Qianlong chao shangyu dang*, vol. 14, p. 139 n. 419 (QL53/1/26 = 3 March 1788)

pp. 58–59: Declaration impériale (Imperial declaration): Floods in various districts in Anhui: *Qing shilu*, vol. 25, p. 407 (*juan* 1296) (QL53/1/丙寅 [= 3] = 9 Febr. 1788); *Qianlong chao shangyu dang*, vol. 14, p. 126 n. 377 (QL53/1/3 = 9 Febr. 1788)

pp. 59–61: Memorial (Memorial): Concerning the publication of *Tongjian* 通鑑 (Comprehensive mirror), *Tongzhi* 通志 (Comprehensive records), and *Wenxian tongkao* 文献通考 (Comprehensive examination of written sources): not yet found

QL53/2/7 = 14 March 1788

pp. 61–70: Declaration impériale (Imperial declaration): General Chang-qing 常青 (?–1793) about Heng-rui 恒瑞 not attacking the enemy in the north of Taiwan and his dismissal:
Qing shilu, vol. 25, pp. 417–419 (*juan* 1296) (QL53/1/乙亥 [= 12] = 18 Febr. 1788)

QL53/2/8 = 15 March 1788

pp. 70–72: Declaration impériale (Imperial declaration): Dismissal of general Chang-qing 常青: not yet found
p. 72: In kien (Presentation of new officials): not yet found
p. 72: In kien (Presentation of new officials): not yet found
p. 72: In kien (Presentation of new officials): not yet found

QL53/2/9 = 16 March 1788

pp. 73–77: Declaration impériale (Imperial declaration): Dismissal of general Chang-qing 常青:
Qing shilu, vol. 25, pp. 429–430 (*juan* 1297) (QL53/1/丙戌 [= 23] = 29 Febr. 1788)
pp. 77–78: Declaration impériale (Imperial declaration): Xu Siceng 徐嗣曾 reports on the escape of five criminals:
Qing shilu, vol. 25, p. 425 (*juan* 1297) (QL53/1/庚辰 [= 17] = 23 Febr. 1788); *Qianlong chao shangyu dang*, vol. 14, pp. 135–136 n. 406 (QL53/1/17 = 23 Febr. 1788)

QL53/2/10 = 17 March 1788

p. 79: Continuation of previous gazette:
Qing shilu, vol. 25, pp. 438–440 (*juan* 1297) (QL53/1/癸巳 [= 30] = 7 March 1788)

QL53/2/11 = 18 March 1788

pp. 79–81: Sur l'examen des letters (On the examination of the scholars): during an audience with the emperor, Peng Yuanrui 彭元瑞 (1731–1803) reports on the tricks and deceit during the provincial and metropolitan exams (*xiangshi* 鄉試 and *huishi* 會試):
Qing shilu, vol. 25, p. 364 (*juan* 1294) (QL52/12/乙未 [= 2] = 9 Jan. 1788); *Qianlong chao shangyu dang*, vol. 14, p. 90 n. 256 (QL52/12/2 = 9 Jan. 1788); *Qianlong di qijuzhu*, vol. 36, p. 361 (QL52/12/2 = 9 Jan. 1788)

QL53/2/12 = 19 March 1788

pp. 81–86: Suite de la precedente Declaration impériale (Continuation of the previous Imperial declaration): In total 11 rules for the composition of the essay during the exams (*kechang tiaoli* 科場條例):
Qing shilu, vol. 25, pp. 392–395 (*juan* 1295) (QL52/12/丁巳 [= 24] = 31 Jan. 1788); *Qianlong chao shangyu dang*, vol. 14, pp. 121–122 n. 366 (QL52/12/24 = 31 Jan. 1788); *Qianlong di qijuzhu*, vol. 36, pp. 416–418 (QL52/12/24 = 31 Jan. 1788)

QL53/2/13 = 20 March 1788

p. 86: Not translated; also concerning the rules for exams

QL53/2/14 = 21 March 1788

p. 86: Not translated; also concerning the rules for exams

QL53/2/15 = 22 March 1788

pp. 86–87: Appointments: not yet found

pp. 87–88: Declaration impériale (Imperial declaration): Li Shiyao 李侍堯 on the arrest of Zhang Maqiu 張媽求 and other thieves in Zhangpu xian 漳浦縣:
Qing shilu, vol. 25, pp. 436–437 (*juan* 1297) (QL53/1/己丑 [= 26] = 3 March 1788)

pp. 88–89: Remerciement (Thanksgiving): Thanksgiving by Zhang Ruojing 張若渟 (?) (1726–1802) for relief efforts in Anhui: not yet found

QL53/2/16 = 23 March 1788

pp. 89–91: Declaration impériale (Imperial declaration): On the failures and punishment of lieutenants Huang Shijian 黃仕簡 (1722–1789) and Ren Cheng'en 任承恩 (1730–1798) in Taiwan:
Qing shilu, vol. 25, pp. 445–446 (*juan* 1298) (QL53/2/乙未 [= 2] = 9 March 1788)

pp. 91–92: Declaration impériale (Imperial declaration): Quan-de 全德 reports on the gifts by salt merchants to Taiwan:
Qing shilu, vol. 25, p. 427 (*juan* 1297) (QL53/1/壬午 [= 19] = 25 Febr. 1788); *Qianlong chao shangyu dang*, vol. 14, p. 136 n. 408 (QL53/1/19 = 25 Febr. 1788)

p. 92: Declaration impériale (Imperial declaration): Wang Chang 王昶 (1725–1806), the Provincial Administration Commissioner (*buzheng shi* 布政使) in Yunnan, is replaced because of age and illness:

Qing shilu, vol. 25, p. 436 (*juan* 1297) (QL53/1/戊子 [= 25] = 2 March 1788); *Qianlong chao shangyu dang*, vol. 14, p. 138 n. 417 (QL53/1/25 = 2 March 1788)

p. 92: Declaration impériale (Imperial declaration): Peng Yuanrui 彭元瑞 is allowed to enter the palace on his horse:
Qing shilu, vol. 25, p. 446 (*juan* 1298) (QL53/2/乙未 [= 2] = 9 March 1788); *Qianlong chao shangyu dang*, vol. 14, p. 143 n. 431 (QL53/2/2 = 9 March 1788); *Qianlong di qijuzhu*, vol. 37, p. 9 (QL53/2/2 = 9 March 1788)

pp. 92–94: Declaration impériale (Imperial declaration): On the report by Fu-gang 富綱 (1737–1800), Governor-General of Yunnan and Guizhou, and Tan Shangzhong 譚尚忠 (1724–1797), Governor of Yunnan, on the misbehaviour of officials in the provinces:
Qing shilu, vol. 25, pp. 432–433 (*juan* 1297) (QL53/1/戊子 [= 25] = 2 March 1788); *Qianlong chao shangyu dang*, vol. 14, p. 139 n. 418 (QL53/1/25 = 2 March 1788)

QL53/2/17 = 24 March 1788

p. 95: Declaration impériale (Imperial declaration): Appointment: not yet found

pp. 95–96: Declaration impériale (Imperial declaration): Building of temples for deceased in Taiwan:
Qing shilu, vol. 25, pp. 445–446 (*juan* 1298) (QL53/2/乙未 [= 2] = 9 March 1788); *Qianlong di qijuzhu*, vol. 37, p. 89 (QL53/2/2 = 9 March 1788)

pp. 96–98: Declaration impériale (Imperial declaration): Liu E 劉峩 (1723–1795), Governor of Beizhili, on filling the position of magistrate in Shuntian fu 順天府:
Qing shilu, vol. 25, p. 452 (*juan* 1298) (QL53/2/庚子 [= 7] = 14 March 1788); *Qianlong chao shangyu dang*, vol. 14, p. 136 n. 439–440 (QL53/2/7 = 14 March 1788); *Qianlong di qijuzhu*, vol. 37, p. 21 (QL53/2/7 = 14 March 1788)

p. 98: Declaration impériale (Imperial declaration): Jing-an 景安 (?–1823) appointed as Provincial Administration Commissioner (*buzhengshi* 布政使) in Henan:
Qing shilu, vol. 25, p. 454 (*juan* 1298) (QL53/2/辛丑 [= 8] = 15 March 1788); *Qianlong chao shangyu dang*, vol. 14, p. 148 n. 444 (QL53/2/8 = 15 March 1788); *Qianlong di qijuzhu*, vol. 37, p. 22 (QL53/2/8 = 15 March 1788)

QL53/2/18 = 25 March 1788

pp. 98–99: Declaration impériale (Imperial declaration): Rewards for Fu-kang-an 福康安 because of the successful suppression of the rebellion and the arrest of Lin Shuangwen 林爽文:
Qing shilu, vol. 25, p. 447 (*juan* 1298) (QL53/2/戊戌 [= 5] = 12 March 1788); *Qianlong di qijuzhu*, vol. 37, p. 17 (QL53/2/5 = 12 March 1788)

p. 100: In kien (Preparations des Mandarins) (In kien (Preparations of the Mandarins)): Presentation of new officials: not yet found

pp. 100–101: Declaration impériale (Imperial declaration): Appointments: not yet found

pp. 101–104: Memorial (Memorial): Memorial by Shu-lin 書麟: not yet found

QL53/2/19 = 26 March 1788

p. 104: Declaration impériale (Imperial declaration): Zhu Huaying 朱化英 (?–1786), Chen Ruzhi 陳汝志, and troops drowned at sea:
Qing shilu, vol. 25, pp. 447–448 (*juan* 1298) (QL53/2/戊戌 [= 5] = 12 March 1788); *Qianlong di qijuzhu*, vol. 37, pp. 16–17 (QL53/2/5 = 12 March 1788)

p. 105: Declaration impériale (Imperial declaration): Liang-han 琅玕 (1744–1804), Governor of Zhejiang, reporting the financial contribution of salt merchants for the compensation of the damage done by rebels in Taiwan:
Qing shilu, vol. 25, pp. 419–420 (*juan* 1296) (QL53/1/丁丑 [= 14] = 20 Febr. 1788); *Qianlong chao shangyu dang*, vol. 14, p.133 n. 399 (QL53/1/14 = 20 Febr. 1788)

pp. 105–108: Accusation: Charge by Zhang Yongqing 孫永清 (?–1790), Governor of Guangxi, against a magistrate: not yet found

QL53/2/20 = 27 March 1788

pp. 108–113: Declaration impériale (Imperial declaration): the emperor attributes the victory in Taiwan to himself:
Qianlong di qijuzhu, vol. 37, p. 13 (QL53/2/1 = 8 March 1788)

QL53/2/21 = 28 March 1788

p. 113: Partial continuation of a previous case (punishment of lieutenants with bad conduct in Taiwan):

Qing shilu, repetition of vol. 25, pp. 445–446 (*juan* 1298) (QL53/2/乙未 [= 2] = 9 March 1788); *Qianlong di qijuzhu*, vol. 37, p. 89 (QL53/2/2 = 9 March 1788)

QL53/2/22 = 29 March 1788

pp. 113–121: Accusation: Charge by Li Shiyao 李侍堯 against Chai Daji 柴大紀 (1732–1788), Regional Commander (*zhenzongbing* 鎮總兵) in Taiwan, for having contributed to the rebellion:
Qing shilu, in edict of the Emperor in vol. 25, pp. 429–431 (*juan* 1297) (QL53/1/丙戌 [= 23] = 29 Febr. 1788); *Qianlong chao shangyu dang*, vol. 14, p. 140 n. 422 (QL53/1/30 = 7 March 1788)

QL53/2/23 = 30 March 1788

pp. 121–125: Memorial (Memorial): Memorial by Minister He [? He-shen 和珅 (1750–1799)] concerning the expenses for the reparation of dikes and the role of A-gui 阿桂 (1717–1797) in this project: not yet found

QL53/2/24 = 31 March 1788

p. 126: Continuation of previous gazette on drowned soldiers:
Qing shilu, vol. 25, pp. 453–454 (*juan* 1298) (QL53/2/辛丑 [= 8] = 15 March 1788); *Qianlong di qijuzhu*, vol. 37, p. 22 (QL53/2/8 = 15 March 1788)

QL53/2/25 = 1 April 1788

p. 126: Repetition of arrest of thieves: not yet found

QL53/2/26 = 2 April 1788

pp. 126–127: Declaration impériale (Imperial declaration): Prince Yongzhang 永璋 (1736–1787) has died:
Qianlong chao shangyu dang, vol. 14, p. 162 n. 451 (QL53/2/10 = 17 March 1788); *Qianlong di qijuzhu*, vol. 37, p. 26 (QL53/2/10 = 17 March 1788)

QL53/2/27 = 3 April 1788

pp. 127–140: Ministry of Justice on the condemnation of General Gui-lin 奎林 (?–1792):
Qianlong chao shangyu dang, vol. 14, pp. 148–160 n. 445 (QL53/2/8 = 15 March 1788) (summary)

pp. 140–144: Declaration impériale (Imperial declaration): In Yili 伊犁, Hai-lu 海祿 accuses Gui-lin 奎林 of brutality; both were sentenced:

Qing shilu, vol. 25, pp. 454–455 (*juan* 1298) (QL53/2/壬寅 [= 9] = 16 March 1788); *Qianlong chao shangyu dang*, pp. 160–161 n. 447 (QL53/2/9 = 16 March 1788); *Qianlong di qijuzhu*, vol. 37, pp. 23–24 (QL53/2/9 = 16 March 1788)

QL53/2/28 = 4 April 1788

p. 144: Continuation of the previous case ("the gazette was fully filled with the preceding story of Gui-lin and Hai-lu")

QL53/2/29 = 5 April 1788

pp. 144–145: The Ministry of Rites recommends change in hats for winter and summer: not yet found

pp. 145–147: Representation d'un yu che (Censeur de l'empire) (Memorial by a yu che (Censor of the empire)): Censor (*yushi* 御史) Feng Feng Yingliu 馮應榴 (1740–1800) on the fraud at the special examination of officials during the imperial visit to Tianjin:
Qing shilu, vol. 25, p. 459 (*juan* 1298) (QL53/2/戊申 [= 15] = 22 March 1788)

QL53/3/1 = 6 April 1788

pp. 148–151: Examen triennal des mandarins (Three-yearly examination of the mandarins): Three-yearly examinations of officials (*daji* 大計); followed by: Catalogue du Tribunal des Mandarins (Catalogue of the Tribunal of the Mandarins): Catalogue with the result of the three-yearly examination
Qing shilu, vol. 25, p. 461 (*juan* 1299) (QL53/2/辛亥 [= 18] = 25 March 1788); *Qianlong di qijuzhu*, vol. 37, pp. 38–42 (QL53/2/18 = 25 March 1788) (response of the emperor at the end)

QL53/3/2 = 7 April 1788

pp. 151–154: Memorial accusation (Memorial charge): Memorial concerning the horse shops in Beijing: not yet found

pp. 155–157: Accusation (Charge): Charge by the censor about the arrest of a criminal in West Beijing: not yet found

QL53/3/3 = 8 April 1788

p. 157: Continuation of a previous case on a wine cellar: not yet found

QL53/3/4 = 9 April 1788
p. 157: Continuation of the description of the three-yearly examination of officials

QL53/3/5 = 10 April 1788
pp. 158–160: Declaration impériale (Imperial declaration): Ming Xing 明興 (?–1791), Governor of Shanxi, accuses Lin Langfeng 林琅奉, Magistrate of Xugou xian 徐溝縣:
Qing shilu, vol. 25, pp. 457–458 (*juan* 1298) (QL53/2/丙午 [= 13] = 20 March 1788); *Qianlong chao shangyu dang*, vol. 14, p. 166 n. 463 (QL53/2/13 = 20 March 1788); *Qianlong di qijuzhu*, vol. 37, p. 30 (QL53/2/13 = 20 March 1788)

QL53/3/6 = 11 April 1788
pp. 160–161: Declaration impériale (Imperial declaration): Favours to the salt merchants of Changlu 長蘆 (near Tianjin):
Qing shilu, vol. 25, pp. 461–462 (*juan* 1299) (QL53/2/壬子 [= 19] = 26 March 1788); *Qianlong chao shangyu dang*, vol. 14, p. 178 n. 488 (QL53/2/19 = 26 March 1788); *Qianlong di qijuzhu*, vol. 37, p. 44 (QL53/2/19 = 26 March 1788)

QL53/3/7 = 12 April 1788
p. 161: Continuation of the description of the three-yearly examination of officials

QL53/3/8 = 13 April 1788
pp. 161–162: Declaration impériale (Imperial declaration): Imperial visit to Tianjin 天津 and Wutai 五臺:
Qing shilu, vol. 25, p. 461 (*juan* 1299) (QL53/2/辛亥 [= 18] = 25 March 1788); *Qianlong chao shangyu dang*, vol. 14, p. 176 n. 482 (QL53/2/18 = 25 March 1788); *Qianlong di qijuzhu*, vol. 37, p. 37 (QL53/2/18 = 25 March 1788)
pp. 162–163: Declaration impériale (Imperial declaration): On the payment of the sailors to Tianjin:
Qing shilu, vol. 25, p. 463 (*juan* 1299) (QL53/2/甲寅 [= 21] = 28 March 1788); *Qianlong chao shangyu dang*, vol. 14, p. 182 n. 494 (QL53/2/21 = 28 March 1788); *Qianlong di qijuzhu*, vol. 37, p. 44 (QL53/2/21 = 28 March 1788)
p. 163: Declaration impériale (Imperial declaration): On the reduction of taxes in the neighbourhood of Tianjin:

Qing shilu, vol. 25, p. 461 (*juan* 1299) (QL53/2/辛亥 [= 18] = 25 March 1788); *Qianlong chao shangyu dang*, vol. 14, p. 176 n. 480 (QL53/2/18 = 25 March 1788); *Qianlong di qijuzhu*, vol. 37, p. 37 (QL53/2/18 = 25 March 1788)

QL53/3/9 = 14 April 1788

p. 163: On the early exposure of a red banner as a sign of victory at the conquest of Taiwan (this is a summary, not a quotation): repetition of an earlier gazette
Qing shilu, vol. 25, pp. 414–415 (*juan* 1296) (QL53/1/壬申 [= 9] = 15 Febr. 1788)

QL53/3/10 = 15 April 1788

p. 163: Continuation of the description of the three-yearly examination of officials

QL53/3/11 = 16 April 1788

p. 164: Punishments and appointments by the Ministry of Personnel: a.o. for the failure to search for Europeans:
Qianlong di qijuzhu, vol. 37, p. 47 (QL53/2/24 = 31 March 1788) (brief mention)

pp. 164–165: Punishments and appointments by the Ministry of Personnel: Quan-kui 全魁 (?–1791):
Qianlong di qijuzhu, vol. 37, p. 38 (QL53/2/18 = 25 March 1788) (brief mention)

pp. 166–167: Accusation: Charge by Liu E 劉峩 against a magistrate
Qianlong chao shangyu dang, vol. 14, p. 177 n. 484 (QL53/2/18 = 25 March 1788) (imperial decision)

QL53/3/12 = 17 April 1788

pp. 167–169: Representation (Memorial): Fu-kang-an 福康安 on rewards for local leaders in Taiwan: not yet found

QL53/3/13 = 18 April 1788

p. 169: Declaration impériale (Imperial declaration): Tax exemption in Xuanhua 宣化 because of heavy rain:
Qianlong chao shangyu dang, vol. 14, p. 181 n. 492 (QL53/2/20 = 27 March 1788); *Qianlong di qijuzhu*, vol. 37, p. 45 (QL53/2/23 = 30 March 1788)

pp. 169–170: Declaration impériale (Imperial declaration): Another tax exemption on the way to Tianjin:
Qing shilu, vol. 25, p. 470 (*juan* 1299) (QL53/2/辛酉 [= 28] = 4 April 1788); *Qianlong chao shangyu dang*, vol. 14, p. 190 n. 517 (QL53/2/28 = 4 April 1788); *Qianlong di qijuzhu*, vol. 37, p. 53 (QL53/2/28 = 4 April 1788)

pp. 170–174: Declaration impériale (Imperial declaration): Fu-kang-an 福康安 on the arrest of rebel Zhuang Datian 莊大田 (1734–1788) in Taiwan:
Qing shilu, vol. 25, pp. 467–469 (*juan* 1299) (QL53/2/庚申 [= 27] = 3 April 1788); *Qianlong di qijuzhu*, vol. 37, pp. 50–52 (QL53/2/27 = 3 April 1788)

QL53/3/14 = 19 April 1788

p. 175: Declaration impériale (Imperial declaration): Compensation for civil and military officials involved in Taiwan: those who were degraded are restored to their rank, and the others are increased by one rank:
Qing shilu, vol. 25, p. 472 (*juan* 1299) (QL53/2/壬戌 [= 29] = 5 April 1788); *Qianlong chao shangyu dang*, vol. 14, p. 191 n. 520 (QL53/2/29 = 5 April 1788); *Qianlong di qijuzhu*, vol. 37, p. 55 (QL53/2/29 = 5 April 1788)

p. 175: Declaration impériale (Imperial declaration): Extra subsidy on trip to Tianjin:
Qing shilu, vol. 25, p. 464 (*juan* 1299) (QL53/2/丙辰 [= 23] = 30 March 1788); *Qianlong chao shangyu dang*, vol. 14, p. 182 n. 495 (QL53/2/23 = 30 March 1788); *Qianlong di qijuzhu*, vol. 37, p. 49 (QL53/2/23 = 30 March 1788)

p. 176: Declaration impériale (Imperial declaration): Compensation for villages in Taiwan:
Qing shilu, vol. 25, p. 475 (*juan* 1300) (QL53/3/癸亥 [= 1] = 6 April 1788)

QL53/3/15 = 20 April 1788

p. 177: Two topics included: compensation for Taiwan and continuation of the description of the three-yearly examination of officials (summary)

QL53/3/16 = 21 April 1788

p. 177: Compensation for victory at Douliumen 斗六門: not yet found

pp. 177–178: Declaration impériale (Imperial declaration): Filling of vacant positions:
Qing shilu, vol. 25, pp. 466–467 (*juan* 1299) (QL53/2/己未 [= 26] = 2 April 1788); *Qianlong chao shangyu dang*, vol. 14, pp. 185–186 n. 504

(QL53/2/26 = 2 April 1788); *Qianlong di qijuzhu*, vol. 37, p. 50 (QL53/2/26 = 2 April 1788)

pp. 178–182: Declaration impériale (Imperial declaration): Liang-han 琅玕 and the confiscation of the house of Chai Daji 柴大紀:
Qianlong di qijuzhu, vol. 37, pp. 55–57 (QL53/2/29 = 5 April 1788) [*Qianlong di qijuzhu*, QL53/3/1–15: absent]

pp. 182–183: Declaration impériale (Imperial declaration): Special examinations during the visit to Tianjin:
Qing shilu, vol. 25, p. 474 (*juan* 1300) (QL53/3/癸亥 [= 1] = 6 April 1788); *Qianlong chao shangyu dang*, vol. 14, p. 193 n. 529 (QL53/3/1 = 6 April 1788)

QL53/3/17 = 22 April 1788

pp. 183–184: Representation (Memorial): Liu E 劉峩 about the wrong appointment of Wang Hao 王灝: not yet found

pp. 184–187: Representation (Memorial): Lan Dixi 蘭第錫 (1736–1797), Governor-General of the two Jiang provinces and Bi Yuan 畢沅 (1730–1797), Governor of Hunan, on vacant positions: not yet found

QL53/3/18 = 23 April 1788

p. 187: Continuation of the case of the five criminals who escaped (summary)

pp. 188–189: Representation (Memorial): Chang-lin 長麟 on salt official He Zechuan 何澤傳:
Qianlong chao shangyu dang, vol. 14, p. 191 n. 521 (QL53/2/29 = 5 April 1788); *Qianlong di qijuzhu*, vol. 37, p. 57 (QL53/2/29 = 5 April 1788)

QL53/3/19 = 24 April 1788

pp. 189–190: Presentation d'un mandarin (Presentation of a mandarin): He Yucheng 何裕城 about the magistrate of Dasou 大庾 not fulfilling his duty (not arresting a missionary): not yet found

p. 190: Declaration impériale (Imperial declaration): Soldiers receiving one month salary for accompanying the trip to Tianjin:
Qing shilu, vol. 25, p. 474 (*juan* 1300) (QL53/3/癸亥 [= 1] = 6 April 1788); *Qianlong chao shangyu dang*, vol. 14, p. 193 n. 525 (QL53/3/1 = 6 April 1788)

p. 190: Declaration impériale (Imperial declaration): Gifts to elderly underway to Tianjin:

Qing shilu, vol. 25, p. 474 (*juan* 1300) (QL53/3/癸亥 [= 1] = 6 April 1788); *Qianlong chao shangyu dang*, vol. 14, p. 193 n. 526 (QL53/3/1 = 6 April 1788)

pp. 190–191: Presentation d'un mandarin (Presentation of a mandarin): Appointment of Na-la-tai 納蘭泰: not yet found

QL53/3/20 = 25 April 1788

pp. 191–192: Declaration impériale (Imperial declaration): Rewards for lower officials related to the war in Taiwan: not yet found

QL53/3/21 = 26 April 1788

p. 192: On an official who has not taken action against heterodox religion: not yet found

pp. 193–194: Accusation: Charge by Shang An 尚安 concerning the merchant Yong Chun 永春, who was robbed and ill-treated by Torghuts: *Qing shilu*, vol. 25, p. 465 (*juan* 1299) (QL53/2/丁巳 [= 24] = 31 March 1788); *Qianlong di qijuzhu*, vol. 37, pp. 45–47 (QL53/2/24 = 31 March 1788)

QL53/3/22 = 27 April 1788

pp. 195–202: Jugement du Tribunal des Crimes (Judgement of the Criminal Tribunal): Crimes and condemnations of Lin Shuangwen 林爽文:

not yet found [vol. 25, p. 484 (*juan* 1300)] (QL53/4/壬申 [= 10] = 15 May 1788)]

QL53/3/23 = 28 April 1788

pp. 203–205: Declaration impériale (Imperial declaration): On the celebration of eightieth birthday of the emperor (*baxun wanshou* 八旬萬壽) in the year Qianlong 55:

Qing shilu, vol. 25, p. 490 (*juan* 1300) (QL53/3/丙子 [= 14] = 19 April 1788); *Qianlong chao shangyu dang*, vol. 14, p. 205 n. 553 (QL53/3/14 = 19 April 1788)

pp. 205–209: Declaration impériale (Imperial declaration): Sun Yongqing 孫永清 (?–1790), Governor of Guangxi, on the escaped prisoner who should not have been executed:

Qing shilu, vol. 25, pp. 480–481 (*juan* 1300) (QL53/3/己巳 [= 7] = 12 April 1788); *Qianlong chao shangyu dang*, vol. 14, pp. 200–201 n. 547 (QL53/3/7 = 12 April 1788)

QL53/3/24 = 29 April 1788

pp. 209–214: Representation du viceroi (Representation of the viceroy): Wu-la-na 伍拉納 (1739–1795), Governor of Fujian, on the prisoner Lü Chen 呂辰 who escaped by having himself replaced by someone else: *Qing shilu*, vol. 25, p. 467 (*juan* 1300) (QL53/3/甲子 [= 2] = 7 April 1788); *Qianlong chao shangyu dang*, vol. 14, pp. 194–195 n. 532 (QL53/3/2 = 7 April 1788)

QL53/3/25 = 30 April 1788

p. 214: Declaration impériale (Imperial declaration): On the examination of the examinators:

Qianlong chao shangyu dang, vol. 14, p. 209 n. 564 (QL53/3/16 = 21 April 1788)

p. 214: Comment asserting that there is nothing of interest to Europe in the remaining gazettes

QL53/3/26 = 1 May 1788

p. 214: In this and following gazettes: On the *yinjian*: nothing interesting any more for Europe

5 Existing Copies of *tizou shijian* 題奏事件

Chinese date	European date	Days	Location
QL35/3/4–30	30 March–25 April 1770	27	Nanjing Library
QL35/5/2–16	26 May–9 June 1770	15	National Library of China
QL35/run 5/8	30 June 1770	1	National Library of China
QL35/run 5/9–18	1–10 July 1770	10	Nanjing Library
QL35/run 5/18–29	10–21 July 1770	12	National Library of China
QL35/6/1–25	22 July–15 August 1770	25	Princeton Univ. Library
QL35/6/26–30	16–20 August 1770	5	Nanjing Library
QL35/7/1–2	21–22 August 1770	2	Nanjing Library
QL35/7/4–14	24 August–3 September 1770	11	Nanjing Library
QL35/7/15–29	4–18 September 1770	15	Capital Library of China
QL35/9/4–25	22 October–12 November 1770	22	Nanjing Library

(*cont.*)

Chinese date	European date	Days	Location
QL35/10/17–30	3–16 December 1770	14	Princeton Univ. Library
QL35/11/1–5	17–21 December 1770	5	Princeton Univ. Library
QL35/11/6–23	22 December 1770–8 January 1771	18	Princeton Univ. Library
QL36/6/24–29	4–9 August 1771	6	National Diet Library
QL37/3/10–14	12–16 April 1772	5	National Library of China
QL37/3/28	30 April 1772	1	National Library of China
QL37/4/9–14	11–16 May 1772	6	Tian Tao
QL37/7/2–29	31 July–27 August 1772	28	National Library of China
QL37/12/1–20	24 December 1772–12 January 1773	20	Princeton Univ. Library
QL37/12/22–??	14 January 1773	1	Princeton Univ. Library
QL38/7/4–21	21 August–7 September 1773	20	National Diet Library
QL38/8/9–15	24–30 September 1773	7	National Diet Library
QL38/8/16–22	1–7 October 1773	7	National Library of China
QL38/10/3	16 November 1773	1	Nanjing Library
QL38/10/5–10	18–23 November 1773	6	Nanjing Library
QL38/11/22–25	4–7 January 1774	4	Nanjing Library
QL38/11/26–29	8–11 January 1774	4	National Diet Library
QL39/3/	[11 April–9 May 1774]	1	Historical Museum of China
QL40/7/1–5	27–31 July 1775	5	National Diet Library
QL40/10/16–23	8–15 November 1775	8	National Diet Library
QL41/3/21	8 May 1776	1	National Diet Library
QL41/3/23–26	10–13 May 1776	4	National Diet Library
QL41/6/9–15	23–29 July 1776	7	National Diet Library
QL41/6/16–22	30 July–5 August 1776	7	Tokyo University
QL41/7/3–28	16 August–10 September 1776	26	National Library of China
QL41/8/	[13 September–11 October 1776]	1	Historical Museum of China
QL42/2/22–30	30 March–7 April 1777	9	Nanjing Library
QL42/7/3–13	5–15 August 1777	11	Princeton Univ. Library
QL42/12/1–6	30 December–4 January 1778	6	Nanjing Library

(*cont.*)

Chinese date	European date	Days	Location
QL43/4/7	3 May 1778	1	Bibliothèque nat. de France
QL43/4/29	25 May 1778	1	Bibliothèque nat. de France
QL43/6/10	7 November 1778	1	Bibliothèque nat. de France
QL43/9/29	17 November 1778	1	Bibliothèque nat. de France
QL43/10/8	26 November 1778	1	Bibliothèque nat. de France
QL43/10/10	28 November 1778	1	Bibliothèque nat. de France
QL44/2/10	27 March 1779	1	Bibliothèque nat. de France
QL44/4/1	16 May 1779	1	Bibliothèque nat. de France
QL44/5/19–20	2–3 July 1779	2	Bibliothèque nat. de France
JQ6/8/30	7 October 1801	1	National Diet Library
JQ6/9/1	8 October 1801	1	National Diet Library
JQ6/9/5	12 October 1801	1	National Diet Library
JQ6/9/8–9	15–16 October 1801	2	Tokyo University
JQ6/9/14	21 October 1801	1	National Diet Library
JQ6/9/16	23 October 1801	1	National Diet Library
JQ6/9/21–22	28–29 October 1801	2	Tokyo University
JQ6/9/26	2 November 1801	1	National Diet Library
JQ6/9/28	4 November 1801	1	National Diet Library
JQ6/10/6	11 November 1801	1	National Diet Library
JQ6/11/7–18	12–23 December 1801	12	National Library of China
JQ6/11/20	25 December 1801	1	National Library of China
JQ6/11/22–27	27 December 1801–1 January 1802	6	National Library of China
	Total number of days:	425	

QL36/1/27–12/26	14 March 1760–31 January 1761	201 excerpts from 181 different days in *Hwanbo sanjeol* 環報刪節	181	Kyujanggak Institute
QL37/12	[24 December 1772–22 January 1773]	*wenxuandan* 文選單, *wuxuandan* 武選單, 1 fol. each	1	Princeton Univ. Library
QL39	? 1774	one page	1	Princeton Univ. Library
QL42/2	[9 March–7 April 1777]	*wenxuandan* 文選單, *wuxuandan* 武選單, 1 page	1	Nanjing Library
?		unknown		Cultural Relics Bureau?
?		? unknown		Fang Hanqi

Sources: Martin Heijdra, personal communication; Pan Tianzhen (1992), p. 85; Ma Ting (1993), p. 118; Kong Zhengyi & Zhang Lu (2014), pp. 171–172; Yin Qing (2018), p. 1811; *Zhongguo guji zongmu: Shibu* (2009), vol. 6, p. 3558, no. *shi* 61247900; Princeton University Library: "Ti zou shi jian" (https://catalog.princeton.edu/catalog/4093844), last accessed 14 October 2020; see also Yale Project: "Exploring the Peking Gazette (*jingbao* 京報)," ed. Michael Hunter (https://tenthousandrooms.yale.edu/project/exploring-peking-gazette-jingbao-jing-bao/ti-zou-shi-jian), last accessed 14 October 2020; National Library of China (http://www.nlc.cn/newen/)

Location:
Beijing Library = Beijing tushuguan 北京图书馆, Beijing
Bibliothèque nat. de France = Bibliothèque nationale de France (BnF) , Paris
Capital Library of China = Shoudu tushuguan 首都图书馆
Cultural Relics Bureau = Beijing wenwuju 北京文物局, Beijing
Fang Hanqi = private collector Fang Hanqi 方汉奇
Historical Museum of China = Zhongguo lishi bowuguan 中国历史博物馆 (renamed Zhongguo guojia bowuguan 中国国家博物馆)
Kyujanggak Institute = Kyujanggak Institute of Korean Studies Collection, Seoul National University
Nanjing Library = Nanjing tushuguan 南京图书馆, Nanjing
National Diet Library = Kokuritsu Kokkaitoshokan 国立国会図書館, Tokyo
National Library of China = Zhongguo guojia tushuguan 中国国家图书馆, Beijing (= former Beijing Library: Beijing tushuguan 北京图书馆)
Princeton Univ. Library = Princeton University Library, Princeton
Tian Tao = private collector Tian Tao 田濤
Tokyo University = Tōkyōdaigaku tōyō bunka kenkyūjo 東京大学東洋文化研究所 Institute of Advanced Studies on Asia, Tokyo University, Tokyo

Bibliography

Abbreviations

ARSI, Jap. Sin.	Archivum Romanum Societatis Iesu, Japonica-Sinica Collection, Rome. See also: Albert Chan, *Chinese Books and Documents in the Jesuit Archives in Rome: A Descriptive Catalogue: Japonica-Sinica I–IV*, New York: M.E. Sharpe, 2002.
APF	Archivio Storico "de Propaganda Fide," Rome.
	SOCP Scritture Originali delle Congregazioni Particolari dell'Indie orientali e Cina
	SC Scritture riferite nei Congressi
BAV	Biblioteca Apostolica Vaticana, Rome.
BnF	Bibliothèque nationale de France, Paris.
ECCP	*Eminent Chinese of the Ch'ing Period (1644–1912)*, 2 vols., ed. by Arthur W. Hummel, Washington: US Government Printing Office, 1943–1944.
HCC	*Handbook of Christianity in China: Volume One (635–1800)*, ed. by Nicolas Standaert, Leiden: Brill, 2001.
Inst.	Institut de France, Paris.
LEC	*Lettres édifiantes et curieuses, écrites des missions étrangères par quelques missionnaires de la Compagnie de Jésus*, 34 vols., Paris: Nicolas Le Clerc (etc.), 1703–1776.
LEC	*Lettres édifiantes et curieuses, écrites des missions étrangères*, 26 vols., Toulouse: Noel-Etienne Sens – Auguste Gaude, 1810–1811.
MCC	*Mémoires concernant l'histoire, les sciences, les arts, les mœurs, les usages, &c. des Chinois, par les missionnaires de Pékin*, 17 vols., Paris: Nyon Libraire – Treuttel et Würtz, 1776–1814.
SKQS	(*Wenyuange*) *Siku quanshu* (文淵閣) 四庫全書, 1500 vols., Taibei: Commercial Press, 1983–1986.

Primary and Secondary Sources

Ai Junchuan 艾俊川, "Tizou shijian bu shi laban yinshuapin: Jian tan 'Qingdai shiyong laban yinshua' shuofa yiju buzu" 《题奏事件》不是蜡版印刷品 – 兼谈"清代使用蜡版印刷"说法依据不足 (The *Tizou Shijian* Is Not a Wax Block Printing: With Some Critical Remarkes on the Theory That Wax Block Printing Was Used in the Qing Dynasties), *Beijing yinshua xueyuan xuebao* 北京印刷学院学报 (2009:6), pp. 11–13.

Barrow, John, *Travels in China*, 2nd edition, London: T. Cadell & W. Davies, 1806.

Barten, J. [Jan], "Hollandse kooplieden op bezoek bij concilievaders," *Archief voor de geschiedenis van de katholieke kerk in Nederland* 12 (1970), pp. 75–121.

Barthélemy, Sarah, "Français et jésuite: Les *Lettres Édifiantes et Curieuses* de Chine, entreprise éditoriale de la mission jésuite française (1702–1783)," *Revue d'histoire ecclésiastique* 114:1–2 (2019), pp. 224–264.

Beurdeley, Michel, *Peintres jésuites en Chine au XVIIIe siècle*, Arcueil: Anthèse, 1997.

Blair, Ann M., *Too Much To Know: Managing Scholarly Information before the Modern Age*, New Haven: Yale Univ. Press, 2010.

Blair, Ann & Devin Fitzgerald, "A Revolution in Information?," in *The Oxford Handbook of Early Modern European History, 1350–1750: Volume I: Peoples and Place*, ed. by Hamish Scott, Oxford: Oxford Univ. Press, 2015, pp. 244–265.

Bosmans, Henri, "Documents relatifs à Ferdinand Verbiest: Les lettres annuelles de la vice-province de la Compagnie de Jésus en Chine, année 1669, par Adrien Grelon," *Annales de la Société d'Émulation de Bruges* 62 (1912), pp. 15–61.

Britton, Roswell S., *The Chinese Periodical Press, 1800–1912*, (Shanghai: Kelly & Walsh, 1933), Taipei: Ch'eng-Wen, 1976.

Burson, Jeffrey D., "Chinese Novices, Jesuit Missionaries and the Accidental Construction of Sinophobia in Enlightenment France," *French History* 27.1 (March 2013), pp. 21–44.

Cartier, Michel, "Le despotisme chinois: Montesquieu et Quesnay, lecteurs de Du Halde," in *La Chine entre amour et haine: Actes du VIIIe colloque de sinologie de Chantilly*, ed. by Michel Cartier, Paris: Desclée de Brouwer, 1998, pp. 15–32.

Censer, Jack R., *The French Press in the Age of Enlightenment*, London: Routledge, 1994.

Ch'ing Administrative Terms: A Translation of the Terminology of the Six Boards with Explanatory Notes, trans. E-tu Zen Sun, Cambridge (Mass.): Harvard Univ. Press, 1961.

Choi, Kee Il Jr., "Portraits of Virtue: Henri-Léonard Bertin, Joseph Amiot and the 'Great Man' of China," *Transactions of the Oriental Ceramic Society* 80 (2015), pp. 49–65.

Collani, Claudia von, "Une légation à Rome manquée: Joachim Bouvet et Sabino Mariani," in *Actes du VIe colloque international de sinologie Chantilly. Images de la Chine: le contexte occidental de la sinologie naissante*, ed. by E. Malatesta & Y. Raguin, Taipei/Paris: Institut Ricci, 1995, pp. 277–301.

Cordier, Henri, "Giuseppe Panzi: Peintre italien à Pé-kin (XVIIIe siècle)," in *Mélanges offerts à M. Émile Picot, membre de l'Institut, par ses amis et ses élèves*, Paris: Édouard Rahir, 1913, vol. 1, pp. 429–443.

Couplet, Philippe, *Tabula chronologica Monarchiae Sinicae juxta cyclos annorum LX, Ab anno ante Christum 2952, ad annum post Christum 1683*, appended at the end of *Confucius Sinarum Philosophus*, Paris: Daniel Horthemels, 1686/87.

Courant, Maurice, *Catalogue des livres chinois, coréens, japonais, etc.*, 8 vols., Paris: Ernest Leroux, 1902–1912.

DaQing wuchao huidian 大清五朝會典, 24 vols., ed. by Yi Xing 易行, Beijing: Xianzhuang shuju, 2006.

D'Arelli, Francesco, "Manuscript Notes of Carlo Horatii Da Castorano O.F.M. and Francesco da Ottaviano O.F.M. on Some Of Aleni's Chinese Writings," in *Scholar from the West: Giulio Aleni S.J. (1582–1649) and the Dialogue between Christianity and China*, ed. by Tiziana Lippiello & Roman Malek, Nettetal: Steyler Verlag, 1997, pp. 433–452.

Dehergne, Joseph, "Les deux Chinois de Bertin: L'enquête industrielle de 1764 et les débuts de la collaboration technique franco-chinoise," Ph.D. diss. ('Thèse de 3e cycle') Univ. of Paris, 1965.

Dehergne, Joseph, *Répertoire des jésuites de Chine de 1552 à 1800*, Rome: Institutum Historicum S.I., 1973.

Dehergne, Joseph, "Pour une édition critique des 'Lettres édifiantes': Les lettres concernant la Chine," *Actes du XXIXe Congrès International des Orientalistes: La Chine antique*, Paris: L'Asiathèque, 1977, pp. 97–102.

Dehergne, Joseph, "Une grande collection: Mémoires concernant les Chinois (1776–1814)," *Bulletin de l'École française d'Extrême-Orient* 72 (1983), pp. 267–297.

Description géographique, historique, chronologique, politique, et physique de l'empire de la Chine et de la Tartarie chinoise, 4 vols., ed. by Jean-Baptiste Du Halde, Paris: P.G. Le Mercier, 1735.

De Weerdt, Hilde, "'Court Gazettes' and 'Short Reports': Official Views and Unofficial Readings of Court News," *Hanxue yanjiu* 漢學研究 27:2 (2009), pp. 167–200.

De Weerdt, Hilde, *Information, Territory, and Networks: The Crisis and Maintenance of Empire in Song China*, Cambridge (Mass.) / London: Harvard Univ. Asia Center, 2015.

Dictionary of Official Titles in Imperial China, ed. by Charles O. Hucker, Stanford: Stanford Univ. Press, 1985.

Dijkstra, Trude, "It is said that...: The Chinese Rites Controversy in Dutch Newspapers and Periodicals in the Seventeenth Century," *Jaarboek voor Nederlandse boekgeschiedenis* 23 (2016), pp. 172–191.

Dijkstra, Trude, "De *Opregte Haerlemsche Courant* en het nieuws uit China," in *Barbaren & wijsgeren: Het beeld van China in de Gouden Eeuw*, ed. by Thijs Weststeijn & Menoo Jonker, Nijmegen: Vantilt, 2017, pp. 59–64.

Ding Chennan 丁晨楠, "Myeongcheongsidae Joseon-ui jung-gugjeongbo sujib: 'Sinmunlyu sosigji' leul jungsim-eulo" 明清時代 朝鮮의 중국정보 수집 – '新聞類 소식지'를 중심으로 (Joseon's Intelligence-Gathering about China during the Ming-Qing Dynasties: Focusing on the Chinese Gazettes), Ph.D. diss. Yonsei Univ. 延世大學校, 2018.

Ding Chennan, "MingQing dinggeqi Chaoxian de Mingchao tangbao souji yu yingdui" 明清鼎革期朝鲜的明朝塘报搜集与应对, *Hanguo yanjiu luncong* 韩国研究论丛 (2019:1), pp. 17–28.

Dooley, Brendan & Sabrina A. Baron, eds., *The Politics of Information in Early Modern Europe*, London: Routledge, 2001.

Dudink, Ad, *Catalogue of Chinese Documents in the "Propaganda Fide" Historical Archives (1622–1830)*, Rome: Urbaniana Univ. Press, 2022.

Elliott, Mark C., *Emperor Qianlong: Son of Heaven, Man of the World*, New York: Longman, 2009.

Encyclopédie, ou Dictionnaire raisonné des sciences, des arts et des métiers par une société de gens de lettres, 35 vols., ed. by Denis Diderot & Jean le Rond d'Alembert, Neuchâtel: Samuel Faulche et Compagnie, 1751–1780.

Fairbank, John K. & S.Y. Têng, "On The Types and Uses of Ch'ing Documents," *Harvard Journal of Asiatic Studies* 5:1 (1940), pp. 1–71.

Fan, T.C., "Chinese Fables and Anti-Walpole Journalism," *The Review of English Studies* 25, no. 98 (April 1949), pp. 141–151.

Fang, Basilia, *Sinica-Sammlung der Österreichische Nationalbibliothek*, Wien: Österreichische Nationalbibliothek, 1992.

Fang Hanqi 方汉奇, ed., *Zhongguo xinwen shiye tongshi* 中国新闻事业通史, 3 vols., Beijing: Renmin daxue chubanshe, 1992–1999.

Fang Hanqi 方汉奇, ed., *Zhongguo xinwen shiye biannian shi* 中国新闻事業编年史, 3 vols., Fuzhou: Fujian renmin chubanshe, 2000.

Fang Hanqi 方汉奇, "'Qingshi – baokan biao' zhong you guan gudai baozhi de jige wenti" 《清史 报刊表》中有关古代报纸的几个问题 (Some Questions Concerning Ancient Newspapers in the Qing History), *Lishi dang'an* 历史档案 (2007:2), pp. 10–15.

Fang Hanqi 方汉奇, ed., *A History of Journalism in China: Volume 1*, Singapore: Silkroad Press, 2013.

Finlay, John R., *Henri Bertin and the Representation of China in Eighteenth-Century France*, New York: Routledge; 2020.

Gaubil, Antoine, *Correspondance de Pékin, 1722–1759*, Genève: Libraire Droz, 1970.

Ge Gongzhen 戈公振, *Zhongguo baoxue shi* 中國報學史, (Shanghai: Commercial Press, 1927, 1928, 1931), Taipei: Xuesheng shuju, 1964.

The General History of China, Containing a Geographical, Historical, Chronological, Political and Physical Description of the Empire of China, Chinese-Tartary, Corea and Thibet, 4 vols., ed. by [J.-B.] Du Halde, London: John Watts, 1736.

Golvers, Noël, *Libraries of Western Learning for China: Circulation of Western books between Europe and China in the Jesuit Mission (ca. 1650–1750). Vol. 3: Of Books and Readers*, Leuven: Ferdinand Verbiest Institute, 2015.

Golvers, Noël, "The Earliest Examples of Chinese Characters Printed in the Southern Low Countries (Leuven, 1672; Antwerp, 1683)," *De Gulden Passer (Tijdschrift voor boekwetenschap / Journal for book history)* 94:2 (2016), pp. 319–333.

Golvers, Noël, *Letters of a Peking Jesuit: The Correspondence of Ferdinand Verbiest, SJ (1623–1688), Revised and Expanded*, Leuven: Ferdinand Verbiest Institute, 2017.

Goto Sueo 後藤末雄, *Kenryu tei den* 乾隆帝伝, (originally 1942) revised and annotated by Nii Yōko 新居洋子, Tokyo: Kokusho kanko kai, 2016.

Gu Keyong 顾克勇 & Ding Xin 丁鑫, "Dibao yanjiu shuping" 邸报研究述评 (Research Review of Dibao), *Zhejiang ligong daxue xuebao* 浙江理工大学学报 (2016:4), pp. 389–395.

Han Qi 韩琦 & Wu Min 吴旻, *Ouzhou suocang Yongzheng Qianlong chao tianzhujiao wenxian huibian* 欧洲所藏雍正乾隆朝天主教文献汇编, Shanghai: Shanghai renmin chubanshe, 2008.

Harris, Lane J., *The Peking Gazette: A Reader in Nineteenth-Century Chinese History*, Leiden: Brill, 2018.

Hau Kiou Choaan, or The Pleasing History, 4 vols., [ed. by Thomas Percy], London: R. and J. Dodsley, 1761.

Herdtrich, Christian Wolfgang, "Lettera del Padre Christiano Herdtrich Austriaco della Compagnia di Giesù, scritta dalla Cina à 23. di Nouembre 1670. Al P. Prospero Intorcetta della medesima Compagnia," in Prospero Intorcetta, *Compendiosa narratione dello stato della missione Cinese, cominciãdo dall'anno 1581. fino al 1669*, Roma: Francesco Tizzoni, 1672, pp. 115–126.

Hermans, Michel, "Joseph-Marie Amiot, une figure de la rencontre de 'l'autre' au temps des lumières," in Yves Lenoir & Nicolas Standaert, eds., *Les danses rituelles chinoises d'après Joseph-Marie Amiot: Aux sources de l'ethnochoréographie*, Namur: Presses universitaires de Namur – Éditions Lessius, 2005, pp. 11–77.

Hermans, Michel, "Amiot's Life," transl. Alison Oliver, in *The Mandate of Heaven: Strategy, Revolution, and the First European Translation of Sunzi's Art of War (1772)*, ed. by Adam Parr, Leiden-Boston: Brill, 2019, pp. 224–274.

Huard, Pierre, Jacqueline Sonolet & Ming Wong, *Médecine en Extrême Orient*, (*Catalogue de l'exposition, Hôpital de la Salpetrière*), Paris: La Salpetrière, 1959.

Huard, Pierre & Ming Wong, "Les enquêtes scientifiques françaises sur la science et la technologie chinoises au XVIIIe siècle," *Bulletin de l'École française d'Extrême-Orient* 53:1 (1966), pp. 137–226.

Huang, Pei, *Autocracy at Work: A Study of the Yung-cheng Period, 1723–1735*, Bloomington: Indiana Univ. Press, 1974.

Hwang Ja 黄梓, *Gugyeog Gabin yeonhaengnok* 국역갑인연행록 (甲寅燕行録), transl. Seo Han-seok 서한석, Seoul: Sejong Daewang Ginyeom Saeophoe, 2015.

Hwang Ja 黄梓, *Gugyeog Gabin yeonhaeng byeollok* 국역 갑인연행별록 (甲寅燕行別録), transl. Sin No-sa 신로사, Seoul: Sejong Daewang Ginyeom Saeophoe, 2015.

Intorcetta, Prospero, *Compendiosa narratione dello stato della missione Cinese, cominciãdo dall'anno 1581. fino al 1669*, Roma: Francesco Tizzoni, 1672.

Kahn, Harold L., *Monarchy in the Emperor's Eyes: Image and Reality in the Ch'ien-lung Reign*, Cambridge (Mass.): Harvard Univ. Press, 1971.

Kangxi qijuzhu 康熙起居注, 3 vols., Beijing: Zhonghua shuju, 1984; facsimile ed. *Qingdai qiju zhuce: Kangxi chao* 清代起居注冊：康熙朝, 32 vols. Beijing: Zhonghua shuju, 2009.

Kelly, Edward Thomas, "The Anti-Christian Persecution of 1616–1617 in Nanking," Ph.D. diss. Columbia Univ., 1971.

Keulemans, Paize, "Tales of an Open World: The Fall of the Ming Dynasty as Dutch Tragedy, Chinese Gossip, and Global News," *Frontiers of Literary Studies in China* 9:2 (2015), pp. 190–234.

Koito Chūgo 小糸忠吾, "Chūgoku seihō-kan no kōryū to tei-hō – jūhasseiki-sue made no shinten o saguru "中国・西方間の交流と邸報 - 十八世紀末までの進展を探る (Chinese Western Contacts and the Court Gazette: Developments until the Eighteenth Century), *Sofia* ソフィア (Sophia) 27:3 (1978), pp. 236–250.

Kong Zhengyi 孔正毅 & Chen Chen 陈晨, "Mingdai 'jingbao' kaolun" 明代"京报"考论, *Guoji xinwenjie* 国际新闻界 (2012:2), pp. 122–127.

Kong Zhengyi 孔正毅 & Zhang Lu 张露, "Qingdai dibao wenxian de xitong kaocha" 清代邸报文献的系统考察 (The Systematic Study of Dibao Literature in the Qing Dynasty), *Xinwen yu chuanbo pinglun* 新闻与传播评论 (2014), pp. 170–184.

Kong Zhengyi 孔正毅 & Wang Shuchuan 王书川, "Qingdai 'dibao' banben wenti chutan" 清代"邸报"版本问题初探 (A Preliminary Study of Dibao Versions in the Qing Dynasty), *Xinwen yu chuanbo pinglun* 新闻与传播评论 (2015:1), pp. 93–106. (2015a).

Kong Zhengyi 孔正毅 & Wang Shuchuan 王书川, "Shilun Qingdai dibao de faxing tixi" 试论清代邸报的发行体系 (On Distribution System of Dibao in the Qing Dynasty), *Nanchang daxue xuebao* 南昌大学学报 (2015:1), pp. 132–139. (2015b)

Landry-Deron, Isabelle, *La preuve par la Chine: La « Description » de J.-B. Du Halde, Jésuite, 1735*, Paris: Editions de l'Ecole des hautes études en sciences sociales, 2002.

Lee, Chao Ying, *Visions de l'Empire du Milieu au 18e siècle en France: Illustrations des* Mémoires concernant les Chinois *1776–1791*, Louvain-la-Neuve: Academia-L'Harmattan, 2016.

Lim, Jongtae, "Tributary Relations between the Chosŏn and Ch'ing Courts to 1800," in *The Cambridge History of China: Volume 9: The Ch'ing Empire to 1800, Part Two*, ed. by Willard J. Peterson, Cambridge: Cambridge Univ. Press, 2016, pp. 146–196.

Long Yun 龍云, *Qian Deming: 18 shiji Zhong Fa jian de wenhua shizhe* 錢德明：18世紀中法間的文化使者, Beijing: Beijing daxue chubanshe, 2015.

Ly-Tio-Fane Madeleine, *Pierre Sonnerat, 1748–1814, An Account of His Life and Work*, Mauritius: Imprimerie et Papeterie Commerciale, 1976.

Ming Qing dang'an 明清檔案, 370 vols., Taibei: Lianjing, 1986–1995.

Ma, Li, *L'art de gouverner chinois dans les périodiques de langue française de 1750 à 1789*, Montpellier: Presses universitaires de la Méditerranée, 2019.

Ma Ting 馬挺, "Chūgoku saiko no insatsu shinbun *daisō jiken* ni tsuite" 中国最古の印刷新聞『題奏事件』について (The Characteristics of Ticou Shijan), *Masu komyunikēshon kenkyū* マス・コミュニケーション研究 (Journal of Mass-Communication Studies) 43 (1993), pp. 117–131, 210–209.

Ma Ting 馬挺, "Chūgoku no shinbun shimen kenkyū ni tsuite no kōsatsu" 中国の新聞紙面研究についての考察 (Researches on the Layout of Chinese Newspaper), *Meisei daigaku kenkyū kiyō* 明星大学研究紀要 (Bulletin of Meisei University) 10 (2002), pp. 69–81; 11 (2003), pp. 99–108.

Ma Ting 馬挺, "Chūgokugo shinbun no shimen henshū no shiteki kōsatsu" 中国語新聞の紙面編集の史的考察 (Historical Researches on the Layout of Chinese Newspaper), *Meiseidaigaku kenkyū kiyō* 明星大学研究紀要 (Bulletin of Meisei University) 12 (2004), pp. 137–170; 13 (2005), pp. 119–134.

Mailla, Joseph-Anne-Marie de Moyriac de, *Histoire générale de la Chine, ou Annales de cet Empire, traduites du Tong-kien-kang-mou*, 13 vols., Paris: Ph.-D. Pierres et Clousier, 1777–1785.

Marinescu, Jocelyn M.N., "The *Ruijianlu* 睿鑑錄 (*Record of Sage Scrutiny*) and its Role in the Defense of Christianity in the Early Qianlong Era," *Sino-Western Cultural Relations Journal* XVIII (2006), pp. 19–36.

Marsy, François-Marie de, *Histoire moderne des Chinois, des Japonnois, des Indiens, des Persans, des Turcs, des Russiens, &c.*, 30 vols., Paris: Chez Desaint & Saillant, 1755–1771.

Martini, Martino, *Opera omnia: Vol. III: Novus atlas Sinensis*, 2 vols., ed. by Franco Demarchi & Giuliano Bertuccioli, Trento: Università degli studi di Trento, 2002.

Meng, Hua, "Chine," in *Dictionnaire général de Voltaire*, ed. by Raymond Trousson & Jeroom Vercruysse, Paris: Champion, 2003, pp. 198–203.

Milsky, Marie-Françoise, "L'intérêt pour la Chine en France au xviiie siècle," Ph.D. diss. École des hautes études en sciences sociales et université Paris VII, 1977.

Mittler, Barbara, *A Newspaper for China?: Power, Identity, and Change in Shanghai's News Media, 1872–1912*, Cambridge (Mass.): Harvard Univ. Asia Center, 2004.

Mokros, Emily C., "Communication, Empire, and Authority in the Qing Gazette," Ph.D. diss. Johns Hopkins Univ., 2016.

Mokros, Emily C., *The Peking Gazette in Late Imperial China: State News and Political Authority*, Seattle: Univ. of Washington Press, 2021.

Montesquieu, Charles de Secondat, baron de, *Geographica* (*Œuvres complètes de Montesquieu* 16), Oxford: Voltaire Foundation, 2007.

Montesquieu, Charles de Secondat, baron de, *Esprit des lois*, Paris: Firmin Didot frères, 1849.

Montesquieu, Charles de Secondat, baron de, *The Spirit of Laws*, in *Complete Works*, London: T. Evans, 1777, vol. 1.

Nii Yōko 新居洋子, "Iezusu kaishi Amiot no mita Kenryu tei to Shincho kanryo" イエズス会士アミオのみた乾隆帝と清朝官僚 (Emperor Qianlong and Qing Officials in the Eyes of a Jesuit Amiot (1718–1793)), *Chūgoku: Shakai to bunka* 中国: 社会と文化 26 (July 2011), pp. 107–123.

Nii Yōko 新居洋子, *Iezusu-kai-shi to fuhen no teikoku: Zai hana senkyōshi ni yoru bunmei no hon'yaku* イエズス会士と普遍の帝国: 在華宣教師による文明の翻訳 (Jesuit Missionaries and Universal Empire: Translation of China by Jean Joseph Marie Amiot), Nagoya: Nagoya daigaku shuppankai, 2017.

Ocko, Jonathan, "The British Museum's Peking Gazette," *Ch'ing-shih wen-t'i* 2:9 (1973), pp. 35–49.

Osterhammel, Jürgen, *Unfabling the East: The Enlightenment's Encounter with Asia*, transl. Robert Savage, Princeton: Princeton Univ. Press, 2018.

Ozouf, Mona, "Le concept d'opinion publique au XVIIIe siècle," *Sociologie de la communication* 1 (1997), pp. 349–365.

Pan Tianzhen 潘天祯, "Qianlong, Jiaqing jian suoyin ribao 'Tizou shijian' de faxian" 乾隆、嘉庆间所印日报《题奏事件》的发现, *Wenwu* 文物 (1992:3), pp. 82–91.

Pereira, Jacques, *Montesquieu et la Chine*, Paris: L'Harmattan, 2008.

Pettegree, Andrew, *The Invention of News: How the World Came to Know about Itself*, New Haven: Yale Univ. Press, 2014.

Pfister, Louis, *Notices biographiques et bibliographiques sur les Jésuites de l'ancienne mission de Chine, 1552–1773*, 2 vols., Shanghai: Imprimerie de la Mission, 1932–1934.

Picard, René, *Les Peintres jésuites à la cour de Chine*, Grenoble: Éditions des 4 seigneurs, 1973.

Pinot, Virgile, *La Chine et la formation de l'esprit philosophique en France (1640–1740)*, Paris: P. Geuthner, 1932.

Porter, David, *The Chinese Taste in Eighteenth-Century England*, Cambridge: Cambridge Univ. Press, 2010.

Qianlong chao junjichu suishou dengji dang 乾隆朝軍機處隨手登記檔, 46 vols., ed. by Zhongguo di yi lishi dang'an guan 中國第一歷史檔案館, Guilin: Guangxi shifan daxue chubanshe, 2000.

Qianlong chao shangyu dang 乾隆朝上諭檔, 18 vols., ed. by Zhongguo di yi lishi dang'an guan 中國第一歷史檔案館, Guilin: Guangxi shifan daxue chubanshe, 2008.

Qianlong di qijuzhu 乾隆帝起居注, 42 vols., ed. by Zhongguo di yi lishi dang'an guan 中國第一歷史檔案館, Guilin: Guangxi shifan daxue chubanshe, 2002.

Qinding Siku quanshu zongmu 钦定四库全书总目, 2 vols., Beijing: Zhonghua shuju, 1997.

Qingdai renwu shengzu nianbiao 清代人物生卒年表, ed. by Jiang Qingbo 江庆柏, Beijing: Renmin chubanshe, 2005.

Qingdai qijuzhu ce: Guoli Gugong bowuyuan zhencang. Yongzheng chao 清代起居注册: 國立故宮博物院珍藏. 雍正朝, 23 vols., ed. by Guoli Gugong bowu yuan 國立故宮博物院, Taibei: Lianjing chuban shiye gongsi, 2015.

Qingdai zhiguan nianbiao 清代職官年表, 4 vols., ed. by Qiang Sifu 錢實甫, Beijing: Zhonghua shuju, 1980.

Qingshi biannian 清史编年, 12 vols. ed. by Zhongguo renmin daxue Qingshi yanjiusuo 中国人民大学清史研究所, Beijing: Zhongguo renmin daxue chubanshe, 1985–2000.

Qingshi gao 清史稿, 48 vols., Beijing: Zhonghua shuju, 1977.

Qing shilu 清實錄, 60 vols., Beijing: Zhonghua shuju, 1982.

[Quesnay, François], M.A., "Despotisme de la Chine," *Éphémérides du citoyen, ou Chronique de l'esprit national* (1767): Tome III.1, pp. 3–88; IV.1, pp. 5–77; V.1, pp. 5–65; VI.1, pp. 5–75.

Quesnay, François, "Despotisme de la Chine," in *Oeuvres économiques et philosophiques: accompagnées des éloges et d'autres travaux biographiques sur Quesnay par différents auteurs*, ed. by Auguste Oncken, Aalen: Scientia, 1965 (reprint of Francfort ed. 1888), pp. 563–660.

Reed, Marcia, "The Qianlong Emperor's Copperplate Engravings," *Harvard Library Bulletin* 28:1 (Spring 2017), pp. 1–24.

Rosso, Antonio Sisto, *Apostolic Legations to China of the Eighteenth Century*, South Pasadena: P.D. and Ione Perkins, 1948.

Rougemont, François de, *Historia Tartaro-Sinica Nova*, Lovanii: Typis Martini Hullegaerde, 1673.

Roux, Pierre-Emmanuel, "The Catholic Experience of Chosŏn Envoys in Beijing: A Contact Zone and the Circulation of Religious Knowledge in the Eighteenth Century," *Acta Koreana* 19:1 (June 2016), pp. 9–44.

Rowbotham, Arnold H., "Voltaire, Sinophile," *PMLA* (*Publication of the Modern Language Association*) 47:4 (Dec. 1932), pp. 1050–1065.

Rydholm, Lena, "China and the World's First Freedom of Information Act: The Swedish Freedom of the Press Act of 1766," *Javnost – The Public* 20:4 (2013), pp. 45–63.

Sacy, Jacques Silvestre de & Michel Antoine, *Henri Bertin dans le sillage de la Chine (1720–1792)*, Paris: Cathasia / Les Belles Lettres, 1970.

Shengchao poxieji 聖朝破邪集, ed. by Xia Guiqi 夏瑰琦, Hong Kong: Jiandao shenxueyuan, 1996.

Shepherd, John Robert, "Taiwan Prefecture in the Eighteenth Century," in *The Cambridge History of China: Volume 9: The Ch'ing Empire to 1800, Part Two*, ed. by Willard J. Peterson, Cambridge: Cambridge Univ. Press, 2016, pp. 77–110.

Shi Yuanyuan 史媛媛, *Qingdai qianzhongqi xinwen chuanbo shi* 清代前中期新闻传播史, Fuzhou: Fujian renmin chubanshe, 2008.

Shizong xianhuangdi shangyu baqi 世宗憲皇帝上諭八旗 (YZ9 = 1731) (13 + 12 + 13 *juan*), *SKQS*, vol. 413.

Shizong xianhuangdi shangyu neige 世宗憲皇帝上諭内閣 (YZ9 = 1731) (159 *juan*), *SKQS*, vols. 414–415.

Shizong xianhuangdi shengxun 世宗憲皇帝聖訓 (QL9 = 1744) (36 *juan*), *SKQS*, vol. 412.

Shizong xianhuangdi zhupi yuzhi 世宗憲皇帝硃批諭旨 (QL3 = 1738) (360 *juan*), SKQS, vols. 416–425.

Sonnerat, Pierre, *Voyage aux Indes orientales et a la Chine, fait par ordre du Roi, depuis 1774 jusqu'en 1781*, 2 vols., Paris: Auteur & Froullé, 1782.

Spence, Jonathan D., *The Death of Woman Wang*, Harmondsworth: Penguin books, 1980.

Spence, Jonathan D., "The K'ang-hsi Reign," in *The Cambridge History of China: Volume 9: The Ch'ing Empire to 1800, Part One*, ed. by Willard J. Peterson, Cambridge: Cambridge Univ. Press, 2002, pp. 120–182.

Standaert, Nicolas, *Chinese Voices in the Rites Controversy: Travelling Books, Community Networks, Intercultural Arguments*, (*Bibliotheca Instituti Historici S.I.* 75), Rome: Institutum Historicum Societatis Iesu, 2012. (2012a)

Standaert, Nicolas, "The 'Edict of Tolerance' (1692): A Textual History and Reading," in Artur K. Wardega & António Vasconcelos de Saldanha, eds., *In the Light and Shadow of an Emperor: Tomás Pereira, SJ (1645–1708), the Kangxi Emperor and the Jesuit Mission in China*, Newcastle upon Tyne (UK): Cambridge Scholars Publishing, 2012, pp. 308–358. (2012b)

Standaert, Nicolas, *The Intercultural Weaving of Historical Texts: Chinese and European Stories about Emperor Ku and His Concubines*, (*Leiden Series in Comparative Historiography* 9), Leiden: Brill, 2016.

Standaert, Nicolas, (Zhong Mingdan 钟鸣旦), "18 shiji jinru quanqiu gonggong lingyu de Zhongguo *dibao*" 18世纪进入全球公共领域的中国《邸报》 (The Chinese Gazette Joining the Global Public in the Eighteenth Century), transl. Hu Hanhan 胡涵菡, *Fudan xuebao* 复旦学报 (2020:5), pp. 1–18.

Standaert, Nicolas, "The Chinese Gazette in European Sources from the Late Qianlong period: The Case of the *Siku Quanshu*," *T'oung Pao* 通報 107 (2021), pp. 133–187.

Staunton, George, *An Authentic Account of an Embassy from the King of Great Britain to the Emperor of China*, 2 vols., London: W. Bulmer, 1797.

Stumpf, Kilian, *The Acta Pekinensia or Historical Records of the Maillard de Tournon Legation: Volume I: December 1705–August 1706*, ed. by Paul Rule and Claudia von Collani, Rome-Macau, IHSI-MRI, 2015.

Tancheng xianzhi 郯城縣志 (12 + 1 juan; QL28 = 1763), ed. By Wang Zhi 王植 & Zhang Jincheng 張金城 (Zhongguo fangzhi congshu 中國方志叢書, Huabei difang 華北地方, Shandong 山東, vol. 378), Taipei: Chengwen, 1976.

Touboul Bouyeure, Frédérique, "La Chine dans le *Journal des Savants* (1688–1765)," in *Succès et échec de la rencontre Chine et Occident du XVIe au XXe siècle: Actes du Ve colloque de sinologie de Chantilly*, ed. by Edward J. Malatesta & Yves Raguin, Taipei / Paris, Ricci Institute / Institut Ricci, 1993, pp. 237–255.

Van Kley, Edwin J., "News from China: Seventeenth Century European Notices of the Manchu Conquest," *Journal of Modern History* 45:4 (1973), pp. 561–582.

Vissière, Isabelle & Jean-Louis, eds., *Lettres édifiantes et curieuses de Chine par des missionnaires jésuites, 1702–1776*, Paris: Garnier-Flammarion, 1979.

Voltaire, *La Philosophie de l'histoire*, (*Les œuvres complètes de Voltaire* 59), Oxford: Voltaire Foundation, 1969.

Voltaire, *Œuvres alphabétiques I*, (*Les œuvres complètes de Voltaire* 33), Oxford: Voltaire Foundation, 1987.

Voltaire, *Œuvres de 1768 (II)*, (*Les œuvres complètes de Voltaire* 66), Oxford: Voltaire Foundation, 1999.

Voltaire, *Essai sur les mœurs et l'esprit des nations: Tome 2: Avant-propos et chapitres 1–37*, (*Les œuvres complètes de Voltaire* 22), Oxford: Voltaire Foundation, 2009.

Voltaire, *Corpus des notes marginales de Voltaire: Tome III: Dale-Frisi*, (*Les œuvres complètes de Voltaire* 138), Oxford: Voltaire Foundation, 2010.

Voltaire, *Corpus des notes marginales de Voltaire: Tome V: La Barre – Muyart de Vouglans*, (*Les œuvres complètes de Voltaire* 140A), Oxford: Voltaire Foundation, 2012.

Voltaire, *Essai sur les mœurs et l'esprit des nations: Tome 8: Chapitres 177–197*, (*Les œuvres complètes de Voltaire* 26C), Oxford: Voltaire Foundation, 2015.

Voltaire, *Siècle de Louis XIV: Tome 6: chapitres 31–39*, (*Les œuvres complètes de Voltaire* 13D), Oxford: Voltaire Foundation, 2016.

Wagner, Rudolf G., ed., *Joining the Global Public: Word, Image and City in Early Chinese Newspapers, 1870–1910*, Albany: State Univ. of New York Press, 2007.

Wagner, Rudolf G., "The Early Chinese Press and the Agency of Its Readers: The Dynamics of the Transcultural Spread of the 'Press' as an Institution," *Itinerario* 44:2 (2020), pp. 412–434.

Walravens, Hartmut & Marion Steinicke, "Miszellen zu Giuseppe Panzi: Ein Jesuitenkünstler am Hof des Qianlong-Kaisers," *Ostasiatische Zeitschrift* 27 (2014), pp. 52–68.

Walter, Xavier, *La troisieme mort des missions de Chine, 1773–1838*, Paris: F.-X. de Guibert, 2008.

Wang Fan-sen 王汎森, "MingQing yilai de yulun shehui" 明清以來的輿論社會, *Hanxue yanjiu tongxun* 漢學研究通訊 37:3 (2018), pp. 1–6.

Wang Hung-tai 王鴻泰, "MingQing de zixun chuanbo, shehui xiangxiang yu gongzhong shehui" 明清的資訊傳播、社會想像與公眾社會, *Mingdai yanjiu* 明代研究 12 (2009:6), pp. 41–92.

Wang Hung-tai 王鴻泰, "Information Media, Social Imagination, and Public Society during the Ming and Qing Dynasties," transl. Luke Hambleton, *Frontiers of History in China* 5:2 (2010), pp. 169–216.

Wang Shizhen 王士禎, *Chibei outan* 池北偶談, (*Qingdai shiliao biji congkan* 清代史料筆記叢刊), 2 vols., Beijing: Zhonghua shuju, 1982.

Wilkinson, Endymion P., *Chinese History: A New Manual*, Cambridge: Harvard Univ. Asia Center, 2018.

Will, Pierre-Étienne, "Le mandarinat entre admiration et détestation: De Ricci à Magalhães à Du Halde," in *Rencontres et médiations entre la Chine, l'Occident et les Amériques: Missionnaires, chamanes et intermédiaires culturels*, ed. by Frédéric Laugrand, Li Shenwen & Peng Nansheng, Québec: Presses de l'Université de Laval, 2015, pp. 153–178.

Woodside, Alexander, "The Ch'ien-lung Reign," in *The Cambridge History of China: Volume 9: The Ch'íng Empire to 1800, Part One*, ed. by Willard J. Peterson, Cambridge: Cambridge Univ. Press, 2002, pp. 230–309.

Wu Boya 吴伯娅, "Yeshuhuishi bixia de Qingdai dibao" 耶稣会士笔下的清代邸报, *MingQing luncong* 明清论丛 (2015:1), pp. 368–375.

Wu Huiyi, *Traduire la Chine au XVIIIe siècle: Les jésuites traducteurs de textes chinois et le renouvellement des connaissances européennes sur la Chine (1687–ca. 1740)*, Paris: Honoré Champion, 2017.

Xiao Shi 蕭奭, *Yong xianlu* 永憲錄, ed. by Zhu Nanxian 朱南銑, Beijing: Zhonghua shuju, 1997.

Xu Guangqi 徐光啓, *Xu Guangqi ji* 徐光啓集, 2 vols., ed. by Wang Zhongmin 王重民, Shanghai: Shanghai guji chubanshe, 1984.

Xu Zilin 徐紫琳, "'Dibao' mingcheng shouci chuxian shijian xintan" "邸报"名称首次出现时间新探, *Xinwen yanjiu daokan* 新闻研究导刊 10:19 (2019), pp. 44–45.

Yan Zonglin 阎宗临, *ZhongXi jiaotong shi* 中西交通史, Guilin: Guangxi shifan daxue chubanshe, 2007.

Yazawa Toshihiko 矢澤利彥, ed., *Iezusukaishi chūgoku shokan shū: 4 Shakaihen* イエズス会士中国書簡集: 4 社會編, Tōkyō: Heibonsha, 1973.

Yin Qing 殷晴, "Shindai ni okeru tei-hō no hakkō to ryūtsū: Shinchō chūō jōhō no denpa no ichisokumen" 清代における邸報の発行と流通: 清朝中央情報の伝播の一側面 (The Dissemination of Court News of the Qing Dynasty: The Publication and Circulation of the *Peking Gazette*), *Shigaku zasshi* 史学雑誌 127:12 (2018), pp. 1807–1844.

Yin Wenjuan 尹文涓, "Yesuhuishi yu xinjiao chuanjiaoshi dui *Jingbao* de jieyi" 耶稣会士与新教传教士对《京报》的节译 (Selected Translation of Peking Gazette by Jesuits and Protestant Missionaries"), *Shijie zongjiao yanjiu* 世界宗教研究 (2005:2), pp. 71–82.

Yin Yungong 尹韵公, *Zhongguo Mingdai xinwen chuanbo shi* 中国明代新闻传播史, Chongqing: Zhongqing chubanshe, 1990.

Yin Yungong 尹韵公, "Yiwei shiba shiji Faguo xuezhe bixia de Zhongguo gudai dibao" 一位十八世纪法国学者笔下的中国古代邸报, *Xinwen zhanxian* 新闻战线 (1993:2), p. 46.

Yongzheng chao hanwen yuzhi huibian 雍正朝漢文諭旨匯編, 10 vols., ed. by Zhongguo di yi lishi dang'an guan 中國第一歷史檔案館, Guilin: Guangxi shifan daxue chubanshe, 1999.

Yongzheng chao qijuzhu ce 雍正朝起居注冊, 5 vols., ed. by Zhongguo diyi lishi dang'an guan 中國第一歷史檔案館, Beijing: Zhonghua shuju, 1993.

Yuan Zhongdao 袁中道, *Kexuezhai ji* 珂雪斋集, ed. by Qian Bocheng 钱伯城, Shanghai: Shanghai guji chubanshe, 2007.

Zelin, Madeleine, "The Yung-cheng Reign," in *The Cambridge History of China: Volume 9: The Ch'ing Empire to 1800, Part One*, ed. by Willard J. Peterson, Cambridge: Cambridge Univ. Press, 2002, pp. 182–229.

Zhang, De'er & Gaston Demarée, "Northern China Maximum Temperature in the Summer of 1743: A Historical Event of Burning Summer in a Relatively Warm Climate Background," *Chinese Science Bulletin* 49:23 (December 1, 2004), pp. 2508–2514.

Zhang Xiaoguang 张晓光, ed., *Qingdai tongban zhangongtu quanbian* 清代铜版战功图全编, Beijing: Xueyuan chuban she, 2003.

Zhang Xiumin 张秀民, *Zhongguo yinshua shi* 中国印刷史, revised by Han Qi 韩琦, Hangzhou: Zhejiang guji chubanshe, 2006.

Zhang Xiumin 张秀民, *The History of Chinese Printing*, revised by Han Qi, Paramus: Homa & Sekey Books, 2009.

Zhongguo guji zongmu: Shibu 中國古籍總目: 史部, 8 vols., ed. by Zhongguo guji zongmu bianzuan weiyuanhui 中國古籍總目編纂委員會, Shanghai: Shanghai guji chubanshe, 2009.

Zhongguo jibao jingpin 中国集报精品, ed. by Zhongguo baoye xiehui 中国报业协会, Beijing: Renmin ribao chubanshe, 2013.

Databases

Chine ancienne: https://www.chineancienne.fr/.

CCT-Database: Ad Dudink & Nicolas Standaert, Chinese Christian Texts Database (CCT-Database) (http://www.arts.kuleuven.be/sinology/cct).

Diaolong Full-text Database of Chinese & Japanese Ancient Books 雕龙中日古籍全文检索数据库 (China Educational Publications): 古今圖書集成; 清代史料; 中國地方誌; 中國地方誌續集; 日本古典書籍庫; 續修四庫全書; 四庫全書; 全四庫存目; 四庫未收書; 四庫禁毀書.

Dictionnaire des journaux 1600–1789: https://dictionnaire-journaux.gazettes18e.fr/.

Édition Numérique Collaborative et CRitique de l'Encyclopédie: http://enccre.academie-sciences.fr/encyclopedie/.

Gallica: BnF Digital Library, Bibliothèque nationale de France, Paris: https://gallica.bnf.fr/.

Internet Archive: https://archive.org/.

Le gazetier universel: Liste des titres de périodiques: http://gazetier-universel.gazettes18e.fr/.

Scripta Sinica: Hanji dianzi wenxian 漢籍電子文獻 (Chinese Electronic Texts), Academia Sinica.

(Wenyuange) Siku quanshu (文淵閣) 四庫全書 (Complete Books in the Four Treasuries (Wenyuan Pavilion Edition)).

Translations of the Peking Gazette Online, compiled by Lane J. Harris, BrillOnline Primary Sources: https://primarysources.brillonline.com/browse/the-peking-gazette.

Zhongguo fangzhi ku 中國方志庫 (Database of Gazetteers from China).

Zhongguo jiben guji ku 中國基本古籍庫 (Database of Basic Ancient Works from China).

Index